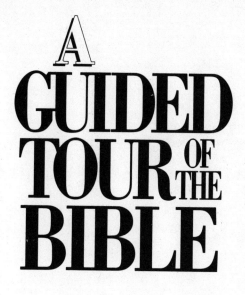

A GUIDED TOUR OF THE BIBLE

Other Books by Philip Yancey

Disappointment With God
Fearfully and Wonderfully Made (with Paul W. Brand)
In His Image (with Paul W. Brand)
Editor of The Student's Guide to the Bible (with Tim Stafford)
Where Is God When It Hurts?

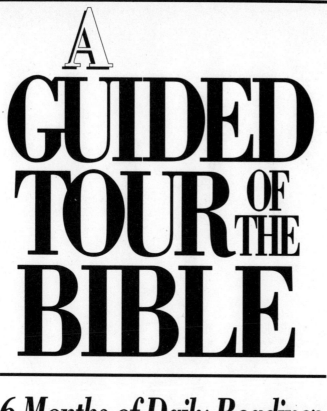

A GUIDED TOUR OF THE BIBLE

6 Months of Daily Readings

PHILIP YANCEY

Daybreak Books
Zondervan Publishing House
Grand Rapids, Michigan

A GUIDED TOUR of the BIBLE
Copyright © 1989 by Philip Yancey

Daybreak Books
are published by
Zondervan Publishing House
1415 Lake Dr., S.E.
Grand Rapids, MI 49506

Library of Congress Cataloging-in-Publication Data

Bible. English. New International. Selections. 1989.
   A guided tour of the Bible : 6 months of daily readings / Philip
Yancey.
   p. cm.
   Bible selections are from the New International Version.
North American ed.
   ISBN 0-310-51650-1
   1. Bible—Meditations. I. Yancey, Philip. II. Title.
BS390.Y36 1989
220.5'208—dc20   89–16430
                                                              CIP

Unless otherwise noted, Scripture quotations are taken from the *Holy Bible: New International Version* (North American Edition), copyright © 1973, 1978, 1984 by The International Bible Society. Used by permission of Zondervan Bible Publishers.

Printed in the United States of America

89 90 91 92 93 94 / AF / 10 9 8 7 6 5 4 3 2 1

Special thanks to
Nia Jones, who directed the editing of this project,
Susan McQuilkin, who assisted in the editing, and
Nancy Wilson, who oversaw a complicated typesetting assignment.

Contents

PAUL'S LEGACY

VITAL LETTERS

Preface

Before beginning work on *The Student Bible*, Tim Stafford and I commissioned a research team to study Bible-reading habits. Of the people surveyed, everyone owned a Bible and nearly all of them wanted to read it regularly. Yet many had simply given up out of a sense of discouragement.

Little wonder. The Bible is a big book, about 1000 pages long. Moreover, it consists of sixty-six different parts written by several dozen authors. Readers who approach it like any other book—beginning with page 1 and proceeding toward the end—soon find themselves lost in a bewildering maze of ancient history.

Commonly, we found, such readers abandon the straight-through method in favor of the "hunt and peck" method, showing a distinct partiality toward Psalms and certain letters in the New Testament. As an author, I cringe to think what would happen if people read my books in the same way they read the Bible. What if a reader picked up one of my books and arbitrarily turned to a stray sentence or paragraph on page 127? Probably it would not make sense; possibly the passage, wrenched out of its context, might convey the opposite of what I intended to communicate.

In view of these problems, I have concluded that *orientation* is one of the greatest needs facing Bible readers. A sense of what the whole book is about would shed light on each of the individual parts. And that's exactly what I hope to accomplish with *A Guided Tour of the Bible*. The readings (adapted from "Track 3" in *The Student Bible*) present an overview of the entire Bible through 180 selected passages. They include at least one chapter from each of the Bible's sixty-six books.

The comments accompanying each reading provide continuity, and help to bridge the 2000-year gap back to when the Bible was written. Taken together, the daily readings and comments will provide a good foundation of Bible understanding. Readers of *The Student Bible* will note that *A Guided Tour* uses the same basic approach as that edition of the Bible, and in some cases draws from *The Student Bible* notes.

This "Guided Tour" is exactly that, a guide-assisted tour of the Bible's highlights, with the goal of presenting the underlying story or "plot." Such a plan is no substitute for mastering the whole Bible, of course, but it may help lower barriers and point the way down a path for further study. Think of it as something like an introductory tour through a great art museum. You won't get to see every painting in the museum, but you will learn the basic layout, and may also acquire a taste for art that will entice you to return and browse at a more leisurely pace.

Since *A Guided Tour* is arranged in 180 separate readings, most people will find it convenient to read one designated passage each day, along with the introductory notes. If you miss a few days, don't worry. Just resume reading when you can. In 180 total days you will get the full overview.

With a few exceptions, I have arranged the biblical material in rough chronological order. You will read the psalms attributed to David as you read about David's life, and the Prophets as you read about their background history. Portions from the Gospels, too, are interspersed, giving a composite picture of Jesus' life on earth; and Paul's letters are scattered throughout the record of his life. This unconventional arrangement should help convey the Bible's "plot."

I readily acknowledge the disadvantages of reading the Bible in a "chopped-up" format. You will miss the flow and overall impact of individual books. And since the readings comprise less than fifteen percent of the Bible, you will miss many of the most familiar and rewarding passages. But I fervently hope that the program of this book will be one step in helping prepare you for a lifetime habit of Bible reading. The Bible is the most important book ever written—a gift to us from God himself. The meaning we get out of it corresponds directly to the energy we put into it.

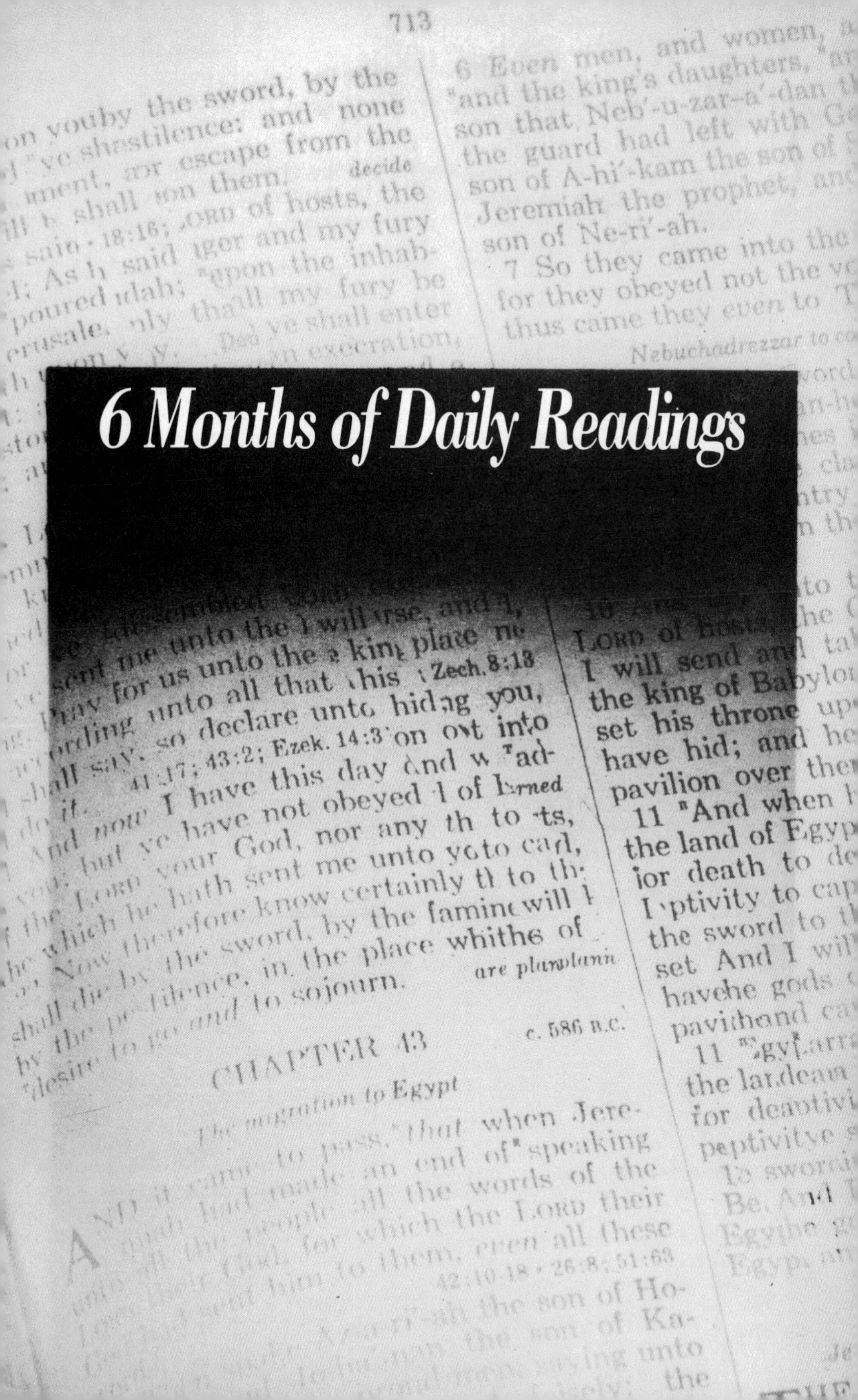

6 Months of Daily Readings

When It All Began

Genesis 1

Everything, truly everything, begins here. The story of the Bible—more, the history of the universe—starts with the simple statement, "In the beginning God created," and the rest of the chapter fills in what he created: stars, oceans, plants, birds, fish, mammals, and finally man and woman.

Genesis 1 says little about the processes God used in creation; you'll find no explanations of DNA or the scientific principles behind creation. But the opening chapter of the Bible does insist on two facts:

1. Creation was God's work. "And God said. . . . And God said. . . . And God said"—the phrase beats in cadence all the way through the chapter, a chapter that mentions the word *God* thirty times. And in this first chapter, the very first glimpse we have of God is as an artist. Butterflies, waterfalls, bottlenose dolphins, praying mantises, kangaroos—they were all his idea. This entire magnificent world we live in is the product of his creative work. God, no one else, is the master of the universe, and all that follows in the Bible reinforces the message of Genesis 1: Behind all of history, there is God.

2. Creation was good. Another sentence tolls softly, like a bell, throughout this chapter: "And God saw that it was good." In our day, we hear alarming reports about nature: the greenhouse effect, polluted oceans, vanishing species, the destruction of rain forests. Much has changed, much has been spoiled since that first moment of creation. Genesis 1 describes the world as God wanted it, before any spoiling. Whatever beauty we sense in nature today is a faint echo of that pristine state.

Captain Frank Borman, one of America's Apollo astronauts, read this chapter on a telecast from outer space on Christmas Eve. As he gazed out of his window, he saw earth as a brightly colored ball hanging alone in the darkness of space. It looked at once awesomely beautiful, and terribly fragile. It looked like the view from Genesis 1.

> **To Reflect On:** *When was the last time you noticed, really noticed, the beauty of the natural world?*

GENESIS 1

The Beginning

1 In the beginning God created the heavens and the earth. ²Now the earth was formless and empty, darkness was over the surface of the deep, and the Spirit of God was hovering over the waters.

³And God said, "Let there be light," and there was light. ⁴God saw that the light was good, and he separated the light from the darkness. ⁵God called the light "day," and the darkness he called "night." And there was evening, and there was morning—the first day.

⁶And God said, "Let there be an expanse between the waters to separate water from water." ⁷So God made the expanse and separated the water under the expanse from the water above it. And it was so. ⁸God called the expanse "sky." And there was evening, and there was morning—the second day.

⁹And God said, "Let the water under the sky be gathered to one place, and let dry ground appear." And it was so. ¹⁰God called the dry ground "land," and the gathered waters he called "seas." And God saw that it was good.

11 Then God said, "Let the land produce vegetation: seed-bearing plants and trees on the land that bear fruit with seed in it, according to their various kinds." And it was so. 12 The land produced vegetation: plants bearing seed according to their kinds and trees bearing fruit with seed in it according to their kinds. And God saw that it was good. 13 And there was evening, and there was morning—the third day.

14 And God said, "Let there be lights in the expanse of the sky to separate the day from the night, and let them serve as signs to mark seasons and days and years, 15 and let them be lights in the expanse of the sky to give light on the earth." And it was so. 16 God made two great lights—the greater light to govern the day and the lesser light to govern the night. He also made the stars. 17 God set them in the expanse of the sky to give light on the earth, 18 to govern the day and the night, and to separate light from darkness. And God saw that it was good. 19 And there was evening, and there was morning—the fourth day.

20 And God said, "Let the water teem with living creatures, and let birds fly above the earth across the expanse of the sky." 21 So God created the great creatures of the sea and every living and moving thing with which the water teems, according to their kinds, and every winged bird according to its kind. And God saw that it was good. 22 God blessed them and said, "Be fruitful and increase in number and fill the water in the seas, and let the birds increase on the earth." 23 And there was evening, and there was morning—the fifth day.

24 And God said, "Let the land produce living creatures according to their kinds: livestock, creatures that move along the ground, and wild animals, each according to its kind." And it was so. 25 God made the wild animals according to their kinds, the livestock according to their kinds, and all the creatures that move along the ground according to their kinds. And God saw that it was good.

26 Then God said, "Let us make man in our image, in our likeness, and let them rule over the fish of the sea and the birds of the air, over the livestock, over all the earth, and over all the creatures that move along the ground."

27 So God created man in his own image,
    in the image of God he created him;
    male and female he created them.

28 God blessed them and said to them, "Be fruitful and increase in number; fill the earth and subdue it. Rule over the fish of the sea and the birds of the air and over every living creature that moves on the ground."

29 Then God said, "I give you every seed-bearing plant on the face of the whole earth and every tree that has fruit with seed in it. They will be yours for food. 30 And to all the beasts of the earth and all the birds of the air and all the creatures that move on the ground—everything that has the breath of life in it—I give every green plant for food." And it was so.

31 God saw all that he had made, and it was very good. And there was evening, and there was morning—the sixth day.

Human Close-up

Genesis 2

The Bible begins and ends with the same setting: a garden watered by a river, the Tree of Life, human beings in the actual presence of God. Eden, where the first human beings lived, was paradise in the fullest sense of the word, and the last book, Revelation, promises that God will someday restore that Paradise. The two scenes are like brackets of perfection around the history of a badly scarred planet.

After presenting the cosmic view in chapter 1, Genesis 2 repeats the story of creation, narrowing the focus to human beings. They alone, of all God's works, are made "in God's image." People have disagreed over the years on what, exactly, that phrase "image of God" means. Is it immortality? Intelligence? Creativity? Relationship? Perhaps the best way to understand is to think of "the image of God" as a mirror. God created human beings so that when he looked upon them he would see reflected something of himself.

Genesis makes the point that human beings are profoundly different from all of God's other creations. We recognize that difference instinctively: You won't go to jail for running over a dog or cat, but you might go to jail for running over a man or woman. Human life is somehow different, more "sacred." Alone of all creation, human beings received the breath of life from God himself.

Human history is just getting underway, and in a compact space Genesis 2 tells the origin of much of human activity. Marriage begins here. Even in a state of perfection, Adam felt loneliness and desire, and God provided woman. From then on, marriage would take priority over all other relationships.

Work begins here, too. Adam was set in a role of authority over the animals and plants. He named them and tended to the plants and creatures of the Garden. Ever since, humans have had a kind of mastery over the rest of creation.

Only the slightest hint of foreboding clouds this blissful scene of Paradise. It appears in verse 17, in the form of a single negative command from God. Adam enjoyed perfect freedom—with this one small exception—a test of obedience.

Throughout history, artists have tried to recreate in words and images what a perfect world would look like, a world of love and beauty, a world without guilt or suffering or shame. Genesis 1–2 describes such a world. For a time, the universe was at peace. When God looked at all he had created, he paid humanity its highest compliment. "Very good," he pronounced, satisfied. Creation was now complete.

To Reflect On: *If you could design a paradise, what would it look like?*

———————————◆———————————

GENESIS 2

2 Thus the heavens and the earth were completed in all their vast array.
²By the seventh day God had finished the work he had been doing; so on the seventh day he rested from all his work. ³And God blessed the seventh day and made it holy, because on it he rested from all the work of creating that he had done.

Adam and Eve

⁴This is the account of the heavens and the earth when they were created.

When the LORD God made the earth and the heavens—⁵and no shrub of the field had yet appeared on the earth and no plant of the field had yet sprung up, for the LORD God had not sent rain on the earth and there was no man to work the ground, ⁶but streams came up from the earth and watered the whole surface of the ground—⁷the LORD God formed the man from the dust of the ground and breathed into his nostrils the breath of life, and the man became a living being.
⁸Now the LORD God had planted a garden in the east, in Eden; and there he put the man he had formed. ⁹And the LORD God made all kinds of trees grow out of the ground—trees that were pleasing to the eye and good for food. In the middle of the garden were the tree of life and the tree of the knowledge of good and evil.
¹⁰A river watering the garden flowed from Eden; from there it was separated into four headwaters. ¹¹The name of the first is the Pishon; it winds through the entire land of Havilah, where there is gold. ¹²(The gold of that land is good; aromatic resin and onyx are also there.) ¹³The name of the second river is the Gihon; it winds through the

entire land of Cush. ¹⁴The name of the third river is the Tigris; it runs along the east side of Asshur. And the fourth river is the Euphrates.

¹⁵The LORD God took the man and put him in the Garden of Eden to work it and take care of it. ¹⁶And the LORD God commanded the man, "You are free to eat from any tree in the garden; ¹⁷but you must not eat from the tree of the knowledge of good and evil, for when you eat of it you will surely die."

¹⁸The LORD God said, "It is not good for the man to be alone. I will make a helper suitable for him."

¹⁹Now the LORD God had formed out of the ground all the beasts of the field and all the birds of the air. He brought them to the man to see what he would name them; and whatever the man called each living creature, that was its name. ²⁰So the man gave names to all the livestock, the birds of the air and all the beasts of the field.

But for Adam no suitable helper was found. ²¹So the LORD God caused the man to fall into a deep sleep; and while he was sleeping, he took one of the man's ribs and closed up the place with flesh. ²²Then the LORD God made a woman from the rib he had taken out of the man, and he brought her to the man.

²³The man said,

"This is now bone of my bones
    and flesh of my flesh;
she shall be called 'woman,'
    for she was taken out of man."

²⁴For this reason a man will leave his father and mother and be united to his wife, and they will become one flesh.
²⁵The man and his wife were both naked, and they felt no shame.

The Crash

Genesis 3

The fall of man" theologians call it, but really it was more like a crash. Adam and Eve, living in Paradise, had everything a person could want, and yet still a thought nagged them, "Are we somehow missing out? Is God keeping something from us?" Like any human being, like every human being who has ever lived, they could not resist the temptation to reach for what lay beyond them.

"There is only one doctrine that can be empirically verified," said George Bernard Shaw, "the doctrine of original sin." Genesis gives few details about that first sin. Only one thing mattered: God had labeled one tree, just one, off-limits. Many people mistakenly assume sex was involved, but in fact something far more basic was at stake. The real issue was: Who will set the rules—the humans or God? Adam and Eve decided in favor of themselves, and the world has never been the same.

Adam and Eve reacted to their sin like anybody reacts to sin. They rationalized, explained themselves, and looked for someone else to take the blame. The author of Genesis pointedly notes that they also felt the need to hide. They hid from each other, sensing for the first time a feeling of shame over their nakedness. Perhaps the greatest change of all, however, occurred in their relationship with God. Previously they had walked and talked with God in the Garden, as with a friend. Now, when they heard his voice, they hid in the brush.

Genesis 3 tells of other profound changes that affected the world when the creatures chose against their Creator. Suffering multiplied. Work became harder, more like drudgery. A new word, *death*, entered human vocabulary. In short, the scene of perfection was permanently spoiled.

The underlying message of Genesis goes against some common assumptions about human history. According to these chapters, the world and humanity have not been gradually evolving toward a better and better state. Long ago, we wrecked against the rocks of our own pride and stubbornness. We're still bearing the consequences: all wars, all violence, all broken relationships, all grief and sadness trace back to that one monumental day in the Garden of Eden.

> **To Reflect On:** *Have you ever felt hemmed-in or stifled by one of God's commands? How did you respond?*

GENESIS 3

The Fall of Man

3 Now the serpent was more crafty than any of the wild animals the LORD God had made. He said to the woman, "Did God really say, 'You must not eat from any tree in the garden'?"

²The woman said to the serpent, "We may eat fruit from the trees in the garden, ³but God did say, 'You must not eat fruit from the tree that is in the middle of the garden, and you must not touch it, or you will die.'"

⁴"You will not surely die," the serpent said to the woman. ⁵"For God knows that when you eat of it your eyes will be opened, and you will be like God, knowing good and evil."

⁶When the woman saw that the fruit of the tree was good for food and pleasing to the eye, and also desirable for gaining wisdom, she took some and ate it. She also gave some to her husband, who was with her, and he ate it. ⁷Then the eyes of both of them were opened, and they realized they were naked; so they sewed fig leaves together and made coverings for themselves.

⁸Then the man and his wife heard the sound of the LORD God as he was walking in the garden in the cool of the day, and they hid from the LORD God among the trees of the garden. ⁹But the LORD God called to the man, "Where are you?"

¹⁰He answered, "I heard you in the garden, and I was afraid because I was naked; so I hid."

¹¹And he said, "Who told you that you were naked? Have you eaten from the tree that I commanded you not to eat from?"

¹²The man said, "The woman you put here with me—she gave me some fruit from the tree, and I ate it."

¹³Then the LORD God said to the woman, "What is this you have done?"

The woman said, "The serpent deceived me, and I ate."

¹⁴So the LORD God said to the serpent, "Because you have done this,

"Cursed are you above all the livestock
    and all the wild animals!

You will crawl on your belly
    and you will eat dust
    all the days of your life.

¹⁵And I will put enmity
    between you and the woman,
    and between your offspring and hers;
he will crush your head,
    and you will strike his heel."

¹⁶To the woman he said,

"I will greatly increase your pains in
    childbearing;
    with pain you will give birth to
    children.
Your desire will be for your husband,
    and he will rule over you."

¹⁷To Adam he said, "Because you listened to your wife and ate from the tree about which I commanded you, 'You must not eat of it,'

"Cursed is the ground because of you;
    through painful toil you will eat of it
    all the days of your life.

¹⁸It will produce thorns and thistles for
        you,
    and you will eat the plants of the
        field.

¹⁹By the sweat of your brow
    you will eat your food
until you return to the ground,
    since from it you were taken;
for dust you are
    and to dust you will return."

²⁰Adam named his wife Eve, because she would become the mother of all the living.

²¹The LORD God made garments of skin for Adam and his wife and clothed them. ²²And the LORD God said, "The man has now become like one of us, knowing good and evil. He must not be allowed to reach out his hand and take also from the tree of life and eat, and live forever." ²³So the LORD God banished him from the Garden of Eden to work the ground from which he had been taken. ²⁴After he drove the man out, he placed on the east side of the Garden of Eden cherubim and a flaming sword flashing back and forth to guard the way to the tree of life.

Crouching at the Door

Genesis 4:1–24

Creation, the origins of man and woman, a fall into sin—in three chapters Genesis has set the stage for human history, and now that history begins to play itself out. The first childbirth—imagine the shock!—the first formal worship, the first division of labor, the first extended families and cities and signs of culture all appear in chapter 4. But one "first" overshadows all the others: the first death of a human being, a death by murder.

It took just one generation for sin to enter the world, and by the second generation people were already killing each other; the malignant results of the Fall spread that quickly. The early part of Genesis shows God intervening often in response. Here, unable to ignore the horrible changes that have crept into his world, God steps in once again with a custom-designed punishment. Cain was to bear the resulting mark with shame the rest of his life, but a few generations later a man named Lamech would brag about his murders.

Not all the news was bad. Civilization progressed rather quickly, with some people learning agriculture, some choosing to work with tools of bronze and iron, and some discovering music and the arts. In this way, human beings began to fulfill the role assigned them as masters over the created world. But despite these advances, history was sliding along another track as well. Every person who followed Adam and Eve faced the same choice of whether or not to obey God's word. And, with numbing monotony, all chose like their original parents.

God's warning to Cain applied to everyone who followed, "If you do not do what is right, sin is crouching at your door; it desires to have you, but you must master it." The next few chapters tell of an ever-worsening spiral of rebellion and evil.

To Reflect On: *Note Cain's response when God confronted him. What do you think you would say if God appeared in person to confront you over some sin?*

GENESIS 4:1–24

Cain and Abel

4 Adam lay with his wife Eve, and she became pregnant and gave birth to Cain. She said, "With the help of the LORD I have brought forth a man." ²Later she gave birth to his brother Abel.

Now Abel kept flocks, and Cain worked the soil. ³In the course of time Cain brought some of the fruits of the soil as an offering to the LORD. ⁴But Abel brought fat portions from some of the firstborn of his flock. The LORD looked with favor on Abel and his offering, ⁵but on Cain and his offering he did not look with favor. So Cain was very angry, and his face was downcast.

⁶Then the LORD said to Cain, "Why are you angry? Why is your face downcast? ⁷If you do what is right, will you not be accepted? But if you do not do what is right, sin is crouching at your door; it desires to have you, but you must master it."

⁸Now Cain said to his brother Abel, "Let's go out to the field." And while they were in the field, Cain attacked his brother Abel and killed him.

⁹Then the LORD said to Cain, "Where is your brother Abel?"

"I don't know," he replied. "Am I my brother's keeper?"

¹⁰The LORD said, "What have you done? Listen! Your brother's blood cries out to me from the ground. ¹¹Now you are under a curse and driven from the ground, which opened its mouth to receive your brother's blood from your hand. ¹²When you work the ground, it will no longer yield its crops for you. You will be a restless wanderer on the earth."

¹³Cain said to the LORD, "My punishment is more than I can bear. ¹⁴Today you are driving me from the land, and I will be hidden from your presence; I will be a restless wanderer on the earth, and whoever finds me will kill me."

¹⁵But the LORD said to him, "Not so; if anyone kills Cain, he will suffer vengeance seven times over." Then the LORD put a mark on Cain so that no one who found him would kill him. ¹⁶So Cain went out from the LORD's presence and lived in the land of Nod, east of Eden.

¹⁷Cain lay with his wife, and she became pregnant and gave birth to Enoch. Cain was then building a city, and he named it after his son Enoch. ¹⁸To Enoch was born Irad, and Irad was the father of Mehujael, and Mehujael was the father of Methushael, and Methushael was the father of Lamech.

¹⁹Lamech married two women, one named Adah and the other Zillah. ²⁰Adah gave birth to Jabal; he was the father of those who live in tents and raise livestock. ²¹His brother's name was Jubal; he was the father of all who play the harp and flute. ²²Zillah also had a son, Tubal-Cain, who forged all kinds of tools out of bronze and iron. Tubal-Cain's sister was Naamah.

²³Lamech said to his wives,

"Adah and Zillah, listen to me;
  wives of Lamech, hear my words.
I have killed a man for wounding me,
  a young man for injuring me.
²⁴If Cain is avenged seven times,
  then Lamech seventy-seven times."

Under Water

Genesis 7

The downward cycle of sin and rebellion continued until, finally, God reached a fateful decision. Genesis 6 records it in what is surely the most poignant sentence ever written, "The LORD was grieved that he had made man on the earth, and his heart was filled with pain." It seemed clear that the human experiment had failed. God, who had taken such pride in his creation, was now ready to destroy it. He could no longer tolerate the violence that had spread across his world.

Legends of a great flood exist in the records of cultures in the Middle East, in Asia, and in South America. One Babylonian document in particular ("The Epic of Gilgamesh") has many parallels to the account in this chapter. But Genesis presents the flood not merely as an accident of geography or climate; it was an act of God. The churning waters described in this chapter stand as a symbol of how far humankind had fallen. Torrents of water swept through towns and cities, forests and deserts, destroying every living or man-made thing.

But Noah's ark—a huge, ungainly boat riding out the storm—stands as a symbol, too: a symbol of mercy. God had resolved to give earth a second chance, which explains why he ordered Noah to meticulously preserve representatives from every species.

Genesis underscores one message above all: The first human beings on earth made a mess of things. Beginning with the rebellion in Genesis 3, the humans had brought on the downfall of all creation. And when the time of judgment came, only eight survived: Noah and his wife and their sons and wives.

To Reflect On: *Many people have the idea that human nature is basically good. Do you agree?*

GENESIS 7

7 The LORD then said to Noah, "Go into the ark, you and your whole family, because I have found you righteous in this generation. ²Take with you seven of every kind of clean animal, a male and its mate, and two of every kind of unclean animal, a male and its mate, ³and also seven of every kind of bird, male and female, to keep their various kinds alive throughout the earth. ⁴Seven days from now I will send rain on the earth for forty days and forty nights, and I will wipe from the face of the earth every living creature I have made."

⁵And Noah did all that the LORD commanded him.

⁶Noah was six hundred years old when the floodwaters came on the earth. ⁷And Noah and his sons and his wife and his sons' wives entered the ark to escape the waters of the flood. ⁸Pairs of clean and unclean animals, of birds and of all creatures that move along the ground, ⁹male and female, came to Noah and entered the ark, as God had commanded Noah. ¹⁰And after the seven days the floodwaters came on the earth.

¹¹In the six hundredth year of Noah's life, on the seventeenth day of the second month—on that day all the springs of the great deep burst forth, and the floodgates of the heavens were opened. ¹²And rain fell on the earth forty days and forty nights.

¹³On that very day Noah and his sons, Shem, Ham and Japheth, together with his wife and the wives of his three sons, entered the ark. ¹⁴They had with them every wild animal according to its kind, all livestock according to their kinds, every creature that moves along the ground according to its kind and every bird according to its kind, everything with wings. ¹⁵Pairs of all creatures that have the breath of life in them came to Noah and entered the ark. ¹⁶The animals going in were male and female of every living thing, as God had commanded Noah. Then the LORD shut him in.

¹⁷For forty days the flood kept coming on the earth, and as the waters increased they lifted the ark high above the earth. ¹⁸The waters rose and increased greatly on the earth, and the ark floated on the surface of the water. ¹⁹They rose greatly on the earth, and all the high mountains under the entire heavens were covered. ²⁰The waters rose and covered the mountains to a depth of more than twenty feet. ²¹Every living thing that moved on the earth perished—birds, livestock, wild animals, all the creatures that swarm over the earth, and all mankind. ²²Everything on dry land that had the breath of life in its nostrils died. ²³Every living thing on the face of the earth was wiped out; men and animals and the creatures that move along the ground and the birds of the air were wiped from the earth. Only Noah was left, and those with him in the ark.

²⁴The waters flooded the earth for a hundred and fifty days.

A New Start

Genesis 8:1–9:7

The gloomy tone of Genesis 7 brightens almost immediately. The next chapter tells of Noah and his family landing on an earth fresh-scrubbed and sprouting new life. All the people who had so grievously offended God had died off. For the first time in years, human beings sought to please God: In his first act on land, Noah made an offering of thanksgiving.

God showed his pleasure by responding with a solemn promise, the first of several *covenants* in the Bible. The terms of the covenant reveal how deeply Adam's fall had affected all of creation. Man had cast a shadow across all nature, a shadow of fear and dread that would continue to spread throughout the animal kingdom. God's covenant recognized certain sad adjustments to the original design of the world. It took for granted that human beings would continue to kill, not only the animals, but also each other.

Despite these adjustments God promised, regardless of what might happen, that never again would he destroy life on such a massive scale. He vowed, in effect, to find another way to deal with the rebellion and violence of man, "though every inclination of his heart is evil from childhood."

An appropriate symbol—the rainbow—marked this first recorded covenant by God. Noah, like Adam before him, had a chance for a brand-new start. Honored by God's special approval, he had the opportunity to set civilization on a whole new course. But before long, Noah went the way of his predecessors—the last glimpse Genesis gives of him, he is sprawled in his tent, drunken and naked.

What seemed like a brand-new story turns out to be a tired recapitulation of the same old story of human failure.

To Reflect On: *What does God's covenant with Noah teach about the uniqueness of human life?*

GENESIS 8:1–9:7

8 But God remembered Noah and all the wild animals and the livestock that were with him in the ark, and he sent a wind over the earth, and the waters receded. ²Now the springs of the deep and the floodgates of the heavens had been closed, and the rain had stopped falling from the sky. ³The water receded steadily from the earth. At the end of the hundred and fifty days the water had gone down, ⁴and on the seventeenth day of the seventh month the ark came to rest on the mountains of Ararat. ⁵The waters continued to recede until the tenth month, and on the first day of the tenth month the tops of the mountains became visible.

⁶After forty days Noah opened the window he had made in the ark ⁷and sent out a raven, and it kept flying back and forth until the water had dried up from the earth. ⁸Then he sent out a dove to see if the water had receded from the surface of the ground. ⁹But the dove could find no place to set its feet because there was water over all the surface of the earth; so it returned to Noah in the ark. He reached out his hand and took the dove and brought it back to himself in the ark. ¹⁰He waited seven more days and again sent out the dove from the ark. ¹¹When the dove returned to him in the evening, there in its beak was a freshly plucked olive leaf! Then Noah knew that the water had receded from the earth. ¹²He waited seven more days and sent the dove out again, but this time it did not return to him.

¹³By the first day of the first month of Noah's six hundred and first year, the water had dried up from the earth. Noah then removed the covering from the ark and saw that the surface of the ground was dry. ¹⁴By the twenty-seventh day of the second month the earth was completely dry.

¹⁵Then God said to Noah, ¹⁶"Come out of the ark, you and your wife and your sons and their wives. ¹⁷Bring out every kind of living creature that is with you—the birds, the animals, and all the creatures that move along the ground—so they can multiply on the earth and be fruitful and increase in number upon it."

¹⁸So Noah came out, together with his sons and his wife and his sons' wives. ¹⁹All the animals and all the creatures that move along the ground and all the birds—everything that moves on the earth—came out of the ark, one kind after another.

²⁰Then Noah built an altar to the LORD and, taking some of all the clean animals and clean birds, he sacrificed burnt offerings on it. ²¹The LORD smelled the pleasing aroma and said in his heart: "Never again will I curse the ground because of man, even though every inclination of his heart is evil from childhood. And never again will I destroy all living creatures, as I have done.

> ²²"As long as the earth endures,
> seedtime and harvest,
> cold and heat,
> summer and winter,
> day and night
> will never cease."

God's Covenant With Noah

9 Then God blessed Noah and his sons, saying to them, "Be fruitful and increase in number and fill the earth. ²The fear and dread of you will fall upon all the beasts of the earth and all the birds of the air, upon every creature that moves along the ground, and upon all the fish of the sea; they are given into your hands. ³Everything that lives and moves will be food for you. Just as I gave you the green plants, I now give you everything.

⁴"But you must not eat meat that has its lifeblood still in it. ⁵And for your lifeblood I will surely demand an accounting. I will demand an accounting from every animal. And from each man, too, I will demand an accounting for the life of his fellow man.

> ⁶"Whoever sheds the blood of man,
> by man shall his blood be shed;
> for in the image of God
> has God made man.

⁷As for you, be fruitful and increase in number; multiply on the earth and increase upon it."

The Plan

Genesis 15

Many times God had intervened directly in human history, but almost always for the sake of punishment—in Adam's day, and Cain's, and in the days of Noah, and at Babel. After scanning these centuries of dismal failure, Genesis changes dramatically at chapter 12. It leaves the big picture of world history and settles on one lonely individual, not a great king or a wealthy landowner, but a childless nomad named Abraham.

It's almost impossible to exaggerate the importance of Abraham in the Bible. To the Jews, he represents the father of a nation, but to all of us he represents far more. He was a singular man of faith whose relationship to God was so close that for many centuries God himself was known as "the God of Abraham."

In effect, God was narrowing the scope of his activity on earth by separating out one group of people he could have a unique relationship with. They would be set apart from other men and women as God's peculiar treasures, his kingdom of priests. This special group would by example teach the rest of the world the advantages of loving and serving God. And Abraham was the father of this new humanity.

Dozens of other passages in the Old Testament set forth the details of God's covenant, or contract, with his chosen people. (The word *testament* means covenant.) Here is what God promised Abraham:

A new land to live in. Trusting God, Abraham left his home and traveled hundreds of miles toward Canaan.

A large and prosperous family. This dream obsessed Abraham and, when its fulfillment seemed long in coming, tested his faith severely.

A great nation. It took many centuries after Abraham for this promise to come true, but finally, in the days of David and Solomon, the Jews at last became a nation.

A blessing to the whole world. From the beginning, God made clear that he chose the Jews not as an end, but as a means to the end goal of reaching other nations.

Genesis 12 records God's first announcement of the plan to Abraham. In this chapter, God responds to Abraham's faltering faith with a fiery vision that seals the promise.

> **To Reflect On:** *Do people still rely on "covenants," or contracts today? What purpose do they serve?*

———————•———————

GENESIS 15

God's Covenant With Abram

15 After this, the word of the LORD came to Abram in a vision:

"Do not be afraid, Abram.
  I am your shield,
  your very great reward."

²But Abram said, "O Sovereign LORD, what can you give me since I remain childless and the one who will inherit my estate is Eliezer of Damascus?" ³And Abram said, "You have given me no children; so a servant in my household will be my heir." ⁴Then the word of the LORD came to him: "This man will not be your heir, but a son coming from your own body will be your heir." ⁵He took him outside and said, "Look up at the heavens and count the stars—if indeed you can count them." Then he said to him, "So shall your offspring be."

⁶Abram believed the LORD, and he credited it to him as righteousness.

⁷He also said to him, "I am the LORD, who brought you out of Ur of the Chaldeans to give you this land to take possession of it."

⁸But Abram said, "O Sovereign LORD, how can I know that I will gain possession of it?"

⁹So the LORD said to him, "Bring me a heifer, a goat and a ram, each three years old, along with a dove and a young pigeon."

¹⁰Abram brought all these to him, cut them in two and arranged the halves opposite each other; the birds, however, he did not cut in half. ¹¹Then birds of prey came down on the carcasses, but Abram drove them away.

¹²As the sun was setting, Abram fell into a deep sleep, and a thick and dreadful darkness came over him. ¹³Then the LORD said to him, "Know for certain that your descendants will be strangers in a country not their own, and they will be enslaved and mistreated four hundred years. ¹⁴But I will punish the nation they serve as slaves, and afterward they will come out with great possessions. ¹⁵You, however, will go to your fathers in peace and be buried at a good old age. ¹⁶In the fourth generation your descendants will come back here, for the sin of the Amorites has not yet reached its full measure."

¹⁷When the sun had set and darkness had fallen, a smoking firepot with a blazing torch appeared and passed between the pieces. ¹⁸On that day the LORD made a covenant with Abram and said, "To your descendants I give this land, from the river of Egypt to the great river, the Euphrates— ¹⁹the land of the Kenites, Kenizzites, Kadmonites, ²⁰Hittites, Perizzites, Rephaites, ²¹Amorites, Canaanites, Girgashites and Jebusites."

Sodom and Gomorrah

Genesis 19

Like a photo negative, this chapter shows by contrast what Abraham was up against in his efforts to found a new and godly nation. His own brother lived in the city of Sodom, a sordid place that saw visiting strangers—angels, as it turned out—as prime targets for gang rape. Sexual violence was just one of Sodom's problems; Ezekiel 16:49 says that Sodom was "arrogant, overfed, and unconcerned; they did not help the poor and needy."

Despite Sodom's woeful condition, God was willing to let the city survive if Abraham could locate a mere ten righteous people there. Ten such people did not exist, and God's patience finally ran out. Once more he stepped in with direct punishment, not to destroy the whole world, but to wipe out two centers of evil.

In typical style, the Bible doesn't bother with scientific explanations of the destruction. Was it a volcanic eruption? The Bible does not say, and the area, now apparently at the bottom of the Dead Sea, cannot easily be investigated. Genesis stresses not how it happened, but why.

According to this chapter, Lot did not learn a lesson from Sodom. Later, in a drunken state, he committed incest with his daughters, producing two family lines that would be traditional enemies of Abraham's family, the Jews.

Jesus later used the account of Sodom and Gomorrah as a warning to people who saw his miracles, but ignored them (Matthew 11). God may not always intervene so spectacularly, but this story serves as a warning that his tolerance for evil has a limit.

To Reflect On: *Are any catastrophes of our time punishments from God? How would you know?*

GENESIS 19

Sodom and Gomorrah Destroyed

19 The two angels arrived at Sodom in the evening, and Lot was sitting in the gateway of the city. When he saw them, he got up to meet them and bowed down with his face to the ground. 2"My lords," he said, "please turn aside to your servant's house. You can wash your feet and spend the night and then go on your way early in the morning."

"No," they answered, "we will spend the night in the square."

3But he insisted so strongly that they did go with him and entered his house. He prepared a meal for them, baking bread without yeast, and they ate. 4Before they had gone to bed, all the men from every part of the city of Sodom—both young and old—surrounded the house. 5They called to Lot, "Where are the men who came to you tonight? Bring them out to us so that we can have sex with them."

6Lot went outside to meet them and shut the door behind him 7and said, "No, my friends. Don't do this wicked thing. 8Look, I have two daughters who have never slept with a man. Let me bring them out to you, and you can do what you like with them. But don't do anything to these men, for they have come under the protection of my roof."

9"Get out of our way," they replied. And they said, "This fellow came here as an alien, and now he wants to play the judge! We'll treat you worse than them." They kept bringing pressure on Lot and moved forward to break down the door.

10But the men inside reached out and pulled Lot back into the house and shut the door. 11Then they struck the men who were at the door of the house, young and old, with blindness so that they could not find the door.

12The two men said to Lot, "Do you have anyone else here—sons-in-law, sons or daughters, or anyone else in the city who belongs to you? Get them out of here, 13because we are going to destroy this place. The outcry to the LORD against its people is so great that he has sent us to destroy it."

14So Lot went out and spoke to his sons-in-law, who were pledged to marry his daughters. He said, "Hurry and get out of this place, because the LORD is about to destroy the city!" But his sons-in-law thought he was joking.

15With the coming of dawn, the angels urged Lot, saying, "Hurry! Take your wife and your two daughters who are here, or you will be swept away when the city is punished."

16When he hesitated, the men grasped his hand and the hands of his wife and of his two daughters and led them safely out of the city, for the LORD was merciful to them. 17As soon as they had brought them out, one of them said, "Flee for your lives! Don't look back, and don't stop anywhere in the plain! Flee to the mountains or you will be swept away!"

18But Lot said to them, "No, my lords, please! 19Your servant has found favor in your eyes, and you have shown great kindness to me in sparing my life. But I can't flee to the mountains; this disaster will overtake me, and I'll die. 20Look, here is a town near enough to run to, and it is small. Let me flee to it—it is very small, isn't it? Then my life will be spared."

21He said to him, "Very well, I will grant this request too; I will not overthrow the town you speak of. 22But flee there quickly, because I cannot do anything until you reach it." (That is why the town was called Zoar.)

23By the time Lot reached Zoar, the sun had risen over the land. 24Then the LORD rained down burning sulfur on Sodom and Gomorrah—from the LORD out of the heavens. 25Thus he overthrew those cities and the entire plain, including all those living in the cities—and also the vegetation in the land. 26But Lot's wife looked back, and she became a pillar of salt.

27Early the next morning Abraham got up and returned to the place where he had stood before the LORD. 28He looked down toward Sodom and Gomorrah, toward all the land of the plain, and he saw dense smoke rising from the land, like smoke from a furnace.

29So when God destroyed the cities of the plain, he remembered Abraham, and he brought Lot out of the catastrophe that overthrew the cities where Lot had lived.

Lot and His Daughters

30Lot and his two daughters left Zoar and settled in the mountains, for he was afraid to stay in Zoar. He and his two daughters lived in a cave. 31One day the older daughter said to the younger, "Our father is old, and there is no man around here to lie with us, as is the custom all over the earth. 32Let's get our father to drink wine and then lie with him and preserve our family line through our father."

33That night they got their father to drink wine, and the older daughter went in and lay with him. He was not aware of it when she lay down or when she got up.

34The next day the older daughter said to the younger, "Last night I lay with my father. Let's get him to drink wine again tonight, and you go in and lie with him so we can preserve our family line through our father." 35So they got their father to drink wine that night also, and the younger daughter went and lay with him. Again he was not aware of it when she lay down or when she got up.

36So both of Lot's daughters became pregnant by their father. 37The older daughter had a son, and she named him Moab; he is the father of the Moabites of today. 38The younger daughter also had a son, and she named him Ben-Ammi; he is the father of the Ammonites of today.

Final Exam

Genesis 22:1–19

Abraham is renowned for his faith, but that faith didn't come easily. Although God had shown Abraham his overall plan for the future in spectacular fashion, the working out of that plan was to include many bumps and pitfalls.

God had told Abraham to claim the land of Canaan, but the land he found there was so drought-stricken and its people so famished that he fled with his family to Egypt. There, he failed a test of faith by lying about his wife to save his own skin (chapter 12).

God had also promised Abraham many descendants, and that also led to a crisis of faith. Nothing gave Abraham more delight than his dreams of a tent filled with the sounds of children—his children—at play. But was that promise a cruel joke God had dangled before him? At the age of eighty-five, Abraham gave up on his wife and slept with a female servant. At least he would have one child he could call his own. At ninety-nine, when he heard God reconfirm the original promise, Abraham laughed in his face. Sarah pregnant at ninety?

What kind of game was God playing? Whatever did he want? God wanted faith, the Bible says, which means complete trust against all odds, and Abraham finally learned that lesson. As it happened, God kept his promise and a son was born to Abraham and Sarah. They never lived to see tents filled with happy children, nor their descendants multiply like the stars in the sky. But they had one beloved son, whom they named Isaac, or "laughter," as if to remind them of the very absurdity, the *miracle*, of childbirth at their ages.

Then God asked one thing more, the test of faith recorded in this chapter, a trial so severe that it made all the others seem like kindergarten games. The Bible makes clear that God never intended to let Abraham go through with his plan of child sacrifice. (Years later, when the Israelites actually committed infant sacrifice, God would call it "something I did not command or mention, nor did it enter my mind," Jeremiah 19.) All along, God had provided another sacrifice, a ram caught by its horns in a thicket. But Abraham could not know these things as he climbed the steep mountain with his only son. He had to follow God's orders in the dark.

Too many times Abraham had doubted God. This time he would obey no matter what. The angel of the Lord tells clearly what Abraham's decision meant to God. It had taken more than a hundred years, but Abraham finally learned to trust. Ever since, he's been known as a man of faith.

> **To Reflect On:** *What is the hardest "test of faith" you have ever been through?*

GENESIS 22:1–19

Abraham Tested

22 Some time later God tested Abraham. He said to him, "Abraham!" "Here I am," he replied.

²Then God said, "Take your son, your only son, Isaac, whom you love, and go to the region of Moriah. Sacrifice him there as a burnt offering on one of the mountains I will tell you about."

³Early the next morning Abraham got up and saddled his donkey. He took with him two of his servants and his son Isaac. When he had cut enough wood for the burnt offering, he set out for the place God had told him about. ⁴On the third day Abraham looked up and saw the place in the distance. ⁵He said to his servants, "Stay here with the donkey while I and the boy go over there. We will worship and then we will come back to you."

⁶Abraham took the wood for the burnt offering and placed it on his son Isaac, and he himself carried the fire and the knife. As the two of them went on together, ⁷Isaac spoke up and said to his father Abraham, "Father?"

"Yes, my son?" Abraham replied.

"The fire and wood are here," Isaac said, "but where is the lamb for the burnt offering?"

⁸Abraham answered, "God himself will provide the lamb for the burnt offering, my son." And the two of them went on together.

⁹When they reached the place God had told him about, Abraham built an altar there and arranged the wood on it. He bound his son Isaac and laid him on the altar, on top of the wood. ¹⁰Then he reached out his hand and took the knife to slay his son. ¹¹But the angel of the LORD called out to him from heaven, "Abraham! Abraham!"

"Here I am," he replied.

¹²"Do not lay a hand on the boy," he said. "Do not do anything to him. Now I know that you fear God, because you have not withheld from me your son, your only son."

¹³Abraham looked up and there in a thicket he saw a ram caught by its horns. He went over and took the ram and sacrificed it as a burnt offering instead of his son. ¹⁴So Abraham called that place The LORD Will Provide. And to this day it is said, "On the mountain of the LORD it will be provided."

¹⁵The angel of the LORD called to Abraham from heaven a second time ¹⁶and said, "I swear by myself, declares the LORD, that because you have done this and have not withheld your son, your only son, ¹⁷I will surely bless you and make your descendants as numerous as the stars in the sky and as the sand on the seashore. Your descendants will take possession of the cities of their enemies, ¹⁸and through your offspring all nations on earth will be blessed, because you have obeyed me."

¹⁹Then Abraham returned to his servants, and they set off together for Beersheba. And Abraham stayed in Beersheba.

The Cheater

Genesis 27:1–38

If Abraham is renowned for faith, his grandson Jacob is renowned for treachery. A twin, he was born with one hand grasping the heel of his brother who preceded him, and his parents memorialized that scene by giving him a name meaning "he grasps the heel," or "he deceives."

In ancient times, the oldest son had two clear advantages: He would receive the family birthright and the father's blessing. The *birthright*, like an inheritance document, granted the right to be in charge of the family and its property. Jacob got the birthright away from Esau by striking a bargain with his brother who was on the verge of starvation (chapter 25).

For most people of that day, the *blessing* represented a kind of magical power that conveyed prosperity from one generation to another; for Isaac, it represented far more. He was transferring to his son the covenant blessing passed down from his father Abraham, a blessing that would one day produce a whole nation of God's favored people. This chapter records one of Jacob's most elaborate tricks: a ruse to get from his tottery father the blessing that rightfully belonged to his elder brother.

As you read these stories, you might find your sympathies leaning toward poor Esau, who got tricked out of his blessing and sold his birthright for a hot meal. But the Bible comes down clearly on the side of Jacob. Esau is blamed for "despising his birthright" (Genesis. 25:34; Hebrews 12:16).

Jacob, willing to lie, cheat, and steal to get in on God's blessing, would have flunked anyone's morality test (Genesis surely does not commend those tricks—Jacob had to pay dearly for them). Yet his life offers up an important lesson: God can deal with anyone, no matter how flawed, who passionately pursues him. The story of Jacob gives hope to imperfect people everywhere.

> **To Reflect On:** *In Old Testament times, names like Isaac ("laughter") or Jacob ("grasper") carried great significance. What kind of descriptive name would fit you?*

GENESIS 27:1–38

Jacob Gets Isaac's Blessing

27 When Isaac was old and his eyes were so weak that he could no longer see, he called for Esau his older son and said to him, "My son."

"Here I am," he answered.

²Isaac said, "I am now an old man and don't know the day of my death. ³Now then, get your weapons—your quiver and bow—and go out to the open country to hunt some wild game for me. ⁴Prepare me the kind of tasty food I like and bring it to me to eat, so that I may give you my blessing before I die."

⁵Now Rebekah was listening as Isaac spoke to his son Esau. When Esau left for the open country to hunt game and bring it back, ⁶Rebekah said to her son Jacob, "Look, I overheard your father say to your brother Esau, ⁷'Bring me some game and prepare me some tasty food to eat, so that I may give you my blessing in the presence of the LORD before I die.' ⁸Now, my son, listen carefully and do what I tell you: ⁹Go out to the flock and bring me two choice young goats, so I can prepare some tasty food for your father, just the way he likes it. ¹⁰Then take it to your father to eat, so that he may give you his blessing before he dies."

¹¹Jacob said to Rebekah his mother, "But my brother Esau is a hairy man, and I'm a

man with smooth skin. ¹²What if my father touches me? I would appear to be tricking him and would bring down a curse on myself rather than a blessing."

¹³His mother said to him, "My son, let the curse fall on me. Just do what I say; go and get them for me."

¹⁴So he went and got them and brought them to his mother, and she prepared some tasty food, just the way his father liked it. ¹⁵Then Rebekah took the best clothes of Esau her older son, which she had in the house, and put them on her younger son Jacob. ¹⁶She also covered his hands and the smooth part of his neck with the goatskins. ¹⁷Then she handed to her son Jacob the tasty food and the bread she had made.

¹⁸He went to his father and said, "My father."

"Yes, my son," he answered. "Who is it?"

¹⁹Jacob said to his father, "I am Esau your firstborn. I have done as you told me. Please sit up and eat some of my game so that you may give me your blessing."

²⁰Isaac asked his son, "How did you find it so quickly, my son?"

"The LORD your God gave me success," he replied.

²¹Then Isaac said to Jacob, "Come near so I can touch you, my son, to know whether you really are my son Esau or not."

²²Jacob went close to his father Isaac, who touched him and said, "The voice is the voice of Jacob, but the hands are the hands of Esau." ²³He did not recognize him, for his hands were hairy like those of his brother Esau; so he blessed him. ²⁴"Are you really my son Esau?" he asked.

"I am," he replied.

²⁵Then he said, "My son, bring me some of your game to eat, so that I may give you my blessing."

Jacob brought it to him and he ate; and he brought some wine and he drank. ²⁶Then his father Isaac said to him, "Come here, my son, and kiss me."

²⁷So he went to him and kissed him. When Isaac caught the smell of his clothes, he blessed him and said,

"Ah, the smell of my son

is like the smell of a field
    that the LORD has blessed.
²⁸May God give you of heaven's dew
    and of earth's richness—
an abundance of grain and new
    wine.
²⁹May nations serve you
    and peoples bow down to you.
Be lord over your brothers,
    and may the sons of your mother
        bow down to you.
May those who curse you be cursed
    and those who bless you be
        blessed."

³⁰After Isaac finished blessing him and Jacob had scarcely left his father's presence, his brother Esau came in from hunting. ³¹He too prepared some tasty food and brought it to his father. Then he said to him, "My father, sit up and eat some of my game, so that you may give me your blessing."

³²His father Isaac asked him, "Who are you?"

"I am your son," he answered, "your firstborn, Esau."

³³Isaac trembled violently and said, "Who was it, then, that hunted game and brought it to me? I ate it just before you came and I blessed him—and indeed he will be blessed!"

³⁴When Esau heard his father's words, he burst out with a loud and bitter cry and said to his father, "Bless me—me too, my father!"

³⁵But he said, "Your brother came deceitfully and took your blessing."

³⁶Esau said, "Isn't he rightly named Jacob? He has deceived me these two times: He took my birthright, and now he's taken my blessing!" Then he asked, "Haven't you reserved any blessing for me?"

³⁷Isaac answered Esau, "I have made him lord over you and have made all his relatives his servants, and I have sustained him with grain and new wine. So what can I possibly do for you, my son?"

³⁸Esau said to his father, "Do you have only one blessing, my father? Bless me too, my father!" Then Esau wept aloud.

Something Undeserved

Genesis 28:10–22; 32:22–32

In Romans 9, the apostle Paul uses Jacob as an example of God's *grace*. Why would God choose a cheating rascal like Jacob to carry out his plan of building a holy nation? "I will have mercy on whom I have mercy, and I will have compassion on whom I have compassion" is God's answer. Paul loved the word *grace*—it means "an undeserved gift"—because he had spent the first part of his life fighting against God's will, and yet God loved him anyway.

These two scenes show grace at work in the life of Jacob. At critical moments in Jacob's life, just as he was about to lose heart, God met him in dramatic personal encounters.

The first time, Jacob was crossing a desert alone as a fugitive. Having cheated his brother out of the family birthright, he was running away from Esau and his murderous threats. Yet God came to him with bright promises, not the reproaches he deserved. Jacob had not sought God; rather, God sought him. At that tender moment, God confirmed that all the blessings he had promised Abraham would apply to Jacob, the disgraced runaway.

The next encounter occurred several decades later, the night before Jacob was to attempt a reconciliation with Esau. In the intervening years, he had prospered and had learned many hard lessons, but as he thought about the rendezvous, he trembled in fear. After pleading with God to keep his promises, he received in response a supernatural encounter as strange as any in the Bible. Jacob, the grasper, had met a worthy opponent at last: He was wrestling with God himself. After that strange night, Jacob always walked with a limp, a permanent reminder of the struggle.

Along the way, Jacob picked up a new name, "Israel," a name that put the final seal of God's grace on him. Jacob the cheat became the namesake of God's chosen people, the "Israelites."

> **To Reflect On:** *Not many people have such dramatic encounters with God. How has God met you at a time of need?*

GENESIS 28:10–22; 32:22–32

Jacob's Dream at Bethel

¹⁰Jacob left Beersheba and set out for Haran. ¹¹When he reached a certain place, he stopped for the night because the sun had set. Taking one of the stones there, he put it under his head and lay down to sleep. ¹²He had a dream in which he saw a stairway resting on the earth, with its top reaching to heaven, and the angels of God were ascending and descending on it. ¹³There above it stood the LORD, and he said: "I am the LORD, the God of your father Abraham and the God of Isaac. I will give you and your descendants the land on which you are lying. ¹⁴Your descendants will be like the dust of the earth, and you will spread out to the west and to the east, to the north and to the south. All peoples on earth will be blessed through you and your offspring. ¹⁵I am with you and will watch over you wherever you go, and I will bring you back to this land. I will not leave you until I have done what I have promised you."

¹⁶When Jacob awoke from his sleep, he thought, "Surely the LORD is in this place, and I was not aware of it." ¹⁷He was afraid and said, "How awesome is this place! This is none other than the house of God; this is the gate of heaven."

¹⁸Early the next morning Jacob took the stone he had placed under his head and set it up as a pillar and poured oil on top of it. ¹⁹He called that place Bethel, though the city used to be called Luz.

²⁰Then Jacob made a vow, saying, "If God will be with me and will watch over me on this journey I am taking and will give me food to eat and clothes to wear ²¹so that I return safely to my father's house, then the LORD will be my God and ²²this stone that I have set up as a pillar will be God's house, and of all that you give me I will give you a tenth."

Jacob Wrestles With God

²²That night Jacob got up and took his two wives, his two maidservants and his eleven sons and crossed the ford of the Jabbok. ²³After he had sent them across the stream, he sent over all his possessions. ²⁴So Jacob was left alone, and a man wrestled with him till daybreak. ²⁵When the man saw that he could not overpower him, he touched the socket of Jacob's hip so that his hip was wrenched as he wrestled with the man. ²⁶Then the man said, "Let me go, for it is daybreak."

But Jacob replied, "I will not let you go unless you bless me."

²⁷The man asked him, "What is your name?"

"Jacob," he answered.

²⁸Then the man said, "Your name will no longer be Jacob, but Israel, because you have struggled with God and with men and have overcome."

²⁹Jacob said, "Please tell me your name."

But he replied, "Why do you ask my name?" Then he blessed him there.

³⁰So Jacob called the place Peniel, saying, "It is because I saw God face to face, and yet my life was spared."

³¹The sun rose above him as he passed Peniel, and he was limping because of his hip. ³²Therefore to this day the Israelites do not eat the tendon attached to the socket of the hip, because the socket of Jacob's hip was touched near the tendon.

Blood Brothers

Genesis 37

Nobody fights like brothers and sisters—family closeness seems to rub salt in the wounds of relationships. Genesis tells of several great brotherly rivalries: Cain and Abel, Isaac and his half-brother Ishmael, Jacob and Esau. In this last story, Joseph's story, it was eleven brothers against one.

The pace of Genesis slows down when it gets to Joseph, with the book devoting far more attention to his life story than anyone else's. Little wonder—Joseph lived one of the great adventure stories of history. A stowaway, slave, and condemned prisoner, he rose to become the number-two ruler of the greatest empire on earth. The saga all began with the near-tragic event recorded in this chapter.

As his father's acknowledged favorite, Joseph seemed curiously insensitive to the potential of his brother's jealousy. He may even have been flaunting status by relating two dreams of his family bowing down to him. At the least, he alienated his brothers so strongly that they decided to take revenge.

The brothers' first plan was murder. As a last-second thought, they sold Joseph instead to traveling merchants on their way to Egypt. Neither the brothers nor Joseph's grieving father, Jacob—he swallowed their story of a wild animal attack—ever expected to see him again.

God, however, had other plans. Joseph's strange dreams, which got him into so much trouble at home, would prove to be his salvation in the faraway land of Egypt.

> **To Reflect On:** *Have you ever experienced God bringing good out of what at first seemed like a disaster?*

GENESIS 37

Joseph's Dreams

37 Jacob lived in the land where his father had stayed, the land of Canaan.

² This is the account of Jacob.

Joseph, a young man of seventeen, was tending the flocks with his brothers, the sons of Bilhah and the sons of Zilpah, his father's wives, and he brought their father a bad report about them.

³ Now Israel loved Joseph more than any of his other sons, because he had been born to him in his old age; and he made a richly ornamented robe for him. ⁴ When his brothers saw that their father loved him more than any of them, they hated him and could not speak a kind word to him.

⁵ Joseph had a dream, and when he told it to his brothers, they hated him all the more. ⁶ He said to them, "Listen to this dream I had: ⁷ We were binding sheaves of grain out in the field when suddenly my sheaf rose and stood upright, while your sheaves gathered around mine and bowed down to it."

⁸ His brothers said to him, "Do you intend to reign over us? Will you actually rule us?" And they hated him all the more because of his dream and what he had said.

⁹ Then he had another dream, and he told it to his brothers. "Listen," he said, "I had another dream, and this time the sun and moon and eleven stars were bowing down to me."

¹⁰ When he told his father as well as his brothers, his father rebuked him and said, "What is this dream you had? Will your mother and I and your brothers actually come and bow down to the ground before you?" ¹¹ His brothers were jealous of him, but his father kept the matter in mind.

Joseph Sold by His Brothers

¹² Now his brothers had gone to graze their father's flocks near Shechem, ¹³ and

Israel said to Joseph, "As you know, your brothers are grazing the flocks near Shechem. Come, I am going to send you to them."

"Very well," he replied.

¹⁴So he said to him, "Go and see if all is well with your brothers and with the flocks, and bring word back to me." Then he sent him off from the Valley of Hebron.

When Joseph arrived at Shechem, ¹⁵a man found him wandering around in the fields and asked him, "What are you looking for?"

¹⁶He replied, "I'm looking for my brothers. Can you tell me where they are grazing their flocks?"

¹⁷"They have moved on from here," the man answered. "I heard them say, 'Let's go to Dothan.'"

So Joseph went after his brothers and found them near Dothan. ¹⁸But they saw him in the distance, and before he reached them, they plotted to kill him.

¹⁹"Here comes that dreamer!" they said to each other. ²⁰"Come now, let's kill him and throw him into one of these cisterns and say that a ferocious animal devoured him. Then we'll see what comes of his dreams."

²¹When Reuben heard this, he tried to rescue him from their hands. "Let's not take his life," he said. ²²"Don't shed any blood. Throw him into this cistern here in the desert, but don't lay a hand on him." Reuben said this to rescue him from them and take him back to his father.

²³So when Joseph came to his brothers, they stripped him of his robe—the richly ornamented robe he was wearing— ²⁴and they took him and threw him into the cistern. Now the cistern was empty; there was no water in it.

²⁵As they sat down to eat their meal, they looked up and saw a caravan of Ishmaelites coming from Gilead. Their camels were loaded with spices, balm and myrrh, and they were on their way to take them down to Egypt.

²⁶Judah said to his brothers, "What will we gain if we kill our brother and cover up his blood? ²⁷Come, let's sell him to the Ishmaelites and not lay our hands on him; after all, he is our brother, our own flesh and blood." His brothers agreed.

²⁸So when the Midianite merchants came by, his brothers pulled Joseph up out of the cistern and sold him for twenty shekels of silver to the Ishmaelites, who took him to Egypt.

²⁹When Reuben returned to the cistern and saw that Joseph was not there, he tore his clothes. ³⁰He went back to his brothers and said, "The boy isn't there! Where can I turn now?"

³¹Then they got Joseph's robe, slaughtered a goat and dipped the robe in the blood. ³²They took the ornamented robe back to their father and said, "We found this. Examine it to see whether it is your son's robe."

³³He recognized it and said, "It is my son's robe! Some ferocious animal has devoured him. Joseph has surely been torn to pieces."

³⁴Then Jacob tore his clothes, put on sackcloth and mourned for his son many days. ³⁵All his sons and daughters came to comfort him, but he refused to be comforted. "No," he said, "in mourning will I go down to the grave to my son." So his father wept for him.

³⁶Meanwhile, the Midianites sold Joseph in Egypt to Potiphar, one of Pharaoh's officials, the captain of the guard.

Behind the Scenes
Genesis 41:1–43

Genesis provides a fascinating look at a variety of ways in which God gave guidance to his people. Sometimes, as with Abraham, he would appear spectacularly and in person, or send angelic messengers. For other people, like Jacob, the guidance came in more mysterious forms: a late-night wrestling match, a dream of a ladder reaching into heaven. For Joseph, God's guidance was indirect, and probably quite mystifying.

God communicated to Joseph not through angels, but mainly through dreams, weird dreams that he would hear about from such dubious sources as jail mates and a despotic Egyptian pharaoh. Yet it was because God revealed to Joseph the proper meaning of those dreams that he eventually rose to prominence. Egyptians of that day were fascinated by dreams (Lengthy textbooks on dream interpretations have been unearthed by archaeologists.), and Joseph the dream-interpreter soon found himself at the top of Pharaoh's government.

In Joseph's time, God mostly worked behind the scenes. In fact, on the surface it often seemed that Joseph got the exact opposite of what he deserved. He explained a dream to his brothers, and they threw him in a cistern. He resisted a sexual advance and landed in an Egyptian prison. He interpreted another dream to save a cell mate's life, and the cell mate promptly forgot about him.

Yet, and perhaps this is why Genesis devotes so much space to him, Joseph never stopped trusting God. In his trials he learned that while God may not *prevent* all hardship, he could *redeem* anything that might happen, even the worst hardships. Joseph came to see God's hand in the tragedies of his life. The hardship of being sold into slavery, for example, eventually turned out for good. It led him into a powerful new career, and the opportunity to save his own family from starvation. "So then," he told his brothers, "it was not you who sent me here, but God" (45:8). Choking back tears, Joseph tried to explain his faith to the same brothers who had tried to kill him, "You intended to harm me, but God intended it for good. . ." (50:20).

> **To Reflect On:** *If God has an important message for you, how does he get it across or get your attention so you will understand it?*

GENESIS 41:1–43

Pharaoh's Dreams

41 When two full years had passed, Pharaoh had a dream: He was standing by the Nile, ²when out of the river there came up seven cows, sleek and fat, and they grazed among the reeds. ³After them, seven other cows, ugly and gaunt, came up out of the Nile and stood beside those on the riverbank. ⁴And the cows that were ugly and gaunt ate up the seven sleek, fat cows. Then Pharaoh woke up.

⁵He fell asleep again and had a second dream: Seven heads of grain, healthy and good, were growing on a single stalk. ⁶After them, seven other heads of grain sprouted—thin and scorched by the east wind. ⁷The thin heads of grain swallowed up the seven healthy, full heads. Then Pharaoh woke up; it had been a dream.

⁸In the morning his mind was troubled, so he sent for all the magicians and wise men of Egypt. Pharaoh told them his dreams, but no one could interpret them for him.

⁹Then the chief cupbearer said to Pharaoh, "Today I am reminded of my shortcomings. ¹⁰Pharaoh was once angry with

his servants, and he imprisoned me and the chief baker in the house of the captain of the guard. ¹¹Each of us had a dream the same night, and each dream had a meaning of its own. ¹²Now a young Hebrew was there with us, a servant of the captain of the guard. We told him our dreams, and he interpreted them for us, giving each man the interpretation of his dream. ¹³And things turned out exactly as he interpreted them to us: I was restored to my position, and the other man was hanged."

¹⁴So Pharaoh sent for Joseph, and he was quickly brought from the dungeon. When he had shaved and changed his clothes, he came before Pharaoh.

¹⁵Pharaoh said to Joseph, "I had a dream, and no one can interpret it. But I have heard it said of you that when you hear a dream you can interpret it."

¹⁶"I cannot do it," Joseph replied to Pharaoh, "but God will give Pharaoh the answer he desires."

¹⁷Then Pharaoh said to Joseph, "In my dream I was standing on the bank of the Nile, ¹⁸when out of the river there came up seven cows, fat and sleek, and they grazed among the reeds. ¹⁹After them, seven other cows came up—scrawny and very ugly and lean. I had never seen such ugly cows in all the land of Egypt. ²⁰The lean, ugly cows ate up the seven fat cows that came up first. ²¹But even after they ate them, no one could tell that they had done so; they looked just as ugly as before. Then I woke up.

²²"In my dreams I also saw seven heads of grain, full and good, growing on a single stalk. ²³After them, seven other heads sprouted—withered and thin and scorched by the east wind. ²⁴The thin heads of grain swallowed up the seven good heads. I told this to the magicians, but none could explain it to me."

²⁵Then Joseph said to Pharaoh, "The dreams of Pharaoh are one and the same. God has revealed to Pharaoh what he is about to do. ²⁶The seven good cows are seven years, and the seven good heads of grain are seven years; it is one and the same dream. ²⁷The seven lean, ugly cows that came up afterward are seven years, and so are the seven worthless heads of grain scorched by the east wind: They are seven years of famine.

²⁸"It is just as I said to Pharaoh: God has shown Pharaoh what he is about to do. ²⁹Seven years of great abundance are coming throughout the land of Egypt, ³⁰but seven years of famine will follow them. Then all the abundance in Egypt will be forgotten, and the famine will ravage the land. ³¹The abundance in the land will not be remembered, because the famine that follows it will be so severe. ³²The reason the dream was given to Pharaoh in two forms is that the matter has been firmly decided by God, and God will do it soon.

³³"And now let Pharaoh look for a discerning and wise man and put him in charge of the land of Egypt. ³⁴Let Pharaoh appoint commissioners over the land to take a fifth of the harvest of Egypt during the seven years of abundance. ³⁵They should collect all the food of these good years that are coming and store up the grain under the authority of Pharaoh, to be kept in the cities for food. ³⁶This food should be held in reserve for the country, to be used during the seven years of famine that will come upon Egypt, so that the country may not be ruined by the famine."

³⁷The plan seemed good to Pharaoh and to all his officials. ³⁸So Pharaoh asked them, "Can we find anyone like this man, one in whom is the spirit of God?"

³⁹Then Pharaoh said to Joseph, "Since God has made all this known to you, there is no one so discerning and wise as you. ⁴⁰You shall be in charge of my palace, and all my people are to submit to your orders. Only with respect to the throne will I be greater than you."

Joseph in Charge of Egypt

⁴¹So Pharaoh said to Joseph, "I hereby put you in charge of the whole land of Egypt." ⁴²Then Pharaoh took his signet ring from his finger and put it on Joseph's finger. He dressed him in robes of fine linen and put a gold chain around his neck. ⁴³He had him ride in a chariot as his second-in-command, and men shouted before him, "Make way!" Thus he put him in charge of the whole land of Egypt.

A Long Forgiveness

Genesis 45:1–46:4

The old, lingering rivalry between Joseph and his brothers comes to a dramatic climax in this chapter. First, a famine nudged Joseph's brothers out of Palestine toward Egypt, a country which, thanks to Joseph, had prepared for the emergency. There, the brothers knelt unwittingly before Joseph—so Egyptian by now as to be unrecognizable—and begged for the right to buy food. Thus began a long, anguished struggle of the heart.

Joseph could have disclosed his identity and made up with his brothers on the spot, or he could have gotten revenge by ordering their executions. He did neither. He began a series of elaborate tests, demanding things from them, playing tricks on them, accusing them for nearly *two years.* All these games brought his brothers confusion and fear, and also flashbacks of guilt over their treatment of him years ago. "Surely we are being punished because of our brother. We saw how distressed he was when he pleaded with us for his life, but we would not listen" (42:21).

The drama took an emotional toll on Joseph. Five times, Genesis records, he broke into tears, once with cries loud enough to be overheard in the next room. Joseph was feeling the awful strain of forgiveness. Finally, as this chapter tells, the brothers discovered the stunning truth: The teenager they had sold as a slave, and nearly killed, was now the second-ranking imperial official of Egypt. He held their fate in his hands.

But Joseph had no interest in revenge. At long last he was ready to forgive, and to welcome them all to the haven of Egypt. The brothers' reconciliation opened the way for the children of Israel to become one family of twelve tribes, a single nation. The old man Jacob, back home in Palestine, didn't know what to believe when he heard the news about his "dead" son. But, spurred on by one last personal revelation from God, he, too, headed off for Egypt.

A large family, a nation, a land—God had promised all these to Abraham and to Isaac and to Jacob. As Genesis closes, only the first of the promises has come true: Jacob's twelve sons have produced a flock of children. The Bible makes plain that these twelve were no more holy than any other sons—eleven of them, after all, had betrayed Joseph. But from this starting point, God would build his nation. Joseph never lost hope that the rest of the promises would be fulfilled as well: On his deathbed, he asked that his bones be carried back to the land God had promised to his father (50:25).

To Reflect On: *What makes it so hard for us to forgive others?*

GENESIS 45:1–46:4

Joseph Makes Himself Known

45 Then Joseph could no longer control himself before all his attendants, and he cried out, "Have everyone leave my presence!" So there was no one with Joseph when he made himself known to his brothers. ²And he wept so loudly that the Egyptians heard him, and Pharaoh's household heard about it.

³Joseph said to his brothers, "I am Joseph! Is my father still living?" But his brothers were not able to answer him, because they were terrified at his presence.

⁴Then Joseph said to his brothers, "Come close to me." When they had done so, he said, "I am your brother Joseph, the one you sold into Egypt! ⁵And now, do not be distressed and do not be angry with yourselves for selling me here, because it was to save lives that God sent me ahead of you. ⁶For two years now there has been famine in the land, and for the next five years there will not be plowing and reaping. ⁷But God sent me ahead of you to preserve for you a remnant on earth and to save your lives by a great deliverance.

⁸"So then, it was not you who sent me here, but God. He made me father to Pharaoh, lord of his entire household and ruler of all Egypt. ⁹Now hurry back to my father and say to him, 'This is what your son Joseph says: God has made me lord of all Egypt. Come down to me; don't delay. ¹⁰You shall live in the region of Goshen and be near me—you, your children and grandchildren, your flocks and herds, and all you have. ¹¹I will provide for you there, because five years of famine are still to come. Otherwise you and your household and all who belong to you will become destitute.'

¹²"You can see for yourselves, and so can my brother Benjamin, that it is really I who am speaking to you. ¹³Tell my father about all the honor accorded me in Egypt and about everything you have seen. And bring my father down here quickly."

¹⁴Then he threw his arms around his brother Benjamin and wept, and Benjamin embraced him, weeping. ¹⁵And he kissed all his brothers and wept over them. Afterward his brothers talked with him.

¹⁶When the news reached Pharaoh's palace that Joseph's brothers had come, Phar-aoh and all his officials were pleased. ¹⁷Pharaoh said to Joseph, "Tell your brothers, 'Do this: Load your animals and return to the land of Canaan, ¹⁸and bring your father and your families back to me. I will give you the best of the land of Egypt and you can enjoy the fat of the land.'

¹⁹"You are also directed to tell them, 'Do this: Take some carts from Egypt for your children and your wives, and get your father and come. ²⁰Never mind about your belongings, because the best of all Egypt will be yours.'"

²¹So the sons of Israel did this. Joseph gave them carts, as Pharaoh had commanded, and he also gave them provisions for their journey. ²²To each of them he gave new clothing, but to Benjamin he gave three hundred shekels of silver and five sets of clothes. ²³And this is what he sent to his father: ten donkeys loaded with the best things of Egypt, and ten female donkeys loaded with grain and bread and other provisions for his journey. ²⁴Then he sent his brothers away, and as they were leaving he said to them, "Don't quarrel on the way!"

²⁵So they went up out of Egypt and came to their father Jacob in the land of Canaan. ²⁶They told him, "Joseph is still alive! In fact, he is ruler of all Egypt." Jacob was stunned; he did not believe them. ²⁷But when they told him everything Joseph had said to them, and when he saw the carts Joseph had sent to carry him back, the spirit of their father Jacob revived. ²⁸And Israel said, "I'm convinced! My son Joseph is still alive. I will go and see him before I die."

Jacob Goes to Egypt

46 So Israel set out with all that was his, and when he reached Beersheba, he offered sacrifices to the God of his father Isaac.

²And God spoke to Israel in a vision at night and said, "Jacob! Jacob!"

"Here I am," he replied.

³"I am God, the God of your father," he said. "Do not be afraid to go down to Egypt, for I will make you into a great nation there. ⁴I will go down to Egypt with you, and I will surely bring you back again. And Joseph's own hand will close your eyes."

Time for Action

Exodus 3

The Bible dispenses with almost four hundred years of Israelite history in just two verses (Exodus 1:6–7). These report that Jacob's family, still small enough by the end of Genesis for the Bible to name all its sons, has now grown into a great, swarming tribe. God's plan was slowly progressing, but with one major hitch: The Egyptian empire had turned against the Israelites.

The Hebrews now toiled as slaves under a hostile pharaoh. They were unified, yes, but in the same way oppressed people anywhere are unified—in their misery. God's promises to Abraham, Isaac, and Jacob had been passed down to each new generation, but who believed in the covenant anymore? Were they an independent nation? Daily, they felt the whips of Egyptian taskmasters. As for the vaunted Promised Land, it lay to the east somewhere, carved up under the dominion of a dozen different kings.

At last God had had enough. "I have indeed seen the misery of my people in Egypt," he said. "Now you will see what I will do." The chapters that follow record the most impressive display of God's power unleashed on earth since creation.

First God needed a leader, and for that job he selected Moses, a choice rich with irony. As a child, the Jewish national hero—a George Washington, Thomas Jefferson, and Abraham Lincoln rolled up into one—had floated in the cattails of the Nile a hairbreadth from certain death. God had next arranged for Moses to receive the best classical education available, in the pharaoh's palace, while being nurtured—for pay!— by his own Israelite mother.

It took forty years in Egypt and forty years in the desert to prepare Moses for the leadership role. God's announcement, or "call," was an encounter Moses would never forget: a fiery bush, a voice from nowhere, God introducing himself by name. "I am the God of Abraham, Isaac, and Jacob," he said, drawing a connection to all the promises that had gone before. And now the time for action had arrived. Moses was his handpicked choice to lead that mob from slavery in Egypt to freedom in the Promised Land.

As this chapter shows, Moses was far from an eager recruit. But his own resistance to God's plan was minor compared to that put up by the Israelites . . . and the Egyptians.

> **To Reflect On:** *Why was Moses so reluc-tant to lead? Do you ever wonder if certain shortcomings you perceive about yourself disqualify you for God's service?*

EXODUS 3

Moses and the Burning Bush

3 Now Moses was tending the flock of Jethro his father-in-law, the priest of Midian, and he led the flock to the far side of the desert and came to Horeb, the mountain of God. ²There the angel of the LORD appeared to him in flames of fire from within a bush. Moses saw that though the bush was on fire it did not burn up. ³So Moses thought, "I will go over and see this strange sight—why the bush does not burn up."

⁴When the LORD saw that he had gone over to look, God called to him from within the bush, "Moses! Moses!"

And Moses said, "Here I am."

⁵"Do not come any closer," God said. "Take off your sandals, for the place where you are standing is holy ground." ⁶Then he said, "I am the God of your father, the God of Abraham, the God of Isaac and the God of Jacob." At this, Moses hid his face, because he was afraid to look at God.

⁷The LORD said, "I have indeed seen the misery of my people in Egypt. I have heard them crying out because of their slave drivers, and I am concerned about their suffering. ⁸So I have come down to rescue them from the hand of the Egyptians and to bring them up out of that land into a good and spacious land, a land flowing with milk and honey—the home of the Canaanites, Hittites, Amorites, Perizzites, Hivites and Jebusites. ⁹And now the cry of the Israelites has reached me, and I have seen the way the Egyptians are oppressing them. ¹⁰So now, go. I am sending you to Pharaoh to bring my people the Israelites out of Egypt."

¹¹But Moses said to God, "Who am I, that I should go to Pharaoh and bring the Israelites out of Egypt?"

¹²And God said, "I will be with you. And this will be the sign to you that it is I who have sent you: When you have brought the people out of Egypt, you will worship God on this mountain."

¹³Moses said to God, "Suppose I go to the Israelites and say to them, 'The God of your fathers has sent me to you,' and they ask me, 'What is his name?' Then what shall I tell them?"

¹⁴God said to Moses, "I AM WHO I AM. This is what you are to say to the Israelites: 'I AM has sent me to you.'"

¹⁵God also said to Moses, "Say to the Israelites, 'The LORD, the God of your fathers—the God of Abraham, the God of Isaac and the God of Jacob—has sent me to you.' This is my name forever, the name by which I am to be remembered from generation to generation.

¹⁶"Go, assemble the elders of Israel and say to them, 'The LORD, the God of your fathers—the God of Abraham, Isaac and Jacob—appeared to me and said: I have watched over you and have seen what has been done to you in Egypt. ¹⁷And I have promised to bring you up out of your misery in Egypt into the land of the Canaanites, Hittites, Amorites, Perizzites, Hivites and Jebusites—a land flowing with milk and honey.'

¹⁸"The elders of Israel will listen to you. Then you and the elders are to go to the king of Egypt and say to him, 'The LORD, the God of the Hebrews, has met with us. Let us take a three-day journey into the desert to offer sacrifices to the LORD our God.' ¹⁹But I know that the king of Egypt will not let you go unless a mighty hand compels him. ²⁰So I will stretch out my hand and strike the Egyptians with all the wonders that I will perform among them. After that, he will let you go.

²¹"And I will make the Egyptians favorably disposed toward this people, so that when you leave you will not go empty-handed. ²²Every woman is to ask her neighbor and any woman living in her house for articles of silver and gold and for clothing, which you will put on your sons and daughters. And so you will plunder the Egyptians."

The Ten Plagues

Exodus 10:3–11:10

To liberate the Israelite slaves, God staged a cosmic showdown known as the Ten Plagues, a showdown so dramatic that in modern times it strains the limits of Hollywood special effects crews just to depict it on-screen. A nation was aborning, and the task of uprooting the Israelites from Egypt called for outside intervention.

First, the Israelites themselves had to be convinced of God's power. After all, they had lived through several centuries in Egypt when God seemed silent and unconcerned. Somehow God had to demonstrate that he had not forgotten his chosen people. Then, too, Egypt needed convincing: No empire would let thousands of valuable slaves walk away free. Exodus asserts more than a dozen times that the plagues were given so that the Israelites and Egyptians would recognize the power of Israel's God.

An even more basic issue was at stake: God's personal credibility. Was he just one more tribal god, like the ones the Egyptians worshiped? The plagues were, in effect, God's open warfare against the false gods of Egypt. He declared as much: "I will bring judgment on all the gods of Egypt" (12:12). Some scholars see each plague as a targeted attack against a specific Egyptian idol. Thus, the plague on the Nile River countered the Egyptians' river god; the plague of flies, the sacred fly; the plague of darkness, the sun god Ra; and the plague on livestock, the sacred bull.

The plagues began as irritants—a river turned red, frogs, gnats—and only escalated in response to Pharaoh's hardening heart. As a last resort, God inflicted the terrible plague recorded in chapter 11. The events of that night are remembered to this day by Jews, and also by Christians, who see Jesus as the ultimate Passover Lamb.

In the end, the plagues worked so effectively that thousands of slaves left unhindered, with the wealth of Egypt showered upon them as farewell gifts. That remarkable time became a cherished part of the Israelites' national memory. "I am the God who brought you out of Egypt," God would remind them again and again whenever they were tempted to doubt his power or concern for them.

> **To Reflect On:** *If God declared war on the "gods" of our modern society, what would they be?*

EXODUS 10:3–11:10

The Plague of Locusts

³So Moses and Aaron went to Pharaoh and said to him, "This is what the LORD, the God of the Hebrews, says: 'How long will you refuse to humble yourself before me? Let my people go, so that they may worship me. ⁴If you refuse to let them go, I will bring locusts into your country tomorrow. ⁵They will cover the face of the ground so that it cannot be seen. They will devour what little you have left after the hail, including every tree that is growing in your fields. ⁶They will fill your houses and those of all your officials and all the Egyptians—something neither your fathers nor your forefathers have ever seen from the day they settled in this land till now.'" Then Moses turned and left Pharaoh.

⁷Pharaoh's officials said to him, "How long will this man be a snare to us? Let the people go, so that they may worship the LORD their God. Do you not yet realize that Egypt is ruined?"

⁸Then Moses and Aaron were brought back to Pharaoh. "Go, worship the LORD your God," he said. "But just who will be going?"

⁹Moses answered, "We will go with our young and old, with our sons and daugh-

ters, and with our flocks and herds, because we are to celebrate a festival to the LORD."

¹⁰Pharaoh said, "The LORD be with you— if I let you go, along with your women and children! Clearly you are bent on evil. ¹¹No! Have only the men go; and worship the LORD, since that's what you have been asking for." Then Moses and Aaron were driven out of Pharaoh's presence.

¹²And the LORD said to Moses, "Stretch out your hand over Egypt so that locusts will swarm over the land and devour everything growing in the fields, everything left by the hail."

¹³So Moses stretched out his staff over Egypt, and the LORD made an east wind blow across the land all that day and all that night. By morning the wind had brought the locusts; ¹⁴they invaded all Egypt and settled down in every area of the country in great numbers. Never before had there been such a plague of locusts, nor will there ever be again. ¹⁵They covered all the ground until it was black. They devoured all that was left after the hail—everything growing in the fields and the fruit on the trees. Nothing green remained on tree or plant in all the land of Egypt.

¹⁶Pharaoh quickly summoned Moses and Aaron and said, "I have sinned against the LORD your God and against you. ¹⁷Now forgive my sin once more and pray to the LORD your God to take this deadly plague away from me."

¹⁸Moses then left Pharaoh and prayed to the LORD. ¹⁹And the LORD changed the wind to a very strong west wind, which caught up the locusts and carried them into the Red Sea. Not a locust was left anywhere in Egypt. ²⁰But the LORD hardened Pharaoh's heart, and he would not let the Israelites go.

The Plague of Darkness

²¹Then the LORD said to Moses, "Stretch out your hand toward the sky so that darkness will spread over Egypt—darkness that can be felt." ²²So Moses stretched out his hand toward the sky, and total darkness covered all Egypt for three days. ²³No one could see anyone else or leave his place for three days. Yet all the Israelites had light in the places where they lived.

²⁴Then Pharaoh summoned Moses and said, "Go, worship the LORD. Even your women and children may go with you; only leave your flocks and herds behind."

²⁵But Moses said, "You must allow us to have sacrifices and burnt offerings to present to the LORD our God. ²⁶Our livestock too must go with us; not a hoof is to be left behind. We have to use some of them in worshiping the LORD our God, and until we get there we will not know what we are to use to worship the LORD."

²⁷But the LORD hardened Pharaoh's heart, and he was not willing to let them go. ²⁸Pharaoh said to Moses, "Get out of my sight! Make sure you do not appear before me again! The day you see my face you will die."

²⁹"Just as you say," Moses replied, "I will never appear before you again."

The Plague on the Firstborn

11 Now the LORD had said to Moses, "I will bring one more plague on Pharaoh and on Egypt. After that, he will let you go from here, and when he does, he will drive you out completely. ²Tell the people that men and women alike are to ask their neighbors for articles of silver and gold." ³(The LORD made the Egyptians favorably disposed toward the people, and Moses himself was highly regarded in Egypt by Pharaoh's officials and by the people.)

⁴So Moses said, "This is what the LORD says: 'About midnight I will go throughout Egypt. ⁵Every firstborn son in Egypt will die, from the firstborn son of Pharaoh, who sits on the throne, to the firstborn son of the slave girl, who is at her hand mill, and all the firstborn of the cattle as well. ⁶There will be loud wailing throughout Egypt—worse than there has ever been or ever will be again. ⁷But among the Israelites not a dog will bark at any man or animal.' Then you will know that the LORD makes a distinction between Egypt and Israel. ⁸All these officials of yours will come to me, bowing down before me and saying, 'Go, you and all the people who follow you!' After that I will leave." Then Moses, hot with anger, left Pharaoh.

⁹The LORD had said to Moses, "Pharaoh will refuse to listen to you—so that my wonders may be multiplied in Egypt." ¹⁰Moses and Aaron performed all these wonders before Pharaoh, but the LORD hardened Pharaoh's heart, and he would not let the Israelites go out of his country.

Second Thoughts

Exodus 14

It didn't take long for Pharaoh and the Egyptians to second-guess their decision to release the slaves. Soon a glittering army of chariots and horsemen was charging after the defenseless Israelites.

Nor did it take long for the Israelites to second-guess their decision to leave. At the first sight of Pharaoh's army, they quaked in fear and accused Moses of leading them to certain destruction in the desert.

As this chapter tells it, the Israelites' final confrontation with Egypt was divinely stage-managed to make a point for all time: God himself, no one else, was responsible for the Israelites' liberation. More than anything else, the account of the Exodus underscores that one indisputable fact. No Israelite armies stood against the mighty Egyptians. At the last possible minute, God arranged a spectacular rescue operation, and an equally spectacular defeat of the Egyptian army. The freed captives could only respond with humility and praise; there was no room for pride. For them, independence from Egypt meant dependence on God.

That pattern of depending on God would continue all through the Exodus. When the wilderness wanderers ran out of water, God provided. When food supplies failed, God provided. When raiders attacked, God provided. In fact, the book of Exodus shows a greater proportion of miracles—direct supernatural acts of God—than any part of the Bible except the Gospels. The psalmists would never tire of celebrating these events in music, and the prophets would later hark back to the days of the Exodus to stir the conscience of their nation. The great miracle of the Red Sea merely set the tone for a national history that was from beginning to end an active movement of God.

> **To Reflect On:** *Read through the song commemorating this event in chapter 15:1– 18. It offers a good model for praising and thanking God when he answers a desperate prayer.*

EXODUS 14

14 Then the LORD said to Moses, 2"Tell the Israelites to turn back and encamp near Pi Hahiroth, between Migdol and the sea. They are to encamp by the sea, directly opposite Baal Zephon. 3Pharaoh will think, 'The Israelites are wandering around the land in confusion, hemmed in by the desert.' 4And I will harden Pharaoh's heart, and he will pursue them. But I will gain glory for myself through Pharaoh and all his army, and the Egyptians will know that I am the LORD." So the Israelites did this.

5When the king of Egypt was told that the people had fled, Pharaoh and his officials changed their minds about them and said, "What have we done? We have let the Israelites go and have lost their services!" 6So he had his chariot made ready and took his army with him. 7He took six hundred of the best chariots, along with all the other chariots of Egypt, with officers over all of them. 8The LORD hardened the heart of Pharaoh king of Egypt, so that he pursued the Israelites, who were marching out boldly. 9The Egyptians—all Pharaoh's horses and chariots, horsemen and troops— pursued the Israelites and overtook them as they camped by the sea near Pi Hahiroth, opposite Baal Zephon.

10As Pharaoh approached, the Israelites looked up, and there were the Egyptians, marching after them. They were terrified and cried out to the LORD. ¹¹They said to Moses, "Was it because there were no graves in Egypt that you brought us to the desert to die? What have you done to us by bringing us out of Egypt? ¹²Didn't we say to you in Egypt, 'Leave us alone; let us serve the Egyptians'? It would have been better for us to serve the Egyptians than to die in the desert!"

¹³Moses answered the people, "Do not be afraid. Stand firm and you will see the deliverance the LORD will bring you today. The Egyptians you see today you will never see again. ¹⁴The LORD will fight for you; you need only to be still."

¹⁵Then the LORD said to Moses, "Why are you crying out to me? Tell the Israelites to move on. ¹⁶Raise your staff and stretch out your hand over the sea to divide the water so that the Israelites can go through the sea on dry ground. ¹⁷I will harden the hearts of the Egyptians so that they will go in after them. And I will gain glory through Pharaoh and all his army, through his chariots and his horsemen. ¹⁸The Egyptians will know that I am the LORD when I gain glory through Pharaoh, his chariots and his horsemen."

¹⁹Then the angel of God, who had been traveling in front of Israel's army, withdrew and went behind them. The pillar of cloud also moved from in front and stood behind them, ²⁰coming between the armies of Egypt and Israel. Throughout the night the cloud brought darkness to the one side and light to the other side; so neither went near the other all night long.

²¹Then Moses stretched out his hand over the sea, and all that night the LORD drove the sea back with a strong east wind and turned it into dry land. The waters were divided, ²²and the Israelites went through the sea on dry ground, with a wall of water on their right and on their left.

²³The Egyptians pursued them, and all Pharaoh's horses and chariots and horsemen followed them into the sea. ²⁴During the last watch of the night the LORD looked down from the pillar of fire and cloud at the Egyptian army and threw it into confusion. ²⁵He made the wheels of their chariots come off so that they had difficulty driving. And the Egyptians said, "Let's get away from the Israelites! The LORD is fighting for them against Egypt."

²⁶Then the LORD said to Moses, "Stretch out your hand over the sea so that the waters may flow back over the Egyptians and their chariots and horsemen." ²⁷Moses stretched out his hand over the sea, and at daybreak the sea went back to its place. The Egyptians were fleeing toward it, and the LORD swept them into the sea. ²⁸The water flowed back and covered the chariots and horsemen—the entire army of Pharaoh that had followed the Israelites into the sea. Not one of them survived.

²⁹But the Israelites went through the sea on dry ground, with a wall of water on their right and on their left. ³⁰That day the LORD saved Israel from the hands of the Egyptians, and Israel saw the Egyptians lying dead on the shore. ³¹And when the Israelites saw the great power the LORD displayed against the Egyptians, the people feared the LORD and put their trust in him and in Moses his servant.

A Treaty with God

Exodus 20:1–21

Nearly everyone has heard of the Ten Commandments. For most of us, they represent a central core of morality, "the basics" that God requires. But for the Israelites in the desert, the Ten Commandments represented far more—nothing less than a major breakthrough. Nations around them, who worshiped many different gods, lived in constant fear of the gods' unpredictability. Who could tell what might anger or please them? But now God himself, Maker of the universe, was giving the Israelites a binding treaty signed in his own hand. They would always know exactly what God required and where they stood before him.

God held before them some wonderful guarantees: prosperity, abundant crops, victorious armies, immunity from health problems. In effect, he agreed to remove most of the problems people face in daily existence. In exchange he asked that the Israelites obey the rules outlined in this and the next few chapters. God's original covenant with Abraham he now made formal, and applied to a whole nation. (This middle part of Exodus is known as the Book of the Covenant, for it contains the essence of the Israelites' treaty with God.)

"Although the whole earth is mine, you will be for me a kingdom of priests and a holy nation," God said (19:5–6). He wanted a nation like no other, a model society centered around a commitment to him. All the Israelites waited in anticipation as Moses climbed a dark, smoky mountain to meet with God. No one present could miss the significance of that meeting: It was marked by thunder and lightning, and a loud, piercing trumpet blast, and fire. The ground itself shook as in an earthquake.

Out of that meeting on Mount Sinai came the rules summarized here. The Bible fills in many more details of the treaty, but these Ten Commandments express the kind of behavior God wanted from his people. It was a day of wild hope. "We will do everything the LORD has said," the people all promised with a shout (19:8).

> **To Reflect On:** *Most of the Ten Command-ments are stated in a negative form. Can you restate them positively? What personal rights do they protect?*

EXODUS 20:1–21

The Ten Commandments

20 And God spoke all these words:

2"I am the LORD your God, who brought you out of Egypt, out of the land of slavery.

3"You shall have no other gods before me.

4"You shall not make for yourself an idol in the form of anything in heaven above or on the earth beneath or in the waters below. 5You shall not bow down to them or worship them; for I, the LORD your God, am a jealous God, punishing the children for the sin of the fathers to the third and fourth generation of those who hate me, 6but showing love to a thousand generations of those who love me and keep my commandments.

7"You shall not misuse the name of the LORD your God, for the LORD will not hold anyone guiltless who misuses his name.

8"Remember the Sabbath day by keeping it holy. 9Six days you shall labor and do all your work, 10but the seventh day is a Sabbath to the LORD your God. On it you shall not do any work, neither you, nor your son or daughter, nor your manservant or maidservant, nor your animals, nor the alien within your gates. 11For in six days the LORD made the heavens and the earth, the sea, and all that is in them, but he rested on the seventh day. Therefore the LORD blessed the Sabbath day and made it holy.

12"Honor your father and your mother, so that you may live long in the land the LORD your God is giving you.

13"You shall not murder.

14"You shall not commit adultery.

15"You shall not steal.

16"You shall not give false testimony against your neighbor.

17"You shall not covet your neighbor's house. You shall not covet your neighbor's wife, or his manservant or maidservant, his ox or donkey, or anything that belongs to your neighbor."

18When the people saw the thunder and lightning and heard the trumpet and saw the mountain in smoke, they trembled with fear. They stayed at a distance 19and said to Moses, "Speak to us yourself and we will listen. But do not have God speak to us or we will die."

20Moses said to the people, "Do not be afraid. God has come to test you, so that the fear of God will be with you to keep you from sinning."

21The people remained at a distance, while Moses approached the thick darkness where God was.

Something New, Something Old

Exodus 32

The bright hope of Exodus 20 dies forever in Exodus 32; there is no more jarring contrast in all the Bible. For forty days Moses visited with God on Mount Sinai, receiving the terms of the covenant, or treaty, that would open up an unprecedented closeness between God and human beings. But what happened down below, at the foot of the mountain, almost defies belief.

The Israelites—people who had seen the ten plagues of Egypt, who had crossed the Red Sea on dry ground, who had drunk water from a rock, who were digesting the miracle of manna in their stomachs at that moment—these same people felt boredom, or impatience, or rebellion, or jealousy, or some such mortal urge, and apparently forgot all about their God. By the time Moses descended from Sinai, the Israelites, God's people, were dancing like pagans around a golden statue.

Moses was so mad that he hurled to the ground the tablets of stone signed by God himself. God was so mad that he nearly destroyed the whole cantankerous nation.

This chapter has many parallels with the story of the very first human rebellion in Genesis 3. Both times, people favored by God failed to trust him and struck out instead against his clear command. Both times, the rebels devised elaborate rationalizations to explain their behavior. Both times, they forfeited special privileges and suffered harsh punishment.

It appeared, for a moment, that something new in the history of humanity would take place among the Israelites: an entire nation devoted to following God. Instead, the same old story replayed itself. No matter what terms God came up with, people found ways to break them.

Only one ray of hope shines out of this dark scene. Moses, the stuttering, reluctant leader, seems to grow into his position at last. His eloquent prayers are answered, and God grants the Israelites yet another chance.

> **To Reflect On:** *What do you think was really behind the Israelites' rebellion?*

EXODUS 32

The Golden Calf

32 When the people saw that Moses was so long in coming down from the mountain, they gathered around Aaron and said, "Come, make us gods who will go before us. As for this fellow Moses who brought us up out of Egypt, we don't know what has happened to him."

²Aaron answered them, "Take off the gold earrings that your wives, your sons and your daughters are wearing, and bring them to me." ³So all the people took off their earrings and brought them to Aaron. ⁴He took what they handed him and made it into an idol cast in the shape of a calf, fashioning it with a tool. Then they said,

"These are your gods, O Israel, who brought you up out of Egypt."

⁵When Aaron saw this, he built an altar in front of the calf and announced, "Tomorrow there will be a festival to the Lord." ⁶So the next day the people rose early and sacrificed burnt offerings and presented fellowship offerings. Afterward they sat down to eat and drink and got up to indulge in revelry.

⁷Then the Lord said to Moses, "Go down, because your people, whom you brought up out of Egypt, have become corrupt. ⁸They have been quick to turn away from what I commanded them and have made themselves an idol cast in the shape of a calf. They have bowed down to it

and sacrificed to it and have said, 'These are your gods, O Israel, who brought you up out of Egypt.'

⁹"I have seen these people," the LORD said to Moses, "and they are a stiff-necked people. ¹⁰Now leave me alone so that my anger may burn against them and that I may destroy them. Then I will make you into a great nation."

¹¹But Moses sought the favor of the LORD his God. "O LORD," he said, "why should your anger burn against your people, whom you brought out of Egypt with great power and a mighty hand? ¹²Why should the Egyptians say, 'It was with evil intent that he brought them out, to kill them in the mountains and to wipe them off the face of the earth'? Turn from your fierce anger; relent and do not bring disaster on your people. ¹³Remember your servants Abraham, Isaac and Israel, to whom you swore by your own self: 'I will make your descendants as numerous as the stars in the sky and I will give your descendants all this land I promised them, and it will be their inheritance forever.'" ¹⁴Then the LORD relented and did not bring on his people the disaster he had threatened.

¹⁵Moses turned and went down the mountain with the two tablets of the Testimony in his hands. They were inscribed on both sides, front and back. ¹⁶The tablets were the work of God; the writing was the writing of God, engraved on the tablets.

¹⁷When Joshua heard the noise of the people shouting, he said to Moses, "There is the sound of war in the camp."

¹⁸Moses replied:

"It is not the sound of victory,
  it is not the sound of defeat;
  it is the sound of singing that I
    hear."

¹⁹When Moses approached the camp and saw the calf and the dancing, his anger burned and he threw the tablets out of his hands, breaking them to pieces at the foot of the mountain. ²⁰And he took the calf they had made and burned it in the fire; then he ground it to powder, scattered it on the water and made the Israelites drink it.

²¹He said to Aaron, "What did these people do to you, that you led them into such great sin?"

²²"Do not be angry, my lord," Aaron answered. "You know how prone these people are to evil. ²³They said to me, 'Make us gods who will go before us. As for this fellow Moses who brought us up out of Egypt, we don't know what has happened to him.' ²⁴So I told them, 'Whoever has any gold jewelry, take it off.' Then they gave me the gold, and I threw it into the fire, and out came this calf!"

²⁵Moses saw that the people were running wild and that Aaron had let them get out of control and so become a laughingstock to their enemies. ²⁶So he stood at the entrance to the camp and said, "Whoever is for the LORD, come to me." And all the Levites rallied to him.

²⁷Then he said to them, "This is what the LORD, the God of Israel, says: 'Each man strap a sword to his side. Go back and forth through the camp from one end to the other, each killing his brother and friend and neighbor.'" ²⁸The Levites did as Moses commanded, and that day about three thousand of the people died. ²⁹Then Moses said, "You have been set apart to the LORD today, for you were against your own sons and brothers, and he has blessed you this day."

³⁰The next day Moses said to the people, "You have committed a great sin. But now I will go up to the LORD; perhaps I can make atonement for your sin."

³¹So Moses went back to the LORD and said, "Oh, what a great sin these people have committed! They have made themselves gods of gold. ³²But now, please forgive their sin—but if not, then blot me out of the book you have written."

³³The LORD replied to Moses, "Whoever has sinned against me I will blot out of my book. ³⁴Now go, lead the people to the place I spoke of, and my angel will go before you. However, when the time comes for me to punish, I will punish them for their sin."

³⁵And the LORD struck the people with a plague because of what they did with the calf Aaron had made.

Legal Matters

Leviticus 26:3–43

Leviticus seems very strange to the modern world, so strange that readers intending to read the entire Bible often bog down in this book. Unlike most of the Bible, it has few stories or personalities, and no poetry. It's a book of laws, crammed full of detailed rules and procedures.

A selective "guided tour" of the Bible such as this one can devote very little time to study of the individual laws. For one reason, many of these rules, appropriate to God's goal of calling out a "separate" people, were changed in the New Testament. Yet a study of such laws can prove rewarding, for they express God's priorities on such subjects as care for the land, concern for the poor, and abuses of family and neighbors.

Although the Old Testament laws recorded in Leviticus, Exodus, Numbers, and Deuteronomy may seem long-winded, keep them in perspective. These laws—just over 600 in all—comprised the entire set of regulations for a nation, as far as we know. (Most modern cities have more traffic laws!) And they are brief and clear. You don't have to go to law school to understand them.

The variety of the laws shows that God involved himself in every aspect of the Israelites' life. Laws against witchcraft are mixed in with laws concerning improper haircuts, and tattoos, and prostitution. God was advancing his plan for the Israelites by carving out a separate *culture*. After four centuries in Egypt, the just-freed slaves, more Egyptian than anything else, needed a comprehensive make-over. That is exactly what God gave them. (Many of the laws seem designed primarily to keep the Israelites "different" from their pagan neighbors.)

Surely it sometimes occurred to the Israelites to wonder, "Is it necessary to follow these picky laws? Are they really so important after all?" Chapter 26 answers that question with finality. The Israelites were a unique people, unlike any other nation on earth, called by God to demonstrate holiness and purity to people around them.

As this chapter makes clear, the reward for obeying the laws would make the Israelites the envy of the world. And if they disobeyed? God spells out in frightening detail the punishments they could then expect.

To Reflect On: *Everybody has a code to live by. Where did you get yours?*

LEVITICUS 26:3–43

Reward for Obedience

³ "'If you follow my decrees and are careful to obey my commands, ⁴I will send you rain in its season, and the ground will yield its crops and the trees of the field their fruit. ⁵Your threshing will continue until grape harvest and the grape harvest will continue until planting, and you will eat all the food you want and live in safety in your land.

⁶ "'I will grant peace in the land, and you will lie down and no one will make you afraid. I will remove savage beasts from the land, and the sword will not pass through your country. ⁷You will pursue your enemies, and they will fall by the sword before you. ⁸Five of you will chase a hundred, and a hundred of you will chase ten thousand, and your enemies will fall by the sword before you.

⁹ "'I will look on you with favor and make you fruitful and increase your numbers, and I will keep my covenant with you. ¹⁰You will still be eating last year's harvest when you will have to move it out to make room for the new. ¹¹I will put my dwelling

place among you, and I will not abhor you. [12]I will walk among you and be your God, and you will be my people. [13]I am the LORD your God, who brought you out of Egypt so that you would no longer be slaves to the Egyptians; I broke the bars of your yoke and enabled you to walk with heads held high.

Punishment for Disobedience

[14]" 'But if you will not listen to me and carry out all these commands, [15]and if you reject my decrees and abhor my laws and fail to carry out all my commands and so violate my covenant, [16]then I will do this to you: I will bring upon you sudden terror, wasting diseases and fever that will destroy your sight and drain away your life. You will plant seed in vain, because your enemies will eat it. [17]I will set my face against you so that you will be defeated by your enemies; those who hate you will rule over you, and you will flee even when no one is pursuing you.

[18]" 'If after all this you will not listen to me, I will punish you for your sins seven times over. [19]I will break down your stubborn pride and make the sky above you like iron and the ground beneath you like bronze. [20]Your strength will be spent in vain, because your soil will not yield its crops, nor will the trees of the land yield their fruit.

[21]" 'If you remain hostile toward me and refuse to listen to me, I will multiply your afflictions seven times over, as your sins deserve. [22]I will send wild animals against you, and they will rob you of your children, destroy your cattle and make you so few in number that your roads will be deserted.

[23]" 'If in spite of these things you do not accept my correction but continue to be hostile toward me, [24]I myself will be hostile toward you and will afflict you for your sins seven times over. [25]And I will bring the sword upon you to avenge the breaking of the covenant. When you withdraw into your cities, I will send a plague among you, and you will be given into enemy hands. [26]When I cut off your supply of bread, ten women will be able to bake your bread in one oven, and they will dole out the bread by weight. You will eat, but you will not be satisfied.

[27]" 'If in spite of this you still do not listen to me but continue to be hostile toward me, [28]then in my anger I will be hostile toward you, and I myself will punish you for your sins seven times over. [29]You will eat the flesh of your sons and the flesh of your daughters. [30]I will destroy your high places, cut down your incense altars and pile your dead bodies on the lifeless forms of your idols, and I will abhor you. [31]I will turn your cities into ruins and lay waste your sanctuaries, and I will take no delight in the pleasing aroma of your offerings. [32]I will lay waste the land, so that your enemies who live there will be appalled. [33]I will scatter you among the nations and will draw out my sword and pursue you. Your land will be laid waste, and your cities will lie in ruins. [34]Then the land will enjoy its sabbath years all the time that it lies desolate and you are in the country of your enemies; then the land will rest and enjoy its sabbaths. [35]All the time that it lies desolate, the land will have the rest it did not have during the sabbaths you lived in it.

[36]" 'As for those of you who are left, I will make their hearts so fearful in the lands of their enemies that the sound of a windblown leaf will put them to flight. They will run as though fleeing from the sword, and they will fall, even though no one is pursuing them. [37]They will stumble over one another as though fleeing from the sword, even though no one is pursuing them. So you will not be able to stand before your enemies. [38]You will perish among the nations; the land of your enemies will devour you. [39]Those of you who are left will waste away in the lands of their enemies because of their sins; also because of their fathers' sins they will waste away.

[40]" 'But if they will confess their sins and the sins of their fathers—their treachery against me and their hostility toward me, [41]which made me hostile toward them so that I sent them into the land of their enemies—then when their uncircumcised hearts are humbled and they pay for their sin, [42]I will remember my covenant with Jacob and my covenant with Isaac and my covenant with Abraham, and I will remember the land. [43]For the land will be deserted by them and will enjoy its sabbaths while it lies desolate without them. They will pay for their sins because they rejected my laws and abhorred my decrees.

An Arm Too Short?

Numbers 11:4–23; 31–34

The book of Numbers covers a journey through the desert that should have lasted about fourteen days, but instead lasted forty years. When they first crossed into the Sinai Peninsula, the Israelites were bursting with a spirit of hope and adventure. Free at last from the chains of slavery, they headed toward the Promised Land. But the weeks, months, and then years of wandering in a hostile desert soon wore down all positive feelings.

With relentless honesty, Numbers tells what happened to change a short excursion into a forty-year detour. Petty things seemed to bother the Israelites most, as their constant complaints about food indicate. With a few exceptions, they ate the same thing every day: *manna* (meaning, literally, "What is it?"), which appeared like dew on the ground each morning. A monotonous diet may seem a trivial exchange for freedom from slavery, but read their grumbling for yourself in this chapter.

The rebellion portrayed here was typical of the whole journey. And the more childishly the people acted, the more their leaders were forced to respond like stern parents. As this chapter shows, Moses and God took turns getting exasperated by the Israelites' constant whining.

True, conditions were rigorous: Facing a constant threat from enemy armies, the tribes had to march under a broiling sun through a desert region oppressed by snakes, scorpions, and constant drought. But the underlying issue was a simple test of faith: Would they trust God to see them through such hard circumstances? Would they follow the terms of the covenant he had signed with them and depend on his promised protection? As God himself put it, "Is the LORD's arm too short? You will now see whether or not what I say will come true for you" (11:23).

> **To Reflect On:** *Do you ever "grumble" against God? If so, what tends to make you do so?*

NUMBERS 11:4–23; 31–34

Quail From the Lord

⁴The rabble with them began to crave other food, and again the Israelites started wailing and said, "If only we had meat to eat! ⁵We remember the fish we ate in Egypt at no cost—also the cucumbers, melons, leeks, onions and garlic. ⁶But now we have lost our appetite; we never see anything but this manna!"

⁷The manna was like coriander seed and looked like resin. ⁸The people went around gathering it, and then ground it in a hand-mill or crushed it in a mortar. They cooked it in a pot or made it into cakes. And it tasted like something made with olive oil. ⁹When the dew settled on the camp at night, the manna also came down.

¹⁰Moses heard the people of every family wailing, each at the entrance to his tent. The Lord became exceedingly angry, and Moses was troubled. ¹¹He asked the Lord, "Why have you brought this trouble on your servant? What have I done to displease you that you put the burden of all these people on me? ¹²Did I conceive all these people? Did I give them birth? Why do you tell me to carry them in my arms, as a nurse carries an infant, to the land you promised on oath to their forefathers? ¹³Where can I get meat for all these people? They keep wailing to me, 'Give us meat to eat!' ¹⁴I cannot carry all these people by myself; the burden is too heavy for me. ¹⁵If this is how you are going to treat me, put me to death right now—if I have found favor in your eyes—and do not let me face my own ruin."

¹⁶The Lord said to Moses: "Bring me seventy of Israel's elders who are known to you as leaders and officials among the people. Have them come to the Tent of Meeting, that they may stand there with you. ¹⁷I will come down and speak with you there, and I will take of the Spirit that is on you and put the Spirit on them. They will help you carry the burden of the people so that you will not have to carry it alone.

¹⁸"Tell the people: 'Consecrate yourselves in preparation for tomorrow, when you will eat meat. The Lord heard you when you wailed, "If only we had meat to eat! We were better off in Egypt!" Now the Lord will give you meat, and you will eat it. ¹⁹You will not eat it for just one day, or two days, or five, ten or twenty days, ²⁰but for a whole month—until it comes out of your nostrils and you loathe it—because you have rejected the Lord, who is among you, and have wailed before him, saying, "Why did we ever leave Egypt?"'"

²¹But Moses said, "Here I am among six hundred thousand men on foot, and you say, 'I will give them meat to eat for a whole month!' ²²Would they have enough if flocks and herds were slaughtered for them? Would they have enough if all the fish in the sea were caught for them?"

²³The Lord answered Moses, "Is the Lord's arm too short? You will now see whether or not what I say will come true for you."

³¹Now a wind went out from the Lord and drove quail in from the sea. It brought them down all around the camp to about three feet above the ground, as far as a day's walk in any direction. ³²All that day and night and all the next day the people went out and gathered quail. No one gathered less than ten homers. Then they spread them out all around the camp. ³³But while the meat was still between their teeth and before it could be consumed, the anger of the Lord burned against the people, and he struck them with a severe plague. ³⁴Therefore the place was named Kibroth Hattaavah, because there they buried the people who had craved other food.

Mutiny

Numbers 14:1–44

Most ancient histories record the heroic exploits of mighty warriors and unblemished leaders. The Bible, however, gives a strikingly different picture, as seen in the brutal realism of a book like Numbers. On a dozen different occasions the Israelites lashed out in despair or rose up in rebellion, plotting against their leaders and denouncing God. The spirit of revolt spread to the priests, to the military, to Moses' family, and ultimately to Moses himself.

This chapter recounts the pivotal event of Numbers, the most decisive event since the Exodus from Egypt. The Israelites were poised on the very border of the Promised Land. If they simply trusted God, they could leave the torturous desert and walk into a land abundant with food and water. Military scouts were delivering their final report on what they had seen.

But despite the miracles God had already performed on their behalf, the Israelites chose to distrust him once again. Cowed by the scouting report of potential opposition, they loudly bemoaned the original decision to leave Egypt. In open mutiny, they even conspired to stone Moses and his brother Aaron.

The real object of revolt, the Israelites' God, felt spurned like a cast-off lover. Convinced at last that this band of renegades was unprepared for conquest of the Promised Land, he postponed all plans. The covenant promise of a new nation in a new land would have to wait, at least until all adults of the grumbling generation had died off. And that's why, out of the many thousands who had left Egypt, only two adults, Joshua and Caleb, survived to enter the Promised Land.

The Israelites had lost faith not only in themselves, but in their God. The apostle Paul points out that these failures "happened to them as examples and were written down as warnings for us, on whom the fulfillment of the ages has come. So, if you think you are standing firm, be careful that you don't fall!" (1 Corinthians 10:11–12).

To Reflect On: *What "giants" cause you fear? How do you respond?*

NUMBERS 14:1–44

The People Rebel

14 That night all the people of the community raised their voices and wept aloud. ²All the Israelites grumbled against Moses and Aaron, and the whole assembly said to them, "If only we had died in Egypt! Or in this desert! ³Why is the LORD bringing us to this land only to let us fall by the sword? Our wives and children will be taken as plunder. Wouldn't it be better for us to go back to Egypt?" ⁴And they said to each other, "We should choose a leader and go back to Egypt."

⁵Then Moses and Aaron fell facedown in front of the whole Israelite assembly gathered there. ⁶Joshua son of Nun and Caleb son of Jephunneh, who were among those who had explored the land, tore their clothes ⁷and said to the entire Israelite assembly, "The land we passed through and explored is exceedingly good. ⁸If the LORD is pleased with us, he will lead us into that land, a land flowing with milk and honey, and will give it to us. ⁹Only do not rebel against the LORD. And do not be afraid of the people of the land, because we will swallow them up. Their protection is gone, but the LORD is with us. Do not be afraid of them."

¹⁰But the whole assembly talked about stoning them. Then the glory of the LORD appeared at the Tent of Meeting to all the Israelites. ¹¹The LORD said to Moses, "How

long will these people treat me with contempt? How long will they refuse to believe in me, in spite of all the miraculous signs I have performed among them? 12I will strike them down with a plague and destroy them, but I will make you into a nation greater and stronger than they."

13Moses said to the LORD, "Then the Egyptians will hear about it! By your power you brought these people up from among them. 14And they will tell the inhabitants of this land about it. They have already heard that you, O LORD, are with these people and that you, O LORD, have been seen face to face, that your cloud stays over them, and that you go before them in a pillar of cloud by day and a pillar of fire by night. 15If you put these people to death all at one time, the nations who have heard this report about you will say, 16'The LORD was not able to bring these people into the land he promised them on oath; so he slaughtered them in the desert.'

17"Now may the Lord's strength be displayed, just as you have declared: 18'The LORD is slow to anger, abounding in love and forgiving sin and rebellion. Yet he does not leave the guilty unpunished; he punishes the children for the sin of the fathers to the third and fourth generation.' 19In accordance with your great love, forgive the sin of these people, just as you have pardoned them from the time they left Egypt until now."

20The LORD replied, "I have forgiven them, as you asked. 21Nevertheless, as surely as I live and as surely as the glory of the LORD fills the whole earth, 22not one of the men who saw my glory and the miraculous signs I performed in Egypt and in the desert but who disobeyed me and tested me ten times— 23not one of them will ever see the land I promised on oath to their forefathers. No one who has treated me with contempt will ever see it. 24But because my servant Caleb has a different spirit and follows me wholeheartedly, I will bring him into the land he went to, and his descendants will inherit it. 25Since the Amalekites and Canaanites are living in the valleys, turn back tomorrow and set out toward the desert along the route to the Red Sea."

26The LORD said to Moses and Aaron: 27"How long will this wicked community grumble against me? I have heard the complaints of these grumbling Israelites. 28So tell them, 'As surely as I live, declares the LORD, I will do to you the very things I heard you say: 29In this desert your bodies will fall—every one of you twenty years old or more who was counted in the census and who has grumbled against me. 30Not one of you will enter the land I swore with uplifted hand to make your home, except Caleb son of Jephunneh and Joshua son of Nun. 31As for your children that you said would be taken as plunder, I will bring them in to enjoy the land you have rejected. 32But you—your bodies will fall in this desert. 33Your children will be shepherds here for forty years, suffering for your unfaithfulness, until the last of your bodies lies in the desert. 34For forty years—one year for each of the forty days you explored the land—you will suffer for your sins and know what it is like to have me against you.' 35I, the LORD, have spoken, and I will surely do these things to this whole wicked community, which has banded together against me. They will meet their end in this desert; here they will die."

36So the men Moses had sent to explore the land, who returned and made the whole community grumble against him by spreading a bad report about it— 37these men responsible for spreading the bad report about the land were struck down and died of a plague before the LORD. 38Of the men who went to explore the land, only Joshua son of Nun and Caleb son of Jephunneh survived.

39When Moses reported this to all the Israelites, they mourned bitterly. 40Early the next morning they went up toward the high hill country. "We have sinned," they said. "We will go up to the place the LORD promised."

41But Moses said, "Why are you disobeying the LORD's command? This will not succeed! 42Do not go up, because the LORD is not with you. You will be defeated by your enemies, 43for the Amalekites and Canaanites will face you there. Because you have turned away from the LORD, he will not be with you and you will fall by the sword."

44Nevertheless, in their presumption they went up toward the high hill country, though neither Moses nor the ark of the LORD's covenant moved from the camp.

Never Forget

Deuteronomy 4:7–38

Four decades later the Israelites stood at the edge of the Promised Land, spiritually and physically seasoned by forty years of wilderness wanderings. With the older generation of doubters and grumblers now dead and buried, a new generation chafed to march in and claim the land. Egypt was a faint memory from childhood; God's people finally had their own cultural identity.

There at the border, the old man Moses delivered three speeches that, for their length and emotional power, have no equal in the Bible. It was his last chance to advise and inspire the people he had led for forty tumultuous years. Passionately, deliberately, tearfully, he reviewed their history step by step, occasionally flaring up at a painful memory but more often pouring out the anguished love of a doting parent. An undercurrent of sadness runs through the speeches, for Moses had learned he would not join in the triumph of entering Canaan.

Moses' longest speech (chapters 4–26) reiterated all the laws that the Israelites had agreed to keep as their part of the covenant. But this was no dry recitation of a legal code. Moses reminisced and embellished and preached, filling in the outline of his speech with personal reminders, object lessons, and sudden outbursts of emotion. His central message: Never forget the lessons you learned in the desert.

In this chapter, Moses recalls the hallmark day when God delivered the covenant on Mount Sinai. He remembers aloud the black clouds and deep darkness and blazing fire. *You saw no shape or form of God on that day,* he reminds them. God's Presence cannot be reduced to any mere image. *Remember that. Don't repeat the mistakes of your parents, who melted their gold into an idol even as I met with God on the mountain.*

Besides all the warnings, Moses was giving a kind of pep talk, a final challenge for the Israelites to recognize their unique calling as a nation. If they followed God's laws, all the lavish benefits of the covenant would be theirs. More, every other nation would look to them and want to know their God. "Has anything so great as this ever happened, or has anything like it ever been heard of?" said Moses (4:32). He seemed incurably astonished at all God had done for him and the other Israelites, and this speech represented his last chance to communicate that sense of wonder and thanksgiving.

> **To Reflect On:** *If you reviewed your own history with God, as Moses did for the Israelites, what lessons would you learn? For what are you most grateful?*

DEUTERONOMY 4:7–38

Obedience Commanded

7 What other nation is so great as to have their gods near them the way the LORD our God is near us whenever we pray to him? 8 And what other nation is so great as to have such righteous decrees and laws as this body of laws I am setting before you today?

9 Only be careful, and watch yourselves closely so that you do not forget the things your eyes have seen or let them slip from your heart as long as you live. Teach them to your children and to their children after them. 10 Remember the day you stood before the LORD your God at Horeb, when he said to me, "Assemble the people before me to hear my words so that they may learn to

revere me as long as they live in the land and may teach them to their children." [11]You came near and stood at the foot of the mountain while it blazed with fire to the very heavens, with black clouds and deep darkness. [12]Then the LORD spoke to you out of the fire. You heard the sound of words but saw no form; there was only a voice. [13]He declared to you his covenant, the Ten Commandments, which he commanded you to follow and then wrote them on two stone tablets. [14]And the LORD directed me at that time to teach you the decrees and laws you are to follow in the land that you are crossing the Jordan to possess.

Idolatry Forbidden

[15]You saw no form of any kind the day the LORD spoke to you at Horeb out of the fire. Therefore watch yourselves very carefully, [16]so that you do not become corrupt and make for yourselves an idol, an image of any shape, whether formed like a man or a woman, [17]or like any animal on earth or any bird that flies in the air, [18]or like any creature that moves along the ground or any fish in the waters below. [19]And when you look up to the sky and see the sun, the moon and the stars—all the heavenly array—do not be enticed into bowing down to them and worshiping things the LORD your God has apportioned to all the nations under heaven. [20]But as for you, the LORD took you and brought you out of the iron-smelting furnace, out of Egypt, to be the people of his inheritance, as you now are.

[21]The LORD was angry with me because of you, and he solemnly swore that I would not cross the Jordan and enter the good land the LORD your God is giving you as your inheritance. [22]I will die in this land; I will not cross the Jordan; but you are about to cross over and take possession of that good land. [23]Be careful not to forget the covenant of the LORD your God that he made with you; do not make for yourselves an idol in the form of anything the LORD your God has forbidden. [24]For the LORD your God is a consuming fire, a jealous God.

[25]After you have had children and grandchildren and have lived in the land a long time—if you then become corrupt and make any kind of idol, doing evil in the eyes of the LORD your God and provoking him to anger, [26]I call heaven and earth as witnesses against you this day that you will quickly perish from the land that you are crossing the Jordan to possess. You will not live there long but will certainly be destroyed. [27]The LORD will scatter you among the peoples, and only a few of you will survive among the nations to which the LORD will drive you. [28]There you will worship man-made gods of wood and stone, which cannot see or hear or eat or smell. [29]But if from there you seek the LORD your God, you will find him if you look for him with all your heart and with all your soul. [30]When you are in distress and all these things have happened to you, then in later days you will return to the LORD your God and obey him. [31]For the LORD your God is a merciful God; he will not abandon or destroy you or forget the covenant with your forefathers, which he confirmed to them by oath.

The LORD Is God

[32]Ask now about the former days, long before your time, from the day God created man on the earth; ask from one end of the heavens to the other. Has anything so great as this ever happened, or has anything like it ever been heard of? [33]Has any other people heard the voice of God speaking out of fire, as you have, and lived? [34]Has any god ever tried to take for himself one nation out of another nation, by testings, by miraculous signs and wonders, by war, by a mighty hand and an outstretched arm, or by great and awesome deeds, like all the things the LORD your God did for you in Egypt before your very eyes?

[35]You were shown these things so that you might know that the LORD is God; besides him there is no other. [36]From heaven he made you hear his voice to discipline you. On earth he showed you his great fire, and you heard his words from out of the fire. [37]Because he loved your forefathers and chose their descendants after them, he brought you out of Egypt by his Presence and his great strength, [38]to drive out before you nations greater and stronger than you and to bring you into their land to give it to you for your inheritance, as it is today.

Perils of Success

Deuteronomy 8

When things are bad, we are not ashamed of our God. We are only ashamed of Him when things are going well." Alexander Solzhenitsyn wrote those words to explain why it was in a Siberian concentration camp that he had first learned to pray. He turned to prayer because he had no other hope. Before his arrest, when things were going well, he had seldom given God a thought.

Moses expressed something very similar in his summary speech to the Israelites. They had learned the habit of depending on God in the Sinai wilderness, where they had no choice; they needed his intervention each day just to eat, and drink. But now, on the banks of the Jordan River, they were about to face a more difficult test of faith. After they entered the land of plenty, would they soon forget the God who had given it to them?

Desert-bred, the Israelites knew little about the seductions of other cultures: the alluring sensuality, the exotic religions, the glittering wealth. Now they were preparing to march into a region known for these enticements, and Moses seemed to fear the coming prosperity far more than the rigors of the desert. In the beautiful land, the Promised Land, the Israelites might put God behind them and credit themselves for their success.

"Remember!" Moses kept urging. Remember the days of slavery in Egypt, and God's acts of liberation. Remember the trials of the vast and desolate desert, and God's faithfulness there. Remember your special calling as God's peculiar treasures. Do not forget, as a prosperous nation, what you learned as refugees in the wilderness.

Moses had good reason for concern, for God, who could see the future, had told him plainly what would happen: "When I have brought them into the land flowing with milk and honey, the land I promised on oath to their forefathers, and when they eat their fill and thrive, they will turn to other gods and worship them, rejecting me and breaking my covenant" (31:20). As the books following Deuteronomy relate, all of Moses' fears came true.

Ironically, as Deuteronomy shows, success may make it harder to depend on God. The Israelites proved less faithful to God after they moved into the Promised Land. There is a grave danger in finally getting what you want.

> **To Reflect On:** *Do you think most about God when things are going well or when you are in trouble?*

DEUTERONOMY 8
Do Not Forget the Lord

8 Be careful to follow every command I am giving you today, so that you may live and increase and may enter and possess the land that the Lord promised on oath to your forefathers. ²Remember how the Lord your God led you all the way in the desert these forty years, to humble you and to test you in order to know what was in your heart, whether or not you would keep his commands. ³He humbled you, causing you to hunger and then feeding you with manna, which neither you nor your fathers had known, to teach you that man does not live on bread alone but on every word that comes from the mouth of the Lord. ⁴Your clothes did not wear out and your feet did not swell during these forty years. ⁵Know then in your heart that as a man disciplines his son, so the Lord your God disciplines you.

⁶Observe the commands of the Lord your God, walking in his ways and revering him. ⁷For the Lord your God is bringing you into a good land—a land with streams and pools of water, with springs flowing in the valleys and hills; ⁸a land with wheat and barley, vines and fig trees, pomegranates, olive oil and honey; ⁹a land where bread will not be scarce and you will lack nothing; a land where the rocks are iron and you can dig copper out of the hills.

¹⁰When you have eaten and are satisfied, praise the Lord your God for the good land he has given you. ¹¹Be careful that you do not forget the Lord your God, failing to observe his commands, his laws and his decrees that I am giving you this day. ¹²Otherwise, when you eat and are satisfied, when you build fine houses and settle down, ¹³and when your herds and flocks grow large and your silver and gold increase and all you have is multiplied, ¹⁴then your heart will become proud and you will forget the Lord your God, who brought you out of Egypt, out of the land of slavery. ¹⁵He led you through the vast and dreadful desert, that thirsty and waterless land, with its venomous snakes and scorpions. He brought you water out of hard rock. ¹⁶He gave you manna to eat in the desert, something your fathers had never known, to humble and to test you so that in the end it might go well with you. ¹⁷You may say to yourself, "My power and the strength of my hands have produced this wealth for me." ¹⁸But remember the Lord your God, for it is he who gives you the ability to produce wealth, and so confirms his covenant, which he swore to your forefathers, as it is today. ¹⁹If you ever forget the Lord your God and follow other gods and worship and bow down to them, I testify against you today that you will surely be destroyed. ²⁰Like the nations the Lord destroyed before you, so you will be destroyed for not obeying the Lord your God.

Loud and Clear

Deuteronomy 28:1–29

Archaeologists have turned up samples of Near Eastern treaties that shed light on the covenant between God and the Israelites. Typically, a small nation seeking protection would negotiate a "suzerainty treaty" with a powerful ruler, and Deuteronomy seems to follow closely the pattern of these treaties. It sets down in official form the relationship between the Israelites and God.

The national treaties usually consisted of the following elements:

1. An introduction identifying the parties of the treaty.
2. A capsule history of prior relations between the two parties.
3. Laws defining each party's obligations.
4. Public witnesses to the treaties.
5. Curses and blessings specifying what will take place should one of the parties break the treaty.

Deuteronomy contains every one of those elements, in the proper order. And the last of Moses' three great speeches, beginning in chapter 27, summarizes the curses and blessings.

For once, nearly everyone in the Israelite camp was jubilant. They stood, eager as children, at the edge of the long-awaited land. Moses, however, held back, unable to share the spirit of optimism. For forty years he had led his cranky tribesmen, and he knew them too well to think that a change in scenery would alter their old ways. A doleful sense of fatalism hangs over these last chapters of Deuteronomy. The Israelites had failed far too often; they were doomed to fail again.

Aware of the significance of this, his last chance to impress upon the Israelites the seriousness of their covenant with God, Moses pulled out all the stops. He began with the speech recorded here. The benefits of keeping the covenant Moses defined in simple and elegant terms, but as he related the consequences of breaking it, his language changed in pitch. His descriptions of those consequences are unmatched for their horror.

As if acknowledging that words were not strong enough to communicate to the Israelites, Moses also orchestrated a dramatic sequence of object lessons that would live in their memories forever. First he had the words of the law painted on some large plaster-coated stones, so that the tribes would pass by visual reminders of the covenant as they entered Canaan. Then, pre-selected shouters climbed two mountains with a narrow valley in between to yell out the rules governing the covenant. As the tribes entered the new land, their ears rang with the loud dissonance of wonderful blessings from one side clashing with horrific curses from the other.

Finally, just in case the Israelites didn't get the message, Moses taught them a song given him by God (chapter 32). Everyone memorized it and sang it as they marched into Canaan. Thus at the birth of their nation, euphoric over the crossing of the Jordan River, the Israelites premiered a kind of national anthem, the strangest national anthem that has ever been sung. It had virtually no words of hope, only doom.

> **To Reflect On:** *Do the principles set forth in this chapter—"Do good, get blessed; do evil, get punished"—still apply today? Why or why not?*

DEUTERONOMY 28:1-29

Blessings for Obedience

28 If you fully obey the LORD your God and carefully follow all his commands I give you today, the LORD your God will set you high above all the nations on earth. ²All these blessings will come upon you and accompany you if you obey the LORD your God:

³You will be blessed in the city and blessed in the country.

⁴The fruit of your womb will be blessed, and the crops of your land and the young of your livestock—the calves of your herds and the lambs of your flocks.

⁵Your basket and your kneading trough will be blessed.

⁶You will be blessed when you come in and blessed when you go out.

⁷The LORD will grant that the enemies who rise up against you will be defeated before you. They will come at you from one direction but flee from you in seven.

⁸The LORD will send a blessing on your barns and on everything you put your hand to. The LORD your God will bless you in the land he is giving you.

⁹The LORD will establish you as his holy people, as he promised you on oath, if you keep the commands of the LORD your God and walk in his ways. ¹⁰Then all the peoples on earth will see that you are called by the name of the LORD, and they will fear you. ¹¹The LORD will grant you abundant prosperity—in the fruit of your womb, the young of your livestock and the crops of your ground—in the land he swore to your forefathers to give you.

¹²The LORD will open the heavens, the storehouse of his bounty, to send rain on your land in season and to bless all the work of your hands. You will lend to many nations but will borrow from none. ¹³The LORD will make you the head, not the tail. If you pay attention to the commands of the LORD your God that I give you this day and carefully follow them, you will always be at the top, never at the bottom. ¹⁴Do not turn aside from any of the commands I give you today, to the right or to the left, following other gods and serving them.

Curses for Disobedience

¹⁵However, if you do not obey the LORD your God and do not carefully follow all his commands and decrees I am giving you today, all these curses will come upon you and overtake you:

¹⁶You will be cursed in the city and cursed in the country.

¹⁷Your basket and your kneading trough will be cursed.

¹⁸The fruit of your womb will be cursed, and the crops of your land, and the calves of your herds and the lambs of your flocks.

¹⁹You will be cursed when you come in and cursed when you go out.

²⁰The LORD will send on you curses, confusion and rebuke in everything you put your hand to, until you are destroyed and come to sudden ruin because of the evil you have done in forsaking him. ²¹The LORD will plague you with diseases until he has destroyed you from the land you are entering to possess. ²²The LORD will strike you with wasting disease, with fever and inflammation, with scorching heat and drought, with blight and mildew, which will plague you until you perish. ²³The sky over your head will be bronze, the ground beneath you iron. ²⁴The LORD will turn the rain of your country into dust and powder; it will come down from the skies until you are destroyed.

²⁵The LORD will cause you to be defeated before your enemies. You will come at them from one direction but flee from them in seven, and you will become a thing of horror to all the kingdoms on earth. ²⁶Your carcasses will be food for all the birds of the air and the beasts of the earth, and there will be no one to frighten them away. ²⁷The LORD will afflict you with the boils of Egypt and with tumors, festering sores and the itch, from which you cannot be cured. ²⁸The LORD will afflict you with madness, blindness and confusion of mind. ²⁹At midday you will grope about like a blind man in the dark. You will be unsuccessful in everything you do; day after day you will be oppressed and robbed, with no one to rescue you.

This Time with Courage

Joshua 2

Often, as we have seen, the Israelites offer examples of what *not* to do. The books of Exodus, Numbers, and Deuteronomy contain many negative lessons and Moses' speeches hint at further failures to come. But the Old Testament does contain a few bright spots of hope, with the book of Joshua representing one of the brightest.

Joshua's opening scene replays an earlier scene. After listening to Moses' swan song speeches, the refugees amassed again beside the Jordan River for a test of courage and faith. Were they ready to cross into the Promised Land? Forty years before, their forebears had panicked in fear. Now, without their legendary leader, Moses, would the Israelites panic again? They had no chariots or even horses, only primitive arms, an untested new leader, and the promise of God's protection.

But an entirely new spirit characterized this group, and the spy story in Joshua 2 expresses the difference clearly. Forty years ago, sparking a revolt among the Israelites, only two of the twelve spies had held out any optimism. But the older generation with its fearful slave mentality had died off, and the new generation was now led by one of the original optimistic spies, Joshua.

This time, Joshua handpicked his own scouts, and the report they brought back makes a sharp contrast with the spy report in Numbers (13:31–33). The new scouts concluded, "The LORD has surely given the whole land into our hands; all the people are melting in fear because of us." Thus Joshua begins as a good-news book, a welcome relief from the discouragement of Numbers and the fatalism of Deuteronomy. What a difference forty years had made!

The heroine of this chapter, Rahab the pagan prostitute, became a favorite figure in Jewish stories and was esteemed by Bible writers as well (see Hebrews 11:31 and James 2:25). She proves that God honors true faith from anyone, regardless of race or religious background. In fact, Rahab, survivor of Jericho, became a direct ancestress of Jesus.

> **To Reflect On:** *Two sets of spies (Moses' and Joshua's) surveyed the same land, but brought back radically different reports. When you confront obstacles, are you more likely to see them as problems or as opportunities?*

JOSHUA 2

Rahab and the Spies

2 Then Joshua son of Nun secretly sent two spies from Shittim. "Go, look over the land," he said, "especially Jericho." So they went and entered the house of a prostitute named Rahab and stayed there.

2 The king of Jericho was told, "Look! Some of the Israelites have come here tonight to spy out the land." 3 So the king of Jericho sent this message to Rahab: "Bring out the men who came to you and entered your house, because they have come to spy out the whole land."

4 But the woman had taken the two men and hidden them. She said, "Yes, the men came to me, but I did not know where they had come from. 5 At dusk, when it was time to close the city gate, the men left. I don't know which way they went. Go after them quickly. You may catch up with them." 6 (But she had taken them up to the roof and hidden them under the stalks of flax she had laid out on the roof.) 7 So the men set out in pursuit of the spies on the road that leads to the fords of the Jordan, and as soon as the pursuers had gone out, the gate was shut.

8 Before the spies lay down for the night, she went up on the roof 9 and said to them, "I know that the LORD has given this land to you and that a great fear of you has fallen on us, so that all who live in this country are melting in fear because of you. 10 We have heard how the LORD dried up the water of the Red Sea for you when you came out of Egypt, and what you did to Sihon and Og, the two kings of the Amorites east of the Jordan, whom you completely destroyed. 11 When we heard of it, our hearts melted and everyone's courage failed because of you, for the LORD your God is God in heaven above and on the earth below. 12 Now then, please swear to me by the LORD that you will show kindness to my family, because I have

shown kindness to you. Give me a sure sign 13 that you will spare the lives of my father and mother, my brothers and sisters, and all who belong to them, and that you will save us from death."

14 "Our lives for your lives!" the men assured her. "If you don't tell what we are doing, we will treat you kindly and faithfully when the LORD gives us the land."

15 So she let them down by a rope through the window, for the house she lived in was part of the city wall. 16 Now she had said to them, "Go to the hills so the pursuers will not find you. Hide yourselves there three days until they return, and then go on your way."

17 The men said to her, "This oath you made us swear will not be binding on us 18 unless, when we enter the land, you have tied this scarlet cord in the window through which you let us down, and unless you have brought your father and mother, your brothers and all your family into your house. 19 If anyone goes outside your house into the street, his blood will be on his own head; we will not be responsible. As for anyone who is in the house with you, his blood will be on our head if a hand is laid on him. 20 But if you tell what we are doing, we will be released from the oath you made us swear."

21 "Agreed," she replied. "Let it be as you say." So she sent them away and they departed. And she tied the scarlet cord in the window.

22 When they left, they went into the hills and stayed there three days, until the pursuers had searched all along the road and returned without finding them. 23 Then the two men started back. They went down out of the hills, forded the river and came to Joshua son of Nun and told him everything that had happened to them. 24 They said to Joshua, "The LORD has surely given the whole land into our hands; all the people are melting in fear because of us."

Strange Tactics

Joshua 5:13–6:27

The Israelites' abysmal failures in the Sinai Desert can be traced back to a simple matter of disobedience. Despite unmistakable divine guidance—a dark cloud and a pillar of fire led them each day—they insisted on choosing their own way over God's. Would the new generation respond any differently? Once they had crossed into Canaan, God tested the Israelites' new resolve to follow him, and it must have strained their faith to new limits.

As for the residents of Canaan, who had long heard about the Israelites' plan to conquer the Promised Land, they braced for the worst. Citizens of Jericho, the first city in the invaders' path, barricaded themselves behind stone walls and awaited the feared onslaught. But how did the vaunted Israelites spend their first week in Canaan? They built a stone monument to God, performed circumcision rituals, and held a Passover celebration—not the sort of behavior you'd expect from a conquering army.

The incidents recorded in Joshua seem specially selected to strike home the point that God, no one else, was in charge. Just before the battle of Jericho, a supernatural visitor appeared to Joshua to embolden him and remind him of the true commander of this military campaign. And the bizarre tactics of the Israelites in besieging Jericho left no doubt who was really in charge. An army could hardly take credit for victory when all it did was march around in circles and shout.

Jericho was probably a center for the worship of the moon god in Canaan, and so the destruction of that city—like the Ten Plagues on Egypt—symbolically announced an open warfare between the God of the Israelites and the region's pagan gods. Although measures against the Canaanites may seem harsh, the Bible makes clear that they had forfeited their right to the land. As Moses told the Israelites, "It is not because of your righteousness or your integrity that you are going in to take possession of their land; but on account of the wickedness of these nations, the LORD your God will drive them out before you" (Deuteronomy 9:5). And, as the story of Rahab shows, Canaanites who turned to God were spared.

> **To Reflect On:** *Do you ever feel foolish or strange when following what you are convinced is God's plan for you?*

JOSHUA 5:13–6:27

The Fall of Jericho

¹³Now when Joshua was near Jericho, he looked up and saw a man standing in front of him with a drawn sword in his hand. Joshua went up to him and asked, "Are you for us or for our enemies?"

¹⁴"Neither," he replied, "but as commander of the army of the LORD I have now come." Then Joshua fell facedown to the ground in reverence, and asked him, "What message does my Lord have for his servant?"

¹⁵The commander of the LORD's army replied, "Take off your sandals, for the place where you are standing is holy." And Joshua did so.

6 Now Jericho was tightly shut up because of the Israelites. No one went out and no one came in.

²Then the LORD said to Joshua, "See, I have delivered Jericho into your hands, along with its king and its fighting men. ³March around the city once with all the armed men. Do this for six days. ⁴Have seven priests carry trumpets of rams' horns in front of the ark. On the seventh day,

march around the city seven times, with the priests blowing the trumpets. ⁵When you hear them sound a long blast on the trumpets, have all the people give a loud shout; then the wall of the city will collapse and the people will go up, every man straight in."

⁶So Joshua son of Nun called the priests and said to them, "Take up the ark of the covenant of the LORD and have seven priests carry trumpets in front of it." ⁷And he ordered the people, "Advance! March around the city, with the armed guard going ahead of the ark of the LORD."

⁸When Joshua had spoken to the people, the seven priests carrying the seven trumpets before the LORD went forward, blowing their trumpets, and the ark of the LORD's covenant followed them. ⁹The armed guard marched ahead of the priests who blew the trumpets, and the rear guard followed the ark. All this time the trumpets were sounding. ¹⁰But Joshua had commanded the people, "Do not give a war cry, do not raise your voices, do not say a word until the day I tell you to shout. Then shout!" ¹¹So he had the ark of the LORD carried around the city, circling it once. Then the people returned to camp and spent the night there.

¹²Joshua got up early the next morning and the priests took up the ark of the LORD. ¹³The seven priests carrying the seven trumpets went forward, marching before the ark of the LORD and blowing the trumpets. The armed men went ahead of them and the rear guard followed the ark of the LORD, while the trumpets kept sounding. ¹⁴So on the second day they marched around the city once and returned to the camp. They did this for six days.

¹⁵On the seventh day, they got up at daybreak and marched around the city seven times in the same manner, except that on that day they circled the city seven times. ¹⁶The seventh time around, when the priests sounded the trumpet blast, Joshua commanded the people, "Shout! For the LORD has given you the city! ¹⁷The city and all that is in it are to be devoted to the LORD. Only Rahab the prostitute and all who are

with her in her house shall be spared, because she hid the spies we sent. ¹⁸But keep away from the devoted things, so that you will not bring about your own destruction by taking any of them. Otherwise you will make the camp of Israel liable to destruction and bring trouble on it. ¹⁹All the silver and gold and the articles of bronze and iron are sacred to the LORD and must go into his treasury."

²⁰When the trumpets sounded, the people shouted, and at the sound of the trumpet, when the people gave a loud shout, the wall collapsed; so every man charged straight in, and they took the city. ²¹They devoted the city to the LORD and destroyed with the sword every living thing in it—men and women, young and old, cattle, sheep and donkeys.

²²Joshua said to the two men who had spied out the land, "Go into the prostitute's house and bring her out and all who belong to her, in accordance with your oath to her." ²³So the young men who had done the spying went in and brought out Rahab, her father and mother and brothers and all who belonged to her. They brought out her entire family and put them in a place outside the camp of Israel.

²⁴Then they burned the whole city and everything in it, but they put the silver and gold and the articles of bronze and iron into the treasury of the LORD's house. ²⁵But Joshua spared Rahab the prostitute, with her family and all who belonged to her, because she hid the men Joshua had sent as spies to Jericho—and she lives among the Israelites to this day.

²⁶At that time Joshua pronounced this solemn oath: "Cursed before the LORD is the man who undertakes to rebuild this city, Jericho:

"At the cost of his firstborn son
    will he lay its foundations;
at the cost of his youngest
    will he set up its gates."

²⁷So the LORD was with Joshua, and his fame spread throughout the land.

Slow Learners

Joshua 7

The Bible does not record history for its own sake. Rather, it selects and highlights certain events that yield practical and spiritual lessons. For example, the book of Joshua, which spans a period of approximately seven years, devotes only a few sentences to some extensive military campaigns. But other key events, such as the fall of Jericho, get detailed coverage. That battle established an important pattern: The Israelites would succeed only if they relied on God, not military might.

Perhaps inevitably, the Israelites got cocky after Jericho. Since they had conquered a fortified city without firing an arrow, the next target, the puny town of Ai, should pose no threat at all. A few thousand soldiers strolled toward Ai. A short time later those same soldiers—minus their dead and wounded—were scrambling for home, thoroughly routed.

Clearly, the juxtaposition of these two stories, Jericho and Ai, is meant to convey a lesson. If the Israelites obeyed God and placed their trust in him, no challenge was too great to overcome. On the other hand, if they insisted on their own way, no obstacle was too small to trip them up.

Significantly, Ai stood near the original site where God had appeared to Abraham and revealed the covenant centuries before. A humiliating defeat in that place shook Joshua to the core. He dissolved in fright, earning God's stern rebuke, "Stand up! What are you doing down on your face?"

Without God's protection, Joshua realized, the Israelites were hopelessly vulnerable. After the painful lesson of Ai, he went back to the basics. The public exposure of Achan's sin underscored the need to follow God's orders scrupulously, even in the earthy matter of warfare. God would not tolerate any of the lying or looting typical of invading armies.

In the next chapter, Joshua is shown fulfilling the orders Moses had given before his death. He read aloud all the words of the covenant with God, wrote them in large letters on stones, and divided up the tribes to shout out the blessings and cursings Moses had pronounced. Already, the Israelites needed a refresher course on the law of God.

To Reflect On: *Why would such a seemingly "little" sin, Achan's deceit, have such major consequences?*

JOSHUA 7

Achan's Sin

7 But the Israelites acted unfaithfully in regard to the devoted things; Achan son of Carmi, the son of Zimri, the son of Zerah, of the tribe of Judah, took some of them. So the LORD's anger burned against Israel.

2 Now Joshua sent men from Jericho to Ai, which is near Beth Aven to the east of Bethel, and told them, "Go up and spy out the region." So the men went up and spied out Ai.

3 When they returned to Joshua, they said, "Not all the people will have to go up against Ai. Send two or three thousand men to take it and do not weary all the people, for only a few men are there." 4 So about three thousand men went up; but they were routed by the men of Ai, 5 who killed about thirty-six of them. They chased the Israelites from the city gate as far as the stone quarries and struck them down on the slopes. At this the hearts of the people melted and became like water.

6 Then Joshua tore his clothes and fell facedown to the ground before the ark of

the LORD, remaining there till evening. The elders of Israel did the same, and sprinkled dust on their heads. ⁷And Joshua said, "Ah, Sovereign LORD, why did you ever bring this people across the Jordan to deliver us into the hands of the Amorites to destroy us? If only we had been content to stay on the other side of the Jordan! ⁸O Lord, what can I say, now that Israel has been routed by its enemies? ⁹The Canaanites and the other people of the country will hear about this and they will surround us and wipe out our name from the earth. What then will you do for your own great name?"

¹⁰The LORD said to Joshua, "Stand up! What are you doing down on your face? ¹¹Israel has sinned; they have violated my covenant, which I commanded them to keep. They have taken some of the devoted things; they have stolen, they have lied, they have put them with their own possessions. ¹²That is why the Israelites cannot stand against their enemies; they turn their backs and run because they have been made liable to destruction. I will not be with you anymore unless you destroy whatever among you is devoted to destruction.

¹³"Go, consecrate the people. Tell them, 'Consecrate yourselves in preparation for tomorrow; for this is what the LORD, the God of Israel, says: That which is devoted is among you, O Israel. You cannot stand against your enemies until you remove it.

¹⁴"'In the morning, present yourselves tribe by tribe. The tribe that the LORD takes shall come forward clan by clan; the clan that the LORD takes shall come forward family by family; and the family that the LORD takes shall come forward man by man. ¹⁵He who is caught with the devoted things shall be destroyed by fire, along with all that belongs to him. He has violated the covenant of the LORD and has done a disgraceful thing in Israel!'"

¹⁶Early the next morning Joshua had Israel come forward by tribes, and Judah was taken. ¹⁷The clans of Judah came forward, and he took the Zerahites. He had the clan of the Zerahites come forward by families, and Zimri was taken. ¹⁸Joshua had his family come forward man by man, and Achan son of Carmi, the son of Zimri, the son of Zerah, of the tribe of Judah, was taken. ¹⁹Then Joshua said to Achan, "My son, give glory to the LORD, the God of Israel, and give him the praise. Tell me what you have done; do not hide it from me."

²⁰Achan replied, "It is true! I have sinned against the LORD, the God of Israel. This is what I have done: ²¹When I saw in the plunder a beautiful robe from Babylonia, two hundred shekels of silver and a wedge of gold weighing fifty shekels, I coveted them and took them. They are hidden in the ground inside my tent, with the silver underneath."

²²So Joshua sent messengers, and they ran to the tent, and there it was, hidden in his tent, with the silver underneath. ²³They took the things from the tent, brought them to Joshua and all the Israelites and spread them out before the LORD.

²⁴Then Joshua, together with all Israel, took Achan son of Zerah, the silver, the robe, the gold wedge, his sons and daughters, his cattle, donkeys and sheep, his tent and all that he had, to the Valley of Achor. ²⁵Joshua said, "Why have you brought this trouble on us? The LORD will bring trouble on you today."

Then all Israel stoned him, and after they had stoned the rest, they burned them. ²⁶Over Achan they heaped up a large pile of rocks, which remains to this day. Then the LORD turned from his fierce anger. Therefore that place has been called the Valley of Achor ever since.

Home at Last

Joshua 24

At the end of his life, Joshua, like Moses before him, stood before the Israelites to deliver a farewell address. Things had gone well under his leadership. The Bible gives the remarkable assessment: "Israel served the Lord throughout the lifetime of Joshua." And now Joshua used his final speech to review all that God had done and to remind his people of their obligations under the covenant with God.

"I gave you a land on which you did not toil and cities you did not build"—at every point, Joshua emphasized that *God* was the sole source of their success. He had called out Abraham and blessed him with children, had delivered the Israelites from slavery in Egypt, had carried them across the desert. And in Joshua's own lifetime he had fulfilled one more promise of the covenant: He had given them the Promised Land. It was theirs to live in.

"Choose for yourselves this day whom you will serve," Joshua challenged his listeners in the stirring climax to his speech. All the people present swore their allegiance to God, the God who had kept his covenant with them. Joshua solemnly ratified the covenant and sent the people away, then quietly prepared to die.

The book of Joshua ends with an act of deep symbolism: The Israelites finally buried the remains of Joseph. For well over four centuries those remains had been preserved in Egypt in anticipation of the Israelites' return to their homeland. And during the forty years of wilderness wanderings, the tribes had carried Joseph's bones as a treasured reminder of their past. Now, at last, Abraham's descendants had come home, and even the dead could rest in peace.

> **To Reflect On:** *When you experience success, who do you tend to credit, yourself or God?*

JOSHUA 24

The Covenant Renewed at Shechem

24 Then Joshua assembled all the tribes of Israel at Shechem. He summoned the elders, leaders, judges and officials of Israel, and they presented themselves before God.

²Joshua said to all the people, "This is what the Lord, the God of Israel, says: 'Long ago your forefathers, including Terah the father of Abraham and Nahor, lived beyond the River and worshiped other gods. ³But I took your father Abraham from the land beyond the River and led him throughout Canaan and gave him many descendants. I gave him Isaac, ⁴and to Isaac I gave Jacob and Esau. I assigned the hill country of Seir to Esau, but Jacob and his sons went down to Egypt.

⁵" 'Then I sent Moses and Aaron, and I afflicted the Egyptians by what I did there, and I brought you out. ⁶When I brought your fathers out of Egypt, you came to the sea, and the Egyptians pursued them with chariots and horsemen as far as the Red Sea. ⁷But they cried to the Lord for help, and he put darkness between you and the Egyptians; he brought the sea over them and covered them. You saw with your own eyes what I did to the Egyptians. Then you lived in the desert for a long time.

⁸" 'I brought you to the land of the Amorites who lived east of the Jordan. They fought against you, but I gave them into your hands. I destroyed them from before you, and you took possession of their land. ⁹When Balak son of Zippor, the king of Moab, prepared to fight against Israel, he sent for Balaam son of Beor to put a curse on you. ¹⁰But I would not listen to Balaam, so he blessed you again and again, and I delivered you out of his hand.

11"'Then you crossed the Jordan and came to Jericho. The citizens of Jericho fought against you, as did also the Amorites, Perizzites, Canaanites, Hittites, Girgashites, Hivites and Jebusites, but I gave them into your hands. 12I sent the hornet ahead of you, which drove them out before you—also the two Amorite kings. You did not do it with your own sword and bow. 13So I gave you a land on which you did not toil and cities you did not build; and you live in them and eat from vineyards and olive groves that you did not plant.'

14"Now fear the LORD and serve him with all faithfulness. Throw away the gods your forefathers worshiped beyond the River and in Egypt, and serve the LORD. 15But if serving the LORD seems undesirable to you, then choose for yourselves this day whom you will serve, whether the gods your forefathers served beyond the River, or the gods of the Amorites, in whose land you are living. But as for me and my household, we will serve the LORD."

16Then the people answered, "Far be it from us to forsake the LORD to serve other gods! 17It was the LORD our God himself who brought us and our fathers up out of Egypt, from that land of slavery, and performed those great signs before our eyes. He protected us on our entire journey and among all the nations through which we traveled. 18And the LORD drove out before us all the nations, including the Amorites, who lived in the land. We too will serve the LORD, because he is our God."

19Joshua said to the people, "You are not able to serve the LORD. He is a holy God; he is a jealous God. He will not forgive your rebellion and your sins. 20If you forsake the LORD and serve foreign gods, he will turn and bring disaster on you and make an end of you, after he has been good to you."

21But the people said to Joshua, "No! We will serve the LORD."

22Then Joshua said, "You are witnesses against yourselves that you have chosen to serve the LORD."

"Yes, we are witnesses," they replied.

23"Now then," said Joshua, "throw away the foreign gods that are among you and yield your hearts to the LORD, the God of Israel."

24And the people said to Joshua, "We will serve the LORD our God and obey him."

25On that day Joshua made a covenant for the people, and there at Shechem he drew up for them decrees and laws. 26And Joshua recorded these things in the Book of the Law of God. Then he took a large stone and set it up there under the oak near the holy place of the LORD.

27"See!" he said to all the people. "This stone will be a witness against us. It has heard all the words the LORD has said to us. It will be a witness against you if you are untrue to your God."

Buried in the Promised Land

28Then Joshua sent the people away, each to his own inheritance.

29After these things, Joshua son of Nun, the servant of the LORD, died at the age of a hundred and ten. 30And they buried him in the land of his inheritance, at Timnath Serah in the hill country of Ephraim, north of Mount Gaash.

31Israel served the LORD throughout the lifetime of Joshua and of the elders who outlived him and who had experienced everything the LORD had done for Israel.

32And Joseph's bones, which the Israelites had brought up from Egypt, were buried at Shechem in the tract of land that Jacob bought for a hundred pieces of silver from the sons of Hamor, the father of Shechem. This became the inheritance of Joseph's descendants.

33And Eleazar son of Aaron died and was buried at Gibeah, which had been allotted to his son Phinehas in the hill country of Ephraim.

Leadership Crisis

Judges 6:8–40

The good-news tone of Joshua sours abruptly in the next book, Judges. After an initial spurt of enthusiasm, the Israelites strayed far, very far from the way God had pointed them. Ignoring Joshua's orders to clear the land, they settled in among the pagan occupants instead. These new neighbors practiced an exotic religion that included sex orgies and child sacrifice as a regular part of worship.

Just one generation later, the Israelites had lost their sense of national identity and had forgotten all about their parents' ringing vows to honor the covenant. They, too, were worshiping the idol Baal. Having violated virtually every moral standard, the nation slid toward chaos—much like modern-day Lebanon, Uganda, or Cambodia. The last verse of Judges sums up the scene: "Everyone did as he saw fit."

The Israelites were suffering from a leadership crisis of huge dimensions. For eighty years they had followed Moses and Joshua, two outstanding leaders who proved impossible to replace. When the twelve tribes splintered apart and retreated into separate territories, God turned to more regional leaders called *judges*. The term may be misleading; these were people renowned not for court cases, but for their military campaigns against foreign invaders. (Today they might be called guerrillas or freedom fighters.)

Some judges, such as the hero of this chapter, emerged as models of courage and faith. And yet a close look at the life of Gideon shows the material God had to work with. His family and village worshiped Baal, not the Lord. In the face of God's clear direction, Gideon sputtered, demanded repeated proofs, used delaying tactics, and worshiped at night to avoid detection. He was subject to paralyzing fears, even on the eve of battle. But God, knowing Gideon's potential, step by step brought him to the point of courage.

> **To Reflect On:** *Gideon is often used as an example of God's guidance. But, in light of what you read in this chapter, do you think he's a negative or positive example? Or both?*

JUDGES 6:8–40

Gideon

⁶Midian so impoverished the Israelites that they cried out to the LORD for help.

⁷When the Israelites cried to the LORD because of Midian, ⁸he sent them a prophet, who said, "This is what the LORD, the God of Israel, says: I brought you up out of Egypt, out of the land of slavery. ⁹I snatched you from the power of Egypt and from the hand of all your oppressors. I drove them from before you and gave you their land. ¹⁰I said to you, 'I am the LORD your God; do not worship the gods of the Amorites, in whose land you live.' But you have not listened to me."

¹¹The angel of the LORD came and sat down under the oak in Ophrah that belonged to Joash the Abiezrite, where his son Gideon was threshing wheat in a winepress to keep it from the Midianites. ¹²When the angel of the LORD appeared to Gideon, he said, "The LORD is with you, mighty warrior."

¹³"But sir," Gideon replied, "if the LORD is with us, why has all this happened to us? Where are all his wonders that our fathers told us about when they said, 'Did not the LORD bring us up out of Egypt?' But now the

Lord has abandoned us and put us into the hand of Midian."

¹⁴The Lord turned to him and said, "Go in the strength you have and save Israel out of Midian's hand. Am I not sending you?"

¹⁵"But Lord," Gideon asked, "how can I save Israel? My clan is the weakest in Manasseh, and I am the least in my family."

¹⁶The Lord answered, "I will be with you, and you will strike down all the Midianites together."

¹⁷Gideon replied, "If now I have found favor in your eyes, give me a sign that it is really you talking to me. ¹⁸Please do not go away until I come back and bring my offering and set it before you."

And the Lord said, "I will wait until you return."

¹⁹Gideon went in, prepared a young goat, and from an ephah of flour he made bread without yeast. Putting the meat in a basket and its broth in a pot, he brought them out and offered them to him under the oak.

²⁰The angel of God said to him, "Take the meat and the unleavened bread, place them on this rock, and pour out the broth." And Gideon did so. ²¹With the tip of the staff that was in his hand, the angel of the Lord touched the meat and the unleavened bread. Fire flared from the rock, consuming the meat and the bread. And the angel of the Lord disappeared. ²²When Gideon realized that it was the angel of the Lord, he exclaimed, "Ah, Sovereign Lord! I have seen the angel of the Lord face to face!"

²³But the Lord said to him, "Peace! Do not be afraid. You are not going to die."

²⁴So Gideon built an altar to the Lord there and called it The Lord is Peace. To this day it stands in Ophrah of the Abiezrites.

²⁵That same night the Lord said to him, "Take the second bull from your father's herd, the one seven years old. Tear down your father's altar to Baal and cut down the Asherah pole beside it. ²⁶Then build a proper kind of altar to the Lord your God on the top of this height. Using the wood of the Asherah pole that you cut down, offer the second bull as a burnt offering."

²⁷So Gideon took ten of his servants and did as the Lord told him. But because he was afraid of his family and the men of the town, he did it at night rather than in the daytime.

²⁸In the morning when the men of the town got up, there was Baal's altar, demolished, with the Asherah pole beside it cut down and the second bull sacrificed on the newly built altar!

²⁹They asked each other, "Who did this?"

When they carefully investigated, they were told, "Gideon son of Joash did it."

³⁰The men of the town demanded of Joash, "Bring out your son. He must die, because he has broken down Baal's altar and cut down the Asherah pole beside it."

³¹But Joash replied to the hostile crowd around him, "Are you going to plead Baal's cause? Are you trying to save him? Whoever fights for him shall be put to death by morning! If Baal really is a god, he can defend himself when someone breaks down his altar." ³²So that day they called Gideon "Jerub-Baal," saying, "Let Baal contend with him," because he broke down Baal's altar.

³³Now all the Midianites, Amalekites and other eastern peoples joined forces and crossed over the Jordan and camped in the Valley of Jezreel. ³⁴Then the Spirit of the Lord came upon Gideon, and he blew a trumpet, summoning the Abiezrites to follow him. ³⁵He sent messengers throughout Manasseh, calling them to arms, and also into Asher, Zebulun and Naphtali, so that they too went up to meet them.

³⁶Gideon said to God, "If you will save Israel by my hand as you have promised— ³⁷look, I will place a wool fleece on the threshing floor. If there is dew only on the fleece and all the ground is dry, then I will know that you will save Israel by my hand, as you said." ³⁸And that is what happened. Gideon rose early the next day; he squeezed the fleece and wrung out the dew—a bowlful of water.

³⁹Then Gideon said to God, "Do not be angry with me. Let me make just one more request. Allow me one more test with the fleece. This time make the fleece dry and the ground covered with dew." ⁴⁰That night God did so. Only the fleece was dry; all the ground was covered with dew.

Raw Material

Judges 7

Joshua won the battle of Jericho by following orders that defied all orthodox military tactics. Similarly, when the time came for Gideon to strike a decisive blow for the Israelites, God gave instructions that would have daunted a seasoned general, much less a greenhorn like Gideon. He reduced the size of Gideon's army from 32,000 to 300 men, so as to leave no doubt it was he, God of the Hebrews, who would fight this battle.

In those days the Israelites lived at the mercy of marauding tribes of Bedouins, who would help themselves to the produce and wealth of the local farmers. But by following God's commands, Gideon led a great victory and freed his people from oppression.

Gideon's against-all-odds victory shows a pattern that is repeated throughout the book of Judges. At a time when women were regarded as second-class citizens, God chose Deborah to lead. Jephthah, another judge, had led a gang of outlaws before God chose him. In fact, this pattern appears throughout the Bible. God did not seek the most capable people, nor the most naturally "good." He worked with the most unlikely material so that everyone could see the glory was his and his alone.

The apostle Paul marveled over this principle more than a thousand years later, writing, "Brothers, think of what you were when you were called. Not many of you were wise by human standards; not many were influential; not many were of noble birth. But God chose the foolish things of the world to shame the wise; God chose the weak things of the world to shame the strong. . . . Therefore, as it is written: 'Let him who boasts boast in the Lord' " (1 Corinthians 1:26-31).

> **To Reflect On:** *Why does God so often rely on "cast offs" to accomplish his work? Who are the exceptions?*

JUDGES 7
Gideon Defeats the Midianites

7 Early in the morning, Jerub-Baal (that is, Gideon) and all his men camped at the spring of Harod. The camp of Midian was north of them in the valley near the hill of Moreh. ²The LORD said to Gideon, "You have too many men for me to deliver Midian into their hands. In order that Israel may not boast against me that her own strength has saved her, ³announce now to the people, 'Anyone who trembles with fear may turn back and leave Mount Gilead.' " So twenty-two thousand men left, while ten thousand remained.

⁴But the LORD said to Gideon, "There are still too many men. Take them down to the water, and I will sift them for you there. If I say, 'This one shall go with you,' he shall go; but if I say, 'This one shall not go with you,' he shall not go."

⁵So Gideon took the men down to the water. There the LORD told him, "Separate those who lap the water with their tongues like a dog from those who kneel down to drink." ⁶Three hundred men lapped with their hands to their mouths. All the rest got down on their knees to drink.

⁷The LORD said to Gideon, "With the three hundred men that lapped I will save you and give the Midianites into your hands. Let all the other men go, each to his own place." ⁸So Gideon sent the rest of the Israelites to their tents but kept the three hundred, who took over the provisions and trumpets of the others.

Now the camp of Midian lay below him in the valley. ⁹During that night the LORD said to Gideon, "Get up, go down against the camp, because I am going to give it into your hands. ¹⁰If you are afraid to attack, go down to the camp with your servant Purah

¹¹and listen to what they are saying. Afterward, you will be encouraged to attack the camp." So he and Purah his servant went down to the outposts of the camp. ¹²The Midianites, the Amalekites and all the other eastern peoples had settled in the valley, thick as locusts. Their camels could no more be counted than the sand on the seashore.

¹³Gideon arrived just as a man was telling a friend his dream. "I had a dream," he was saying. "A round loaf of barley bread came tumbling into the Midianite camp. It struck the tent with such force that the tent overturned and collapsed."

¹⁴His friend responded, "This can be nothing other than the sword of Gideon son of Joash, the Israelite. God has given the Midianites and the whole camp into his hands."

¹⁵When Gideon heard the dream and its interpretation, he worshiped God. He returned to the camp of Israel and called out, "Get up! The LORD has given the Midianite camp into your hands." ¹⁶Dividing the three hundred men into three companies, he placed trumpets and empty jars in the hands of all of them, with torches inside.

¹⁷"Watch me," he told them. "Follow my lead. When I get to the edge of the camp, do exactly as I do. ¹⁸When I and all who are with me blow our trumpets, then from all around the camp blow yours and shout, 'For the LORD and for Gideon.'"

¹⁹Gideon and the hundred men with him reached the edge of the camp at the beginning of the middle watch, just after they had changed the guard. They blew their trumpets and broke the jars that were in their hands. ²⁰The three companies blew the trumpets and smashed the jars. Grasping the torches in their left hands and holding in their right hands the trumpets they were to blow, they shouted, "A sword for the LORD and for Gideon!" ²¹While each man held his position around the camp, all the Midianites ran, crying out as they fled.

²²When the three hundred trumpets sounded, the LORD caused the men throughout the camp to turn on each other with their swords. The army fled to Beth Shittah toward Zererah as far as the border of Abel Meholah near Tabbath. ²³Israelites from Naphtali, Asher and all Manasseh were called out, and they pursued the Midianites. ²⁴Gideon sent messengers throughout the hill country of Ephraim, saying, "Come down against the Midianites and seize the waters of the Jordan ahead of them as far as Beth Barah."

So all the men of Ephraim were called out and they took the waters of the Jordan as far as Beth Barah. ²⁵They also captured two of the Midianite leaders, Oreb and Zeeb. They killed Oreb at the rock of Oreb, and Zeeb at the winepress of Zeeb. They pursued the Midianites and brought the heads of Oreb and Zeeb to Gideon, who was by the Jordan.

Superman's Weakness

Judges 16:1–30

The most famous of all the judges makes an appearance toward the end of the book, and the Bible devotes four chapters to the dramatic events of his life. If Gideon shows how a person with limited potential can be greatly used by God, Samson illustrates just the opposite: a person with enormous potential who squanders it.

When Samson entered the picture, the Israelites were once again suffering under foreign domination. An angel announced his birth, making clear that God had great things in store for Samson and wanted him specially set apart.

Indeed, Samson was blessed with extraordinary supernatural gifts. When the Spirit of the Lord came upon him, he could tackle a lion or single-handedly rout an entire army. And yet, as the stories from his youth reveal, Samson wielded that strength in ways more befitting a juvenile delinquent than a spiritual leader.

Like any rebellious teenager, he chose for a wife the kind of woman sure to cause his parents—and God—the most grief. That marriage barely survived a week, and next Samson took up with a Philistine prostitute. This chapter describes how he, stupidly, forfeited his great strength in a dalliance with a third woman, the seductive Delilah. Samson's story is like a morality play. No one in the world could match his physical strength; just about anyone could match his moral strength. His moral lapses would seem almost incomprehensible were they not repeated by spiritual leaders in almost every generation.

In the end, Samson, the designated savior of his people, was led out to perform like a trained bear for his captors. It appeared that the God of the Israelites had been soundly defeated by the pagans and their gods. But Samson, and God, had one last surprise for the Philistine oppressors.

To Reflect On: *In what areas are you living up to your potential? In what areas are you falling short?*

JUDGES 16:1–30

Samson and Delilah

16 One day Samson went to Gaza, where he saw a prostitute. He went in to spend the night with her. ²The people of Gaza were told, "Samson is here!" So they surrounded the place and lay in wait for him all night at the city gate. They made no move during the night, saying, "At dawn we'll kill him."

³But Samson lay there only until the middle of the night. Then he got up and took hold of the doors of the city gate, together with the two posts, and tore them loose, bar and all. He lifted them to his shoulders and carried them to the top of the hill that faces Hebron.

⁴Some time later, he fell in love with a woman in the Valley of Sorek whose name was Delilah. ⁵The rulers of the Philistines went to her and said, "See if you can lure him into showing you the secret of his great strength and how we can overpower him so we may tie him up and subdue him. Each one of us will give you eleven hundred shekels of silver."

⁶So Delilah said to Samson, "Tell me the secret of your great strength and how you can be tied up and subdued."

⁷Samson answered her, "If anyone ties me with seven fresh thongs that have not been dried, I'll become as weak as any other man."

⁸Then the rulers of the Philistines brought her seven fresh thongs that had not been dried, and she tied him with them.

9With men hidden in the room, she called to him, "Samson, the Philistines are upon you!" But he snapped the thongs as easily as a piece of string snaps when it comes close to a flame. So the secret of his strength was not discovered.

10Then Delilah said to Samson, "You have made a fool of me; you lied to me. Come now, tell me how you can be tied."

11He said, "If anyone ties me securely with new ropes that have never been used, I'll become as weak as any other man."

12So Delilah took new ropes and tied him with them. Then, with men hidden in the room, she called to him, "Samson, the Philistines are upon you!" But he snapped the ropes off his arms as if they were threads.

13Delilah then said to Samson, "Until now, you have been making a fool of me and lying to me. Tell me how you can be tied."

He replied, "If you weave the seven braids of my head into the fabric [on the loom] and tighten it with the pin, I'll become as weak as any other man." So while he was sleeping, Delilah took the seven braids of his head, wove them into the fabric 14and tightened it with the pin.

Again she called to him, "Samson, the Philistines are upon you!" He awoke from his sleep and pulled up the pin and the loom, with the fabric.

15Then she said to him, "How can you say, 'I love you,' when you won't confide in me? This is the third time you have made a fool of me and haven't told me the secret of your great strength." 16With such nagging she prodded him day after day until he was tired to death.

17So he told her everything. "No razor has ever been used on my head," he said, "because I have been a Nazirite set apart to God since birth. If my head were shaved, my strength would leave me, and I would become as weak as any other man."

18When Delilah saw that he had told her everything, she sent word to the rulers of the Philistines, "Come back once more; he has told me everything." So the rulers of the Philistines returned with the silver in their hands. 19Having put him to sleep on her lap, she called a man to shave off the seven braids of his hair, and so began to subdue him. And his strength left him.

20Then she called, "Samson, the Philistines are upon you!"

He awoke from his sleep and thought, "I'll go out as before and shake myself free." But he did not know that the LORD had left him.

21Then the Philistines seized him, gouged out his eyes and took him down to Gaza. Binding him with bronze shackles, they set him to grinding in the prison. 22But the hair on his head began to grow again after it had been shaved.

The Death of Samson

23Now the rulers of the Philistines assembled to offer a great sacrifice to Dagon their god and to celebrate, saying, "Our god has delivered Samson, our enemy, into our hands."

24When the people saw him, they praised their god, saying,

"Our god has delivered our enemy
  into our hands,
the one who laid waste our land
  and multiplied our slain."

25While they were in high spirits, they shouted, "Bring out Samson to entertain us." So they called Samson out of the prison, and he performed for them.

When they stood him among the pillars, 26Samson said to the servant who held his hand, "Put me where I can feel the pillars that support the temple, so that I may lean against them." 27Now the temple was crowded with men and women; all the rulers of the Philistines were there, and on the roof were about three thousand men and women watching Samson perform. 28Then Samson prayed to the LORD, "O Sovereign LORD, remember me. O God, please strengthen me just once more, and let me with one blow get revenge on the Philistines for my two eyes." 29Then Samson reached toward the two central pillars on which the temple stood. Bracing himself against them, his right hand on the one and his left hand on the other, 30Samson said, "Let me die with the Philistines!" Then he pushed with all his might, and down came the temple on the rulers and all the people in it. Thus he killed many more when he died than while he lived.

Superman's Weakness   79

Tough Love
Ruth 1

In the days when the judges ruled . . ." begins this charming tale about two scrappy women. It has nothing like the broad sweep of history found in Judges. Rather, Ruth narrows its focus to the story of one family trying to cope during chaotic, tumultuous times. In style, it calls to mind such stories of simple village life as *Fiddler on the Roof*.

Things got so bad in Canaan, especially after a severe famine, that Naomi's Israelite family migrated into enemy territory just to survive. There, her two sons married local pagan women and settled down. Years later, after both those sons and her husband had died, Naomi decided to return to the land of her birth. This book mainly tells of the stubborn loyalty of Naomi's daughter-in-law named Ruth.

Ruth and Naomi were unlikely friends. Ruth was young and strong; Naomi, past middle age and broken-hearted. In addition, they came from completely different ethnic and religious backgrounds. Who would have put them together? But somewhere along the way Ruth had converted to the worship of the true God, and she insisted on returning with Naomi to the land of the Israelites.

In a few brief chapters, Ruth manages to capture a slice of agrarian life in ancient times. The male-dominated society posed problems for unattached women, and these two lived in harsh, trying times. Ruth served awhile as a migrant farm worker, surviving on the gleanings left in the fields by the harvesters. (God's laws required that wealthy farmers help the needy by leaving some grain behind for the poor to harvest.)

You can read this small book in several ways: as a tiny, elegant portrait of life in ancient times, or as a record of God's faithfulness to the needy, or as an inspiring story of undying friendship. Ultimately Ruth does get a loving husband and both women find economic security.) Perhaps the most accurate way to read this story, however, is as a missionary story. God not only accepted Ruth, a member of the despised Moabites, into his family, but also used her to produce Israel's greatest king. Ruth's great-grandson turned out to be David. To anyone who thinks God's love was for the Israelites only, Ruth's life makes a striking contradiction.

> **To Reflect On:** *When has a friend "gone out on a limb" for you?*

RUTH 1

Naomi and Ruth

1 In the days when the judges ruled, there was a famine in the land, and a man from Bethlehem in Judah, together with his wife and two sons, went to live for a while in the country of Moab. ²The man's name was Elimelech, his wife's name Naomi, and the names of his two sons were Mahlon and Kilion. They were Ephrathites from Bethlehem, Judah. And they went to Moab and lived there.

³Now Elimelech, Naomi's husband, died, and she was left with her two sons. ⁴They married Moabite women, one named Orpah and the other Ruth. After they had lived there about ten years, ⁵both Mahlon and Kilion also died, and Naomi was left without her two sons and her husband.

⁶When she heard in Moab that the LORD had come to the aid of his people by providing food for them, Naomi and her daughters-in-law prepared to return home from there. ⁷With her two daughters-in-law she left the place where she had been living and set out on the road that would take them back to the land of Judah.

⁸Then Naomi said to her two daughters-in-law, "Go back, each of you, to your mother's home. May the LORD show kindness to you, as you have shown to your dead and to me. ⁹May the LORD grant that each of you will find rest in the home of another husband."

Then she kissed them and they wept aloud ¹⁰and said to her, "We will go back with you to your people."

¹¹But Naomi said, "Return home, my daughters. Why would you come with me? Am I going to have any more sons, who could become your husbands? ¹²Return home, my daughters; I am too old to have another husband. Even if I thought there was still hope for me—even if I had a husband tonight and then gave birth to sons— ¹³would you wait until they grew up? Would you remain unmarried for them? No, my daughters. It is more bitter for me than for you, because the LORD's hand has gone out against me!"

¹⁴At this they wept again. Then Orpah kissed her mother-in-law good-by, but Ruth clung to her.

¹⁵"Look," said Naomi, "your sister-in-law is going back to her people and her gods. Go back with her."

¹⁶But Ruth replied, "Don't urge me to leave you or to turn back from you. Where you go I will go, and where you stay I will stay. Your people will be my people and your God my God. ¹⁷Where you die I will die, and there I will be buried. May the LORD deal with me, be it ever so severely, if anything but death separates you and me." ¹⁸When Naomi realized that Ruth was determined to go with her, she stopped urging her.

¹⁹So the two women went on until they came to Bethlehem. When they arrived in Bethlehem, the whole town was stirred because of them, and the women exclaimed, "Can this be Naomi?"

²⁰"Don't call me Naomi," she told them. "Call me Mara, because the Almighty has made my life very bitter. ²¹I went away full, but the LORD has brought me back empty. Why call me Naomi? The LORD has afflicted me; the Almighty has brought misfortune upon me."

²²So Naomi returned from Moab accompanied by Ruth the Moabitess, her daughter-in-law, arriving in Bethlehem as the barley harvest was beginning.

All-purpose Leader

1 Samuel 3

By the time of the judges, most terms in the Israelites' covenant with God had already been fulfilled. Abraham's descendants, twelve tribes and many thousands strong, had a land of their own. And yet, something was clearly lacking. No one could begin to call the crazy quilt of tribal territories a unified "nation." In fact, throughout the judges' era the Israelites fought each other as often as they fought their hostile neighbors.

As this book opens, the Philistines, a traditional enemy, were exploiting the Israelites' disunity, pushing ever deeper into their territory. The Philistines had superior weapons—chariots, in particular—and Israel had neither a central administration nor a regular army to mount an effective defense. A crisis of leadership was building, a crisis that threatened the very existence of Israel. The military weakness led to one of the darkest days of Jewish history when the Philistines captured the sacred ark of the covenant. Some wondered whether God had abandoned them and thus forsaken the covenant.

"In those days the word of the LORD was rare; there were not many visions" begins this chapter. But it goes on to relate how God stepped in directly, as he had done with Abraham and Moses before, calling out a leader for his people. "See, I am about to do something in Israel that will make the ears of everyone who hears of it tingle," God announced. He answered the desperate prayer of a barren farm wife and granted her a son, Samuel, who would grow into his role as one of Israel's greatest leaders.

Ultimately, Samuel would serve the Israelites in many capacities. He was both judge and prophet. A priest by training, he also led the nation's worship. When the need arose, he even functioned as a military general, spearheading a victorious recapture of disputed territories. And finally, under God's direction, Samuel anointed Israel's first two kings. By performing these varied roles, Samuel left an important legacy: He managed to unite the tribes for the first time in a century. Under his leadership, Israel came to the very brink of nationhood. God had not forgotten the covenant after all.

> **To Reflect On:** *Have you ever felt "called" by God for a certain task?*

1 SAMUEL 3

The LORD Calls Samuel

3 The boy Samuel ministered before the LORD under Eli. In those days the word of the LORD was rare; there were not many visions.

2 One night Eli, whose eyes were becoming so weak that he could barely see, was lying down in his usual place. 3 The lamp of God had not yet gone out, and Samuel was lying down in the temple of the LORD, where the ark of God was. 4 Then the LORD called Samuel.

Samuel answered, "Here I am." 5 And he ran to Eli and said, "Here I am; you called me."

But Eli said, "I did not call; go back and lie down." So he went and lay down.

6 Again the LORD called, "Samuel!" And Samuel got up and went to Eli and said, "Here I am; you called me."

"My son," Eli said, "I did not call; go back and lie down."

7 Now Samuel did not yet know the LORD: The word of the LORD had not yet been revealed to him.

8 The LORD called Samuel a third time, and Samuel got up and went to Eli and said, "Here I am; you called me."

Then Eli realized that the LORD was calling the boy. 9 So Eli told Samuel, "Go and lie down, and if he calls you, say, 'Speak, LORD, for your servant is listening.'" So Samuel went and lay down in his place.

10 The LORD came and stood there, calling as at the other times, "Samuel! Samuel!"

Then Samuel said, "Speak, for your servant is listening."

11 And the LORD said to Samuel: "See, I am about to do something in Israel that will make the ears of everyone who hears of it tingle. 12 At that time I will carry out against Eli everything I spoke against his family—from beginning to end. 13 For I told him that I would judge his family forever because of the sin he knew about; his sons made themselves contemptible, and he failed to restrain them. 14 Therefore, I swore to the house of Eli, 'The guilt of Eli's house will never be atoned for by sacrifice or offering.'"

15 Samuel lay down until morning and then opened the doors of the house of the LORD. He was afraid to tell Eli the vision, 16 but Eli called him and said, "Samuel, my son."

Samuel answered, "Here I am."

17 "What was it he said to you?" Eli asked. "Do not hide it from me. May God deal with you, be it ever so severely, if you hide from me anything he told you." 18 So Samuel told him everything, hiding nothing from him. Then Eli said, "He is the LORD; let him do what is good in his eyes."

19 The LORD was with Samuel as he grew up, and he let none of his words fall to the ground. 20 And all Israel from Dan to Beersheba recognized that Samuel was attested as a prophet of the LORD. 21 The LORD continued to appear at Shiloh, and there he revealed himself to Samuel through his word.

Tale of Two Kings

1 Samuel 16

The Philistine military threat never entirely went away. As Samuel aged, Israel needed continuing vigorous leadership, but Samuel's sons hardly measured up to the task. What could be done? Looking around them, the tribes saw that virtually every other country had a king. *Aha, that's the answer*, they concluded, and urged Samuel to appoint an Israelite king (8:4–5).

The idea of a king seems to have been popular with everyone except Samuel and God, who sensed in the request an underlying rejection of God's own leadership. Samuel warned the elders bluntly against the problems they might be inviting: tyranny, oppression, a military draft, high taxes, maybe even slavery. But the people begged for a king despite his warnings.

Did God oppose the very notion of a king? Probably not. Many years before, Moses had predicted the Israelites would someday have a king, and God eventually used the royal line to produce his own son Jesus, King of Kings. But the Bible makes one thing clear: God opposed the people's motives, as expressed by the elders, "Then we will be like all the other nations" (8:20). God did not want them to be like all the other nations. He, no human being, was the true ruler of the Israelites.

Israel's first king began his reign with enormous promise. Saul was a perfect physical specimen—handsome, strong, intelligent, a head taller than anyone else. Leadership qualities oozed out of him. But he failed, for one simple reason: He disobeyed God, refusing to acknowledge him as the true ruler. And without hesitation, God ended that royal dynasty and looked elsewhere for a replacement.

The replacement king was utterly unlike the first king. No one had imagined royalty potential in the shepherd boy David—not even his own father. But, as God said, "Man looks at the outward appearance, but the LORD looks at the heart." David had the kind of heart God could work with. Despite his humble beginnings, despite his many flaws, he went on to become the greatest king in the history of the Israelites.

> **To Reflect On:** *Would the leadership qualities God values be an asset or a handicap to someone running for president of the United States?*

1 SAMUEL 16

Samuel Anoints David

16 The LORD said to Samuel, "How long will you mourn for Saul, since I have rejected him as king over Israel? Fill your horn with oil and be on your way; I am sending you to Jesse of Bethlehem. I have chosen one of his sons to be king."

²But Samuel said, "How can I go? Saul will hear about it and kill me."

The LORD said, "Take a heifer with you and say, 'I have come to sacrifice to the LORD.' ³Invite Jesse to the sacrifice, and I will show you what to do. You are to anoint for me the one I indicate."

⁴Samuel did what the LORD said. When he arrived at Bethlehem, the elders of the town trembled when they met him. They asked, "Do you come in peace?"

⁵Samuel replied, "Yes, in peace; I have come to sacrifice to the LORD. Consecrate yourselves and come to the sacrifice with me." Then he consecrated Jesse and his sons and invited them to the sacrifice.

⁶When they arrived, Samuel saw Eliab and thought, "Surely the LORD's anointed stands here before the LORD."

⁷But the LORD said to Samuel, "Do not consider his appearance or his height, for I have rejected him. The LORD does not look at the things man looks at. Man looks at the outward appearance, but the LORD looks at the heart."

⁸Then Jesse called Abinadab and had him pass in front of Samuel. But Samuel said, "The LORD has not chosen this one either." ⁹Jesse then had Shammah pass by, but Samuel said, "Nor has the LORD chosen this one." ¹⁰Jesse had seven of his sons pass before Samuel, but Samuel said to him, "The LORD has not chosen these." ¹¹So he asked Jesse, "Are these all the sons you have?"

"There is still the youngest," Jesse answered, "but he is tending the sheep."

Samuel said, "Send for him; we will not sit down until he arrives."

¹²So he sent and had him brought in. He was ruddy, with a fine appearance and handsome features.

Then the LORD said, "Rise and anoint him; he is the one."

¹³So Samuel took the horn of oil and anointed him in the presence of his brothers, and from that day on the Spirit of the LORD came upon David in power. Samuel then went to Ramah.

David in Saul's Service

¹⁴Now the Spirit of the LORD had departed from Saul, and an evil spirit from the LORD tormented him.

¹⁵Saul's attendants said to him, "See, an evil spirit from God is tormenting you. ¹⁶Let our lord command his servants here to search for someone who can play the harp. He will play when the evil spirit from God comes upon you, and you will feel better."

¹⁷So Saul said to his attendants, "Find someone who plays well and bring him to me."

¹⁸One of the servants answered, "I have seen a son of Jesse of Bethlehem who knows how to play the harp. He is a brave man and a warrior. He speaks well and is a fine-looking man. And the LORD is with him."

¹⁹Then Saul sent messengers to Jesse and said, "Send me your son David, who is with the sheep." ²⁰So Jesse took a donkey loaded with bread, a skin of wine and a young goat and sent them with his son David to Saul.

²¹David came to Saul and entered his service. Saul liked him very much, and David became one of his armor-bearers. ²²Then Saul sent word to Jesse, saying, "Allow David to remain in my service, for I am pleased with him."

²³Whenever the spirit from God came upon Saul, David would take his harp and play. Then relief would come to Saul; he would feel better, and the evil spirit would leave him.

A Shepherd's Song

Psalm 23

David was a well-rounded human being. Although he had enough courage to take on the likes of Goliath, he certainly did not fit any macho warrior mold. In fact, David first gained King Saul's notice for his musical, not military, skills. Initially, he was brought to the army camp because his harp playing soothed the frayed nerves of the troubled king.

Almost half of the 150 psalms in the Bible are credited to David, and it seems only appropriate to read a sampling in conjunction with his life history. This famous psalm reveals at once the secret of David's poetic abilities and the secret of his faith.

In his poetry David tended to start with the scene around him—rocks, caves, stars, battlefields, sheep—and work out from that physical world to express profound thoughts about God. Psalm 23, for instance, stems from his experience as a shepherd boy. A book like *A Shepherd Looks at Psalm 23* explains how this psalm uses the precise metaphors that emerge from the tasks of sheepherding; David was able to reduce those images to a few condensed, beautiful stanzas.

The psalm captures the essence of David's trust in God. Sheep have blind, absolute trust in a leader: If a lead sheep plunges off a cliff, an entire flock will follow. That kind of unshakable trust was what David sought in his walk with God.

Yet, no one can dismiss David as having a rosy, romantic view of life. The preceding song, Psalm 22, shows just how tough, gritty, and ruthlessly honest he could be. Somehow David managed to make God the center of his life, regardless of circumstances—whether he felt specially comforted by God, or cruelly abandoned. "Some trust in chariots and some in horses, but we trust in the name of the LORD our God," wrote this soldier who spent much of his time running from chariots and horses (Psalm 20:7).

The best way to read the psalms is to make these ancient prayers your own by speaking them directly to God. Over the years, millions of people have found comfort and inspiration by "praying" the eloquent words of Psalm 23, written by the shepherd who would be king.

> **To Reflect On:** *Does your faith resemble more the childlike faith of Psalm 23 or the barely-hanging-on faith of Psalm 22?*

PSALM 23

Psalm 23

A psalm of David.

[1] The LORD is my shepherd, I shall not be
  in want.
[2] He makes me lie down in green
    pastures,
  he leads me beside quiet waters,
[3] he restores my soul.
  He guides me in paths of
    righteousness
  for his name's sake.
[4] Even though I walk
    through the valley of the shadow of
    death,

I will fear no evil,
  for you are with me;
your rod and your staff,
  they comfort me.

[5] You prepare a table before me
  in the presence of my enemies.
You anoint my head with oil;
  my cup overflows.
[6] Surely goodness and love will follow
    me
  all the days of my life,
and I will dwell in the house of the
    LORD
  forever.

Giant-killer

1 Samuel 17:4–7, 16–50

King David dominates much of the Old Testament, and much of Jewish history. This exciting story from his boyhood, told in colorful, eyewitness detail is one of the most famous of all Bible stories, a beacon of hope for all out-sized underdogs.

David spent the better part of a decade trying to escape the wrath of King Saul, and much of Saul's enmity probably traced back to this one scene. Saul, leader of a large army, sat in his tent, terrorized by the taunts of the colossal Goliath. Meanwhile David, a mere boy too small for a suit of armor, strode out bravely to meet Goliath's challenge. Little wonder that Saul came to resent and even fear the remarkable youth.

The scenario related here is not as farfetched as it may seem. "Single combat" or "representative" warfare was an acceptable style of settling differences in ancient times. As Tom Wolfe explains it in *The Right Stuff*, "In single combat the mightiest soldier of one army would fight the mightiest soldier of the other army as a substitute for a pitched battle between the entire forces. . . . Originally it had a magical meaning. . . . They believed that the gods determined the outcome of single combat; therefore, it was useless for the losing side to engage in a full-scale battle."

During many lonely hours as a shepherd boy, David had honed his slingshot skills to a state of perfection. But he took no personal credit for the victory. "You come against me with sword and spear and javelin," he shouted to Goliath, "but I come against you in the name of the LORD Almighty, the God of the armies of Israel, whom you have defied." In the tradition of Joshua and Gideon, he placed complete trust in God alone—a lesson that King Saul had never learned.

Once Goliath had fallen, the rest of the Philistines quickly succumbed. Soon the Israelites were dancing in the streets and singing, "Saul has slain his thousands, and David his tens of thousands." The nation was beginning to recognize in David the qualities that had marked him for potential kingship. Saul, however, was not about to relinquish his throne without a fight.

> **To Reflect On:** *Have you ever been forced to rely utterly on God at a time of great fear and danger?*

---

1 SAMUEL 17:4–7, 16–50

David and Goliath

⁴A champion named Goliath, who was from Gath, came out of the Philistine camp. He was over nine feet tall. ⁵He had a bronze helmet on his head and wore a coat of scale armor of bronze weighing five thousand shekels; ⁶on his legs he wore bronze greaves, and a bronze javelin was slung on his back. ⁷His spear shaft was like a weaver's rod, and its iron point weighed six hundred shekels. His shield bearer went ahead of him.

¹⁶For forty days the Philistine came forward every morning and evening and took his stand.

¹⁷Now Jesse said to his son David, "Take this ephah of roasted grain and these ten loaves of bread for your brothers and hurry to their camp. ¹⁸Take along these ten cheeses to the commander of their unit. See how your brothers are and bring back some assurance from them. ¹⁹They are with Saul and all the men of Israel in the Valley of Elah, fighting against the Philistines."

²⁰Early in the morning David left the flock with a shepherd, loaded up and set out, as Jesse had directed. He reached the

camp as the army was going out to its battle positions, shouting the war cry. 21Israel and the Philistines were drawing up their lines facing each other. 22David left his things with the keeper of supplies, ran to the battle lines and greeted his brothers. 23As he was talking with them, Goliath, the Philistine champion from Gath, stepped out from his lines and shouted his usual defiance, and David heard it. 24When the Israelites saw the man, they all ran from him in great fear.

25Now the Israelites had been saying, "Do you see how this man keeps coming out? He comes out to defy Israel. The king will give great wealth to the man who kills him. He will also give him his daughter in marriage and will exempt his father's family from taxes in Israel."

26David asked the men standing near him, "What will be done for the man who kills this Philistine and removes this disgrace from Israel? Who is this uncircumcised Philistine that he should defy the armies of the living God?"

27They repeated to him what they had been saying and told him, "This is what will be done for the man who kills him."

28When Eliab, David's oldest brother, heard him speaking with the men, he burned with anger at him and asked, "Why have you come down here? And with whom did you leave those few sheep in the desert? I know how conceited you are and how wicked your heart is; you came down only to watch the battle."

29"Now what have I done?" said David. "Can't I even speak?" 30He then turned away to someone else and brought up the same matter, and the men answered him as before. 31What David said was overheard and reported to Saul, and Saul sent for him.

32David said to Saul, "Let no one lose heart on account of this Philistine; your servant will go and fight him."

33Saul replied, "You are not able to go out against this Philistine and fight him; you are only a boy, and he has been a fighting man from his youth."

34But David said to Saul, "Your servant has been keeping his father's sheep. When a lion or a bear came and carried off a sheep from the flock, 35I went after it, struck it and rescued the sheep from its mouth. When it turned on me, I seized it by its hair, struck it and killed it. 36Your servant has killed both the lion and the bear; this uncircumcised

Philistine will be like one of them, because he has defied the armies of the living God. 37The LORD who delivered me from the paw of the lion and the paw of the bear will deliver me from the hand of this Philistine."

Saul said to David, "Go, and the LORD be with you."

38Then Saul dressed David in his own tunic. He put a coat of armor on him and a bronze helmet on his head. 39David fastened on his sword over the tunic and tried walking around, because he was not used to them.

"I cannot go in these," he said to Saul, "because I am not used to them." So he took them off. 40Then he took his staff in his hand, chose five smooth stones from the stream, put them in the pouch of his shepherd's bag and, with his sling in his hand, approached the Philistine.

41Meanwhile, the Philistine, with his shield bearer in front of him, kept coming closer to David. 42He looked David over and saw that he was only a boy, ruddy and handsome, and he despised him. 43He said to David, "Am I a dog, that you come at me with sticks?" And the Philistine cursed David by his gods. 44"Come here," he said, "and I'll give your flesh to the birds of the air and the beasts of the field!"

45David said to the Philistine, "You come against me with sword and spear and javelin, but I come against you in the name of the LORD Almighty, the God of the armies of Israel, whom you have defied. 46This day the LORD will hand you over to me, and I'll strike you down and cut off your head. Today I will give the carcasses of the Philistine army to the birds of the air and the beasts of the earth, and the whole world will know that there is a God in Israel. 47All those gathered here will know that it is not by sword or spear that the LORD saves; for the battle is the LORD's, and he will give all of you into our hands."

48As the Philistine moved closer to attack him, David ran quickly toward the battle line to meet him. 49Reaching into his bag and taking out a stone, he slung it and struck the Philistine on the forehead. The stone sank into his forehead, and he fell facedown on the ground.

50So David triumphed over the Philistine with a sling and a stone; without a sword in his hand he struck down the Philistine and killed him.

Outdoor Lessons

Psalm 19

David lived much of his life outdoors, beginning first with his years as a shepherd and continuing on through his time of running from Saul and commanding armies on a battlefield. Not surprisingly a great love, even reverence, for the natural world shows through in many of his psalms.

These psalms present a world that fits together as a whole. At night wild animals hunt; at daybreak humans go out to work. As rain falls, nourishing crops for people and grass for cattle, it also waters the forest where wild animals live. Yet the psalmist doesn't just marvel over the complexity and beauty of nature; behind everything he sees the hand of God. The world works because an intimate, personal God watches over it. Every breath of life depends on his will. So do the weather, the winds and clouds, the very stability of the earth.

Psalm 19 brings together two of David's favorite themes: God's care for the earth, and his care for the chosen people of Israel. He begins with the natural world, marveling at the mantle of stars that covers the whole earth—stars he often slept under at night. Yet, David and the Israelites, unlike their neighbors, did not worship the sun and stars as gods, but rather saw them as the workmanship of a great God who oversees all creation.

In the middle of the psalm, the author turns his attention from nature to the "law of the Lord," which formed the heart of God's covenant with his people. To reflect that change, the poem in Hebrew uses a different, more personal name for God. The first six verses refer to God with a general name that anyone, of any religion, might use, much like our English word *God.* But from verse seven onward, God is called *Yahweh,* the personal name revealed to Moses from the burning bush. The heavens declare the glory of God, but God's law reveals even more—his personal voice to his chosen people.

David wrote some of the psalms as a fugitive, while fleeing the wrath of King Saul. Even though God had promised him the throne of Israel, David had to run for his life. He had many nights of fear and many doubts, but his bedrock trust held firm. He believed that the God who had demonstrated his faithfulness to the natural world, and to the nation David would one day govern, would show that same faithfulness in fulfilling promises to David himself.

To Reflect On: *Does nature reveal "the glory of God" to you?*

PSALM 19

Psalm 19

For the director of music.
A psalm of David.

¹The heavens declare the glory of God;
the skies proclaim the work of his
hands.
²Day after day they pour forth speech;
night after night they display
knowledge.
³There is no speech or language
where their voice is not heard.
⁴Their voice goes out into all the earth,
their words to the ends of the
world.

In the heavens he has pitched a tent
for the sun,
5   which is like a bridegroom coming
forth from his pavilion,
like a champion rejoicing to run his
course.

⁶It rises at one end of the heavens
and makes its circuit to the other;
nothing is hidden from its heat.

⁷The law of the LORD is perfect,
reviving the soul.

The statutes of the LORD are
trustworthy,
making wise the simple.
⁸The precepts of the LORD are right,
giving joy to the heart.
The commands of the LORD are radiant,
giving light to the eyes.
⁹The fear of the LORD is pure,
enduring forever.
The ordinances of the LORD are sure
and altogether righteous.
¹⁰They are more precious than gold,
than much pure gold;
they are sweeter than honey,
than honey from the comb.
¹¹By them is your servant warned;
in keeping them there is great
reward.

¹²Who can discern his errors?
Forgive my hidden faults.
¹³Keep your servant also from willful
sins;
may they not rule over me.
Then will I be blameless,
innocent of great transgression.

¹⁴May the words of my mouth and the
meditation of my heart
be pleasing in your sight,
O LORD, my Rock and my Redeemer.

Struggle for the Throne

1 Samuel 20:4–41

Y ou can sense the force of David's personality by observing the effect he had on people around him. During Davids's fugitive days, a ragtag band of men followed him across rugged hills and deserts, quite willing to give their lives for his sake. And this chapter tells of an undying friendship from his early days, before the radical break with King Saul. The king's son Jonathan valued friendship with David so much that he forfeited his chance at succession to the throne.

Saul revealed his true, murderous intent to Jonathan in a dramatic scene at the dinner table. Jonathan warned David, and thus began the terrible struggle between the competing kings. Saul, the king rejected by God, lived on in luxury while David, secretly anointed as his replacement, lived in the wilderness, scrambling to survive. Saul had a professional army; David, a small band made up of family members and an assortment of outlaws.

The events of the next few years played out the inner character of the two men. Saul knew God's will about the rightful king of Israel, but spent his life resisting it. In contrast, David showed amazing patience waiting for the prophecy to come true. Twice when Saul accidentally fell into his hands, David refused to kill him. He fought not to win but to survive.

In the remainder of 1 Samuel, a long, Shakespearean-style drama unfolds. King Saul, an ancient Macbeth, has lost his grip and is clearly deteriorating. His son has sided with David; his daughter, married to him, has shifted her loyalties as well. Saul, insane with rage, turns up the heat. Can David hold on long enough to outlast him?

At times, David despaired. "One of these days I will be destroyed by the hand of Saul," he said (27:1). For a while he even left Israel to serve as a mercenary for a Philistine king. His position was desperate. David had one precious asset only: God's promise that he would be king. Although his faith in that promise was tested to the extreme, David learned to wait for God's timing. In the end, like the hero of a Shakespearean tragedy, Saul took his own life. Meanwhile, David inherited the throne of Israel.

To Reflect On: *Have you ever had a close same-sex friendship such as David and Jonathan had?*

---

1 SAMUEL 20:4–41

David and Jonathan

⁴Jonathan said to David, "Whatever you want me to do, I'll do for you."

⁵So David said, "Look, tomorrow is the New Moon festival, and I am supposed to dine with the king; but let me go and hide in the field until the evening of the day after tomorrow. ⁶If your father misses me at all, tell him, 'David earnestly asked my permission to hurry to Bethlehem, his hometown, because an annual sacrifice is being made there for his whole clan.' ⁷If he says, 'Very well,' then your servant is safe. But if he loses his temper, you can be sure that he is determined to harm me. ⁸As for you, show kindness to your servant, for you have brought him into a covenant with you before the LORD. If I am guilty, then kill me yourself! Why hand me over to your father?"

⁹"Never!" Jonathan said. "If I had the least inkling that my father was determined to harm you, wouldn't I tell you?"

¹⁰David asked, "Who will tell me if your father answers you harshly?"

¹¹"Come," Jonathan said, "let's go out into the field." So they went there together. ¹²Then Jonathan said to David: "By the LORD, the God of Israel, I will surely sound out my father by this time the day after tomorrow! If he is favorably disposed toward you, will I not send you word and let you know? ¹³But if my father is inclined to harm you, may the LORD deal with me, be it ever so severely, if I do not let you know and send you away safely. May the LORD be with you as he has been with my father. ¹⁴But show me unfailing kindness like that of the LORD as long as I live, so that I may not be killed, ¹⁵and do not ever cut off your kindness from my family—not even when the LORD has cut off every one of David's enemies from the face of the earth."

¹⁶So Jonathan made a covenant with the house of David, saying, "May the LORD call David's enemies to account." ¹⁷And Jonathan had David reaffirm his oath out of love for him, because he loved him as he loved himself.

¹⁸Then Jonathan said to David: "Tomorrow is the New Moon festival. You will be missed, because your seat will be empty. ¹⁹The day after tomorrow, toward evening, go to the place where you hid when this trouble began, and wait by the stone Ezel. ²⁰I will shoot three arrows to the side of it, as though I were shooting at a target. ²¹Then I will send a boy and say, 'Go, find the arrows.' If I say to him, 'Look, the arrows are on this side of you; bring them here,' then come, because, as surely as the LORD lives, you are safe; there is no danger. ²²But if I say to the boy, 'Look, the arrows are beyond you,' then you must go, because the LORD has sent you away. ²³And about the matter you and I discussed—remember, the LORD is witness between you and me forever."

²⁴So David hid in the field, and when the New Moon festival came, the king sat down to eat. ²⁵He sat in his customary place by the wall, opposite Jonathan, and Abner sat next to Saul, but David's place was empty. ²⁶Saul said nothing that day, for he thought, "Something must have happened to David to make him ceremonially unclean—surely he is unclean." ²⁷But the next day, the second day of the month, David's place was empty again. Then Saul said to his son Jonathan, "Why hasn't the son of Jesse come to the meal, either yesterday or today?"

²⁸Jonathan answered, "David earnestly asked me for permission to go to Bethlehem. ²⁹He said, 'Let me go, because our family is observing a sacrifice in the town and my brother has ordered me to be there. If I have found favor in your eyes, let me get away to see my brothers.' That is why he has not come to the king's table."

³⁰Saul's anger flared up at Jonathan and he said to him, "You son of a perverse and rebellious woman! Don't I know that you have sided with the son of Jesse to your own shame and to the shame of the mother who bore you? ³¹As long as the son of Jesse lives on this earth, neither you nor your kingdom will be established. Now send and bring him to me, for he must die!"

³²"Why should he be put to death? What has he done?" Jonathan asked his father. ³³But Saul hurled his spear at him to kill him. Then Jonathan knew that his father intended to kill David.

³⁴Jonathan got up from the table in fierce anger; on that second day of the month he did not eat, because he was grieved at his father's shameful treatment of David.

³⁵In the morning Jonathan went out to the field for his meeting with David. He had a small boy with him, ³⁶and he said to the boy, "Run and find the arrows I shoot." As the boy ran, he shot an arrow beyond him. ³⁷When the boy came to the place where Jonathan's arrow had fallen, Jonathan called out after him, "Isn't the arrow beyond you?" ³⁸Then he shouted, "Hurry! Go quickly! Don't stop!" The boy picked up the arrow and returned to his master. ³⁹(The boy knew nothing of all this; only Jonathan and David knew.) ⁴⁰Then Jonathan gave his weapons to the boy and said, "Go, carry them back to town."

⁴¹After the boy had gone, David got up from the south side of the stone and bowed down before Jonathan three times, with his face to the ground. Then they kissed each other and wept together—but David wept the most.

Ups and Downs

Psalm 27

The psalms open a window into the inner life of King David. That window discloses some surprises, however. David was surely no saint and seldom did he show the peace and serenity normally associated with "spiritual" people. In fact, he often cried out against God, blaming him when things went wrong and begging for relief.

Psalm 27—relatively mild in comparison with other examples—shifts in mood with every stanza. The first stanza opens with a bold declaration of confidence in God from an author who seems downright fearless. The second stanza hints at the author's true condition: Tired of running, he yearns for the day when he can rest safely in God's dwelling, and rise above all his enemies. By the third stanza, all confidence has melted and the psalmist is pleading for help. The psalm ends in a calmer tone, with a word of practical advice David often had opportunity to put into practice, "Wait for the LORD."

The psalms are not pious devotionals. They are filled with accounts of enemies who scheme and gossip and plot violence. For the psalmists, faith in God involved a constant struggle against powerful forces that often seemed more real than God. The writers frequently asked, "Where are you, God? Why don't you help me?" They often felt abandoned, misused, betrayed.

Yet out of such trials, a strong, toughened faith in God emerged. In the years when David was an outlaw from King Saul, his hideouts included a "rock" in the desert and a "stronghold." As an experienced fighter, David knew the value of such defenses. But when he wrote about those days—as in this psalm—he called God his rock and his fortress. He recognized readily that God was the true source of his protection.

Danger did not fade away even after David became king. He faced unceasing hostility from enemies, as well as numerous internal rebellions and coup attempts. But David had learned a pattern of helpless dependence in the wilderness, and practiced it throughout his life.

> **To Reflect On:** *Is your emotional life fairly even, or full of peaks and valleys? What about your spiritual life?*

PSALM 27

Psalm 27

Of David.

¹The LORD is my light and my
salvation—
whom shall I fear?
The LORD is the stronghold of my life—
of whom shall I be afraid?
²When evil men advance against me
to devour my flesh,
when my enemies and my foes attack
me,
they will stumble and fall.
³Though an army besiege me,
my heart will not fear;
though war break out against me,
even then will I be confident.
⁴One thing I ask of the LORD,
this is what I seek:
that I may dwell in the house of the
LORD
all the days of my life,
to gaze upon the beauty of the LORD
and to seek him in his temple.
⁵For in the day of trouble
he will keep me safe in his dwelling;
he will hide me in the shelter of his
tabernacle
and set me high upon a rock.
⁶Then my head will be exalted
above the enemies who surround me;

at his tabernacle will I sacrifice with
shouts of joy;
I will sing and make music to the
LORD.

⁷Hear my voice when I call, O LORD;
be merciful to me and answer me.
⁸My heart says of you, "Seek his face!"
Your face, LORD, I will seek.
⁹Do not hide your face from me,
do not turn your servant away in
anger;
you have been my helper.
Do not reject me or forsake me,
O God my Savior.
¹⁰Though my father and mother forsake
me,
the LORD will receive me.
¹¹Teach me your way, O LORD;
lead me in a straight path
because of my oppressors.
¹²Do not turn me over to the desire of
my foes,
for false witnesses rise up against
me,
breathing out violence.

¹³I am still confident of this:
I will see the goodness of the LORD
in the land of the living.
¹⁴Wait for the LORD;
be strong and take heart
and wait for the LORD.

King of Passion

2 Samuel 6

An unavoidable question dangles over the Bible's account of David's life. How could anyone so obviously flawed—he did, as we shall see, commit adultery and murder—be called "a man after God's own heart"? The central event in this chapter may point to an answer to that question.

David consistently acknowledged that God, not a human king, was the true ruler of Israel, and so in one of his first official acts, he sent for the sacred ark of the Lord that had been captured by the Philistines half a century before. He would install it in Jerusalem, the new capital city he was building, as a symbol of God's reign.

It took a few false starts to get the ark to Jerusalem. Without looking up the regulations given to Moses, the Israelites tried transporting the ark on an ox cart, as the Philistines paraded their gods, rather than on the shoulders of the Levites, as God had commanded. Somebody died, David got mad, and the ark sat in a private home for three months.

Nevertheless, when the ark finally did move to Jerusalem, to the accompaniment of a brass band and the shouts of a huge crowd, King David completely lost control. Bursting with joy, he cartwheeled in the streets, like an Olympic gymnast who has just won the gold medal and is out strutting his stuff.

Needless to say, the scene of a dignified king doing backflips in a scanty robe broke every rule ever devised by a politician's image builders. David's wife, for one, was scandalized. But David set her straight: It was God, no one else, that he was dancing before. And, king or no, he didn't care what anyone else thought as long as that one-person audience could sense his jubilation.

In short, David was a man of *passion*, and he felt more passionately about the God of Israel than about anything else in the world. The message got through to the entire nation. As Frederick Buechner has written, "He had feet of clay like the rest of us if not more so—self-serving and deceitful, lustful and vain—but on the basis of that dance alone, you can see why it was David more than anybody else that Israel lost her heart to and why, when Jesus of Nazareth came riding into Jerusalem on his flea-bitten mule a thousand years later, it was as the Son of David that they hailed him" (*Peculiar Treasures*, p. 24).

> **To Reflect On:** *If you had been in the crowd watching David dance, how would you have responded?*

2 SAMUEL 6

The Ark Brought to Jerusalem

6 David again brought together out of Israel chosen men, thirty thousand in all. ²He and all his men set out from Baalah of Judah to bring up from there the ark of God, which is called by the Name, the name of the LORD Almighty, who is enthroned between the cherubim that are on the ark. ³They set the ark of God on a new cart and brought it from the house of Abinadab, which was on the hill. Uzzah and Ahio, sons of Abinadab, were guiding the new cart ⁴with the ark of God on it, and Ahio was walking in front of it. ⁵David and the whole house of Israel were celebrating with all their might before the LORD, with songs and with harps, lyres, tambourines, sistrums and cymbals.

⁶When they came to the threshing floor of Nacon, Uzzah reached out and took hold of the ark of God, because the oxen stumbled. ⁷The LORD's anger burned against Uzzah because of his irreverent act; therefore God struck him down and he died there beside the ark of God.

⁸Then David was angry because the LORD's wrath had broken out against Uzzah, and to this day that place is called Perez Uzzah.

⁹David was afraid of the LORD that day and said, "How can the ark of the LORD ever come to me?" ¹⁰He was not willing to take the ark of the LORD to be with him in the City of David. Instead, he took it aside to the house of Obed-Edom the Gittite. ¹¹The ark of the LORD remained in the house of Obed-Edom the Gittite for three months, and the LORD blessed him and his entire household.

¹²Now King David was told, "The LORD has blessed the household of Obed-Edom and everything he has, because of the ark of God." So David went down and brought up the ark of God from the house of Obed-Edom to the City of David with rejoicing. ¹³When those who were carrying the ark of the LORD had taken six steps, he sacrificed a bull and a fattened calf. ¹⁴David, wearing a linen ephod, danced before the LORD with all his might, ¹⁵while he and the entire house of Israel brought up the ark of the LORD with shouts and the sound of trumpets.

¹⁶As the ark of the LORD was entering the City of David, Michal daughter of Saul watched from a window. And when she saw King David leaping and dancing before the LORD, she despised him in her heart.

¹⁷They brought the ark of the LORD and set it in its place inside the tent that David had pitched for it, and David sacrificed burnt offerings and fellowship offerings before the LORD. ¹⁸After he had finished sacrificing the burnt offerings and fellowship offerings, he blessed the people in the name of the LORD Almighty. ¹⁹Then he gave a loaf of bread, a cake of dates and a cake of raisins to each person in the whole crowd of Israelites, both men and women. And all the people went to their homes.

²⁰When David returned home to bless his household, Michal daughter of Saul came out to meet him and said, "How the king of Israel has distinguished himself today, disrobing in the sight of the slave girls of his servants as any vulgar fellow would!"

²¹David said to Michal, "It was before the LORD, who chose me rather than your father or anyone from his house when he appointed me ruler over the LORD's people Israel—I will celebrate before the LORD. ²²I will become even more undignified than this, and I will be humiliated in my own eyes. But by these slave girls you spoke of, I will be held in honor."

²³And Michal daughter of Saul had no children to the day of her death.

A Different Kind of House

1 Chronicles 17

After bringing the ark of God to Jerusalem, David began to dream of building a splendid home for it, a temple devoted to the God of the Israelites. In a day when pagan temples ranked among the wonders of the world, he thought it only fitting to lavish the wealth of his kingdom on a "house" for the true God. But God made it clear that David was not the one to build such a temple. Elsewhere (1 Chronicles 22:8), the Bible states the reason: As a warrior, David had shed much blood, and God wanted his house built by a man of peace. That task should be left for David's son.

Although God vetoed the plan to build a temple, he granted David far more. Harking back to his covenant with the Israelites, he promised—in a tender play on words—to build a "house" out of David's descendants that would last forever. Whatever his reservations about the Israelites' demand for a king, God had fully "adopted" the king as his representative within the nation. In a typically humble response, David erupted in a prayer of astonished thanksgiving.

This promise, given in an intimate exchange between God and David, sowed the seed for what would become a long-time hope of the Jews: a royal "Messiah," or Anointed One. Saul's dynasty ended just as it had begun; David's would continue through a long line of kings and culminate in God's own Son, to be born into David's lineage in Bethlehem, the City of David. Has God's promise been fulfilled? The fact that even in modern times people still pore over the lives of David and other kings of tiny Israel—though far grander, more impressive kings have faded from history—and recognize one descendant as the true Messiah should give a hint.

(Note: The books of Samuel, Kings, and Chronicles often overlap, telling the same history from different perspectives. This chapter from 1 Chronicles repeats almost word for word the seventh chapter of 2 Samuel.)

To Reflect On: *When have you felt like giving God a large gift?*

---

1 CHRONICLES 17

God's Promise to David

17 After David was settled in his palace, he said to Nathan the prophet, "Here I am, living in a palace of cedar, while the ark of the covenant of the LORD is under a tent."

²Nathan replied to David, "Whatever you have in mind, do it, for God is with you."

³That night the word of God came to Nathan, saying:

⁴"Go and tell my servant David, 'This is what the LORD says: You are not the one to build me a house to dwell in. ⁵I have not dwelt in a house from the day I brought Israel up out of Egypt to this day. I have moved from one tent site to another, from one dwelling place to another. ⁶Wherever I have moved with all the Israelites, did I ever say to any of their leaders whom I commanded to shepherd my people, "Why have you not built me a house of cedar?" '

⁷"Now then, tell my servant David, 'This is what the LORD Almighty says: I took you from the pasture and from following the flock, to be ruler over my people Israel. ⁸I have been with you wherever you have gone, and I have cut off all your enemies from before you. Now I will make your name like the names of the greatest men of the earth. ⁹And I will provide a place for

my people Israel and will plant them so that they can have a home of their own and no longer be disturbed. Wicked people will not oppress them anymore, as they did at the beginning [10]and have done ever since the time I appointed leaders over my people Israel. I will also subdue all your enemies.

" 'I declare to you that the LORD will build a house for you: [11]When your days are over and you go to be with your fathers, I will raise up your offspring to succeed you, one of your own sons, and I will establish his kingdom. [12]He is the one who will build a house for me, and I will establish his throne forever. [13]I will be his father, and he will be my son. I will never take my love away from him, as I took it away from your predecessor. [14]I will set him over my house and my kingdom forever; his throne will be established forever.' '

[15]Nathan reported to David all the words of this entire revelation.

David's Prayer

[16]Then King David went in and sat before the LORD, and he said:

"Who am I, O LORD God, and what is my family, that you have brought me this far? [17]And as if this were not enough in your sight, O God, you have spoken about the future of the house of your servant. You have looked on me as though I were the most exalted of men, O LORD God.

[18]"What more can David say to you for honoring your servant? For you know your servant, [19]O LORD. For the sake of your servant and according to your will, you have done this great thing and made known all these great promises.

[20]"There is no one like you, O LORD, and there is no God but you, as we have heard with our own ears. [21]And who is like your people Israel—the one nation on earth whose God went out to redeem a people for himself, and to make a name for yourself, and to perform great and awesome wonders by driving out nations from before your people, whom you redeemed from Egypt? [22]You made your people Israel your very own forever, and you, O LORD, have become their God.

[23]"And now, LORD, let the promise you have made concerning your servant and his house be established forever. Do as you promised, [24]so that it will be established and that your name will be great forever. Then men will say, 'The LORD Almighty, the God over Israel, is Israel's God!' And the house of your servant David will be established before you.

[25]"You, my God, have revealed to your servant that you will build a house for him. So your servant has found courage to pray to you. [26]O LORD, you are God! You have promised these good things to your servant. [27]Now you have been pleased to bless the house of your servant, that it may continue forever in your sight; for you, O LORD, have blessed it, and it will be blessed forever."

The Goodness of God

Psalm 103

David never got over a sense of *astonishment* at all God had done for him. As he grew older and reviewed his life, he realized that, despite the hardships, God had always delivered him "from the pit." God had kept his promises. In gratitude, David wrote many psalms praising God for his past faithfulness. The king served, in effect, as a national reservoir of memory for his people; he helped the whole nation remember God's benefits.

When the Israelites praised God, their thoughts centered on God's actions in freeing them from slavery and leading them into a land of their own. Their psalms were like history lessons, designed to summon up the past, especially the hallmark days of deliverance under Moses. They studied those days in the Torah, or five books of Moses, and wrote songs to commemorate them.

The memories weren't all positive, and the Israelites' songs could be brutally frank about the ancestors' rebellions, complaints, and lack of gratitude. Yet, they had one great, happy reason to rejoice: God had kept his promise to love them. To psalm writers like David, the events of Israel's history were unmistakable signs of God's grace. They had done nothing to deserve God's love, and yet he had showered love on them.

This psalm could be titled "The Goodness of God." It reviews the dark times of illness and oppression, of sin and rebellion, and then it points with amazement to the remarkable ways in which God transformed all those dark times. God understands and will not overwhelm human weakness: "He knows how we are formed, he remembers that we are dust." More, despite our failings, he has in store for us an unfathomable eternity of love. 0P1 David has one loud message to celebrate: We do not get what we deserve. We get far more. The psalm ends in a burst of praise, starting with the grand sweep of the universe and spiraling back to the setting of the very first verse—David praising God in his inmost being.

> **To Reflect On:** *When you review your past, do you tend to focus on the victories or the failures?*

PSALM 103

Psalm 103
Of David.

[1] Praise the LORD, O my soul;
all my inmost being, praise his holy
name.
[2] Praise the LORD, O my soul,
and forget not all his benefits—
[3] who forgives all your sins
and heals all your diseases,
[4] who redeems your life from the pit
and crowns you with love and
compassion,
[5] who satisfies your desires with good
things
so that your youth is renewed like
the eagle's.

[6] The LORD works righteousness
and justice for all the oppressed.

[7] He made known his ways to Moses,
his deeds to the people of Israel:
[8] The LORD is compassionate and gracious,
slow to anger, abounding in love.
[9] He will not always accuse,
nor will he harbor his anger forever;
[10] he does not treat us as our sins
deserve
or repay us according to our
iniquities.
[11] For as high as the heavens are above
the earth,
so great is his love for those who
fear him;

[12] as far as the east is from the west,
so far has he removed our
transgressions from us.
[13] As a father has compassion on his
children,
so the LORD has compassion on those
who fear him;
[14] for he knows how we are formed,
he remembers that we are dust.
[15] As for man, his days are like grass,
he flourishes like a flower of the
field;
[16] the wind blows over it and it is gone,
and its place remembers it no more.
[17] But from everlasting to everlasting
the LORD's love is with those who
fear him,
and his righteousness with their
children's children—
[18] with those who keep his covenant
and remember to obey his precepts.

[19] The LORD has established his throne in
heaven,
and his kingdom rules over all.

[20] Praise the LORD, you his angels,
you mighty ones who do his
bidding,
who obey his word.
[21] Praise the LORD, all his heavenly hosts,
you his servants who do his will.
[22] Praise the LORD, all his works
everywhere in his dominion.

Praise the LORD, O my soul.

Kings Will Be Kings

2 Samuel 11

In the spring, at the time when kings go off to war . . ." begins this story, one of the most masterfully told in all the Bible. That spring, however, one particular king named David did not go off to war. Well-entrenched in Jerusalem, he settled into the luxury of the palace and directed the army from afar.

It is the simplest story in the world, this tale of David and Bathsheba: Man sees woman, man sleeps with woman, woman gets pregnant. Nothing unusual there. Every year scandal sheets broadcast modern variations on the same theme. Substitute a politician—or evangelist—for the king, and a beauty queen for Bathsheba. What else is new?

The scandal didn't especially shock David's Israelite subjects. Like most people, they were resigned to the fact that the people on top who make the rules often don't bother to live by them. Lots of leaders in history have followed this course, taking the spoils they want, the money they want, the privileges they want. The Romans had a phrase for such behavior, *rex lex*—the king is law—rather than *lex rex*—the law is king.

Bathsheba's pregnancy complicated the picture somewhat. Today, a leader in David's situation might destroy the evidence with an abortion. David had his own cover-up plan. It started as a clever attempt to deceive, making Bathsheba's husband appear as the likely father. Uriah's scruples, however, put King David to shame, or should have. What ensued was a classic case of "one crime leads to another." In the end, David, the man after God's own heart, broke the 6th, 7th, 9th, and 10th commandments. For his loyalty, David's soldier Uriah got the reward of murder, and many other Israelites fell with him.

This story shows David at his most Machiavellian: cold as iron, ruthless in use of his power. Even so, not a word of protest was filed, though Uriah's general knew the real story. What the king wants the king gets, no questions asked. Such is life.

After a mourning period, Bathsheba moved into the palace and David married her. By then many people must have surmised what had happened—the servants knew, at any rate—but the Bible doesn't report that any of them were displeased. Why expect anything different from a king?

The story of David's infidelity might have ended there, and probably would have, except for one portentous sentence at the close of this chapter. It says merely, "The thing David had done displeased the LORD."

> **To Reflect On:** *Have you ever been caught in the act, like David, and tried to deceive your way out?*

2 SAMUEL 11

David and Bathsheba

11 In the spring, at the time when kings go off to war, David sent Joab out with the king's men and the whole Israelite army. They destroyed the Ammonites and besieged Rabbah. But David remained in Jerusalem.

²One evening David got up from his bed and walked around on the roof of the palace. From the roof he saw a woman bathing. The woman was very beautiful, ³and David sent someone to find out about her. The man said, "Isn't this Bathsheba, the daughter of Eliam and the wife of Uriah the Hittite?" ⁴Then David sent messengers to get her. She came to him, and he slept with her. (She had purified herself from her uncleanness.) Then she went back home. ⁵The woman conceived and sent word to David, saying, "I am pregnant."

⁶So David sent this word to Joab: "Send me Uriah the Hittite." And Joab sent him to David. ⁷When Uriah came to him, David asked him how Joab was, how the soldiers were and how the war was going. ⁸Then David said to Uriah, "Go down to your house and wash your feet." So Uriah left the palace, and a gift from the king was sent after him. ⁹But Uriah slept at the entrance to the palace with all his master's servants and did not go down to his house.

¹⁰When David was told, "Uriah did not go home," he asked him, "Haven't you just come from a distance? Why didn't you go home?" ¹¹Uriah said to David, "The ark and Israel and Judah are staying in tents, and my master Joab and my lord's men are camped in the open fields. How could I go to my house to eat and drink and lie with my wife? As surely as you live, I will not do such a thing!"

¹²Then David said to him, "Stay here one more day, and tomorrow I will send you back." So Uriah remained in Jerusalem that day and the next. ¹³At David's invitation, he ate and drank with him, and David made him drunk. But in the evening Uriah went out to sleep on his mat among his master's servants; he did not go home.

¹⁴In the morning David wrote a letter to Joab and sent it with Uriah. ¹⁵In it he wrote, "Put Uriah in the front line where the fighting is fiercest. Then withdraw from him so he will be struck down and die."

¹⁶So while Joab had the city under siege, he put Uriah at a place where he knew the strongest defenders were. ¹⁷When the men of the city came out and fought against Joab, some of the men in David's army fell; moreover, Uriah the Hittite was dead.

¹⁸Joab sent David a full account of the battle. ¹⁹He instructed the messenger: "When you have finished giving the king this account of the battle, ²⁰the king's anger may flare up, and he may ask you, 'Why did you get so close to the city to fight? Didn't you know they would shoot arrows from the wall? ²¹Who killed Abimelech son of Jerub-Besheth? Didn't a woman throw an upper millstone on him from the wall, so that he died in Thebez? Why did you get so close to the wall?' If he asks you this, then say to him, 'Also, your servant Uriah the Hittite is dead.' "

²²The messenger set out, and when he arrived he told David everything Joab had sent him to say. ²³The messenger said to David, "The men overpowered us and came out against us in the open, but we drove them back to the entrance to the city gate. ²⁴Then the archers shot arrows at your servants from the wall, and some of the king's men died. Moreover, your servant Uriah the Hittite is dead."

²⁵David told the messenger, "Say this to Joab: 'Don't let this upset you; the sword devours one as well as another. Press the attack against the city and destroy it.' Say this to encourage Joab."

²⁶When Uriah's wife heard that her husband was dead, she mourned for him. ²⁷After the time of mourning was over, David had her brought to his house, and she became his wife and bore him a son. But the thing David had done displeased the LORD.

Caught in the Act

2 Samuel 12:1–25

In a society where the ruler makes the laws, who can hold the ruler accountable? All over the globe today, people who live under the thumb of tyrants ask that same question. But from the beginning, God had established Israel as *his* kingdom, with its ruler as his representative, not the final authority. And after David's great sin, God sent the prophet Nathan to confront the king.

It was Nathan who had conveyed to the king God's lavish promise to establish David's "house" (1 Chronicles 17). This time he, a welcome guest of the palace, came with a heartrending tale of poverty, greed, and injustice. He presented the case to David, the highest judge in Israel, for a verdict. David knew exactly how to decide such a case: The man deserved to die! When he said so, Nathan delivered his own devastating verdict, "You are the man!"

In this dramatic scene David's greatness shows itself. There was nothing novel in his saga of lust, greed, adultery, and murder, but very much was novel in his response to Nathan. He could have had Nathan killed. Or he could have laughed and thrown him out of the palace. Instead, David said to Nathan, "I have sinned against the LORD." Immediately, he admitted his guilt, acknowledging God as the true ruler of the land.

To appreciate David's confession, you only have to think of the response of leaders "caught in the act" in our own time: a president squirming before the cameras during Watergate and reluctantly conceding, "Wrongs were committed"; a parade of officials marching before the Senate during the Irangate hearings with alibis, excuses, and rationalizations; a presidential candidate denying well-subtantiated charges of habitual womanizing. In contrast to these accused leaders, King David saw at once the heart of the issue. He had sinned not just against Uriah and his country, but against the Lord.

David was a great king partly because he did not act with the normal pride of a great king. Confronted with the truth, he repented. Forgiveness came in an instant, but the consequences of David's actions would plague the kingdom for a generation. For one thing, he had lost moral authority within his own family. Over the next few years, one of David's sons would rape his sister, and another would kill his brother and launch a coup against David himself. King David had left a legacy of abuse of power, and not all his successors would be so quick to repent.

> **To Reflect On:** *How do you react instinctively when someone confronts you over wrongdoing?*

2 SAMUEL 12:1–25

Nathan Rebukes David

12 The LORD sent Nathan to David. When he came to him, he said, "There were two men in a certain town, one rich and the other poor. ²The rich man had a very large number of sheep and cattle, ³but the poor man had nothing except one little ewe lamb he had bought. He raised it, and it grew up with him and his children. It shared his food, drank from his cup and even slept in his arms. It was like a daughter to him.

⁴"Now a traveler came to the rich man, but the rich man refrained from taking one of his own sheep or cattle to prepare a meal for the traveler who had come to him. Instead, he took the ewe lamb that belonged to the poor man and prepared it for the one who had come to him."

⁵David burned with anger against the man and said to Nathan, "As surely as the LORD lives, the man who did this deserves to die! ⁶He must pay for that lamb four times over, because he did such a thing and had no pity."

⁷Then Nathan said to David, "You are the man! This is what the LORD, the God of Israel, says: 'I anointed you king over Israel, and I delivered you from the hand of Saul. ⁸I gave your master's house to you, and your master's wives into your arms. I gave you the house of Israel and Judah. And if all this had been too little, I would have given you even more. ⁹Why did you despise the word of the LORD by doing what is evil in his eyes? You struck down Uriah the Hittite with the sword and took his wife to be your own. You killed him with the sword of the Ammonites. ¹⁰Now, therefore, the sword will never depart from your house, because you despised me and took the wife of Uriah the Hittite to be your own.

¹¹This is what the LORD says: 'Out of your own household I am going to bring calamity upon you. Before your very eyes I will take your wives and give them to one who is close to you, and he will lie with your wives in broad daylight. ¹²You did it in secret, but I will do this thing in broad daylight before all Israel.'"

¹³Then David said to Nathan, "I have sinned against the LORD."

Nathan replied, "The LORD has taken away your sin. You are not going to die. ¹⁴But because by doing this you have made the enemies of the LORD show utter contempt, the son born to you will die."

¹⁵After Nathan had gone home, the LORD struck the child that Uriah's wife had borne to David, and he became ill. ¹⁶David pleaded with God for the child. He fasted and went into his house and spent the nights lying on the ground. ¹⁷The elders of his household stood beside him to get him up from the ground, but he refused, and he would not eat any food with them.

¹⁸On the seventh day the child died. David's servants were afraid to tell him that the child was dead, for they thought, "While the child was still living, we spoke to David but he would not listen to us. How can we tell him the child is dead? He may do something desperate."

¹⁹David noticed that his servants were whispering among themselves and he realized the child was dead. "Is the child dead?" he asked.

"Yes," they replied, "he is dead."

²⁰Then David got up from the ground. After he had washed, put on lotions and changed his clothes, he went into the house of the LORD and worshiped. Then he went to his own house, and at his request they served him food, and he ate.

²¹His servants asked him, "Why are you acting this way? While the child was alive, you fasted and wept, but now that the child is dead, you get up and eat!"

²²He answered, "While the child was still alive, I fasted and wept. I thought, 'Who knows? The LORD may be gracious to me and let the child live.' ²³But now that he is dead, why should I fast? Can I bring him back again? I will go to him, but he will not return to me."

²⁴Then David comforted his wife Bathsheba, and he went to her and lay with her. She gave birth to a son, and they named him Solomon. The LORD loved him; ²⁵and because the LORD loved him, he sent word through Nathan the prophet to name him Jedidiah.

True Confession

Psalm 51

This poem of remembrance may well be the most impressive outcome of David's sordid affair with Bathsheba. It is one thing for a king to confess a moral lapse in private to a prophet. It is quite another for him to compose a detailed account of that confession that could be sung throughout the land!

All nations have heroes, but Israel may be alone in making epic literature about its greatest hero's failings. This eloquent psalm, possibly used in worship services as a guide for confession, shows that Israel ultimately remembered David more for his devotion to God than for his political achievements.

Step by step, the psalm takes the reader (or singer) through the stages of repentance. It describes the constant mental replays—"Oh, if only I had a chance to do it over"—the gnawing guilt, the shame, and finally the hope for a new beginning that springs from true repentance.

David lived under Old Testament law, which prescribed a harsh punishment for his crimes: death by stoning. But in a remarkable way this psalm transcends the rigid formulas of law and reveals the true nature of sin as a broken *relationship* with God. "Against you, you only, have I sinned," David cried out. He could see that no ritual sacrifices or religious ceremonies would cause his guilt to vanish; the sacrifices God wanted were "a broken spirit, a broken and contrite heart." Those, David had.

In the midst of his prayer, David looks for possible good that might come out of his tragedy, and sees a glimmer of light. He prays for God to use his experience as a moral lesson for others. Perhaps, by reading his story of sin, they might avoid the same pitfalls, or by reading his confession they might gain hope in forgiveness. David's prayer was fully answered and is his greatest legacy as king. The best king of Israel fell the farthest. But neither he, nor anyone, can fall beyond the reach of God's love and forgiveness.

> **To Reflect On:** *Would you lose respect for a leader if he or she admitted failures as openly as David did?*

PSALM 51

Psalm 51

For the director of music. A psalm of
David. When the prophet Nathan came
to him after David had committed adultery with Bathsheba.

¹Have mercy on me, O God,
  according to your unfailing love;
according to your great compassion
  blot out my transgressions.
²Wash away all my iniquity
  and cleanse me from my sin.

³For I know my transgressions,
  and my sin is always before me.
⁴Against you, you only, have I sinned
  and done what is evil in your sight,
 so that you are proved right when you
    speak
  and justified when you judge.
⁵Surely I was sinful at birth,
  sinful from the time my mother
    conceived me.
⁶Surely you desire truth in the inner
    parts;
  you teach me wisdom in the inmost
    place.

⁷Cleanse me with hyssop, and I will be
    clean;
  wash me, and I will be whiter than
    snow.
⁸Let me hear joy and gladness;
  let the bones you have crushed
    rejoice.
⁹Hide your face from my sins

and blot out all my iniquity.

¹⁰Create in me a pure heart, O God,
  and renew a steadfast spirit within
    me.
¹¹Do not cast me from your presence
  or take your Holy Spirit from me.
¹²Restore to me the joy of your salvation
  and grant me a willing spirit, to
    sustain me.

¹³Then I will teach transgressors your
    ways,
  and sinners will turn back to you.
¹⁴Save me from bloodguilt, O God,
  the God who saves me,
  and my tongue will sing of your
    righteousness.
¹⁵O Lord, open my lips,
  and my mouth will declare your
    praise.
¹⁶You do not delight in sacrifice, or I
    would bring it;
  you do not take pleasure in burnt
    offerings.
¹⁷The sacrifices of God are a broken
    spirit;
  a broken and contrite heart,
  O God, you will not despise.

¹⁸In your good pleasure make Zion
    prosper;
  build up the walls of Jerusalem.
¹⁹Then there will be righteous sacrifices,
  whole burnt offerings to delight you;
  then bulls will be offered on your
    altar.

David's Spiritual Secret

Psalm 139

In the end, David—lusty, vengeful King David—gained a reputation as a friend of God. For a time in Israel, Jehovah (or Yahweh) was known as "the God of David"; the two were that closely identified. What was David's secret? This majestic psalm, attributed to David's influence, hints at an answer.

Mainly, Psalm 139 reveals the *intimacy* that existed between David and his God. It's true that he sometimes contemplated running from God. But David concluded that, no matter where he went or what he did, he could never escape God's presence. If God knew his every thought and motive, how could he run away? Throughout his life, David believed, truly believed, that the spiritual world was every bit as real as his physical world of swords and spears and caves and thrones.

The psalms form a record of David's conscious effort to subject his own daily life to the reality of that spiritual world beyond him. Taken together, they show how closely David depended on God. His exploits—killing wild animals bare-handed, felling Goliath, surviving Saul's onslaughts, routing the Philistines—made him a hero in his nation's eyes. But as David himself reflected on those events, and wrote poetry about them, he always found a way to make God the one on center stage. Whatever the phrase "practicing the presence of God" means, David experienced. He intentionally involved God in every detail of his life.

David firmly believed he *mattered* to God. After one narrow escape he wrote, "[God] rescued me because he delighted in me" (Psalm 18:19). Another time he argued, in so many words (Psalm 30), "What good will it do you if I die, Lord? Who will praise you then?" And this psalm, 139, beautifully expresses David's sense of wonder at God's love and concern.

Reading David's psalms, with all their emotional peaks and valleys, it may even seem that he wrote them as a form of spiritual therapy, a way of talking himself into faith when his spirit and emotions were wavering. Now, centuries later, we can use those very same prayers as steps of faith, a path to lead us from an obsession with ourselves to the actual presence of God.

To Reflect On: *How do you "practice the presence of God" in your life?*

PSALM 139

Psalm 139

For the director of music. Of David.
A psalm.

¹O Lᴏʀᴅ, you have searched me
  and you know me.
²You know when I sit and when I rise;
  you perceive my thoughts from afar.
³You discern my going out and my lying
    down;
  you are familiar with all my ways.
⁴Before a word is on my tongue
  you know it completely, O Lᴏʀᴅ.

⁵You hem me in—behind and before;
  you have laid your hand upon me.
⁶Such knowledge is too wonderful for
    me,
  too lofty for me to attain.

⁷Where can I go from your Spirit?
  Where can I flee from your presence?
⁸If I go up to the heavens, you are
    there;
  if I make my bed in the depths, you
    are there.
⁹If I rise on the wings of the dawn,
  if I settle on the far side of the sea,
¹⁰even there your hand will guide me,
  your right hand will hold me fast.

¹¹If I say, "Surely the darkness will hide
    me
  and the light become night around
    me,"
¹²even the darkness will not be dark to
    you;
  the night will shine like the day,
  for darkness is as light to you.

¹³For you created my inmost being;
  you knit me together in my mother's
    womb.

¹⁴I praise you because I am fearfully and
    wonderfully made;
  your works are wonderful,
  I know that full well.
¹⁵My frame was not hidden from you
  when I was made in the secret
    place.
  When I was woven together in the
    depths of the earth,
¹⁶ your eyes saw my unformed body.
  All the days ordained for me
  were written in your book
  before one of them came to be.

¹⁷How precious to me are your
    thoughts, O God!
  How vast is the sum of them!
¹⁸Were I to count them,
  they would outnumber the grains of
    sand.
  When I awake,
  I am still with you.

¹⁹If only you would slay the wicked, O
    God!
  Away from me, you bloodthirsty
    men!
²⁰They speak of you with evil intent;
  your adversaries misuse your name.
²¹Do I not hate those who hate you, O
    Lᴏʀᴅ,
  and abhor those who rise up against
    you?
²²I have nothing but hatred for them;
  I count them my enemies.

²³Search me, O God, and know my
    heart;
  test me and know my anxious
    thoughts.
²⁴See if there is any offensive way in
    me,
  and lead me in the way everlasting.

The Man Who Had Everything

1 Kings 3

The first half of 1 Kings describes a man who got life handed to him on a silver platter. The favored son of King David and Queen Bathsheba, young Solomon grew up in the royal palace. Early on, the precocious prince astounded others with his talent for songwriting and natural history.

Even God lavished special gifts on Solomon. In an incredible dream sequence, Solomon actually got the opportunity every child secretly longs for. God offered him any wish—long life, riches, anything at all—and when Solomon chose wisdom, God added bonus gifts of wealth, honor, and peace.

A mere teenager when he took over the throne of Israel, Solomon soon became the richest, most impressive ruler of his time. In Jerusalem, silver was as common as stones (10:27). And a fleet of trading ships brought exotica for the king's private collections—apes and baboons from Africa, and ivory and gold by the ton. He was called the wisest man in the world, and kings and queens traveled hundreds of miles to meet him. They went away dazzled by the genius of Israel's king and by the prosperity of his nation.

Israel reached its Golden Age under King Solomon, a shining moment of tranquillity in its long, tormented history. Almost all the Promised Land lay in Solomon's domain, and the nation was at peace. Literature and culture flourished. Of the common people, the Bible reports simply that "they ate, they drank and they were happy" (4:20).

Solomon began with every advantage, and at first he served the Lord. But even in the happy days depicted in this chapter, danger signs can be seen. Contrast King David's humble confession before God with Solomon's public spectacle of one thousand burnt offerings. The new king had a penchant for excess that would prove his undoing.

The first verse tells of a shrewd political alliance with Pharaoh of Egypt. Already Solomon was looking to military strength, rather than to God for security. And his passion for foreign-born wives would eventually lead to his downfall. Over time, he married princesses from Moab, Ammon, Edom, Sidon, and other nations—seven hundred wives in all, and three hundred concubines! The entire complexion of the court changed. Eventually, to please his wives, Solomon would take a final, terrible step of building altars to all their gods.

> **To Reflect On:** *Think of people you know who have many natural abilities—do they tend to use those gifts to serve God?*

1 KINGS 3

Solomon Asks for Wisdom

3 Solomon made an alliance with Pharaoh king of Egypt and married his daughter. He brought her to the City of David until he finished building his palace and the temple of the LORD, and the wall around Jerusalem. ²The people, however, were still sacrificing at the high places, because a temple had not yet been built for the Name of the LORD. ³Solomon showed his love for the LORD by walking according to the statutes of his father David, except that he offered sacrifices and burned incense on the high places.

⁴The king went to Gibeon to offer sacrifices, for that was the most important high place, and Solomon offered a thousand burnt offerings on that altar. ⁵At Gibeon the LORD appeared to Solomon during the night in a dream, and God said, "Ask for whatever you want me to give you."

⁶Solomon answered, "You have shown great kindness to your servant, my father David, because he was faithful to you and righteous and upright in heart. You have continued this great kindness to him and have given him a son to sit on his throne this very day.

⁷"Now, O LORD my God, you have made your servant king in place of my father David. But I am only a little child and do not know how to carry out my duties. ⁸Your servant is here among the people you have chosen, a great people, too numerous to count or number. ⁹So give your servant a discerning heart to govern your people and to distinguish between right and wrong. For who is able to govern this great people of yours?"

¹⁰The Lord was pleased that Solomon had asked for this. ¹¹So God said to him, "Since you have asked for this and not for long life or wealth for yourself, nor have asked for the death of your enemies but for discernment in administering justice, ¹²I will do what you have asked. I will give you a wise and discerning heart, so that there will never have been anyone like you, nor will there ever be. ¹³Moreover, I will give you what you have not asked for—both riches and honor—so that in your lifetime you will have no equal among kings. ¹⁴And if you walk in my ways and obey my statutes and commands as David your father did, I will give you a long life." ¹⁵Then Solomon awoke—and he realized it had been a dream.

He returned to Jerusalem, stood before the ark of the Lord's covenant and sacrificed burnt offerings and fellowship offerings. Then he gave a feast for all his court.

A Wise Ruling

¹⁶Now two prostitutes came to the king and stood before him. ¹⁷One of them said, "My lord, this woman and I live in the same house. I had a baby while she was there with me. ¹⁸The third day after my child was born, this woman also had a baby. We were alone; there was no one in the house but the two of us.

¹⁹"During the night this woman's son died because she lay on him. ²⁰So she got up in the middle of the night and took my son from my side while I your servant was asleep. She put him by her breast and put her dead son by my breast. ²¹The next morning, I got up to nurse my son—and he was dead! But when I looked at him closely in the morning light, I saw that it wasn't the son I had borne."

²²The other woman said, "No! The living one is my son; the dead one is yours."

But the first one insisted, "No! The dead one is yours; the living one is mine." And so they argued before the king.

²³The king said, "This one says, 'My son is alive and your son is dead,' while that one says, 'No! Your son is dead and mine is alive.'"

²⁴Then the king said, "Bring me a sword." So they brought a sword for the king. ²⁵He then gave an order: "Cut the living child in two and give half to one and half to the other."

²⁶The woman whose son was alive was filled with compassion for her son and said to the king, "Please, my lord, give her the living baby! Don't kill him!"

But the other said, "Neither I nor you shall have him. Cut him in two!"

²⁷Then the king gave his ruling: "Give the living baby to the first woman. Do not kill him; she is his mother."

²⁸When all Israel heard the verdict the king had given, they held the king in awe, because they saw that he had wisdom from God to administer justice.

High-water Mark

1 Kings 8:1–34

Of Solomon's many accomplishments, one looms large above the rest. He spared no expense in building a place for God to indwell, and Solomon's temple, fashioned by 200,000 workmen, soon ranked as one of the wonders of the world. From a distance, it shone like a snowcapped mountain. Inside, all the walls, and even the floors, were plated with pure gold.

In many ways the scene in this chapter represents the high-water mark of the entire Old Testament, the fulfillment of God's covenant with Israel. Solomon called the nation together to dedicate the temple to God, and as thousands of people looked on in a huge public ceremony, the glory of the Lord came down to fill the temple. Even the priests were driven back by the mighty force.

God was making Solomon's temple the center of his activity on earth, and the crowd spontaneously decided to stay another two weeks to celebrate. Kneeling on a bronze platform, Solomon prayed aloud, "I have indeed built a magnificent temple for you, a place for you to dwell forever." Then he caught himself in astonishment. "But will God really dwell on earth? The heavens, even the highest heaven, cannot contain you. How much less this temple I have built!"

God had done it! His promises to Abraham and Moses had finally come true. In one of the most magnificent prayers ever prayed, Solomon reviewed the history of the covenant, and asked God to seal that agreement with his Presence in the temple. God responded: "I have heard the prayer and plea you have made before me; I have consecrated this temple . . . my eyes and my heart will always be there" (9:3).

The Israelites now had land, a nation with secure boundaries, and a gleaming symbol of God's presence among them. All this came to pass in a land rich with silver and gold. On the famous day of the temple dedication, everyone saw the fire and the cloud of his Presence. No one could doubt God's faithfulness.

To Reflect On: *What promises has God kept for you?*

---

1 KINGS 8:1–34

The Ark Brought to the Temple

8 Then King Solomon summoned into his presence at Jerusalem the elders of Israel, all the heads of the tribes and the chiefs of the Israelite families, to bring up the ark of the LORD's covenant from Zion, the City of David. ²All the men of Israel came together to King Solomon at the time of the festival in the month of Ethanim, the seventh month.

³When all the elders of Israel had arrived, the priests took up the ark, ⁴and they brought up the ark of the LORD and the Tent of Meeting and all the sacred furnishings in it. The priests and Levites carried them up, ⁵and King Solomon and the entire assembly of Israel that had gathered about him were before the ark, sacrificing so many sheep and cattle that they could not be recorded or counted.

⁶The priests then brought the ark of the LORD's covenant to its place in the inner sanctuary of the temple, the Most Holy Place, and put it beneath the wings of the cherubim. ⁷The cherubim spread their wings over the place of the ark and overshadowed the ark and its carrying poles. ⁸These poles were so long that their ends could be seen from the Holy Place in front of the inner sanctuary, but not from outside the Holy Place; and they are still there today. ⁹There was nothing in the ark except the two stone tablets that Moses had placed

in it at Horeb, where the LORD made a covenant with the Israelites after they came out of Egypt.

¹⁰When the priests withdrew from the Holy Place, the cloud filled the temple of the LORD. ¹¹And the priests could not perform their service because of the cloud, for the glory of the LORD filled his temple.

¹²Then Solomon said, "The LORD has said that he would dwell in a dark cloud; ¹³I have indeed built a magnificent temple for you, a place for you to dwell forever."

¹⁴While the whole assembly of Israel was standing there, the king turned around and blessed them. ¹⁵Then he said:

"Praise be to the LORD, the God of Israel, who with his own hand has fulfilled what he promised with his own mouth to my father David. For he said, ¹⁶'Since the day I brought my people Israel out of Egypt, I have not chosen a city in any tribe of Israel to have a temple built for my Name to be there, but I have chosen David to rule my people Israel.'

¹⁷"My father David had it in his heart to build a temple for the Name of the LORD, the God of Israel. ¹⁸But the LORD said to my father David, 'Because it was in your heart to build a temple for my Name, you did well to have this in your heart. ¹⁹Nevertheless, you are not the one to build the temple, but your son, who is your own flesh and blood—he is the one who will build the temple for my Name.'

²⁰The LORD has kept the promise he made: I have succeeded David my father and now I sit on the throne of Israel, just as the LORD promised, and I have built the temple for the Name of the LORD, the God of Israel. ²¹I have provided a place there for the ark, in which is the covenant of the LORD that he made with our fathers when he brought them out of Egypt."

Solomon's Prayer of Dedication

²²Then Solomon stood before the altar of the LORD in front of the whole assembly of Israel, spread out his hands toward heaven ²³and said:

"O LORD, God of Israel, there is no God like you in heaven above or on earth below—you who keep your covenant of love with your servants who continue wholeheartedly in your way. ²⁴You have kept your promise to your servant David my father; with your mouth you have promised and with your hand you have fulfilled it—as it is today.

²⁵"Now LORD, God of Israel, keep for your servant David my father the promises you made to him when you said, 'You shall never fail to have a man to sit before me on the throne of Israel, if only your sons are careful in all they do to walk before me as you have done.' ²⁶And now, O God of Israel, let your word that you promised your servant David my father come true.

²⁷"But will God really dwell on earth? The heavens, even the highest heaven, cannot contain you. How much less this temple I have built! ²⁸Yet give attention to your servant's prayer and his plea for mercy, O LORD my God. Hear the cry and the prayer that your servant is praying in your presence this day. ²⁹May your eyes be open toward this temple night and day, this place of which you said, 'My Name shall be there,' so that you will hear the prayer your servant prays toward this place. ³⁰Hear the supplication of your servant and of your people Israel when they pray toward this place. Hear from heaven, your dwelling place, and when you hear, forgive.

³¹"When a man wrongs his neighbor and is required to take an oath and he comes and swears the oath before your altar in this temple, ³²then hear from heaven and act. Judge between your servants, condemning the guilty and bringing down on his own head what he has done. Declare the innocent not guilty, and so establish his innocence.

³³"When your people Israel have been defeated by an enemy because they have sinned against you, and when they turn back to you and confess your name, praying and making supplication to you in this temple, ³⁴then hear from heaven and forgive the sin of your people Israel and bring them back to the land you gave to their fathers.

More Than a Building

Psalm 84

It is almost impossible to exaggerate the significance of the temple for Jews throughout history. They took pride in its beautiful architecture (as people today might honor the Notre Dame cathedral), but the temple was far more than a grand symbol. Israel's entire national religious life centered around this building, the house of God.

Faithful Jews turned and faced the temple daily in prayer. Each year they made pilgrimages there to celebrate three great festivals honoring God's covenant with them. The Israelites even came to believe that the temple magically protected them against foreign invasion. As long as the temple stood, some said, no foreign armies could enter Jerusalem—a belief the prophet Jeremiah soundly condemned.

This psalm captures some of the intense feelings about the temple. It was written by one of the "Sons of Korah," a priestly choir established by King David to provide music for worship. As the writer travels to the temple on pilgrimage, his joy and anticipation make the desert surroundings seem almost like an oasis. Perhaps using a little humor, he claims to envy the sparrows and swallows that build nests inside the walls of the temple and thus get to live there permanently. He sings, "Better is one day in your courts than a thousand elsewhere."

The object of the psalmist's enthusiasm, the glorious temple built by Solomon, stood for about 380 years, occasionally falling into disrepair. Destroyed by the Babylonians, it was rebuilt just before the time of Ezra and Nehemiah, and then reconstructed by King Herod in Jesus' time. Jesus, who also made pilgrimages to the temple, walked in the temple on "Solomon's Porch," and the early church met on the temple grounds.

Herod's temple eventually fell to the Romans, and years later the Moslems built a mosque on the site. But the temple has never lost its sacred significance for the Jews, and even today some in Israel propose rebuilding the temple.

To Reflect On: *Is the worship of God dull or exciting for you? Why? What religious symbols have intense meaning for you?*

PSALM 84

Psalm 84

For the director of music. According to *gittith.* Of the Sons of Korah. A psalm.

¹How lovely is your dwelling place,
O LORD Almighty!
²My soul yearns, even faints,
for the courts of the LORD;
my heart and my flesh cry out
for the living God.

³Even the sparrow has found a home,
and the swallow a nest for herself,
where she may have her young—
a place near your altar,
O LORD Almighty, my King and my
God.
⁴Blessed are those who dwell in your
house;
they are ever praising you.   *Selah*

⁵Blessed are those whose strength is in
you,
who have set their hearts on
pilgrimage.

⁶As they pass through the Valley of
Baca,
they make it a place of springs;
the autumn rains also cover it with
pools.
⁷They go from strength to strength,
till each appears before God in Zion.

⁸Hear my prayer, O LORD God Almighty;
listen to me, O God of Jacob.   *Selah*
⁹Look upon our shield, O God;
look with favor on your anointed
one.

¹⁰Better is one day in your courts
than a thousand elsewhere;
I would rather be a doorkeeper in the
house of my God
than dwell in the tents of the
wicked.
¹¹For the LORD God is a sun and shield;
the LORD bestows favor and honor;
no good thing does he withhold
from those whose walk is blameless.

¹²O LORD Almighty,
blessed is the man who trusts in
you.

Life Advice

Proverbs 4

The happy days of Solomon's reign did not last. In a pointed editorial aside, the author of 1 Kings notes that after building the temple, Solomon spent twice as much time and energy on the construction of his own palace (7:1). He proved unable to control his extravagant appetite in any area: wealth, power, romance, political intrigue. He seemed obsessed with a desire to outdo anyone who had ever lived, and gradually his devotion to God slipped away. First Kings gives this summation of Solomon's days, "So Solomon did evil in the eyes of the LORD; he did not follow the LORD completely, as David his father had done" (11:6).

Yet, although Solomon ultimately failed to please God, he did use his enormous talent for much good. In the arts, he created many fine works, among them several books of biblical literature. Inspired by God's supernatural gift of wisdom, he composed 1,005 songs and 3000 proverbs—many of which are collected in this book.

This representative chapter captures the pattern of the book of Proverbs: A wise old man, surrounded by eager young admirers, coyly unveils to them the secrets of his life. (A modern parallel: Millions of Americans will buy the latest how-to book by a famous sports figure or business executive—*maybe it will help me achieve that same kind of success*, they think.) Before revealing his secrets, however, the author of Proverbs wants to get one thing straight. The wisdom he is teaching cannot be reduced to a series of "Don't do this; do that" rules. There is no formula for "one-minute wisdom"; true wisdom demands a lifelong quest. The rewards of such a life, however, will repay any sacrifice, "though it cost all you have."

As the author contrasts "the path of the righteous" with "the way of the wicked," one cannot help wondering how Solomon might have fared if he had consistently followed his own advice. Now, his time passing; he could only hope to convey that hard-bitten wisdom to future generations.

> **To Reflect On:** *Do people in modern times pursue "wisdom" with the same desire and energy that this chapter sets forth? Where do people in modern times pursue "wisdom"?*

PROVERBS 4

Wisdom Is Supreme

4 Listen, my sons, to a father's
instruction;
pay attention and gain
understanding.
²I give you sound learning,
so do not forsake my teaching.
³When I was a boy in my father's
house,
still tender, and an only child of my
mother,
⁴he taught me and said,
"Lay hold of my words with all your
heart;
keep my commands and you will
live.
⁵Get wisdom, get understanding;
do not forget my words or swerve
from them.
⁶Do not forsake wisdom, and she will
protect you;
love her, and she will watch over
you.
⁷Wisdom is supreme; therefore get
wisdom.
Though it cost all you have, get
understanding.
⁸Esteem her, and she will exalt you;
embrace her, and she will honor
you.
⁹She will set a garland of grace on your
head
and present you with a crown of
splendor."

¹⁰Listen, my son, accept what I say,
and the years of your life will be
many.
¹¹I guide you in the way of wisdom
and lead you along straight paths.
¹²When you walk, your steps will not be
hampered;
when you run, you will not stumble.
¹³Hold on to instruction, do not let it
go;
guard it well, for it is your life.
¹⁴Do not set foot on the path of the
wicked
or walk in the way of evil men.
¹⁵Avoid it, do not travel on it;
turn from it and go on your way.
¹⁶For they cannot sleep till they do evil;
they are robbed of slumber till they
make someone fall.
¹⁷They eat the bread of wickedness
and drink the wine of violence.

¹⁸The path of the righteous is like the
first gleam of dawn,
shining ever brighter till the full light
of day.
¹⁹But the way of the wicked is like deep
darkness;
they do not know what makes them
stumble.

²⁰My son, pay attention to what I say;
listen closely to my words.
²¹Do not let them out of your sight,
keep them within your heart;
²²for they are life to those who find
them
and health to a man's whole body.
²³Above all else, guard your heart,
for it is the wellspring of life.
²⁴Put away perversity from your mouth;
keep corrupt talk far from your lips.
²⁵Let your eyes look straight ahead,
fix your gaze directly before you.
²⁶Make level paths for your feet
and take only ways that are firm.
²⁷Do not swerve to the right or the left;
keep your foot from evil.

How To Read Proverbs

Proverbs 10

Solomon had the ability to express his great wisdom in a very down-to-earth way. As a result, the book of Proverbs reads like a collection of the folksy, common-sense advice you might get from an uncle or aunt, or a godparent. The practical guidance, intended to help you make your way in the world, skips from topic to topic. It comments on small issues as well as large: blabbermouthing, wearing out your welcome with neighbors, being unbearably cheerful too early in the morning.

Anybody can find exceptions to the generalities in Proverbs. For instance, Proverbs 10:4 says "Lazy hands make a man poor, but diligent hands bring wealth." Yet, farmers who work diligently may go hungry during a drought, and lazy dreamers sometimes hit the lottery jackpot. Proverbs simply tells how life works most of the time; it gives the rule, not the exceptions. (Try to live by the exceptions, though, and you court disaster.) Normally, people who are godly, moral, hardworking, and wise will succeed in life. Fools and scoffers, though they appear successful, will pay a long-term price for their lifestyles.

The advice in Proverbs usually takes the form of a brief, pungent "one-liner," so the book requires a different kind of reading than others in the Bible. It's hard to read several chapters in a row. The proverbs are meant to be taken in small doses, savored, digested, and gradually absorbed.

It helps to have a basic understanding of the structure of the proverbs, especially the style known as "parallelism." That word describes the tendency of Hebrew poetry to repeat a thought in a slightly different way. For example, Proverbs 10:10 uses "synonymous parallelism": "He who winks maliciously causes grief, and a chattering fool comes to ruin." The second half of the proverb underscores and embellishes the message of the first half.

Mostly, however, this chapter uses "antithetical parallelism," in which a thought is followed by its opposite: "Lazy hands make a man poor, but diligent hands bring wealth." The word "but" often connects the two antithetical statements. In both kinds of parallelism, the trick is to compare each phrase with its pair in the other half of the proverb. For instance, in 10:4 "diligent hands" pairs with its opposite, "lazy hands," and "bring wealth" is the opposite of "make a man poor." Sometimes these comparisons bare subtle shades of meaning.

To Reflect On: *Which of the proverbs in this chapter apply most directly to you?*

PROVERBS 10

Proverbs of Solomon

10 The proverbs of Solomon:

A wise son brings joy to his
    father,
but a foolish son grief to his mother.

²Ill-gotten treasures are of no value,
    but righteousness delivers from
        death.

³The LORD does not let the righteous go
        hungry
    but he thwarts the craving of the
        wicked.

⁴Lazy hands make a man poor,
    but diligent hands bring wealth.

⁵He who gathers crops in summer is a
        wise son,
    but he who sleeps during harvest is
        a disgraceful son.

⁶Blessings crown the head of the
righteous,
but violence overwhelms the mouth
of the wicked.

⁷The memory of the righteous will be a
blessing,
but the name of the wicked will rot.

⁸The wise in heart accept commands,
but a chattering fool comes to ruin.

⁹The man of integrity walks securely,
but he who takes crooked paths will
be found out.

¹⁰He who winks maliciously causes grief,
and a chattering fool comes to ruin.

¹¹The mouth of the righteous is a
fountain of life,
but violence overwhelms the mouth
of the wicked.

¹²Hatred stirs up dissension,
but love covers over all wrongs.

¹³Wisdom is found on the lips of the
discerning,
but a rod is for the back of him who
lacks judgment.

¹⁴Wise men store up knowledge,
but the mouth of a fool invites ruin.

¹⁵The wealth of the rich is their fortified
city,
but poverty is the ruin of the poor.

¹⁶The wages of the righteous bring them
life,
but the income of the wicked brings
them punishment.

¹⁷He who heeds discipline shows the
way to life,
but whoever ignores correction leads
others astray.

¹⁸He who conceals his hatred has lying
lips,
and whoever spreads slander is a
fool.

¹⁹When words are many, sin is not
absent,
but he who holds his tongue is wise.

²⁰The tongue of the righteous is choice
silver,
but the heart of the wicked is of
little value.

²¹The lips of the righteous nourish
many,
but fools die for lack of judgment.

²²The blessing of the LORD brings wealth,
and he adds no trouble to it.

²³A fool finds pleasure in evil conduct,
but a man of understanding delights
in wisdom.

²⁴What the wicked dreads will overtake
him;
what the righteous desire will be
granted.

²⁵When the storm has swept by, the
wicked are gone,
but the righteous stand firm forever.

²⁶As vinegar to the teeth and smoke to
the eyes,
so is a sluggard to those who send
him.

²⁷The fear of the LORD adds length to
life,
but the years of the wicked are cut
short.

²⁸The prospect of the righteous is joy,
but the hopes of the wicked come to
nothing.

²⁹The way of the LORD is a refuge for
the righteous,
but it is the ruin of those who do
evil.

³⁰The righteous will never be uprooted,
but the wicked will not remain in
the land.

³¹The mouth of the righteous brings
forth wisdom,
but a perverse tongue will be cut
out.

³²The lips of the righteous know what is
fitting,
but the mouth of the wicked only
what is perverse.

Words about Words

A Proverbs Sampler

Who is the wisest person you know? Probably you'll come up with an elderly person, full of life experience, with a wry twist of humor and a colorful way of putting things. Solomon must have been like that, and he passed down his observations about life in elegant, witty nuggets of insight.

Yet for all its wisdom, Proverbs may well be the most abused book in the Bible. People often quote the proverbs as if they were absolute promises from God or rigid rules for living, when in fact few of them should be read that way. It's best to study the whole book to get its overall point of view on a subject.

Solomon did not sit around all day spouting proverbs in topical sequence. Most likely, those that survive in this book were assembled late in his life, in no strict order. Thus reading Proverbs may at first remind you of reading the dictionary: You'll encounter short, self-contained items in a long list with little or no connection between them.

Even though the one-liners in Proverbs move quickly (and apparently randomly) from one subject to another, there is an overall objective behind the disorder. If you spend enough time in Proverbs, you will gain a subtle and practical understanding of life. Familiar themes keep showing up: the use and abuse of the tongue, wealth and poverty, keeping and losing one's temper, laziness and hard work.

In a "bird's-eye view" survey of the Bible, there is no time for such topical in-depth study. However, the following sampler of proverbs, all dealing with the power of words, shows how such a study might work. Taken together, these proverbs present a wise, balanced view of conversation. They reveal the explosive power— for good or for evil—of ordinary words.

Proverbs on the importance of words: 10:11, 20; 12:14; 15:4; 17:10; 18:21; 25:11.
Proverbs on the wrong way to speak: 6:16–19; 11:9,12, 13; 12:18; 13:3; 16:27, 28; 18:8, 13; 26:23–28; 29:5.
Proverbs on the dangers of words: 10:19; 14:23.

To Reflect On: *Have you said anything recently that you wish you could unsay?*

A PROVERBS SAMPLER

Proverbs on the importance of words

Chapter 10

¹¹The mouth of the righteous is a
    fountain of life,
  but violence overwhelms the mouth
    of the wicked.

²⁰The tongue of the righteous is choice
    silver,
  but the heart of the wicked is of
    little value.

Chapter 12

¹⁴From the fruit of his lips a man is
    filled with good things
  as surely as the work of his hands
    rewards him.

Chapter 15

⁴The tongue that brings healing is a tree
    of life,
  but a deceitful tongue crushes the
    spirit.

Chapter 17

¹⁰A rebuke impresses a man of
    discernment

more than a hundred lashes a fool.

Chapter 18

²¹The tongue has the power of life and
death,
and those who love it will eat its
fruit.

Chapter 25

¹¹A word aptly spoken
is like apples of gold in settings of
silver.

Proverbs on the wrong way to speak
Chapter 6

¹⁶There are six things the LORD hates,
seven that are detestable to him:
¹⁷   haughty eyes,
a lying tongue,
hands that shed innocent blood,
¹⁸   a heart that devises wicked
schemes,
feet that are quick to rush into
evil,
¹⁹   a false witness who pours out lies
and a man who stirs up
dissension among brothers.

Chapter 11

⁹With his mouth the godless destroys his
neighbor,
but through knowledge the righteous
escape.

¹²A man who lacks judgment derides his
neighbor,
but a man of understanding holds
his tongue.

¹³A gossip betrays a confidence,
but a trustworthy man keeps a
secret.

Chapter 12

¹⁸Reckless words pierce like a sword,
but the tongue of the wise brings
healing.

Chapter 13

³He who guards his lips guards his life,
but he who speaks rashly will come
to ruin.

Chapter 16

²⁷A scoundrel plots evil,
and his speech is like a scorching
fire.

²⁸A perverse man stirs up dissension,
and a gossip separates close friends.

Chapter 18

⁸The words of a gossip are like choice
morsels;
they go down to a man's inmost
parts.

¹³He who answers before listening—
that is his folly and his shame.

Chapter 26

²³Like a coating of glaze over
earthenware
are fervent lips with an evil heart.

²⁴A malicious man disguises himself with
his lips,
but in his heart he harbors deceit.
²⁵Though his speech is charming, do not
believe him,
for seven abominations fill his heart.
²⁶His malice may be concealed by
deception,
but his wickedness will be exposed
in the assembly.

²⁷If a man digs a pit, he will fall into it;
if a man rolls a stone, it will roll
back on him.

²⁸A lying tongue hates those it hurts,
and a flattering mouth works ruin.

Chapter 29

⁵Whoever flatters his neighbor
is spreading a net for his feet.

Proverbs on the dangers of words
Chapter 10

¹⁹When words are many, sin is not
absent,
but he who holds his tongue is wise.

Chapter 14

²³All hard work brings a profit,
but mere talk leads only to poverty.

Common Topic, Uncommon Song

Song of Songs 2

Without doubt more songs have been written about romantic love than any other subject. If you question that, just tune your radio to any popular station and listen for fifteen minutes. You'll hear songs about new love, failed love, wild and crazy love, every kind of love. And, to many people's surprise, the Bible itself contains an explicit love song—complete with erotic lyrics.

Solomon, with all his wives and mistresses, was a devoted student of romance. Ultimately, he fell victim to an obsession with it that caused him much grief. But the Song of Songs (also known as the Song of Solomon) celebrates a high form of beautiful love. It shows no embarrassment about lovers enjoying each other's bodies and openly expressing that enjoyment.

Not everyone has felt comfortable with the frankness of this book. In medieval Spain, Saint Teresa of Avila led a campaign to remove all copies of Song of Songs from the Bible and burn them in public bonfires. Priests and teachers who refused were removed from their jobs, and even imprisoned.

Over the centuries, many others have tried to read the song as though it had nothing to do with physical lovers, seeing it instead as an allegory of love between God and his people. But nowadays most scholars believe that the poem was intended to be taken at face value, as a celebration of love between a newly-married couple.

These lovers look without shame on one another, and tell each other what they feel. They revel in the sensuous: the beauty of nature, the scent of perfumes and spices. They are explicit and erotic. Yet, Song of Songs creates a very different atmosphere than most modern love songs. It harks back to the original love in the Garden of Eden, when man and woman were naked and unashamed. You sense no shame or guilt; you feel that God himself smiles upon their love.

> **To Reflect On:** *What similarities do you see between this chapter and modern love songs? What differences?*

SONG OF SONGS 2

Beloved

2 I am a rose of Sharon,
a lily of the valleys.

Lover

²Like a lily among thorns
is my darling among the maidens.

Beloved

³Like an apple tree among the trees of
the forest
is my lover among the young men.
I delight to sit in his shade,
and his fruit is sweet to my taste.
⁴He has taken me to the banquet hall,
and his banner over me is love.
⁵Strengthen me with raisins,
refresh me with apples,
for I am faint with love.
⁶His left arm is under my head,
and his right arm embraces me.
⁷Daughters of Jerusalem, I charge you
by the gazelles and by the does of
the field:
Do not arouse or awaken love until it
so desires.

⁸Listen! My lover!
Look! Here he comes,
leaping across the mountains,
bounding over the hills.
⁹My lover is like a gazelle or a young
stag.
Look! There he stands behind our
wall,
gazing through the windows,
peering through the lattice.

¹⁰My lover spoke and said to me,
"Arise, my darling,
my beautiful one, and come with
me.
¹¹See! The winter is past;
the rains are over and gone.
¹²Flowers appear on the earth;
the season of singing has come,
the cooing of doves
is heard in our land.
¹³The fig tree forms its early fruit;
the blossoming vines spread their
fragrance.
Arise, come, my darling;
my beautiful one, come with me.'

Lover

¹⁴My dove in the clefts of the rock,
in the hiding places on the
mountainside,
show me your face,
let me hear your voice;
for your voice is sweet,
and your face is lovely.
¹⁵Catch for us the foxes,
the little foxes
that ruin the vineyards,
our vineyards that are in bloom.

Beloved

¹⁶My lover is mine and I am his;
he browses among the lilies.
¹⁷Until the day breaks
and the shadows flee,
turn, my lover,
and be like a gazelle
or like a young stag
on the rugged hills.

Dangling

Ecclesiastes 3

People surprised to find a book like Song of Songs in the Bible may be knocked flat by the book of Ecclesiastes. "Meaningless! Meaningless! Everything is meaningless!" cries the author of this bleak capitulation of despair. At first, its message and tone may seem more appropriate for a modern book of grim existentialism.

Although Ecclesiastes mentions no author by name, it contains broad hints that King Solomon was, if not its author, then at least its inspiration. It tells the story of the richest, wisest, most famous man in the world, who follows every pleasure impulse as far as it can lead him. This man, "the Teacher," finally collapses in regret and despair; he has squandered his life.

Because of the mood swings in Ecclesiastes, the book must be read as a whole to grasp its full meaning. But this early chapter gives a capsule summary, beginning with an elegant poem about Time—words made famous in a folk song of the 1960s—and proceeding from there into musings about life typical of the Teacher's search for meaning.

God has laid a "burden" on humanity, the author concludes: a burden that keeps us from finding ultimate satisfaction on earth. After a lifetime spent in the pursuit of pleasure, the Teacher was driven to ask, "Is that all there is?" Even the rare moments of peace and satisfaction he had found were easily spoiled by the onrushing threat of death. According to the Teacher, life doesn't make sense outside of God and will, in fact, never fully make sense because we are not God.

But God has also "set eternity in the hearts of men." We feel longings for something more: pleasures that will last forever; love that won't go sour; fulfillment, not boredom, from our work.

The Teacher thus dangles between two states, feeling a steady drag toward despair but also a tug toward something higher. Much like a personal journal, the book of Ecclesiastes records his search for balance. The tension does not resolve in this chapter, and some readers wonder if it resolves at all. But Ecclesiastes ends with one final word of advice, the summation of all the Teacher's wisdom: "Fear God and keep his commandments, for this is the whole duty of man" (12:13).

> **To Reflect On:** *The Teacher is painfully honest about his doubts and his despair. What portions of this chapter did you especially identify with?*

ECCLESIASTES 3

A Time for Everything

3 There is a time for everything,
and a season for every activity under
heaven:

2 a time to be born and a time to die,
a time to plant and a time to uproot,
3 a time to kill and a time to heal,
a time to tear down and a time to
build,
4 a time to weep and a time to laugh,
a time to mourn and a time to
dance,
5 a time to scatter stones and a time
to gather them,
a time to embrace and a time to
refrain,
6 a time to search and a time to give
up,
a time to keep and a time to throw
away,
7 a time to tear and a time to mend,
a time to be silent and a time to
speak,
8 a time to love and a time to hate,
a time for war and a time for peace.

9 What does the worker gain from his toil? 10 I have seen the burden God has laid on men. 11 He has made everything beautiful in its time. He has also set eternity in the hearts of men; yet they cannot fathom what God has done from beginning to end. 12 I know that there is nothing better for men than to be happy and do good while they live. 13 That everyone may eat and drink, and find satisfaction in all his toil—this is the gift of God. 14 I know that everything God does will endure forever; nothing can be added to it and nothing taken from it. God does it so that men will revere him.

15 Whatever is has already been,
and what will be has been before;
and God will call the past to
account.

16 And I saw something else under the sun:

In the place of judgment—wickedness
was there,
in the place of justice—wickedness
was there.

17 I thought in my heart,

"God will bring to judgment
both the righteous and the wicked,
for there will be a time for every
activity,
a time for every deed."

18 I also thought, "As for men, God tests them so that they may see that they are like the animals. 19 Man's fate is like that of the animals; the same fate awaits them both: As one dies, so dies the other. All have the same breath; man has no advantage over the animal. Everything is meaningless. 20 All go to the same place; all come from dust, and to dust all return. 21 Who knows if the spirit of man rises upward and if the spirit of the animal goes down into the earth?"

22 So I saw that there is nothing better for a man than to enjoy his work, because that is his lot. For who can bring him to see what will happen after him?

New Breed of Heroes

1 Kings 17

The nation of Israel flourished during the Golden Age of David and Solomon, but in the end Solomon's weaknesses seriously eroded the kingdom. His lavish public projects lay a heavy tax burden on its citizens and forced him to conscript some of them as virtual slaves. His moral failures undermined the spiritual unity of the nation, and the brief, shining vision of a covenant nation gradually faded away. After Solomon's death, the nation split in two and slid toward ruin.

The remaining part of the Old Testament can prove especially confusing: the two nations had thirty-nine rulers between them, and a couple dozen prophets besides. To avoid getting hopelessly lost, keep these basic facts in mind: *Israel* was the breakaway Northern Kingdom, with a capital city of Samaria. All its rulers proved unfaithful to God. *Judah* was the Southern Kingdom, with its capital in Jerusalem. In general its rulers, descendants of David, remained more faithful to God and his covenant, and consequently Judah survived 136 years longer.

Although the Bible discusses all thirty-nine rulers by name, its focus clearly moves away from them. The first three kings—Saul, David, and Solomon—are each given lengthy treatment. But after Solomon, stories of the kings speed up into a forgettable blur. God turns instead to his prophets.

Elijah, the wildest and wooliest prophet of all, first makes an appearance in this chapter. He illustrates better than anyone else the decisive change: where King Solomon had worn jewelry and fine clothes and lived luxuriously in a gilded palace, Elijah wore a diaper-like covering of black camel's hair, slept in the wilderness, and had to beg—or pray—for handouts. He came on the scene when Israel (the Northern Kingdom) was thriving politically, but floundering spiritually. Queen Jezebel had just launched a murderous campaign to eliminate all true prophets of God and replace them with nearly a thousand pagan priests.

This chapter shows glimpses of Elijah during his fugitive days. Although he was a moody prophet, subject to bouts of depression and self-doubt, he clearly had God on his side. The tender story of his healing of a widow's son shows that God had not forgotten the "little people." The salvation of Israel would depend on how well they listened to prophets like Elijah.

To Reflect On: *What do you learn about Elijah's personality in this chapter?*

1 KINGS 17

Elijah Fed by Ravens

17 Now Elijah the Tishbite, from Tishbe in Gilead, said to Ahab, "As the LORD, the God of Israel, lives, whom I serve, there will be neither dew nor rain in the next few years except at my word."

²Then the word of the LORD came to Elijah: ³"Leave here, turn eastward and hide in the Kerith Ravine, east of the Jordan. ⁴You will drink from the brook, and I have ordered the ravens to feed you there."

⁵So he did what the LORD had told him. He went to the Kerith Ravine, east of the Jordan, and stayed there. ⁶The ravens brought him bread and meat in the morning and bread and meat in the evening, and he drank from the brook.

The Widow at Zarephath

⁷Some time later the brook dried up because there had been no rain in the land. ⁸Then the word of the LORD came to him: ⁹"Go at once to Zarephath of Sidon and stay there. I have commanded a widow in that place to supply you with food." ¹⁰So he went to Zarephath. When he came to the town gate, a widow was there gathering sticks. He called to her and asked, "Would you bring me a little water in a jar so I may have a drink?" ¹¹As she was going to get it, he called, "And bring me, please, a piece of bread."

¹²"As surely as the LORD your God lives," she replied, "I don't have any bread—only a handful of flour in a jar and a little oil in a jug. I am gathering a few sticks to take home and make a meal for myself and my son, that we may eat it—and die."

¹³Elijah said to her, "Don't be afraid. Go home and do as you have said. But first make a small cake of bread for me from what you have and bring it to me, and then make something for yourself and your son. ¹⁴For this is what the LORD, the God of Israel, says: 'The jar of flour will not be used up and the jug of oil will not run dry until the day the LORD gives rain on the land.' "

¹⁵She went away and did as Elijah had told her. So there was food every day for Elijah and for the woman and her family. ¹⁶For the jar of flour was not used up and the jug of oil did not run dry, in keeping with the word of the LORD spoken by Elijah.

¹⁷Some time later the son of the woman who owned the house became ill. He grew worse and worse, and finally stopped breathing. ¹⁸She said to Elijah, "What do you have against me, man of God? Did you come to remind me of my sin and kill my son?"

¹⁹"Give me your son," Elijah replied. He took him from her arms, carried him to the upper room where he was staying, and laid him on his bed. ²⁰Then he cried out to the LORD, "O LORD my God, have you brought tragedy also upon this widow I am staying with, by causing her son to die?" ²¹Then he stretched himself out on the boy three times and cried to the LORD, "O LORD my God, let this boy's life return to him!"

²²The LORD heard Elijah's cry, and the boy's life returned to him, and he lived. ²³Elijah picked up the child and carried him down from the room into the house. He gave him to his mother and said, "Look, your son is alive!"

²⁴Then the woman said to Elijah, "Now I know that you are a man of God and that the word of the LORD from your mouth is the truth."

Mountaintop Showdown

1 Kings 18:15–46

In ancient Africa, tribes would sometimes fight their battles single-combat style. Great armies lined up across from each other, waving their weapons menacingly and hurling insults back and forth. When tribal hatred reached a kind of critical mass, two warriors—only two—stepped forward to fight on behalf of all the rest. Whoever drew first blood would prove the gods were on his side, and his opponent's army would surrender.

Single-combat warfare cropped up throughout ancient times—remember David and Goliath—and in the Middle Ages in Europe. The pioneer West offered a classic American version: the one-on-one showdown between gunslingers representing the forces of good (white hat) and the forces of evil (dark hat). Something like single-combat warfare took place at a moment of deep crisis in Israel. As usual, the prophet Elijah was on center stage.

Elijah journeyed across Israel to a rugged mountain to confront his pagan enemies. Few scenes in history can match the one that transpired on windswept Mount Carmel. On one side stood a resplendent array of 850 prophets of Baal and Asherah; on the other stood a lone, bedraggled desert prophet of God. Elijah let the pagan prophets have first turn. As they danced around an altar beseeching their gods, he sat back, enjoyed the show, and taunted them to frenzy. "Maybe your god is deep in thought, or traveling, or sleeping," he yelled, and the priests slashed themselves with swords until the blood ran.

Elijah may have been outnumbered, but he proved a worthy adversary. When his time came, he worked the crowd like a master magician. He stacked the odds against a miracle by dousing the site with twelve large jars of water—the most precious commodity in Israel after a three-year drought. Just when it seemed Elijah was perpetrating a huge national joke, the miracle happened: fire fell from heaven. The crowd dropped to the ground in fear and awe. The heat was enough to melt even the stones and soil, and flames licked water from the trenches as if it were fuel.

Elijah's very name meant "The LORD is my God," and, in the final analysis, the showdown on Mount Carmel was no contest at all. Elijah went on to orchestrate one of the greatest outbreaks of miracles in biblical history. It was as if God was sounding a loud, unmistakable final warning to the North—a warning they failed to heed.

> **To Reflect On:** *This chapter shows God revealing himself in a spectacular public display. Have you known him to do such things today? If not, why not?*

---

1 KINGS 18:15–46

¹⁵Elijah said, "As the LORD Almighty lives, whom I serve, I will surely present myself to Ahab today."

Elijah on Mount Carmel

¹⁶So Obadiah went to meet Ahab and told him, and Ahab went to meet Elijah.

¹⁷When he saw Elijah, he said to him, "Is that you, you troubler of Israel?"

¹⁸"I have not made trouble for Israel," Elijah replied. "But you and your father's family have. You have abandoned the LORD's commands and have followed the Baals. ¹⁹Now summon the people from all over Israel to meet me on Mount Carmel. And bring the four hundred and fifty

prophets of Baal and the four hundred prophets of Asherah, who eat at Jezebel's table."

²⁰So Ahab sent word throughout all Israel and assembled the prophets on Mount Carmel. ²¹Elijah went before the people and said, "How long will you waver between two opinions? If the LORD is God, follow him; but if Baal is God, follow him."

But the people said nothing.

²²Then Elijah said to them, "I am the only one of the LORD's prophets left, but Baal has four hundred and fifty prophets. ²³Get two bulls for us. Let them choose one for themselves, and let them cut it into pieces and put it on the wood but not set fire to it. I will prepare the other bull and put it on the wood but not set fire to it. ²⁴Then you call on the name of your god, and I will call on the name of the LORD. The god who answers by fire—he is God."

Then all the people said, "What you say is good."

²⁵Elijah said to the prophets of Baal, "Choose one of the bulls and prepare it first, since there are so many of you. Call on the name of your god, but do not light the fire." ²⁶So they took the bull given them and prepared it.

Then they called on the name of Baal from morning till noon. "O Baal, answer us!" they shouted. But there was no response; no one answered. And they danced around the altar they had made.

²⁷At noon Elijah began to taunt them. "Shout louder!" he said. "Surely he is a god! Perhaps he is deep in thought, or busy, or traveling. Maybe he is sleeping and must be awakened." ²⁸So they shouted louder and slashed themselves with swords and spears, as was their custom, until their blood flowed. ²⁹Midday passed, and they continued their frantic prophesying until the time for the evening sacrifice. But there was no response, no one answered, no one paid attention.

³⁰Then Elijah said to all the people, "Come here to me." They came to him, and he repaired the altar of the LORD, which was in ruins. ³¹Elijah took twelve stones, one for each of the tribes descended from Jacob, to whom the word of the LORD had come, saying, "Your name shall be Israel." ³²With the stones he built an altar in the name of the LORD, and he dug a trench around it

large enough to hold two seahs of seed. ³³He arranged the wood, cut the bull into pieces and laid it on the wood. Then he said to them, "Fill four large jars with water and pour it on the offering and on the wood."

³⁴"Do it again," he said, and they did it again.

"Do it a third time," he ordered, and they did it the third time. ³⁵The water ran down around the altar and even filled the trench.

³⁶At the time of sacrifice, the prophet Elijah stepped forward and prayed: "O LORD, God of Abraham, Isaac and Israel, let it be known today that you are God in Israel and that I am your servant and have done all these things at your command. ³⁷Answer me, O LORD, answer me, so these people will know that you, O LORD, are God, and that you are turning their hearts back again."

³⁸Then the fire of the LORD fell and burned up the sacrifice, the wood, the stones and the soil, and also licked up the water in the trench.

³⁹When all the people saw this, they fell prostrate and cried, "The LORD—he is God! The LORD—he is God!"

⁴⁰Then Elijah commanded them, "Seize the prophets of Baal. Don't let anyone get away!" They seized them, and Elijah had them brought down to the Kishon Valley and slaughtered there.

⁴¹And Elijah said to Ahab, "Go, eat and drink, for there is the sound of a heavy rain." ⁴²So Ahab went off to eat and drink, but Elijah climbed to the top of Carmel, bent down to the ground and put his face between his knees.

⁴³"Go and look toward the sea," he told his servant. And he went up and looked.

"There is nothing there," he said.

Seven times Elijah said, "Go back."

⁴⁴The seventh time the servant reported, "A cloud as small as a man's hand is rising from the sea."

So Elijah said, "Go and tell Ahab, 'Hitch up your chariot and go down before the rain stops you.'"

⁴⁵Meanwhile, the sky grew black with clouds, the wind rose, a heavy rain came on and Ahab rode off to Jezreel. ⁴⁶The power of the LORD came upon Elijah and, tucking his cloak into his belt, he ran ahead of Ahab all the way to Jezreel.

A Worthy Replacement

2 Kings 5

Who could replace a mighty prophet like Elijah? When the time came to choose a successor, Elijah settled on his most faithful companion, a farmer named Elisha. The two had similar names but distinctive styles. Elijah was a loner, and often a fugitive, and preached a stern message of judgment. In contrast, Elisha lived among common people, and stressed life, hope, and God's grace.

Elisha lived a colorful life: He led a school of prophets, served as a military spy, advised kings, and even anointed revolutionaries. Easily recognizable with his bald head and wooden walking staff, he became a famous figure in Israel, especially as reports of his miracles spread. Elisha had asked for a double portion of Elijah's spirit, and the Bible pointedly records about twice as many miracles performed by Elisha. Many of these miracles prefigure the miracles Jesus himself would later perform; they show God caring for the needs of poor and outcast people.

During Elisha's lifetime Israel was reeling—internally from the corruption of King Ahab's reign, and externally from attacks by the neighboring state of Aram (the area known today as Syria). Sometimes Elisha used his special powers to assist Israel's army. But in this chapter he is seen offering assistance to a high-ranking enemy general. Naaman's pilgrimage shows how far Elisha's fame had spread. A pagan king was willing to seek help from God's prophet in order to get a general's health restored.

Elisha's brusque treatment of generals and kings contrasts sharply with the tenderness he showed toward the poor and oppressed. The bizarre procedure he prescribed, along with his refusal to take payment, offended Naaman. Elisha, however, was making it clear that healing came not through magical powers or a shaman's secret technique, but through God—and God required obedience and humility even of five-star generals with piles of gold.

Jesus referred to this story at the beginning of his ministry (Luke 4:27). He made the same point as Elisha: Don't try to "box in" God. He is to be obeyed, on his own terms, not manipulated.

> **To Reflect On:** *One writer has defined the Christian life as "living by God's surprises." Has God ever surprised you?*

2 KINGS 5

Naaman Healed of Leprosy

5 Now Naaman was commander of the army of the king of Aram. He was a great man in the sight of his master and highly regarded, because through him the LORD had given victory to Aram. He was a valiant soldier, but he had leprosy.

²Now bands from Aram had gone out and had taken captive a young girl from Israel, and she served Naaman's wife. ³She said to her mistress, "If only my master would see the prophet who is in Samaria! He would cure him of his leprosy."

⁴Naaman went to his master and told him what the girl from Israel had said. ⁵"By all means, go," the king of Aram replied. "I will send a letter to the king of Israel." So Naaman left, taking with him ten talents of silver, six thousand shekels of gold and ten sets of clothing. ⁶The letter that he took to the king of Israel read: "With this letter I am sending my servant Naaman to you so that you may cure him of his leprosy."

⁷As soon as the king of Israel read the letter, he tore his robes and said, "Am I God? Can I kill and bring back to life? Why does this fellow send someone to me to be

cured of his leprosy? See how he is trying to pick a quarrel with me!"

⁸When Elisha the man of God heard that the king of Israel had torn his robes, he sent him this message: "Why have you torn your robes? Have the man come to me and he will know that there is a prophet in Israel." ⁹So Naaman went with his horses and chariots and stopped at the door of Elisha's house. ¹⁰Elisha sent a messenger to say to him, "Go, wash yourself seven times in the Jordan, and your flesh will be restored and you will be cleansed."

¹¹But Naaman went away angry and said, "I thought that he would surely come out to me and stand and call on the name of the LORD his God, wave his hand over the spot and cure me of my leprosy. ¹²Are not Abana and Pharpar, the rivers of Damascus, better than any of the waters of Israel? Couldn't I wash in them and be cleansed?" So he turned and went off in a rage.

¹³Naaman's servants went to him and said, "My father, if the prophet had told you to do some great thing, would you not have done it? How much more, then, when he tells you, 'Wash and be cleansed'!" ¹⁴So he went down and dipped himself in the Jordan seven times, as the man of God had told him, and his flesh was restored and became clean like that of a young boy.

¹⁵Then Naaman and all his attendants went back to the man of God. He stood before him and said, "Now I know that there is no God in all the world except in Israel. Please accept now a gift from your servant."

¹⁶The prophet answered, "As surely as the LORD lives, whom I serve, I will not accept a thing." And even though Naaman urged him, he refused.

¹⁷"If you will not," said Naaman, "please let me, your servant, be given as much earth as a pair of mules can carry, for your servant will never again make burnt offerings and sacrifices to any other god but the LORD. ¹⁸But may the LORD forgive your servant for this one thing: When my master

enters the temple of Rimmon to bow down and he is leaning on my arm and I bow there also—when I bow down in the temple of Rimmon, may the LORD forgive your servant for this."

¹⁹"Go in peace," Elisha said.

After Naaman had traveled some distance, ²⁰Gehazi, the servant of Elisha the man of God, said to himself, "My master was too easy on Naaman, this Aramean, by not accepting from him what he brought. As surely as the LORD lives, I will run after him and get something from him."

²¹So Gehazi hurried after Naaman. When Naaman saw him running toward him, he got down from the chariot to meet him. "Is everything all right?" he asked.

²²"Everything is all right," Gehazi answered. "My master sent me to say, 'Two young men from the company of the prophets have just come to me from the hill country of Ephraim. Please give them a talent of silver and two sets of clothing.'"

²³"By all means, take two talents," said Naaman. He urged Gehazi to accept them, and then tied up the two talents of silver in two bags, with two sets of clothing. He gave them to two of his servants, and they carried them ahead of Gehazi. ²⁴When Gehazi came to the hill, he took the things from the servants and put them away in the house. He sent the men away and they left. ²⁵Then he went in and stood before his master Elisha.

"Where have you been, Gehazi?" Elisha asked.

"Your servant didn't go anywhere," Gehazi answered.

²⁶But Elisha said to him, "Was not my spirit with you when the man got down from his chariot to meet you? Is this the time to take money, or to accept clothes, olive groves, vineyards, flocks, herds, or menservants and maidservants? ²⁷Naaman's leprosy will cling to you and to your descendants forever." Then Gehazi went from Elisha's presence and he was leprous, as white as snow.

The Day the Earth Will Shake

Joel 2:1–19

Scenes from the lives of Elijah and Elisha—fire on Mount Carmel, the widow's oil, Naaman's healing, the chariots of fire—are among the most familiar of Old Testament stories. But in a sense those two prophets represented the last of a dying breed. The prophets who followed them performed few miracles, relying less on spectacular displays of power and more on the power of the Word.

The prophet Joel provides a brief introduction to the style of the writing prophets. No one knows for sure when he delivered his messages—they could have come anywhere within a four-century span. No one is even sure whether he lived in Israel of the North or Judah of the South. But in gripping prose he warned his people of a terrible disaster to come. This one chapter captures as well as any the essential message of all the prophets.

1. A day of judgment. Nearly every prophet begins with words meant to inspire fear and dread. Some warned of invading armies, and some of natural disasters. For example, Joel paints vivid pictures of an army of locusts.

The locusts could symbolically represent human armies, but may also be taken literally. People who have lived through a locust invasion never forget the experience. Here is how author Isak Dinesen recalls such an event in Africa:

> I saw, along the Northern horizon, a shadow on the sky, like a long stretch of smoke, a town burning, "a million-peopled city vomiting smoke in the bright air," I thought, or like a thin cloud rising.
>
> "What is that?" I asked.
>
> "Grasshoppers," said the Indian. . . .
>
> The next morning as I opened my door and looked out, the whole landscape outside was the colour of pale dull terra cotta. The grasshoppers were sitting there. While I stood and looked at it, all the scenery began to quiver and break, the grasshoppers moved and lifted. . . . They had broken a couple of big trees in my drive simply by sitting on them, and when you looked at the trees and remembered that each of the grasshoppers could only weigh a tenth of an ounce, you began to conceive the number of them.

2. A call to repentance. The prophets raise alarm with good reason, for they see such disasters as a consequence of their nation's unfaithfulness to God. They urgently call on their people to turn from their evil ways. Joel 2:13 could stand as a single, eloquent summary of the heart of the prophets' message.

3. A future of hope. Every biblical prophet, no matter how dour, gets around to a word of hope. Taken together, they tell of a time when God will make right everything wrong with the earth, a time when The World As It Is will finally match The World As God Wants It.

Joel 2 is a fine capsule summary of this threefold message.

> **To Reflect On:** *Peter applied Joel's prophecy about "the day of the LORD" to the events of Pentecost (Acts 2:17–21). Have all of Joel's prophecies already been fulfilled?*

JOEL 2:1–19

An Army of Locusts

2 Blow the trumpet in Zion;
sound the alarm on my holy hill.

Let all who live in the land tremble,
   for the day of the LORD is coming.
It is close at hand—
2   a day of darkness and gloom,
   a day of clouds and blackness.
Like dawn spreading across the moun-
      tains
   a large and mighty army comes,
such as never was of old
   nor ever will be in ages to come.

3 Before them fire devours,
   behind them a flame blazes.
Before them the land is like the garden
      of Eden,
   behind them, a desert waste—
   nothing escapes them.
4 They have the appearance of horses;
   they gallop along like cavalry.
5 With a noise like that of chariots
   they leap over the mountaintops,
like a crackling fire consuming stubble,
   like a mighty army drawn up for
      battle.

6 At the sight of them, nations are in
      anguish;
   every face turns pale.
7 They charge like warriors;
   they scale walls like soldiers.
They all march in line,
   not swerving from their course.
8 They do not jostle each other;
   each marches straight ahead.
They plunge through defenses
   without breaking ranks.
9 They rush upon the city;
   they run along the wall.
They climb into the houses;
   like thieves they enter through the
      windows.
10 Before them the earth shakes,
   the sky trembles,
the sun and moon are darkened,
   and the stars no longer shine.
11 The LORD thunders
   at the head of his army;
his forces are beyond number,
   and mighty are those who obey his
      command.
The day of the LORD is great;

it is dreadful.
Who can endure it?

Rend Your Heart

12 "Even now," declares the LORD,
   "return to me with all your heart,
   with fasting and weeping and
      mourning."

13 Rend your heart
   and not your garments.
Return to the LORD your God,
   for he is gracious and compassionate,
slow to anger and abounding in love,
   and he relents from sending
      calamity.
14 Who knows? He may turn and have
      pity
   and leave behind a blessing—
grain offerings and drink offerings
   for the LORD your God.

15 Blow the trumpet in Zion,
   declare a holy fast,
   call a sacred assembly.
16 Gather the people,
   consecrate the assembly;
bring together the elders,
   gather the children,
   those nursing at the breast.
Let the bridegroom leave his room
   and the bride her chamber.
17 Let the priests, who minister before
      the LORD,
   weep between the temple porch and
      the altar.
Let them say, "Spare your people, O
      LORD.
   Do not make your inheritance an
      object of scorn,
   a byword among the nations.
Why should they say among the
      peoples,
   'Where is their God?'"

The LORD's Answer

18 Then the LORD will be jealous for his
      land
   and take pity on his people.

19 The LORD will reply to them:

"I am sending you grain, new wine
      and oil,
   enough to satisfy you fully;
never again will I make you
   an object of scorn to the nations.

Beloved Enemies

Jonah 3–4

Occasionally a natural disaster, such as that described by Joel, wracked the tiny kingdoms of Israel and Judah. But far more often, almost constantly, the Israelites faced the threat of invasion by great powers. Egypt, Assyria, and Babylon all cast giant shadows of fear across the land, and Israel and her neighbors scrambled to form alliances to counter the threat.

The prophet Jonah lived during a period when Assyria was the enemy most feared. This book about him is unique among the prophets for two reasons:

1. It takes the form of a short story, not a transcription of a sermon or prophetic message. In fact, the book contains but one line of formal prophecy (3:4).

2. Jonah delivered his message not to Israel, or to Judah, but rather to the hated Assyrians.

Nearly everyone knows about the misadventures that befell Jonah on his journey to Nineveh: the ocean storm and the detour in the belly of a whale. But readers of Jonah often miss the central point, the reason for Jonah's misadventures in the first place. He was rebelling against God's mercy. Jonah offers a true-life study of how hard it is to follow the biblical command, "Love your enemies." While many people admire that command, few find it easy to put into practice.

Jonah had understandable reason to balk at God's orders to preach in Nineveh, for that city was the capital of an empire renowned for its cruelty. Assyrian soldiers had no qualms about "scorched earth" military tactics. Typically, after destroying an enemy's fields and cities, they would slaughter the conquered peoples or hammer iron hooks through their noses or lower lips and lead them away as slaves. Jonah wanted no part in giving such bullies a chance to repent. But amazingly, God loved Nineveh and wanted to save the city, not destroy it. He knew the people were ripe for change.

The book of Jonah powerfully expresses God's yearning to forgive, and these two brief chapters fill in the lesser-known details of Jonah's mission. To the prophet's disgust, a simple announcement of doom sparked a spiritual revival in pagan Nineveh. And Jonah, sulking under a shriveled vine, admitted he had suspected God's soft heart all along. He could not trust God—could not, that is, trust him to be harsh and unrelenting toward Nineveh. As Robert Frost summed up the book, "After Jonah, you could never trust God not to be merciful again."

The book also reveals God's ultimate purpose for his chosen people: He wanted them, like Jonah, to reach out to other people and demonstrate his love and forgiveness. Nineveh's wholehearted response put the Israelites to shame, for not once did they respond to a prophet like these Assyrians did.

To Reflect On: *Have you ever consciously tried to love the "enemies" in your life?*

JONAH 3–4

Jonah Goes to Nineveh

3 Then the word of the LORD came to Jonah a second time: ²"Go to the great city of Nineveh and proclaim to it the message I give you."

³Jonah obeyed the word of the LORD and went to Nineveh. Now Nineveh was a very important city—a visit required three days. ⁴On the first day, Jonah started into the city. He proclaimed: "Forty more days and Nineveh will be overturned." ⁵The Ninevites believed God. They declared a fast, and all of them, from the greatest to the least, put on sackcloth.

⁶When the news reached the king of Nineveh, he rose from his throne, took off his royal robes, covered himself with sackcloth and sat down in the dust. ⁷Then he issued a proclamation in Nineveh:

"By the decree of the king and his nobles:

Do not let any man or beast, herd or flock, taste anything; do not let them eat or drink. ⁸But let man and beast be covered with sackcloth. Let everyone call urgently on God. Let them give up their evil ways and their violence. ⁹Who knows? God may yet relent and with compassion turn from his fierce anger so that we will not perish."

¹⁰When God saw what they did and how they turned from their evil ways, he had compassion and did not bring upon them the destruction he had threatened.

Jonah's Anger at the LORD's Compassion

4 But Jonah was greatly displeased and became angry. ²He prayed to the LORD, "O LORD, is this not what I said when I was still at home? That is why I was so quick to flee to Tarshish. I knew that you are a gracious and compassionate God, slow to anger and abounding in love, a God who relents from sending calamity. ³Now, O LORD, take away my life, for it is better for me to die than to live."

⁴But the LORD replied, "Have you any right to be angry?"

⁵Jonah went out and sat down at a place east of the city. There he made himself a shelter, sat in its shade and waited to see what would happen to the city. ⁶Then the LORD God provided a vine and made it grow up over Jonah to give shade for his head to ease his discomfort, and Jonah was very happy about the vine. ⁷But at dawn the next day God provided a worm, which chewed the vine so that it withered. ⁸When the sun rose, God provided a scorching east wind, and the sun blazed on Jonah's head so that he grew faint. He wanted to die, and said, "It would be better for me to die than to live."

⁹But God said to Jonah, "Do you have a right to be angry about the vine?"

"I do," he said. "I am angry enough to die."

¹⁰But the LORD said, "You have been concerned about this vine, though you did not tend it or make it grow. It sprang up overnight and died overnight. ¹¹But Nineveh has more than a hundred and twenty thousand people who cannot tell their right hand from their left, and many cattle as well. Should I not be concerned about that great city?"

Street-corner Prophet

Amos 4

Biblical prophets represented a wide spectrum of social backgrounds and personality types, but modern-day cartoonists tend to perpetuate a single stereotyped image. And the fact is, Amos fits the stereotype. He was the kind to stand on street corners with a signboard and rail against the whole miserable world.

Ironically, Amos appeared on the scene when Israel, the Northern Kingdom, was booming. They had beaten back all their traditional enemies and even invaded neighboring Judah, taking land and prisoners. For a change, the government was stable: King Jeroboam II presided over a half-century of prosperity and strength. People were too busy enjoying the good life to listen to the rantings of a prophet, and for precisely that reason Amos spoke in italics and exclamation points.

Unlike Jonah, Amos was not a professional prophet. He was a man of the land, a shepherd and a tender of sycamore trees. A migrant to Israel from the South, he spoke with a rural accent and was probably the butt of many jokes by city sophisticates.

Amos the peasant could not get over what he found in the Northern cities. The luxurious lifestyles shocked him: gorgeous couches, beds of carved ivory, summer homes, top-grade meat, fine wine. It seemed obvious to Amos that this extravagance was built on a foundation of injustice: oppression of the poor, slavery, dishonest business practices, court bribes, privilege bought with money. The pampered rich women—half of them alcoholics—reminded Amos of the "cows of Bashan" that would be fattened up just before butchering.

People considered themselves properly religious, but they couldn't wait for Sabbath to end so they could dash back to work and cheat someone else.

Lulled into security by their powerful, victorious army, the Israelites thought they were safe for generations. But, as Amos warned, Israel could not forever push God into a small corner of their lives, to be brought out like a magic charm whenever they needed him. God is a lion, not a pet, and in the book of Amos, he roars.

Apparently, no one took Amos's ravings seriously. "Prepare to meet your God, O Israel," he shouted from the street corners, but those words had about as much impact in his day as they do in ours. Nevertheless, the prophet's warnings proved true: in a remarkably short time, Israel fell apart. Five kings lost the throne in thirteen years, four of them by assassination. A mere thirty years after Jeroboam II's reign, the Northern Kingdom of Israel ceased to exist.

Amos is not a comfortable book to read—its message hits too close to our own time, when nations judge success by the size of gross national product and military forces. For that reason alone, it deserves a close look.

To Reflect On: *What parallels do you see between Amos's time and our own?*

AMOS 4

Israel Has Not Returned to God

4 Hear this word, you cows of Bashan on Mount Samaria,
you women who oppress the poor
and crush the needy
and say to your husbands, "Bring us
some drinks!"
²The Sovereign LORD has sworn by his
holiness:
"The time will surely come
when you will be taken away with
hooks,
the last of you with fishhooks.
³You will each go straight out
through breaks in the wall,
and you will be cast out toward
Harmon,"
declares the LORD.
⁴"Go to Bethel and sin;
go to Gilgal and sin yet more.
Bring your sacrifices every morning,
your tithes every three years.
⁵Burn leavened bread as a thank offering
and brag about your freewill
offerings—
boast about them, you Israelites,
for this is what you love to do,"
declares the Sovereign LORD.
⁶"I gave you empty stomachs in every
city
and lack of bread in every town,
yet you have not returned to me,"
declares the LORD.

⁷"I also withheld rain from you
when the harvest was still three
months away.
I sent rain on one town,
but withheld it from another.
One field had rain;
another had none and dried up.

⁸People staggered from town to town for
water
but did not get enough to drink,
yet you have not returned to me,"
declares the LORD.

⁹"Many times I struck your gardens and
vineyards,
I struck them with blight and
mildew.
Locusts devoured your fig and olive
trees,
yet you have not returned to me,"
declares the LORD.

¹⁰"I sent plagues among you
as I did to Egypt.
I killed your young men with the
sword,
along with your captured horses.
I filled your nostrils with the stench of
your camps,
yet you have not returned to me,"
declares the LORD.

¹¹"I overthrew some of you
as I overthrew Sodom and
Gomorrah.
You were like a burning stick snatched
from the fire,
yet you have not returned to me,"
declares the LORD.

¹²"Therefore this is what I will do to
you, Israel,
and because I will do this to you,
prepare to meet your God, O Israel."

¹³He who forms the mountains,
creates the wind,
and reveals his thoughts to man,
he who turns dawn to darkness,
and treads the high places of the
earth—
the LORD God Almighty is his name.

Human Object Lesson

Hosea 2:4–3:5

God sent prophets to Israel and Judah to meet the need of the moment. When people were cocky, self-indulgent, and spiritually deaf, a screamer like Amos appeared on the scene. But suffering people called for another tone. Just a few years after Amos, as Israel was breaking apart and sliding toward chaos, a word from God came to Hosea. To a shattered nation, Hosea brought a hope-filled message of grace and forgiveness.

Most books of the prophets focus on the audience and all the things they've done wrong. Hosea, in contrast, shines the spotlight on God. What is it like to be God? How must he feel when his chosen people reject him and go panting after false gods? As if words alone were too weak to convey his passion, God asked the brave prophet Hosea to act out a living parable. He married a loose woman named Gomer, who, true to form, soon ran away and committed adultery. Only by living out that drama could Hosea understand, and then express, something of how Israel's rebuke felt to God.

Poor Hosea lived a soap-opera existence. After Gomer had wandered off, fallen for another man, and then moved out, God instructed Hosea simply to invite her back and forgive her. The pattern hopelessly repeated itself. Gomer bore two children—but was Hosea really their father? According to the Mosaic Law, he should have turned his adulterous wife out on the street, or had her tried in court. What Hosea did, and God did, was unheard of.

Hosea is one of the most emotional books in the Bible, an outpouring of suffering love from God's heart. Read aloud, this chapter sounds like a fight between a husband and wife overheard through thin walls. The book of Hosea, in fact, represents the first time God's covenant with Israel was described in terms of marriage. It shows that God longs for his people with the tenderness and hunger that a lover feels toward his bride.

In the covenant, Israel had agreed to love and obey God no matter what, "till death do us part." But as they prospered in the new land, that flame of love died. The old covenant was fractured. As Hosea tells it, the death of their love broke God's heart. God could only promise another chance, with a new covenant at a future time when "you will call me 'my husband'; you will no longer call me 'my master'."

> **To Reflect On:** *Hosea describes various stages in Israel's relationship to God: during courtship and engagement, as newlyweds, when unfaithful, when separated. What stage are you in with God?*

HOSEA 2:4–3:5

⁴I will not show my love to her
    children,
    because they are the children of
      adultery.
⁵Their mother has been unfaithful
    and has conceived them in disgrace.
  She said, 'I will go after my lovers,
    who give me my food and my
      water,
my wool and my linen, my oil and
    my drink.'
⁶Therefore I will block her path with
    thornbushes;
  I will wall her in so that she cannot
    find her way.
⁷She will chase after her lovers but not
    catch them;
  she will look for them but not find
    them.
Then she will say,

'I will go back to my husband as at
first,
for then I was better off than now.'
⁸She has not acknowledged that I was
the one
who gave her the grain, the new
wine and oil,
who lavished on her the silver and
gold—
which they used for Baal.

⁹"Therefore I will take away my grain
when it ripens,
and my new wine when it is ready.
I will take back my wool and my linen,
intended to cover her nakedness.
¹⁰So now I will expose her lewdness
before the eyes of her lovers;
no one will take her out of my
hands.
¹¹I will stop all her celebrations:
her yearly festivals, her New Moons,
her Sabbath days—all her appointed
feasts.
¹²I will ruin her vines and her fig trees,
which she said were her pay from
her lovers;
I will make them a thicket,
and wild animals will devour them.
¹³I will punish her for the days
she burned incense to the Baals;
she decked herself with rings and
jewelry,
and went after her lovers,
but me she forgot,"
declares the LORD.

¹⁴"Therefore I am now going to allure
her;
I will lead her into the desert
and speak tenderly to her.
¹⁵There I will give her back her
vineyards,
and will make the Valley of Achor a
door of hope.
There she will sing as in the days of
her youth,
as in the day she came up out of
Egypt.

¹⁶"In that day," declares the LORD,
"you will call me 'my husband';
you will no longer call me 'my
master.'
¹⁷I will remove the names of the Baals
from her lips;

no longer will their names be
invoked.
¹⁸In that day I will make a covenant for
them
with the beasts of the field and the
birds of the air
and the creatures that move along
the ground.
Bow and sword and battle
I will abolish from the land,
so that all may lie down in safety.
¹⁹I will betroth you to me forever;
I will betroth you in righteousness
and justice,
in love and compassion.
²⁰I will betroth you in faithfulness,
and you will acknowledge the LORD.

²¹"In that day I will respond,"
declares the LORD—
"I will respond to the skies,
and they will respond to the earth;
²²and the earth will respond to the
grain,
the new wine and oil,
and they will respond to Jezreel.
²³I will plant her for myself in the land;
I will show my love to the one I
called 'Not my loved one.'
I will say to those called 'Not my
people,' 'You are my people';
and they will say, 'You are my
God.'"

Hosea's Reconciliation With His Wife

3 The LORD said to me, "Go, show your
love to your wife again, though she is
loved by another and is an adulteress. Love
her as the LORD loves the Israelites, though
they turn to other gods and love the sacred
raisin cakes."

²So I bought her for fifteen shekels of
silver and about a homer and a lethek of
barley. ³Then I told her, "You are to live
with me many days; you must not be a
prostitute or be intimate with any man, and
I will live with you."

⁴For the Israelites will live many days
without king or prince, without sacrifice or
sacred stones, without ephod or idol. ⁵Af-
terward the Israelites will return and seek
the LORD their God and David their king.
They will come trembling to the LORD and to
his blessings in the last days.

Wounded Lover

Hosea 11:1–11

Many people carry around the image of God as an impersonal Force, something akin to the law of gravity. Hosea portrays almost the opposite: a God of passion and fury and tears and love. A God in mourning over Israel's rejection of him.

God used Hosea's unhappy story to illustrate his own whipsaw emotions. That first blush of love when he found Israel, he said, was like finding grapes in the desert. But as Israel broke his trust again and again, he had to endure the awful shame of a wounded lover. God's words carry a tone surprisingly like self-pity: "I am like a moth to Ephraim, like rot to the people of Judah" (5:12).

The powerful image of a jilted lover explains why, in a chapter like Hosea 11, God's emotions seem to vacillate so. He is preparing to obliterate Israel—wait, now he is weeping, holding out open arms—no, he is sternly pronouncing judgment again. Those shifting moods seem hopelessly irrational, except to anyone who has been jilted by a lover.

Is there a more powerful human feeling than that of betrayal? Ask a high school girl whose boyfriend has just dumped her for a pretty cheerleader. Or tune your radio to a country-western station and listen to the lyrics of infidelity. Or check out the murders reported in the daily newspaper; an amazing proportion trace back to a fight with an estranged lover. Hosea, and God, demonstrate in living color exactly what it is like to love someone desperately, and get nothing in return. Not even God, with all his power, can force a human being to love him.

Virtually every chapter of Hosea talks about the "prostitution" or "adultery" of God's people. God the lover will not share his bride with anyone else. Yet, amazingly, even when she turns her back on him, he sticks with her. He is willing to suffer, in hope that someday she will change. Hosea proves that God longs not to punish, but to love.

> **To Reflect On:** *What is your strongest memory of feeling betrayed?*

HOSEA 11:1–11

God's Love for Israel

11 "When Israel was a child,
I loved him,
and out of Egypt I called my son.
²But the more I called Israel,
the further they went from me.
They sacrificed to the Baals
and they burned incense to images.
³It was I who taught Ephraim to walk,
taking them by the arms;
but they did not realize
it was I who healed them.
⁴I led them with cords of human
kindness,
with ties of love;
I lifted the yoke from their neck
and bent down to feed them.

⁵"Will they not return to Egypt
and will not Assyria rule over them
because they refuse to repent?
⁶Swords will flash in their cities,
will destroy the bars of their gates
and put an end to their plans.
⁷My people are determined to turn from
me.

Even if they call to the Most High,
he will by no means exalt them.

⁸"How can I give you up, Ephraim?
How can I hand you over, Israel?
How can I treat you like Admah?
How can I make you like Zeboiim?
My heart is changed within me;
all my compassion is aroused.
⁹I will not carry out my fierce anger,
nor will I turn and devastate
Ephraim.
For I am God, and not man—
the Holy One among you.
I will not come in wrath.
¹⁰They will follow the LORD;
he will roar like a lion.
When he roars,
his children will come trembling from
the west.
¹¹They will come trembling
like birds from Egypt,
like doves from Assyria.
I will settle them in their homes,"
declares the LORD.

National Postmortem

2 Kings 17:1–23; 35–41

An impressive lineup of prophets all tried their hand at convincing Israel to change its ways. But nothing, not the miracles of Elijah and Elisha nor the shouts of Amos nor the impassioned pleas of Hosea, had much effect. When times of trouble came, the nation turned toward the gods of their neighbors, and frantically signed up military allies; they never turned wholeheartedly to God.

The day of judgment so harrowingly foretold by the prophets is here recorded in the flat, matter-of-fact language of history. Second Kings 17 gives a postmortem on the Northern Kingdom of Israel, a kingdom that has disappeared from the map. The end came when Israel's kings, against all the prophets' advice, sought to purchase political protection, first from Assyria, and then from Egypt. Discovering the double cross, Assyria sent an invasion force against Israel.

In early wars Assyrian conquerors had exterminated their enemies, but in later years they adopted the new technique of deporting their victims and replacing them with foreigners from other conquered territories. The radical disruption of their societies tended to keep conquered peoples from regrouping and rising up as a new threat. In keeping with that policy, Assyria deported 27,290 captives from the land of Israel, dispersing the "ten lost tribes of Israel."

These emigrés the Assyrians replaced with foreigners who formed a new identity as "Samaritans," a group that existed in New Testament times and, in fact, can still be found in modern Israel. Samaritan settlers combined their native religions with some reverence for the true God.

After this chapter, the Bible's attention turns south toward Judah, the collective name for the two surviving tribes of Israelites. Why did the Assyrian tragedy happen? Second Kings diagnoses idolatry as the chief cause of Israel's moral collapse. Unfortunately, the practice had already gained a foothold in the Southern Kingdom as well.

To Reflect On: *Why do you think God viewed idolatry as such a serious crime?*

---

2 KINGS 17:1–23; 35–41

Hoshea Last King of Israel

17 In the twelfth year of Ahaz king of Judah, Hoshea son of Elah became king of Israel in Samaria, and he reigned nine years. ²He did evil in the eyes of the LORD, but not like the kings of Israel who preceded him.

³Shalmaneser king of Assyria came up to attack Hoshea, who had been Shalmaneser's vassal and had paid him tribute. ⁴But the king of Assyria discovered that Hoshea was a traitor, for he had sent envoys to So king of Egypt, and he no longer paid tribute to the king of Assyria, as he had done year by year. Therefore Shalmaneser seized him and put him in prison. ⁵The king of Assyria invaded the entire land, marched against Samaria and laid siege to it for three years. ⁶In the ninth year of Hoshea, the king of Assyria captured Samaria and deported the Israelites to Assyria. He settled them in Halah, in Gozan on the Habor River and in the towns of the Medes.

Israel Exiled Because of Sin

⁷All this took place because the Israelites had sinned against the LORD their God, who had brought them up out of Egypt from under the power of Pharaoh king of Egypt. They worshiped other gods ⁸and followed the practices of the nations the LORD had

driven out before them, as well as the practices that the kings of Israel had introduced. ⁹The Israelites secretly did things against the LORD their God that were not right. From watchtower to fortified city they built themselves high places in all their towns. ¹⁰They set up sacred stones and Asherah poles on every high hill and under every spreading tree. ¹¹At every high place they burned incense, as the nations whom the LORD had driven out before them had done. They did wicked things that provoked the LORD to anger. ¹²They worshiped idols, though the LORD had said, "You shall not do this." ¹³The LORD warned Israel and Judah through all his prophets and seers: "Turn from your evil ways. Observe my commands and decrees, in accordance with the entire Law that I commanded your fathers to obey and that I delivered to you through my servants the prophets."

¹⁴But they would not listen and were as stiff-necked as their fathers, who did not trust in the LORD their God. ¹⁵They rejected his decrees and the covenant he had made with their fathers and the warnings he had given them. They followed worthless idols and themselves became worthless. They imitated the nations around them although the LORD had ordered them, "Do not do as they do," and they did the things the LORD had forbidden them to do.

¹⁶They forsook all the commands of the LORD their God and made for themselves two idols cast in the shape of calves, and an Asherah pole. They bowed down to all the starry hosts, and they worshiped Baal. ¹⁷They sacrificed their sons and daughters in the fire. They practiced divination and sorcery and sold themselves to do evil in the eyes of the LORD, provoking him to anger. ¹⁸So the LORD was very angry with Israel and removed them from his presence. Only

the tribe of Judah was left, ¹⁹and even Judah did not keep the commands of the LORD their God. They followed the practices Israel had introduced. ²⁰Therefore the LORD rejected all the people of Israel; he afflicted them and gave them into the hands of plunderers, until he thrust them from his presence.

²¹When he tore Israel away from the house of David, they made Jeroboam son of Nebat their king. Jeroboam enticed Israel away from following the LORD and caused them to commit a great sin. ²²The Israelites persisted in all the sins of Jeroboam and did not turn away from them ²³until the LORD removed them from his presence, as he had warned through all his servants the prophets. So the people of Israel were taken from their homeland into exile in Assyria, and they are still there.

³⁵When the LORD made a covenant with the Israelites, he commanded them: "Do not worship any other gods or bow down to them, serve them or sacrifice to them. ³⁶But the LORD, who brought you up out of Egypt with mighty power and outstretched arm, is the one you must worship. To him you shall bow down and to him offer sacrifices. ³⁷You must always be careful to keep the decrees and ordinances, the laws and commands he wrote for you. Do not worship other gods. ³⁸Do not forget the covenant I have made with you, and do not worship other gods. ³⁹Rather, worship the LORD your God; it is he who will deliver you from the hand of all your enemies."

⁴⁰They would not listen, however, but persisted in their former practices. ⁴¹Even while these people were worshiping the LORD, they were serving their idols. To this day their children and grandchildren continue to do as their fathers did.

Meanwhile in Jerusalem

2 Chronicles 20:1–30

So far our readings have sampled the 200-year history of Israel, which began sliding away from God from the very first days of its birth as a nation. But the Bible devotes far more space to the kings and prophets of the Southern Kingdom. Judah proved more faithful in living up to the covenant with God, and chiefly for that reason it outlasted Israel by nearly a century and a half.

With a corrupt government in place, presiding over a population barely one-fifth the size of Israel's, Judah at the time of partition faced formidable obstacles. But the Southern Kingdom held certain advantages as well. Its rulers, all descendants of David, were mostly immune from the assassination plots and political intrigues that plagued the North. The temple in Jerusalem provided a strong unifying force. And, of the nineteen men and one woman who ruled Judah, at least a handful demonstrated a quality of spiritual leadership unmatched in the Northern Kingdom.

This chapter, for example, tells of the extraordinary king named Jehoshaphat, one of Judah's early rulers. No ruler of Judah had a wholly peaceful reign, and as a result much of the action in 2 Chronicles takes place, like this story, on a battlefield. Here is the book's philosophy of war in a nutshell: *If you trust in your own military might or that of powerful neighbors, you will lose. Instead, humble yourself and rely totally on God—regardless of the odds against you.*

As the kings of Judah demonstrated with monotonous regularity, it took uncommon courage to rely on God alone at a moment of great peril. Even the best of them dipped into the royal treasury to purchase help from neighboring allies. But King Jehoshaphat provides a textbook example of the proper response. When invading armies threatened, he called the entire nation together in a giant prayer meeting. On the day of battle, he sent a choir in front of his army to sing praises to God.

Jehoshaphat's tactics may seem more suitable for a summer camp meeting than a battlefield, but they worked. The enemy forces all turned against each other, and Judah's army marched home victorious.

This bright moment of national faith shines out from a very mottled historical record. By his public prayer and personal example, King Jehoshaphat showed what could happen when a leader placed complete trust in God.

To Reflect On: *Have any modern leaders demonstrated inspiring faith?*

---

2 CHRONICLES 20:1–30

Jehoshaphat Defeats Moab and Ammon

20 After this, the Moabites and Ammonites with some of the Meunites came to make war on Jehoshaphat.

²Some men came and told Jehoshaphat, "A vast army is coming against you from Edom, from the other side of the Sea. It is already in Hazazon Tamar" (that is, En Gedi). ³Alarmed, Jehoshaphat resolved to inquire of the LORD, and he proclaimed a fast for all Judah. ⁴The people of Judah came together to seek help from the LORD; indeed, they came from every town in Judah to seek him.

⁵Then Jehoshaphat stood up in the assembly of Judah and Jerusalem at the temple of the LORD in the front of the new courtyard ⁶and said:

"O LORD, God of our fathers, are you not the God who is in heaven? You rule over all the kingdoms of the nations. Power and might are in your hand, and no one can withstand you. 7O our God, did you not drive out the inhabitants of this land before your people Israel and give it forever to the descendants of Abraham your friend? 8They have lived in it and have built in it a sanctuary for your Name, saying, 9'If calamity comes upon us, whether the sword of judgment, or plague or famine, we will stand in your presence before this temple that bears your Name and will cry out to you in our distress, and you will hear us and save us.'

10"But now here are men from Ammon, Moab and Mount Seir, whose territory you would not allow Israel to invade when they came from Egypt; so they turned away from them and did not destroy them. 11See how they are repaying us by coming to drive us out of the possession you gave us as an inheritance. 12O our God, will you not judge them? For we have no power to face this vast army that is attacking us. We do not know what to do, but our eyes are upon you."

13All the men of Judah, with their wives and children and little ones, stood there before the LORD. 14Then the Spirit of the LORD came upon Jahaziel son of Zechariah, the son of Benaiah, the son of Jeiel, the son of Mattaniah, a Levite and descendant of Asaph, as he stood in the assembly.

15He said: "Listen, King Jehoshaphat and all who live in Judah and Jerusalem! This is what the LORD says to you: 'Do not be afraid or discouraged because of this vast army. For the battle is not yours, but God's. 16Tomorrow march down against them. They will be climbing up by the Pass of Ziz, and you will find them at the end of the gorge in the Desert of Jeruel. 17You will not have to fight this battle. Take up your positions; stand firm and see the deliverance the LORD will give you, O Judah and Jerusalem. Do not be afraid; do not be discouraged. Go out to face them tomorrow, and the LORD will be with you.'"

18Jehoshaphat bowed with his face to the ground, and all the people of Judah and Jerusalem fell down in worship before the LORD. 19Then some Levites from the Kohathites and Korahites stood up and praised the LORD, the God of Israel, with very loud voice.

20Early in the morning they left for the Desert of Tekoa. As they set out, Jehoshaphat stood and said, "Listen to me, Judah and people of Jerusalem! Have faith in the LORD your God and you will be upheld; have faith in his prophets and you will be successful." 21After consulting the people, Jehoshaphat appointed men to sing to the LORD and to praise him for the splendor of his holiness as they went out at the head of the army, saying:

"Give thanks to the LORD,
    for his love endures forever."

22As they began to sing and praise, the LORD set ambushes against the men of Ammon and Moab and Mount Seir who were invading Judah, and they were defeated. 23The men of Ammon and Moab rose up against the men from Mount Seir to destroy and annihilate them. After they finished slaughtering the men from Seir, they helped to destroy one another.

24When the men of Judah came to the place that overlooks the desert and looked toward the vast army, they saw only dead bodies lying on the ground; no one had escaped. 25So Jehoshaphat and his men went to carry off their plunder, and they found among them a great amount of equipment and clothing and also articles of value—more than they could take away. There was so much plunder that it took three days to collect it. 26On the fourth day they assembled in the Valley of Beracah, where they praised the LORD. This is why it is called the Valley of Beracah to this day.

27Then, led by Jehoshaphat, all the men of Judah and Jerusalem returned joyfully to Jerusalem, for the LORD had given them cause to rejoice over their enemies. 28They entered Jerusalem and went to the temple of the LORD with harps and lutes and trumpets.

29The fear of God came upon all the kingdoms of the countries when they heard how the LORD had fought against the enemies of Israel. 30And the kingdom of Jehoshaphat was at peace, for his God had given him rest on every side.

Rumors of Destruction

Micah 6

Not every king of Judah had Jehoshaphat's faith and courage. As the years ground on, the same decadence that had characterized the Northern Kingdom of Israel spread like an epidemic through Judah. Other parts of the Bible detail Judah's faults: one notorious king, Ahaz, set up foreign altars, offered his own children in human sacrifice, and shuttered the Lord's temple. Along with the religious corruption came every other kind of sin: dishonesty, greed, bribery, injustice.

Around the same time Amos was blasting Israel in the North, another country preacher, Micah, was called by God to deliver similar words of warning to Judah. Micah got emotionally caught up in his message:

> Because of this I will weep and wail;
> > I will go about barefoot and naked.
> I will howl like a jackal
> > and moan like an owl.
> For her wound is incurable;
> > It has come to Judah.
> It has reached the very gate of my people,
> > even to Jerusalem itself (1:8–9).

Micah lived in tumultuous times. Once, Judah lost 120,000 soldiers in a single day (2 Chronicles 28:6). The nation watched in fear as Assyria, the chief power of the day, brutally smashed the Northern Kingdom. What would keep Judah from a similar fate? That very prospect of judgment was what made Micah howl like a jackal and moan like an owl.

This chapter opens with an impassioned plea from God. "My people, what have I done to you?" God asks. He reviews the history of his chosen people, reminding them of his great works on their behalf. In his rhetorical response, Micah makes clear that God desires true, heartfelt changes, not just a veneer of religion: "And what does the LORD require of you? To act justly and to love mercy and to walk humbly with your God."

Micah concludes darkly that his people, afflicted with the same sickness as their relatives to the North, would meet the same end. Even so, Micah saw light ahead. Amid graphic predictions of destruction, Micah gives clear predictions of the Messiah, the future leader from the tiny town of Bethlehem who would offer new hope to the earth (5:2).

To Reflect On: *Imagine God personally addressing your church, spelling out exactly what changes he wants. What would he say?*

MICAH 6

The LORD's Case Against Israel

6 Listen to what the LORD says:

"Stand up, plead your case before the
    mountains;
  let the hills hear what you have to
    say.
2 Hear, O mountains, the LORD's
    accusation;
  listen, you everlasting foundations of
    the earth.
For the LORD has a case against his
    people;
  he is lodging a charge against Israel.

3 "My people, what have I done to you?
  How have I burdened you? Answer
    me.
4 I brought you up out of Egypt
  and redeemed you from the land of
    slavery.
I sent Moses to lead you,
  also Aaron and Miriam.
5 My people, remember
  what Balak king of Moab counseled
  and what Balaam son of Beor
    answered.
Remember [your journey] from Shittim
    to Gilgal,
  that you may know the righteous
    acts of the LORD."

6 With what shall I come before the LORD
  and bow down before the exalted
    God?
Shall I come before him with burnt
    offerings,
  with calves a year old?
7 Will the LORD be pleased with thousands
    of rams,
  with ten thousand rivers of oil?
Shall I offer my firstborn for my
    transgression,
  the fruit of my body for the sin of
    my soul?

8 He has showed you, O man, what is
    good.
  And what does the LORD require of
    you?
To act justly and to love mercy
  and to walk humbly with your God.

Israel's Guilt and Punishment

9 Listen! The LORD is calling to the city—
  and to fear your name is wisdom—
  "Heed the rod and the One who
    appointed it.
10 Am I still to forget, O wicked house,
  your ill-gotten treasures
  and the short ephah, which is
    accursed?
11 Shall I acquit a man with dishonest
    scales,
  with a bag of false weights?
12 Her rich men are violent;
  her people are liars
  and their tongues speak deceitfully.
13 Therefore, I have begun to destroy
    you,
  to ruin you because of your sins.
14 You will eat but not be satisfied;
  your stomach will still be empty.
You will store up but save nothing,
  because what you save I will give to
    the sword.
15 You will plant but not harvest;
  you will press olives but not use the
    oil on yourselves,
  you will crush grapes but not drink
    the wine.
16 You have observed the statutes of
    Omri
  and all the practices of Ahab's
    house,
  and you have followed their
    traditions.
Therefore I will give you over to ruin
  and your people to derision;
  you will bear the scorn of the
    nations."

Happy Days Are Here Again

2 Chronicles 30

Toward the end of Micah's career, just as the situation in Judah was deteriorating, another great king took the throne. In fact, 2 Chronicles spends more time on Hezekiah than on anyone else. The very first year of his reign he led a program to restore the temple, which had fallen into disrepair from lack of use. Hezekiah turned the tables on Judah's priests: He stood in the temple square and delivered a rousing sermon to *them*.

When Hezekiah decided to sponsor a huge religious festival, the idea at first met with scorn and ridicule. But a king's proclamation carries certain weight, and the nation finally did come together in a remarkable scene of happiness and unity. Hezekiah even sent "missionary" couriers to the devastated land to the North, and some survivors of the Assyrian scourge made their way to Jerusalem.

This chapter closely resembles 1 Kings 8 and its story of Solomon's dedication of the temple. Hezekiah was intent on renewing the covenant with God in hopes of forestalling God's judgment. The details of the festival celebration show just how badly Judah had neglected the covenant: There was a shortage of priests, and Hezekiah had to bend the rules or not enough worshipers would have been properly purified.

It was no accident that Hezekiah organized his festival around the Passover. That day marked the birth of a nation, when God freed his people from slavery in Egypt. In a real sense, the Passover had sealed the covenant, and Hezekiah determined to remind the nation of its heritage.

Despite the initial skepticism, the people of Judah got caught up in the celebration and, as in Solomon's day, spontaneously decided to stay another seven days. "There was great joy in Jerusalem," the Bible reports, "for since the days of Solomon son of David king of Israel there had been nothing like this in Jerusalem."

> **To Reflect On:** *When you hear about a religious renewal or "revival," do you tend to be (a) skeptical, (b) cautious, (c) open-minded, (d) enthusiastic?*

---

2 CHRONICLES 30

Hezekiah Celebrates the Passover

30 Hezekiah sent word to all Israel and Judah and also wrote letters to Ephraim and Manasseh, inviting them to come to the temple of the LORD in Jerusalem and celebrate the Passover to the LORD, the God of Israel. ² The king and his officials and the whole assembly in Jerusalem decided to celebrate the Passover in the second month. ³ They had not been able to celebrate it at the regular time because not enough priests had consecrated themselves and the people had not assembled in Jerusalem. ⁴ The plan seemed right both to the king and to the whole assembly. ⁵ They decided to send a proclamation throughout Israel, from Beer-sheba to Dan, calling the people to come to Jerusalem and celebrate the Passover to the LORD, the God of Israel. It had not been celebrated in large numbers according to what was written.

⁶ At the king's command, couriers went throughout Israel and Judah with letters from the king and from his officials, which read:

"People of Israel, return to the LORD, the God of Abraham, Isaac and Israel, that he may return to you who are left, who have escaped from the hand of the kings of Assyria. ⁷ Do not be like your fathers and brothers, who were unfaithful to the LORD, the God of their fathers, so that he made them an object of horror, as you see. ⁸Do not be stiff-necked, as your fathers were; submit to the LORD. Come to the sanctuary, which he has consecrated forever. Serve the LORD your God, so that his fierce anger will turn away from you. ⁹If you return to the LORD, then your brothers and your children will be shown compassion by their captors and will come back to this land, for the LORD your God is gracious and compassionate. He will not turn his face from you if you return to him."

¹⁰The couriers went from town to town in Ephraim and Manasseh, as far as Zebulun, but the people scorned and ridiculed them. ¹¹Nevertheless, some men of Asher, Manasseh and Zebulun humbled themselves and went to Jerusalem. ¹²Also in Judah the hand of God was on the people to give them unity of mind to carry out what the king and his officials had ordered, following the word of the LORD.

¹³A very large crowd of people assembled in Jerusalem to celebrate the Feast of Unleavened Bread in the second month. ¹⁴They removed the altars in Jerusalem and cleared away the incense altars and threw them into the Kidron Valley.

¹⁵They slaughtered the Passover lamb on the fourteenth day of the second month. The priests and the Levites were ashamed and consecrated themselves and brought burnt offerings to the temple of the LORD. ¹⁶Then they took up their regular positions as prescribed in the Law of Moses the man of God. The priests sprinkled the blood handed to them by the Levites. ¹⁷Since many in the crowd had not consecrated themselves, the Levites had to kill the Passover lambs for all those who were not ceremonially clean and could not consecrate [their lambs] to the LORD. ¹⁸Although most

of the many people who came from Ephraim, Manasseh, Issachar and Zebulun had not purified themselves, yet they ate the Passover, contrary to what was written. But Hezekiah prayed for them, saying, "May the LORD, who is good, pardon everyone ¹⁹who sets his heart on seeking God—the LORD, the God of his fathers—even if he is not clean according to the rules of the sanctuary." ²⁰And the LORD heard Hezekiah and healed the people.

²¹The Israelites who were present in Jerusalem celebrated the Feast of Unleavened Bread for seven days with great rejoicing, while the Levites and priests sang to the LORD every day, accompanied by the LORD's instruments of praise.

²²Hezekiah spoke encouragingly to all the Levites, who showed good understanding of the service of the LORD. For the seven days they ate their assigned portion and offered fellowship offerings and praised the LORD, the God of their fathers.

²³The whole assembly then agreed to celebrate the festival seven more days; so for another seven days they celebrated joyfully. ²⁴Hezekiah king of Judah provided a thousand bulls and seven thousand sheep and goats for the assembly, and the officials provided them with a thousand bulls and ten thousand sheep and goats. A great number of priests consecrated themselves. ²⁵The entire assembly of Judah rejoiced, along with the priests and Levites and all who had assembled from Israel, including the aliens who had come from Israel and those who lived in Judah. ²⁶There was great joy in Jerusalem, for since the days of Solomon son of David king of Israel there had been nothing like this in Jerusalem. ²⁷The priests and the Levites stood to bless the people, and God heard them, for their prayer reached heaven, his holy dwelling place.

Power behind the Throne

Isaiah 6

This chapter flashes back to a scene that took place two decades before Hezekiah became king. The prophet Isaiah, a giant of Jewish history, received a direct, dramatic call from God.

When Isaiah began his work, Judah seemed strong and wealthy. But Isaiah saw signs of grave danger—the very same signs that had alarmed his contemporary, the prophet Micah. Men went around drunk; women cared more about their clothes than about their neighbors' hunger. People gave lip service to God and kept up the outward appearance of religion, but little more.

External dangers loomed even larger: on all sides; monster empires were burgeoning. The nation of Judah, said Isaiah, stood at a crossroads. It could either regain its footing or begin a perilous slide downward.

Two kings, Jotham and Ahaz, paid Isaiah little heed. Ahaz sold off temple treasures to buy protection from Assyria; and it was he who erected foreign idols in Jerusalem and sacrificed his own sons as part of a pagan ritual. Isaiah breathed fire during those dark days, and the collection of his early sermons still gives off heat. But, in a remarkable turnaround, the new king Hezekiah made Isaiah one of his most trusted advisers. In any moment of crisis, he called upon the prophet.

Not every prophet blasted the establishment from street corners. Isaiah spent his days in the corridors of power, offering political advice and helping set the course of his nation. (Second Chronicles 26:22 even credits him with writing an official royal history.) Although he sometimes stood alone against a crowd of contrary advisers, he never tempered his message. Isaiah outlasted four kings, but he finally offended one beyond repair. Tradition records that the last, King Manasseh, had Isaiah killed by fastening him between two planks of wood and sawing his body in half.

It seems likely that much of Hezekiah's zeal for reform traces back to the influence of the prophet Isaiah. The divine call recorded in this chapter shows where Isaiah got the courage and commitment that made him such an important force in Judah's history.

To Reflect On: *When have you "volunteered" for a difficult task for God?*

ISAIAH 6

6 In the year that King Uzziah died, I saw the Lord seated on a throne, high and exalted, and the train of his robe filled the temple. ²Above him were seraphs, each with six wings: With two wings they covered their faces, with two they covered their feet, and with two they were flying. ³And they were calling to one another:

"Holy, holy, holy is the LORD Almighty;
the whole earth is full of his glory."

⁴At the sound of their voices the door-posts and thresholds shook and the temple was filled with smoke.

⁵"Woe to me!" I cried. "I am ruined! For I am a man of unclean lips, and I live among a people of unclean lips, and my eyes have seen the King, the LORD Almighty."

⁶Then one of the seraphs flew to me with a live coal in his hand, which he had taken with tongs from the altar. ⁷With it he touched my mouth and said, "See, this has touched your lips; your guilt is taken away and your sin atoned for."

⁸Then I heard the voice of the Lord saying, "Whom shall I send? And who will go for us?" And I said, "Here am I. Send me!"

⁹He said, "Go and tell this people:

" 'Be ever hearing, but never
understanding;
be ever seeing, but never perceiving.'
¹⁰Make the heart of this people
calloused;
make their ears dull
and close their eyes.
Otherwise they might see with their
eyes,
hear with their ears,
understand with their hearts,
and turn and be healed."
¹¹Then I said, "For how long, O Lord?"
And he answered:

"Until the cities lie ruined
and without inhabitant,
until the houses are left deserted
and the fields ruined and ravaged,
¹²until the LORD has sent everyone far
away
and the land is utterly forsaken.
¹³And though a tenth remains in the
land,
it will again be laid waste.
But as the terebinth and oak
leave stumps when they are cut
down,
so the holy seed will be the stump
in the land."

Eloquent Hope

Isaiah 25:1–26:6

In addition to his role as adviser to kings, Isaiah was a writer of enormous talent, the Milton or Shakespeare of Hebrew literature. No other biblical author can match his rich vocabulary and use of imagery, and the New Testament quotes him more than all the other prophets combined. Many of his majestic phrases have become a familiar part of the English vocabulary.

Using his great ability, Isaiah tried to awaken Judah from its spiritual slump. Like most of the prophets, he preached a two-part message of (1) **Judgment** to come unless people radically change their ways; and (2) **Hope** in a future when God will restore not only the Israelites, but the whole world.

During the period when Judah was fat, self-indulgent, and reveling in luxury, Isaiah warned of a reckoning day. But later, when Jerusalem was surrounded by foreign troops, Isaiah offered stirring words of hope. World-class tyrants didn't intimidate Isaiah; he knew that God could toss them aside like twigs.

Isaiah summons up latent human longings for a better world. He had no doubt that God will one day transform this pockmarked planet into a new earth that has no tears, no pain, no death. In the future world as pictured by Isaiah, wild animals will lie beside each other in peace. Weapons will be melted into farm tools.

At a given point in history, God may appear powerless, or blithely unconcerned about the violence and evil that plague this planet. The people of Jerusalem certainly questioned his concern in the face of the Assyrian invasion. Isaiah gave them a local message of hope: entrust your future to God alone. And he expanded that message to encompass the entire world.

Isaiah 24–27 gives a preview of the end of all history. First will come a difficult time, when God purifies the stained earth. Like a woman in childbirth, the earth will undergo pain and struggle. But what follows next will be a future life so wonderful we can barely imagine it. In chapters like this one, Isaiah helps us imagine it.

> **To Reflect On:** *What gives you hope about the future?*

ISAIAH 25:1–26:6

Praise to the LORD

25 O LORD, you are my God;
I will exalt you and praise your
name,
for in perfect faithfulness
you have done marvelous things,
things planned long ago.
2 You have made the city a heap of
rubble,
the fortified town a ruin,
the foreigners' stronghold a city no
more;
it will never be rebuilt.
3 Therefore strong peoples will honor
you;
cities of ruthless nations will revere
you.
4 You have been a refuge for the poor,
a refuge for the needy in his distress,
a shelter from the storm
and a shade from the heat.
For the breath of the ruthless
is like a storm driving against a wall
5 and like the heat of the desert.
You silence the uproar of foreigners;
as heat is reduced by the shadow of
a cloud,
so the song of the ruthless is stilled.

6 On this mountain the LORD Almighty
will prepare
a feast of rich food for all peoples,
a banquet of aged wine—
the best of meats and the finest of
wines.
7 On this mountain he will destroy
the shroud that enfolds all peoples,
the sheet that covers all nations;
8 he will swallow up death forever.
The Sovereign LORD will wipe away the
tears
from all faces;
he will remove the disgrace of his
people
from all the earth.
                    The LORD has spoken.

9 In that day they will say,

"Surely this is our God;
we trusted in him, and he saved us.
This is the LORD, we trusted in him;
let us rejoice and be glad in his
salvation."

10 The hand of the LORD will rest on this
mountain;
but Moab will be trampled under
him
as straw is trampled down in the
manure.
11 They will spread out their hands in it,
as a swimmer spreads out his hands
to swim.
God will bring down their pride
despite the cleverness of their hands.
12 He will bring down your high fortified
walls
and lay them low;
he will bring them down to the
ground,
to the very dust.

A Song of Praise

26 In that day this song will be sung in
the land of Judah:

We have a strong city;
God makes salvation
its walls and ramparts.
2 Open the gates
that the righteous nation may enter,
the nation that keeps faith.
3 You will keep in perfect peace
him whose mind is steadfast,
because he trusts in you.
4 Trust in the LORD forever,
for the LORD, the LORD, is the Rock
eternal.
5 He humbles those who dwell on high,
he lays the lofty city low;
he levels it to the ground
and casts it down to the dust.
6 Feet trample it down—
the feet of the oppressed,
the footsteps of the poor.

City under Siege

2 Chronicles 32:1–31

It was the greatest crisis that Hezekiah and Isaiah ever faced. The very survival of Judah was in peril, and what happened next had such significance that the Bible gives three different accounts: in this chapter, in 2 Kings 18–19, and in Isaiah 36–37.

Assyria, ever thirsty for more conquests, had just rolled into Judah, leveling forty-six walled cities and taking 200,150 captives. The Assyrian king demanded huge sums of money from Hezekiah, whom he mockingly described as "a bird in a cage." Hezekiah might as well have been in a cage, for siege armies completely surrounded his city. (In anticipation of the siege, Hezekiah had fortified Jerusalem's walls and secured water supplies by digging a long tunnel to channel water from a spring to an underground reservoir. A tremendous engineering feat in its day, the tunnel was rediscovered in the late 1800s and is now a tourist spot in Jerusalem.)

Cowering behind his city's walls, Hezekiah once more turned to Isaiah for advice. Should he surrender? Negotiate? Outside, the Assyrians were directing a barrage of propaganda at Jerusalem's demoralized citizens. They scoffed at Israelite hopes for a miracle from God. No gods had helped any other nation withstand the Assyrian juggernaut.

Isaiah, however, refused to panic. Against all odds, he calmly advised prayer and reliance on the power of God. *Have faith,* he said. *Don't surrender, and don't fear. Assyria will return home, wounded.*

Jerusalem looked like a doomed city during the siege by Assyria. But two things happened to fulfill Isaiah's prophecy. First, a great plague struck the Assyrians (Isaiah 37), a plague also recorded by the historian Herodotus. Later, the murder of Assyria's leader brought internal chaos to that country and canceled out the Assyrian threat.

The miraculous deliverance saved Judah, but only temporarily. In his latter days, Hezekiah foolishly flaunted his country's wealth before envoys from Babylon, a rising power in the East. The citizens of Judah grew proud as well; they became convinced that Jerusalem, God's city, was indestructible—a belief that would be proven tragically false.

> **To Reflect On:** *Two verses from this chapter (v. 7 and v. 31) show that God may sometimes seem close, and sometimes distant. What makes the difference?*

---

2 CHRONICLES 32:1–31

Sennacherib Threatens Jerusalem

32 After all that Hezekiah had so faithfully done, Sennacherib king of Assyria came and invaded Judah. He laid siege to the fortified cities, thinking to conquer them for himself. ²When Hezekiah saw that Sennacherib had come and that he intended to make war on Jerusalem, ³he consulted with his officials and military staff about blocking off the water from the springs outside the city, and they helped him. ⁴A large force of men assembled, and they blocked all the springs and the stream that flowed through the land. "Why should the kings of Assyria come and find plenty of water?" they said. ⁵Then he worked hard repairing all the broken sections of the wall and building towers on it. He built another wall outside that one and reinforced the supporting terraces of the City of David. He also made large numbers of weapons and shields.

⁶He appointed military officers over the people and assembled them before him in the square at the city gate and encouraged them with these words: ⁷"Be strong and courageous. Do not be afraid or discouraged because of the king of Assyria and the vast army with him, for there is a greater power with us than with him. ⁸With him is only the arm of flesh, but with us is the LORD our God to help us and to fight our battles." And the people gained confidence from what Hezekiah the king of Judah said.

⁹Later, when Sennacherib king of Assyria and all his forces were laying siege to Lachish, he sent his officers to Jerusalem with this message for Hezekiah king of Judah and for all the people of Judah who were there:

¹⁰"This is what Sennacherib king of Assyria says: On what are you basing your confidence, that you remain in Jerusalem under siege? ¹¹When Hezekiah says, 'The LORD our God will save us from the hand of the king of Assyria,' he is misleading you, to let you die of hunger and thirst. ¹²Did not Hezekiah himself remove this god's high places and altars, saying to Judah and Jerusalem, 'You must worship before one altar and burn sacrifices on it'?

¹³"Do you not know what I and my fathers have done to all the peoples of the other lands? Were the gods of those nations ever able to deliver their land from my hand? ¹⁴Who of all the gods of these nations that my fathers destroyed has been able to save his people from me? How then can your god deliver you from my hand? ¹⁵Now do not let Hezekiah deceive you and mislead you like this. Do not believe him, for no god of any nation or kingdom has been able to deliver his people from my hand or the hand of my fathers. How much less will your god deliver you from my hand!"

¹⁶Sennacherib's officers spoke further against the LORD God and against his servant Hezekiah. ¹⁷The king also wrote letters insulting the LORD, the God of Israel, and saying this against him: "Just as the gods of the peoples of the other lands did not rescue their people from my hand, so the god of Hezekiah will not rescue his people from my hand." ¹⁸Then they called out in

Hebrew to the people of Jerusalem who were on the wall, to terrify them and make them afraid in order to capture the city. ¹⁹They spoke about the God of Jerusalem as they did about the gods of the other peoples of the world—the work of men's hands.

²⁰King Hezekiah and the prophet Isaiah son of Amoz cried out in prayer to heaven about this. ²¹And the LORD sent an angel, who annihilated all the fighting men and the leaders and officers in the camp of the Assyrian king. So he withdrew to his own land in disgrace. And when he went into the temple of his god, some of his sons cut him down with the sword.

²²So the LORD saved Hezekiah and the people of Jerusalem from the hand of Sennacherib king of Assyria and from the hand of all others. He took care of them on every side. ²³Many brought offerings to Jerusalem for the LORD and valuable gifts for Hezekiah king of Judah. From then on he was highly regarded by all the nations.

Hezekiah's Pride, Success and Death

²⁴In those days Hezekiah became ill and was at the point of death. He prayed to the LORD, who answered him and gave him a miraculous sign. ²⁵But Hezekiah's heart was proud and he did not respond to the kindness shown him; therefore the LORD's wrath was on him and on Judah and Jerusalem. ²⁶Then Hezekiah repented of the pride of his heart, as did the people of Jerusalem; therefore the LORD's wrath did not come upon them during the days of Hezekiah.

²⁷Hezekiah had very great riches and honor, and he made treasuries for his silver and gold and for his precious stones, spices, shields and all kinds of valuables. ²⁸He also made buildings to store the harvest of grain, new wine and oil; and he made stalls for various kinds of cattle, and pens for the flocks. ²⁹He built villages and acquired great numbers of flocks and herds, for God had given him very great riches.

³⁰It was Hezekiah who blocked the upper outlet of the Gihon spring and channeled the water down to the west side of the City of David. He succeeded in everything he undertook. ³¹But when envoys were sent by the rulers of Babylon to ask him about the miraculous sign that had occurred in the land, God left him to test him and to know everything that was in his heart.

Enemy Justice

Nahum 1

Nahum had one distinct advantage over most biblical prophets: he was addressing an enemy. Prophets like Micah and Isaiah sometimes collapsed in grief as they thought about the judgments that would befall their own people. But Nahum lowered the boom on Assyria, a nation that had just obliterated the Northern Kingdom of Israel and, except for God's miraculous intervention in ,Hezekiah's day, would have done the same to Nahum's homeland of Judah.

Assyria was an easy enemy to hate—something along the line of Hitler's Germany. Its soldiers decimated cities, led captives away with hooks in their noses, and plowed salt into fertile ground. In fact, Assyria's very obnoxiousness lay at the heart of what Nahum had to say.

A question nagged at the citizens of Judah, who had experienced the full force of Assyria's "endless cruelty." Assyria had trampled a huge, crescent-shaped path of destruction across the Middle East, from the region of modern-day Turkey down the Persian Gulf all the way to Egypt. Judah, in contrast, was a tiny vassal state barely clinging to existence. Why would God hold Judah accountable but allow Assyria to go unpunished?

Nahum brashly predicted that even mighty Assyria would meet its end. Its people had repented once, in Jonah's day, but had reverted to old patterns that would bring on God's judgment. Undoubtedly, the people of Judah applauded Nahum's prophecies—but who could believe them? Assyria, the most powerful empire in the world for two hundred years, would not simply disappear.

Nahum delivered these prophecies sometime around 700 B.C., not long after the siege of Jerusalem. In 612 B.C., Nineveh, the last Assyrian stronghold, fell to the Babylonians and Persians. Over time a carpet of grass covered the pile of rubble marking what had been the greatest city of its time. Years later, both Alexander the Great and Napoleon would camp nearby, with no clue that a city had ever been there.

Like all the biblical prophets, Nahum saw beyond the intimidating forces of history. He knew that behind the rise and fall of empires an even greater force was at work, determining the ultimate outcome. Though God's justice may seem slow, nothing can finally escape it. As Nahum put it, "The LORD is good, a refuge in times of trouble. He cares for those who trust in him, but . . . he will pursue his foes into darkness."

> **To Reflect On:** *What modern-day injustices seem to be going unpunished?*

NAHUM 1

1 An oracle concerning Nineveh. The book of the vision of Nahum the Elkoshite.

The LORD's Anger Against Nineveh

²The LORD is a jealous and avenging
God;
the LORD takes vengeance and is
filled with wrath.
The LORD takes vengeance on his foes
and maintains his wrath against his
enemies.
³The LORD is slow to anger and great in
power;
the LORD will not leave the guilty
unpunished.
His way is in the whirlwind and the
storm,
and clouds are the dust of his feet.
⁴He rebukes the sea and dries it up;
he makes all the rivers run dry.
Bashan and Carmel wither
and the blossoms of Lebanon fade.
⁵The mountains quake before him
and the hills melt away.
The earth trembles at his presence,
the world and all who live in it.
⁶Who can withstand his indignation?
Who can endure his fierce anger?
His wrath is poured out like fire;
the rocks are shattered before him.

⁷The LORD is good,
a refuge in times of trouble.
He cares for those who trust in him,
⁸ but with an overwhelming flood
he will make an end of [Nineveh];
he will pursue his foes into
darkness.

⁹Whatever they plot against the LORD
he will bring to an end;
trouble will not come a second time.
¹⁰They will be entangled among thorns
and drunk from their wine;
they will be consumed like dry
stubble.
¹¹From you, [O Nineveh,] has one come
forth
who plots evil against the LORD
and counsels wickedness.

¹²This is what the LORD says:

"Although they have allies and are
numerous,
they will be cut off and pass away.
Although I have afflicted you, [O
Judah,]
I will afflict you no more.
¹³Now I will break their yoke from your
neck
and tear your shackles away."

¹⁴The LORD has given a command
concerning you, [Nineveh]:
"You will have no descendants to
bear your name.
I will destroy the carved images and
cast idols
that are in the temple of your gods.
I will prepare your grave,
for you are vile."

¹⁵Look, there on the mountains,
the feet of one who brings good
news,
who proclaims peace!
Celebrate your festivals, O Judah,
and fulfill your vows.
No more will the wicked invade you;
they will be completely destroyed.

Rotten Ruling Class
Zephaniah 3

Through the influence of prophets like Micah and Isaiah, King Hezekiah helped set the land of Judah back on course. But if a good king like Hezekiah was rare, having two good kings in a row was virtually unheard of. Hezekiah's death vacated the throne for Manasseh, who proved to be one of Judah's all-time worst kings. In his fifty-year reign—the longest of any king of Israel or Judah—Manasseh reversed all the good that Hezekiah had accomplished.

An unabashed tyrant, Manasseh filled the streets of Jerusalem with blood. (It was he who, according to tradition, had Isaiah sawn in two.) He made child sacrifice common practice, built astrology altars in God's temple, and encouraged male prostitution as part of religious ritual. By the time he died, very few reminders of the covenant with God remained in Judah. Public shrines abounded, and storefronts in Jerusalem were advertising household gods, mediums, and spiritists. God's chosen people had out-paganized the pagans.

The next king, Amon, started out in his father's footsteps, but this time his own officials rose up in revolt and assassinated him after two years. The nation of Judah, cut loose from its moorings, was drifting toward total anarchy. And Josiah, the pint-size prince crowned by Amon's supporters, hardly represented much reason for optimism.

In the early days of Josiah's reign, the prophet Zephaniah spoke out against the decadence spreading throughout Judah. Other prophets had come from peasant stock; Zephaniah proudly traced his ancestry back to King Hezekiah. Yet, unlike others of high social standing, he didn't try to defend the upper classes. Rather, he accused them of chief responsibility for the decay in Judah. The officials, the priests, the rulers, the judges, even the prophets—these are the targets of Zephaniah's rage.

The leaders of Judah were pointing the entire nation on a course of self-destruction. Unless they reversed directions, Jerusalem would face the same fate as many of its fallen neighbors.

To Reflect On: *Zephaniah begins with gloom but ends with joy. What gives him reason for hope?*

ZEPHANIAH 3

The Future of Jerusalem

3 Woe to the city of oppressors,
rebellious and defiled!

2She obeys no one,
she accepts no correction.
She does not trust in the LORD,
she does not draw near to her God.
3Her officials are roaring lions,
her rulers are evening wolves,
who leave nothing for the morning.
4Her prophets are arrogant;
they are treacherous men.
Her priests profane the sanctuary
and do violence to the law.
5The LORD within her is righteous;
he does no wrong.
Morning by morning he dispenses his
justice,
and every new day he does not fail,
yet the unrighteous know no shame.

6"I have cut off nations;
their strongholds are demolished.
I have left their streets deserted,
with no one passing through.
Their cities are destroyed;
no one will be left—no one at all.
7I said to the city,
'Surely you will fear me

and accept correction!'
Then her dwelling would not be cut
off,
nor all my punishments come upon
her.
But they were still eager
to act corruptly in all they did.
8Therefore wait for me," declares the
LORD,
"for the day I will stand up to
testify.
I have decided to assemble the nations,
to gather the kingdoms
and to pour out my wrath on them—
all my fierce anger.
The whole world will be consumed
by the fire of my jealous anger.

9"Then will I purify the lips of the
peoples,
that all of them may call on the
name of the LORD
and serve him shoulder to shoulder.
10From beyond the rivers of Cush
my worshipers, my scattered people,
will bring me offerings.
11On that day you will not be put to
shame
for all the wrongs you have done to
me,
because I will remove from this city
those who rejoice in their pride.
Never again will you be haughty
on my holy hill.
12But I will leave within you
the meek and humble,
who trust in the name of the LORD.
13The remnant of Israel will do no
wrong;
they will speak no lies,
nor will deceit be found in their
mouths.

They will eat and lie down
and no one will make them afraid."

14Sing, O Daughter of Zion;
shout aloud, O Israel!
Be glad and rejoice with all your heart,
O Daughter of Jerusalem!
15The LORD has taken away your
punishment,
he has turned back your enemy.
The LORD, the King of Israel, is with
you;
never again will you fear any harm.
16On that day they will say to
Jerusalem,
"Do not fear, O Zion;
do not let your hands hang limp.
17The LORD your God is with you,
he is mighty to save.
He will take great delight in you,
he will quiet you with his love,
he will rejoice over you with
singing."

18"The sorrows for the appointed feasts
I will remove from you;
they are a burden and a reproach to
you.
19At that time I will deal
with all who oppressed you;
I will rescue the lame
and gather those who have been
scattered.
I will give them praise and honor
in every land where they were put
to shame.
20At that time I will gather you;
at that time I will bring you home.
I will give you honor and praise
among all the peoples of the earth
when I restore your fortunes
before your very eyes,"
says the LORD.

Judah's Boy Wonder

2 Kings 22:1–23:3

The Bible does not record what specific effect Zephaniah's words had within Judah. But it does give a thrilling account of a turnaround that occurred during his days, led by King Josiah.

King Josiah took over at the age of eight, in the midst of a crisis seemingly beyond all healing. But Josiah was no ordinary eight year old. Raised by a wicked king in a wicked time, he somehow emerged with a spiritual vision that had no equal. The Bible's judgment is unequivocal: "Neither before nor after Josiah was there a king like him who turned to the LORD as he did—with all his heart and with all his soul and with all his strength, in accordance with all the Law of Moses" (2 Kings 23:25). Against the odds, Josiah steered his nation back toward God.

Josiah devoted much time and energy to a favorite public works project, repairing the temple. And one busy day, as carpenters sawed new joists and beams, and masons carved new stones for the temple walls, and workmen hauled off rubble from the idols Josiah had smashed—in the midst of that din and clutter, a priest made an amazing discovery. He found a scroll that looked like—*could it be?*—the Book of the Covenant, the original record of the agreement between the Israelites and their God. (Most scholars believe the scroll contained part or all of the book of Deuteronomy.)

The neglect of such an important document, long buried and forgotten, shows the extent of Judah's slide away from God. And Josiah's response shows the depth of his commitment. Hearing those sacred words for the first time, he tore his robes in shame and repentance. And after a prophetess had confirmed the scroll's authenticity, Josiah pledged himself and his nation to the terms of the long-lost covenant.

This chapter tells the story of the dramatic discovery, and the next tells of Josiah's fervent campaign to call his nation back to God. His actions would change the landscape of Judah and stave off certain destruction. All this came about because a young king took seriously the words of God.

To Reflect On: *When have you experienced an "awakening" similar to King Josiah's?*

---

2 KINGS 22:1–23:3

The Book of the Law Found

22 Josiah was eight years old when he became king, and he reigned in Jerusalem thirty-one years. His mother's name was Jedidah daughter of Adaiah; she was from Bozkath. ²He did what was right in the eyes of the LORD and walked in all the ways of his father David, not turning aside to the right or to the left.

³In the eighteenth year of his reign, King Josiah sent the secretary, Shaphan son of Azaliah, the son of Meshullam, to the temple of the LORD. He said: ⁴"Go up to Hilkiah the high priest and have him get ready the money that has been brought into the temple of the LORD, which the doorkeepers have collected from the people. ⁵Have them entrust it to the men appointed to supervise the work on the temple. And have these men pay the workers who repair the temple of the LORD— ⁶the carpenters, the builders and the masons. Also have them purchase timber and dressed stone to repair the temple. ⁷But they need not account for the money entrusted to them, because they are acting faithfully."

⁸Hilkiah the high priest said to Shaphan the secretary, "I have found the Book of the Law in the temple of the LORD." He gave it to Shaphan, who read it. ⁹Then Shaphan the secretary went to the king and reported to him: "Your officials have paid out the money that was in the temple of the LORD and have entrusted it to the workers and supervisors at the temple." ¹⁰Then Shaphan the secretary informed the king, "Hilkiah the priest has given me a book." And Shaphan read from it in the presence of the king.

¹¹When the king heard the words of the Book of the Law, he tore his robes. ¹²He gave these orders to Hilkiah the priest, Ahikam son of Shaphan, Acbor son of Micaiah, Shaphan the secretary and Asaiah the king's attendant: ¹³"Go and inquire of the LORD for me and for the people and for all Judah about what is written in this book that has been found. Great is the LORD's anger that burns against us because our fathers have not obeyed the words of this book; they have not acted in accordance with all that is written there concerning us."

¹⁴Hilkiah the priest, Ahikam, Acbor, Shaphan and Asaiah went to speak to the prophetess Huldah, who was the wife of Shallum son of Tikvah, the son of Harhas, keeper of the wardrobe. She lived in Jerusalem, in the Second District.

¹⁵She said to them, "This is what the LORD, the God of Israel, says: Tell the man who sent you to me, ¹⁶'This is what the LORD says: I am going to bring disaster on this place and its people, according to everything written in the book the king of Judah has read. ¹⁷Because they have forsaken me and burned incense to other gods and provoked me to anger by all the idols their hands have made, my anger will burn against this place and will not be quenched.' ¹⁸Tell the king of Judah, who sent you to inquire of the LORD, 'This is what the LORD, the God of Israel, says concerning the words you heard: ¹⁹Because your heart was responsive and you humbled yourself before the LORD when you heard what I have spoken against this place and its people, that they would become accursed and laid waste, and because you tore your robes and wept in my presence, I have heard you, declares the LORD. ²⁰Therefore I will gather you to your fathers, and you will be buried in peace. Your eyes will not see all the disaster I am going to bring on this place.' "

So they took her answer back to the king.

Josiah Renews the Covenant

23 Then the king called together all the elders of Judah and Jerusalem. ²He went up to the temple of the LORD with the men of Judah, the people of Jerusalem, the priests and the prophets—all the people from the least to the greatest. He read in their hearing all the words of the Book of the Covenant, which had been found in the temple of the LORD. ³The king stood by the pillar and renewed the covenant in the presence of the LORD—to follow the LORD and keep his commands, regulations and decrees with all his heart and all his soul, thus confirming the words of the covenant written in this book. Then all the people pledged themselves to the covenant.

National Adultery

Jeremiah 2:2b–27

Zephaniah was not the only prophet active during King Josiah's days. Just as Josiah was reaching adulthood, the doleful voice of Jeremiah began to be heard in the streets of Jerusalem. Later, Jeremiah's messages were collected into a book that is the Bible's longest, and easily its most passionate. Jeremiah was subject to violent swings of mood, and his book reflects that same emotional temperament. The English word *jeremiad*, which means "a long complaint," conveys something of his tone.

This chapter, full of strong images and rhetorical blasts, typifies Jeremiah's style. He uses sexual imagery to present Judah's crisis as a kind of lover's quarrel between God and Judah. She is like a prostitute who lies down under every spreading tree; like a rutting she-camel; like a donkey in heat driven wild with desire.

But what is the object of Judah's desire? Incredibly, she is trading the glory of God for worthless idols of wood and stone. She is exchanging a spring of living water for a leaky well. God, the wounded lover, cannot comprehend his people's actions, and neither can Jeremiah.

Jeremiah had two main complaints against Judah: She prostituted herself both through idol worship and through alliances with foreign nations. When a military threat loomed, Judah turned to empires like Assyria, Egypt, or Babylon for help, not to God.

Josiah, one of Judah's all-time best kings, led a mostly successful campaign to rid the nation of idols. But even Josiah succumbed to the temptation of foreign entanglements. Against Jeremiah's counsel, he thrust himself into international politics by leading an ill-advised march against Egyptian armies. Josiah died in that battle, and his death shocked the nation. A grieving Jeremiah wrote laments in honor of the king.

Judah would never recover from Josiah's fatal mistake. Egypt installed a puppet king over Judah, and from then on no one had the ability to rally Judah's religious or political strength. Jeremiah lived through the reigns of four weakling kings, and the messages collected in this book heap scorn upon them.

To Reflect On: *To whom do you show the most consistent loyalty? Are you loyal to God?*

JEREMIAH 2:2b–27

Israel Forsakes God

" 'I remember the devotion of your
   youth,
   how as a bride you loved me
and followed me through the desert,
   through a land not sown.
³Israel was holy to the Lord,
   the firstfruits of his harvest;
all who devoured her were held guilty,
   and disaster overtook them,' "
                              declares the Lord.

⁴Hear the word of the Lord, O house of
   Jacob,

all you clans of the house of Israel.

⁵This is what the Lord says:

"What fault did your fathers find in me,
   that they strayed so far from me?
They followed worthless idols
   and became worthless themselves.
⁶They did not ask, 'Where is the Lord,
   who brought us up out of Egypt
and led us through the barren
   wilderness,
   through a land of deserts and rifts,
a land of drought and darkness,
   a land where no one travels and no
      one lives?'

⁷I brought you into a fertile land
   to eat its fruit and rich produce.
But you came and defiled my land
   and made my inheritance detestable.
⁸The priests did not ask,
   'Where is the LORD?'
Those who deal with the law did not
      know me;
   the leaders rebelled against me.
The prophets prophesied by Baal,
   following worthless idols.

⁹"Therefore I bring charges against you
      again,"
                     declares the LORD.
   "And I will bring charges against
      your children's children.
¹⁰Cross over to the coasts of Kittim and
      look,
   send to Kedar and observe closely;
   see if there has ever been anything
      like this:
¹¹Has a nation ever changed its gods?
   (Yet they are not gods at all.)
But my people have exchanged their
      Glory
   for worthless idols.
¹²Be appalled at this, O heavens,
   and shudder with great horror,"
                     declares the LORD.
¹³"My people have committed two sins:
They have forsaken me,
   the spring of living water,
and have dug their own cisterns,
   broken cisterns that cannot hold
      water.
¹⁴Is Israel a servant, a slave by birth?
   Why then has he become plunder?
¹⁵Lions have roared;
   they have growled at him.
They have laid waste his land;
   his towns are burned and deserted.
¹⁶Also, the men of Memphis and
      Tahpanhes
   have shaved the crown of your head.
¹⁷Have you not brought this on
      yourselves
   by forsaking the LORD your God
   when he led you in the way?
¹⁸Now why go to Egypt
   to drink water from the Shihor?
And why go to Assyria
   to drink water from the River?

¹⁹Your wickedness will punish you;
   your backsliding will rebuke you.
Consider then and realize
   how evil and bitter it is for you
when you forsake the LORD your God
   and have no awe of me,"
   declares the Lord, the LORD Almighty.

²⁰"Long ago you broke off your yoke
   and tore off your bonds;
   you said, 'I will not serve you!'
Indeed, on every high hill
   and under every spreading tree
   you lay down as a prostitute.
²¹I had planted you like a choice vine
   of sound and reliable stock.
How then did you turn against me
   into a corrupt, wild vine?
²²Although you wash yourself with soda
   and use an abundance of soap,
   the stain of your guilt is still before
      me,"
            declares the Sovereign LORD.
²³"How can you say, 'I am not defiled;
   I have not run after the Baals'?
See how you behaved in the valley;
   consider what you have done.
You are a swift she-camel
   running here and there,
²⁴a wild donkey accustomed to the
      desert,
   sniffing the wind in her craving—
   in her heat who can restrain her?
Any males that pursue her need not
      tire themselves;
   at mating time they will find her.
²⁵Do not run until your feet are bare
   and your throat is dry.
But you said, 'It's no use!
   I love foreign gods,
   and I must go after them.'

²⁶"As a thief is disgraced when he is
      caught,
   so the house of Israel is disgraced—
they, their kings and their officials,
   their priests and their prophets.
²⁷They say to wood, 'You are my
      father,'
   and to stone, 'You gave me birth.'
They have turned their backs to me
   and not their faces;
yet when they are in trouble, they say,
   'Come and save us!' "

Balky Prophet

Jeremiah 15

For most of his life Jeremiah had to deliver a gloomy message, and no one felt the weight of that message more than he. "Since my people are crushed, I am crushed; I mourn, and horror grips me. . . . Oh that my head were a spring of water and my eyes a fountain of tears" (8:21, 9:1). That spirit comes through so strongly in his writings that Jeremiah has become known as "the weeping prophet."

More than Judah's future caused Jeremiah alarm; he feared for his own personal safety. From the very beginning he argued with God about his assignment as a prophet, and throughout his career he remained reluctant, insecure, and often unhappy.

God made harsh demands on Jeremiah, and he responded to those demands in typical fashion: by whining, complaining, feeling sorry for himself, and even lashing out against God's cruelty. The book includes a remarkable series of conversations—more like arguments—in which Jeremiah tells God exactly how he feels. "O LORD, you deceived me," he accuses (20:7). He calls into question God's ability: "Why are you like a man taken by surprise, like a warrior powerless to save?" (14:9). Jeremiah did not appreciate his own or his country's predicament and he let God know it.

This chapter includes one such conversation with God. Quotation marks surround God's speeches: He begins by pronouncing judgment on the nation of Judah. But at verse 10 Jeremiah butts in with his agenda. What will people think of a prophet delivering a message like that? His name is a national swear word already. He'd be better off unborn. God resumes his solemn pronouncement in verse 12, only to be interrupted again by Jeremiah's self-piteous complaints. To him, God seems unreliable, like a brook that dries up, a spring that fails.

Despite Jeremiah's fits and protests, God never gave up on him. In this chapter he promises to make the weepy prophet "a fortified wall of bronze," able to stand against the whole land. Likewise, Jeremiah, for all his diatribes, never gave up on God. The word of God was inside him and he couldn't stop talking about it, no matter how hard he tried. "But if I say, 'I will not mention him or speak any more in his name,' his word is in my heart like a fire, a fire shut up in my bones. I am weary of holding it in; indeed, I cannot."

> **To Reflect On:** *What "complaints" would you bring to God? Do you, like Jeremiah, ever feel unappreciated by God?*

JEREMIAH 15

15 Then the LORD said to me: "Even if Moses and Samuel were to stand before me, my heart would not go out to this people. Send them away from my presence! Let them go! 2 And if they ask you, 'Where shall we go?' tell them, 'This is what the LORD says:

" 'Those destined for death, to death;
those for the sword, to the sword;
those for starvation, to starvation;
those for captivity, to captivity.'

3 "I will send four kinds of destroyers against them," declares the LORD, "the sword to kill and the dogs to drag away and the birds of the air and the beasts of the earth to devour and destroy. 4 I will make them abhorrent to all the kingdoms of the earth because of what Manasseh son of Hezekiah king of Judah did in Jerusalem.

5 "Who will have pity on you, O
Jerusalem?

Who will mourn for you?
Who will stop to ask how you are?
⁶You have rejected me, declares the
LORD.
"You keep on backsliding.
So I will lay hands on you and destroy
you;
I can no longer show compassion.
⁷I will winnow them with a winnowing
fork
at the city gates of the land.
I will bring bereavement and destruction
on my people,
for they have not changed their
ways.
⁸I will make their widows more
numerous
than the sand of the sea.
At midday I will bring a destroyer
against the mothers of their young
men;
suddenly I will bring down on them
anguish and terror.
⁹The mother of seven will grow faint
and breathe her last.
Her sun will set while it is still day;
she will be disgraced and humiliated.
I will put the survivors to the sword
before their enemies,"
declares the LORD.

¹⁰Alas, my mother, that you gave me
birth,
a man with whom the whole land
strives and contends!
I have neither lent nor borrowed,
yet everyone curses me.

¹¹The LORD said,

"Surely I will deliver you for a good
purpose;
surely I will make your enemies
plead with you
in times of disaster and times of
distress.
¹²"Can a man break iron—
iron from the north—or bronze?
¹³Your wealth and your treasures
I will give as plunder, without
charge,

because of all your sins
throughout your country.
¹⁴I will enslave you to your enemies
in a land you do not know,
for my anger will kindle a fire
that will burn against you."

¹⁵You understand, O LORD;
remember me and care for me.
Avenge me on my persecutors.
You are long-suffering—do not take
me away;
think of how I suffer reproach for
your sake.
¹⁶When your words came, I ate them;
they were my joy and my heart's
delight,
for I bear your name,
O LORD God Almighty.
¹⁷I never sat in the company of revelers,
never made merry with them;
I sat alone because your hand was on
me
and you had filled me with
indignation.
¹⁸Why is my pain unending
and my wound grievous and
incurable?
Will you be to me like a deceptive
brook,
like a spring that fails?

¹⁹Therefore this is what the LORD says:

"If you repent, I will restore you
that you may serve me;
if you utter worthy, not worthless,
words,
you will be my spokesman.
Let this people turn to you,
but you must not turn to them.
²⁰I will make you a wall to this people,
a fortified wall of bronze;
they will fight against you
but will not overcome you,
for I am with you
to rescue and save you,"
declares the LORD.
²¹"I will save you from the hands of the
wicked
and redeem you from the grasp of
the cruel."

No Dead End

Jeremiah 31:12–34

Trained as a priest, Jeremiah learned at an early age the story of the covenant between God and his chosen people. Yet he also knew the more recent history of ten Israelite tribes being dispersed by the Assyrians. Suddenly he learned—and was ordered to prophesy—that the two surviving tribes in Judah would undergo a similar trial. In Jeremiah's own lifetime, enemy armies from Babylon would desecrate the holy city of Jerusalem and take captive many more Israelites.

Has God abandoned the covenant? Has he cast aside his chosen people? Every generation of Jews since Jeremiah's day has asked those very questions. (For an example, see the Apostle Paul's passionate discussion in Romans 9–11.) In this chapter, Jeremiah receives a dream sequence that hints at an answer.

Jeremiah saw that a "remnant" would survive the Babylonian invasion. God had not permanently rejected his people, but was allowing them to go through a time of temporary punishment for the sake of purging. More, God promised that the future of the Israelites would be far grander than anything in the past.

Bible interpreters disagree on the full meaning of these promises. Some things are clear: For example, God promised a "new covenant" to replace and improve on the old, broken one. Hebrews 8 quotes a key passage from this chapter in Jeremiah and applies the prophecy to Jesus, who made possible the *new* covenant and its grand forgiveness.

But what of the predictions that seem to apply, geographically, to the land of Palestine? Some of the exiled Israelites, led by Ezra and Nehemiah, did eventually return from captivity in Babylon, but that sparse resettlement of a devastated land hardly calls to mind the glorious new society described here. Jewish scholars disagree on the meaning: some point to the modern-day state of Israel as a direct fulfillment of this prophecy, while others violently disagree. And some Christian theologians believe that these promises, under the new covenant, apply to the Church in a more general sense, and not to the Jewish race and its settlement of the land.

Jeremiah did not get a detailed blueprint of future history, but he did get a resounding confirmation of how God feels about his people.

To Reflect On: *Does God have a "covenant" with us today? What does it promise?*

JEREMIAH 31:12–34

¹²"They will come and shout for joy on
the heights of Zion;
they will rejoice in the bounty of the
LORD—
the grain, the new wine and the oil,
the young of the flocks and herds.
They will be like a well-watered
garden,
and they will sorrow no more.
¹³Then maidens will dance and be glad,
young men and old as well.

I will turn their mourning into
gladness;
I will give them comfort and joy
instead of sorrow.
¹⁴I will satisfy the priests with
abundance,
and my people will be filled with my
bounty,

declares the LORD.

¹⁵This is what the LORD says:

"A voice is heard in Ramah,
mourning and great weeping,

Rachel weeping for her children
and refusing to be comforted,
because her children are no more."

16 This is what the LORD says:

"Restrain your voice from weeping
and your eyes from tears,
for your work will be rewarded,"
declares the LORD.
"They will return from the land of
the enemy.
17 So there is hope for your future,"
declares the LORD.
"Your children will return to their
own land.

18 "I have surely heard Ephraim's
moaning:
'You disciplined me like an unruly
calf,
and I have been disciplined.
Restore me, and I will return,
because you are the LORD my God.
19 After I strayed,
I repented;
after I came to understand,
I beat my breast.
I was ashamed and humiliated
because I bore the disgrace of my
youth.'
20 Is not Ephraim my dear son,
the child in whom I delight?
Though I often speak against him,
I still remember him.
Therefore my heart yearns for him;
I have great compassion for him,"
declares the LORD.

21 "Set up road signs;
put up guideposts.
Take note of the highway,
the road that you take.
Return, O Virgin Israel,
return to your towns.
22 How long will you wander,
O unfaithful daughter?
The LORD will create a new thing on
earth—
a woman will surround a man."

23 This is what the LORD Almighty, the
God of Israel, says: "When I bring them
back from captivity, the people in the land
of Judah and in its towns will once again use
these words: 'The LORD bless you, O righteous dwelling, O sacred mountain.' 24 People will live together in Judah and all its
towns—farmers and those who move about
with their flocks. 25 I will refresh the weary
and satisfy the faint."

26 At this I awoke and looked around. My
sleep had been pleasant to me.
27 "The days are coming," declares the
LORD, "when I will plant the house of Israel
and the house of Judah with the offspring of
men and of animals. 28 Just as I watched
over them to uproot and tear down, and to
overthrow, destroy and bring disaster, so I
will watch over them to build and to plant,"
declares the LORD. 29 "In those days people
will no longer say,

'The fathers have eaten sour grapes,
and the children's teeth are set on
edge.'

30 Instead, everyone will die for his own
sin; whoever eats sour grapes—his own
teeth will be set on edge.

31 "The time is coming," declares the
LORD,
"when I will make a new covenant
with the house of Israel
and with the house of Judah.
32 It will not be like the covenant
I made with their forefathers
when I took them by the hand
to lead them out of Egypt,
because they broke my covenant,
though I was a husband to them,"
declares the LORD.
33 "This is the covenant I will make with
the house of Israel
after that time," declares the LORD.
"I will put my law in their minds
and write it on their hearts.
I will be their God,
and they will be my people.
34 No longer will a man teach his
neighbor,
or a man his brother, saying, 'Know
the LORD,'
because they will all know me,
from the least of them to the
greatest,"
declares the LORD.
"For I will forgive their wickedness
and will remember their sins no
more."

Prophet's Perils

Jeremiah 38

An ironic Jewish curse goes like this: "May you live in interesting times." It seems that the more "interesting" the times, the more the Jews suffered. And, as this chapter indicates, Jeremiah assuredly lived in interesting times. Jeremiah had very good reason for being a weeping, balky prophet. "I get no respect!" he could rightfully claim.

Four kings succeeded Josiah, but each of them served as puppet for a larger empire, and each of them gave the prophet Jeremiah a hard time. One king scheduled a private reading of Jeremiah's prophecies in his winter apartment. As each scroll was read, the king casually hacked it to pieces with a knife and tossed it into the fireplace (36:23). On other occasions the prophet himself was beaten and put in stocks, or locked in a dungeon, or, as this chapter relates, thrown in a well. The best state Jeremiah could hope for was house arrest or confinement in the king's courtyard.

The mistreatment only served to harden Jeremiah's resolve. He would curse his tormentors even as they released him from the stocks. Evidently, he reserved his fears and doubts for God's ears alone.

The events in this chapter took place in Jerusalem, in the midst of a terrible two-year siege by the Babylonians. The city's starving residents, barely clinging to survival, had resorted to cannibalism. City officials were frantically trying to improve morale and whip up courage. Little wonder they objected to Jeremiah's dour advice: "We're going to lose anyway—might as well defect over the walls, or open the gates and let the Babylonians in."

The following chapter (39) tells of Jeremiah's prophecies coming true. Babylon's army did breach the walls, and then captured and tortured the weak King Zedekiah. The conquerors treated Jeremiah with respect, however, having heard of his counsel to surrender.

But Jeremiah's trials did not end with the fall of Jerusalem. Not long afterward, a gang of Israelites rebelled against their captors and ran to Egypt, with the angry prophet in tow. They thought they had reached safety. But in his last recorded words, Jeremiah, a browbeaten seventy-year-old, announced that those refugees would meet a tragic end. They ignored him—just like everyone else in Jeremiah's hapless career.

To Reflect On: *What do you think Jeremiah would have said about the "prosperity theology" some Christians preach today?*

JEREMIAH 38

Jeremiah Thrown Into a Cistern

38 Shephatiah son of Mattan, Gedaliah son of Pashhur, Jehucal son of Shelemiah, and Pashhur son of Malkijah heard what Jeremiah was telling all the people when he said, ²"This is what the LORD says: 'Whoever stays in this city will die by the sword, famine or plague, but whoever goes over to the Babylonians will live. He will escape with his life; he will live.' ³And this is what the LORD says: 'This city will certainly be handed over to the army of the king of Babylon, who will capture it.'"

⁴Then the officials said to the king, "This man should be put to death. He is discouraging the soldiers who are left in this city, as well as all the people, by the things he is saying to them. This man is not seeking the good of these people but their ruin."

⁵"He is in your hands," King Zedekiah answered. "The king can do nothing to oppose you."

⁶So they took Jeremiah and put him into the cistern of Malkijah, the king's son, which was in the courtyard of the guard. They lowered Jeremiah by ropes into the cistern; it had no water in it, only mud, and Jeremiah sank down into the mud.

⁷But Ebed-Melech, a Cushite, an official in the royal palace, heard that they had put Jeremiah into the cistern. While the king was sitting in the Benjamin Gate, ⁸Ebed-Melech went out of the palace and said to him, ⁹"My lord the king, these men have acted wickedly in all they have done to Jeremiah the prophet. They have thrown him into a cistern, where he will starve to death when there is no longer any bread in the city."

¹⁰Then the king commanded Ebed-Melech the Cushite, "Take thirty men from here with you and lift Jeremiah the prophet out of the cistern before he dies."

¹¹So Ebed-Melech took the men with him and went to a room under the treasury in the palace. He took some old rags and worn-out clothes from there and let them down with ropes to Jeremiah in the cistern. ¹²Ebed-Melech the Cushite said to Jeremiah, "Put these old rags and worn-out clothes under your arms to pad the ropes." Jeremiah did so, ¹³and they pulled him up with the ropes and lifted him out of the cistern. And Jeremiah remained in the courtyard of the guard.

Zedekiah Questions Jeremiah Again

¹⁴Then King Zedekiah sent for Jeremiah the prophet and had him brought to the third entrance to the temple of the LORD. "I am going to ask you something," the king said to Jeremiah. "Do not hide anything from me."

¹⁵Jeremiah said to Zedekiah, "If I give you an answer, will you not kill me? Even if I did give you counsel, you would not listen to me."

¹⁶But King Zedekiah swore this oath secretly to Jeremiah: "As surely as the LORD lives, who has given us breath, I will neither kill you nor hand you over to those who are seeking your life."

¹⁷Then Jeremiah said to Zedekiah, "This is what the LORD God Almighty, the God of Israel, says: 'If you surrender to the officers of the king of Babylon, your life will be spared and this city will not be burned down; you and your family will live. ¹⁸But if you will not surrender to the officers of the king of Babylon, this city will be handed over to the Babylonians and they will burn it down; you yourself will not escape from their hands.'"

¹⁹King Zedekiah said to Jeremiah, "I am afraid of the Jews who have gone over to the Babylonians, for the Babylonians may hand me over to them and they will mistreat me."

²⁰"They will not hand you over," Jeremiah replied. "Obey the LORD by doing what I tell you. Then it will go well with you, and your life will be spared. ²¹But if you refuse to surrender, this is what the LORD has revealed to me: ²²All the women left in the palace of the king of Judah will be brought out to the officials of the king of Babylon. Those women will say to you:

" 'They misled you and overcame
        you—
    those trusted friends of yours.
Your feet are sunk in the mud;
    your friends have deserted you.'

²³"All your wives and children will be brought out to the Babylonians. You yourself will not escape from their hands but will be captured by the king of Babylon; and this city will be burned down."

²⁴Then Zedekiah said to Jeremiah, "Do not let anyone know about this conversation, or you may die. ²⁵If the officials hear that I talked with you, and they come to you and say, 'Tell us what you said to the king and what the king said to you; do not hide it from us or we will kill you,' ²⁶then tell them, 'I was pleading with the king not to send me back to Jonathan's house to die there.'"

²⁷All the officials did come to Jeremiah and question him, and he told them everything the king had ordered him to say. So they said no more to him, for no one had heard his conversation with the king.

²⁸And Jeremiah remained in the courtyard of the guard until the day Jerusalem was captured.

Debating God

Habakkuk 1

Everyone has a built-in sense of justice. If, in the Olympic games, a basketball referee calls thirty-nine fouls against the U.S. team and none against the Soviets, fans are outraged. *That's not fair!* If a careless driver runs down a small child and nonchalantly drives on, other drivers will follow in hot pursuit. *He can't get away with that!* We may disagree on specific rules of fairness, but we all follow some inner code.

And, frankly, often life seems unfair. What child "deserves" to grow up in the slums of Calcutta, or Rio de Janeiro, or the East Bronx? Why should people like Adolf Hitler, and Pol Pot get away with tyrannizing millions of people? Why are some kind, gentle people struck down in the prime of life while other meaner people live into cantankerous old age?

We all ask different versions of such questions. The prophet named Habakkuk asked them of God directly, and got a no-holds-barred reply. Like his contemporary Jeremiah, Habakkuk did not mince words. He began with a series of blustery accusations in which he demanded that God explain why he wasn't responding to the injustice, violence, and evil that the prophet could clearly see around him.

God answered with the same message he had told Jeremiah, that he would send the Babylonians to punish Judah. But such words hardly reassured Habakkuk, for the Babylonians were ruthless, savage people. Could this be justice—using an even more evil nation to punish Judah?

The book of Habakkuk does not solve the problem of evil. But Habakkuk's conversations with God convinced him of one certainty: God had not lost control. As a God of justice, he could not let evil win. First, he would deal with the Babylonians on their own terms. Then, later, he would intervene with great force, shaking the very foundations of the earth until no sign of injustice remained.

"The earth will be filled with the knowledge of the glory of the LORD, as the waters cover the sea," God promised Habakkuk (2:14). A glimpse of that powerful glory changed the prophet's attitude from outrage to joy. In the course of his "debate" with God, Habakkuk learned new lessons about faith, which are beautifully expressed in the last chapter. God's answers so satisfied Habakkuk that his book, which begins with a complaint, ends with one of the most beautiful songs in the Bible.

> **To Reflect On:** *What do you find most troubling about God's answer to Habakkuk? Most satisfying? Do you have questions similar to Habakkuk's? How do you think God would answer them if he spoke to you directly? Have you ever asked God these questions? What did he answer?*

HABAKKUK 1

1 The oracle that Habakkuk the prophet received.

Habakkuk's Complaint

²How long, O LORD, must I call for help,
  but you do not listen?
Or cry out to you, "Violence!"
  but you do not save?
³Why do you make me look at injustice?
  Why do you tolerate wrong?
Destruction and violence are before me;
  there is strife, and conflict abounds.
⁴Therefore the law is paralyzed,
  and justice never prevails.
The wicked hem in the righteous,
  so that justice is perverted.

The LORD's Answer

⁵"Look at the nations and watch—
  and be utterly amazed.
For I am going to do something in
    your days
  that you would not believe,
  even if you were told.
⁶I am raising up the Babylonians,
  that ruthless and impetuous people,
who sweep across the whole earth
  to seize dwelling places not their
    own.
⁷They are a feared and dreaded people;
  they are a law to themselves
  and promote their own honor.
⁸Their horses are swifter than leopards,
  fiercer than wolves at dusk.
Their cavalry gallops headlong;
  their horsemen come from afar.
They fly like a vulture swooping to
    devour;
⁹ they all come bent on violence.

Their hordes advance like a desert wind
  and gather prisoners like sand.
¹⁰They deride kings
  and scoff at rulers.
They laugh at all fortified cities;
  they build earthen ramps and capture
    them.
¹¹Then they sweep past like the wind
    and go on—
  guilty men, whose own strength is
    their god."

Habakkuk's Second Complaint

¹²O LORD, are you not from everlasting?
  My God, my Holy One, we will not
    die.
O LORD, you have appointed them to
    execute judgment;
  O Rock, you have ordained them to
    punish.
¹³Your eyes are too pure to look on evil;
  you cannot tolerate wrong.
Why then do you tolerate the
    treacherous?
  Why are you silent while the wicked
  swallow up those more righteous
    than themselves?
¹⁴You have made men like fish in the
    sea,
  like sea creatures that have no ruler.
¹⁵The wicked foe pulls all of them up
    with hooks,
  he catches them in his net,
he gathers them up in his dragnet;
  and so he rejoices and is glad.
¹⁶Therefore he sacrifices to his net
  and burns incense to his dragnet,
for by his net he lives in luxury
  and enjoys the choicest food.
¹⁷Is he to keep on emptying his net,
  destroying nations without mercy?

In Shock

Lamentations 3:1–40

I am the man who has seen affliction . . ." begins this chapter, and that doleful sentence captures the mood of this entire book. Judah's king is now shackled and blinded, his princes slaughtered. Jerusalem—the capital city, the holy city—is no more. The poet writes in a state of dazed grief. He wanders the empty streets, piled high with corpses, and tries to make sense of a tragedy that defies all comprehension.

In some ways, Lamentations reads like a modern book, for our own century has seen many books "lamenting" great tragedies: Jewish memoirs from the Holocaust, Solzhenitsyn's recounting of the Gulag, eyewitness reports from Dresden, and Hiroshima, and, more recently, from Ethiopia and Cambodia. The horror in those accounts echoes the horror described in Lamentations.

But beyond the human tragedy, a different kind of distress gnawed at the author. Babylonian soldiers had entered the temple—pagans in the Most Holy Place!—looted it, then burned it to the ground. The dream of the covenant died on that day. Historians record that as the Babylonians entered the temple they swept the empty air with their spears, seeking the unseen Jewish God. But they found nothing. God had given up; he had fled the premises. Jews still mourn the event: Each year on the anniversary of the day the temple was destroyed, the Orthodox read the book of Lamentations aloud.

The tone of this anonymous book may sound familiar, for the prophet Jeremiah is the likely author. He is an old man, with shriveled skin and broken bones. He has been hunted, jailed, tortured, thrown in a pit and left for dead. Yet nothing can match the grief he feels now as he stares, not at his own wounds, but at the gaping wounds of Jerusalem.

God is an enemy, the prophet concludes, in an outburst familiar to any reader of Jeremiah. He lets his venom spill out. And yet, in the middle of this dark chapter, the author remembers what he once learned about God in brighter, happier times. He recalls the goodness of God, the love, the compassion. In the midst of this bleak book come words that a writer later crafted into a hymn: "Great is Thy Faithfulness." At the moment of terrible tragedy, those qualities of God may seem very far away—but where else can we turn? As Lamentations shows, without God's hope, there is no hope.

> **To Reflect On:** *In your darkest times, do your thoughts turn to God? What helps you find relief?*

LAMENTATIONS 3:1–40

3 I am the man who has seen
affliction
by the rod of his wrath.
²He has driven me away and made me
walk
in darkness rather than light;
³indeed, he has turned his hand against
me
again and again, all day long.

⁴He has made my skin and my flesh
grow old
and has broken my bones.
⁵He has besieged me and surrounded
me
with bitterness and hardship.
⁶He has made me dwell in darkness
like those long dead.

⁷He has walled me in so I cannot
escape;
he has weighed me down with
chains.
⁸Even when I call out or cry for help,
he shuts out my prayer.

⁹He has barred my way with blocks of
stone;
he has made my paths crooked.

¹⁰Like a bear lying in wait,
like a lion in hiding,
¹¹he dragged me from the path and
mangled me
and left me without help.
¹²He drew his bow
and made me the target for his
arrows.

¹³He pierced my heart
with arrows from his quiver.
¹⁴I became the laughingstock of all my
people;
they mock me in song all day long.
¹⁵He has filled me with bitter herbs
and sated me with gall.

¹⁶He has broken my teeth with gravel;
he has trampled me in the dust.
¹⁷I have been deprived of peace;
I have forgotten what prosperity is.
¹⁸So I say, "My splendor is gone
and all that I had hoped from the
LORD."

¹⁹I remember my affliction and my
wandering,
the bitterness and the gall.
²⁰I well remember them,
and my soul is downcast within me.
²¹Yet this I call to mind
and therefore I have hope:

²²Because of the LORD's great love we
are not consumed,
for his compassions never fail.
²³They are new every morning;
great is your faithfulness.
²⁴I say to myself, "The LORD is my
portion;
therefore I will wait for him."

²⁵The LORD is good to those whose hope
is in him,
to the one who seeks him;
²⁶it is good to wait quietly
for the salvation of the LORD.
²⁷It is good for a man to bear the yoke
while he is young.

²⁸Let him sit alone in silence,
for the LORD has laid it on him.
²⁹Let him bury his face in the dust—
there may yet be hope.
³⁰Let him offer his cheek to one who
would strike him,
and let him be filled with disgrace.

³¹For men are not cast off
by the Lord forever.
³²Though he brings grief, he will show
compassion,
so great is his unfailing love.
³³For he does not willingly bring
affliction
or grief to the children of men.

³⁴To crush underfoot
all prisoners in the land,
³⁵to deny a man his rights
before the Most High,
³⁶to deprive a man of justice—
would not the Lord see such things?

³⁷Who can speak and have it happen
if the Lord has not decreed it?
³⁸Is it not from the mouth of the Most
High
that both calamities and good things
come?
³⁹Why should any living man complain
when punished for his sins?

⁴⁰Let us examine our ways and test
them,
and let us return to the LORD.

No Room To Gloat

Obadiah

Remember, O LORD, what the Edomites did on the day Jerusalem fell. 'Tear it down,' they cried, 'tear it down to its foundations!' " (Psalm 137:7) Survivors of the sacking of Jerusalem would never forget the reactions of their neighbors the Edomites, who had watched the carnage with open glee. The Edomites cheered the conquering Babylonian army, looted the fleeing refugees, and helped plunder Jerusalem. Psalm 137, one of the saddest passages in the Bible, voices the Israelites' acrid bitterness over this offense.

To rub salt in Judah's wounds, the Edomites were actually distant relatives. Their nation traced back to the feud between twin brothers Jacob and Esau. While Jacob fathered the Israelites, Esau, having traded away his birthright for a meal, moved to desolate mountain country and founded the nation of Edom. The twins' descendants continued the quarrel for hundreds of years, and now the Edomites were gloating over the Israelites' calamity. True sons of Esau, they thought primarily of the immediate gain available to them from plunder.

The Edomites' attitude contrasts sharply with the sorrow expressed in the book of Lamentations. And Obadiah, the shortest book in the Old Testament, makes clear that the Edomites would pay for their callousness and cruelty: "As you have done, it will be done to you." Those who had betrayed Judah would be repaid with treachery from their own allies.

Obadiah predicted opposite futures for Israel and Edom. According to him, downtrodden Israel would rise again, but Edom would disappear from the face of the earth. History bore out the latter prediction in 70 A.D., when Roman legions destroyed the last remnant of Edomites during a siege of Jerusalem.

> **To Reflect On:** *Edom was basing its security on its strategic location "on the heights" and "in the clefts of the rocks." What do people around you base their security on?*

OBADIAH

¹The vision of Obadiah.

This is what the Sovereign LORD says about Edom—

We have heard a message from the
  LORD:
  An envoy was sent to the nations to
    say,
  "Rise, and let us go against her for
    battle"—
²"See, I will make you small among the
    nations;
  you will be utterly despised.
³The pride of your heart has deceived
    you,
  you who live in the clefts of the
    rocks
  and make your home on the heights,

you who say to yourself,
  'Who can bring me down to the
    ground?'
⁴Though you soar like the eagle
  and make your nest among the stars,
  from there I will bring you down,"
                declares the LORD.
⁵"If thieves came to you,
  if robbers in the night—
Oh, what a disaster awaits you—
  would they not steal only as much
    as they wanted?
If grape pickers came to you,
  would they not leave a few grapes?
⁶But how Esau will be ransacked,
  his hidden treasures pillaged!
⁷All your allies will force you to the
    border;

your friends will deceive and
    overpower you;
those who eat your bread will set a
    trap for you,
    but you will not detect it.

8"In that day," declares the LORD,
    "will I not destroy the wise men of
    Edom,
    men of understanding in the
    mountains of Esau?
9Your warriors, O Teman, will be
    terrified,
    and everyone in Esau's mountains
    will be cut down in the slaughter.
10Because of the violence against your
    brother Jacob,
    you will be covered with shame;
    you will be destroyed forever.
11On the day you stood aloof
    while strangers carried off his wealth
and foreigners entered his gates
    and cast lots for Jerusalem,
    you were like one of them.
12You should not look down on your
    brother
    in the day of his misfortune,
nor rejoice over the people of Judah
    in the day of their destruction,
nor boast so much
    in the day of their trouble.
13You should not march through the
    gates of my people
    in the day of their disaster,
nor look down on them in their
    calamity
    in the day of their disaster,
nor seize their wealth
    in the day of their disaster.
14You should not wait at the crossroads
    to cut down their fugitives,
nor hand over their survivors
    in the day of their trouble.

15"The day of the LORD is near
    for all nations.
As you have done, it will be done to
    you;
    your deeds will return upon your
    own head.
16Just as you drank on my holy hill,
    so all the nations will drink
    continually;
they will drink and drink
    and be as if they had never been.
17But on Mount Zion will be deliverance;
    it will be holy,
and the house of Jacob
    will possess its inheritance.
18The house of Jacob will be a fire
    and the house of Joseph a flame;
the house of Esau will be stubble,
    and they will set it on fire and
    consume it.
There will be no survivors
    from the house of Esau."
                  The LORD has spoken.

19People from the Negev will occupy
    the mountains of Esau,
and people from the foothills will
    possess
    the land of the Philistines.
They will occupy the fields of Ephraim
    and Samaria,
    and Benjamin will possess Gilead.
20This company of Israelite exiles who
    are in Canaan
    will possess [the land] as far as
    Zarephath;
the exiles from Jerusalem who are in
    Sepharad
    will possess the towns of the Negev.
21Deliverers will go up on Mount Zion
    to govern the mountains of Esau.
    And the kingdom will be the LORD's.

Prophet in Exile

Ezekiel 1

About the same time that Jeremiah, Habakkuk, and Obadiah were prophesying in Judah, a man named Ezekiel received a dramatic call to minister to their unfortunate countrymen in exile. The Babylonian army had been pillaging Judah for twenty years before the fall of Jerusalem, and Ezekiel was among the first wave of captives taken to Babylon, nearly 500 miles away. He lived with the Israelites in a refugee settlement beside a river.

Like refugees everywhere, those in Babylon longed for nothing more than a chance to return to their homeland. They received letters of advice and comfort from the prophet Jeremiah. They cringed at reports of rebellion by Judah's kings, fearful that any rebellion might arouse the wrath of Babylon. They wondered anxiously whether their beleaguered nation could survive. Would the Babylonians lose patience and destroy the holy city of Jerusalem? Would God possibly allow such a thing?

An uprooted, dispirited people such as these needed a strong, authoritative voice, and in Ezekiel they got exactly that. As a young man in training for the priesthood, he had found his career plans interrupted by the foreign deportations. What good was a priest in Babylon when the temple was in Jerusalem? Chapter 1 records how God summoned Ezekiel to a new role, as prophet to the Jews in exile.

Ezekiel begins with a description so unearthly that some have suggested the prophet saw a UFO. Indeed, there are some similarities: glowing lights, quick movements, inhuman figures. But, there are differences, too, in this account of a "close encounter," this majestic being was not mysteriously rushing off to disappear. He wanted to be known by everyone. And he had chosen the prophet Ezekiel as the one privileged to make him known.

Confronted with such splendor, Ezekiel fell on his face. But the Spirit of God raised him to his feet and gave him an assignment. After that vision, Ezekiel would never again wonder about a question that often bothered the other refugees: Had God abandoned them? Ezekiel's encounter of the closest kind convinced him permanently that God still cared about his people—even the exiles in Babylon.

> **To Reflect On:** *Have you ever felt "abandoned" by God? What helped you feel less so?*

EZEKIEL 1

The Living Creatures and the Glory of the LORD

1 In the thirtieth year, in the fourth month on the fifth day, while I was among the exiles by the Kebar River, the heavens were opened and I saw visions of God.

²On the fifth of the month—it was the fifth year of the exile of King Jehoiachin— ³the word of the LORD came to Ezekiel the priest, the son of Buzi, by the Kebar River in the land of the Babylonians. There the hand of the LORD was upon him.

⁴I looked, and I saw a windstorm coming out of the north—an immense cloud with flashing lightning and surrounded by brilliant light. The center of the fire looked like glowing metal, ⁵and in the fire was what looked like four living creatures. In appearance their form was that of a man, ⁶but each of them had four faces and four wings. ⁷Their legs were straight; their feet were like those of a calf and gleamed like burnished bronze. ⁸Under their wings on their four sides they had the hands of a man. All four of them had faces and wings, ⁹and their wings touched one another. Each one went straight ahead; they did not turn as they moved.

¹⁰Their faces looked like this: Each of the four had the face of a man, and on the right side each had the face of a lion, and on the left the face of an ox; each also had the face of an eagle. ¹¹Such were their faces. Their wings were spread out upward; each had two wings, one touching the wing of another creature on either side, and two wings covering its body. ¹²Each one went straight ahead. Wherever the spirit would go, they would go, without turning as they went. ¹³The appearance of the living creatures was like burning coals of fire or like torches. Fire moved back and forth among the creatures; it was bright, and lightning flashed out of it. ¹⁴The creatures sped back and forth like flashes of lightning.

¹⁵As I looked at the living creatures, I saw a wheel on the ground beside each creature with its four faces. ¹⁶This was the appearance and structure of the wheels: They sparkled like chrysolite, and all four looked alike. Each appeared to be made like a wheel intersecting a wheel. ¹⁷As they moved, they would go in any one of the four directions the creatures faced; the wheels did not turn about as the creatures went. ¹⁸Their rims were high and awesome, and all four rims were full of eyes all around.

¹⁹When the living creatures moved, the wheels beside them moved; and when the living creatures rose from the ground, the wheels also rose. ²⁰Wherever the spirit would go, they would go, and the wheels would rise along with them, because the spirit of the living creatures was in the wheels. ²¹When the creatures moved, they also moved; when the creatures stood still, they also stood still; and when the creatures rose from the ground, the wheels rose along with them, because the spirit of the living creatures was in the wheels.

²²Spread out above the heads of the living creatures was what looked like an expanse, sparkling like ice, and awesome. ²³Under the expanse their wings were stretched out one toward the other, and each had two wings covering its body. ²⁴When the creatures moved, I heard the sound of their wings, like the roar of rushing waters, like the voice of the Almighty, like the tumult of an army. When they stood still, they lowered their wings.

²⁵Then there came a voice from above the expanse over their heads as they stood with lowered wings. ²⁶Above the expanse over their heads was what looked like a throne of sapphire, and high above on the throne was a figure like that of a man. ²⁷I saw that from what appeared to be his waist up he looked like glowing metal, as if full of fire, and that from there down he looked like fire; and brilliant light surrounded him. ²⁸Like the appearance of a rainbow in the clouds on a rainy day, so was the radiance around him.

This was the appearance of the likeness of the glory of the LORD. When I saw it, I fell facedown, and I heard the voice of one speaking.

Toughening Up

Ezekiel 2–3

Orthodox Jewish rabbis forbid anyone under the age of thirty to read the first three chapters of Ezekiel. No young person, they reason, is ready for such a direct encounter with the glory of the Lord. Indeed, Ezekiel himself barely survived the experience. He kept falling on his face, and was knocked speechless for seven days.

Such exalted revelations were part of God's training regimen, a process of toughening up the prophet for a demanding task. With Isaiah sawn in two and Jeremiah thrown in a well, the prophets of Judah had plenty of reason for alarm. What might befall Ezekiel as he took the word of God to an ornery people in the heart of enemy territory? To embolden him, God gave Ezekiel an experience he would never forget or doubt, no matter what difficulties he might confront.

God warned Ezekiel that few Israelites, if any, would listen to his message. He had to become as stubborn and unyielding as the audience he addressed. As a result, Ezekiel lived a lonely life. People thought of him as a dreamy storyteller, and scoffed at his pessimistic predictions of Jerusalem's fall. Still, despite the negative tone of his prophecies, Ezekiel never once lost hope. He could see past the tragedies of the present day to a future time when God would restore his people and his temple.

Ezekiel's faith could not be shaken, because he had received a vision of the glory of the Lord. Due to his priestly training, he undoubtedly recognized the light, the fire, and the glow—Israelites had seen those images in the pillar of fire in the wilderness, and in the cloud that descended into Solomon's temple. Now the nation was in shambles, its chief citizens in exile. But even there, in Babylon, the glory of the Lord appeared to Ezekiel.

Ezekiel looked upon that glory not once, but twice, at the beginning of his ministry. That experience alone gave him the courage he would need to fight off the enemies— "briers and thorns and scorpions"—that surrounded him.

> **To Reflect On:** *What obstacles do people face today when they try to deliver a message from God?*

EZEKIEL 2–3

Ezekiel's Call

2 He said to me, "Son of man, stand up on your feet and I will speak to you." ²As he spoke, the Spirit came into me and raised me to my feet, and I heard him speaking to me.

³He said: "Son of man, I am sending you to the Israelites, to a rebellious nation that has rebelled against me; they and their fathers have been in revolt against me to this very day. ⁴The people to whom I am sending you are obstinate and stubborn. Say to them, 'This is what the Sovereign LORD says.' ⁵And whether they listen or fail to listen—for they are a rebellious house—

they will know that a prophet has been among them. ⁶And you, son of man, do not be afraid of them or their words. Do not be afraid, though briers and thorns are all around you and you live among scorpions. Do not be afraid of what they say or terrified by them, though they are a rebellious house. ⁷You must speak my words to them, whether they listen or fail to listen, for they are rebellious. ⁸But you, son of man, listen to what I say to you. Do not rebel like that rebellious house; open your mouth and eat what I give you."

⁹Then I looked, and I saw a hand stretched out to me. In it was a scroll, ¹⁰which he unrolled before me. On both

sides of it were written words of lament and mourning and woe.

3 And he said to me, "Son of man, eat what is before you, eat this scroll; then go and speak to the house of Israel." ²So I opened my mouth, and he gave me the scroll to eat.

³Then he said to me, "Son of man, eat this scroll I am giving you and fill your stomach with it." So I ate it, and it tasted as sweet as honey in my mouth.

⁴He then said to me: "Son of man, go now to the house of Israel and speak my words to them. ⁵You are not being sent to a people of obscure speech and difficult language, but to the house of Israel— ⁶not to many peoples of obscure speech and difficult language, whose words you cannot understand. Surely if I had sent you to them, they would have listened to you. ⁷But the house of Israel is not willing to listen to you because they are not willing to listen to me, for the whole house of Israel is hardened and obstinate. ⁸But I will make you as unyielding and hardened as they are. ⁹I will make your forehead like the hardest stone, harder than flint. Do not be afraid of them or terrified by them, though they are a rebellious house."

¹⁰And he said to me, "Son of man, listen carefully and take to heart all the words I speak to you. ¹¹Go now to your countrymen in exile and speak to them. Say to them, 'This is what the Sovereign Lord says,' whether they listen or fail to listen."

¹²Then the Spirit lifted me up, and I heard behind me a loud rumbling sound— May the glory of the Lord be praised in his dwelling place!— ¹³the sound of the wings of the living creatures brushing against each other and the sound of the wheels beside them, a loud rumbling sound. ¹⁴The Spirit then lifted me up and took me away, and I went in bitterness and in the anger of my spirit, with the strong hand of the Lord upon me. ¹⁵I came to the exiles who lived at Tel Abib near the Kebar River. And there, where they were living, I sat among them for seven days—overwhelmed.

Warning to Israel

¹⁶At the end of seven days the word of the Lord came to me: ¹⁷"Son of man, I have made you a watchman for the house of Israel; so hear the word I speak and give them warning from me. ¹⁸When I say to a wicked man, 'You will surely die,' and you do not warn him or speak out to dissuade him from his evil ways in order to save his life, that wicked man will die for his sin, and I will hold you accountable for his blood. ¹⁹But if you do warn the wicked man and he does not turn from his wickedness or from his evil ways, he will die for his sin; but you will have saved yourself.

²⁰"Again, when a righteous man turns from his righteousness and does evil, and I put a stumbling block before him, he will die. Since you did not warn him, he will die for his sin. The righteous things he did will not be remembered, and I will hold you accountable for his blood. ²¹But if you do warn the righteous man not to sin and he does not sin, he will surely live because he took warning, and you will have saved yourself."

²²The hand of the Lord was upon me there, and he said to me, "Get up and go out to the plain, and there I will speak to you." ²³So I got up and went out to the plain. And the glory of the Lord was standing there, like the glory I had seen by the Kebar River, and I fell facedown. ²⁴Then the Spirit came into me and raised me to my feet. He spoke to me and said: "Go, shut yourself inside your house. ²⁵And you, son of man, they will tie with ropes; you will be bound so that you cannot go out among the people. ²⁶I will make your tongue stick to the roof of your mouth so that you will be silent and unable to rebuke them, though they are a rebellious house. ²⁷But when I speak to you, I will open your mouth and you shall say to them, 'This is what the Sovereign Lord says.' Whoever will listen let him listen, and whoever will refuse let him refuse; for they are a rebellious house."

Draw Large and Shout

Ezekiel 4

When someone asked Flannery O'Connor why she populated her novels with such exaggerated, eccentric characters she replied, "To the hard of hearing you shout, and for the almost-blind you draw large and startling figures." The same answer may help explain the oddities of Ezekiel. He, too, faced a stubborn, dense audience who had little tolerance for his message. And, at God's instruction, he employed some bizarre methods to get that message across.

The book records twelve public "object lessons" acted out by the prophet. For example, one year he lay on his side every day, bound by ropes and facing a clay model of Jerusalem. Strange? When a car is headed toward the edge of a cliff, you may scream and gesture so wildly that people think you insane. So it was with Ezekiel, who would do anything to force people to pay attention. (These same people, after all, had ignored God's other messengers, including Jeremiah, a master of weird communication techniques.)

The first part of Ezekiel mainly concerns the political situation back in the homeland of Judah. False prophets were assuring the exiles that God would never allow his temple or holy city to be destroyed. Ezekiel blasted these phony optimists and broadcasted God's plan of judgment in strong words and public protests. He took no great delight in the doomsday message. Twice, seeing the future, he fell down, crying out in horror (9:8; 11:13). In this chapter, when God tells him to cook food on human excrement as a symbolic act, he is too shocked to agree.

At great personal sacrifice, Ezekiel delivered an undiluted message from God, presenting it in a way that the Israelites could not ignore. The exaggerated style says less about Ezekiel than it does about the One who gave the orders. God would not let go of his people until he had done all in his power to turn them around. No device was too undignified, no carnival ploy too corny, as long as he had the slightest hope of breaking through. "As surely as I live, declares the Sovereign LORD, I take no pleasure in the death of the wicked, but rather that they turn from their ways and live. Turn! Turn from your evil ways! Why will you die, O house of Israel?" (33:11).

> **To Reflect On:** *How does God get your attention?*

EZEKIEL 4

Siege of Jerusalem Symbolized

4 "Now, son of man, take a clay tablet, put it in front of you and draw the city of Jerusalem on it. ²Then lay siege to it: Erect siege works against it, build a ramp up to it, set up camps against it and put battering rams around it. ³Then take an iron pan, place it as an iron wall between you and the city and turn your face toward it. It will be under siege, and you shall besiege it. This will be a sign to the house of Israel.

⁴"Then lie on your left side and put the sin of the house of Israel upon yourself. You are to bear their sin for the number of days you lie on your side. ⁵I have assigned you the same number of days as the years of their sin. So for 390 days you will bear the sin of the house of Israel.

⁶"After you have finished this, lie down again, this time on your right side, and bear the sin of the house of Judah. I have assigned you 40 days, a day for each year. ⁷Turn your face toward the siege of Jerusalem and with bared arm prophesy against her. ⁸I will tie you up with ropes so that you cannot turn from one side to the other until you have finished the days of your siege.

⁹"Take wheat and barley, beans and lentils, millet and spelt; put them in a storage jar and use them to make bread for yourself. You are to eat it during the 390 days you lie on your side. ¹⁰Weigh out twenty shekels of food to eat each day and eat it at set times. ¹¹Also measure out a sixth of a hin of water and drink it at set times. ¹²Eat the food as you would a barley cake; bake it in the sight of the people, using human excrement for fuel." ¹³The LORD said, "In this way the people of Israel will eat defiled food among the nations where I will drive them."

¹⁴Then I said, "Not so, Sovereign LORD! I have never defiled myself. From my youth until now I have never eaten anything found dead or torn by wild animals. No unclean meat has ever entered my mouth."

¹⁵"Very well," he said, "I will let you bake your bread over cow manure instead of human excrement."

¹⁶He then said to me: "Son of man, I will cut off the supply of food in Jerusalem. The people will eat rationed food in anxiety and drink rationed water in despair, ¹⁷for food and water will be scarce. They will be appalled at the sight of each other and will waste away because of their sin.

Dry Bones

Ezekiel 37

It's easy to sum up the message of Ezekiel in a phrase, for the book repeats this line more than sixty times: "Then they will know that I am the LORD." Why would Jerusalem be destroyed? Why would all Judah's enemies come to a violent end? So that they would "know that I am the LORD." In a sudden change of tone, God used that same phrase to explain why he would bring about a time of future happiness.

After all the gloom, Ezekiel at last got to pronounce words of great joy and hope. In the early days, he alone had prophesied doom, and no one had listened. Then, for a period of seven years he maintained a virtual silence. But now—ironically, soon after Jerusalem's destruction—he opened his mouth again, and bright words of hope issued forth.

Ezekiel experienced a sudden surge in popularity among the exiles, since he alone had predicted current events accurately. As people flocked to hear his words, he first scolded them for their unchanged hearts, but then confirmed the rumor of good news to come. Life would be restored.

No part of Ezekiel captures that message of hope more effectively, or has achieved more lasting fame, than this startling vision of the valley of dry bones. Even today, that vivid image lives on in song. Like a graveyard of scattered, bleached bones coming gloriously to life, the deadest of the dead will live.

Ezekiel's original audience was still trying to absorb the staggering news that the temple had been razed, with God apparently departed. But Ezekiel assured them God had not given up; the split kingdoms of Judah and Israel would join together again at last. God was coming back to his home, to live with his people.

The book ends with a shining vision of a new Jerusalem arising from the ruins of the old. Scholars disagree on whether Ezekiel's words apply literally, or symbolically, to the nation of Israel. But it is clear that the good news will affect the whole world. The triumphant name of that new city says it all: "And the name of the city from that time on will be: THE LORD IS THERE."

To Reflect On: *Where are you spiritually? With the dry bones? Barely stirring? Alive and well?*

EZEKIEL 37

The Valley of Dry Bones

37 The hand of the LORD was upon me, and he brought me out by the Spirit of the LORD and set me in the middle of a valley; it was full of bones. ²He led me back and forth among them, and I saw a great many bones on the floor of the valley, bones that were very dry. ³He asked me, "Son of man, can these bones live?"

I said, "O Sovereign LORD, you alone know."

⁴Then he said to me, "Prophesy to these bones and say to them, 'Dry bones, hear the word of the LORD! ⁵This is what the Sovereign LORD says to these bones: I will make breath enter you, and you will come to life. ⁶I will attach tendons to you and make flesh come upon you and cover you with skin; I will put breath in you, and you will come to life. Then you will know that I am the LORD.'"

⁷So I prophesied as I was commanded. And as I was prophesying, there was a noise, a rattling sound, and the bones came together, bone to bone. ⁸I looked, and tendons and flesh appeared on them and skin covered them, but there was no breath in them.

⁹Then he said to me, "Prophesy to the breath; prophesy, son of man, and say to it, 'This is what the Sovereign LORD says: Come from the four winds, O breath, and breathe into these slain, that they may live.'" ¹⁰So I prophesied as he commanded me, and breath entered them; they came to life and stood up on their feet—a vast army.

¹¹Then he said to me: "Son of man, these bones are the whole house of Israel. They say, 'Our bones are dried up and our hope is gone; we are cut off.' ¹²Therefore prophesy and say to them: 'This is what the Sovereign LORD says: O my people, I am going to open your graves and bring you up from them; I will bring you back to the land of Israel. ¹³Then you, my people, will know that I am the LORD, when I open your graves and bring you up from them. ¹⁴I will put my Spirit in you and you will live, and I will settle you in your own land. Then you will know that I the LORD have spoken, and I have done it, declares the LORD.'"

One Nation Under One King

¹⁵The word of the LORD came to me: ¹⁶"Son of man, take a stick of wood and write on it, 'Belonging to Judah and the Israelites associated with him.' Then take another stick of wood, and write on it, 'Ephraim's stick, belonging to Joseph and all the house of Israel associated with him.' ¹⁷Join them together into one stick so that they will become one in your hand.

¹⁸"When your countrymen ask you, 'Won't you tell us what you mean by this?' ¹⁹say to them, 'This is what the Sovereign LORD says: I am going to take the stick of Joseph—which is in Ephraim's hand—and of the Israelite tribes associated with him, and join it to Judah's stick, making them a single stick of wood, and they will become one in my hand.' ²⁰Hold before their eyes the sticks you have written on ²¹and say to them, 'This is what the Sovereign LORD says: I will take the Israelites out of the nations where they have gone. I will gather them from all around and bring them back into their own land. ²²I will make them one nation in the land, on the mountains of Israel. There will be one king over all of them and they will never again be two nations or be divided into two kingdoms. ²³They will no longer defile themselves with their idols and vile images or with any of their offenses, for I will save them from all their sinful backsliding, and I will cleanse them. They will be my people, and I will be their God.

²⁴"'My servant David will be king over them, and they will all have one shepherd. They will follow my laws and be careful to keep my decrees. ²⁵They will live in the land I gave to my servant Jacob, the land where your fathers lived. They and their children and their children's children will live there forever, and David my servant will be their prince forever. ²⁶I will make a covenant of peace with them; it will be an everlasting covenant. I will establish them and increase their numbers, and I will put my sanctuary among them forever. ²⁷My dwelling place will be with them; I will be their God, and they will be my people. ²⁸Then the nations will know that I the LORD make Israel holy, when my sanctuary is among them forever.'"

Enemy Employers

Daniel 1

The prophets Daniel and Ezekiel had much in common. Both came from solid families in Judah, had first-rate minds, and showed leadership potential at an early age. They could have anticipated an outstanding future in Jerusalem—except for the rude interruption of an invasion by Babylon. Both were subsequently taken hostage and deported to the enemy capital, and there the similarity between their lives ends. Whereas Ezekiel spent his days preaching (and acting out) sermons to the Jewish exiles, Daniel was recruited for a job in the king's palace.

In fact, Daniel's life in the palace more closely resembles that of the ancient character Joseph, who also rose to a position of prominence in a foreign government. As this chapter underscores, Daniel achieved success without bending his own principles of integrity. Somehow he managed to thrive in an environment marked by ambition and intrigue, while still holding to his high-minded Jewish ideals.

The Babylonians did their best to purge the young Jews of their heritage. They forced on them new, pagan names, and plied them with wine and food that had been offered to idols. Even the study course for diplomats-in-training was distasteful to a Jew: It covered sorcery, magic, and a pagan, multigod religion. Daniel and his three friends overcame these obstacles and excelled enough to attract the attention of the king. He had to take notice: They were ten times more impressive than anyone else in the kingdom.

Taken together, the biblical prophets offer not one, but many models of how a person can serve both God and the state. On the one extreme stand men like Amos and Elijah, who, as outsiders, railed against the evils of society. Others, such as Jeremiah and Nathan, gave occasional counsel to kings, but kept a safe distance. Isaiah and Samuel, however, became the official advisers of kings. And in this book the prophet Daniel shows that a person can keep pure even while working within a tyrannical regime.

For at least sixty-six years, Daniel served pagan kings with great diligence and resourcefulness. Yet he never once compromised his faith, even when threatened with death. The Bible offers no better model of how to live among people who do not share or respect your beliefs.

To Reflect On: *When have you taken a difficult or unpopular stand as a matter of integrity?*

DANIEL 1

Daniel's Training in Babylon

1 In the third year of the reign of Jehoiakim king of Judah, Nebuchadnezzar king of Babylon came to Jerusalem and besieged it. ²And the Lord delivered Jehoiakim king of Judah into his hand, along with some of the articles from the temple of God. These he carried off to the temple of his god in Babylonia and put in the treasure house of his god.

³Then the king ordered Ashpenaz, chief of his court officials, to bring in some of the Israelites from the royal family and the nobility— ⁴young men without any physical defect, handsome, showing aptitude for every kind of learning, well informed, quick to understand, and qualified to serve in the king's palace. He was to teach them the language and literature of the Babylonians. ⁵The king assigned them a daily amount of food and wine from the king's table. They were to be trained for three years, and after that they were to enter the king's service.

⁶Among these were some from Judah: Daniel, Hananiah, Mishael and Azariah. ⁷The chief official gave them new names: to Daniel, the name Belteshazzar; to Hananiah, Shadrach; to Mishael, Meshach; and to Azariah, Abednego.

⁸But Daniel resolved not to defile himself with the royal food and wine, and he asked the chief official for permission not to defile himself this way. ⁹Now God had caused the official to show favor and sympathy to Daniel, ¹⁰but the official told Daniel, "I am afraid of my lord the king, who has assigned your food and drink. Why should he see you looking worse than the other young men your age? The king would then have my head because of you."

¹¹Daniel then said to the guard whom the chief official had appointed over Daniel, Hananiah, Mishael and Azariah, ¹²"Please test your servants for ten days: Give us nothing but vegetables to eat and water to drink. ¹³Then compare our appearance with that of the young men who eat the royal food, and treat your servants in accordance with what you see." ¹⁴So he agreed to this and tested them for ten days.

¹⁵At the end of the ten days they looked healthier and better nourished than any of the young men who ate the royal food. ¹⁶So the guard took away their choice food and the wine they were to drink and gave them vegetables instead.

¹⁷To these four young men God gave knowledge and understanding of all kinds of literature and learning. And Daniel could understand visions and dreams of all kinds.

¹⁸At the end of the time set by the king to bring them in, the chief official presented them to Nebuchadnezzar. ¹⁹The king talked with them, and he found none equal to Daniel, Hananiah, Mishael and Azariah; so they entered the king's service. ²⁰In every matter of wisdom and understanding about which the king questioned them, he found them ten times better than all the magicians and enchanters in his whole kingdom.

²¹And Daniel remained there until the first year of King Cyrus.

Well-timed Rescue

Daniel 3:1–29

Stories from Daniel have become famous, and in fact any of the first six chapters would make a script for a thriller. This chapter begins with an egocentric decree by a Babylonian ruler so puffed-up that he commissions a skyscraper-size statue of himself. It ends with a rescue so sensational it nearly persuades that ruler to convert to Judaism.

Daniel does not appear in this story (possibly he was away on a diplomatic mission); clearly, if he had been around he would have chosen the same course as his three friends. They saw Nebuchadnezzar's decree as a bottom-line issue of spiritual integrity that brought their dual loyalties into irreconcilable conflict. In this instance, they could not serve both the kingdom of God and the kingdom of Babylon. There could be no compromise.

Idolatry was, in fact, the stubborn sin of Judah that had brought on the Babylonian punishment in the first place. The Jews could never expect God's blessing if they chose to bow down to Nebuchadnezzar and his gold image. The uncompromising response of Daniel's friends shows that the Babylonian captivity was having a "refiner's fire" effect on a whole generation of Jewish exiles.

The book of Daniel makes for exciting reading because, at this most precarious time in Israelite history, God let loose with a burst of miraculous activity: supernatural dreams, handwriting on the wall, rescues from a fiery furnace and a lions' den. Not since Elisha's day had the Israelites seen such signs and wonders.

The story of the fiery furnace has a happy ending, far beyond anything the three courageous Jews might have hoped for. Not only did they survive; the event ensured that Nebuchadnezzar would treat the Jewish religion with tolerance throughout his reign.

The Israelites were still thinking of God in terms of their own small community, their capital city and the temple there. But God had never intended for his blessings to stop with the Jews. He had the world in mind. When he had first revealed the covenant to Abraham, he had promised that Abraham's offspring would bless the whole earth (Genesis 12:3). Over the years, the Jews had found it difficult enough to keep their own faith, let alone spread it to other nations.

Ironically, at a time of deep humiliation, while living as unwilling captives in Babylon, the Jews began to convince others that their God deserved honor. The proclamations by Nebuchadnezzar and later Darius (6:26–27) honored God more than anything a king of Judah had done in years.

> **To Reflect On:** *What do you learn about faith from the reply of Daniel's friends (vv. 15–18)?*

DANIEL 3:1–29

The Image of Gold and the Fiery Furnace

3 King Nebuchadnezzar made an image of gold, ninety feet high and nine feet wide, and set it up on the plain of Dura in the province of Babylon. ²He then summoned the satraps, prefects, governors, advisers, treasurers, judges, magistrates and all the other provincial officials to come to the dedication of the image he had set up. ³So the satraps, prefects, governors, advisers, treasurers, judges, magistrates and all the other provincial officials assembled for the dedication of the image that King Nebuchadnezzar had set up, and they stood before it.

⁴Then the herald loudly proclaimed, "This is what you are commanded to do, O peoples, nations and men of every language: ⁵As soon as you hear the sound of the horn, flute, zither, lyre, harp, pipes and all kinds of music, you must fall down and worship the image of gold that King Nebuchadnezzar has set up. ⁶Whoever does not fall down and worship will immediately be thrown into a blazing furnace."

⁷Therefore, as soon as they heard the sound of the horn, flute, zither, lyre, harp and all kinds of music, all the peoples, nations and men of every language fell down and worshiped the image of gold that King Nebuchadnezzar had set up.

⁸At this time some astrologers came forward and denounced the Jews. ⁹They said to King Nebuchadnezzar, "O king, live forever! ¹⁰You have issued a decree, O king, that everyone who hears the sound of the horn, flute, zither, lyre, harp, pipes and all kinds of music must fall down and worship the image of gold, ¹¹and that whoever does not fall down and worship will be thrown into a blazing furnace. ¹²But there are some Jews whom you have set over the affairs of the province of Babylon—Shadrach, Meshach and Abednego—who pay no attention to you, O king. They neither serve your gods nor worship the image of gold you have set up."

¹³Furious with rage, Nebuchadnezzar summoned Shadrach, Meshach and Abednego. So these men were brought before the king, ¹⁴and Nebuchadnezzar said to them, "Is it true, Shadrach, Meshach and Abednego, that you do not serve my gods or worship the image of gold I have set up? ¹⁵Now when you hear the sound of the horn, flute, zither, lyre, harp, pipes and all kinds of music, if you are ready to fall down and worship the image I made, very good. But if you do not worship it, you will be thrown immediately into a blazing furnace. Then what god will be able to rescue you from my hand?"

¹⁶Shadrach, Meshach and Abednego replied to the king, "O Nebuchadnezzar, we do not need to defend ourselves before you in this matter. ¹⁷If we are thrown into the blazing furnace, the God we serve is able to save us from it, and he will rescue us from

your hand, O king. ¹⁸But even if he does not, we want you to know, O king, that we will not serve your gods or worship the image of gold you have set up."

¹⁹Then Nebuchadnezzar was furious with Shadrach, Meshach and Abednego, and his attitude toward them changed. He ordered the furnace heated seven times hotter than usual ²⁰and commanded some of the strongest soldiers in his army to tie up Shadrach, Meshach and Abednego and throw them into the blazing furnace. ²¹So these men, wearing their robes, trousers, turbans and other clothes, were bound and thrown into the blazing furnace. ²²The king's command was so urgent and the furnace so hot that the flames of the fire killed the soldiers who took up Shadrach, Meshach and Abednego, ²³and these three men, firmly tied, fell into the blazing furnace.

²⁴Then King Nebuchadnezzar leaped to his feet in amazement and asked his advisers, "Weren't there three men that we tied up and threw into the fire?"

They replied, "Certainly, O king."

²⁵He said, "Look! I see four men walking around in the fire, unbound and unharmed, and the fourth looks like a son of the gods."

²⁶Nebuchadnezzar then approached the opening of the blazing furnace and shouted, "Shadrach, Meshach and Abednego, servants of the Most High God, come out! Come here!"

So Shadrach, Meshach and Abednego came out of the fire, ²⁷and the satraps, prefects, governors and royal advisers crowded around them. They saw that the fire had not harmed their bodies, nor was a hair of their heads singed; their robes were not scorched, and there was no smell of fire on them.

²⁸Then Nebuchadnezzar said, "Praise be to the God of Shadrach, Meshach and Abednego, who has sent his angel and rescued his servants! They trusted in him and defied the king's command and were willing to give up their lives rather than serve or worship any god except their own God. ²⁹Therefore I decree that the people of any nation or language who say anything against the God of Shadrach, Meshach and Abednego be cut into pieces and their houses be turned into piles of rubble, for no other god can save in this way."

Like Father, Like Son

Daniel 5

A miracle may make someone sit up and take notice, but it surely does not guarantee long-term change. Despite Nebuchadnezzar's new-found enthusiasm for the God of the Hebrews, in time he apparently forgot all about his religious zeal. Not until a fit of insanity drove him to eat grass like an ox did an alarm sound in his memory (chapter 4).

The king's son Belshazzar, who had grown up in the midst of the flurry of miracles, had an even shorter memory. Chapter 5 introduces the new king at a state orgy as he boozes it up with a thousand nobles and assorted women. They were carousing in a kind of "hurricane party" to show their disdain over reports of enemy armies advancing on the capital. The party even included a religious element, after a fashion: They worshiped idols, and used sacred relics stolen from the temple in Jerusalem to hold their wine.

Belshazzar's raucous party provided the setting for a scene straight out of a horror film: human fingers, eerily disconnected from any hand, wrote a message on the wall. The king trembled and turned pale, but it took the queen to remember the supernatural gifts of an old Jewish prophet. Daniel hadn't changed a bit over the years. He respectfully declined the king's bribes, but interpreted the dream anyway, after delivering an impromptu sermon.

That night, Daniel got another high-ranking appointment to the government of a tyrant. But the job didn't last long. The same night, Babylon fell victim to a sneak attack, and Darius the Mede took over the kingdom.

A phrase has come down from this story—"That's the handwriting on the wall"—to signify a final warning just before the end. The prophets of Israel and Judah had tried to interpret God's "handwriting" for their countrymen, with little success, and God had used Babylon to punish them. Now Babylon, having ignored the warnings of a spiritual giant like Daniel, was itself due for punishment. They had ignored handwriting on the wall long enough.

> **To Reflect On:** *What "handwriting on the wall" might our society be ignoring?*

DANIEL 5

The Writing on the Wall

5 King Belshazzar gave a great banquet for a thousand of his nobles and drank wine with them. ²While Belshazzar was drinking his wine, he gave orders to bring in the gold and silver goblets that Nebuchadnezzar his father had taken from the temple in Jerusalem, so that the king and his nobles, his wives and his concubines might drink from them. ³So they brought in the gold goblets that had been taken from the temple of God in Jerusalem, and the king and his nobles, his wives and his concubines drank from them. ⁴As they drank the wine, they praised the gods of gold and silver, of bronze, iron, wood and stone.

⁵Suddenly the fingers of a human hand appeared and wrote on the plaster of the wall, near the lampstand in the royal palace. The king watched the hand as it wrote. ⁶His face turned pale and he was so frightened that his knees knocked together and his legs gave way.

⁷The king called out for the enchanters, astrologers and diviners to be brought and said to these wise men of Babylon, "Whoever reads this writing and tells me what it means will be clothed in purple and have a gold chain placed around his neck, and he

will be made the third highest ruler in the kingdom."

⁸Then all the king's wise men came in, but they could not read the writing or tell the king what it meant. ⁹So King Belshazzar became even more terrified and his face grew more pale. His nobles were baffled.

¹⁰The queen, hearing the voices of the king and his nobles, came into the banquet hall. "O king, live forever!" she said. "Don't be alarmed! Don't look so pale! ¹¹There is a man in your kingdom who has the spirit of the holy gods in him. In the time of your father he was found to have insight and intelligence and wisdom like that of the gods. King Nebuchadnezzar your father— your father the king, I say—appointed him chief of the magicians, enchanters, astrologers and diviners. ¹²This man Daniel, whom the king called Belteshazzar, was found to have a keen mind and knowledge and understanding, and also the ability to interpret dreams, explain riddles and solve difficult problems. Call for Daniel, and he will tell you what the writing means."

¹³So Daniel was brought before the king, and the king said to him, "Are you Daniel, one of the exiles my father the king brought from Judah? ¹⁴I have heard that the spirit of the gods is in you and that you have insight, intelligence and outstanding wisdom. ¹⁵The wise men and enchanters were brought before me to read this writing and tell me what it means, but they could not explain it. ¹⁶Now I have heard that you are able to give interpretations and to solve difficult problems. If you can read this writing and tell me what it means, you will be clothed in purple and have a gold chain placed around your neck, and you will be made the third highest ruler in the kingdom."

¹⁷Then Daniel answered the king, "You may keep your gifts for yourself and give your rewards to someone else. Nevertheless, I will read the writing for the king and tell him what it means.

¹⁸"O king, the Most High God gave your father Nebuchadnezzar sovereignty and greatness and glory and splendor. ¹⁹Because of the high position he gave him, all the peoples and nations and men of every language dreaded and feared him. Those the king wanted to put to death, he put to death; those he wanted to spare, he spared; those he wanted to promote, he promoted; and those he wanted to humble, he humbled. ²⁰But when his heart became arrogant and hardened with pride, he was deposed from his royal throne and stripped of his glory. ²¹He was driven away from people and given the mind of an animal; he lived with the wild donkeys and ate grass like cattle; and his body was drenched with the dew of heaven, until he acknowledged that the Most High God is sovereign over the kingdoms of men and sets over them anyone he wishes.

²²"But you his son, O Belshazzar, have not humbled yourself, though you knew all this. ²³Instead, you have set yourself up against the Lord of heaven. You had the goblets from his temple brought to you, and you and your nobles, your wives and your concubines drank wine from them. You praised the gods of silver and gold, of bronze, iron, wood and stone, which cannot see or hear or understand. But you did not honor the God who holds in his hand your life and all your ways. ²⁴Therefore he sent the hand that wrote the inscription.

²⁵"This is the inscription that was written:

MENE, MENE, TEKEL, PARSIN

²⁶"This is what these words mean:

Mene: God has numbered the days of your reign and brought it to an end.
²⁷*Tekel:* You have been weighed on the scales and found wanting.
²⁸*Peres:* Your kingdom is divided and given to the Medes and Persians."

²⁹Then at Belshazzar's command, Daniel was clothed in purple, a gold chain was placed around his neck, and he was proclaimed the third highest ruler in the kingdom.

³⁰That very night Belshazzar, king of the Babylonians, was slain, ³¹and Darius the Mede took over the kingdom, at the age of sixty-two.

The Lions' Den

Daniel 6:1–27

This chapter opens with the news that Daniel has a new boss. It is a measure of the prophet's amazing skill that he, an alien, could distinguish himself under two capricious Babylonian regimes, and then under the occupation forces of Medo-Persia. Nevertheless, when news leaked that Daniel would govern the entire kingdom, the palace conspiracy machine kicked into motion.

Daniel must have been in his eighties when the events of this chapter took place. After six decades of service, he finally faced a situation like the one his three friends in the fiery furnace had faced—an unresolvable conflict between the law of God and the law of the land. During those years Daniel had lost much of his Jewish heritage and had even taken on a Babylonian name. Yet, although he could hardly worship God in the way he wished, at the temple in Jerusalem, his devotion to God never wavered. In defiance of the king's new law, the old prophet kept on pointing himself toward Jerusalem three times a day in prayer.

The story of Daniel in the lions' den has special meaning for both Jews and Christians because, sadly, history has repeated itself so often. The Roman Empire, Stalin's Russia, Hitler's Germany, China, Muslim sheikdoms—they've all taken their turn at restricting worship, often enforcing the laws with punishments as cruel as the one described here. Yet the church has survived, and even thrived, during times of intense persecution. Not everyone who undergoes religious persecution receives miraculous deliverance like Daniel's. But, all together, the martyrs have given a witness to the watching world that true faith cannot be stamped out, no matter what the penalty.

A miracle spared Daniel's life. Perhaps an even greater miracle took place in those around him. Stirred by Daniel's faith, the Persian ruler issued a proclamation that everyone in his kingdom must fear and reverence "the God of Daniel." Soon, the very same empire that had passed laws against Jewish worship would escort the Jewish exiles back to their homeland, with official sanction to rebuild the temple.

The harsh times in Babylon had their effect on the Jewish community as well. Led by the examples of people such as Daniel, they began a new practice of meeting together in "synagogues" to study the Law and to pray. And they would return to Palestine purged of the sin that had brought them so much anguish: Jews never again were known to practice idolatry. The refining fire had done its work.

> **To Reflect On:** *Do you know of any irreconcilable conflicts between the law of the land and the law of God today?*

DANIEL 6:1–27

Daniel in the Den of Lions

6 It pleased Darius to appoint 120 satraps to rule throughout the kingdom, ²with three administrators over them, one of whom was Daniel. The satraps were made accountable to them so that the king might not suffer loss. ³Now Daniel so distinguished himself among the administrators and the satraps by his exceptional qualities that the king planned to set him over the whole kingdom. ⁴At this, the administrators and the satraps tried to find grounds for charges against Daniel in his conduct of government affairs, but they were unable to do so. They could find no corruption in him, because he was trustworthy and neither corrupt nor negligent. ⁵Finally these men said, "We will never find any basis for charges against this man Daniel unless it has something to do with the law of his God."

6So the administrators and the satraps went as a group to the king and said: "O King Darius, live forever! 7The royal administrators, prefects, satraps, advisers and governors have all agreed that the king should issue an edict and enforce the decree that anyone who prays to any god or man during the next thirty days, except to you, O king, shall be thrown into the lions' den. 8Now, O king, issue the decree and put it in writing so that it cannot be altered—in accordance with the laws of the Medes and Persians, which cannot be repealed." 9So King Darius put the decree in writing.

10Now when Daniel learned that the decree had been published, he went home to his upstairs room where the windows opened toward Jerusalem. Three times a day he got down on his knees and prayed, giving thanks to his God, just as he had done before. 11Then these men went as a group and found Daniel praying and asking God for help. 12So they went to the king and spoke to him about his royal decree: "Did you not publish a decree that during the next thirty days anyone who prays to any god or man except to you, O king, would be thrown into the lions' den?"

The king answered, "The decree stands—in accordance with the laws of the Medes and Persians, which cannot be repealed."

13Then they said to the king, "Daniel, who is one of the exiles from Judah, pays no attention to you, O king, or to the decree you put in writing. He still prays three times a day." 14When the king heard this, he was greatly distressed; he was determined to rescue Daniel and made every effort until sundown to save him.

15Then the men went as a group to the king and said to him, "Remember, O king, that according to the law of the Medes and Persians no decree or edict that the king issues can be changed."

16So the king gave the order, and they brought Daniel and threw him into the lions' den. The king said to Daniel, "May your God, whom you serve continually, rescue you!"

17A stone was brought and placed over the mouth of the den, and the king sealed it with his own signet ring and with the rings of his nobles, so that Daniel's situation might not be changed. 18Then the king returned to his palace and spent the night without eating and without any entertainment being brought to him. And he could not sleep.

19At the first light of dawn, the king got up and hurried to the lions' den. 20When he came near the den, he called to Daniel in an anguished voice, "Daniel, servant of the living God, has your God, whom you serve continually, been able to rescue you from the lions?"

21Daniel answered, "O king, live forever! 22My God sent his angel, and he shut the mouths of the lions. They have not hurt me, because I was found innocent in his sight. Nor have I ever done any wrong before you, O king."

23The king was overjoyed and gave orders to lift Daniel out of the den. And when Daniel was lifted from the den, no wound was found on him, because he had trusted in his God.

24At the king's command, the men who had falsely accused Daniel were brought in and thrown into the lions' den, along with their wives and children. And before they reached the floor of the den, the lions overpowered them and crushed all their bones.

25Then King Darius wrote to all the peoples, nations and men of every language throughout the land:

"May you prosper greatly!

26"I issue a decree that in every part of my kingdom people must fear and reverence the God of Daniel.

"For he is the living God
  and he endures forever;
 his kingdom will not be destroyed,
  his dominion will never end.
27He rescues and he saves;
  he performs signs and wonders
  in the heavens and on the earth.
He has rescued Daniel
  from the power of the lions."

Back in Jerusalem

Ezra 3:1–4:5

For more than half a century Jewish exiles, among them Daniel and Ezekiel, were held captive in Babylon. Some, like Daniel, prospered in the foreign land; but no true Israelite ever felt totally at peace there. Always, a longing gnawed inside, a longing for home, and for the temple of God. As one poet in exile wrote, "If I forget you, O Jerusalem, may my right hand forget its skill. May my tongue cling to the roof of my mouth if I do not remember you, if I do not consider Jerusalem my highest joy" (Psalm 137:5).

Daniel's new boss, in keeping with the Persian policy of religious tolerance, granted permission for the first wave of Jewish exiles to return to Jerusalem, and the book of Ezra tells their story. The prophets' hopeful visions of a return to the land were coming true at last. And yet the sight that greeted the returning exiles in Jerusalem made them very sad: The city was a ghost town, burned and pillaged years before by the conquering Babylonians. The temple of God was a mound of rubble.

As this chapter relates, the settlers went to work at once, setting temple reconstruction as their highest priority. They had hope: The Persians had even given back the pilfered silver and gold temple articles. When the Jews finally laid the foundation, the sound of their shouting could be heard from far away. The temple, after all, was the place where they would meet God and, as such, symbolized a new start with him.

Yet the shouts of joy mingled with loud cries of weeping as well. The older returnees, those who remembered Solomon's temple in all its splendor, wept at the comparison. They had lost political independence, and needed permission from a foreign government just to rebuild the temple. The Jews had regained only a tiny portion of their former territory. They were very far from the glory days of David and Solomon.

The book of Ezra thus introduces a new period in the Israelites' history—a period in which they became more like a "church" than a nation. Their leaders focused energy not on fighting enemy armies, but on fighting sin and spiritual compromise. They feared repeating the mistakes that had sent them into exile.

To Reflect On: *If a modern city burned to the ground, what buildings would likely be replaced first?*

———————◆———————

EZRA 3:1–4:5

Rebuilding the Altar

3 When the seventh month came and the Israelites had settled in their towns, the people assembled as one man in Jerusalem. ²Then Jeshua son of Jozadak and his fellow priests and Zerubbabel son of Shealtiel and his associates began to build the altar of the God of Israel to sacrifice burnt offerings on it, in accordance with what is written in the Law of Moses the man of God. ³Despite their fear of the peoples around them, they built the altar on its foundation and sacrificed burnt offerings on it to the LORD, both the morning and evening sacrifices. ⁴Then in accordance with what is written, they celebrated the Feast of Tabernacles with the required number of burnt offerings prescribed for each day. ⁵After that, they presented the regular burnt offerings, the New Moon sacrifices and the sacrifices for all the appointed sacred feasts of the LORD, as well as those brought as freewill offerings to the LORD. ⁶On the first day of the seventh month they began to offer burnt offerings to the LORD, though the foundation of the LORD's temple had not yet been laid.

Rebuilding the Temple

⁷Then they gave money to the masons and carpenters, and gave food and drink and oil to the people of Sidon and Tyre, so that they would bring cedar logs by sea from Lebanon to Joppa, as authorized by Cyrus king of Persia.

⁸In the second month of the second year after their arrival at the house of God in Jerusalem, Zerubbabel son of Shealtiel, Jeshua son of Jozadak and the rest of their brothers (the priests and the Levites and all who had returned from the captivity to Jerusalem) began the work, appointing Levites twenty years of age and older to supervise the building of the house of the LORD. ⁹Jeshua and his sons and brothers and Kadmiel and his sons (descendants of Hodaviah) and the sons of Henadad and their sons and brothers—all Levites—joined together in supervising those working on the house of God.

¹⁰When the builders laid the foundation of the temple of the LORD, the priests in their vestments and with trumpets, and the Levites (the sons of Asaph) with cymbals, took their places to praise the LORD, as prescribed by David king of Israel. ¹¹With praise and thanksgiving they sang to the LORD:

"He is good;
his love to Israel endures forever."

And all the people gave a great shout of praise to the LORD, because the foundation of the house of the LORD was laid. ¹²But many of the older priests and Levites and family heads, who had seen the former temple, wept aloud when they saw the foundation of this temple being laid, while many others shouted for joy. ¹³No one could distinguish the sound of the shouts of joy from the sound of weeping, because the people made so much noise. And the sound was heard far away.

Opposition to the Rebuilding

4 When the enemies of Judah and Benjamin heard that the exiles were building a temple for the LORD, the God of Israel, ²they came to Zerubbabel and to the heads of the families and said, "Let us help you build because, like you, we seek your God and have been sacrificing to him since the time of Esarhaddon king of Assyria, who brought us here."

³But Zerubbabel, Jeshua and the rest of the heads of the families of Israel answered, "You have no part with us in building a temple to our God. We alone will build it for the LORD, the God of Israel, as King Cyrus, the king of Persia, commanded us."

⁴Then the peoples around them set out to discourage the people of Judah and make them afraid to go on building. ⁵They hired counselors to work against them and frustrate their plans during the entire reign of Cyrus king of Persia and down to the reign of Darius king of Persia.

A Needed Boost

Haggai 1:1–2:5

The burst of energy described in Ezra did not last long. Opposition soon arose among the tribes bordering Israel, who did not look kindly on the resurgence of a traditional enemy. The temple project especially alarmed them, in view of all the stories they had heard about the miraculous power of Israel's God. And surely, they reasoned, a rebuilt temple would only inflame the Israelites' religious zeal. Even Israel's protector, Persia, began to waver on its promises to the Jews.

In the face of this stiff opposition, the Jews lost enthusiasm, or rather redirected their enthusiasm toward other projects. Just a few years after the exiles' return, work on the temple ground to a halt. The Jews began to concentrate instead on building their own homes and regaining their former prosperity. They had forgotten the original motive for returning to Jerusalem.

About twenty years after the first migration, a prophet named Haggai appeared in Jerusalem to confront the growing apathy and confusion. He did not rage like Jeremiah or act out public object lessons like Ezekiel. He simply urged these pioneers to give careful thought to their situation. "Is it a time for you yourselves to be living in your paneled houses, while this house [the temple] remains a ruin?" he asked.

Haggai put things simply and logically. The settlers had worked hard, but what had it earned them? Their crops were unsuccessful. Their money disappeared as soon as they earned it. Haggai's diagnosis: mistaken priorities. The Israelites needed to put God first, and for starters that meant rebuilding his temple. God's reputation was at stake. If the temple symbolized God's presence, how could he be properly honored when his house lay in ruins?

A statement made by Jesus years later summarizes Haggai's message well: "Do not worry, saying, 'What shall we eat?' or 'What shall we drink?' or 'What shall we wear? . . . But seek first his [God's] kingdom and his righteousness, and all these things will be given to you as well" (Matthew 6:33). Amazingly, Haggai struck an immediate chord of response in his audience. Prophets before him, such as Amos, Isaiah, or Jeremiah, had spoken for decades without seeing such a heartfelt reaction.

To Reflect On: *What tends to distract us from spiritual priorities?*

HAGGAI 1:1–2:5

A Call to Build the House of the LORD

1 In the second year of King Darius, on the first day of the sixth month, the word of the LORD came through the prophet Haggai to Zerubbabel son of Shealtiel, governor of Judah, and to Joshua son of Jehozadak, the high priest:

²This is what the LORD Almighty says: "These people say, 'The time has not yet come for the LORD's house to be built.'"

³Then the word of the LORD came through the prophet Haggai: ⁴"Is it a time for you yourselves to be living in your paneled houses, while this house remains a ruin?"

⁵Now this is what the LORD Almighty says: "Give careful thought to your ways. ⁶You have planted much, but have harvested little. You eat, but never have enough. You drink, but never have your fill. You put on clothes, but are not warm. You earn wages, only to put them in a purse with holes in it."

⁷This is what the LORD Almighty says: "Give careful thought to your ways. ⁸Go up into the mountains and bring down timber and build the house, so that I may take pleasure in it and be honored," says the LORD. ⁹"You expected much, but see, it turned out to be little. What you brought home, I blew away. Why?" declares the LORD Almighty. "Because of my house, which remains a ruin, while each of you is busy with his own house. ¹⁰Therefore, because of you the heavens have withheld their dew and the earth its crops. ¹¹I called for a drought on the fields and the mountains, on the grain, the new wine, the oil and whatever the ground produces, on men and cattle, and on the labor of your hands."

¹²Then Zerubbabel son of Shealtiel, Joshua son of Jehozadak, the high priest, and the whole remnant of the people obeyed the voice of the LORD their God and the message of the prophet Haggai, because the LORD their God had sent him. And the people feared the LORD.

¹³Then Haggai, the LORD's messenger, gave this message of the LORD to the people: "I am with you," declares the LORD. ¹⁴So the LORD stirred up the spirit of Zerubbabel son of Shealtiel, governor of Judah, and the spirit of Joshua son of Jehozadak, the high priest, and the spirit of the whole remnant of the people. They came and began to work on the house of the LORD Almighty, their God, ¹⁵on the twenty-fourth day of the sixth month in the second year of King Darius.

The Promised Glory of the New House

2 On the twenty-first day of the seventh month, the word of the LORD came through the prophet Haggai: ²"Speak to Zerubbabel son of Shealtiel, governor of Judah, to Joshua son of Jehozadak, the high priest, and to the remnant of the people. Ask them, ³'Who of you is left who saw this house in its former glory? How does it look to you now? Does it not seem to you like nothing? ⁴But now be strong, O Zerubbabel,' declares the LORD. 'Be strong, O Joshua son of Jehozadak, the high priest. Be strong, all you people of the land,' declares the LORD, 'and work. For I am with you,' declares the LORD Almighty. ⁵'This is what I covenanted with you when you came out of Egypt. And my Spirit remains among you. Do not fear.'"

Raising Sights

Zechariah 8

Another, younger prophet named Zechariah joined Haggai in his campaign to lift the spirits of the settlers in Jerusalem (Ezra 5:1 lists both these prophets by name). The two had a similar message, but a different approach. Whereas Haggai asked the Jews to look around at their current conditions and then make some needed changes, Zechariah called them to look beyond the present and envision a new Jerusalem, a "City of Truth."

At the time, the pioneers were focusing on immediate goals: the next planting of crops, basic shelter for their families, repopulating the deserted city. Zechariah lifted their sights toward a far more glorious future, when Jerusalem would be a light to the world and people from many nations would stream to the city "because we have heard that God is with you." The prophet gives his prescription for reaching such a state: The new society must be built on justice, honesty, integrity, and peace.

It took years to rebuild the city of Jerusalem, and centuries for Israel to regain some form of political independence. The Jews who labored so hard must have asked themselves often, "Is this all God has in mind for us?" Zechariah replied with a resounding "No!" He insisted that the small refugee community in fact held the key to the world's future: Their new beginning would lead the way to a Messiah who would bring hope to the whole earth.

Following Haggai's lead, Zechariah seized upon the need to rebuild the temple as a vital first step. These prophets saw that as long as the temple lay in ruins, Israel's distinctive character as a people of God was suspect. Together, the two men had a remarkable effect on their countrymen. At their urging, the Jews organized to build again, and within four years the temple was complete. Once more the nation had a central reminder of its original covenant with God.

To Reflect On: *How well does your community measure up to the society God describes in this chapter?*

ZECHARIAH 8

The LORD Promises to Bless Jerusalem

8 Again the word of the LORD Almighty came to me. ²This is what the LORD Almighty says: "I am very jealous for Zion; I am burning with jealousy for her."

³This is what the LORD says: "I will return to Zion and dwell in Jerusalem. Then Jerusalem will be called the City of Truth, and the mountain of the LORD Almighty will be called the Holy Mountain."

⁴This is what the LORD Almighty says: "Once again men and women of ripe old age will sit in the streets of Jerusalem, each with cane in hand because of his age. ⁵The city streets will be filled with boys and girls playing there."

⁶This is what the LORD Almighty says: "It may seem marvelous to the remnant of this people at that time, but will it seem marvelous to me?" declares the LORD Almighty.

⁷This is what the LORD Almighty says: "I will save my people from the countries of the east and the west. ⁸I will bring them back to live in Jerusalem; they will be my people, and I will be faithful and righteous to them as their God."

⁹This is what the LORD Almighty says: "You who now hear these words spoken by the prophets who were there when the foundation was laid for the house of the LORD Almighty, let your hands be strong so that the temple may be built. ¹⁰Before that time there were no wages for man or beast. No one could go about his business safely because of his enemy, for I had turned every man against his neighbor. ¹¹But now I will not deal with the remnant of this people as I did in the past," declares the LORD Almighty.

¹²"The seed will grow well, the vine will yield its fruit, the ground will produce its crops, and the heavens will drop their dew. I will give all these things as an inheritance to the remnant of this people. ¹³As you have been an object of cursing among the nations, O Judah and Israel, so will I save you, and you will be a blessing. Do not be afraid, but let your hands be strong."

¹⁴This is what the LORD Almighty says: "Just as I had determined to bring disaster upon you and showed no pity when your fathers angered me," says the LORD Almighty, ¹⁵"so now I have determined to do good again to Jerusalem and Judah. Do not be afraid. ¹⁶These are the things you are to do: Speak the truth to each other, and render true and sound judgment in your courts; ¹⁷do not plot evil against your neighbor, and do not love to swear falsely. I hate all this," declares the LORD.

¹⁸Again the word of the LORD Almighty came to me. ¹⁹This is what the LORD Almighty says: "The fasts of the fourth, fifth, seventh and tenth months will become joyful and glad occasions and happy festivals for Judah. Therefore love truth and peace."

²⁰This is what the LORD Almighty says: "Many peoples and the inhabitants of many cities will yet come, ²¹and the inhabitants of one city will go to another and say, 'Let us go at once to entreat the LORD and seek the LORD Almighty. I myself am going.' ²²And many peoples and powerful nations will come to Jerusalem to seek the LORD Almighty and to entreat him."

²³This is what the LORD Almighty says: "In those days ten men from all languages and nations will take firm hold of one Jew by the hem of his robe and say, 'Let us go with you, because we have heard that God is with you.'"

A Man for All Seasons

Nehemiah 2

Sixty-five years passed. The Jews had a temple in Jerusalem, yes, but very little beyond that. The holy city was sparsely occupied; most Jews had settled in the outlying villages and towns rather than inside its crumbling walls. Indeed, with all the intermarriage and mixing with foreigners, the entire community seemed on the verge of losing its unique identity. The Jews' cultural and religious heritage was slipping away.

What could stop the downhill slide? One man, a Jewish exile who had stayed behind in Babylon, had an idea. Like Daniel before him, Nehemiah had risen in the ranks of a foreign government (Persia), and was prospering. Nevertheless, his heart was with his countrymen back in Jerusalem, and when he heard the dismaying reports from that city he felt compelled to act. He obtained the king's permission to lead an expedition to Jerusalem with the goal of rebuilding the city's wall.

You would have to live in the ancient world, or in medieval Europe, to fully appreciate the importance of a city wall. In an age when nomadic warriors posed a constant danger, a wall offered a city its only security. It was for lack of a wall that the Jews had scattered among their neighbors and were now facing permanent assimilation into other cultures. By constructing a wall, Nehemiah could help make Jerusalem into a sacred city again and protect its Jewish residents by controlling who else came and went.

Nehemiah stands in a long line of remarkable Israelite leaders such as Moses, Samuel, David, Hezekiah, and Josiah. Strictly speaking, he was not a prophet, although he was surely a man of God. He did not act without prayer, and he did not pray without acting. Although he had enormous skills in management and leadership, he did not seek after earthly status—if he had, he never would have left Persia.

Nehemiah improvised as he went, meeting each new challenge with a combination of business savvy, courage, and dependence on God. He mobilized work crews, fought off opposition, reformed the court system, purified religious practices, and, when necessary, rallied the troops with stirring speeches. And he did all this while ''on leave'' from his responsibilities as statesman in the Persian court.

> **To Reflect On:** *Do you see any secrets of success in this record of Nehemiah's actions?*

NEHEMIAH 2

Artaxerxes Sends Nehemiah to Jerusalem

2 In the month of Nisan in the twentieth year of King Artaxerxes, when wine was brought for him, I took the wine and gave it to the king. I had not been sad in his presence before; ²so the king asked me, "Why does your face look so sad when you are not ill? This can be nothing but sadness of heart."

I was very much afraid, ³but I said to the king, "May the king live forever! Why should my face not look sad when the city where my fathers are buried lies in ruins, and its gates have been destroyed by fire?"

⁴The king said to me, "What is it you want?"

Then I prayed to the God of heaven, ⁵and I answered the king, "If it pleases the king and if your servant has found favor in his sight, let him send me to the city in Judah where my fathers are buried so that I can rebuild it."

⁶Then the king, with the queen sitting beside him, asked me, "How long will your journey take, and when will you get back?" It pleased the king to send me; so I set a time.

⁷I also said to him, "If it pleases the king, may I have letters to the governors of Trans-Euphrates, so that they will provide me safe-conduct until I arrive in Judah? ⁸And may I have a letter to Asaph, keeper of the king's forest, so he will give me timber to make beams for the gates of the citadel by the temple and for the city wall and for the residence I will occupy?" And because the gracious hand of my God was upon me, the king granted my requests. ⁹So I went to the governors of Trans-Euphrates and gave them the king's letters. The king had also sent army officers and cavalry with me.

¹⁰When Sanballat the Horonite and Tobiah the Ammonite official heard about this, they were very much disturbed that someone had come to promote the welfare of the Israelites.

Nehemiah Inspects Jerusalem's Walls

¹¹I went to Jerusalem, and after staying there three days ¹²I set out during the night with a few men. I had not told anyone what my God had put in my heart to do for Jerusalem. There were no mounts with me except the one I was riding on.

¹³By night I went out through the Valley Gate toward the Jackal Well and the Dung Gate, examining the walls of Jerusalem, which had been broken down, and its gates, which had been destroyed by fire. ¹⁴Then I moved on toward the Fountain Gate and the King's Pool, but there was not enough room for my mount to get through; ¹⁵so I went up the valley by night, examining the wall. Finally, I turned back and reentered through the Valley Gate. ¹⁶The officials did not know where I had gone or what I was doing, because as yet I had said nothing to the Jews or the priests or nobles or officials or any others who would be doing the work.

¹⁷Then I said to them, "You see the trouble we are in: Jerusalem lies in ruins, and its gates have been burned with fire. Come, let us rebuild the wall of Jerusalem, and we will no longer be in disgrace." ¹⁸I also told them about the gracious hand of my God upon me and what the king had said to me.

They replied, "Let us start rebuilding." So they began this good work.

¹⁹But when Sanballat the Horonite, Tobiah the Ammonite official and Geshem the Arab heard about it, they mocked and ridiculed us. "What is this you are doing?" they asked. "Are you rebelling against the king?"

²⁰I answered them by saying, "The God of heaven will give us success. We his servants will start rebuilding, but as for you, you have no share in Jerusalem or any claim or historic right to it."

Mourning into Joy

Nehemiah 7:73b–8:18

Nehemiah alone was an impressive leader, but when paired with Ezra he was downright indomitable. The two made a perfect combination. Nehemiah, emboldened by good political connections, inspired others with his hands-on management style and his fearless optimism. Ezra relied more on moral force than on personality. He could trace his priestly lineage all the way back to Moses' brother Aaron, and he seemed singularly determined to restore integrity to that office.

On his arrival in Jerusalem some years before, Ezra had been shocked by the Jews' spiritual apathy. Rather than mounting a soapbox and scolding them for their failures, he tore his hair and beard, threw himself on the ground, and began a fast of repentance (see Ezra 9). His remarkable display of contrition so startled the Jewish settlers that they all agreed to repent and change their ways. Ezra had that kind of moral influence over people.

The action in this chapter takes place after Nehemiah has completed the arduous task of repairing the wall. The Jews, safe at last from their enemies, gather together in hopes of regaining some sense of national identity. As spiritual leader, Ezra is chosen to address the huge crowd. He stands on a newly built platform and begins to read from a document nearly 1000 years old, the scroll that contains the Israelites' original covenant with God.

As Ezra reads the ancient words, a sound begins to rise, spreading through the multitude. It is the sound of weeping. The Bible does not explain the reason for the tears. Were the people feeling guilt over their long history of breaking that covenant? Or nostalgia over the favored days when Israel had full independence? Whatever the reason, this was no time for tears. Nehemiah and Ezra sent out orders to prepare for a huge feast and celebration. God wanted joy, not mourning. His chosen people were being rebuilt, just as surely as the stone walls of Jerusalem had been rebuilt.

The central image of this chapter—a lone figure atop a wooden platform reading from a scroll—came to symbolize the Jewish race. They were becoming "people of the Book." The Jews had not regained the territory and splendor their nation once enjoyed under David and Solomon. The temple they had painstakingly constructed would eventually fall to looters, just like the one it replaced. But they would never forget the lesson of Ezra. He became the prototype for a new leader of the Jews: the scribe, a student of Scripture.

> **To Reflect On:** *How important is the Bible in your own life?*

Do Not Weep - Rejoice

NEHEMIAH 7:73b–8:18

Ezra Reads the Law

When the seventh month came and the

8 Israelites had settled in their towns, ¹all the people assembled as one man in the square before the Water Gate. They told Ezra the scribe to bring out the Book of the Law of Moses, which the Lord had commanded for Israel.

²So on the first day of the seventh month Ezra the priest brought the Law before the assembly, which was made up of men and women and all who were able to understand. ³He read it aloud from daybreak till noon as he faced the square before the Water Gate in the presence of the men, women and others who could understand. And all the people listened attentively to the Book of the Law.

⁴Ezra the scribe stood on a high wooden platform built for the occasion. Beside him on his right stood Mattithiah, Shema, Anaiah, Uriah, Hilkiah and Maaseiah; and on his left were Pedaiah, Mishael, Malkijah, Hashum, Hashbaddanah, Zechariah and Meshullam.

⁵Ezra opened the book. All the people could see him because he was standing above them; and as he opened it, the people all stood up. ⁶Ezra praised the Lord, the great God; and all the people lifted their hands and responded, "Amen! Amen!" Then they bowed down and worshiped the Lord with their faces to the ground.

⁷The Levites—Jeshua, Bani, Sherebiah, Jamin, Akkub, Shabbethai, Hodiah, Maaseiah, Kelita, Azariah, Jozabad, Hanan and Pelaiah—instructed the people in the Law while the people were standing there. ⁸They read from the Book of the Law of God, making it clear and giving the meaning so that the people could understand what was being read.

⁹Then Nehemiah the governor, Ezra the priest and scribe, and the Levites who were instructing the people said to them all,

"This day is sacred to the Lord your God. Do not mourn or weep." For all the people had been weeping as they listened to the words of the Law.

¹⁰Nehemiah said, "Go and enjoy choice food and sweet drinks, and send some to those who have nothing prepared. This day is sacred to our Lord. Do not grieve, for the joy of the Lord is your strength."

¹¹The Levites calmed all the people saying, "Be still, for this is a sacred day. Do not grieve."

¹²Then all the people went away to eat and drink, to send portions of food and to celebrate with great joy, because they now understood the words that had been made known to them.

¹³On the second day of the month, the heads of all the families, along with the priests and the Levites, gathered around Ezra the scribe to give attention to the words of the Law. ¹⁴They found written in the Law, which the Lord had commanded through Moses, that the Israelites were to live in booths during the feast of the seventh month ¹⁵and that they should proclaim this word and spread it throughout their towns and in Jerusalem: "Go out into the hill country and bring back branches from olive and wild olive trees, and from myrtles, palms and shade trees, to make booths"—as it is written.

¹⁶So the people went out and brought back branches and built themselves booths on their own roofs, in their courtyards, in the courts of the house of God and in the square by the Water Gate and the one by the Gate of Ephraim. ¹⁷The whole company that had returned from exile built booths and lived in them. From the days of Joshua son of Nun until that day, the Israelites had not celebrated it like this. And their joy was very great.

¹⁸Day after day, from the first day to the last, Ezra read from the Book of the Law of God. They celebrated the feast for seven days, and on the eighth day, in accordance with the regulation, there was an assembly.

Jews Who Stayed Behind

Esther 3:8—4:17

Not every Jewish exile took the opportunity to return to the homeland. Some had put down roots during the half-century of Babylonian Captivity, and when the more tolerant Persian regime took over, many of these decided to stay. (Communities of Jews in present-day Iraq and Syria still trace their ancestry to this group of exiles.) This adventure story concerns one such Jew who stayed behind, a beautiful woman named Esther.

The Jews in Persia faced a grave crisis. Their success had attracted so much jealousy that a powerful man was leading a conspiracy to kill every Jew in the land. Tragically, the underlying "plot" of Esther is an old and familiar one to Jews, for throughout history—Roman campaigns, medieval Jew-hunts, Russian pogroms, Hitler's "final solution"—no other group has faced such a constant threat of extermination.

Although the book of Esther never once mentions the word *God*, the story highlights the many "coincidences" that worked together on the Jews' behalf. By the "accident" of her beauty and the "accident" of the former queen's dismissal, Esther had risen from obscurity to become queen of the Persian Empire, one of the greatest powers of the world. She alone, of all the Jews, had access to the king. As her cousin Mordecai put it, "Who knows but that you have come to royal position for such a time as this?"

Yet in those days, a queen did not easily stand up to her husband—especially a husband like Xerxes, who had already summarily dismissed one queen for insubordination. By intervening for the sake of her race, Esther might be putting her own life in jeopardy. This portion of the book spells out Esther's dilemma, and tells the decision she finally reached. The rest of the book records a series of twists of plot: The Jews are spared, even honored, and the original conspirator is hanged in their place.

Esther's story is a thrilling chapter in the story of God's love for the Jews. While no other group has been so persecuted, no other group has shown the Jews' ability to overcome adversity. How? Esther reveals God's exquisite timing, combined with the courage of individuals who "happened" to be in the right place at the right time.

> **To Reflect On:** *Someone has called coincidences "God's way of working anonymously." Do you tend to give God credit for the "coincidences" in your life?*

ESTHER 3:8–4:17

Haman's Plot to Destroy the Jews

⁸Then Haman said to King Xerxes, "There is a certain people dispersed and scattered among the peoples in all the provinces of your kingdom whose customs are different from those of all other people and who do not obey the king's laws; it is not in the king's best interest to tolerate them. ⁹If it pleases the king, let a decree be issued to destroy them, and I will put ten thousand talents of silver into the royal treasury for the men who carry out this business."

¹⁰So the king took his signet ring from his finger and gave it to Haman son of Hammedatha, the Agagite, the enemy of the Jews. ¹¹"Keep the money," the king said to Haman, "and do with the people as you please."

¹²Then on the thirteenth day of the first month the royal secretaries were summoned. They wrote out in the script of each province and in the language of each people all Haman's orders to the king's satraps, the governors of the various provinces and the nobles of the various peoples. These were written in the name of King Xerxes himself and sealed with his own ring. ¹³Dispatches were sent by couriers to all the king's provinces with the oder to destroy, kill and annihilate all the Jews—young and old, women and little children—on a single day, the thirteenth day of the twelfth month, the month of Adar, and to plunder their goods. ¹⁴A copy of the text of the edict was to be issued as law in every province and made known to the people of every nationality so they would be ready for that day.

¹⁵Spurred on by the king's command, the couriers went out, and the edict was issued in the citadel of Susa. The king and Haman sat down to drink, but the city of Susa was bewildered.

Mordecai Persuades Esther to Help

4 When Mordecai learned of all that had been done, he tore his clothes, put on sackcloth and ashes, and went out into the city, wailing loudly and bitterly. ²But he went only as far as the king's gate, because no one clothed in sackcloth was allowed to enter it. ³In every province to which the edict and order of the king came, there was great mourning among the Jews, with fasting, weeping and wailing. Many lay in sackcloth and ashes.

⁴When Esther's maids and eunuchs came and told her about Mordecai, she was in great distress. She sent clothes for him to put on instead of his sackcloth, but he would not accept them. ⁵Then Esther summoned Hathach, one of the king's eunuchs assigned to attend her, and ordered him to find out what was troubling Mordecai and why.

⁶So Hathach went out to Mordecai in the open square of the city in front of the king's gate. ⁷Mordecai told him everything that had happened to him, including the exact amount of money Haman had promised to pay into the royal treasury for the destruction of the Jews. ⁸He also gave him a copy of the text of the edict for their annihilation, which had been published in Susa, to show to Esther and explain it to her, and he told him to urge her to go into the king's presence to beg for mercy and plead with him for her people.

⁹Hathach went back and reported to Esther what Mordecai had said. ¹⁰Then she instructed him to say to Mordecai, ¹¹"All the king's officials and the people of the royal provinces know that for any man or woman who approaches the king in the inner court without being summoned the king has but one law: that he be put to death. The only exception to this is for the king to extend the gold scepter to him and spare his life. But thirty days have passed since I was called to go to the king."

¹²When Esther's words were reported to Mordecai, ¹³he sent back this answer: "Do not think that because you are in the king's house you alone of all the Jews will escape. ¹⁴For if you remain silent at this time, relief and deliverance for the Jews will arise from another place, but you and your father's family will perish. And who knows but that you have come to royal position for such a time as this?"

¹⁵Then Esther sent this reply to Mordecai: ¹⁶"Go, gather together all the Jews who are in Susa, and fast for me. Do not eat or drink for three days, night or day. I and my maids will fast as you do. When this is done, I will go to the king, even though it is against the law. And if I perish, I perish."

¹⁷So Mordecai went away and carried out all of Esther's instructions.

Crushed Hopes

Malachi 2:17–3:18

Malachi is the last Old Testament voice, and his book serves as a good prelude to the next 400 years of biblical silence. From the Israelites' point of view, those four centuries could be termed "the era of lowered expectations." They had returned to the land, but that land remained a backwater province under the domination of Persia (then Greece, then Rome—imperial armies took turns tramping through Israel). The grand future of triumph and world peace described by the prophets seemed a distant pipe dream. Even the restored temple caused stabs of nostalgic pain: It hardly rivaled Solomon's majestic building, and no one had seen God's glory descend on this new temple as it had in Solomon's day.

A general malaise set in among the Jews, a low-grade disappointment with God that showed in their complaints and also in their actions. They were not "big" sinners like the people before the Exile, who had practiced child sacrifice and brought idols into the temple. People in Malachi's time went through the motions of their religion, but they had lost contact with the God whom the religion was all about.

Malachi is written in the form of a dialogue, with the "children" of Israel bringing their grievances to God, the Father. They were questioning God's love and his fairness. One gripe bothered them more than any: "It is futile to serve God. What did we gain by carrying out his requirements?" Following God had not brought the anticipated reward.

In reply, Malachi calls his people to rise above their selfishness and to trust the God of the covenant; he has not abandoned his treasured possession. "Test me," says God, "and see if I will not throw open the floodgates of heaven and pour out so much blessing that you will not have room enough for it."

At least some of Malachi's message took hold. During the next 400 years, reform movements like the Pharisees became increasingly devoted to keeping the Law. Unfortunately, many of them would cling fiercely to that Law even when Jesus, the "messenger of the covenant" prophesied by Malachi, brought a new message of forgiveness and grace.

> **To Reflect On:** *What treatments does God offer for the Israelites' "lukewarm" faith?*

MALACHI 2:17–3:18

The Day of Judgment

¹⁷You have wearied the Lord with your words.

"How have we wearied him?" you ask.

By saying, "All who do evil are good in the eyes of the LORD, and he is pleased with them" or "Where is the God of justice?"

3 "See, I will send my messenger, who will prepare the way before me. Then suddenly the Lord you are seeking will come to his temple; the messenger of the covenant, whom you desire, will come," says the LORD Almighty.

²But who can endure the day of his coming? Who can stand when he appears? For he will be like a refiner's fire or a launderer's soap. ³He will sit as a refiner and purifier of silver; he will purify the Levites and refine them like gold and silver. Then the LORD will have men who will bring offerings in righteousness, ⁴and the offerings of Judah and Jerusalem will be acceptable to the LORD, as in days gone by, as in former years.

⁵"So I will come near to you for judgment. I will be quick to testify against sorcerers, adulterers and perjurers, against those who defraud laborers of their wages, who oppress the widows and the fatherless, and deprive aliens of justice, but do not fear me," says the LORD Almighty.

Robbing God

⁶"I the LORD do not change. So you, O descendants of Jacob, are not destroyed. ⁷Ever since the time of your forefathers you have turned away from my decrees and have not kept them. Return to me, and I will return to you," says the LORD Almighty.

"But you ask, 'How are we to return?' ⁸"Will a man rob God? Yet you rob me.

"But you ask, 'How do we rob you?'

"In tithes and offerings. ⁹You are under a curse—the whole nation of you—because you are robbing me. ¹⁰Bring the whole tithe into the storehouse, that there may be food in my house. Test me in this," says the LORD Almighty, "and see if I will not throw open the floodgates of heaven and pour out so much blessing that you will not have room enough for it. ¹¹I will prevent pests from devouring your crops, and the vines in your fields will not cast their fruit," says the LORD Almighty. ¹²"Then all the nations will call you blessed, for yours will be a delightful land," says the LORD Almighty.

¹³"You have said harsh things against me," says the LORD.

"Yet you ask, 'What have we said against you?'

¹⁴"You have said, 'It is futile to serve God. What did we gain by carrying out his requirements and going about like mourners before the LORD Almighty? ¹⁵But now we call the arrogant blessed. Certainly the evildoers prosper, and even those who challenge God escape.'"

¹⁶Then those who feared the LORD talked with each other, and the LORD listened and heard. A scroll of remembrance was written in his presence concerning those who feared the LORD and honored his name.

¹⁷"They will be mine," says the LORD Almighty, "in the day when I make up my treasured possession. I will spare them, just as in compassion a man spares his son who serves him. ¹⁸And you will again see the distinction between the righteous and the wicked, between those who serve God and those who do not."

Is God Unfair?

Job 1–2:10

One book of the Bible is virtually ageless. It relates the story of Job, a rich "patriarch" who could have lived in Abraham's time, but whose story was probably reduced to this poetic form hundreds of years later, during Israel's literary Golden Age. Regardless, the book raises questions so urgent and universal that it speaks to every era. In recent times, authors like Robert Frost, Archibald MacLeish, and Muriel Spark have all tried their hand at retelling the story of Job.

In the period between the Old and New Testaments, Job became a favorite of the Jews (as proven by the ancient commentaries archaeologists have unearthed). His story centers around a question that haunted the Jews from the earliest days, when they were first chosen as God's covenant people. Somehow, they expected better treatment. Job had the courage to voice the question aloud—*Is God unfair?*—and no one has asked that question more eloquently or profoundly.

The book seems meant to explore the outer limits of unfairness. Job, the most upright, outstanding man in all the earth, must endure the worst calamities. He suffers unbearable punishment—but for what? What has he done wrong?

The book reads like a detective story in which the readers know far more than the central characters. The very first chapter answers Job's main concern: He has done nothing to deserve such suffering. We, the readers, know that, but nobody tells Job and his friends. As the prologue reveals, Job was involved in a cosmic test, a contest proposed in heaven but staged on earth.

People in Malachi's day had asked, "What do we gain by following God?" and that question gets at the heart of Job's test. Satan had claimed that people love God *only* because of his good gifts. According to Satan, no one would ever follow God apart from some selfish gain. *Of course*, Job was blameless and upright; he was also rich and healthy. Remove those good things from Job's life, Satan challenged, and watch Job's faith melt away. Or so Satan thought.

God's reputation is on the line in this book; it rests suspensefully on the response of a devastated, miserable man. Will Job continue to trust God, even as his world crashes down around him? Will he believe in a God of justice, even when life seems grotesquely unfair?

To Reflect On: *When have you questioned "why bad things happen to good people"?*

JOB 1–2:10

Prologue

1 In the land of Uz there lived a man whose name was Job. This man was blameless and upright; he feared God and shunned evil. ²He had seven sons and three daughters, ³and he owned seven thousand sheep, three thousand camels, five hundred yoke of oxen and five hundred donkeys, and had a large number of servants. He was the greatest man among all the people of the East.

⁴His sons used to take turns holding feasts in their homes, and they would invite their three sisters to eat and drink with them. ⁵When a period of feasting had run its course, Job would send and have them purified. Early in the morning he would sacrifice a burnt offering for each of them, thinking, "Perhaps my children have sinned

and cursed God in their hearts." This was Job's regular custom.

Job's First Test

⁶One day the angels came to present themselves before the Lord, and Satan also came with them. ⁷The Lord said to Satan, "Where have you come from?"

Satan answered the Lord, "From roaming through the earth and going back and forth in it."

⁸Then the Lord said to Satan, "Have you considered my servant Job? There is no one on earth like him; he is blameless and upright, a man who fears God and shuns evil."

⁹"Does Job fear God for nothing?" Satan replied. ¹⁰"Have you not put a hedge around him and his household and everything he has? You have blessed the work of his hands, so that his flocks and herds are spread throughout the land. ¹¹But stretch out your hand and strike everything he has, and he will surely curse you to your face."

¹²The Lord said to Satan, "Very well, then, everything he has is in your hands, but on the man himself do not lay a finger."

Then Satan went out from the presence of the Lord.

¹³One day when Job's sons and daughters were feasting and drinking wine at the oldest brother's house, ¹⁴a messenger came to Job and said, "The oxen were plowing and the donkeys were grazing nearby, ¹⁵and the Sabeans attacked and carried them off. They put the servants to the sword, and I am the only one who has escaped to tell you!"

¹⁶While he was still speaking, another messenger came and said, "The fire of God fell from the sky and burned up the sheep and the servants, and I am the only one who has escaped to tell you!"

¹⁷While he was still speaking, another messenger came and said, "The Chaldeans formed three raiding parties and swept down on your camels and carried them off. They put the servants to the sword, and I am the only one who has escaped to tell you!"

¹⁸While he was still speaking, yet another messenger came and said, "Your sons and daughters were feasting and drinking wine at the oldest brother's house, ¹⁹when suddenly a mighty wind swept in from the desert and struck the four corners of the house. It collapsed on them and they are dead, and I am the only one who has escaped to tell you!"

²⁰At this, Job got up and tore his robe and shaved his head. Then he fell to the ground in worship ²¹and said:

"Naked I came from my mother's
  womb,
  and naked I will depart.
The Lord gave and the Lord has taken
  away;
  may the name of the Lord be
  praised."

²²In all this, Job did not sin by charging God with wrongdoing.

Job's Second Test

2 On another day the angels came to present themselves before the Lord, and Satan also came with them to present himself before him. ²And the Lord said to Satan, "Where have you come from?"

Satan answered the Lord, "From roaming through the earth and going back and forth in it."

³Then the Lord said to Satan, "Have you considered my servant Job? There is no one on earth like him; he is blameless and upright, a man who fears God and shuns evil. And he still maintains his integrity, though you incited me against him to ruin him without any reason."

⁴"Skin for skin!" Satan replied. "A man will give all he has for his own life. ⁵But stretch out your hand and strike his flesh and bones, and he will surely curse you to your face."

⁶The Lord said to Satan, "Very well, then, he is in your hands; but you must spare his life."

⁷So Satan went out from the presence of the Lord and afflicted Job with painful sores from the soles of his feet to the top of his head. ⁸Then Job took a piece of broken pottery and scraped himself with it as he sat among the ashes.

⁹His wife said to him, "Are you still holding on to your integrity? Curse God and die!"

¹⁰He replied, "You are talking like a foolish woman. Shall we accept good from God, and not trouble?"

In all this, Job did not sin in what he said.

Blast from the Storm

Job 38

It seems a travesty to skip thirty-five chapters and rush to the conclusion, for those middle chapters of Job express the human dilemma as well as it has ever been expressed. Like all grieving persons, Job drifted on emotional currents, alternately whining, exploding, cajoling, and collapsing into self-pity. Sometimes he agreed with his friends, who blamed Job himself for his suffering, and sometimes he violently disagreed. Occasionally, in the midst of deepest despair, he would come up with a statement of brilliant hope.

Nearly every argument on the problem of pain appears somewhere in the book of Job, but the arguing never seemed to help Job much. His was a crisis of relationship more than a crisis of intellectual doubt. *Could he trust God?* Job wanted one thing above all else: an appearance by the one Person who could explain his miserable fate. He wanted to meet God himself, face to face.

Eventually, as this chapter relates, Job got his wish. God showed up in person. He timed his entrance with perfect irony, just as Elihu was expounding on why Job had no right to expect a visit from God.

No one—not Job, nor any of his friends—was prepared for what God had to say. Job had saved up a long list of questions, but it was God, not Job, who asked the questions. "Brace yourself like a man," he began; "I will question you, and you shall answer me." Brushing aside thirty-five chapters' worth of debates on the problem of pain, God plunged instead into a majestic poem on the wonders of the natural world. He guided Job through the gallery of creation, pointing out with pride such favorites as mountain goats, wild donkeys, ostriches, and eagles.

Above all, God's speech defined the vast difference between a God of all creation and one puny man like Job. "Do you have an arm like God's?" he asked at one point (40:9). God reeled off natural phenomena—the solar system, constellations, thunderstorms, wild animals—that Job could not begin to explain. God's point was obvious: If you can't comprehend the visible world you live in, how dare you expect to comprehend a world you cannot even see!

To Reflect On: *Does God's reply to Job surprise you? In Job's place, what kind of answer would you have wanted from God?*

JOB 38

The LORD Speaks

38 Then the LORD answered Job out of the storm. He said:

2 "Who is this that darkens my counsel
  with words without knowledge?
3 Brace yourself like a man;
  I will question you,
  and you shall answer me.

4 "Where were you when I laid the
    earth's foundation?
  Tell me, if you understand.
5 Who marked off its dimensions? Surely
      you know!
  Who stretched a measuring line
    across it?
6 On what were its footings set,
  or who laid its cornerstone—
7 while the morning stars sang together
  and all the angels shouted for joy?

8 "Who shut up the sea behind doors
  when it burst forth from the womb,
9 when I made the clouds its garment
  and wrapped it in thick darkness,

¹⁰when I fixed limits for it
    and set its doors and bars in place,
¹¹when I said, 'This far you may come
    and no farther;
    here is where your proud waves
        halt'?

¹²"Have you ever given orders to the
        morning,
    or shown the dawn its place,
¹³that it might take the earth by the
        edges
    and shake the wicked out of it?
¹⁴The earth takes shape like clay under
    a seal;
    its features stand out like those of a
        garment.
¹⁵The wicked are denied their light,
    and their upraised arm is broken.

¹⁶"Have you journeyed to the springs of
        the sea
    or walked in the recesses of the
        deep?
¹⁷Have the gates of death been shown
    to you?
    Have you seen the gates of the
        shadow of death?
¹⁸Have you comprehended the vast
        expanses of the earth?
    Tell me, if you know all this.

¹⁹"What is the way to the abode of
        light?
    And where does darkness reside?
²⁰Can you take them to their places?
    Do you know the paths to their
        dwellings?
²¹Surely you know, for you were already
        born!
    You have lived so many years!

²²"Have you entered the storehouses of
        the snow
    or seen the storehouses of the hail,
²³which I reserve for times of trouble,
    for days of war and battle?
²⁴What is the way to the place where
        the lightning is dispersed,
    or the place where the east winds
        are scattered over the earth?

²⁵Who cuts a channel for the torrents of
        rain,
    and a path for the thunderstorm,
²⁶to water a land where no man lives,
    a desert with no one in it,
²⁷to satisfy a desolate wasteland
    and make it sprout with grass?
²⁸Does the rain have a father?
    Who fathers the drops of dew?
²⁹From whose womb comes the ice?
    Who gives birth to the frost from the
        heavens
³⁰when the waters become hard as
        stone,
    when the surface of the deep is
        frozen?

³¹"Can you bind the beautiful Pleiades?
    Can you loose the cords of Orion?
³²Can you bring forth the constellations
        in their seasons
    or lead out the Bear with its cubs?
³³Do you know the laws of the heavens?
    Can you set up [God's] dominion
        over the earth?

³⁴"Can you raise your voice to the
        clouds
    and cover yourself with a flood of
        water?
³⁵Do you send the lightning bolts on
        their way?
    Do they report to you, 'Here we
        are'?
³⁶Who endowed the heart with wisdom
    or gave understanding to the mind?
³⁷Who has the wisdom to count the
        clouds?
    Who can tip over the water jars of
        the heavens
³⁸when the dust becomes hard
    and the clods of earth stick together?

³⁹"Do you hunt the prey for the lioness
    and satisfy the hunger of the lions
⁴⁰when they crouch in their dens
    or lie in wait in a thicket?
⁴¹Who provides food for the raven
    when its young cry out to God
    and wander about for lack of food?

Job's Happy Ending

Job 42

The impact of God's speech on Job was almost as amazing as the speech itself. Although his complaints about suffering and unfairness did not even come up, Job seemed satisfied—humiliated, actually—by the blast from the storm. What God said was not nearly so important as the mere fact that he showed up. His presence spectacularly answered Job's biggest question: Is anybody out there? "Surely I spoke of things I did not understand," Job confessed, "things too wonderful for me to know." Catching sight of the big picture at last, Job repented in dust and ashes.

God had some words of correction for Job: No one, not Job and especially not his friends, had the evidence needed to make judgments about how he ran the world. But mainly God praised Job, calling him "my servant." (Ezekiel 14:14 mentions Job in God's list of the finest human examples of righteousness.)

Satan had wagered with God that Job would "surely curse you to your face." He lost that wager. Despite all that happened, Job did not curse God. He clung to his belief in a just God even though everything in his experience seemed to contradict it. Significantly, Job spoke his contrite words *before* any of his losses had been restored, while still sitting in a pile of ashes, naked, covered with sores. He had learned to believe even in the dark, with no hope of reward.

The book of Job ends with some surprising twists. Job's friends, who had spouted all the right pieties and cliches, had to plead for forgiveness. Job, who had raged and cried out, received twice as much as he ever had before: 14,000 sheep, 6000 camels, 1000 donkeys, and 10 new children.

The book of Job gave much comfort to Jews during the harsh period between the Old and New Testaments. It demonstrated the important lesson that not all suffering comes as punishment; a person's trials may, in fact, be used to win a great spiritual victory. And the happy ending of Job also echoed the promises of the prophets, awakening hopes for a future time of peace and restoration.

Christians, looking back, see yet another message in Job, who stands as an early prototype of the Messiah. Job, the best man of his day, suffered terribly; Jesus, a perfect man, would suffer even more.

To Reflect On: *Have you experienced any Job-like trials in your life? What was their result?*

JOB 42

Job

42 Then Job replied to the LORD:

2"I know that you can do all things;
no plan of yours can be thwarted.
3[You asked,] 'Who is this that obscures
my counsel without
knowledge?'
Surely I spoke of things I did not
understand,
things too wonderful for me to
know.

4["You said,] 'Listen now, and I will
speak;
I will question you,
and you shall answer me.'
5My ears had heard of you
but now my eyes have seen you.
6Therefore I despise myself
and repent in dust and ashes."

Epilogue

7After the LORD had said these things to
Job, he said to Eliphaz the Temanite, "I am
angry with you and your two friends,
because you have not spoken of me what is
right, as my servant Job has. 8So now take
seven bulls and seven rams and go to my
servant Job and sacrifice a burnt offering for
yourselves. My servant Job will pray for
you, and I will accept his prayer and not
deal with you according to your folly. You
have not spoken of me what is right, as my
servant Job has." 9So Eliphaz the Temanite,
Bildad the Shuhite and Zophar the Naam-
athite did what the LORD told them; and the
LORD accepted Job's prayer.

10After Job had prayed for his friends,
the LORD made him prosperous again and
gave him twice as much as he had before.
11All his brothers and sisters and everyone
who had known him before came and ate
with him in his house. They comforted and
consoled him over all the trouble the LORD
had brought upon him, and each one gave
him a piece of silver and a gold ring.

12The LORD blessed the latter part of Job's
life more than the first. He had fourteen
thousand sheep, six thousand camels, a
thousand yoke of oxen and a thousand
donkeys. 13And he also had seven sons and
three daughters. 14The first daughter he
named Jemimah, the second Keziah and the
third Keren-Happuch. 15Nowhere in all the
land were there found women as beautiful
as Job's daughters, and their father granted
them an inheritance along with their
brothers.

16After this, Job lived a hundred and
forty years; he saw his children and their
children to the fourth generation. 17And so
he died, old and full of years.

Who's in Charge?

Isaiah 40:6b–31

The book of Job concerns the sufferings of one man. The prophets of Israel and Judah spoke to the sufferings of an entire race. Their history had begun with God's covenant with Abraham and had culminated in a splendid nation centered in Jerusalem, where God dwelt in a temple. But now the Jews were scattered across the Middle East, dispersed by Assyrian and Babylonian armies. The minority who had returned to Jerusalem lived under the total domination of a foreign government in Persia. The same questions Job had asked while scratching himself with shards of pottery, the Jews asked about their race. Had God abandoned them? Would they have a future?

The Jews' hope for the future centered in a Messiah, who had been promised by almost all the prophets. After Malachi, as the years dragged on, the Jews scoured the scrolls of these prophets, seeking clues into their destiny. Of all the prophets, Isaiah gives perhaps the clearest picture of what the Jews might expect. His earlier messages blasted his nation's sin and unfaithfulness. But beginning with chapter 40, Isaiah shifts into a new key. Gone are the bleak predictions of judgment. Instead, a message of hope and joy breaks in. "Speak tenderly to Jerusalem, and proclaim to her that her hard service has been completed. . . ."

According to Isaiah, what happened to Judah was not God's defeat. God had in mind a new thing, a plan far more wonderful than anything seen before. In words that have become familiar, the book of Isaiah explains why the future holds hope—not just for the Jews, but for the whole world. A mysterious figure called "the servant" would, through his suffering, provide a means of rescue. Later, in a faraway time, God would usher in peace for all in a new heaven and new earth.

Chapter 40 introduces this last section of Isaiah with the sweeping declaration that God reigns over all. In many ways, these soaring words restate in global terms God's personal message to Job. "Surely the nations are like a drop in a bucket. . . . He sits enthroned above the circle of the earth, and its people are like grasshoppers." God shows himself master of nature, of history, indeed, of the entire universe.

> **To Reflect On:** *Why are there so many rhetorical questions in this chapter? What effect is the author trying to produce?*

ISAIAH 40:6b–31

Comfort for God's People

"All men are like grass,
  and all their glory is like the flowers
    of the field.
7 The grass withers and the flowers fall,
  because the breath of the LORD blows
    on them.
  Surely the people are grass.
8 The grass withers and the flowers fall,
  but the word of our God stands
    forever."

9 You who bring good tidings to Zion,
  go up on a high mountain.
You who bring good tidings to
    Jerusalem,
  lift up your voice with a shout,
lift it up, do not be afraid;
  say to the towns of Judah,
  "Here is your God!"
10 See, the Sovereign LORD comes with
    power,
  and his arm rules for him.
See, his reward is with him,
  and his recompense accompanies
    him.
11 He tends his flock like a shepherd:

He gathers the lambs in his arms
and carries them close to his heart;
he gently leads those that have
young.

¹²Who has measured the waters in the
hollow of his hand,
or with the breadth of his hand
marked off the heavens?
Who has held the dust of the earth in
a basket,
or weighed the mountains on the
scales
and the hills in a balance?
¹³Who has understood the mind of the
LORD,
or instructed him as his counselor?
¹⁴Whom did the LORD consult to
enlighten him,
and who taught him the right way?
Who was it that taught him knowledge
or showed him the path of
understanding?

¹⁵Surely the nations are like a drop in a
bucket;
they are regarded as dust on the
scales;
he weighs the islands as though they
were fine dust.
¹⁶Lebanon is not sufficient for altar fires,
nor its animals enough for burnt
offerings.
¹⁷Before him all the nations are as
nothing;
they are regarded by him as
worthless
and less than nothing.

¹⁸To whom, then, will you compare
God?
What image will you compare him
to?
¹⁹As for an idol, a craftsman casts it,
and a goldsmith overlays it with gold
and fashions silver chains for it.
²⁰A man too poor to present such an
offering
selects wood that will not rot.
He looks for a skilled craftsman
to set up an idol that will not
topple.

²¹Do you not know?
Have you not heard? ·
Has it not been told you from the
beginning?

Have you not understood since the
earth was founded?
²²He sits enthroned above the circle of
the earth,
and its people are like grasshoppers.
He stretches out the heavens like a
canopy,
and spreads them out like a tent to
live in.
²³He brings princes to naught
and reduces the rulers of this world
to nothing.
²⁴No sooner are they planted,
no sooner are they sown,
no sooner do they take root in the
ground,
than he blows on them and they
wither,
and a whirlwind sweeps them away
like chaff.

²⁵"To whom will you compare me?
Or who is my equal?" says the Holy
One.
²⁶Lift your eyes and look to the
heavens:
Who created all these?
He who brings out the starry host one
by one,
and calls them each by name.
Because of his great power and mighty
strength,
not one of them is missing.

²⁷Why do you say, O Jacob,
and complain, O Israel,
"My way is hidden from the LORD;
my cause is disregarded by my
God"?
²⁸Do you not know?
Have you not heard?
The LORD is the everlasting God,
the Creator of the ends of the earth.
He will not grow tired or weary,
and his understanding no one can
fathom.
²⁹He gives strength to the weary
and increases the power of the weak.
³⁰Even youths grow tired and weary,
and young men stumble and fall;
³¹but those who hope in the LORD
will renew their strength.
They will soar on wings like eagles;
they will run and not grow weary,
they will walk and not be faint.

Who's in Charge? 213

Suffering Servant

Isaiah 52

Isaiah's four songs about a "suffering servant" are among the richest, and most closely studied, passages in the Old Testament. This chapter illustrates why the servant songs sparked fierce debates among the ancient rabbis seeking to understand them. The first part of the chapter stirs anticipation for a glorious time when God will restore Jerusalem and prove to all, "Your God reigns!" It looks like Israel will gain revenge on their enemies at last.

But the author explains how God will "redeem Jerusalem" by introducing the mysterious figure of the suffering servant, whose appearance was "disfigured beyond that of any man . . . marred beyond human likeness." Who is this suffering servant? And how will such a wounded person bring about a great victory?

Jewish scholars puzzled over these passages for centuries. They seemed to have grave significance, but what exactly did the prophet mean? Some of the servant songs refer to the nation of Israel as a whole, but passages like this one portray the servant as a specific individual, a great leader who suffers terribly. Although Isaiah holds him up as the deliverer of all humankind, he resembles more a tragic figure than a hero.

Some Jewish scholars speculated the prophet was describing himself or perhaps a colleague, such as Jeremiah. Still others focused their hopes on a Messiah to come. They looked for a king from humble origins, one whose power would depend not on swords, but on the spirits of people committed to him. In general, however, the idea of the suffering servant never really caught on within the Jewish nation. They longed for a victorious Messiah, not a suffering one.

The image of the suffering servant went underground, as it were, lying dormant for centuries. Then, in a dramatic scene early in his ministry, Jesus quoted from one of Isaiah's servant passages. After reading aloud in the synagogue, Jesus "rolled up the scroll, gave it back to the attendant and sat down. The eyes of everyone in the synagogue were fastened on him, and he began by saying to them, 'Today this scripture is fulfilled in your hearing'" (Luke 4:20–21).

At last, a link snapped into place for some, but not all, of Jesus' listeners. The Messiah had come at last—not as a conquering general, but as a humble peasant, a carpenter's son from Nazareth.

> **To Reflect On:** *If you had been a Jew in Jesus' day, would you have been disappointed in the Messiah?*

ISAIAH 52

52 Awake, awake, O Zion,
clothe yourself with strength.
Put on your garments of splendor,
O Jerusalem, the holy city.
The uncircumcised and defiled
will not enter you again.
²Shake off your dust;
rise up, sit enthroned, O Jerusalem.
Free yourself from the chains on your
neck,
O captive Daughter of Zion.

³For this is what the LORD says:

"You were sold for nothing,
and without money you will be
redeemed."

⁴For this is what the Sovereign LORD says:

"At first my people went down to Egypt
to live;
lately, Assyria has oppressed them.

⁵"And now what do I have here?" declares the LORD.

"For my people have been taken away
for nothing,
and those who rule them mock,"
declares the LORD.
"And all day long
my name is constantly blasphemed.
⁶Therefore my people will know my
name;
therefore in that day they will know
that it is I who foretold it.
Yes, it is I."

⁷How beautiful on the mountains
are the feet of those who bring good
news,
who proclaim peace,
who bring good tidings,
who proclaim salvation,
who say to Zion,
"Your God reigns!"
⁸Listen! Your watchmen lift up their
voices;
together they shout for joy.
When the LORD returns to Zion,
they will see it with their own eyes.
⁹Burst into songs of joy together,
you ruins of Jerusalem,
for the LORD has comforted his people,
he has redeemed Jerusalem.
¹⁰The LORD will lay bare his holy arm
in the sight of all the nations,
and all the ends of the earth will see
the salvation of our God.

¹¹Depart, depart, go out from there!
Touch no unclean thing!
Come out from it and be pure,
you who carry the vessels of the
LORD.
¹²But you will not leave in haste
or go in flight;
for the LORD will go before you,
the God of Israel will be your rear
guard.

The Suffering and Glory of the Servant

¹³See, my servant will act wisely;
he will be raised and lifted up and
highly exalted.
¹⁴Just as there were many who were
appalled at him—
his appearance was so disfigured
beyond that of any man
and his form marred beyond human
likeness—
¹⁵so will he sprinkle many nations,
and kings will shut their mouths
because of him.
For what they were not told, they will
see,
and what they have not heard, they
will understand.

The Wounded Healer

Isaiah 53

New Testament writers leave no doubt as to the identity of the suffering servant: at least ten times they apply Isaiah's four songs directly to Jesus. In one instance, Philip corrected an Ethiopian official who had wondered if the suffering servant referred to an ancient prophet (Acts 8:26–35).

Isaiah 53 reads almost like an eyewitness account of Jesus' last days on earth. The physical description—the Bible contains no other physical description of Jesus—is shocking. The servant "had no beauty or majesty to attract us to him"; he was "like one from whom men hide their faces." As this chapter foretells, Jesus did not open his mouth to answer his accusers at his trial. He left no descendants. He was cut off in the prime of life and, thanks to a gracious friend, was buried in a rich man's tomb. But that was not the end. After three days he saw "the light of life."

According to Isaiah, the servant died for a very specific purpose: "He was pierced for our transgressions." He took on pain for the sake of others, for *our* sakes. His wounds, an apparent defeat, made possible a great victory. His death sealed a future triumph when all that is wrong on earth will be set right. Significantly, the book of Isaiah does not end with the suffering servant image, but goes on to describe that wonderful life in a new heaven and new earth. But the time of travail was a necessary first step, for the servant absorbed in himself the punishment that was due for all the evils of the world.

Isaiah 53 forms an underlying foundation for much New Testament theology. In addition, these detailed prophecies, recorded many centuries before Jesus' birth, offer convincing proof that God was revealing his plan for the ages through the ancient prophets. He had not permanently severed his covenant with the Jews. Rather, out of Jewish roots—King David's own stock—he would bring forth a new king, a king like no other, to reclaim all the earth.

> **To Reflect On:** *Why did Jesus choose to come in the form described here?*

ISAIAH 53

53 Who has believed our message
and to whom has the arm of the LORD
been revealed?
2 He grew up before him like a tender
shoot,
and like a root out of dry ground.
He had no beauty or majesty to attract
us to him,
nothing in his appearance that we
should desire him.
3 He was despised and rejected by men,
a man of sorrows, and familiar with
suffering.
Like one from whom men hide their
faces
he was despised, and we esteemed
him not.

4 Surely he took up our infirmities
and carried our sorrows,
yet we considered him stricken by God,
smitten by him, and afflicted.
5 But he was pierced for our
transgressions,
he was crushed for our iniquities;
the punishment that brought us peace
was upon him,
and by his wounds we are healed.
6 We all, like sheep, have gone astray,
each of us has turned to his own
way;
and the LORD has laid on him
the inquity of us all.

7 He was oppressed and afflicted,
yet he did not open his mouth;
he was led like a lamb to the slaughter,
and as a sheep before her shearers is
silent,

so he did not open his mouth.
8 By oppression and judgment he was
taken away.
And who can speak of his
descendants?
For he was cut off from the land of the
living;
for the transgression of my people
he was stricken.
9 He was assigned a grave with the
wicked,
and with the rich in his death,
though he had done no violence,
nor was any deceit in his mouth.

10 Yet it was the LORD's will to crush him
and cause him to suffer,
and though the LORD makes his life a
guilt offering,
he will see his offspring and prolong
his days,
and the will of the LORD will prosper
in his hand.
11 After the suffering of his soul,
he will see the light of life and be
satisfied;
by his knowledge my righteous servant
will justify many,
and he will bear their iniquities.
12 Therefore I will give him a portion
among the great,
and he will divide the spoils with
the strong,
because he poured out his life unto
death,
and was numbered with the
transgressors.
For he bore the sin of many,
and made intercession for the
transgressors.

The End of It All

Isaiah 55

Even though Isaiah lived in tumultuous times, when the Jews were at the mercy of foreign powers, his writing lacks the tone of impassioned complaint that sometimes colors the other prophets. Isaiah had seen a glimpse of the future, and that glimpse convinced him that good news lay ahead. No invading armies, no terrible calamities could interfere with God's final purpose for the earth.

"For a brief moment I abandoned you, but with deep compassion I will bring you back," God says to Israel (54:7). Isaiah foretells a time when the ruined holy city, rebuilt, will achieve an unprecedented level of greatness. Yet the promise in these chapters goes far beyond what has ever been realized in Jerusalem. It merges into a vision of a future state where sin and sorrow no longer exist and we live in final peace with God.

The last part of Isaiah, addressed to a people facing deep despair, opens the door for the Jews to become a gift to all people. According to Isaiah, word about God will go out to nations nearby and faraway, and to distant islands that have never heard of him (66:18–21). This prophecy saw fulfillment in Jesus, who recruited disciples to carry his message worldwide. Through his life and death, the suffering servant indeed introduced the gospel to the entire world.

In this and other soaring chapters, Isaiah described the future with such eloquence that New Testament books like Revelation could not improve on the language; they merely quoted Isaiah. Whatever longings we feel on earth—for peace, for an end to suffering, for an unspoiled planet—will some day be fulfilled. Isaiah assures us that one day our very best dreams, all of them, will come true.

We may not understand the process the world must go through to arrive at that future time: "'For my thoughts are not your thoughts, neither are your ways my ways,' declares the LORD." But, as this chapter makes clear, God's covenant with his people is everlasting. Nothing can cancel it.

Such visions of the future seeped inside the Jewish consciousness. As the decades, even centuries passed, empires—Babylon, Persia, Egypt, Greece, Syria, Rome—rose and fell, their armies chasing each other across the plains of Palestine. Each new empire subjugated the Jews with ease. Sometimes the entire race verged on extinction. Four centuries separate the last words of the prophets in the Old Testament and the first words of Matthew in the New Testament—"the 400 silent years," they are called. Did God care? Was he even alive? In desperation the common people waited for a Messiah; they had no other hope.

To Reflect On: *What would you most like to see changed in the world? Does Isaiah speak to that change?*

ISAIAH 55

Invitation to the Thirsty

55 "Come, all you who are thirsty,
come to the waters;
and you who have no money,
come, buy and eat!
Come, buy wine and milk
without money and without cost.
²Why spend money on what is not
bread,
and your labor on what does not
satisfy?
Listen, listen to me, and eat what is
good,
and your soul will delight in the
richest of fare.
³Give ear and come to me;
hear me, that your soul may live.
I will make an everlasting covenant
with you,
my faithful love promised to David.
⁴See, I have made him a witness to the
peoples,
a leader and commander of the
peoples.
⁵Surely you will summon nations you
know not,
and nations that do not know you
will hasten to you,
because of the LORD your God,
the Holy One of Israel,
for he has endowed you with
splendor."

⁶Seek the LORD while he may be found;
call on him while he is near.
⁷Let the wicked forsake his way
and the evil man his thoughts.
Let him turn to the LORD, and he will
have mercy on him,
and to our God, for he will freely
pardon.

⁸"For my thoughts are not your
thoughts,
neither are your ways my ways,"
declares the LORD.
⁹"As the heavens are higher than the
earth,
so are my ways higher than your
ways
and my thoughts than your
thoughts.
¹⁰As the rain and the snow
come down from heaven,
and do not return to it
without watering the earth
and making it bud and flourish,
so that it yields seed for the sower
and bread for the eater,
¹¹so is my word that goes out from my
mouth:
It will not return to me empty,
but will accomplish what I desire
and achieve the purpose for which I
sent it.
¹²You will go out in joy
and be led forth in peace;
the mountains and hills
will burst into song before you,
and all the trees of the field
will clap their hands.
¹³Instead of the thornbush will grow the
pine tree,
and instead of briers the myrtle will
grow.
This will be for the LORD's renown,
for an everlasting sign,
which will not be destroyed."

Breakout

Luke 1:8–52

Does any human emotion run as deep as hope? Fairy tales, for example, pass down from generation to generation a belief in the impossibly happy ending, an irrepressible sense that in the end the forces of evil will lose the struggle and the brave and good will somehow triumph.

For the Jews in Palestine 2000 years ago, all hope seemed like a fairy tale. As Middle Eastern empires rose and fell, the tiny nation of Israel could never break free from the domination of greater powers. No prophet had spoken to them in 400 years. At the end of the Old Testament, God was in hiding. He had long threatened to hide his face, and as he did so a dark shadow fell across the planet. This is how one Jewish poet expressed the mood of the times:

> We are given no miraculous signs;
>   no prophets are left,
>   and none of us knows how long this will be.
> How long will the enemy mock you, O God? (Ps. 74:9–10).

For four centuries, the 400 years of God's silence, the Jews waited and wondered. God seemed passive, unconcerned, and deaf to their prayers. Only one hope remained, the ancient promise of a Messiah; on that promise the Jews staked everything. And then something momentous happened. The birth of a baby was announced—a birth unlike any that had come before.

You can catch the excitement just by watching the reactions of people in this chapter. The way Luke tells it, events surrounding Jesus' birth resembled a joy-filled musical. Characters crowded into the scene: a white-haired great uncle, an astonished virgin, a tottery old prophetess. They all smiled broadly and, as likely as not, burst into song. Once Mary overcame the shock from seeing an angel, she let loose with a beautiful hymn. Even an unborn cousin kicked for joy inside his mother's womb.

Luke takes care to make direct connections to Old Testament promises of a Messiah; the angel Gabriel even called John the Baptist an "Elijah" sent to prepare the way for the Lord. Clearly, something was brewing on planet earth. Among dreary, defeated villagers in a remote corner of the Roman Empire, something climactically good was breaking out.

To Reflect On: *If an angel appeared to you, would you respond like Zechariah, or like Mary?*

LUKE 1:8–52

⁸Once when Zechariah's division was on duty and he was serving as priest before God, ⁹he was chosen by lot, according to the custom of the priesthood, to go into the temple of the Lord and burn incense. ¹⁰And when the time for the burning of incense came, all the assembled worshipers were praying outside.

¹¹Then an angel of the Lord appeared to him, standing at the right side of the altar of incense. ¹²When Zechariah saw him, he was startled and was gripped with fear. ¹³But the angel said to him: "Do not be afraid, Zechariah; your prayer has been heard. Your wife Elizabeth will bear you a son, and you are to give him the name John. ¹⁴He will be a joy and delight to you, and many will rejoice because of his birth, ¹⁵for

he will be great in the sight of the Lord. He is never to take wine or other fermented drink, and he will be filled with the Holy Spirit even from birth. ¹⁶Many of the people of Israel will he bring back to the Lord their God. ¹⁷And he will go on before the Lord, in the spirit and power of Elijah, to turn the hearts of the fathers to their children and the disobedient to the wisdom of the righteous—to make ready a people prepared for the Lord."

¹⁸Zechariah asked the angel, "How can I be sure of this? I am an old man and my wife is well along in years."

¹⁹The angel answered, "I am Gabriel. I stand in the presence of God, and I have been sent to speak to you and to tell you this good news. ²⁰And now you will be silent and not able to speak until the day this happens, because you did not believe my words, which will come true at their proper time."

²¹Meanwhile, the people were waiting for Zechariah and wondering why he stayed so long in the temple. ²²When he came out, he could not speak to them. They realized he had seen a vision in the temple, for he kept making signs to them but remained unable to speak.

²³When his time of service was completed, he returned home. ²⁴After this his wife Elizabeth became pregnant and for five months remained in seclusion. ²⁵"The Lord has done this for me," she said. "In these days he has shown his favor and taken away my disgrace among the people."

The Birth of Jesus Foretold

²⁶In the sixth month, God sent the angel Gabriel to Nazareth, a town in Galilee, ²⁷to a virgin pledged to be married to a man named Joseph, a descendant of David. The virgin's name was Mary. ²⁸The angel went to her and said, "Greetings, you who are highly favored! The Lord is with you."

²⁹Mary was greatly troubled at his words and wondered what kind of greeting this might be. ³⁰But the angel said to her, "Do not be afraid, Mary, you have found favor with God. ³¹You will be with child and give birth to a son, and you are to give him the name Jesus. ³²He will be great and will be called the Son of the Most High. The Lord God will give him the throne of his father David, ³³and he will reign over the house of Jacob forever; his kingdom will never end."

³⁴"How will this be," Mary asked the angel, "since I am a virgin?"

³⁵The angel answered, "The Holy Spirit will come upon you, and the power of the Most High will overshadow you. So the holy one to be born will be called the Son of God. ³⁶Even Elizabeth your relative is going to have a child in her old age, and she who was said to be barren is in her sixth month. ³⁷For nothing is impossible with God."

³⁸"I am the Lord's servant," Mary answered. "May it be to me as you have said." Then the angel left her.

Mary Visits Elizabeth

³⁹At that time Mary got ready and hurried to a town in the hill country of Judea, ⁴⁰where she entered Zechariah's home and greeted Elizabeth. ⁴¹When Elizabeth heard Mary's greeting, the baby leaped in her womb, and Elizabeth was filled with the Holy Spirit. ⁴²In a loud voice she exclaimed: "Blessed are you among women, and blessed is the child you will bear! ⁴³But why am I so favored, that the mother of my Lord should come to me? ⁴⁴As soon as the sound of your greeting reached my ears, the baby in my womb leaped for joy. ⁴⁵Blessed is she who has believed that what the Lord has said to her will be accomplished!"

Mary's Song

⁴⁶And Mary said:

"My soul glorifies the Lord
⁴⁷ and my spirit rejoices in God my
　　Savior,
⁴⁸for he has been mindful
　of the humble state of his servant.
From now on all generations will call
　me blessed,
⁴⁹ for the Mighty One has done great
　　things for me—
　holy is his name.
⁵⁰His mercy extends to those who fear
　him,
　from generation to generation.
⁵¹He has performed mighty deeds with
　his arm;
　he has scattered those who are
　　proud in their inmost thoughts.
⁵²He has brought down rulers from their
　thrones
　but has lifted up the humble.

God's Disguise

Luke 2:1–40

Nearly every time an angel appears in the Bible, the first words he says are "Don't be afraid!" The angel Gabriel began his announcements to Zechariah and Mary that way, as did most angels in the Old Testament. Little wonder. When the supernatural made contact with planet earth, it usually left the human observers flat on their faces, in catatonic fear.

But Luke tells of God making an appearance on earth in a form that would not frighten. In Jesus, born in a barn and laid in a feeding trough, God found at last a mode of approach that we need not fear. What could be less scary than a newborn baby with jerky limbs and eyes that do not quite focus? Something brand-new was underway. Imagine becoming a baby again: giving up language and muscle coordination, and the ability to eat solid food and control your bladder. That gives just a hint of the "emptying" that God went through.

According to the Bible, Jesus was both God and man. As God, he could work miracles, forgive sins, conquer death, and predict the future. Jesus did all that, provoking awe in the people around him. But for Jews accustomed to images of God as a bright cloud or pillar of fire, Jesus also caused much confusion. How could a baby in Bethlehem, a carpenter's son, a man from Nazareth, be the Messiah from God? Jesus' skin got in the way.

Puzzled skeptics would stalk Jesus throughout his ministry. But this chapter shows that God confirmed Jesus' identity from his earliest days. A group of shepherds in a field had no doubt—they heard the message of good news straight from a choir of angels. And an old prophet and prophetess recognized him also. Even the skeptical teachers in the temple had to scratch their heads in amazement.

Why did God empty himself and take on human form? The Bible gives many reasons, some densely theological and some quite practical. The scene of Jesus as an adolescent lecturing rabbis in the temple (2:41–5:2) gives one clue. For the first time, ordinary people could hold a conversation, a debate, with God in visible form. Jesus could talk to anyone—his parents, a rabbi, a poor widow—without first having to announce "Don't be afraid!" In Jesus, God came close.

> **To Reflect On:** *The scene in the temple (the only biblical glimpse of Jesus' boyhood) reveals a communication gap between Jesus and his parents. What other problems do you think he faced by being both God and man?*

LUKE 2:1–40

The Birth of Jesus

2 In those days Caesar Augustus issued a decree that a census should be taken of the entire Roman world. ²(This was the first census that took place while Quirinius was governor of Syria.) ³And everyone went to his own town to register.

⁴So Joseph also went up from the town of Nazareth in Galilee to Judea, to Bethlehem the town of David, because he belonged to the house and line of David. ⁵He went there to register with Mary, who was pledged to be married to him and was expecting a child. ⁶While they were there, the time came for the baby to be born, ⁷and she gave birth to her firstborn, a son. She wrapped

him in cloths and placed him in a manger, because there was no room for them in the inn.

The Shepherds and the Angels

[8] And there were shepherds living out in the fields nearby, keeping watch over their flocks at night. [9] An angel of the Lord appeared to them, and the glory of the Lord shone around them, and they were terrified. [10] But the angel said to them, "Do not be afraid. I bring you good news of great joy that will be for all the people. [11] Today in the town of David a Savior has been born to you; he is Christ the Lord. [12] This will be a sign to you: You will find a baby wrapped in cloths and lying in a manger."

[13] Suddenly a great company of the heavenly host appeared with the angel, praising God and saying,

[14] "Glory to God in the highest,
   and on earth peace to men on
      whom his favor rests."

[15] When the angels had left them and gone into heaven, the shepherds said to one another, "Let's go to Bethlehem and see this thing that has happened, which the Lord has told us about."

[16] So they hurried off and found Mary and Joseph, and the baby, who was lying in the manger. [17] When they had seen him, they spread the word concerning what had been told them about this child, [18] and all who heard it were amazed at what the shepherds said to them. [19] But Mary treasured up all these things and pondered them in her heart. [20] The shepherds returned, glorifying and praising God for all the things they had heard and seen, which were just as they had been told.

Jesus Presented in the Temple

[21] On the eighth day, when it was time to circumcise him, he was named Jesus, the name the angel had given him before he had been conceived.

[22] When the time of their purification according to the Law of Moses had been completed, Joseph and Mary took him to Jerusalem to present him to the Lord [23] (as it is written in the Law of the Lord, "Every firstborn male is to be consecrated to the Lord"), [24] and to offer a sacrifice in keeping with what is said in the Law of the Lord: "a pair of doves or two young pigeons."

[25] Now there was a man in Jerusalem called Simeon, who was righteous and devout. He was waiting for the consolation of Israel, and the Holy Spirit was upon him. [26] It had been revealed to him by the Holy Spirit that he would not die before he had seen the Lord's Christ. [27] Moved by the Spirit, he went into the temple courts. When the parents brought in the child Jesus to do for him what the custom of the Law required, [28] Simeon took him in his arms and praised God, saying:

[29] "Sovereign Lord, as you have
      promised,
   you now dismiss your servant in
      peace.
[30] For my eyes have seen your salvation,
[31]   which you have prepared in the
         sight of all people,
[32] a light for revelation to the Gentiles
   and for glory to your people Israel."

[33] The child's father and mother marveled at what was said about him. [34] Then Simeon blessed them and said to Mary, his mother: "This child is destined to cause the falling and rising of many in Israel, and to be a sign that will be spoken against, [35] so that the thoughts of many hearts will be revealed. And a sword will pierce your own soul too."

[36] There was also a prophetess, Anna, the daughter of Phanuel, of the tribe of Asher. She was very old; she had lived with her husband seven years after her marriage, [37] and then was a widow until she was eighty-four. She never left the temple but worshiped night and day, fasting and praying. [38] Coming up to them at that very moment, she gave thanks to God and spoke about the child to all who were looking forward to the redemption of Jerusalem.

[39] When Joseph and Mary had done everything required by the Law of the Lord, they returned to Galilee to their own town of Nazareth. [40] And the child grew and became strong; he was filled with wisdom, and the grace of God was upon him.

Immediate Impact

Mark 1

Although the four Gospels all cover basically the same ground, each one looks at Jesus' life from a unique angle. Matthew and Luke both begin with three chapters of historical background, taking pains to verify Jesus' Old Testament connections. Mark, however, plunges right in to report on Jesus' ministry, covering his baptism and temptation, the calling of the disciples, and a series of miracles in the first chapter alone.

Mark reads like a newspaper account, jam-packed with action, and with little room left over for parables, speeches, or editorial comments. Thus the book gives an ideal "bird's eye view" of Jesus' life. Its style—simple sentences without complicated transitions or long speeches—makes understanding easier.

After John the Baptist had fanned enthusiasm for Jesus—so much enthusiasm, in fact, that John landed in jail—Jesus openly announced his ministry. He had some surprises in store for the eager audience. For one thing, Jesus did not go to Jerusalem, the natural center of activity for any aspiring leader, but to the small towns in the hill country of Galilee. (He had grown up nearby, in the obscure town of Nazareth, which led some sophisticates to scoff, "Nazareth! Can anything good come from there?")

In other ways, too, Jesus did not fit the expected image of a prophet. His cousin John personified that severe ascetic image: He lived in a desert, ate insects, and preached a harsh message of judgment. But Jesus lived in the midst of people, dined in their homes, and brought a message of the good news of God.

When Jesus began healing people, however, his reputation swelled overnight. Mark shows gymnasium-size crowds pressing around Jesus so tightly that he had to plan escape routes. News of his miraculous powers spread even when he tried to hush it up. Wherever he went, the crowds followed, buzzing about his remarkable life. "Is he the Holy One of God?" "Is he mad?" "Isn't this the carpenter's boy?" The word was out.

> **To Reflect On:** *Based just on what you read in this chapter, what words would you use to describe Jesus?*

MARK 1

John the Baptist Prepares the Way

1 The beginning of the gospel about Jesus Christ, the Son of God.

²It is written in Isaiah the prophet:
"I will send my messenger ahead of
    you,
  who will prepare your way"—
³"a voice of one calling in the desert,
 'Prepare the way for the Lord,
    make straight paths for him.'"

⁴And so John came, baptizing in the desert region and preaching a baptism of repentance for the forgiveness of sins. ⁵The whole Judean countryside and all the people of Jerusalem went out to him. Confessing their sins, they were baptized by him in the Jordan River. ⁶John wore clothing made of camel's hair, with a leather belt around his waist, and he ate locusts and wild honey. ⁷And this was his message: "After me will come one more powerful than I, the thongs of whose sandals I am not worthy to stoop down and untie. ⁸I baptize you with water, but he will baptize you with the Holy Spirit."

The Baptism and Temptation of Jesus

⁹At that time Jesus came from Nazareth in Galilee and was baptized by John in the

Jordan. [10]As Jesus was coming up out of the water, he saw heaven being torn open and the Spirit descending on him like a dove. [11]And a voice came from heaven: "You are my Son, whom I love; with you I am well pleased."

[12]At once the Spirit sent him out into the desert, [13]and he was in the desert forty days, being tempted by Satan. He was with the wild animals, and angels attended him.

The Calling of the First Disciples

[14]After John was put in prison, Jesus went into Galilee, proclaiming the good news of God. [15]"The time has come," he said. "The kingdom of God is near. Repent and believe the good news!"

[16]As Jesus walked beside the Sea of Galilee, he saw Simon and his brother Andrew casting a net into the lake, for they were fishermen. [17]"Come, follow me," Jesus said, "and I will make you fishers of men." [18]At once they left their nets and followed him.

[19]When he had gone a little farther, he saw James son of Zebedee and his brother John in a boat, preparing their nets. [20]Without delay he called them, and they left their father Zebedee in the boat with the hired men and followed him.

Jesus Drives Out an Evil Spirit

[21]They went to Capernaum, and when the Sabbath came, Jesus went into the synagogue and began to teach. [22]The people were amazed at his teaching, because he taught them as one who had authority, not as the teachers of the law. [23]Just then a man in their synagogue who was possessed by an evil spirit cried out, [24]"What do you want with us, Jesus of Nazareth? Have you come to destroy us? I know who you are—the Holy One of God!"

[25]"Be quiet!" said Jesus sternly. "Come out of him!" [26]The evil spirit shook the man violently and came out of him with a shriek.

[27]The people were all so amazed that they asked each other, "What is this? A new teaching—and with authority! He even gives orders to evil spirits and they obey him." [28]News about him spread quickly over the whole region of Galilee.

Jesus Heals Many

[29]As soon as they left the synagogue, they went with James and John to the home of Simon and Andrew. [30]Simon's mother-in-law was in bed with a fever, and they told Jesus about her. [31]So he went to her, took her hand and helped her up. The fever left her and she began to wait on them.

[32]That evening after sunset the people brought to Jesus all the sick and demon-possessed. [33]The whole town gathered at the door, [34]and Jesus healed many who had various diseases. He also drove out many demons, but he would not let the demons speak because they knew who he was.

Jesus Prays in a Solitary Place

[35]Very early in the morning, while it was still dark, Jesus got up, left the house and went off to a solitary place, where he prayed. [36]Simon and his companions went to look for him, [37]and when they found him, they exclaimed: "Everyone is looking for you!"

[38]Jesus replied, "Let us go somewhere else—to the nearby villages—so I can preach there also. That is why I have come." [39]So he traveled throughout Galilee, preaching in their synagogues and driving out demons.

A Man With Leprosy

[40]A man with leprosy came to him and begged him on his knees, "If you are willing, you can make me clean."

[41]Filled with compassion, Jesus reached out his hand and touched the man. "I am willing," he said. "Be clean!" [42]Immediately the leprosy left him and he was cured.

[43]Jesus sent him away at once with a strong warning: [44]"See that you don't tell this to anyone. But go, show yourself to the priest and offer the sacrifices that Moses commanded for your cleansing, as a testimony to them." [45]Instead he went out and began to talk freely, spreading the news. As a result, Jesus could no longer enter a town openly but stayed outside in lonely places. Yet the people still came to him from everywhere.

Signal Fires of Opposition

Mark 2

When a new leader starts making waves, opposition is sure to follow. Anyone who declares for the candidacy of the U.S. presidency, for example, must brace for a long, dreary campaign of rumor, innuendo, and mud-slinging. While on earth, Jesus made a claim more extravagant than any politician's: He claimed to be the Messiah, sent from God. And opposition to him sprang up soon after the wild surge of popularity in Galilee. This chapter tells of three different criticisms that people would make against Jesus throughout his life.

1. **He blasphemes.** The teachers of the Law were scandalized by Jesus' forgiving sins. "He's blaspheming!" they muttered. "Who can forgive sins but God alone?" Jesus readily agreed that only God could forgive sins—that was his point exactly.

Throughout his life, Jesus faced strongest opposition from the most pious followers of Old Testament law. They could never accept that the awesome, distant God of Israel could take up residence inside a human body. Eventually, they had Jesus executed for making that claim. (People who accept Jesus as a "good man and enlightened teacher" today often overlook the scenes where Jesus blatantly identifies himself with God. When the Pharisees reacted violently to Jesus, it was because they had heard him correctly—they simply refused to believe him.)

2. **He keeps disreputable company.** Everyone wants to be on the side of a popular leader; the rich and powerful, especially, expect certain favors and courtesies from "the new kid on the block." But Jesus showed a distinct preference for the most unseemly sort of people. He offended politicians and religious leaders by calling them names. Even after becoming famous he would dine with an outcast tax collector and his low-life friends. On hearing the gossip about this strange behavior, Jesus said simply, "It is not the healthy who need a doctor, but the sick. I have not come to call the righteous, but sinners."

3. **He goes against tradition.** Jesus didn't require from his disciples anything like the strictness observed by John the Baptist's disciples. To the Pharisees, it seemed Jesus' disciples were even playing fast and loose with the holy Sabbath. Jesus' response: It's time for a new cloth; the old one has been patched together long enough. Before long, he would introduce the "new covenant." God had some major changes in store for the human race, and the narrow, confining covenant with the Israelites simply couldn't hold all those changes.

> **To Reflect On:** *Try to project yourself back into Jesus' time. What might have shocked you?*

MARK 2

Jesus Heals a Paralytic

2 A few days later, when Jesus again entered Capernaum, the people heard that he had come home. ²So many gathered that there was no room left, not even outside the door, and he preached the word to them. ³Some men came, bringing to him a paralytic, carried by four of them. ⁴Since they could not get him to Jesus because of the crowd, they made an opening in the roof above Jesus and, after digging through it, lowered the mat the paralyzed man was lying on. ⁵When Jesus saw their faith, he said to the paralytic, "Son, your sins are forgiven."

⁶Now some teachers of the law were sitting there, thinking to themselves, ⁷"Why does this fellow talk like that? He's blaspheming! Who can forgive sins but God alone?"

⁸Immediately Jesus knew in his spirit that this was what they were thinking in their hearts, and he said to them, "Why are you thinking these things? ⁹Which is easier: to say to the paralytic, 'Your sins are forgiven,' or to say, 'Get up, take your mat and walk'? ¹⁰But that you may know that the Son of Man has authority on earth to forgive sins . . . ." He said to the paralytic, ¹¹"I tell you, get up, take your mat and go home." ¹²He got up, took his mat and walked out in full view of them all. This amazed everyone and they praised God, saying, "We have never seen anything like this!"

The Calling of Levi

¹³Once again Jesus went out beside the lake. A large crowd came to him, and he began to teach them. ¹⁴As he walked along, he saw Levi son of Alphaeus sitting at the tax collector's booth. "Follow me," Jesus told him, and Levi got up and followed him.

¹⁵While Jesus was having dinner at Levi's house, many tax collectors and "sinners" were eating with him and his disciples, for there were many who followed him. ¹⁶When the teachers of the law who were Pharisees saw him eating with the "sinners" and tax collectors, they asked his disciples: "Why does he eat with tax collectors and 'sinners'?"

¹⁷On hearing this, Jesus said to them, "It is not the healthy who need a doctor, but the sick. I have not come to call the righteous, but sinners."

Jesus Questioned About Fasting

¹⁸Now John's disciples and the Pharisees were fasting. Some people came and asked Jesus, "How is it that John's disciples and the disciples of the Pharisees are fasting, but yours are not?"

¹⁹Jesus answered, "How can the guests of the bridegroom fast while he is with them? They cannot, so long as they have him with them. ²⁰But the time will come when the bridegroom will be taken from them, and on that day they will fast.

²¹"No one sews a patch of unshrunk cloth on an old garment. If he does, the new piece will pull away from the old, making the tear worse. ²²And no one pours new wine into old wineskins. If he does, the wine will burst the skins, and both the wine and the wineskins will be ruined. No, he pours new wine into new wineskins."

Lord of the Sabbath

²³One Sabbath Jesus was going through the grainfields, and as his disciples walked along, they began to pick some heads of grain. ²⁴The Pharisees said to him, "Look, why are they doing what is unlawful on the Sabbath?"

²⁵He answered, "Have you never read what David did when he and his companions were hungry and in need? ²⁶In the days of Abiathar the high priest, he entered the house of God and ate the consecrated bread, which is lawful only for priests to eat. And he also gave some to his companions."

²⁷Then he said to them, "The Sabbath was made for man, not man for the Sabbath. ²⁸So the Son of Man is Lord even of the Sabbath."

Late-night Conversation

John 3

Reading Mark 2 and John 3 back-to-back reveals a chief difference between Mark's and John's gospels. Mark gives the panoramic view: action, crowds, short scenes spliced together to create an overall impact. John tightens the camera angle, closing in on a few individual faces—a woman at a well, a blind man, a member of the Jewish ruling council—to compose a more intimate, in-depth portrait.

A simple word or phrase with a profound meaning—that is the style of Jesus' teaching as presented in John. No biblical author used simpler, more commonplace words: *water, world, light, life, birth, love, truth.* Yet John used them with such depth and skill that hundreds of authors since have tried to plumb their meaning.

Take this conversation with Nicodemus, for instance. He came to Jesus at night, in order to avoid detection. He risked his reputation and safety by even meeting with Jesus, whom his fellow Pharisees had sworn to kill. But Nicodemus had questions, burning questions, the most important questions anyone could ask: *Who are you, Jesus? Have you really come from God?* Jesus responded with the image of a second birth, in words we now recognize as among the most familiar in the Bible.

Evidently, some of Jesus' words to Nicodemus must have sunk in. Later he would stand up for Jesus at the Jewish ruling council and, after the crucifixion, help prepare Jesus' body for burial.

John follows this conversation with a report from John the Baptist. People were questioning him, too, about the new teacher across the river who was drawing all the crowds. In words that echo Jesus' own, John confirmed that Jesus held the keys to eternal life. He was indeed the one John had come to announce: "He must become greater; I must become less."

> **To Reflect On:** *How would you explain the phrase "born again" to someone who had never heard it?*

JOHN 3

Jesus Teaches Nicodemus

3 Now there was a man of the Pharisees named Nicodemus, a member of the Jewish ruling council. ²He came to Jesus at night and said, "Rabbi, we know you are a teacher who has come from God. For no one could perform the miraculous signs you are doing if God were not with him."

³In reply Jesus declared, "I tell you the truth, no one can see the kingdom of God unless he is born again."

⁴"How can a man be born when he is old?" Nicodemus asked. "Surely he cannot enter a second time into his mother's womb to be born!"

⁵Jesus answered, "I tell you the truth, no one can enter the kingdom of God unless he is born of water and the Spirit. ⁶Flesh gives birth to flesh, but the Spirit gives birth to spirit. ⁷You should not be surprised at my saying, 'You must be born again.' ⁸The wind blows wherever it pleases. You hear its sound, but you cannot tell where it comes from or where it is going. So it is with everyone born of the Spirit."

⁹"How can this be?" Nicodemus asked.

¹⁰"You are Israel's teacher," said Jesus, "and do you not understand these things? ¹¹I tell you the truth, we speak of what we know, and we testify to what we have seen, but still you people do not accept our testimony. ¹²I have spoken to you of earthly things and you do not believe; how then will you believe if I speak of heavenly things? ¹³No one has ever gone into heaven except the one who came from heaven—the Son of Man. ¹⁴Just as Moses lifted up the snake in the desert, so the Son of Man must be lifted up, ¹⁵that everyone who believes in him may have eternal life.

¹⁶"For God so loved the world that he gave his one and only Son, that whoever believes in him shall not perish but have eternal life. ¹⁷For God did not send his Son into the world to condemn the world, but to save the world through him. ¹⁸Whoever believes in him is not condemned, but whoever does not believe stands condemned already because he has not believed in the name of God's one and only Son. ¹⁹This is the verdict: Light has come into the world, but men loved darkness instead of light because their deeds were evil. ²⁰Everyone who does evil hates the light, and will not come into the light for fear that his deeds will be exposed. ²¹But whoever lives by the truth comes into the light, so that it may be seen plainly that what he has done has been done through God."

John the Baptist's Testimony About Jesus

²²After this, Jesus and his disciples went out into the Judean countryside, where he spent some time with them, and baptized. ²³Now John also was baptizing at Aenon near Salim, because there was plenty of water, and people were constantly coming to be baptized. ²⁴(This was before John was put in prison.) ²⁵An argument developed between some of John's disciples and a certain Jew over the matter of ceremonial washing. ²⁶They came to John and said to him, "Rabbi, that man who was with you on the other side of the Jordan—the one you testified about—well, he is baptizing, and everyone is going to him."

²⁷To this John replied, "A man can receive only what is given him from heaven. ²⁸You yourselves can testify that I said, 'I am not the Christ but am sent ahead of him.' ²⁹The bride belongs to the bridegroom. The friend who attends the bridegroom waits and listens for him, and is full of joy when he hears the bridegroom's voice. That joy is mine, and it is now complete. ³⁰He must become greater; I must become less.

³¹"The one who comes from above is above all; the one who is from the earth belongs to the earth, and speaks as one from the earth. The one who comes from heaven is above all. ³²He testifies to what he has seen and heard, but no one accepts his testimony. ³³The man who has accepted it has certified that God is truthful. ³⁴For the one whom God has sent speaks the words of God, for God gives the Spirit without limit. ³⁵The Father loves the Son and has placed everything in his hands. ³⁶Whoever believes in the Son has eternal life, but whoever rejects the Son will not see life, for God's wrath remains on him."

Miracles and Magic

Mark 3

The Gospels record some three dozen miracles performed by Jesus, and he stated plainly why he did them: "Believe me when I say that I am in the Father and the Father is in me; or at least believe on the evidence of the miracles themselves" (John 10:38). They served as convincing proofs that he was the Messiah, the Son of God.

As Mark shows, large crowds flocked from far away as word of Jesus' powers spread. Some people came for healing; others, just to witness the extraordinary phenomena. Who but a messenger from God could perform such works? Yet Jesus himself had an odd ambivalence toward miracles. He never did "tricks" on demand, like a magician. "A wicked and adulterous generation looks for a miraculous sign," he said to those who sought a display of magic (Matthew 12:39).

Jesus seemed not to trust miracles to produce the kind of faith he was interested in. Mark reports that on seven separate occasions he warned a person just healed, "Tell no one!" He was suspicious of the popular acclaim that his miracles stirred up, for he had a hard message of obedience and sacrifice, and miracles tended to attract gawkers and sensation-seekers.

Mainly, Jesus used his powers in compassionate response to human needs. Every time someone asked directly, he healed. When his disciples grew frightened on a stormy lake, he walked to them across the water or calmed the wind. When his audience got hungry he fed them, and when wedding guests grew thirsty he made wine. Often he instructed the awed onlookers not to spread the word.

Much like people today, Jesus' contemporaries looked for ways to explain away his powers, even when faced with irrefutable evidence. Here, the Pharisees seek to credit the miracles to Satan's power. On another occasion they arranged a formal tribunal, complete with judges and witnesses, to examine a man Jesus had healed. The man's parents confirmed his story ("One thing I do know. I was blind but now I see!"), but still the doubters hurled insults and threw him out of court (John 9).

This chapter mentions a murder plot hatched by people angry over one of Jesus' healings. Later, in perhaps the most remarkable cover-up of all, religious leaders similarly tried to counteract the effect of Jesus' raising of Lazarus from the dead. The incident had caused quite a stir, occurring as it did before a crowd, four days after Lazarus' funeral. Hard evidence of an astonishing miracle was walking free around the town of Bethany. But the religious establishment simply made plans to destroy that evidence by putting both Jesus and Lazarus to death (John 11).

In short, the crowd's mixed responses bore out Jesus' suspicions about the limited value of miracles. They rarely created faith, but rather affirmed it in true seekers.

> **To Reflect On:** *Would people be more likely to believe God if miracles were more common today?*

MARK 3

3 Another time he went into the synagogue, and a man with a shriveled hand was there. [2]Some of them were looking for a reason to accuse Jesus, so they watched him closely to see if he would heal him on the Sabbath. [3]Jesus said to the man with the shriveled hand, "Stand up in front of everyone."

[4]Then Jesus asked them, "Which is lawful on the Sabbath: to do good or to do evil, to save life or to kill?" But they remained silent.

[5]He looked around at them in anger and, deeply distressed at their stubborn hearts, said to the man, "Stretch out your hand." He stretched it out, and his hand was completely restored. [6]Then the Pharisees went out and began to plot with the Herodians how they might kill Jesus.

Crowds Follow Jesus

[7]Jesus withdrew with his disciples to the lake, and a large crowd from Galilee followed. [8]When they heard all he was doing, many people came to him from Judea, Jerusalem, Idumea, and the regions across the Jordan and around Tyre and Sidon. [9]Because of the crowd he told his disciples to have a small boat ready for him, to keep the people from crowding him. [10]For he had healed many, so that those with diseases were pushing forward to touch him. [11]Whenever the evil spirits saw him, they fell down before him and cried out, "You are the Son of God." [12]But he gave them strict orders not to tell who he was.

The Appointing of the Twelve Apostles

[13]Jesus went up on a mountainside and called to him those he wanted, and they came to him. [14]He appointed twelve—designating them apostles—that they might be with him and that he might send them out to preach [15]and to have authority to drive out demons. [16]These are the twelve he appointed: Simon (to whom he gave the name Peter); [17]James son of Zebedee and his brother John (to them he gave the name Boanerges, which means Sons of Thunder); [18]Andrew, Philip, Bartholomew, Matthew, Thomas, James son of Alphaeus, Thaddaeus, Simon the Zealot [19]and Judas Iscariot, who betrayed him.

Jesus and Beelzebub

[20]Then Jesus entered a house, and again a crowd gathered, so that he and his disciples were not even able to eat. [21]When his family heard about this, they went to take charge of him, for they said, "He is out of his mind."

[22]And the teachers of the law who came down from Jerusalem said, "He is possessed by Beelzebub! By the prince of demons he is driving out demons."

[23]So Jesus called them and spoke to them in parables: "How can Satan drive out Satan? [24]If a kingdom is divided against itself, that kingdom cannot stand. [25]If a house is divided against itself, that house cannot stand. [26]And if Satan opposes himself and is divided, he cannot stand; his end has come. [27]In fact, no one can enter a strong man's house and carry off his possessions unless he first ties up the strong man. Then he can rob his house. [28]I tell you the truth, all the sins and blasphemies of men will be forgiven them. [29]But whoever blasphemes against the Holy Spirit will never be forgiven; he is guilty of an eternal sin."

[30]He said this because they were saying, "He has an evil spirit."

Jesus' Mother and Brothers

[31]Then Jesus' mother and brothers arrived. Standing outside, they sent someone in to call him. [32]A crowd was sitting around him, and they told him, "Your mother and brothers are outside looking for you."

[33]"Who are my mother and my brothers?" he asked.

[34]Then he looked around at those seated in a circle around him and said, "Here are my mother and my brothers! [35]Whoever does God's will is my brother and sister and mother."

Hard Soil

Mark 4

The story about the sower of seed summarizes well the mixed results Jesus himself got while on earth. We who live 2000 years later, with such events as Christmas and Easter marked plainly on our calendars, may easily miss the sheer incredulity that greeted Jesus in the flesh.

Neighbors. They had watched him play in the streets with their own children; Jesus was simply too familiar for them to believe he was sent from God. "Isn't this the carpenter?" they asked. "Isn't this Mary's son and the brother of James, Joseph, Judas and Simon? . . . What's this wisdom that has been given him, that he even does miracles?" (Mark 6:3, 2).

Family. Mark casually mentions that one time Jesus' mother and brothers arrived to take charge of him because they had concluded, "He is out of his mind" (4:21) Not even his mother and brothers could easily reconcile the wondrous and the ordinary.

Religious experts. The scribes and Pharisees, who pored over the prophets, should have had the clearest notion of what the Messiah would look like. But no group caused Jesus more trouble. They criticized his theology, his lifestyle, and his choice of friends. When he performed miracles, they attributed his power to Satan and demons.

The crowds. Common people seemed unable to make up their minds about Jesus. One moment they judged him "demon-possessed and raving mad" (John 10:20); the next, they forcibly tried to crown him king.

How could Jesus, God's Son, worker of astounding miracles in broad daylight, go unrecognized? The incident that ends this chapter may provide a clue. When a storm nearly capsized the boat transporting Jesus, he yelled into the wind and spray, "Quiet! Be still!" The disciples shrank back in terror. What kind of person could shout down the weather, as if correcting an unruly child?

That scene helped convince them Jesus was unlike anyone else on earth. Yet it may also help suggest a reason for their confusion about him. Jesus had, after all, fallen asleep in the boat from sheer fatigue, a symptom of his human frailty. And the Son of God, the creator of weather, was—but for this one instance of miracle—one of its victims.

The early church argued for three centuries about exactly what happened when God became man, but their creeds did little to dispel the sense of mystery. In a way, Jesus was just like everyone else—he had a race, an occupation, a family background, a body shape. In a way he was something entirely new in the history of the universe. In between his humanity and deity lies the mystery that never completely goes away.

> **To Reflect On:** *In Jesus' story of the sower and the soil, what kind of "soil" best represents your own response to the gospel?*

MARK 4

The Parable of the Sower

4 Again Jesus began to teach by the lake. The crowd that gathered around him was so large that he got into a boat and sat in it out on the lake, while all the people were along the shore at the water's edge. ²He taught them many things by parables, and in his teaching said: ³"Listen! A farmer went out to sow his seed. ⁴As he was scattering the seed, some fell along the path, and the birds came and ate it up. 5Some fell on rocky places, where it did not have much soil. It sprang up quickly, because the soil was shallow. 6But when the sun came up, the plants were scorched, and they withered because they had no root. 7Other seed fell among thorns, which grew up and choked the plants, so that they did not bear grain. 8Still other seed fell on good soil. It came up, grew and produced a crop, multiplying thirty, sixty, or even a hundred times.

9Then Jesus said, "He who has ears to hear, let him hear."

10When he was alone, the Twelve and the others around him asked him about the parables. 11He told them, "The secret of the kingdom of God has been given to you. But to those on the outside everything is said in parables 12so that,

" 'they may be ever seeing but never
        perceiving,
    and ever hearing but never
        understanding;
    otherwise they might turn and be
        forgiven!' "

13Then Jesus said to them, "Don't you understand this parable? How then will you understand any parable? 14The farmer sows the word. Some people are like seed along the path, where the word is sown. As soon as they hear it, Satan comes and takes away the word that was sown in them. 16Others, like seed sown on rocky places, hear the word and at once receive it with joy. 17But since they have no root, they last only a short time. When trouble or persecution comes because of the word, they quickly fall away. 18Still others, like seed sown among thorns, hear the word; 19but the worries of this life, the deceitfulness of wealth and the desires for other things come in and choke the word, making it unfruitful. 20Others, like seed sown on good soil, hear the word, accept it, and produce a crop—thirty, sixty or even a hundred times what was sown."

A Lamp on a Stand

21He said to them, "Do you bring in a lamp to put it under a bowl or a bed? Instead, don't you put it on its stand? 22For whatever is hidden is meant to be disclosed, and whatever is concealed is meant to be brought out into the open. 23If anyone has ears to hear, let him hear."

24"Consider carefully what you hear," he continued. "With the measure you use, it will be measured to you—and even more. 25Whoever has will be given more; whoever does not have, even what he has will be taken from him."

The Parable of the Growing Seed

26He also said, "This is what the kingdom of God is like. A man scatters seed on the ground. 27Night and day, whether he sleeps or gets up, the seed sprouts and grows, though he does not know how. 28All by itself the soil produces grain—first the stalk, then the head, then the full kernel in the head. 29As soon as the grain is ripe, he puts the sickle to it, because the harvest has come."

The Parable of the Mustard Seed

30Again he said, "What shall we say the kingdom of God is like, or what parable shall we use to describe it? 31It is like a mustard seed, which is the smallest seed you plant in the ground. 32Yet when planted, it grows and becomes the largest of all garden plants, with such big branches that the birds of the air can perch in its shade."

33With many similar parables Jesus spoke the word to them, as much as they could understand. 34He did not say anything to them without using a parable. But when he was alone with his own disciples, he explained everything.

Jesus Calms the Storm

35That day when evening came, he said to his disciples, "Let us go over to the other side." 36Leaving the crowd behind, they took him along, just as he was, in the boat. There were also other boats with him. 37A furious squall came up, and the waves broke over the boat, so that it was nearly swamped. 38Jesus was in the stern, sleeping on a cushion. The disciples woke him and said to him, "Teacher, don't you care if we drown?"

39He got up, rebuked the wind and said to the waves, "Quiet! Be still!" Then the wind died down and it was completely calm.

40He said to his disciples, "Why are you so afraid? Do you still have no faith?"

41They were terrified and asked each other, "Who is this? Even the wind and the waves obey him!"

Jesus and Illness

Mark 5

At one point some of the controversy about Jesus even affected John the Baptist, the prophet who more than anyone had raised the people's hopes about a Messiah. It was he who had baptized Jesus and pronounced him the Son of God. But two years later, as he languished on death row, John the Baptist himself began to wonder. He sent Jesus a direct question: "Are you the one who was to come, or should we expect someone else?"

This was Jesus' reply: "Go back and report to John what you have seen and heard: The blind receive sight, the lame walk, those who have leprosy are cured, the deaf hear, the dead are raised, and the Good News is preached to the poor. Blessed is the man who does not fall away on account of me" (Luke 7). Clearly, Jesus saw his miracles of healing as important proofs of who he was.

The healings did something else as well: They overturned common notions about how God views sick people. At that time, the Pharisees taught a very strict principle (along the lines of Job's friends' beliefs) that "All suffering comes from sin." They judged a deranged or demon-possessed person as permanently cursed by God. They saw God's hand of punishment in natural disasters, birth defects, and such long-term conditions as blindness and paralysis. Leprosy victims were unclean, excluded even from worship.

But Jesus contradicted such teaching. This chapter shows him curing a demon-possessed man, touching and healing an "unclean" woman, and resurrecting a child. On other occasions, he directly refuted the doctrine about sin and suffering. He denied that a man's blindness came from his own or his parents' sin, and he dismissed the common opinion that tragedies happen to those who deserve them (see John 9 and Luke 13).

Jesus did not heal everyone on earth, or even in Palestine. But his treatment of the sick and needy shows they are especially loved, not cursed, by God. The healings also provide a "sign" of what will happen in the future, when all diseases, and even death, will be destroyed.

> **To Reflect On:** *Do Christians around you still harbor the notion that a suffering person "got what he deserved"?*

MARK 5

The Healing of a Demon-possessed Man

5 They went across the lake to the region of the Gerasenes. ²When Jesus got out of the boat, a man with an evil spirit came from the tombs to meet him. ³This man lived in the tombs, and no one could bind him any more, not even with a chain. ⁴For he had often been chained hand and foot, but he tore the chains apart and broke the irons on his feet. No one was strong enough to subdue him. ⁵Night and day among the tombs and in the hills he would cry out and cut himself with stones.

⁶When he saw Jesus from a distance, he ran and fell on his knees in front of him. ⁷He shouted at the top of his voice, "What do you want with me, Jesus, Son of the Most High God? Swear to God that you won't torture me!" ⁸For Jesus had said to him, "Come out of this man, you evil spirit!"

⁹Then Jesus asked him, "What is your name?"

"My name is Legion," he replied, "for we are many." [10] And he begged Jesus again and again not to send them out of the area.

[11] A large herd of pigs was feeding on the nearby hillside. [12] The demons begged Jesus, "Send us among the pigs; allow us to go into them." [13] He gave them permission, and the evil spirits came out and went into the pigs. The herd, about two thousand in number, rushed down the steep bank into the lake and were drowned.

[14] Those tending the pigs ran off and reported this in the town and countryside, and the people went out to see what had happened. [15] When they came to Jesus, they saw the man who had been possessed by the legion of demons, sitting there, dressed and in his right mind; and they were afraid. [16] Those who had seen it told the people what had happened to the demon-possessed man—and told about the pigs as well. [17] Then the people began to plead with Jesus to leave their region.

[18] As Jesus was getting into the boat, the man who had been demon-possessed begged to go with him. [19] Jesus did not let him, but said, "Go home to your family and tell them how much the Lord has done for you, and how he has had mercy on you." [20] So the man went away and began to tell in the Decapolis how much Jesus had done for him. And all the people were amazed.

A Dead Girl and a Sick Woman

[21] When Jesus had again crossed over by boat to the other side of the lake, a large crowd gathered around him while he was by the lake. [22] Then one of the synagogue rulers, named Jairus, came there. Seeing Jesus, he fell at his feet [23] and pleaded earnestly with him, "My little daughter is dying. Please come and put your hands on her so that she will be healed and live." [24] So Jesus went with him.

A large crowd followed and pressed around him. [25] And a woman was there who had been subject to bleeding for twelve years. [26] She had suffered a great deal under the care of many doctors and had spent all she had, yet instead of getting better she grew worse. [27] When she heard about Jesus, she came up behind him in the crowd and touched his cloak, [28] because she thought, "If I just touch his clothes, I will be healed." [29] Immediately her bleeding stopped and she felt in her body that she was freed from her suffering.

[30] At once Jesus realized that power had gone out from him. He turned around in the crowd and asked, "Who touched my clothes?"

[31] "You see the people crowding against you," his disciples answered, "and yet you can ask, 'Who touched me?'"

[32] But Jesus kept looking around to see who had done it. [33] Then the woman, knowing what had happened to her, came and fell at his feet and, trembling with fear, told him the whole truth. [34] He said to her, "Daughter, your faith has healed you. Go in peace and be freed from your suffering."

[35] While Jesus was still speaking, some men came from the house of Jairus, the synagogue ruler. "Your daughter is dead," they said. "Why bother the teacher any more?"

[36] Ignoring what they said, Jesus told the synagogue ruler, "Don't be afraid; just believe."

[37] He did not let anyone follow him except Peter, James and John the brother of James. [38] When they came to the home of the synagogue ruler, Jesus saw a commotion, with people crying and wailing loudly. [39] He went in and said to them, "Why all this commotion and wailing? The child is not dead but asleep." [40] But they laughed at him.

After he put them all out, he took the child's father and mother and the disciples who were with him, and went in where the child was. [41] He took her by the hand and said to her, "Talitha koum!" (which means, "Little girl, I say to you, get up!"). [42] Immediately the girl stood up and walked around (she was twelve years old). At this they were completely astonished. [43] He gave strict orders not to let anyone know about this, and told them to give her something to eat.

Inflammatory Word

Matthew 5:1–37

If Jesus had avoided one emotionally charged word, *kingdom*, everything might have been different. Whenever he said it, images would dance in the minds of his audience: bright banners, glittering armies, the gold and ivory of Solomon's day, the nation of Israel restored to glory. Jesus often used this word that quickened the pulse of Israel, starting with his very first message, "Repent, for the kingdom of heaven is near" (4:17).

By boldly comparing himself to Israel's most powerful king—"The Queen of the South . . . came from the ends of the earth to listen to Solomon's wisdom, and now one greater than Solomon is here" (12:42)—Jesus tapped into the reservoir of his nation's deepest longings. More, he claimed that the extravagant promises of the prophets were coming true in him. What was about to happen, he said, was a new thing, and would far surpass anything from the past: "For I tell you that many prophets and kings wanted to see what you see but did not see it, and to hear what you hear but did not hear it" (Luke 10:24).

The expectations raised by such statements led to confusion and, finally, angry rejection. The initial excitement over Jesus' miracles was displaced by disappointment when he failed to restore the long-awaited kingdom. For, as it turned out, the word *kingdom*" meant one thing to the crowd and quite another to Jesus.

Winds of change were blowing through Israel as Jesus spoke. Guerrilla fighters called Zealots hung on the edges of the crowds—one of them penetrated his inner circle of twelve disciples—awaiting the signal. Armed and well-organized, they were spoiling for a fight against oppressive Rome. But the signal for revolt never came. To their dismay, it gradually became clear that Jesus was not talking about a political or military kingdom at all.

Jesus indicated that two kinds of history are going on simultaneously. We live in a visible world of families and people and cities and nations, "the kingdom of this world." But he called for people to commit their lives to an invisible kingdom, the "kingdom of heaven," more important and more valuable than anything in the visible world. It is like the finest pearl in the world, he said, worth selling everything you have to invest in it.

Success in the kingdom of heaven involves a great reversal of values, as seen in this major address, the Sermon on the Mount. "Blessed are the poor in spirit," Jesus said, and also those who mourn, and the meek, and those who hunger and thirst, and the persecuted . . . "for theirs is the kingdom of heaven." Status in this world is no guarantee of status in the kingdom of heaven.

To Reflect On: *How does Jesus' formula for success compare with modern America's?*

MATTHEW 5:1–37

The Beatitudes

5 Now when he saw the crowds, he went up on a mountainside and sat down. His disciples came to him, ²and he began to teach them, saying:

³"Blessed are the poor in spirit,
  for theirs is the kingdom of heaven.

⁴Blessed are those who mourn,
  for they will be comforted.
⁵Blessed are the meek,
  for they will inherit the earth.
⁶Blessed are those who hunger and
    thirst for righteousness,
  for they will be filled.
⁷Blessed are the merciful,
  for they will be shown mercy.

⁸Blessed are the pure in heart,
  for they will see God.
⁹Blessed are the peacemakers,
  for they will be called sons of God.
¹⁰Blessed are those who are persecuted
      because of righteousness,
  for theirs is the kingdom of heaven.

¹¹"Blessed are you when people insult you, persecute you and falsely say all kinds of evil against you because of me. ¹²Rejoice and be glad, because great is your reward in heaven, for in the same way they persecuted the prophets who were before you.

Salt and Light

¹³"You are the salt of the earth. But if the salt loses its saltiness, how can it be made salty again? It is no longer good for anything, except to be thrown out and trampled by men.

¹⁴"You are the light of the world. A city on a hill cannot be hidden. ¹⁵Neither do people light a lamp and put it under a bowl. Instead they put it on its stand, and it gives light to everyone in the house. ¹⁶In the same way, let your light shine before men, that they may see your good deeds and praise your Father in heaven.

The Fulfillment of the Law

¹⁷"Do not think that I have come to abolish the Law or the Prophets; I have not come to abolish them but to fulfill them. ¹⁸I tell you the truth, until heaven and earth disappear, not the smallest letter, not the least stroke of a pen, will by any means disappear from the Law until everything is accomplished. ¹⁹Anyone who breaks one of the least of these commandments and teaches others to do the same will be called least in the kingdom of heaven, but whoever practices and teaches these commands will be called great in the kingdom of heaven. ²⁰For I tell you that unless your righteousness surpasses that of the Pharisees and the teachers of the law, you will certainly not enter the kingdom of heaven.

Murder

²¹"You have heard that it was said to the people long ago, 'Do not murder, and anyone who murders will be subject to judgment.' ²²But I tell you that anyone who is angry with his brother will be subject to judgment. Again, anyone who says to his brother, 'Raca,' is answerable to the Sanhedrin. But anyone who says, 'You fool!' will be in danger of the fire of hell.

²³"Therefore, if you are offering your gift at the altar and there remember that your brother has something against you, ²⁴leave your gift there in front of the altar. First go and be reconciled to your brother; then come and offer your gift.

²⁵"Settle matters quickly with your adversary who is taking you to court. Do it while you are still with him on the way, or he may hand you over to the judge, and the judge may hand you over to the officer, and you may be thrown into prison. ²⁶I tell you the truth, you will not get out until you have paid the last penny.

Adultery

²⁷"You have heard that it was said, 'Do not commit adultery.' ²⁸But I tell you that anyone who looks at a woman lustfully has already committed adultery with her in his heart. ²⁹If your right eye causes you to sin, gouge it out and throw it away. It is better for you to lose one part of your body than for your whole body to be thrown into hell. ³⁰And if your right hand causes you to sin, cut it off and throw it away. It is better for you to lose one part of your body than for your whole body to go into hell.

Divorce

³¹"It has been said, 'Anyone who divorces his wife must give her a certificate of divorce.' ³²But I tell you that anyone who divorces his wife, except for marital unfaithfulness, causes her to become an adulteress, and anyone who marries the divorced woman commits adultery.

Oaths

³³"Again, you have heard that it was said to the people long ago, 'Do not break your oath, but keep the oaths you have made to the Lord.' ³⁴But I tell you, Do not swear at all: either by heaven, for it is God's throne; ³⁵or by the earth, for it is his footstool; or by Jerusalem, for it is the city of the Great King. ³⁶And do not swear by your head, for you cannot make even one hair white or black. ³⁷Simply let your 'Yes' be 'Yes,' and your 'No,' 'No'; anything beyond this comes from the evil one.

Savings Account

Matthew 6

Matthew 6, a continuation of the Sermon on the Mount, contains The Lord's Prayer, perhaps the most famous prayer of all. Jesus gave it as a model of prayer, and it captures well the message of the kingdom: "Your kingdom come, your will be done on earth as it is in heaven." Jesus sought to bring the two worlds together, and the Sermon on the Mount explains how.

At first glance, some of the advice may seem downright foolish: Give to everyone who asks, love your enemies, turn the other cheek, grant interest-free loans, don't worry about clothes or food. Can such idealism ever work in the "real," or visible, world? That was Jesus' point precisely: Break your obsession with safety, security, thriftiness, self-righteousness. Depend instead on the Father, letting him take care of the personal injustices that come your way, trusting him to look after your daily needs. In a nutshell, the message of the kingdom is this: Live for God and not other people.

The message applies to rewards as well. Most of us look to friends and colleagues for our rewards: a slap on the back, a hero medal, applause, a lavish compliment. But according to Jesus, by far the more important rewards await us after death. Therefore, the most significant human acts of all may be carried out in secret, seen by no one but God.

As Jesus explained it, we are accumulating a kind of savings account, "storing up treasures" in heaven rather than on earth. Treasures so great that they will pay back any amount of suffering in this life. The Old Testament had dropped a few scant hints about an afterlife, but Jesus spoke plainly about a place where "the righteous will shine like the sun in the kingdom of the Father" (13:43).

In their quest for a kingdom, the Jews had been looking for signs of God's approval in this life, primarily through prosperity and political power. Beginning with this speech, Jesus changed the focus to the life to come. He discounted success in this visible world. Invest in the future life, he cautioned; after all, rust, a thief, or a lowly insect can destroy all else that we accumulate.

> **To Reflect On:** *Of the people you know, who best puts these principles into practice?*

MATTHEW 6

Giving to the Needy

6 "Be careful not to do your 'acts of righteousness' before men, to be seen by them. If you do, you will have no reward from your Father in heaven.

²"So when you give to the needy, do not announce it with trumpets, as the hypocrites do in the synagogues and on the streets, to be honored by men. I tell you the truth, they have received their reward in full. ³But when you give to the needy, do not let your left hand know what your right hand is doing, ⁴so that your giving may be in secret. Then your Father, who sees what is done in secret, will reward you.

Prayer

⁵"And when you pray, do not be like the hypocrites, for they love to pray standing in the synagogues and on the street corners to be seen by men. I tell you the truth, they have received their reward in full. ⁶But when you pray, go into your room, close the door and pray to your Father, who is unseen. Then your Father, who sees what is done in secret, will reward you. ⁷And when you pray, do not keep on babbling like

pagans, for they think they will be heard because of their many words. [8]Do not be like them, for your Father knows what you need before you ask him.

[9]"This, then, is how you should pray:

" 'Our Father in heaven,
hallowed be your name,
[10]your kingdom come,
your will be done
on earth as it is in heaven.
[11]Give us today our daily bread.
[12]Forgive us our debts,
as we also have forgiven our
debtors.
[13]And lead us not into temptation,
but deliver us from the evil one.'

[14]For if you forgive men when they sin against you, your heavenly Father will also forgive you. [15]But if you do not forgive men their sins, your Father will not forgive your sins.

Fasting

[16]"When you fast, do not look somber as the hypocrites do, for they disfigure their faces to show men they are fasting. I tell you the truth, they have received their reward in full. [17]But when you fast, put oil on your head and wash your face, [18]so that it will not be obvious to men that you are fasting, but only to your Father, who is unseen; and your Father, who sees what is done in secret, will reward you.

Treasures in Heaven

[19]"Do not store up for yourselves treasures on earth, where moth and rust destroy, and where thieves break in and steal. [20]But store up for yourselves treasures in heaven, where moth and rust do not destroy, and where thieves do not break in and steal. [21]For where your treasure is, there your heart will be also.

[22]"The eye is the lamp of the body. If your eyes are good, your whole body will be full of light. [23]But if your eyes are bad, your whole body will be full of darkness. If then the light within you is darkness, how great is that darkness!

[24]"No one can serve two masters. Either he will hate the one and love the other, or he will be devoted to the one and despise the other. You cannot serve both God and Money.

Do Not Worry

[25]"Therefore I tell you, do not worry about your life, what you will eat or drink; or about your body, what you will wear. Is not life more important than food, and the body more important than clothes? [26]Look at the birds of the air; they do not sow or reap or store away in barns, and yet your heavenly Father feeds them. Are you not much more valuable than they? [27]Who of you by worrying can add a single hour to his life?

[28]"And why do you worry about clothes? See how the lilies of the field grow. They do not labor or spin. [29]Yet I tell you that not even Solomon in all his splendor was dressed like one of these. [30]If that is how God clothes the grass of the field, which is here today and tomorrow is thrown into the fire, will he not much more clothe you, O you of little faith? [31]So do not worry, saying, 'What shall we eat?' or 'What shall we drink?' or 'What shall we wear?' [32]For the pagans run after all these things, and your heavenly Father knows that you need them. [33]But seek first his kingdom and his righteousness, and all these things will be given to you as well. [34]Therefore do not worry about tomorrow, for tomorrow will worry about itself. Each day has enough trouble of its own.

Kingdom Tales

Matthew 13:24–58

Sometimes, as in the Sermon on the Mount, Jesus would deliver a long, topically organized speech. More often, though, he relied on the parable, a compact short story with a moral. Writers have long marveled at his skill in communicating profound truth in such simple, everyday stories.

The parables served Jesus' purposes perfectly. When he first told the stories in this chapter, he was floating offshore in a boat, shouting to the large crowds that had gathered. Because the stories concerned their daily lives—farming, baking bread, hunting buried treasure, fishing—he was able to hold their attention. And yet the parables simultaneously allowed Jesus to train his disciples "privately"; later on, he could take the disciples aside and explain the deeper meaning.

As Jesus told his disciples, parables also helped to winnow the audience. Spectators seeking entertainment could go home with a few stories to mull over, but more serious inquirers would need to come back for further interpretation. Parables also helped preserve his message: Years later, as people reflected on what Jesus taught, his parables came to mind in vivid detail.

Matthew 13 collects several of Jesus' stories about the "kingdom of heaven." Although Jesus never concisely defined the term, he gave many clues about the nature of his kingdom. Unlike, say, Greece or China or Spain, it has no geographical boundaries and can't be charted on a map. Its followers live right among their enemies, not separated from them by a moat or a wall. Still Jesus predicted that the kingdom would show remarkable growth even in an evil environment bent on its destruction.

In summary, the "kingdom of heaven" consists of the rule of God in the world. It comprises people of all races and from all nations who loyally follow God's will. The disciples, accustomed to more traditional images of power and leadership, couldn't quite grasp Jesus' concept of the kingdom. They kept asking him to explain his parables even as they jockeyed vainly for status. Not until he died, and then came back, did they comprehend his mission on earth.

> **To Reflect On:** *Jesus addressed peasants and fishermen. Choose one of these parables and think about how you would express it in the terms of modern, technological society.*

MATTHEW 13:24–58

The Parable of the Weeds

24Jesus told them another parable: "The kingdom of heaven is like a man who sowed good seed in his field. 25But while everyone was sleeping, his enemy came and sowed weeds among the wheat, and went away. 26When the wheat sprouted and formed heads, then the weeds also appeared.

27"The owner's servants came to him and said, 'Sir didn't you sow good seed in your field? Where then did the weeds come from?'

28" 'An enemy did this,' he replied.

"The servants asked him, 'Do you want us to go and pull them up?'

29" 'No,' he answered, 'because while you are pulling the weeds, you may root up the wheat with them. 30Let both grow together until the harvest. At that time I will tell the harvesters: First collect the weeds and tie them in bundles to be burned; then gather the wheat and bring it into my barn.' "

The Parables of the Mustard Seed and the Yeast

³¹He told them another parable: "The kingdom of heaven is like a mustard seed, which a man took and planted in his field. ³²Though it is the smallest of all your seeds, yet when it grows, it is the largest of garden plants and becomes a tree, so that the birds of the air come and perch in its branches."

³³He told them still another parable: "The kingdom of heaven is like yeast that a woman took and mixed into a large amount of flour until it worked all through the dough."

³⁴Jesus spoke all these things to the crowd in parables; he did not say anything to them without using a parable. ³⁵So was fulfilled what was spoken through the prophet:

"I will open my mouth in parables,
I will utter things hidden since the
creation of the world."

The Parable of the Weeds Explained

³⁶Then he left the crowd and went into the house. His disciples came to him and said, "Explain to us the parable of the weeds in the field."

³⁷He answered, "The one who sowed the good seed is the Son of Man. ³⁸The field is the world, and the good seed stands for the sons of the kingdom. The weeds are the sons of the evil one, ³⁹and the enemy who sows them is the devil. The harvest is the end of the age, and the harvesters are angels.

⁴⁰"As the weeds are pulled up and burned in the fire, so it will be at the end of the age. ⁴¹The Son of Man will send out his angels, and they will weed out of his kingdom everything that causes sin and all who do evil. ⁴²They will throw them into the fiery furnace, where there will be weeping and gnashing of teeth. ⁴³Then the righteous will shine like the sun in the kingdom of their Father. He who has ears, let him hear.

The Parables of the Hidden Treasure and the Pearl

⁴⁴"The kingdom of heaven is like treasure hidden in a field. When a man found it, he hid it again, and then in his joy went and sold all he had and bought that field.

⁴⁵"Again, the kingdom of heaven is like a merchant looking for fine pearls. ⁴⁶When he found one of great value, he went away and sold everything he had and bought it.

The Parable of the Net

⁴⁷"Once again, the kingdom of heaven is like a net that was let down into the lake and caught all kinds of fish. ⁴⁸When it was full, the fishermen pulled it up on the shore. Then they sat down and collected the good fish in baskets, but threw the bad away. ⁴⁹This is how it will be at the end of the age. The angels will come and separate the wicked from the righteous ⁵⁰and throw them into the fiery furnace, where there will be weeping and gnashing of teeth.

⁵¹"Have you understood all these things?" Jesus asked.

"Yes," they replied.

⁵²He said to them, "Therefore every teacher of the law who has been instructed about the kingdom of heaven is like the owner of a house who brings out of his storeroom new treasures as well as old."

A Prophet Without Honor

⁵³When Jesus had finished these parables, he moved on from there. ⁵⁴Coming to his hometown, he began teaching the people in their synagogue, and they were amazed. "Where did this man get this wisdom and these miraculous powers?" they asked. ⁵⁵"Isn't this the carpenter's son? Isn't his mother's name Mary, and aren't his brothers James, Joseph, Simon and Judas? ⁵⁶Aren't all his sisters with us? Where then did this man get all these things?" ⁵⁷And they took offense at him.

But Jesus said to them, "Only in his hometown and in his own house is a prophet without honor."

⁵⁸And he did not do many miracles there because of their lack of faith.

Contrast in Power

Mark 6:14b–56

In this chapter, Mark brings together scenes that illustrate very different kinds of power in the two kingdoms. Herod, ruler of Galilee, personified one kind. He was rich and ruthless, and had legions of Roman soldiers to carry out his every command. He left impressive monuments all over Palestine. Mark tells how Herod used power: He stole his brother's wife, locked up John the Baptist, and then had the prophet beheaded as a party trick. Killing John wasn't Herod's preference, but he had to honor a careless vow in order to protect his image.

Jesus, too, was a leader—a king, in fact—but one who broke stereotypes. His power was undeniable; yet he used that power compassionately, to feed the hungry and heal the sick. At the beginning of his ministry, Jesus had declined a tempting offer of glory and territory, and after that he seemed to give no thought to cultivating an image of power or importance. He spent his time telling stories, not raising an army. He sought to please God, not to satisfy people's false expectations.

Herod had built a lavish palace in Jesus' home province of Galilee, but Jesus carefully avoided that fashionable area. As Herod wined and dined prominent guests in the resort town of Tiberias, Jesus roamed the countryside with his ragtag followers. He too served a banquet, of sorts, to 5000 unexpected guests. His simple message of love, forgiveness, and healing had its own kind of power. Mark tells of crowds chasing Jesus around a lake, running to fetch their sick friends, pressing in close to touch the Teacher.

Jesus had contemptuously dismissed Herod as "that fox." But as talk about Jesus spread, Herod longed for a chance to meet him. Eventually he got his chance, at Jesus' trial. Eager to see a miracle, Herod used charm, ridicule, and military force to try to coax some response from Jesus. He failed—Jesus never once succumbed to that kind of power.

To Reflect On: *Which kind of power are most people attracted to? Which kind are you attracted to?*

———◆———

MARK 6:14b–56

Jesus Sends Out the Twelve

Some were saying, "John the Baptist has been raised from the dead, and that is why miraculous powers are at work in him."

[15]Others said, "He is Elijah."

And still others claimed, "He is a prophet, like one of the prophets of long ago."

[16]But when Herod heard this, he said, "John, the man I beheaded, has been raised from the dead!"

[17]For Herod himself had given orders to have John arrested, and he had him bound and put in prison. He did this because of Herodias, his brother Philip's wife, whom he had married. [18]For John had been saying to Herod, "It is not lawful for you to have your brother's wife." [19]So Herodias nursed a grudge against John and wanted to kill him. But she was not able to, [20]because Herod feared John and protected him, knowing him to be a righteous and holy man. When Herod heard John, he was greatly puzzled; yet he liked to listen to him.

[21]Finally the opportune time came. On his birthday Herod gave a banquet for his high officials and military commanders and the leading men of Galilee. [22]When the daughter of Herodias came in and danced, she pleased Herod and his dinner guests.

The king said to the girl, "Ask me for anything you want, and I'll give it to you." ²³And he promised her with an oath, "Whatever you ask I will give you, up to half my kingdom."

²⁴She went out and said to her mother, "What shall I ask for?"

"The head of John the Baptist," she answered.

²⁵At once the girl hurried in to the king with the request: "I want you to give me right now the head of John the Baptist on a platter."

²⁶The king was greatly distressed, but because of his oaths and his dinner guests, he did not want to refuse her. ²⁷So he immediately sent an executioner with orders to bring John's head. The man went, beheaded John in the prison, ²⁸and brought back his head on a platter. He presented it to the girl, and she gave it to her mother. ²⁹On hearing of this, John's disciples came and took his body and laid it in a tomb.

Jesus Feeds the Five Thousand

³⁰The apostles gathered around Jesus and reported to him all they had done and taught. ³¹Then, because so many people were coming and going that they did not even have a chance to eat, he said to them, "Come with me by your selves to a quiet place and get some rest."

³²So they went away by themselves in a boat to a solitary place. ³³But many who saw them leaving recognized them and ran on foot from all the towns and got there ahead of them. ³⁴When Jesus landed and saw a large crowd, he had compassion on them, because they were like sheep without a shepherd. So he began teaching them many things.

³⁵By this time it was late in the day, so his disciples came to him. "This is a remote place," they said, "and it's already very late. ³⁶Send the people away so they can go to the surrounding countryside and villages and buy themselves something to eat."

³⁷But he answered, "You give them something to eat."

They said to him, "That would take eight months of a man's wages! Are we to go and spend that much on bread and give it to them to eat?"

³⁸"How many loaves do you have?" he asked. "Go and see."

When they found out, they said, "Five— and two fish."

³⁹Then Jesus directed them to have all the people sit down in groups on the green grass. ⁴⁰So they sat down in groups of hundreds and fifties. ⁴¹Taking the five loaves and the two fish and looking up to heaven, he gave thanks and broke the loaves. Then he gave them to his disciples to set before the people. He also divided the two fish among them all. ⁴²They all ate and were satisfied, ⁴³and the disciples picked up twelve basketfuls of broken pieces of bread and fish. ⁴⁴The number of the men who had eaten was five thousand.

Jesus Walks on the Water

⁴⁵Immediately Jesus made his disciples get into the boat and go on ahead of him to Bethsaida, while he dismissed the crowd. ⁴⁶After leaving them, he went up on a mountainside to pray.

⁴⁷When evening came, the boat was in the middle of the lake, and he was alone on land. ⁴⁸He saw the disciples straining at the oars, because the wind was against them. About the fourth watch of the night he went out to them, walking on the lake. He was about to pass by them, ⁴⁹but when they saw him walking on the lake, they thought he was a ghost. They cried out, ⁵⁰because they all saw him and were terrified.

Immediately he spoke to them and said, "Take courage! It is I. Don't be afraid." ⁵¹Then he climbed into the boat with them, and the wind died down. They were completely amazed, ⁵²for they had not understood about the loaves; their hearts were hardened.

⁵³When they had crossed over, they landed at Gennesaret and anchored there. ⁵⁴As soon as they got out of the boat, people recognized Jesus. ⁵⁵They ran throughout that whole region and carried the sick on mats to wherever they heard he was. ⁵⁶And wherever he went—into villages, towns or countryside—they placed the sick in the marketplaces. They begged him to let them touch even the edge of his cloak, and all who touched him were healed.

Of Two Worlds

Luke 16

A story is told about Rabbi Joseph Schneerson, a Hasidic leader during the early days of the Russian revolution. The rabbi spent much time in jail, persecuted for his faith. One morning in 1927, as he prayed in a Leningrad synagogue, secret police rushed in and arrested him. They took him to a police station and worked him over, demanding that he give up his religious activities. He refused. The interrogator brandished a gun in his face and said, "This little toy has made many a man change his mind." Rabbi Schneerson answered, "This little toy can intimidate only that kind of man who has many gods and but one world. Because I have only one God and two worlds, I am not impressed by this little toy."

The theme of "two worlds," or two kingdoms, emerges often in Jesus' teaching, and two stories in this chapter draw a sharp distinction between the two worlds. "What is highly valued among men is detestable in God's sight," Jesus said, commenting on the first story. The second story, of the rich man and Lazarus, elaborates on that difference in values between the two worlds. The rich man prospered in this world, yet neglected to make any provision for eternal life and thus suffered the consequences. Meanwhile, a half-starved beggar, who by any standard would be judged a failure in this life, received an eternal reward.

Jesus told such stories to a Jewish audience with a tradition of wealthy patriarchs, strong kings, and victorious heroes. But Jesus kept emphasizing his stunning reversal of values. People who have little value in this world (the poor, the persecuted—people like Lazarus) may, in fact, have great stature in God's kingdom. Consistently he presented the visible world as a place to invest for the future, to store up treasure for the life to come.

Jesus once asked a question that brings the two worlds starkly together: "What good will it be for a man if he gains the whole world, yet forfeits his soul?" (Matthew 16:26).

> **To Reflect On:** *How would you rate yourself, using the standards of success and failure in this world? What if you used Jesus' standards?*

LUKE 16

The Parable of the Shrewd Manager

16 Jesus told his disciples: "There was a rich man whose manager was accused of wasting his possessions. ²So he called him in and asked him, 'What is this I hear about you? Give an account of your management, because you cannot be manager any longer.'

³"The manager said to himself, 'What shall I do now? My master is taking away my job. I'm not strong enough to dig, and I'm ashamed to beg—⁴I know what I'll do so that, when I lose my job here, people will welcome me into their houses.'

⁵"So he called in each one of his master's debtors. He asked the first, 'How much do you owe my master?'

⁶" 'Eight hundred gallons of olive oil,' he replied.

"The manager told him, 'Take your bill, sit down quickly, and make it four hundred.'

⁷"Then he asked the second, 'And how much do you owe?'

" 'A thousand bushels of wheat,' he repied.

"He told him, 'Take your bill and make it eight hundred.'

8"The master commended the dishonest manager because he had acted shrewdly. For the people of this world are more shrewd in dealing with their own kind than are the people of the light. 9I tell you, use worldly wealth to gain friends for yourselves, so that when it is gone, you will be welcomed into eternal dwellings.

10"Whoever can be trusted with very little can also be trusted with much, and whoever is dishonest with very little will also be dishonest with much. 11So if you have not been trustworthy in handling worldly wealth, who will trust you with true riches? 12And if you have not been trustworthy with someone else's property, who will give you property of your own?

13"No servant can serve two masters. Either he will hate the one and love the other, or he will be devoted to the one and despise the other. You cannot serve both God and Money."

14The Pharisees, who loved money, heard all this and were sneering at Jesus. 15He said to them, "You are the ones who justify yourselves in the eyes of men, but God knows your hearts. What is highly valued among men is detestable in God's sight.

Additional Teachings

16"The Law and the Prophets were proclaimed until John. Since that time, the good news of the kingdom of God is being preached, and everyone is forcing his way into it. 7It is easier for heaven and earth to disappear than for the least stroke of a pen to drop out of the Law.

18"Anyone who divorces his wife and marries another woman commits adultery, and the man who marries a divorced woman commits adultery.

The Rich Man and Lazarus

19"There was a rich man who was dressed in purple and fine linen and lived in luxury every day. 20At his gate was laid a beggar named Lazarus, covered with sores 21and longing to eat what fell from the rich man's table. Even the dogs came and licked his sores.

22"The time came when the beggar died and the angels carried him to Abraham's side. The rich man also died and was buried. 23In hell, where he was in torment, he looked up and saw Abraham far away, with Lazarus by his side. 24So he called to him, 'Father Abraham, have pity on me and send Lazarus to dip the tip of his finger in water and cool my tongue, because I am in agony in this fire.'

25"But Abraham replied, 'Son, remember that in your lifetime you received your good things, while Lazarus received bad things, but now he is comforted here and you are in agony. 26And besides all this, between us and you a great chasm has been fixed, so that those who want to go from here to you cannot, nor can anyone cross over from there to us.'

27"He answered, 'Then I beg you, father, send Lazarus to my father's house, 28for I have five brothers. Let him warn them, so that they will not also come to this place of torment.'

29"Abraham replied, 'They have Moses and the Prophets; let them listen to them.'

30"'No, father Abraham,' he said, 'but if someone from the dead goes to them, they will repent.'

31"He said to him, 'If they do not listen to Moses and the Prophets, they will not be convinced even if someone rises from the dead.'"

Jesus on Money

Luke 12:13–48

Jesus had more to say on money than almost any other topic. Yet two thousand years later, Christians have trouble agreeing on exactly what he *did* say. One reason is that he rarely gave "practical" advice. He avoided comment on specific economic systems and, as in this chapter, refused to get involved in personal disputes about finances. Jesus saw money primarily as a *spiritual* force.

One pastor boils down money issues into three questions:

1. How did you get it? (Did it involve injustice, cheating, oppression of the poor?)
2. What are you doing with it? (Are you hoarding it? Exploiting others? Wasting it on needless luxuries?)
3. What is it doing to you?

Although Jesus spoke to all three of those issues, he concentrated on the last one. As he explained it, money operates much like idolatry. It can catch hold and dominate a person's life, diverting attention away from God. Jesus challenged people to break free of money's power—even if it meant giving it all away.

This chapter offers a good summary of Jesus' attitude toward money. He did not condemn all possessions ("your Father knows that you need [food, drink, and clothes"]). But he strongly warned against putting faith in money to secure the future. As his story of the rich man shows, money will ultimately fail to solve life's biggest problems.

Jesus urged his listeners to seek treasure in the kingdom of God, for such treasure could benefit them in this life and the next one, too. "Do not worry," he said. Rather, trust God to provide your basic needs. To emphasize his point, he brought up the example of King Solomon, the richest man in the Old Testament. To most nationalistic Jews, Solomon was a hero, but Jesus saw him in a different light: Solomon's wealth had long since vanished, and even in his prime he was no more impressive than a common wildflower. Better to trust in the God who lavishes care on the whole earth than to spend your life worrying about money and possessions.

To Reflect On: *How do you fit together Jesus' teaching and our culture's emphasis on financial security for the future?*

LUKE 12:13–48

The Parable of the Rich Fool

¹³Someone in the crowd said to him, "Teacher, tell my brother to divide the inheritance with me."

¹⁴Jesus replied, "Man, who appointed me a judge or an arbiter between you?" ¹⁵Then he said to them, "Watch out! Be on your guard against all kinds of greed; a man's life does not consist in the abundance of his possessions."

¹⁶And he told them this parable: "The ground of a certain rich man produced a good crop. ¹⁷He thought to himself, 'What shall I do? I have no place to store my crops.'

¹⁸"Then he said, 'This is what I'll do. I will tear down my barns and build bigger ones, and there I will store all my grain and my goods. ¹⁹And I'll say to myself, "You have plenty of good things laid up for many years. Take life easy; eat, drink and be merry."'

²⁰"But God said to him, 'You fool! This very night your life will be demanded from

you. Then who will get what you have prepared for yourself?'

²¹"This is how it will be with anyone who stores up things for himself but is not rich toward God."

Do Not Worry

²²Then Jesus said to his disciples: "Therefore I tell you, do not worry about your life, what you will eat; or about your body, what you will wear. ²³Life is more than food, and the body more than clothes. ²⁴Consider the ravens: They do not sow or reap, they have no storeroom or barn; yet God feeds them. And how much more valuable you are than birds! ²⁵Who of you by worrying can add a single hour to his life? ²⁶Since you cannot do this very little thing, why do you worry about the rest?

²⁷"Consider how the lilies grow. They do not labor or spin. Yet I tell you, not even Solomon in all his splendor was dressed like one of these. ²⁸If that is how God clothes the grass of the field, which is here today, and tomorrow is thrown into the fire, how much more will he clothe you, O you of little faith! ²⁹And do not set your heart on what you will eat or drink; do not worry about it. ³⁰For the pagan world runs after all such things, and your Father knows that you need them. ³¹But seek his kingdom, and these things will be given to you as well.

³²"Do not be afraid, little flock, for your Father has been pleased to give you the kingdom. ³³Sell your possessions and give to the poor. Provide purses for yourselves that will not wear out, a treasure in heaven that will not be exhausted, where no thief comes near and no moth destroys. ³⁴For where your treasure is, there your heart will be also.

Watchfulness

³⁵"Be dressed ready for service and keep your lamps burning, ³⁶like men waiting for their master to return from a wedding banquet, so that when he comes and knocks they can immediately open the door for him. ³⁷It will be good for those servants whose master finds them watching when he comes. I tell you the truth, he will dress himself to serve, will have them recline at the table and will come and wait on them. ³⁸It will be good for those servants whose master finds them ready, even if he comes in the second or third watch of the night. ³⁹But understand this: If the owner of the house had known at what hour the thief was coming, he would not have let his house be broken into. ⁴⁰You also must be ready, because the Son of Man will come at an hour when you do not expect him."

⁴¹Peter asked, "Lord are you telling this parable to us, or to everyone?"

⁴²The Lord answered, "Who then is the faithful and wise manager, whom the master puts in charge of his servants to give them their food allowance at the proper time? ⁴³It will be good for that servant whom the master finds doing so when he returns. ⁴⁴I tell you the truth, he will put him in charge of all his possessions. ⁴⁵But suppose the servant says to himself, 'My master is taking a long time in coming,' and he then begins to beat the menservants and maidservants and to eat and drink and get drunk. ⁴⁶The master of that servant will come on a day when he does not expect him and at an hour he is not aware of. He will cut him to pieces and assign him a place with the unbelievers.

⁴⁷"That servant who knows his master's will and does not get ready or does not do what his master wants will be beaten with many blows. ⁴⁸But the one who does not know and does things deserving punishment will be beaten with few blows. From everyone who has been given much, much will be demanded; and from the one who has been entrusted with much, much more will be asked.

How to Succeed without Really Trying

Luke 18:1-30

A series of vignettes in this chapter reinforces the message about money, and about two worlds. In Luke's typical style, the stories feature underdogs: a mistreated widow, a despised tax collector, little children, a blind beggar. A rich man makes an appearance, but, like the rich man in the story of Lazarus, only as a negative example.

Even Jesus' closest disciples had trouble swallowing his teaching that money represents a grave danger. Yet Jesus sternly warned that wealth can keep people from the kingdom of God by tempting them to depend on themselves rather than on God. The story of the Pharisee and the tax collector expands that message. Not only wealth, but *any* form of pride or self-dependence tends to lead away from God.

An effort to become "holy," for example, may accomplish just the opposite if it results in spiritual pride and a feeling of superiority. Human beings have an incurable tendency to feed their own egos, to take credit, to compete. The way to God, said Jesus, is just the opposite: Trust God like a little child, admit wrong, let go.

Jesus reveals the key to true success in the very first story in this collection, a parable illustrating why we "should always pray and not give up." The persistent widow endured much frustration and apparent injustice before the judge finally granted her request. Similarly, Jesus implied, we may go through desert periods when it looks like God is ignoring our heartfelt requests. But in the end God himself will settle accounts. And all those whose faith holds firm, even in the hard times, will see justice.

> **To Reflect On:** *When have you resembled the Pharisee in Jesus' story? The tax collector?*

LUKE 18:1–30

The Parable of the Persistent Widow

18 Then Jesus told his disciples a parable to show them that they should always pray and not give up. ²He said: "In a certain town there was a judge who neither feared God nor cared about men. ³And there was a widow in that town who kept coming to him with the plea, 'Grant me justice against my adversary.'

⁴"For some time he refused. But finally he said to himself, 'Even though I don't fear God or care about men, ⁵yet because this widow keeps bothering me, I will see that she gets justice, so that she won't eventually wear me out with her coming!' "

⁶And the Lord said, "Listen to what the unjust judge says. ⁷And will not God bring about justice for his chosen ones, who cry out to him day and night? Will he keep putting them off? ⁸I tell you, he will see that they get justice, and quickly. However, when the Son of Man comes, will he find faith on the earth?"

The Parable of the Pharisee and the Tax Collector

⁹To some who were confident of their own righteousness and looked down on everybody else, Jesus told this parable: ¹⁰"Two men went up to the temple to pray, one a Pharisee and the other a tax collector. ¹¹The Pharisee stood up and prayed about himself: 'God, I thank you that I am not like other men—robbers, evildoers, adulterers—or even like this tax collector. ¹²I fast twice a week and give a tenth of all I get.'

¹³"But the tax collector stood at a distance. He would not even look up to heaven, but beat his breast and said, 'God have mercy on me, a sinner.'

¹⁴"I tell you that this man, rather than the other, went home justified before God. For everyone who exalts himself will be humbled, and he who humbles himself will be exalted."

The Little Children and Jesus

¹⁵People were also bringing babies to Jesus to have him touch them. When the disciples saw this, they rebuked them. ¹⁶But Jesus called the children to him and said, "Let the little children come to me, and do not hinder them, for the kingdom of God belongs to such as these. ¹⁷I tell you the truth, anyone who will not receive the kingdom of God like a little child will never enter it."

The Rich Ruler

¹⁸A certain ruler asked him, "Good teacher, what must I do to inherit eternal life?"

¹⁹"Why do you call me good?" Jesus answered. "No one is good—except God alone. ²⁰You know the commandments: 'Do not commit adultery, do not murder, do not steal, do not give false testimony, honor your father and mother.' "

²¹"All these I have kept since I was a boy," he said.

²²When Jesus heard this, he said to him, "You still lack one thing. Sell everything you have and give to the poor, and you will have treasure in heaven. Then come, follow me."

²³When he heard this, he became very sad, because he was a man of great wealth. ²⁴Jesus looked at him and said, "How hard it is for the rich to enter the kingdom of God! ²⁵Indeed, it is easier for a camel to go through the eye of a needle than for a rich man to enter the kingdom of God."

²⁶Those who heard this asked, "Who then can be saved?"

²⁷Jesus replied, "What is impossible with men is possible with God."

²⁸Peter said to him, "We have left all we had to follow you!"

²⁹"I tell you the truth," Jesus said to them, "no one who has left home or wife or brothers or parents or children for the sake of the kingdom of God ³⁰will fail to receive many times as much in this age and, in the age to come, eternal life."

Master Storyteller

Luke 15

The chief priests, the teachers of the Law and the leaders among the people were trying to kill him. Yet they could not find any way to do it, because all the people hung on his words" (Luke 19:47–48). Using simple, homespun images, Jesus expressed profound truths in a way that held his audience captive. His parables, or concise short stories, have won high praise even from literary experts who do not accept their message. Some of the most famous of these parables, including these three, appear only in Luke's gospel.

Although trained as a physician, Luke demonstrated great skill as a writer. The introduction to his book mentions that he carefully investigated reports from eyewitnesses before writing the book that bears his name. Using the finest Greek found in the New Testament, he brought characters and scenes vividly to life.

Luke especially excels at conveying the plight of the poor and the outcast. Women, largely ignored by ancient historians, play a large role in his book—he introduces thirteen mentioned nowhere else—as do children. It may seem strange that a man belonging to the upper class would emerge as a champion of the underdog—evidently, Jesus' own compassion had affected Luke deeply.

The three stories in this chapter all stir up feelings for the underdog. A shepherd scours the hillside in a frantic search for a missing sheep. A woman turns her house upside down over a lost silver coin. A runaway son thumbs his nose at a life of comfort and ends up half-starved in a pigpen. In a few brief sentences, the parables tug at feelings of loss and remorse that lie buried just beneath the surface in all of us. And yet all three parables end the same: Spectacular good news floods in to replace the sadness, and partying breaks out.

The word *gospel* itself comes from the Old English word *godspell*. It means, simply, "good news"—a message that Luke never lost sight of. Even for the saddest story, there can be a happy ending after all.

> **To Reflect On:** *In the story of the lost son, which of the two brothers do you most resemble?*

LUKE 15

The Parable of the Lost Sheep

15 Now the tax collectors and "sinners" were all gathering around to hear him. ²But the Pharisees and the teachers of the law muttered, "This man welcomes sinners and eats with them."

³Then Jesus told them this parable: ⁴"Suppose one of you has a hundred sheep and loses one of them. Does he not leave the ninety-nine in the open country and go after the lost sheep until he finds it? ⁵And when he finds it, he joyfully puts it on his shoulders ⁶and goes home. Then he calls his friends and neighbors together and says, 'Rejoice with me; I have found my lost sheep.' ⁷I tell you that in the same way there will be more rejoicing in heaven over one sinner who repents than over ninety-nine righteous persons who do not need to repent.

The Parable of the Lost Coin

⁸"Or suppose a woman has ten silver coins and loses one. Does she not light a lamp, sweep the house and search carefully until she finds it? ⁹And when she finds it, she calls her friends and neighbors together and says, 'Rejoice with me; I have found my lost coin.' ¹⁰In the same way, I tell you, there is rejoicing in the presence of the angels of God over one sinner who repents."

The Parable of the Lost Son

¹¹Jesus continued: "There was a man who had two sons. ¹²The younger one said to his father, 'Father, give me my share of the estate.' So he divided his property between them.

¹³"Not long after that, the younger son got together all he had, set off for a distant country and there squandered his wealth in wild living. ¹⁴After he had spent everything, there was a severe famine in that whole country, and he began to be in need. ¹⁵So he went and hired himself out to a citizen of that country, who sent him to his fields to feed pigs. ¹⁶He longed to fill his stomach with the pods that the pigs were eating, but no one gave him anything.

¹⁷"When he came to his senses, he said, 'How many of my father's hired men have food to spare, and here I am starving to death! ¹⁸I will set out and go back to my father and say to him: Father, I have sinned against heaven and against you. ¹⁹I am no longer worthy to be called your son; make me like one of your hired men.' ²⁰So he got up and went to his father.

"But while he was still a long way off, his father saw him and was filled with compassion for him; he ran to his son, threw his arms around him and kissed him.

²¹"The son said to him, 'Father, I have sinned against heaven and against you. I am no longer worthy to be called your son.'

²²"But the father said to his servants, 'Quick! Bring the best robe and put it on him. Put a ring on his finger and sandals on his feet. ²³Bring the fattened calf and kill it. Let's have a feast and celebrate. ²⁴For this son of mine was dead and is alive again; he was lost and is found.' So they began to celebrate.

²⁵"Meanwhile, the older son was in the field. When he came near the house, he heard music and dancing. ²⁶So he called one of the servants and asked him what was going on. ²⁷'Your brother has come,' he replied, 'and your father has killed the fattened calf because he has him back safe and sound.'

²⁸"The older brother became angry and refused to go in. So his father went out and pleaded with him. ²⁹But he answered his father, 'Look! All these years I've been slaving for you and never disobeyed your orders. Yet you never gave me even a young goat so I could celebrate with my friends. ³⁰But when this son of yours who has squandered your property with prostitutes comes home, you kill the fattened calf for him.'

³¹"'My son,' the father said, 'you are always with me, and everything I have is yours. ³²But we had to celebrate and be glad, because this brother of yours was dead and is alive again; he was lost and is found.'"

Food That Endures

John 6:22–71

All four gospels include an account of the feeding of the 5000, but John adds the most detail. He describes the effect of the miracle on the ordinary people who saw it. At first, dazzled by the miracle, they tried to crown Jesus king. Characteristically, he slipped away, but the persistent crowd commandeered boats and sailed across a lake in pursuit.

The next day when the crowds caught up with him, Jesus met them with a blunt warning, "I tell you the truth, you are looking for me, not because you saw miraculous signs but because you ate the loaves and had your fill. Do not work for food that spoils, but for food that endures to eternal life, which the Son of Man will give you."

That response shows why Jesus distrusted sensation-seeking crowds: They cared far more for physical spectacle than for spiritual truth. And what happened next certainly bears out his suspicion. As he was interpreting the spiritual meaning of the miracle, all the enthusiasm of the previous day melted away. The crowd grew downright restless when he openly avowed his true identity as the one sent from God. They could not reconcile such exalted claims ("I have come down from heaven.") with their knowledge that he was a local man, whose mother and father they knew.

Jesus used the miracle they had seen firsthand as a way of introducing his topic of the bread of life (his words were later applied to the Lord's Supper). But in the end the crowd—who had proof of Jesus' supernatural power digesting in their bellies—abandoned him, unbelieving. Many of his disciples turned back too, never to follow him again.

> **To Reflect On:** *Why did the crowd take offense at Jesus? Why do people take offense at him today?*

JOHN 6:22–71

Jesus Walks on the Water

²²The next day the crowd that had stayed on the opposite shore of the lake realized that only one boat had been there, and that Jesus had not entered it with his disciples, but that they had gone away alone. ²³Then some boats from Tiberias landed near the place where the people had eaten the bread after the Lord had given thanks. ²⁴Once the crowd realized that neither Jesus nor his disciples were there, they got into the boats and went to Capernaum in search of Jesus.

Jesus the Bread of Life

²⁵When they found him on the other side of the lake, they asked him, "Rabbi, when did you get here?"

²⁶Jesus answered, "I tell you the truth, you are looking for me, not because you saw miraculous signs but because you ate the loaves and had your fill. ²⁷Do not work for food that spoils, but for food that endures to eternal life, which the Son of Man will give you. On him God the Father has placed his seal of approval."

²⁸Then they asked him, "What must we do to do the works God requires?"

²⁹Jesus answered, "The work of God is this: to believe in the one he has sent."

³⁰So they asked him, "What miraculous sign then will you give that we may see it and believe you? What will you do? ³¹Our forefathers ate the manna in the desert; as it is written; 'He gave them bread from heaven to eat.' "

³²Jesus said to them, "I tell you the truth, it is not Moses who has given you the bread from heaven, but it is my Father who gives you the true bread from heaven. ³³For the bread of God is he who comes down from heaven and gives life to the world."

34 "Sir," they said, "from now on give us this bread."

35 Then Jesus declared, "I am the bread of life. He who comes to me will never go hungry, and he who believes in me will never be thirsty. 36 But as I told you, you have seen me and still you do not believe. 37 All that the Father gives me will come to me, and whoever comes to me I will never drive away. 38 For I have come down from heaven not to do my will but to do the will of him who sent me. 39 And this is the will of him who sent me, that I shall lose none of all that he has given me, but raise them up at the last day. 40 For my Father's will is that everyone who looks to the Son and believes in him shall have eternal life, and I will raise him up at the last day."

41 At this the Jews began to grumble about him because he said, "I am the bread that came down from heaven." 42 They said, "Is this not Jesus, the son of Joseph, whose father and mother we know? How can he now say, 'I came down from heaven'?"

43 "Stop grumbling among yourselves," Jesus answered. 44 "No one can come to me unless the Father who sent me draws him, and I will raise him up at the last day. 45 It is written in the Prophets: 'They will all be taught by God.' Everyone who listens to the Father and learns from him comes to me. 46 No one has seen the Father except the one who is from God; only he has seen the Father. 47 I tell you the truth, he who believes has everlasting life. 48 I am the bread of life. 49 Your forefathers ate the manna in the desert, yet they died. 50 But here is the bread that comes down from heaven, which a man may eat and not die. 51 I am the living bread that came down from heaven. If anyone eats of this bread, he will live forever. This bread is my flesh, which I will give for the life of the world."

52 Then the Jews began to argue sharply among themselves, "How can this man give us his flesh to eat?"

53 Jesus said to them, "I tell you the truth, unless you eat the flesh of the Son of Man and drink his blood, you have no life in you. 54 Whoever eats my flesh and drinks my blood has eternal life, and I will raise him up at the last day. 55 For my flesh is real food and my blood is real drink. 56 Whoever eats my flesh and drinks my blood remains in me, and I in him. 57 Just as the living Father sent me and I live because of the Father, so the one who feeds on me will live because of me. 58 This is the bread that came down from heaven. Your forefathers ate manna and died, but he who feeds on this bread will live forever." 59 He said this while teaching in the synagogue in Capernaum.

Many Disciples Desert Jesus

60 On hearing it, many of his disciples said, "This is a hard teaching. Who can accept it?"

61 Aware that his disciples were grumbling about this, Jesus said to them, "Does this offend you? 62 What if you see the Son of Man ascend to where he was before! 63 The Spirit gives life; the flesh counts for nothing. The words I have spoken to you are spirit and they are life. 64 Yet there are some of you who do not believe." For Jesus had known from the beginning which of them did not believe and who would betray him. 65 He went on to say, "This is why I told you that no one can come to me unless the Father has enabled him."

66 From this time many of his disciples turned back and no longer followed him.

67 "You do not want to leave too, do you?" Jesus asked the Twelve.

68 Simon Peter answered him, "Lord, to whom shall we go? You have the words of eternal life. 69 We believe and know that you are the Holy One of God."

70 Then Jesus replied, "Have I not chosen you, the Twelve? Yet one of you is a devil!" 71 (He meant Judas, the son of Simon Iscariot, who, though one of the Twelve, was later to betray him.)

Poles Apart

Mark 7

Although the crowds sometimes had difficulty swallowing Jesus' message, they would tag along as long as he kept on healing people. On the other hand, the religious, political, and intellectual establishments all strongly opposed Jesus, but could not manage to loosen his grip upon the common people. The Pharisees, in particular, tried to trap him in a major blunder that might turn the people—or the government—against him.

In many ways, the Pharisees made for an odd set of enemies. They were, in fact, among the most religious people of Jesus' day. More than any other group, they strove to follow the letter of the Old Testament law. But Jesus could see right through the Pharisees' pious behavior. He blasted them for focusing on the "outside" while neglecting the far greater dangers from within.

Pharisees were strict legalists who proudly embellished Jewish law with their own traditions. For example, they determined that a person could ride a donkey without breaking the Sabbath rules, but not use a switch to speed up the animal. It was permissible to give to a beggar on the Sabbath only if the beggar stuck his hand inside the home, so the giver needn't reach outside. A woman could not look in the mirror on the Sabbath for she might see a gray hair and be tempted to pull it out.

Jesus reacted with surprising harshness to such seemingly petty matters. By concentrating on all the rules, the Pharisees risked missing the whole point of the gospel. Such external, showy forms of legalism did not get anyone closer to God; just the opposite, they tended to make people proud and cliquish and self-righteous.

One way Jesus exposed the hypocrisy in the Pharisees' attitude was by publicly healing people on the sacred Sabbath. Fully aware that such acts would scandalize strict Pharisees, he went ahead anyway, insisting that compassion for needy people must take precedence over any tradition.

To Reflect On: *What Pharisee-like qualities exist in your church? In you?*

MARK 7

Clean and Unclean

7 The Pharisees and some of the teachers of the law who had come from Jerusalem gathered around Jesus and ²saw some of his disciples eating food with hands that were "unclean," that is, unwashed. ³(The Pharisees and all the Jews do not eat unless they give their hands a ceremonial washing, holding to the tradition of the elders. ⁴When they come from the marketplace they do not eat unless they wash. And they observe many other traditions, such as the washing of cups, pitchers and kettles.)

⁵So the Pharisees and teachers of the law asked Jesus, "Why don't your disciples live according to the tradition of the elders instead of eating their food with 'unclean' hands?"

⁶He replied, "Isaiah was right when he prophesied about you hypocrites; as it is written:

" 'These people honor me with their
   lips,
   but their hearts are far from me.
⁷They worship me in vain;
   their teachings are but rules taught
   by men.'

⁸You have let go of the commands of God and are holding on to the traditions of men."

⁹And he said to them: "You have a fine way of setting aside the commands of God

in order to observe your own traditions! [10]For Moses said, 'Honor your father and your mother,' and, 'Anyone who curses his father or mother must be put to death.' [11]But you say that if a man says to his father or mother: 'Whatever help you might otherwise have received from me is Corban' (that is, a gift devoted to God), [12]then you no longer let him do anything for his father or mother. [13]Thus you nullify the word of God by your tradition that you have handed down. And you do many things like that."

[14]Again Jesus called the crowd to him and said, "Listen to me, everyone, and understand this. [15]Nothing outside a man can make him 'unclean' by going into him. Rather, it is what comes out of a man that makes him 'unclean.'"

[17]After he had left the crowd and entered the house, his disciples asked him about this parable. [18]"Are you so dull?" he asked. "Don't you see that nothing that enters a man from the outside can make him 'unclean'? [19]For it doesn't go into his heart but into his stomach, and then out of his body." (In saying this, Jesus declared all foods "clean.")

[20]He went on: "What comes out of a man is what makes him 'unclean.' [21]For from within, out of men's hearts, come evil thoughts, sexual immorality, theft, murder, adultery, [22]greed, malice, deceit, lewdness, envy, slander, arrogance and folly. [23]All these evils come from inside and make a man 'unclean.'"

The Faith of a Syrophoenician Woman

[24]Jesus left that place and went to the vicinity of Tyre. He entered a house and did not want anyone to know it; yet he could not keep his presence secret. [25]In fact, as soon as she heard about him, a woman whose little daughter was possessed by an evil spirit came and fell at his feet. [26]The woman was a Greek, born in Syrian Phoenicia. She begged Jesus to drive the demon out of her daughter.

[27]"First let the children eat all they want," he told her, "for it is not right to take the children's bread and toss it to their dogs."

[28]"Yes, Lord," she replied, "but even the dogs under the table eat the children's crumbs."

[29]Then he told her, "For such a reply, you may go; the demon has left your daughter."

[30]She went home and found her child lying on the bed, and the demon gone.

The Healing of a Deaf and Mute Man

[31]Then Jesus left the vicinity of Tyre and went through Sidon, down to the Sea of Galilee and into the region of the Decapolis. [32]There some people brought to him a man who was deaf and could hardly talk, and they begged him to place his hand on the man.

[33]After he took him aside, away from the crowd, Jesus put his fingers into the man's ears. Then he spit and touched the man's tongue. [34]He looked up to heaven and with a deep sigh said to him, "*Ephphatha!*" (which means, "Be opened!"). [35]At this, the man's ears were opened, his tongue was loosened and he began to speak plainly.

[36]Jesus commanded them not to tell anyone. But the more he did so, the more they kept talking about it. [37]People were overwhelmed with amazement. "He has done everything well," they said. "He even makes the deaf hear and the mute speak."

The Mathematics of Legalism

Matthew 18:21–19:12

Legalists, people who follow strict rules of conduct, at first glance may seem "righteous." But Jesus warned against the subtle dangers of legalism. Oddly, it tends to lower a person's view of God. If I manage to meet all the requirements of a strict rule book, I may begin to feel secure about my own goodness. I may think that I have earned God's approval through my own efforts.

People who questioned Jesus in person—both his enemies the Pharisees and his friends the disciples—sought a precise list of rules so that they could strive to meet those obligations and thus feel satisfied. To such people, Jesus shouts a loud "No!" We never outgrow our need for God; we never *arrive* in the Christian life. We survive spiritually only if we constantly depend on God.

In the first story in this passage, Peter tries almost ludicrously to reduce forgiveness to a mathematical formula: *Let's see, exactly how many times must I forgive someone? Six? Seven?* Jesus mocks the question and then tells a profound story about God's forgiveness, so great and all-encompassing that it defies all mathematics.

Next, the Pharisees try to pin down a formula for divorce. Once again Jesus avoids the answer they want to hear and points instead to the principles that undergird all marriages.

These examples illustrate how Jesus usually handled questions about specific problems. When a pious man asked which neighbors he should go about loving, Jesus told of the Good Samaritan who showed love even to his enemies. Jesus didn't tell a rich person to give away 18.5 percent of his belongings; he said to give them all away. He didn't restrict adultery to the act of intercourse; he connected it to lust, adultery of the heart. Murder? In principle, that's no different from anger.

In short, Jesus always refused to lower the sights. He lashed out at every form of legalism, every human attempt to accumulate a list of credits. The credit goes to God, not us. The chief danger facing legalists is that they risk missing the whole point of the gospel: It is a gift freely given by God to people who don't deserve it.

To Reflect On: *When has it been hard for you to forgive someone?*

MATTHEW 18:21–19:12

The Parable of the Unmerciful Servant

21 Then Peter came to Jesus and asked, "Lord, how many times shall I forgive my brother when he sins against me? Up to seven times?"

22 Jesus answered, "I tell you, not seven times, but seventy-seven times.

23 "Therefore, the kingdom of heaven is like a king who wanted to settle accounts with his servants. 24 As he began the settlement, a man who owed him ten thousand talents was brought to him. 25 Since he was not able to pay, the master ordered that he and his wife and his children and all that he had be sold to repay the debt.

26 "The servant fell on his knees before him. 'Be patient with me,' he begged, 'and I will pay back everything.' 27 The servant's master took pity on him, canceled the debt and let him go.

28 "But when that servant went out, he found one of his fellow servants who owed him a hundred denarii. He grabbed him and began to choke him. 'Pay back what you owe me!' he demanded.

29 "His fellow servant fell to his knees and begged him, 'Be patient with me, and I will pay you back.'

30 "But he refused. Instead, he went off and had the man thrown into prison until he could pay the debt. 31 When the other servants saw what had happened, they were greatly distressed and went and told their master everything that had happened.

32 "Then the master called the servant in. 'You wicked servant,' he said, 'I canceled all that debt of yours because you begged me to. 33 Shouldn't you have had mercy on your fellow servant just as I had on you?' 34 In anger his master turned him over to the jailers to be tortured, until he should pay back all he owed.

35 "This is how my heavenly Father will treat each of you unless you forgive your brother from your heart."

Divorce

19 When Jesus had finished saying these things, he left Galilee and went into the region of Judea to the other side of the Jordan. 2 Large crowds followed him, and he healed them there.

3 Some Pharisees came to him to test him. They asked, "Is it lawful for a man to divorce his wife for any and every reason?"

4 "Haven't you read," he replied, "that at the beginning the Creator 'made them male and female,' 5 and said, 'For this reason a man will leave his father and mother and be united to his wife, and the two will become one flesh'? 6 So they are no longer two, but one. Therefore what God has joined together, let man not separate."

7 "Why then," they asked, "did Moses command that a man give his wife a certificate of divorce and send her away?"

8 Jesus replied, "Moses permitted you to divorce your wives because your hearts were hard. But it was not this way from the beginning. 9 I tell you that anyone who divorces his wife, except for marital unfaithfulness, and marries another woman commits adultery."

10 The disciples said to him, "If this is the situation between a husband and wife, it is better not to marry."

11 Jesus replied, "Not everyone can accept this word, but only those to whom it has been given. 12 For some are eunuchs because they were born that way; others were made that way by men; and others have renounced marriage because of the kingdom of heaven. The one who can accept this should accept it."

Coming Clean

John 10

Every few years an author or movie director comes out with a new work raising questions about Jesus' identity. Often such portrayals show him wandering around the earth in a daze, trying to figure out why he came and what he is supposed to be doing. Nothing could be further from the account given us by John, Jesus' closest friend. According to him, Jesus was no "man who fell to earth," but God's Son, sent on a mission from the Father. "I know where I came from and where I am going," Jesus said (8:14).

Of the four gospel writers, John dwells most prominently on Jesus' identity as the true Messiah, the Son of God. He states his purpose in writing very clearly: "These are written that you may believe that Jesus is the Christ, the Son of God, and that by believing you may have life in his name" (20:31). His book includes incidents from no more than twenty days in Jesus' life, arranged so as to demonstrate who Jesus is. Significantly, most of these incidents come from the final days of Jesus' life, when he was declaring his mission openly.

"I am the gate," Jesus says in this chapter; "I am the good shepherd." Jews who heard those words undoubtedly thought back to Old Testament kings like David, who were known as the shepherds of Israel. When some challenged him bluntly, "If you are the Christ, tell us plainly," Jesus answered with equal bluntness, "I and the Father are one." The pious Jews understood him perfectly: They picked up stones to execute him for blasphemy.

Not even these hostile reactions surprised Jesus. He expected opposition, even execution. As he explained, a truly good shepherd, unlike a hired hand, "lays down his life for the sheep." He was the only person in history who chose to be born, chose to die, and chose to come back again. This chapter explains why he made those choices.

> **To Reflect On:** *What difference does it make that Jesus is God and not just a man?*

JOHN 10

The Shepherd and His Flock

10 "I tell you the truth, the man who does not enter the sheep pen by the gate, but climbs in by some other way, is a thief and a robber. ²The man who enters by the gate is the shepherd of his sheep. ³The watchman opens the gate for him, and the sheep listen to his voice. He calls his own sheep by name and leads them out. ⁴When he has brought out all his own, he goes on ahead of them, and his sheep follow him because they know his voice. ⁵But they will never follow a stranger; in fact, they will run away from him because they do not recognize a stranger's voice." ⁶Jesus used this figure of speech, but they did not understand what he was telling them.

⁷Therefore Jesus said again, "I tell you the truth, I am the gate for the sheep. ⁸All who ever came before me were thieves and robbers, but the sheep did not listen to them. ⁹I am the gate; whoever enters through me will be saved. He will come in and go out, and find pasture. ¹⁰The thief comes only to steal and kill and destroy; I have come that they may have life, and have it to the full.

¹¹"I am the good shepherd. The good shepherd lays down his life for the sheep. ¹²The hired hand is not the shepherd who owns the sheep. So when he sees the wolf coming, he abandons the sheep and runs away. Then the wolf attacks the flock and scatters it. ¹³The man runs away because he is a hired hand and cares nothing for the sheep.

¹⁴"I am the good shepherd; I know my sheep and my sheep know me— ¹⁵just as the Father knows me and I know the Father—and I lay down my life for the sheep. ¹⁶I have other sheep that are not of this sheep pen. I must bring them also. They too will listen to my voice, and there shall be one flock and one shepherd. ¹⁷The reason my Father loves me is that I lay down my life—only to take it up again. ¹⁸No one takes it from me, but I lay it down of my own accord. I have authority to lay it down and authority to take it up again. This command I received from my Father."

¹⁹At these words the Jews were again divided. ²⁰Many of them said, "He is demon-possessed and raving mad. Why listen to him?"

²¹But others said, "These are not the sayings of a man possessed by a demon. Can a demon open the eyes of the blind?"

The Unbelief of the Jews

²²Then came the Feast of Dedication at Jerusalem. It was winter, ²³and Jesus was in the temple area walking in Solomon's Colonnade. ²⁴The Jews gathered around him, saying, "How long will you keep us in suspense? If you are the Christ, tell us plainly."

²⁵Jesus answered, "I did tell you, but you do not believe. The miracles I do in my Father's name speak for me, ²⁶but you do not believe because you are not my sheep. ²⁷My sheep listen to my voice; I know them, and they follow me. ²⁸I give them eternal life, and they shall never perish; no one can snatch them out of my hand. ²⁹My Father, who has given them to me, is greater than all; no one can snatch them out of my Father's hand. ³⁰I and the Father are one."

³¹Again the Jews picked up stones to stone him, ³²but Jesus said to them, "I have shown you many great miracles from the Father. For which of these do you stone me?'

³³"We are not stoning you for any of these," replied the Jews, "but for blasphemy, because you, a mere man, claim to be God."

³⁴Jesus answered them, "Is it not written in your Law, 'I have said you are gods'? ³⁵If he called them 'gods,' to whom the word of God came—and the Scripture cannot be broken— ³⁶what about the one whom the Father set apart as his very own and sent into the world? Why then do you accuse me of blasphemy because I said, 'I am God's Son'? ³⁷Do not believe me unless I do what my Father does. ³⁸But if I do it, even though you do not believe me, believe the miracles, that you may know and understand that the Father is in me, and I in the Father." ³⁹Again they tried to seize him, but he escaped their grasp.

⁴⁰Then Jesus went back across the Jordan to the place where John had been baptizing in the early days. Here he stayed ⁴¹and many people came to him. They said, "Though John never performed a miraculous sign, all that John said about this man was true." ⁴²And in that place many believed in Jesus.

Turning Point

Mark 8

As this chapter opens, Jesus is exasperated with his disciples. They had seen him feed 5000 people, and then 4000, and yet still they worried about their next meal. "Do you have eyes but fail to see, and ears but fail to hear?" he asked reproachfully. Still, for all their denseness, the disciples had grasped something about Jesus that eluded most others. The crowds saw him as a reincarnation of a prophet: Elijah, maybe, or John the Baptist. But in this scene, Peter boldly pronounces Jesus the "Christ," the very *Messiah* long predicted by the prophets.

It would be impossible to exaggerate the importance of that single word to first-century Jews. Ground down by centuries of foreign domination, they staked all their hopes in a *Messiah* who would lead their nation back to glory. Matthew records that Jesus, pleased by Peter's impulsive declaration, lavished praise on him (16:17–19). But, Peter's brightest moment was immediately followed by one of his dullest—a few paragraphs later Jesus identifies Peter with Satan. What transpired between those two scenes marks an important turning point in the story of Jesus' life.

To Peter and the other disciples, "Messiah" stood for wealth and fame and political power, the very temptations of an earthly kingdom that Jesus had resisted from Satan. Jesus knew that the true Messiah would first have to endure scorn, humiliation, suffering, and even death. He was the Suffering Servant prophesied by Isaiah. He would take up an executioner's cross, not a worldly position of honor.

Jesus accepted Peter's designation; he was indeed the true Messiah. But from that moment on, Jesus made a strategic shift. He left Galilee and headed toward the capital of Jerusalem. Instead of addressing the crowds, he narrowed his scope to the twelve disciples and worked to prepare them for the suffering and death to come. Peter may have grasped Jesus' identity, but he had much to learn about his mission. He wanted Jesus to avoid pain, not understanding that the pain of the cross would bring salvation to the whole world.

To Reflect On: *If someone asked you who Jesus is, what would you say?*

MARK 8

Jesus Feeds the Four Thousand

8 During those days another large crowd gathered. Since they had nothing to eat, Jesus called his disciples to him and said, 2"I have compassion for these people; they have already been with me three days and have nothing to eat. 3If I send them home hungry, they will collapse on the way, because some of them have come a long distance."

4His disciples answered, "But where in this remote place can anyone get enough bread to feed them?"

5"How many loaves do you have?" Jesus asked.

"Seven," they replied.

6He told the crowd to sit down on the ground. When he had taken the seven loaves and given thanks, he broke them and gave them to his disciples to set before the people, and they did so. 7They had a few small fish as well; he gave thanks for them also and told the disciples to distribute them. 8The people ate and were satisfied. Afterward the disciples picked up seven basketfuls of broken pieces that were left over. 9About four thousand men were present. And having sent them away, 10he got into the boat with his disciples and went to the region of Dalmanutha.

11The Pharisees came and began to question Jesus. To test him, they asked him for a sign from heaven. ¹²He sighed deeply and said, "Why does this generation ask for a miraculous sign? I tell you the truth, no sign will be given to it." ¹³Then he left them, got back into the boat and crossed to the other side.

The Yeast of the Pharisees and Herod

¹⁴The disciples had forgotten to bring bread, except for one loaf they had with them in the boat. ¹⁵"Be careful," Jesus warned them. "Watch out for the yeast of the Pharisees and that of Herod."

¹⁶They discussed this with one another and said, "It is because we have no bread."

¹⁷Aware of their discussion, Jesus asked them: "Why are you talking about having no bread? Do you still not see or understand? Are your hearts hardened? ¹⁸Do you have eyes but fail to see, and ears but fail to hear? And don't you remember? ¹⁹When I broke the five loaves for the five thousand, how many basketfuls of pieces did you pick up?"

"Twelve," they replied.

²⁰"And when I broke the seven loaves for the four thousand, how many basketfuls of pieces did you pick up?"

They answered, "Seven."

²¹He said to them, "Do you still not understand?"

The Healing of a Blind Man at Bethsaida

²²They came to Bethsaida, and some people brought a blind man and begged Jesus to touch him. ²³He took the blind man by the hand and led him outside the village. When he had spit on the man's eyes and put his hands on him, Jesus asked, "Do you see anything?"

²⁴He looked up and said, "I see people; they look like trees walking around."

²⁵Once more Jesus put his hands on the man's eyes. Then his eyes were opened, his sight was restored, and he saw everything clearly. ²⁶Jesus sent him home, saying, "Don't go into the village."

Peter's Confession of Christ

²⁷Jesus and his disciples went on to the villages around Caesarea Philippi. On the way he asked them, "Who do people say I am?"

²⁸They replied, "Some say John the Baptist; others say Elijah; and still others, one of the prophets."

²⁹"But what about you?" he asked. "Who do you say I am?"

Peter answered, "You are the Christ."

³⁰Jesus warned them not to tell anyone about him.

Jesus Predicts His Death

³¹He then began to teach them that the Son of Man must suffer many things and be rejected by the elders, chief priests and teachers of the law, and that he must be killed and after three days rise again. ³²He spoke plainly about this, and Peter took him aside and began to rebuke him.

³³But when Jesus turned and looked at his disciples, he rebuked Peter. "Get behind me, Satan!" he said. "You do not have in mind the things of God, but the things of men."

³⁴Then he called the crowd to him along with the disciples and said: "If anyone would come after me, he must deny himself and take up his cross and follow me. ³⁵For whoever wants to save his life will lose it, but whoever loses his life for me and for the gospel will save it. ³⁶What good is it for a man to gain the whole world, yet forfeit his soul? ³⁷Or what can a man give in exchange for his soul? ³⁸If anyone is ashamed of me and my words in this adulterous and sinful generation, the Son of Man will be ashamed of him when he comes in his Father's glory with the holy angels."

Dull Disciples

Mark 9:1–41

Despite the increased attention, Jesus' closest disciples, the Twelve, did not distinguish themselves—to put it mildly. "Are you so dull?" Jesus asked them at one point, and later sighed in exasperation, "How long shall I put up with you?" This chapter alone shows the disciples bungling a work of healing, misunderstanding Jesus' hints about his coming death and resurrection, squabbling about status, and trying to shut down the work of another disciple. Obviously, there was much in Jesus' mission they failed to comprehend.

Three of the disciples observed a dramatic scene that should have quelled any lingering doubts. "The Transfiguration," reported in vivid detail by Matthew, Mark, and Luke, afforded absolute proof of God's approval. Jesus' face shone like the sun and his clothes became dazzling, "whiter than anyone in the world could bleach them." A cloud enveloped the disciples and inside that cloud, to their astonishment, they found two long-dead giants of Jewish history: Moses and Elijah. It was too much to take; when God spoke audibly in the cloud, the disciples fell down, terrified. (Most scholars believe Mark got his details from Peter, one of the eyewitnesses. Peter describes the long-term impact of this experience in 2 Peter 1:16–18.)

Yet what impact did such a stupendous event have on the disciples? Did it permanently silence their questions and fill them with solid faith? A few weeks later, each one of the Twelve—including the three eyewitnesses of the Transfiguration—abandoned Jesus in his hour of deepest need. Somehow the import of who Jesus was, God in flesh, never really sank in until after he had left and then come back.

Actually, the fact of the disciples' abrupt change makes compelling evidence for Jesus' resurrection. The cowering disciples portrayed in Mark hardly resemble the bold, confident figures in the book of Acts. Something incredible had to happen to turn this bunch of bumblers into heroes of the faith.

> **To Reflect On:** *This chapter includes both "highs" and "lows" in the disciples' experience. What would a graph of your spiritual journey look like?*

MARK 9:1–41

9 And he said to them, "I tell you the truth, some who are standing here will not taste death before they see the kingdom of God come with power."

The Transfiguration

²After six days Jesus took Peter, James and John with him and led them up a high mountain, where they were all alone. There he was transfigured before them. ³His clothes became dazzling white, whiter than anyone in the world could bleach them. ⁴And there appeared before them Elijah and Moses, who were talking with Jesus.

⁵Peter said to Jesus, "Rabbi, it is good for us to be here. Let us put up three shelters—one for you, one for Moses and one for Elijah." ⁶(He did not know what to say, they were so frightened.)

⁷Then a cloud appeared and enveloped them, and a voice came from the cloud: "This is my Son, whom I love. Listen to him!"

⁸Suddenly, when they looked around, they no longer saw anyone with them except Jesus.

⁹As they were coming down the mountain, Jesus gave them orders not to tell anyone what they had seen until the Son of

Man had risen from the dead. ¹⁰They kept the matter to themselves, discussing what "rising from the dead" meant.

¹¹And they asked him, "Why do the teachers of the law say that Elijah must come first?"

¹²Jesus replied, "To be sure, Elijah does come first, and restores all things. Why then is it written that the Son of Man must suffer much and be rejected? ¹³But I tell you, Elijah has come, and they have done to him everything they wished, just as it is written about him."

The Healing of a Boy With an Evil Spirit

¹⁴When they came to the other disciples, they saw a large crowd around them and the teachers of the law arguing with them. ¹⁵As soon as all the people saw Jesus, they were overwhelmed with wonder and ran to greet him.

¹⁶"What are you arguing with them about?" he asked.

¹⁷A man in the crowd answered, "Teacher, I brought you my son, who is possessed by a spirit that has robbed him of speech. ¹⁸Whenever it seizes him, it throws him to the ground. He foams at the mouth, gnashes his teeth and becomes rigid. I asked your disciples to drive out the spirit, but they could not."

¹⁹"O unbelieving generation," Jesus replied, "how long shall I stay with you? How long shall I put up with you? Bring the boy to me."

²⁰So they brought him. When the spirit saw Jesus, it immediately threw the boy into a convulsion. He fell to the ground and rolled around, foaming at the mouth.

²¹Jesus asked the boy's father, "How long has he been like this?"

"From childhood," he answered. ²²"It has often thrown him into fire or water to kill him. But if you can do anything, take pity on us and help us."

²³"'If you can'?" said Jesus. "Everything is possible for him who believes."

²⁴Immediately the boy's father exclaimed, "I do believe; help me overcome my unbelief!"

²⁵When Jesus saw that a crowd was running to the scene, he rebuked the evil spirit. "You deaf and mute spirit," he said, "I command you, come out of him and never enter him again."

²⁶The spirit shrieked, convulsed him violently and came out. The boy looked so much like a corpse that many said, "He's dead." ²⁷But Jesus took him by the hand and lifted him to his feet, and he stood up.

²⁸After Jesus had gone indoors, his disciples asked him privately, "Why couldn't we drive it out?"

²⁹He replied, "This kind can come out only by prayer."

³⁰They left that place and passed through Galilee. Jesus did not want anyone to know where they were, ³¹because he was teaching his disciples. He said to them, "The Son of Man is going to be betrayed into the hands of men. They will kill him, and after three days he will rise." ³²But they did not understand what he meant and were afraid to ask him about it.

Who Is the Greatest?

³³They came to Capernaum. When he was in the house, he asked them, "What were you arguing about on the road?" ³⁴But they kept quiet because on the way they had argued about who was the greatest.

³⁵Sitting down, Jesus called the Twelve and said, "If anyone wants to be first, he must be the very last, and the servant of all."

³⁶He took a little child and had him stand among them. Taking him in his arms, he said to them, ³⁷"Whoever welcomes one of these little children in my name welcomes me; and whoever welcomes me does not welcome me but the one who sent me."

Whoever Is Not Against Us Is for Us

³⁸"Teacher," said John, "we saw a man driving out demons in your name and we told him to stop, because he was not one of us."

³⁹"Do not stop him," Jesus said. "No one who does a miracle in my name can in the next moment say anything bad about me, ⁴⁰for whoever is not against us is for us. ⁴¹I tell you the truth, anyone who gives you a cup of water in my name because you belong to Christ will certainly not lose his reward.

Mission Improbable

Luke 10

Jesus' time on earth was running out. Only a few weeks remained for him to prepare others to carry on his work, and he used that time for a crash training course. The opening scene in this chapter shows a major advance in his plan of "turning over" his work to his followers. This time he commissioned seventy-two, not twelve, followers in a hazardous assignment.

A seismic change was rumbling. As Jesus described the mission of the seventy-two, he did not disguise his alarm. "Go! I am sending you out like lambs among wolves," he said. Finally, in a voice that commanded attention, he gave this mysterious charge: "He who listens to you listens to me; he who rejects you rejects me."

Luke's next view of Jesus is almost unprecedented in the Gospels. Nowhere else will you find Jesus so happy, so bubbling with joy. The caution in his face had turned to exuberance: "Many prophets and kings wanted to see what you see but did not see it, and to hear what you hear but did not hear it." It had really worked, the dangerous mission into the hill country, and Jesus celebrated the enormous breakthrough with those seventy-two disciples.

In that triumphant response Jesus reveals the significance of the final days of his mission. He had come to earth to establish a *church*, a group of people who would carry on his will after his departure. And while those seventy-two disciples were plodding the dusty roads of Judea, knocking on doors, explaining the Messiah, praying for the sick, Jesus watched Satan fall like lightning from heaven. Their actions won a cosmic victory. Jesus' own mission—more, his own life—was being lived out through seventy-two very ordinary human beings.

The sending of the seventy-two disciples is only one of three stories in this rich chapter. Taken together, the three provide a full picture of what following Jesus might include. For the seventy-two, it meant boldly proclaiming the kingdom of God; for the Good Samaritan, it meant binding the wounds of a robbery victim; for Mary, it meant total absorption in the words of Jesus.

> **To Reflect On:** *Of the three ways of following Jesus described in this chapter, which do you do best?*

LUKE 10

Jesus Sends Out the Seventy-two

10 After this the Lord appointed seventy-two others and sent them two by two ahead of him to every town and place where he was about to go. ²He told them, "The harvest is plentiful, but the workers are few. Ask the Lord of the harvest, therefore, to send out workers into his harvest field. ³Go! I am sending you out like lambs among wolves. ⁴Do not take a purse or bag or sandals; and do not greet anyone on the road.

⁵"When you enter a house, first say, 'Peace to this house.' ⁶If a man of peace is there, your peace will rest on him; if not, it will return to you. ⁷Stay in that house, eating and drinking whatever they give you, for the worker deserves his wages. Do not move around from house to house.

⁸"When you enter a town and are welcomed, eat what is set before you. ⁹Heal the sick who are there and tell them, 'The kingdom of God is near you.' ¹⁰But when you enter a town and are not welcomed, go into its streets and say, ¹¹'Even the dust of your town that sticks to our feet we wipe off

against you. Yet be sure of this: The kingdom of God is near.' ¹²I tell you, it will be more bearable on that day for Sodom than for that town.

¹³"Woe to you, Korazin! Woe to you, Bethsaida! For if the miracles that were performed in you had been performed in Tyre and Sidon, they would have repented long ago, sitting in sackcloth and ashes. ¹⁴But it will be more bearable for Tyre and Sidon at the judgment than for you. ¹⁵And you, Capernaum, will you be lifted up to the skies? No, you will go down to the depths.

¹⁶"He who listens to you listens to me; he who rejects you rejects me; but he who rejects me rejects him who sent me."

¹⁷The seventy-two returned with joy and said, "Lord, even the demons submit to us in your name."

¹⁸He replied, "I saw Satan fall like lightning from heaven. ¹⁹I have given you authority to trample on snakes and scorpions and to overcome all the power of the enemy; nothing will harm you. ²⁰However, do not rejoice that the spirits submit to you, but rejoice that your names are written in heaven."

²¹At that time Jesus, full of joy through the Holy Spirit, said, "I praise you, Father, Lord of heaven and earth, because you have hidden these things from the wise and learned, and revealed them to little children. Yes, Father, for this was your good pleasure.

²²"All things have been committed to me by my Father. No one knows who the Son is except the Father, and no one knows who the Father is except the Son and those to whom the Son chooses to reveal him."

²³Then he turned to his disciples and said privately, "Blessed are the eyes that see what you see. ²⁴For I tell you that many prophets and kings wanted to see what you see but did not see it, and to hear what you hear but did not hear it."

The Parable of the Good Samaritan

²⁵On one occasion an expert in the law stood up to test Jesus. "Teacher," he asked, "what must I do to inherit eternal life?"

²⁶"What is written in the Law?" he replied. "How do you read it?"

²⁷He answered: "'Love the Lord your God with all your heart and with all your soul and with all your strength and with all your mind'; and, 'Love your neighbor as yourself.'"

²⁸"You have answered correctly," Jesus replied. "Do this and you will live."

²⁹But he wanted to justify himself, so he asked Jesus, "And who is my neighbor?"

³⁰In reply Jesus said: "A man was going down from Jerusalem to Jericho, when he fell into the hands of robbers. They stripped him of his clothes, beat him and went away, leaving him half dead. ³¹A priest happened to be going down the same road, and when he saw the man, he passed by on the other side. ³²So too, a Levite, when he came to the place and saw him, passed by on the other side. ³³But a Samaritan, as he traveled, came where the man was; and when he saw him, he took pity on him. ³⁴He went to him and bandaged his wounds, pouring on oil and wine. Then he put the man on his own donkey, took him to an inn and took care of him. ³⁵The next day he took out two silver coins and gave them to the innkeeper. 'Look after him,' he said, 'and when I return, I will reimburse you for any extra expense you may have.'

³⁶"Which of these three do you think was a neighbor to the man who fell into the hands of robbers?"

³⁷The expert in the law replied, "The one who had mercy on him."

Jesus told him, "Go and do likewise."

At the Home of Martha and Mary

³⁸As Jesus and his disciples were on their way, he came to a village where a woman named Martha opened her home to him. ³⁹She had a sister called Mary, who sat at the Lord's feet listening to what he said. ⁴⁰But Martha was distracted by all the preparations that had to be made. She came to him and asked, "Lord, don't you care that my sister has left me to do the work by myself? Tell her to help me!"

⁴¹"Martha, Martha," the Lord answered, "you are worried and upset about many things, ⁴²but only one thing is needed. Mary has chosen what is better, and it will not be taken away from her."

Servant Leadership

Mark 10:32–11:11

This scene opens with yet another prediction of Jesus' death. Showing incredible insensitivity, two of the disciples immediately lapsed into a petty dispute about status. They could not grasp the message Jesus patiently repeated for them: In his kingdom, the greatest is the one who *serves*.

Jesus used curious techniques to gain recruits for his kingdom. His job descriptions included such words as "cross" and "slave"—rather like a Marine Corps recruiter displaying photos of war amputees and dead soldiers. Not even his closest friends could comprehend how the ugly image of an executioner's cross fit their dreams of a new kingdom. No matter how many times Jesus explained the way of the cross, it never seemed to sink in.

As the group reached Jerusalem, however, Jesus did permit one great display of public adulation. Always before, he had shrunk away from the crowds who tried to coronate him. But in the "triumphal entry," he let people honor him as the conquering Messiah.

In some ways, the procession was a slapstick affair compared to the lavish processions of the Romans—Jesus rode on a donkey, after all, not on a stallion or in a gilded chariot. But the event, foretold by the prophets, had deep meaning for the Jews. Jesus was openly declaring himself as Messiah, and the triumphal entry set all of Jerusalem astir.

Jewish leaders who opposed Jesus raised an alarm, and even the Romans took note of a man claiming to be a king. The rest of the Gospels, however, demonstrate how tragically short-lived Jesus' public acceptance proved to be. The crowds, like the disciples, were wholly unprepared for Jesus' style of kingdom. Its demands were too hard; its rewards too vague.

> **To Reflect On:** *How can a person demonstrate "servant leadership" today?*

MARK 10:32–11:11

Jesus Again Predicts His Death

³²They were on their way up to Jerusalem, with Jesus leading the way, and the disciples were astonished, while those who followed were afraid. Again he took the Twelve aside and told them what was going to happen to him. ³³"We are going up to Jerusalem," he said, "and the Son of Man will be betrayed to the chief priests and teachers of the law. They will condemn him to death and will hand him over to the Gentiles, ³⁴who will mock him and spit on him, flog him and kill him. Three days later he will rise."

The Request of James and John

³⁵Then James and John, the sons of Zebedee, came to him. "Teacher," they said, "we want you to do for us whatever we ask."

³⁶"What do you want me to do for you?" he asked.

³⁷They replied, "Let one of us sit at your right and the other at your left in your glory."

³⁸"You don't know what you are asking," Jesus said. "Can you drink the cup I drink or be baptized with the baptism I am baptized with?"

³⁹"We can," they answered.

Jesus said to them, "You will drink the cup I drink and be baptized with the baptism I am baptized with, ⁴⁰but to sit at my right or left is not for me to grant. These places belong to those for whom they have been prepared."

⁴¹When the ten heard about this, they became indignant with James and John. ⁴²Jesus called them together and said, "You know that those who are regarded as rulers of the Gentiles lord it over them, and their high officials exercise authority over them. ⁴³Not so with you. Instead, whoever wants to become great among you must be your servant, ⁴⁴and whoever wants to be first must be slave of all. ⁴⁵For even the Son of Man did not come to be served, but to serve, and to give his life as a ransom for many."

Blind Bartimaeus Receives His Sight

⁴⁶Then they came to Jericho. As Jesus and his disciples, together with a large crowd, were leaving the city, a blind man, Bartimaeus (that is, the Son of Timaeus), was sitting by the roadside begging. ⁴⁷When he heard that it was Jesus of Nazareth, he began to shout, "Jesus, Son of David, have mercy on me!"

⁴⁸Many rebuked him and told him to be quiet, but he shouted all the more, "Son of David, have mercy on me!"

⁴⁹Jesus stopped and said, "Call him."

So they called to the blind man, "Cheer up! On your feet! He's calling you." ⁵⁰Throwing his cloak aside, he jumped to his feet and came to Jesus.

⁵¹"What do you want me to do for you?" Jesus asked him.

The blind man said, "Rabbi, I want to see."

⁵²"Go," said Jesus, "your faith has healed you." Immediately he received his sight and followed Jesus along the road.

The Triumphal Entry

11 As they approached Jerusalem and came to Bethphage and Bethany at the Mount of Olives, Jesus sent two of his disciples, ²saying to them, "Go to the village ahead of you, and just as you enter it, you will find a colt tied there, which no one has ever ridden. Untie it and bring it here. ³If anyone asks you, 'Why are you doing this?' tell him, 'The Lord needs it and will send it back here shortly.'"

⁴They went and found a colt outside in the street, tied at a doorway. As they untied it, ⁵some people standing there asked, "What are you doing, untying that colt?" ⁶They answered as Jesus had told them to, and the people let them go. ⁷When they brought the colt to Jesus and threw their cloaks over it, he sat on it. ⁸Many people spread their cloaks on the road, while others spread branches they had cut in the fields. ⁹Those who went ahead and those who followed shouted,

"Hosanna!"

"Blessed is he who comes in the name of the Lord!"

¹⁰"Blessed is the coming kingdom of our father David!"

"Hosanna in the highest!"

¹¹Jesus entered Jerusalem and went to the temple. He looked around at everything, but since it was already late, he went out to Bethany with the Twelve.

Opposition Heats Up

Mark 11:12–12:12

The last few weeks of Jesus' life show a mounting sense of urgency, as seen in several dramatic confrontations at the temple. That sacred site, supposedly the center for worship of God, had taken on a commercial cast. Merchants, who sold sacrificial animals to pilgrims and foreigners at inflated prices, seemed more interested in profit than in true worship. In the spirit of the Old Testament prophets, Jesus branded them "robbers" and forcibly drove them out.

Mark folds that scene into an account of a fig tree cursed by Jesus because of its lack of fruit. He was probably drawing a direct parallel to the religious establishment of the day. It, too, was "withered," and Jesus was about to take decisive action against it.

Jesus did nothing to temper his harsh message. On the contrary, he told a parable that seemed deliberately provocative. He presented himself as God's last resort, his final attempt to break through stubborn resistance. But he, too, would be killed, by the same people whose ancestors had mocked and killed the prophets.

Battle lines were drawn. On one side was Jesus, kept safe only by his widespread popularity. On the other were leaders of the religious and political establishments. Threatened by Jesus' radical message of repentance and reform, they determined to find a way to trap Jesus and turn the crowd against him.

> **To Reflect On:** *How would you label Jesus' primary emotion in each of the stories of this passage?*

MARK 11:12–12:12

Jesus Clears the Temple

¹²The next day as they were leaving Bethany, Jesus was hungry. ¹³Seeing in the distance a fig tree in leaf, he went to find out if it had any fruit. When he reached it, he found nothing but leaves, because it was not the season for figs. ¹⁴Then he said to the tree, "May no one ever eat fruit from you again." And his disciples heard him say it.

¹⁵On reaching Jerusalem, Jesus entered the temple area and began driving out those who were buying and selling there. He overturned the tables of the money changers and the benches of those selling doves, ¹⁶and would not allow anyone to carry merchandise through the temple courts. ¹⁷And as he taught them, he said, "Is it not written:

" 'My house will be called
a house of prayer for all nations'?

But you have made it 'a den of robbers.' "

¹⁸The chief priests and the teachers of the law heard this and began looking for a way to kill him, for they feared him, because the whole crowd was amazed at his teaching.

¹⁹When evening came, they went out of the city.

The Withered Fig Tree

²⁰In the morning, as they went along, they saw the fig tree withered from the roots. ²¹Peter remembered and said to Jesus, "Rabbi, look! The fig tree you cursed has withered!"

²²"Have faith in God," Jesus answered. ²³"I tell you the truth, if anyone says to this mountain, 'Go, throw yourself into the sea,' and does not doubt in his heart but believes that what he says will happen, it will be done for him. ²⁴Therefore I tell you, whatever you ask for in prayer, believe that you have received it, and it will be yours. ²⁵And when you stand praying, if you hold anything against anyone, forgive him, so that your Father in heaven may forgive you your sins."

The Authority of Jesus Questioned

27They arrived again in Jerusalem, and while Jesus was walking in the temple courts, the chief priests, the teachers of the law and the elders came to him. 28"By what authority are you doing these things?" they asked. "And who gave you authority to do this?"

29Jesus replied, "I will ask you one question. Answer me, and I will tell you by what authority I am doing these things. 30John's baptism—was it from heaven, or from men? Tell me!"

31They discussed it among themselves and said, "If we say, 'From heaven,' he will ask, 'Then why didn't you believe him?' 32But if we say, 'From men' . . . . " (they feared the people, for everyone held that John really was a prophet.)

33So they answered Jesus, "We don't know."

Jesus said, "Neither will I tell you by what authority I am doing these things."

The Parable of the Tenants

12 He then began to speak to them in parables: "A man planted a vineyard. He put a wall around it, dug a pit for the winepress and built a watchtower. Then he rented the vineyard to some farmers and went away on a journey. 2At harvest time he sent a servant to the tenants to collect from them some of the fruit of the vineyard. 3But they seized him, beat him and sent him away empty-handed. 4Then he sent another servant to them; they struck this man on the head and treated him shamefully. 5He sent still another, and that one they killed. He sent many others; some of them they beat, others they killed.

6"He had one left to send, a son, whom he loved. He sent him last of all, saying, 'They will respect my son.'

7"But the tenants said to one another, 'This is the heir. Come, let's kill him, and the inheritance will be ours.' 8So they took him and killed him, and threw him out of the vineyard.

9"What then will the owner of the vineyard do? He will come and kill those tenants and give the vineyard to others. 10Haven't you read this scripture:

" 'The stone the builders rejected
has become the capstone;
11the Lord has done this,
and it is marvelous in our eyes'?"

12Then they looked for a way to arrest him because they knew he had spoken the parable against them. But they were afraid of the crowd; so they left him and went away.

Baiting Jesus

Mark 12:13–44

Mark 12 records three different skirmishes between Jesus and the groups seeking to trap him.

The Pharisees, allied with a party following Herod, cynically praised Jesus, and then sprang on him a double-bind question: "Is it right to pay taxes to Caesar or not?" If Jesus said "Pay the taxes," he would lose popular support, for the independence-minded Jews despised Roman occupation forces. If he said "Don't pay," he could be turned in to Rome for breaking the law.

Next, a small but powerful religious group tried to stump Jesus with a theological question. The Sadducees, who did not believe in an afterlife, proposed a complicated riddle about life after death.

Finally, Jesus' perennial enemies the Pharisees took their turn. Jewish rabbis counted 613 commandments in the Law, and various splinter groups bickered over which ones were most important. The teacher of the Law asked Jesus to select just one as the greatest commandment of all, knowing his choice would offend some of those groups.

Jesus avoided each of the verbal traps, succeeding so brilliantly that Mark concludes, "And from then on no one dared ask him any more questions." In all these skirmishes, Jesus did not try to placate his adversaries. Instead, he used the occasions of conflict to warn his disciples and the watching crowds against those adversaries, whose fury only increased.

After he had fended off the last critic, Jesus pointed to a poor widow who had just made a tiny but sacrificial offering for the temple treasury. Her faithfulness, said Jesus, was far more impressive than that of the greedy religious establishment, who "devour widows' houses and for a show make lengthy prayers."

> **To Reflect On:** *What can you learn from Jesus' style in handling his enemies? How do you tend to respond to people who oppose you?*

MARK 12:13–44

Paying Taxes to Caesar

¹³Later they sent some of the Pharisees and Herodians to Jesus to catch him in his words. ¹⁴They came to him and said, "Teacher, we know you are a man of integrity. You aren't swayed by men, because you pay no attention to who they are; but you teach the way of God in accordance with the truth. Is it right to pay taxes to Caesar or not? ¹⁵Should we pay or shouldn't we?"

But Jesus knew their hypocrisy. "Why are you trying to trap me?" he asked. "Bring me a denarius and let me look at it." ¹⁶They brought the coin, and he asked them, "Whose portrait is this? And whose inscription?"

"Caesar's," they replied.

¹⁷Then Jesus said to them, "Give to Caesar what is Caesar's and to God what is God's."

And they were amazed at him.

Marriage at the Resurrection

¹⁸Then the Sadducees, who say there is no resurrection, came to him with a question. ¹⁹"Teacher," they said, "Moses wrote for us that if a man's brother dies and leaves a wife but no children, the man must marry the widow and have children for his brother. ²⁰Now there were seven brothers.

The first one married and died without leaving any children. ²¹The second one married the widow, but he also died, leaving no child. It was the same with the third. ²²In fact, none of the seven left any children. Last of all, the woman died too. ²³At the resurrection whose wife will she be, since the seven were married to her?"

²⁴Jesus replied, "Are you not in error because you do not know the Scriptures or the power of God? ²⁵When the dead rise, they will neither marry nor be given in marriage; they will be like the angels in heaven. ²⁶Now about the dead rising— have you not read in the book of Moses, in the account of the bush, how God said to him, 'I am the God of Abraham, the God of Isaac, and the God of Jacob'? ²⁷He is not the God of the dead, but of the living. You are badly mistaken!"

The Greatest Commandment

²⁸One of the teachers of the law came and heard them debating. Noticing that Jesus had given them a good answer, he asked him, "Of all the commandments, which is the most important?"

²⁹"The most important one," answered Jesus, "Is this: 'Hear, O Israel, the Lord our God, the Lord is one. ³⁰Love the Lord your God with all your heart and with all your soul and with all your mind and with all your strength.' ³¹The second is this: 'Love your neighbor as yourself.' There is no commandment greater than these."

³²"Well said, teacher," the man replied. "You are right in saying that God is one and there is no other but him. ³³To love him with all your heart, with all your understanding and with all your strength, and to love your neighbor as yourself is more important than all burnt offerings and sacrifices."

³⁴When Jesus saw that he had answered wisely, he said to him, "You are not far from the kingdom of God." And from then on no one dared ask him any more questions.

Whose Son Is the Christ?

³⁵While Jesus was teaching in the temple courts, he asked, "How is it that the teachers of the law say that the Christ is the son of David? ³⁶David himself, speaking by the Holy Spirit, declared:

" 'The Lord said to my Lord:
"Sit at my right hand
until I put your enemies
under your feet.' "

³⁷David himself calls him 'Lord.' How then can he be his son?"

The large crowd listened to him with delight.

³⁸As he taught, Jesus said, "Watch out for the teachers of the law. They like to walk around in flowing robes and be greeted in the marketplaces, ³⁹and have the most important seats in the synagogues and the places of honor at banquets. ⁴⁰They devour widows' houses and for a show make lengthy prayers. Such men will be punished most severely."

The Widow's Offering

⁴¹Jesus sat down opposite the place where the offerings were put and watched the crowd putting their money into the temple treasury. Many rich people threw in large amounts. ⁴²But a poor widow came and put in two very small copper coins, worth only a fraction of a penny.

⁴³Calling his disciples to him, Jesus said, "I tell you the truth, this poor widow has put more into the treasury than all the others. ⁴⁴They all gave out of their wealth; but she, out of her poverty, put in everything—all she had to live on."

A Day To Dread

Mark 13

Move forward a few days, beyond the events of this chapter, as Jesus is prodded by Roman soldiers toward the place of execution. A group of women follows behind, hysterical with grief. Suddenly Jesus turns and silences them with these words, "Daughters of Jerusalem, do not weep for me; weep for yourselves and for your children. . . . For if men do these things when the tree is green, what will happen when it is dry?" (Luke 23:29, 31).

Even in Jesus' childhood, rumors about him had provoked a king's bloody campaign of infanticide. And as this chapter spells out in grim detail, Jesus did not expect the war against God's kingdom to end with his own death. He predicted that evil would only intensify until at last, in one final spasm of rebellion, the earth would give way to God's final restoration.

The words of this chapter echo, and quote from, the Old Testament prophets. "Before we can hear the last word," said Dietrich Bonhoeffer, "we must listen to the next-to-the-last word," and in the Bible that consists of dreadful apocalyptic visions. At the end of time, God will take off all the wraps. And when Jesus returns, he will appear in a new form—not as a helpless babe in a manger, not nailed to a crosspiece of wood, but as "the Son of Man coming in clouds with great power and glory."

Some of Jesus' dire predictions found fulfillment in A.D. 70, when Roman soldiers broke through the walls of Jerusalem and demolished Herod's temple—the same temple Jesus' disciples were admiring when Jesus first spoke these words. Other predictions, clearly, have not yet been fulfilled. In this passage, Jesus gives direct clues to events that will precede his second coming. But, notably, he ends with a warning that no one can calculate the precise time of his return to earth.

It didn't take long for doubters to appear on the scene. Just a few decades later scoffers were already mocking the notion of the "second coming" of Christ. "Where is this 'coming' he promised? Ever since our fathers died, everything goes on as it has since the beginning of creation" (2 Peter 3:4). For all such scoffers, Jesus and the prophets have one ominous word of advice: Just wait. God will not remain silent forever. One day, earth and sky will flee from his presence.

> **To Reflect On:** *What response did Jesus want from the disciples who first heard these words? What response does he want from us?*

MARK 13

Signs of the End of the Age

13 As he was leaving the temple, one of his disciples said to him, "Look, Teacher! What massive stones! What magnificent buildings!"

2 "Do you see all these great buildings?" replied Jesus. "Not one stone here will be left on another; every one will be thrown down."

3 As Jesus was sitting on the Mount of Olives opposite the temple, Peter, James, John and Andrew asked him privately, 4 "Tell us, when will these things happen? And what will be the sign that they are all about to be fulfilled?"

5 Jesus said to them: "Watch out that no one deceives you. 6 Many will come in my name, claiming, 'I am he,' and will deceive many. 7 When you hear of wars and rumors of wars, do not be alarmed. Such things must happen, but the end is still to come. 8 Nation will rise against nation, and kingdom against kingdom. There will be earthquakes in various places, and famines. These are the beginning of birth pains.

9 "You must be on your guard. You will be handed over to the local councils and flogged in the synagogues. On account of me you will stand before governors and kings as witnesses to them. 10 And the gospel must first be preached to all nations. 11 Whenever you are arrested and brought to trial, do not worry beforehand about what to say. Just say whatever is given you at the time, for it is not you speaking, but the Holy Spirit.

12 "Brother will betray brother to death, and a father his child. Children will rebel against their parents and have them put to death. 13 All men will hate you because of me, but he who stands firm to the end will be saved.

14 "When you see 'the abomination that causes desolation' standing where it does not belong—let the reader understand—then let those who are in Judea flee to the mountains. 15 Let no one on the roof of his house go down or enter the house to take anything out. 16 Let no one in the field go back to get his cloak. 17 How dreadful it will be in those days for pregnant women and nursing mothers! 18 Pray that this will not take place in winter, 19 because those will be days of distress unequaled from the beginning, when God created the world, until now—and never to be equaled again. 20 If the Lord had not cut short those days, no one would survive. But for the sake of the elect, whom he has chosen, he has shortened them. 21 At that time if anyone says to you, 'Look, here is the Christ!' or, 'Look, there he is!' do not believe it. 22 For false Christs and false prophets will appear and perform signs and miracles to deceive the elect—if that were possible. 23 So be on your guard; I have told you everything ahead of time.

24 "But in those days, following that distress,

" 'the sun will be darkened,
    and the moon will not give its light;
25 the stars will fall from the sky,
    and the heavenly bodies will be
        shaken.'

26 "At that time men will see the Son of Man coming in clouds with great power and glory. 27 And he will send his angels and gather his elect from the four winds, from the ends of the earth to the ends of the heavens.

28 "Now learn this lesson from the fig tree: As soon as its twigs get tender and its leaves come out, you know that summer is near. 29 Even so, when you see these things happening, you know that it is near, right at the door. 30 I tell you the truth, this generation will certainly not pass away until all these things have happened. 31 Heaven and earth will pass away, but my words will never pass away.

The Day and Hour Unknown

32 "No one knows about that day or hour, not even the angels in heaven, nor the Son, but only the Father. 33 Be on guard! Be alert! You do not know when that time will come. 34 It's like a man going away: He leaves his house and puts his servants in charge, each with his assigned task, and tells the one at the door to keep watch.

35 "Therefore keep watch because you do not know when the owner of the house will come back—whether in the evening, or at midnight, or when the rooster crows, or at dawn. 36 If he comes suddenly, do not let him find you sleeping. 37 What I say to you, I say to everyone: 'Watch!' "

A Day To Dread 273

A Scent of Doom

Mark 14:1–31

The Passover, an annual commemoration of the Israelites' deliverance from Egypt, was one of the high points of the Jewish calendar. All males older than twelve traveled to Jerusalem for the holiday, filling the city with hundreds of thousands of pilgrims.

Jesus had entered that festive scene in a moment of triumph on Palm Sunday, but very soon a sense of doom stole in. He seemed obsessed with death. When a woman splashed him with expensive perfume, he called it a form of burial preparation.

All four gospels report on the disciples' final meal with Jesus. Passover festivities culminated in a solemn meal, where family and close friends gathered to remember the Exodus, the time of liberation. They tasted morsels of food, sipped wine, and read aloud the stories from the Old Testament. They also selected a lamb to take to the temple and offer as a sacrifice to God. Thus, the holiday ended on a sad and bloody note (as many as a quarter of a million Passover lambs were sacrificed in Jesus' day).

Outside the room, Jesus' enemies were stalking, waiting for an occasion to seize him. Inside, the disciples swore loyalty to their leader, even as he insisted that, down to a man, all would soon forsake him. It was at this somber meal that Jesus made a profound declaration. "This is the blood of the new covenant," he said as he poured the wine. "Take it, this is my body," he said, breaking bread.

Something new was happening in the history of the Jews, something the disciples would not fully understand for many days. A dream was dying, a two-thousand-year-old dream traceable back to Abraham—a dream of a mighty nation, God's covenant nation.

Jesus was announcing a new covenant, sealed not with the blood of lambs, but with his own blood. The new kingdom, the kingdom of God, would not be led by Jewish generals and kings, but rather by the scared band of disciples gathered around the table—the very disciples who would soon betray him.

Today, virtually all Christian churches continue the practice of Communion (Mass, Eucharist, or Lord's Supper) in some form. That solemn ceremony dates back to this original Passover meal when Jesus instituted the new covenant.

To Reflect On: *How does the tone of the Lord's Supper in your church resemble, or differ from, this original scene?*

MARK 14:1–31

Jesus Anointed at Bethany

14 Now the Passover and the Feast of Unleavened Bread were only two days away, and the chief priests and the teachers of the law were looking for some sly way to arrest Jesus and kill him. ²"But not during the Feast," they said, "or the people may riot."

³While he was in Bethany, reclining at the table in the home of a man known as Simon the Leper, a woman came with an alabaster jar of very expensive perfume, made of pure nard. She broke the jar and poured the perfume on his head.

⁴Some of those present were saying indignantly to one another, "Why this waste of perfume? ⁵It could have been sold for more than a year's wages and the money given to the poor." And they rebuked her harshly.

⁶"Leave her alone," said Jesus. "Why are you bothering her? She has done a beautiful thing to me. ⁷The poor you will always have with you, and you can help them any time you want. But you will not always have me. ⁸She did what she could. She poured perfume on my body beforehand to prepare for my burial. ⁹I tell you the truth, wherever the gospel is preached throughout the world, what she has done will also be told, in memory of her."

¹⁰Then Judas Iscariot, one of the Twelve, went to the chief priests to betray Jesus to them. ¹¹They were delighted to hear this and promised to give him money. So he watched for an opportunity to hand him over.

The Lord's Supper

¹²On the first day of the Feast of Unleavened Bread, when it was customary to sacrifice the Passover lamb, Jesus' disciples asked him, "Where do you want us to go and make preparations for you to eat the Passover?"

¹³So he sent two of his disciples, telling them, "Go into the city, and a man carrying a jar of water will meet you. Follow him. ¹⁴Say to the owner of the house he enters, 'The Teacher asks: Where is my guest room, where I may eat the Passover with my disciples?' ¹⁵He will show you a large upper room, furnished and ready. Make preparations for us there."

¹⁶The disciples left, went into the city and found things just as Jesus had told them. So they prepared the Passover.

¹⁷When evening came, Jesus arrived with the Twelve. ¹⁸While they were reclining at the table eating, he said, "I tell you the truth, one of you will betray me—one who is eating with me."

¹⁹They were saddened, and one by one they said to him, "Surely not I?"

²⁰"It is one of the Twelve," he replied, "one who dips bread into the bowl with me. ²¹The Son of Man will go just as it is written about him. But woe to that man who betrays the Son of Man! It would be better for him if he had not been born."

²²While they were eating, Jesus took bread, gave thanks and broke it, and gave it to his disciples, saying, "Take it; this is my body."

²³Then he took the cup, gave thanks and offered it to them, and they all drank from it.

²⁴"This is my blood of the covenant, which is poured out for many," he said to them. ²⁵"I tell you the truth, I will not drink again of the fruit of the vine until that day when I drink it anew in the kingdom of God."

²⁶When they had sung a hymn, they went out to the Mount of Olives.

Jesus Predicts Peter's Denial

²⁷"You will all fall away," Jesus told them, "for it is written:

" 'I will strike the shepherd,
   and the sheep will be scattered.'

²⁸But after I have risen, I will go ahead of you into Galilee."

²⁹Peter declared, "Even if all fall away, I will not."

³⁰"I tell you the truth," Jesus answered, "today—yes, tonight—before the rooster crows twice you yourself will disown me three times."

³¹But Peter insisted emphatically, "Even if I have to die with you, I will never disown you." And all the others said the same.

One Final Meal Together

John 14

The apostle John devoted one-third of his gospel to the last twenty-four hours of Jesus' life. The Passover meal that Mark covered in a few brief paragraphs, John stretched out over five chapters (13–17), and nothing like these chapters exists elsewhere in the Bible. Their slow-motion, realistic detail provides an intimate memoir of Jesus' most anguished evening on earth.

Leonardo da Vinci immortalized the setting of The Last Supper in his famous painting, arranging the participants on one side of the table as if they were posing for the artist. John avoids physical details and presents instead the maelstrom of human emotions. He holds a light to the disciples' faces, and you can almost see the awareness flickering in their eyes. All that Jesus had told them over the past three years was settling in.

Never before had Jesus been so direct with them. It was his last chance to communicate to them the significance of his life and his death. He refrained from parables and painstakingly answered the disciples' redundant questions. The world was about to undergo a convulsive trauma, and the eleven fearful men with him were his hope for that world.

"I am going away, and I am coming back to you," Jesus kept repeating, until at last the disciples showed signs of comprehension. God's Son had entered the world to reside in one body. He was now leaving earth to return to the Father. But someone else—the Spirit of truth, the Counselor—would come to take up residence in many bodies, in *their* bodies.

Jesus was planning to die, yes. He was leaving them. But in some mysterious way, he was not leaving. He would not stay dead. For the disciples, caught up in the excitement of the Passover, sobered by Jesus' haunting obsession with death, it was all too much to grasp. That night, Jesus gave them an intimacy with the Father such as they had never known; even so, he promised an even greater intimacy to come. He seemed aware that much of what they nodded their heads at now would not sink in until later.

To Reflect On: *This chapter contains many promises. Which have been fulfilled in your life?*

JOHN 14
Jesus Comforts His Disciples

14 "Do not let your hearts be troubled. Trust in God; trust also in me. ²In my Father's house are many rooms; if it were not so, I would have told you. I am going there to prepare a place for you. ³And if I go and prepare a place for you, I will come back and take you to be with me that you also may be where I am. ⁴You know the way to the place where I am going."

Jesus the Way to the Father

⁵Thomas said to him, "Lord, we don't know where you are going, so how can we know the way?"

⁶Jesus answered, "I am the way and the truth and the life. No one comes to the Father except through me. ⁷If you really knew me, you would know my Father as well. From now on, you do know him and have seen him."

⁸Philip said, "Lord, show us the Father and that will be enough for us."

⁹Jesus answered: "Don't you know me, Philip, even after I have been among you such a long time? Anyone who has seen me has seen the Father. How can you say, 'Show us the Father'? ¹⁰Don't you believe that I am in the Father, and that the Father is in me? The words I say to you are not just my own. Rather, it is the Father, living in me, who is doing his work. ¹¹Believe me when I say that I am in the Father and the Father is in me; or at least believe on the evidence of the miracles themselves. ¹²I tell you the truth, anyone who has faith in me will do what I have been doing. He will do even greater things than these, because I am going to the Father. ¹³And I will do whatever you ask in my name, so that the Son may bring glory to the Father. ¹⁴You may ask me for anything in my name, and I will do it.

Jesus Promises the Holy Spirit

¹⁵"If you love me, you will obey what I command. ¹⁶And I will ask the Father, and he will give you another Counselor to be with you forever—¹⁷the Spirit of truth. The world cannot accept him, because it neither sees him nor knows him. But you know him, for he lives with you and will be in you. ¹⁸I will not leave you as orphans; I will come to you. ¹⁹Before long, the world will not see me anymore, but you will see me. Because I live, you also will live. ²⁰On that day you will realize that I am in my Father, and you are in me, and I am in you. ²¹Whoever has my commands and obeys them, he is the one who loves me. He who loves me will be loved by my Father, and I too will love him and show myself to him."

²²Then Judas (not Judas Iscariot) said, "But, Lord, why do you intend to show yourself to us and not to the world?"

²³Jesus replied, "If anyone loves me, he will obey my teaching. My Father will love him, and we will come to him and make our home with him. ²⁴He who does not love me will not obey my teaching. These words you hear are not my own; they belong to the Father who sent me.

²⁵"All this I have spoken while still with you. ²⁶But the Counselor, the Holy Spirit, whom the Father will send in my name, will teach you all things and will remind you of everything I have said to you. ²⁷Peace I leave with you; my peace I give you. I do not give to you as the world gives. Do not let your hearts be troubled and do not be afraid.

²⁸"You heard me say, 'I am going away and I am coming back to you.' If you loved me, you would be glad that I am going to the Father, for the Father is greater than I. ²⁹I have told you now before it happens, so that when it does happen you will believe. ³⁰I will not speak with you much longer, for the prince of this world is coming. He has no hold on me, ³¹but the world must learn that I love the Father and that I do exactly what my Father has commanded me.

"Come now; let us leave.

The Vital Link

John 15:1–16:4

The sense of urgency grew inside the stuffy, crowded room. Jesus had just a few more hours to prepare his disciples for the tumult that lay ahead. More, they were his closest friends in all the world, and he was about to leave them. "He showed them the full extent of his love," John says (13:1).

In this passage, Jesus envisions what will happen to the little band—so quick with their affirmations of loyalty now, so quick with their denials later—after his departure. He foresees fierce opposition, and hatred, and beatings, and executions. The disciples would face all these trials on his behalf, and without his physical presence to protect them.

As he had done so often, Jesus searched for an allegory, a parable from nature to drive home his point. Just outside Jerusalem, rows of vineyards covered the hills— probably, he and his disciples had walked through them on their way to the city—and Jesus summoned up two images from those vineyards.

First, the image of lush, juicy grapes. Not long before, the disciples had drunk the product of those grapes as they listened to Jesus' deeply symbolic words about the blood of the covenant. In order to bear fruit, Jesus said, one thing was essential: They must remain in intimate connection with the vine. "I am the vine; you are the branches. If a man remains in me and I in him, he will bear much fruit; apart from me you can do nothing." Jesus reminded the Twelve that he had handpicked them for a specific mission: "to go and bear fruit—fruit that will last."

Then Jesus mentioned one more image: a pile of dead sticks at the edge of the vineyard. Somehow, these branches had lost their connection with the vine, the source of nourishment. A farmer had snapped them off and thrown them in a heap for burning. They no longer had a useful function.

Most likely, Jesus' disciples did not fully understand his meaning that night. But the symbol, with its abrupt contrast between juicy grapes and withered branches, would stay with them. It would surface directly whenever they gathered together to celebrate the Lord's Supper. The spectacular history of the early church gives certain proof that they eventually heeded his heartfelt words about "remaining" in him.

To Reflect On: *In what ways do you work at "remaining" in Jesus?*

JOHN 15:1–16:4

The Vine and the Branches

15 "I am the true vine, and my Father is the gardener. ²He cuts off every branch in me that bears no fruit, while every branch that does bear fruit he prunes so that it will be even more fruitful. ³You are already clean because of the word I have spoken to you. ⁴Remain in me, and I will remain in you. No branch can bear fruit by itself; it must remain in the vine. Neither can you bear fruit unless you remain in me.

⁵"I am the vine; you are the branches. If a man remains in me and I in him, he will bear much fruit; apart from me you can do nothing. ⁶If anyone does not remain in me, he is like a branch that is thrown away and withers; such branches are picked up, thrown into the fire and burned. ⁷If you remain in me and my words remain in you, ask whatever you wish, and it will be given you. ⁸This is to my Father's glory, that you bear much fruit, showing yourselves to be my disciples.

⁹"As the Father has loved me, so have I loved you. Now remain in my love. ¹⁰If you obey my commands, you will remain in my love, just as I have obeyed my Father's commands and remain in his love. ¹¹I have told you this so that my joy may be in you and that your joy may be complete. ¹²My command is this: Love each other as I have loved you. ¹³Greater love has no one than this, that he lay down his life for his friends. ¹⁴You are my friends if you do what I command. ¹⁵I no longer call you servants, because a servant does not know his master's business. Instead, I have called you friends, for everything that I learned from my Father I have made known to you. ¹⁶You did not choose me, but I chose you and appointed you to go and bear fruit— fruit that will last. Then the Father will give you whatever you ask in my name. ¹⁷This is my command: Love each other.

The World Hates the Disciples

¹⁸"If the world hates you, keep in mind that it hated me first. ¹⁹If you belonged to the world, it would love you as its own. As it is, you do not belong to the world, but I have chosen you out of the world. That is why the world hates you. ²⁰Remember the words I spoke to you: 'No servant is greater than his master.' If they persecuted me, they will persecute you also. If they obeyed my teaching, they will obey yours also. ²¹They will treat you this way because of my name, for they do not know the One who sent me. ²²If I had not come and spoken to them, they would not be guilty of sin. Now, however, they have no excuse for their sin. ²³He who hates me hates my Father as well. ²⁴If I had not done among them what no one else did, they would not be guilty of sin. But now they have seen these miracles, and yet they have hated both me and my Father. ²⁵But this is to fulfill what is written in their Law: 'They hated me without reason.'

²⁶"When the Counselor comes, whom I will send to you from the Father, the Spirit of truth who goes out from the Father, he will testify about me. ²⁷And you also must testify, for you have been with me from the beginning.

16 "All this I have told you so that you will not go astray. ²They will put you out of the synagogue; in fact, a time is coming when anyone who kills you will think he is offering a service to God. ³They will do such things because they have not known the Father or me. ⁴I have told you this, so that when the time comes you will remember that I warned you. I did not tell you this at first because I was with you.

Turning Bad into Good

John 16:5–33

After the allegory of the vine and branches, Jesus turned from word pictures and spoke directly about what would happen to the disciples. Never was he more "theological" with them. Some of it they understood; some of it they did not. John shows them whispering to each other, trying to figure out his meaning.

Perhaps the strangest words of all were these: "It is for your good that I am going away." Good? How could it possibly be good for him to abandon them, thus dashing their hopes of a restored kingdom? Jesus tried to explain the advantages to come, when the Spirit would live inside them, but the disciples were too busy discussing what he meant by "going away" to comprehend.

Jesus' analogy of childbirth gave a further clue. Although childbirth may involve great pain, the pain is not a dead end, like pain caused by cancer. The effort of giving birth produces something—new life!—and results in joy. In the same way, the great sorrow he and the disciples were about to undergo would not be a dead end. His pain would bring about the salvation of the world; their grief would turn to joy.

Jesus concluded his words that fateful evening with a ringing declaration, "Take heart! I have overcome the world." How hollow this statement would seem the next evening when his pale, abused body hung on an executioner's cross, and the disciples slunk away in the darkness. Their emotions, and faith, were to rise and plummet in one unforgettable day—just as Jesus had predicted in his analogy of childbirth.

> **To Reflect On:** *How would the world be different if Jesus had stayed on earth instead of going away?*

JOHN 16:5–33

The Work of the Holy Spirit

5 "Now I am going to him who sent me, yet none of you asks me, 'Where are you going?' 6 Because I have said these things, you are filled with grief. 7 But I tell you the truth: It is for your good that I am going away. Unless I go away, the Counselor will not come to you; but if I go, I will send him to you. 8 When he comes, he will convict the world of guilt in regard to sin and righteousness and judgment: 9 in regard to sin, because men do not believe in me; 10 in regard to righteousness, because I am going to the Father, where you can see me no longer; 11 and in regard to judgment, because the prince of this world now stands condemned.

12 "I have much more to say to you, more than you can now bear. 13 But when he, the Spirit of truth, comes, he will guide you into all truth. He will not speak on his own; he will speak only what he hears, and he will tell you what is yet to come. 14 He will bring glory to me by taking from what is mine and making it known to you. 15 All that belongs to the Father is mine. That is why I said the Spirit will take from what is mine and make it known to you.

16 "In a little while you will see me no more, and then after a little while you will see me."

The Disciples' Grief Will Turn to Joy

17 Some of his disciples said to one another, "What does he mean by saying, 'In a little while you will see me no more, and then after a little while you will see me,' and 'Because I am going to the Father'?" 18 They kept asking, "What does he mean by 'a little while'? We don't understand what he is saying."

19 Jesus saw that they wanted to ask him about this, so he said to them, "Are you asking one another what I meant when I said, 'In a little while you will see me no more, and then after a little while you will see me'? 20 I tell you the truth, you will weep and mourn while the world rejoices. You will grieve, but your grief will turn to joy. 21 A woman giving birth to a child has pain because her time has come; but when her baby is born she forgets the anguish because of her joy that a child is born into the world. 22 So with you: Now is your time of grief, but I will see you again and you will rejoice, and no one will take away your joy. 23 In that day you will no longer ask me anything. I tell you the truth, my Father will give you whatever you ask in my name. 24 Until now you have not asked for anything in my name. Ask and you will receive, and your joy will be complete.

25 "Though I have been speaking figuratively, a time is coming when I will no longer use this kind of language but will tell you plainly about my Father. 26 In that day you will ask in my name. I am not saying that I will ask the Father on your behalf. 27 No, the Father himself loves you because you have loved me and have believed that I came from God. 28 I came from the Father and entered the world; now I am leaving the world and going back to the Father."

29 Then Jesus' disciples said, "Now you are speaking clearly and without figures of speech. 30 Now we can see that you know all things and that you do not even need to have anyone ask you questions. This makes us believe that you came from God."

31 "You believe at last!" Jesus answered. 32 "But a time is coming, and has come, when you will be scattered, each to his own home. You will leave me all alone. Yet I am not alone, for my Father is with me.

33 "I have told you these things, so that in me you may have peace. In this world you will have trouble. But take heart! I have overcome the world."

Commissioning

John 17

When the disciples responded to Jesus' speech with the bold pronouncement, "This makes us believe that you came from God," it seemed to settle something in Jesus' mind. "You believe at last!" he said, with obvious relief, and then concluded the intimate get-together with this, his longest recorded prayer. In it, Jesus summed up his feelings and his plans for the tight circle of friends gathered around him.

Their previous missions, the preaching and healing ministries in the countryside, had been mere warm-up exercises. Now he was turning everything over to them. "I confer on you a kingdom, just as my Father conferred one on me," he said (Luke 22:29). His prayer represented a kind of commissioning or graduation.

Using language full of mystery, Jesus told them that he must leave the world but they must remain in it to proclaim him. They would now attract the hatred and hostility that had previously been directed against him. And yet, although they lived "in the world," they were not quite "of the world." Something set them apart from the world and bound them together with him in unity with God—a unity so close as to defy all explanation.

Jesus prayed, too, for the other believers who would follow them, stretching in an unbroken chain throughout history. "I pray . . . that all of them may be one, Father, just as you are in me and I am in you. May they also be in us so that the world may believe that you have sent me." And then he led the frightened little band to his appointment with death.

> **To Reflect On:** *Based on this prayer, how would you sum up Jesus' goals for the church? How well does your church fulfill those goals?*

JOHN 17

Jesus Prays for Himself

17 After Jesus said this, he looked toward heaven and prayed:

"Father, the time has come. Glorify your Son, that your Son may glorify you. ²For you granted him authority over all people that he might give eternal life to all those you have given him. ³Now this is eternal life: that they may know you, the only true God, and Jesus Christ, whom you have sent. ⁴I have brought you glory on earth by completing the work you gave me to do. ⁵And now, Father, glorify me in your presence with the glory I had with you before the world began.

Jesus Prays for His Disciples

⁶"I have revealed you to those whom you gave me out of the world. They were yours; you gave them to me and they have obeyed your word. ⁷Now they know that everything you have given me comes from you. ⁸For I gave them the words you gave me and they accepted them. They knew with certainty that I came from you, and they believed that you sent me. ⁹I pray for them. I am not praying for the world, but for those you have given me, for they are yours. ¹⁰All I have is yours, and all you have is mine. And glory has come to me through them. ¹¹I will remain in the world no longer, but they are still in the world, and I am coming to you. Holy Father, protect them by the power of your name—the name you gave me—so that they may be one as we are one. ¹²While I was with them, I protected them and kept them safe by that name you gave me. None has been lost except the one

doomed to destruction so that Scripture would be fulfilled.

¹³"I am coming to you now, but I say these things while I am still in the world, so that they may have the full measure of my joy within them. ¹⁴I have given them your word and the world has hated them, for they are not of the world any more than I am of the world. ¹⁵My prayer is not that you take them out of the world but that you protect them from the evil one. ¹⁶They are not of the world, even as I am not of it. ¹⁷Sanctify them by the truth; your word is truth. ¹⁸As you sent me into the world, I have sent them into the world. ¹⁹For them I sanctify myself, that they too may be truly sanctified.

Jesus Prays for All Believers

²⁰"My prayer is not for them alone. I pray also for those who will believe in me through their message, ²¹that all of them may be one, Father, just as you are in me and I am in you. May they also be in us so that the world may believe that you have sent me. ²²I have given them the glory that you gave me, that they may be one as we are one: ²³I in them and you in me. May they be brought to complete unity to let the world know that you sent me and have loved them even as you have loved me.

²⁴"Father, I want those you have given me to be with me where I am, and to see my glory, the glory you have given me because you loved me before the creation of the world.

²⁵"Righteous Father, though the world does not know you, I know you, and they know that you have sent me. ²⁶I have made you known to them, and will continue to make you known in order that the love you have for me may be in them and that I myself may be in them."

Appointment with Destiny

Matthew 26:36–68

It is a stroke of bitter irony that in the Gospels the intimate scene of the Last Supper butts up against the scene of betrayal in Gethsemane. The ordeal began with Jesus praying in a quiet, cool grove of olive trees, with three of his disciples waiting sleepily outside. Inside the garden all was peaceful; outside, the forces of hell itself were on the loose.

A large armed mob made its way toward the garden to seize and torture Jesus. He felt afraid, and abandoned. Falling facedown on the ground, he prayed for some way out. The future of the human race and of the entire universe came down to this one weeping figure. His sweat fell to the ground in large drops, like blood.

All the deep ironies of Jesus' life came crashing together that evening in the garden when the one whom wise men had crossed a continent to worship was sold, like a slave, for thirty pieces of silver. Jesus' disciples showed that they still had not come to terms with the kind of "kingdom" Jesus wanted to establish. Blustery Peter was prepared to install a kingdom the traditional way—by force. When a scuffle broke out, he hacked off a guard's ear. But Jesus stopped the violence and performed, notably, his last miracle: He healed the guard.

With a single prayer, Jesus reminded his friends, he could dispatch squads of angels. He had the power to defend himself, but he would not use it. When the reality dawned on the disciples that they could expect no last-minute rescue operations from the invisible world, they all fled. Their last flicker of hope had been extinguished. If Jesus would not protect himself, how could he protect them?

Matthew's account of what transpired in Gethsemane and before the Sanhedrin shows that, in an odd inversion, the "victim" dominated all that took place. Jesus, not Judas, not the mob, and not the high priest, acted like one truly in control. When they put him on the stand and accused him, he maintained a regal silence. "Tell us if you are the Christ [Messiah], the Son of God," they demanded. He finally answered with a simple "Yes, it is as you say."

That single admission condemned Jesus to death, for the Sanhedrin had a different expectation of the Messiah. They wanted a conqueror to set them free by force. Jesus knew that only one thing—his death—would truly set them free. For that reason he had come to earth.

> **To Reflect On:** *If you had been in the garden with Jesus, how would you have reacted to the scene of confrontation?*

MATTHEW 26:36–68

Gethsemane

³⁶Then Jesus went with his disciples to a place called Gethsemane, and he said to them, "Sit here while I go over there and pray." ³⁷He took Peter and the two sons of Zebedee along with him, and he began to be sorrowful and troubled. ³⁸Then he said to them, "My soul is overwhelmed with sorrow to the point of death. Stay here and keep watch with me."

³⁹Going a little farther, he fell with his face to the ground and prayed, "My Father, if it is possible, may this cup be taken from me. Yet not as I will, but as you will."

⁴⁰Then he returned to his disciples and found them sleeping. "Could you men not keep watch with me for one hour?" he asked Peter. ⁴¹"Watch and pray so that you will not fall into temptation. The spirit is willing, but the body is weak."

⁴²He went away a second time and prayed, "My Father, if it is not possible for this cup to be taken away unless I drink it, may your will be done."

⁴³When he came back, he again found them sleeping, because their eyes were heavy. ⁴⁴So he left them and went away once more and prayed the third time, saying the same thing.

⁴⁵Then he returned to the disciples and said to them, "Are you still sleeping and resting? Look, the hour is near, and the Son of Man is betrayed into the hands of sinners. ⁴⁶Rise, let us go! Here comes my betrayer!"

Jesus Arrested

⁴⁷While he was still speaking, Judas, one of the Twelve, arrived. With him was a large crowd armed with swords and clubs, sent from the chief priests and the elders of the people. ⁴⁸Now the betrayer had arranged a signal with them: "The one I kiss is the man; arrest him." ⁴⁹Going at once to Jesus, Judas said, "Greetings, Rabbi!" and kissed him.

⁵⁰Jesus replied, "Friend, do what you came for."

Then the men stepped forward, seized Jesus and arrested him. ⁵¹With that, one of Jesus' companions reached for his sword, drew it out and struck the servant of the high priest, cutting off his ear.

⁵²"Put your sword back in its place," Jesus said to him, "for all who draw the sword will die by the sword. ⁵³Do you think I cannot call on my Father, and he will at once put at my disposal more than twelve legions of angels? ⁵⁴But how then would the Scriptures be fulfilled that say it must happen in this way?"

⁵⁵At that time Jesus said to the crowd, "Am I leading a rebellion, that you have come out with swords and clubs to capture me? Every day I sat in the temple courts teaching, and you did not arrest me. ⁵⁶But this has all taken place that the writings of the prophets might be fulfilled." Then all the disciples deserted him and fled.

Before the Sanhedrin

⁵⁷Those who had arrested Jesus took him to Caiaphas, the high priest, where the teachers of the law and the elders had assembled. ⁵⁸But Peter followed him at a distance, right up to the courtyard of the high priest. He entered and sat down with the guards to see the outcome.

⁵⁹The chief priests and the whole Sanhedrin were looking for false evidence against Jesus so that they could put him to death. ⁶⁰But they did not find any, though many false witnesses came forward.

Finally two came forward ⁶¹and declared, "This fellow said, 'I am able to destroy the temple of God and rebuild it in three days.'"

⁶²Then the high priest stood up and said to Jesus, "Are you not going to answer? What is this testimony that these men are bringing against you?" ⁶³But Jesus remained silent.

The high priest said to him, "I charge you under oath by the living God: Tell us if you are the Christ, the Son of God."

⁶⁴"Yes, it is as you say," Jesus replied. "But I say to all of you: In the future you will see the Son of Man sitting at the right hand of the Mighty One and coming on the clouds of heaven."

⁶⁵Then the high priest tore his clothes and said, "He has spoken blasphemy! Why do we need any more witnesses? Look, now you have heard the blasphemy. ⁶⁶What do you think?"

"He is worthy of death," they answered.

⁶⁷Then they spit in his face and struck him with their fists. Others slapped him ⁶⁸and said, "Prophesy to us, Christ. Who hit you?"

No Justice

Matthew 27:1–31

The Gospels record a pass-the-buck sequence in Jesus' encounter with "justice." Roman law had granted the Jews many freedoms, including the right to their own court system, the Sanhedrin. When Jesus identified himself as the Messiah, the Sanhedrin convicted him of the religious charge of blasphemy, a capital offense. However, the Sanhedrin had no authority to carry out a death sentence; that required the sanction of Roman justice. Thus Jesus' opponents sent him to Pilate, the Roman governor of Judea.

Somewhere along the way, the accusers changed the charge against Jesus from a religious one (which would not have impressed Pilate) to a political one. They portrayed Jesus as a dangerous revolutionary who had declared himself king of the Jews in defiance of Roman rule. Pilate had grave misgivings about the charge, and his wife's premonitions compounded his sense of uneasiness.

Luke records that Pilate at first declared Jesus innocent despite pressure from the crowd. Then he sought a way out of his dilemma by deferring the case to Herod, who had jurisdiction over Jesus' home region. Herod toyed with Jesus for a while, but, disappointed by Jesus' silence and his refusal to perform miracles, ultimately sent him back to Pilate.

As Pilate tried three different times to get the Jewish leaders to release their prisoner, the fury of the crowd against Jesus only swelled. At last, facing a mob scene, the canny governor yielded to their demands, but only after ceremoniously washing his hands of innocent blood.

Through all these legal proceedings, as the central drama of history was being played out, Jesus kept an almost unbroken silence. He was acknowledged king at last—with a crown of thorns jammed onto his head, and a royal robe draped across his bloodied back. Pilate seemed to recognize, at some level, the enormity of the injustice he had participated in. He prepared a notice of Jesus' "crime" to be fastened to the cross, which read, in three languages, "JESUS OF NAZARETH, THE KING OF THE JEWS." When the chief priests protested that it should read only that Jesus *claimed* to be king, Pilate answered, "What I have written, I have written" (John 19).

To Reflect On: *What was it about Jesus that stirred up such strong feelings in his opponents?*

———————◆———————

MATTHEW 27:1–31

Judas Hangs Himself

27 Early in the morning, all the chief priests and the elders of the people came to the decision to put Jesus to death. ²They bound him, led him away and handed him over to Pilate, the governor.

³When Judas, who had betrayed him, saw that Jesus was condemned, he was seized with remorse and returned the thirty silver coins to the chief priests and the elders. ⁴"I have sinned," he said, "for I have betrayed innocent blood."

"What is that to us?" they repiled. "That's your responsibility."

⁵So Judas threw the money into the temple and left. Then he went away and hanged himself.

⁶The chief priests picked up the coins and said, "It is against the law to put this into the treasury, since it is blood money." ⁷So they decided to use the money to buy the potter's field as a burial place for foreigners. ⁸That is why it has been called the Field of Blood to this day. ⁹Then what was spoken by Jeremiah the prophet was fulfilled: "They took the thirty silver coins, the price set on him by the people of Israel, ¹⁰and they used them to buy the potter's field, as the Lord commanded me."

Jesus Before Pilate

¹¹Meanwhile Jesus stood before the governor, and the governor asked him, "Are you the king of the Jews?"

"Yes, it is as you say," Jesus replied. ¹²When he was accused by the chief priests and the elders, he gave no answer. ¹³Then Pilate asked him, "Don't you hear the testimony they are bringing against you?" ¹⁴But Jesus made no reply, not even to a single charge—to the great amazement of the governor.

¹⁵Now it was the governor's custom at the Feast to release a prisoner chosen by the crowd. ¹⁶At that time they had a notorious prisoner, called Barabbas. ¹⁷So when the crowd had gathered, Pilate asked them, "Which one do you want me to release to you: Barabbas, or Jesus who is called Christ?" ¹⁸For he knew it was out of envy that they had handed Jesus over to him.

¹⁹While Pilate was sitting on the judge's seat, his wife sent him this message: "Don't have anything to do with that innocent man, for I have suffered a great deal today in a dream because of him."

²⁰But the chief priests and the elders persuaded the crowd to ask for Barabbas and to have Jesus executed.

²¹"Which of the two do you want me to release to you?" asked the governor.

"Barabbas," they answered.

²²"What shall I do, then, with Jesus who is called Christ?" Pilate asked.

They all answered, "Crucify him!"

²³"Why? What crime has he committed?" asked Pilate.

But they shouted all the louder, "Crucify him!"

²⁴When Pilate saw that he was getting nowhere, but that instead an uproar was starting, he took water and washed his hands in front of the crowd. "I am innocent of this man's blood," he said. "It is your responsibility!"

²⁵All the people answered, "Let his blood be on us and on our children!"

²⁶Then he released Barabbas to them. But he had Jesus flogged, and handed them over to be crucified.

The Soldiers Mock Jesus

²⁷Then the governor's soldiers took Jesus into the Praetorium and gathered the whole company of soldiers around him. ²⁸They stripped him and put a scarlet robe on him, ²⁹and then twisted together a crown of thorns and set it on his head. They put a staff in his right hand and knelt in front of him and mocked him. "Hail, king of the Jews!" they said. ³⁰They spit on him, and took the staff and struck him on the head again and again. ³¹After they had mocked him, they took off the robe and put his own clothes on him. Then they led him away to crucify him.

The Last Temptation

Mark 15:21–47

Long before, at the very beginning of his ministry, Jesus had resisted Satan's temptation toward an easier path of safety and physical comfort. Now, as the moment of truth drew near, that temptation must have seemed more alluring than ever.

Everybody, it seemed, was demanding a miracle. At the Sanhedrin trial, the priests who slapped Jesus challenged him, "Prophesy! Who hit you?" Pilate and Herod, who had heard rumors about Jesus' powers, begged for a show. The grieving women, who had followed Jesus all the way from Galilee, yearned for a miracle of rescue. The disciples, cowering in fear, ached for one.

On the cross, a criminal at Jesus' left taunted him, "Aren't you the Christ? Then save yourself and us." The crowd milling about the site took up the cry: "Let him come down from the cross, and we will believe in him. . . . Let God rescue him now if he wants him."

But there was no rescue, no miracle. There was only silence. The Father had turned his back, or so it seemed, letting history take its course, letting everything evil in the world triumph over everything good. How could Jesus save others when, quite simply, he could not save himself?

Why did Jesus have to die? Theologians who ponder such things have debated various theories of "the Atonement" for centuries, with little agreement. Somehow it required love, sacrificial love, to win what could not be won by force.

Mark's account presents the facts, not the theology, but one detail he includes may provide a clue. Jesus had just uttered the awful cry, "My God, my God, why have you forsaken me?" He, God's Son, identified so closely with the human race—taking on their sin!—that God the Father had to turn away. The gulf was that great. But, Mark adds, just as Jesus breathed his last, "The curtain of the temple was torn in two from top to bottom."

That massive curtain served to seal off the Most Holy Place, where God's Presence dwelled. No one except the high priest was allowed inside, and he could enter only once a year, on a designated day. As the author of Hebrews would later note (Hebrews 10), the tearing of that curtain showed beyond doubt exactly what was accomplished by Jesus' death on the cross. No more sacrifices would ever be required. Jesus won for all of us—ordinary people, not just priests—immediate access to God's presence. By taking on the burden of human sin, and bearing its punishment, Jesus removed forever the barrier between God and us.

> **To Reflect On:** *When have you most wanted a "miracle" in your life and been disappointed? What did you learn from that experience?*

———————————◆———————————

MARK 15:21-47

The Crucifixion

²¹A certain man from Cyrene, Simon, the Father of Alexander and Rufus, was passing by on his way in from the country, and they forced him to carry the cross. ²²They brought Jesus to the place called Golgotha (which means The Place of the Skull). ²³Then they offered him wine mixed with myrrh, but he did not take it. ²⁴And they crucified him. Dividing up his clothes, they cast lots to see what each would get.

²⁵It was the third hour when they crucified him. ²⁶The written notice of the charge against him read: THE KING OF THE JEWS. ²⁷They crucified two robbers with him, one on his right and one on his left. ²⁹Those who passed by hurled insults at him, shaking their heads and saying, "So! You who are going to destroy the temple and build it in three days, ³⁰come down from the cross and save yourself!"

³¹In the same way the chief priests and the teachers of the law mocked him among themselves. "He saved others," they said, "but he can't save himself! ³²Let this Christ, this King of Israel, come down now from the cross that we may see and believe." Those crucified with him also heaped insults on him.

The Death of Jesus

³³At the sixth hour darkness came over the whole land until the ninth hour. ³⁴And at the ninth hour Jesus cried out in a loud voice, *"Eloi, Eloi, lama sabachthani?"*—which means, "My God, my God, why have you forsaken me?"

³⁵When some of those standing near heard this, they said, "Listen, he's calling Elijah."

³⁶One man ran, filled a sponge with wine vinegar, put it on a stick, and offered it to Jesus to drink. "Now leave him alone. Let's see if Elijah comes to take him down," he said.

³⁷With a loud cry, Jesus breathed his last.

³⁸The curtain of the temple was torn in two from top to bottom. ³⁹And when the centurion, who stood there in front of Jesus, heard his cry and saw how he died, he said, "Surely this man was the Son of God!"

⁴⁰Some women were watching from a distance. Among them were Mary Magdalene, Mary the mother of James the younger and of Joses, and Salome. ⁴¹In Galilee these women had followed him and cared for his needs. Many other women who had come up with him to Jerusalem were also there.

The Burial of Jesus

⁴²It was Preparation Day (that is, the day before the Sabbath). So as evening approached, ⁴³Joseph of Arimathea, a prominent member of the Council, who was himself waiting for the kingdom of God, went boldly to Pilate and asked for Jesus' body. ⁴⁴Pilate was surprised to hear that he was already dead. Summoning the centurion, he asked him if Jesus had already died. ⁴⁵When he learned from the centurion that it was so, he gave the body to Joseph. ⁴⁶So Joseph bought some linen cloth, took down the body, wrapped it in the linen, and placed it in a tomb cut out of rock. Then he rolled a stone against the entrance of the tomb. ⁴⁷Mary Magdalene and Mary the mother of Joses saw where he was laid.

Signs of Life

Matthew 27:62–28:15

When the greatest miracle of all history occurred, the only eyewitnesses were soldiers standing guard outside Jesus' tomb. When the earth shook and an angel appeared, bright as lightning, these guards trembled and became like dead men. Then, with an incurably human reflex, they fled to the authorities to report the disturbance.

But here is an astounding fact: Later that afternoon the soldiers, who had seen proof of the Resurrection with their own eyes, changed their story. The resurrection of the Son of God did not seem nearly as significant as, say, stacks of freshly minted silver.

A few women, grieving friends of Jesus, were next to learn of the Miracle of Miracles. Matthew reports that when an angel broke the news of Jesus' resurrection, the women hurried away "afraid yet filled with joy." *Fear*, the reflexive human response to a supernatural encounter—when the women heard from a glowing angel firsthand news of an event beyond comprehension, of course they felt afraid. *Yet filled with joy*—the news they heard was the best news of all, news too good to be true, news so good it had to be true. Jesus was back! He had returned, as promised. The dreams of the Messiah all came surging back as the women ran fearfully and joyfully to tell the disciples.

Even as the women ran, the soldiers were rehearsing an alibi, their part in an elaborate cover-up scheme. Like everything else in Jesus' life, his resurrection drew forth two contrasting responses. Those who believed were transformed, finding enough hope and courage to go out and change the world. But those who chose not to believe found ways to ignore evidence they had seen with their own eyes.

> **To Reflect On:** *What makes you believe, or not believe, in Jesus?*

———————◆———————

MATTHEW 27:62–28:15

The Guard at the Tomb

⁶²The next day, the one after Preparation Day, the chief priests and the Pharisees went to Pilate. ⁶³"Sir," they said, "we remember that while he was still alive that deceiver said, 'After three days I will rise again.' ⁶⁴So give the order for the tomb to be made secure until the third day. Otherwise, his disciples may come and steal the body and tell the people that he has been raised from the dead. This last deception will be worse than the first."

⁶⁵"Take a guard," Pilate answered. "Go, make the tomb as secure as you know how." ⁶⁶So they went and made the tomb secure by putting a seal on the stone and posting the guard.

28 After the Sabbath, at dawn on the first day of the week, Mary Magdalene and the other Mary went to look at the tomb.

²There was a violent earthquake, for an angel of the Lord came down from heaven and, going to the tomb, rolled back the stone and sat on it. ³His appearance was like lightning, and his clothes were white as snow. ⁴The guards were so afraid of him that they shook and became like dead men.

⁵The angel said to the women, "Do not be afraid, for I know that you are looking for Jesus, who was crucified. ⁶He is not here; he has risen, just as he said. Come and see the place where he lay. ⁷Then go quickly and tell his disciples: 'He has risen from the dead and is going ahead of you into Galilee. There you will see him.' Now I have told you."

⁸So the women hurried away from the tomb, afraid yet filled with joy, and ran to tell his disciples. ⁹Suddenly Jesus met them. "Greetings," he said. They came to him, clasped his feet and worshiped him. ¹⁰Then Jesus said to them, "Do not be afraid. Go and tell my brothers to go to Galilee; there they will see me."

The Guards' Report

¹¹While the women were on their way, some of the guards went into the city and reported to the chief priests everything that had happened. ¹²When the chief priests had met with the elders and devised a plan, they gave the soldiers a large sum of money, ¹³telling them, "You are to say, 'His disciples came during the night and stole him away while we were asleep.' ¹⁴If this report gets to the governor, we will satisfy him and keep you out of trouble." ¹⁵So the soldiers took the money and did as they were instructed. And this story has been widely circulated among the Jews to this very day.

The Rumor Confirmed

John 20

People who discount the Resurrection tend to portray the disciples in one of two ways: (1) as gullible country bumpkins with a weakness for ghost stories, or (2) as shrewd conspirators who hatch a resurrection plot to attract popular support for their movement. The Bible presents a radically different picture. It shows Jesus' followers themselves as the ones most skeptical of rumors about a risen Jesus.

Mary Magdalene was still bewildered and afraid even after an angel broke the news plainly to her. When she met Jesus himself near the tomb, she didn't recognize him until he spoke her name.

Reports from the women of an empty tomb failed to convince the disciples—"their words seemed to them like nonsense" (Luke 24)—and so Peter and another ran to the graveyard to see for themselves. That same night all the disciples huddled in a locked room, afraid of the Jews, apparently still skeptical.

For his part, Jesus went out of his way to allay the disciples' fears and suspicions. In broad daylight he visited and fished with them. Once he asked a dubious Thomas to test his scarred skin by touch. Another time he ate a piece of broiled fish in their presence to prove he was not a ghost (Luke 24). This was no mirage, no hallucination; it was Jesus their master, no one else.

The appearances of the risen Christ recorded in the Bible, fewer than a dozen, show a clear pattern. With one exception, he visited small groups of people closeted indoors or in a remote area. By the garden tomb, in a locked room, on the road to Emmaus, beside the Sea of Galilee, atop the Mount of Olives—such private encounters bolstered the faith of people who already believed in Jesus. But as far as we know, not a single unbeliever saw Jesus after his death.

What would have happened if Jesus had reappeared on Pilate's porch or before the Sanhedrin, this time with a withering blast against those who had ordered his death? Surely such a public scene would have caused a sensation. But would it have kindled faith? Jesus had already answered that question in a poignant prophecy contained in his story of the rich man and Lazarus: "If they do not listen to Moses and the Prophets, they will not be convinced even if someone rises from the dead" (Luke 16).

Jesus chose another way: to let the disciples themselves spread the word, as his witnesses.

> **To Reflect On:** *Would you have greeted the news of Jesus' resurrection like Mary? Like Peter? Like Thomas?*

JOHN 20

The Empty Tomb

20 Early on the first day of the week, while it was still dark, Mary Magdalene went to the tomb and saw that the stone had been removed from the entrance. ²So she came running to Simon Peter and the other disciple, the one Jesus loved, and said, "They have taken the Lord out of the tomb, and we don't know where they have put him!"

³So Peter and the other disciple started for the tomb. ⁴Both were running, but the other disciple outran Peter and reached the tomb first. ⁵He bent over and looked in at the strips of linen lying there but did not go in. ⁶Then Simon Peter, who was behind him, arrived and went into the tomb. He saw the strips of linen lying there, ⁷as well as the burial cloth that had been around Jesus' head. The cloth was folded up by itself, separate from the linen. ⁸Finally the other disciple, who had reached the tomb first, also went inside. He saw and believed. ⁹(They still did not understand from Scripture that Jesus had to rise from the dead.)

Jesus Appears to Mary Magdalene

¹⁰Then the disciples went back to their homes, ¹¹but Mary stood outside the tomb crying. As she wept, she bent over to look into the tomb ¹²and saw two angels in white, seated where Jesus' body had been, one at the head and the other at the foot.

¹³They asked her, "Woman, why are you crying?"

"They have taken my Lord away," she said, "and I don't know where they have put him." ¹⁴At this, she turned around and saw Jesus standing there, but she did not realize that it was Jesus.

¹⁵"Woman," he said, "why are you crying? Who is it you are looking for?"

Thinking he was the gardener, she said, "Sir, if you have carried him away, tell me where you have put him, and I will get him."

¹⁶Jesus said to her, "Mary."

She turned toward him and cried out in Aramaic, "Rabboni!" (which means Teacher).

¹⁷Jesus said, "Do not hold on to me, for I have not yet returned to the Father. Go instead to my brothers and tell them, 'I am returning to my Father and your Father, to my God and your God.'"

¹⁸Mary Magdalene went to the disciples with the news: "I have seen the Lord!" And she told them that he had said these things to her.

Jesus Appears to His Disciples

¹⁹On the evening of that first day of the week, when the disciples were together, with the doors locked for fear of the Jews, Jesus came and stood among them and said, "Peace be with you!" ²⁰After he said this, he showed them his hands and side. The disciples were overjoyed when they saw the Lord.

²¹Again Jesus said, "Peace be with you! As the Father has sent me, I am sending you." ²²And with that he breathed on them and said, "Receive the Holy Spirit. ²³If you forgive anyone his sins, they are forgiven; if you do not forgive them, they are not forgiven."

Jesus Appears to Thomas

²⁴Now Thomas (called Didymus), one of the Twelve, was not with the disciples when Jesus came. ²⁵So the other disciples told him, "We have seen the Lord!"

But he said to them, "Unless I see the nail marks in his hands and put my finger where the nails were, and put my hand into his side, I will not believe it."

²⁶A week later his disciples were in the house again, and Thomas was with them. Though the doors were locked, Jesus came and stood among them and said, "Peace be with you!" ²⁷Then he said to Thomas, "Put your finger here; see my hands. Reach out your hand and put it into my side. Stop doubting and believe."

²⁸Thomas said to him, "My Lord and my God!"

²⁹Then Jesus told him, "Because you have seen me, you have believed; blessed are those who have not seen and yet have believed."

³⁰Jesus did many other miraculous signs in the presence of his disciples, which are not recorded in this book. ³¹But these are written that you may believe that Jesus is the Christ, the Son of God, and that by believing you may have life in his name.

Roadside Encounter

Luke 24:13–49

This scene at the end of Luke's gospel captures the swirl of emotions in Jesus' disciples the fateful week of his execution. Two followers were walking away from Jerusalem, downhearted and perplexed. Their dream of "the one who was going to redeem Israel" had died along with their leader on the cross. And yet they too had heard the crazy rumors of an empty tomb. What did it all mean?

A stranger appeared beside the two forlorn disciples. At first he seemed the only man alive who hadn't heard about the incredible week in Jerusalem. But as he talked it became clear that he knew more about what had happened than anyone. Painstakingly, he traced the whole story of the gospel, beginning with Moses and the prophets. According to him, the prophets had predicted all along that the Messiah would suffer these things.

The stranger fascinated them, so much so that they begged him to stay longer. Then at mealtime, he made a hauntingly familiar gesture and the last link snapped into place. It was Jesus sitting at their table! No one else. Without a doubt, he was alive.

They were two ordinary people, not even counted among the twelve intimates of Jesus. But the encounter with the risen Christ changed them forever. "Were not our hearts burning within us while he talked with us on the road and opened the Scriptures to us?" they recalled. They dashed to meet the Twelve (now Eleven, with Judas's betrayal) only to learn that Peter, too, had seen Jesus. Suddenly, in the midst of that chaotic scene of joy and confusion, Jesus himself appeared. He explained once and for all that his death and resurrection were not unforeseen, but rather lay at the heart of God's plan all along.

Jesus had one last promise to keep: He departed from earth, and in his place he left the band of believers to carry out his mission. These people, common people with more than a touch of cowardice, had followed Jesus, listened to him, and watched him die (from a distance for safety's sake). But seeing Jesus alive changed all that. They returned to Jerusalem with great joy, and before long they were out telling the world the good news.

To Reflect On: *How did the truth about Jesus "dawn" on you?*

LUKE 24:13-49

On the Road to Emmaus

¹³Now that same day two of them were going to a village called Emmaus, about seven miles from Jerusalem. ¹⁴They were talking with each other about everything that had happened. ¹⁵As they talked and discussed these things with each other, Jesus himself came up and walked along with them; ¹⁶but they were kept from recognizing him.

¹⁷He asked them, "What are you discussing together as you walk along?"

They stood still, their faces downcast. ¹⁸One of them, named Cleopas, asked him, "Are you only a visitor to Jerusalem and do not know the things that have happened there in these days?"

¹⁹"What things?" he asked.

"About Jesus of Nazareth," they replied. "He was a prophet, powerful in word and deed before God and all the people. ²⁰The chief priests and our rulers handed him over to be sentenced to death, and they crucified him; ²¹but we had hoped that he was the one who was going to redeem Israel. And what is more, it is the third day since all this took place. ²²In addition, some of our women amazed us. They went to the tomb early this morning ²³but didn't find his body. They came and told us that they had seen a vision of angels, who said he was alive. ²⁴Then some of our companions went to the tomb and found it just as the women had said, but him they did not see."

²⁵He said to them, "How foolish you are, and how slow of heart to believe all the prophets have spoken! ²⁶Did not the Christ have to suffer these things and then encounter his glory?" ²⁷And beginning with Moses and all the Prophets, he explained to them what was said in all the Scriptures concerning himself.

²⁸As they approached the village to which they were going, Jesus acted as if he were going farther. ²⁹But they urged him strongly, "Stay with us, for it is nearly evening; the day is almost over." So he went in to stay with them.

³⁰When he was at the table with them, he took bread, gave thanks, broke it and began to give it to them. ³¹Then their eyes were opened and they recognized him, and he disappeared from their sight. ³²They asked each other, "Were not our hearts burning within us while he talked with us on the road and opened the Scriptures to us?"

³³They got up and returned at once to Jerusalem. There they found the Eleven and those with them, assembled together ³⁴and saying, "It is true! The Lord has risen and has appeared to Simon." ³⁵Then the two told what had happened on the way, and how Jesus was recognized by them when he broke the bread.

Jesus Appears to the Disciples

³⁶While they were still talking about this, Jesus himself stood among them and said to them, "Peace be with you."

³⁷They were startled and frightened, thinking they saw a ghost. ³⁸He said to them, "Why are you troubled, and why do doubts rise in your minds? ³⁹Look at my hands and my feet. It is I myself! Touch me and see; a ghost does not have flesh and bones, as you see I have."

⁴⁰When he had said this, he showed them his hands and feet. ⁴¹And while they still did not believe it because of joy and amazement, he asked them, "Do you have anything here to eat?" ⁴²They gave him a piece of broiled fish, ⁴³and he took it and ate it in their presence.

⁴⁴He said to them, "This is what I told you while I was still with you: Everything must be fulfilled that is written about me in the Law of Moses, the Prophets and the Psalms."

⁴⁵Then he opened their minds so they could understand the Scriptures. ⁴⁶He told them, "This is what is written: The Christ will suffer and rise from the dead on the third day, ⁴⁷and repentance and forgiveness of sins will be preached in his name to all nations, beginning at Jerusalem. ⁴⁸You are witnesses of these things. ⁴⁹I am going to send you what my Father has promised; but stay in the city until you have been clothed with power from on high."

Departed, But Not Gone

Acts 1

The disciples, expecting a kingdom along the lines of the nation of Israel in the Old Testament, wanted what people have always sought in a visible kingdom: a chicken in every pot, full employment, a strong army to deter invaders. No matter how many times Jesus explained the invisible kingdom, and the way of the cross, it never seemed to sink in.

The disciples' obsession with Israel's restored kingdom did not fade even after Jesus had died and come back to life. For forty days after the Resurrection he appeared and disappeared seemingly at will. When he came, his followers listened eagerly to his explanations of all that had happened. When he left, they plotted the structure of the new kingdom that he would surely inaugurate. Think of it: Jerusalem free at last from Roman domination.

Jesus gave some mystifying orders, however. He told his followers to return to Jerusalem and simply wait. Something more was needed. Do not leave the city, he said, until the Holy Spirit comes. At last, one of the disciples put to Jesus the question they had all been debating together, "Lord, are you at this time going to restore the kingdom to Israel?"

No one was prepared for Jesus' reaction. He seemed to brush the question aside, deflecting attention away from Israel toward neighboring countries, all the way to the ends of the earth. He mentioned the Holy Spirit again, and then, to everyone's utter amazement, his body lifted off the ground, suspended there for a moment, then disappeared into a cloud. And they never saw him again.

Christians believe that all of history revolves around the life of Jesus the Christ. But the plain fact is that Jesus left earth after thirty-three years. Furthermore, he declared it a good thing: "You are filled with grief. But I tell you the truth: It is for your good that I am going away. Unless I go away, the Counselor will not come to you" (John 16).

The book of Acts, written by the same author as the gospel of Luke, tells what happened after Jesus' departure when the counselor came at last. First, the disciples began adjusting to new realities: They selected a replacement for Judas, made plans to follow Jesus' final instructions, and returned to Jerusalem to await the Holy Spirit.

> **To Reflect On:** *Project yourself back to the forty-day period after Jesus' resurrection. What would you have been expecting Jesus to do?*

ACTS 1

Jesus Taken Up Into Heaven

1 In my former book, Theophilus, I wrote about all that Jesus began to do and to teach ²until the day he was taken up to heaven, after giving instructions through the Holy Spirit to the apostles he had chosen. ³After his suffering, he showed himself to these men and gave many convincing proofs that he was alive. He appeared to them over a period of forty days and spoke about the kingdom of God. ⁴On one occasion, while he was eating with them, he gave them this command: "Do not leave Jerusalem, but wait for the gift my Father promised, which you have heard me speak about. ⁵For John baptized with water, but in a few days you will be baptized with the Holy Spirit."

⁶So when they met together, they asked him, "Lord, are you at this time going to restore the kingdom to Israel?"

⁷He said to them: "It is not for you to know the times or dates the Father has set by his own authority. ⁸But you will receive power when the Holy Spirit comes on you; and you will be my witnesses in Jerusalem, and in all Judea and Samaria, and to the ends of the earth."

⁹After he said this, he was taken up before their very eyes, and a cloud hid him from their sight.

¹⁰They were looking intently up into the sky as he was going, when suddenly two men dressed in white stood beside them. ¹¹"Men of Galilee," they said, "why do you stand here looking into the sky? This same Jesus, who has been taken from you into heaven, will come back in the same way you have seen him go into heaven."

Matthias Chosen to Replace Judas

¹²Then they returned to Jerusalem from the hill called the Mount of Olives, a Sabbath day's walk from the city. ¹³When they arrived, they went upstairs to the room where they were staying. Those present were Peter, John, James and Andrew; Philip and Thomas, Bartholomew and Matthew; James son of Alphaeus and Simon the Zealot, and Judas son of James. ¹⁴They all joined together constantly in prayer, along with the women and Mary the mother of Jesus, and with his brothers.

¹⁵In those days Peter stood up among the believers (a group numbering about a hundred and twenty) ¹⁶and said, "Brothers, the Scripture had to be fulfilled which the Holy Spirit spoke long ago through the mouth of David concerning Judas, who served as guide for those who arrested Jesus—¹⁷he was one of our number and shared in this ministry."

¹⁸(With the reward he got for his wickedness, Judas bought a field; there he fell headlong, his body burst open and all his intestines spilled out. ¹⁹Everyone in Jerusalem heard about this, so they called that field in their language Akeldama, that is, Field of Blood.)

²⁰"For," said Peter, "it is written in the book of Psalms,

" 'May his place be deserted;
    let there be no one to dwell in it,'

and,

" 'May another take his place of
    leadership.'

²¹Therefore it is necessary to choose one of the men who have been with us the whole time the Lord Jesus went in and out among us, ²²beginning from John's baptism to the time when Jesus was taken up from us. For one of these must become a witness with us of his resurrection.

²³So they proposed two men: Joseph called Barsabbas (also known as Justus) and Matthias. ²⁴Then they prayed, "Lord, you know everyone's heart. Show us which of these two you have chosen ²⁵to take over this apostolic ministry, which Judas left to go where he belongs." ²⁶Then they cast lots, and the lot fell to Matthias; so he was added to the eleven apostles.

Explosion

Acts 2:1–41

On the feast day of Pentecost, the disciples got what they had been waiting for. Perhaps half a million pilgrims were milling about in Jerusalem on that Jewish holiday. The believers, in accord with Jesus' instructions, had gathered in a small group indoors, where they patiently awaited what had been promised. Then, with a sound like a violent wind and a sight like tongues of fire, it happened. The Holy Spirit, the Presence of God himself, took up residence inside ordinary bodies—their bodies.

The disciples hit the streets with a bold new style that the world has never recovered from. Soon everyone in Jerusalem was talking about the Jesus-followers. A few mocked them as drunks. But clearly, something was afoot. To their amazement, pilgrims from all over the world heard the Galileans' message in their own native languages.

There was Peter, coward apostle who had denied Christ three times to save his own neck, brazenly taking on both Jewish and Roman authorities. Quoting from King David and the prophet Joel, he proclaimed that they had just lived through the most important event of all history. "God has raised this Jesus to life, and we are all witnesses of this fact," he said, and went on to declare Jesus as the very Messiah, the fulfillment of the Jews' long-awaited dream. Three thousand people responded to Peter's powerful message on that first day. And thus the Christian church was born.

Beginning with that boisterous scene in Jerusalem, Luke weaves a historical adventure tale. The group of new believers, at first a mere annoyance to the Jews and the Romans, would not stop growing. Just as Jesus had predicted, the message spread throughout Judea, and Samaria, and in less than one generation had penetrated into Rome, the center of civilization. In an era when new religions were a dime a dozen, the Christian faith became a worldwide phenomenon. It all began with this scene on the day of Pentecost.

> **To Reflect On:** *In this chapter, search for all the positive qualities that helped attract others to the new group of believers.*

ACTS 2:1–41

The Holy Spirit Comes at Pentecost

2 When the day of Pentecost came, they were all together in one place. [2]Suddenly a sound like the blowing of a violent wind came from heaven and filled the whole house where they were sitting. [3]They saw what seemed to be tongues of fire that separated and came to rest on each of them. [4]All of them were filled with the Holy Spirit and began to speak in other tongues as the Spirit enabled them.

[5]Now there were staying in Jerusalem God-fearing Jews from every nation under heaven. [6]When they heard this sound, a crowd came together in bewilderment, because each one heard them speaking in his own language. [7]Utterly amazed, they asked: "Are not all these men who are speaking Galileans? [8]Then how is it that each of us hears them in his own native language? [9]Parthians, Medes and Elamites; residents of Mesopotamia, Judea and Cappadocia, Pontus and Asia, [10]Phrygia and Pamphylia, Egypt and the parts of Libya near Cyrene; visitors from Rome [11](both Jews and converts to Judaism); Cretans and Arabs—we hear them declaring the wonders of God in our own tongues!" [12]Amazed and perplexed, they asked one another, "What does this mean?"

[13]Some, however, made fun of them and said, "They have had too much wine."

Peter Addresses the Crowd

[14] Then Peter stood up with the Eleven, raised his voice and addressed the crowd: "Fellow Jews and all of you who live in Jerusalem, let me explain this to you; listen carefully to what I say. [15] These men are not drunk, as you suppose. It's only nine in the morning! [16] No, this is what was spoken by the prophet Joel:

[17] " 'In the last days, God says,
I will pour out my Spirit on all
     people.
Your sons and daughters will prophesy,
     your young men will see visions,
     your old men will dream dreams.
[18] Even on my servants, both men and
          women,
     I will pour out my Spirit in those
          days,
     and they will prophesy.
[19] I will show wonders in the heaven
          above
     and signs on the earth below,
     blood and fire and billows of smoke.
[20] The sun will be turned to darkness
     and the moon to blood
     before the coming of the great and
          glorious day of the Lord.
[21] And everyone who calls
     on the name of the Lord will be
          saved.

[22] "Men of Israel, listen to this: Jesus of Nazareth was a man accredited by God to you by miracles, wonders and signs, which God did among you through him, as you yourselves know. [23] This man was handed over to you by God's set purpose and foreknowledge; and you, with the help of wicked men, put him to death by nailing him to the cross. [24] But God raised him from the dead, freeing him from the agony of death, because it was impossible for death to keep its hold on him. [25] David said about him:

" 'I saw the Lord always before me.
     Because he is at my right hand,
     I will not be shaken.
[26] Therefore my heart is glad and my
          tongue rejoices;

my body also will live in hope,
[27] because you will not abandon me to
          the grave,
     nor will you let your Holy One see
          decay.
[28] You have made known to me the
          paths of life;
     you will fill me with joy in your
          presence.'

[29] "Brothers, I can tell you confidently that the patriarch David died and was buried, and his tomb is here to this day. [30] But he was a prophet and knew that God had promised him on oath that he would place one of his descendants on the throne. [31] Seeing what was ahead, he spoke of the resurrection of the Christ, that he was not abandoned to the grave, nor did his body see decay. [32] God has raised this Jesus to life, and we are all witnesses of the fact. [33] Exalted to the right hand of God, he has received from the Father the promised Holy Spirit and has poured out what you now see and hear. [34] For David did not ascend to heaven, and yet he said,

" 'The Lord said to my Lord:
     "Sit at my right hand
[35] until I make your enemies
     a footstool for your feet.' "

[36] "Therefore let all Israel be assured of this: God has made this Jesus, whom you crucified, both Lord and Christ."

[37] When the people head this, they were cut to the heart and said to Peter and the other apostles, "Brothers, what shall we do?"

[38] Peter replied, "Repent and be baptized, every one of you, in the name of Jesus Christ for the forgiveness of your sins. And you will receive the gift of the Holy Spirit. [39] The promise is for you and your children and for all who are far off—for all whom the Lord our God will call."

[40] With many other words he warned them; and he pleaded with them, "Save yourselves from this corrupt generation." [41] Those who accepted his message were baptized, and about three thousand were added to their number that day.

Shock Waves

Acts 5

The disciples, newly empowered with the Holy Spirit, started acting a lot like Jesus. They went to the temple and preached sermons; they healed the sick; they met the needs of the poor. To many bystanders, the message of new life in Jesus sounded wonderful, like the first note of music to people born deaf. Five thousand men believed, including some priests. The followers were soon organizing and electing officers.

Acts also shows that problems sprang up alongside the successes. The church became popular, an "in" place to belong. Sorcerers and magicians dropped in, drawn by the reports of healings and other wonders. Wealthy people, like Ananias and Sapphira, saw the church as a place to gain applause for their benevolence. Such opportunists learned that the apostles, not to mention God, would not tolerate corruption in the fledgling church.

Before long, the focus of concern shifted away from internal problems to outside opposition. The same forces that had conspired against Jesus—temple officers, the Sadducees, the high priest, the Sanhedrin, Roman guards—aligned themselves against the new phenomenon of the church. Every so often they would haul in the leaders, but for what could they prosecute them—healing the sick? Inciting people to praise God? The Christians hardly resembled dangerous conspirators; they usually met openly on the temple porch.

Even so, religious leaders beat and jailed the apostles on trumped-up charges. What happened next should have given the establishment a clue into exactly what they were up against: The apostles responded to the beatings with praise to God for the privilege of suffering in his name, and an angel of the Lord sprang them free from jail.

Gamaliel, a wise old Pharisee, had perhaps the best advice of all (vv. 38–39). He could not have been more prophetic.

> **To Reflect On:** *What internal problems threaten the church today? What dangers come from outside?*

ACTS 5

Ananias and Sapphira

5 Now a man named Ananias, together with his wife Sapphira, also sold a piece of property. [2] With his wife's full knowledge he kept back part of the money for himself, but brought the rest and put it at the apostles' feet.

[3] Then Peter said, "Ananias, how is it that Satan has so filled your heart that you have lied to the Holy Spirit and have kept for yourself some of the money you received for the land?

[4] Didn't it belong to you before it was sold? And after it was sold, wasn't the money at your disposal? What made you think of doing such a thing? You have not lied to men but to God."

[5] When Ananias heard this, he fell down and died. And great fear seized all who heard what had happened. [6] Then the young men came forward, wrapped up his body, and carried him out and buried him.

[7] About three hours later his wife came in, not knowing what had happened. [8] Peter asked her, "Tell me, is this the price you and Ananias got for the land?"

"Yes," she said, "that is the price."

[9] Peter said to her, "How could you agree to test the Spirit of the Lord? Look! The feet of the men who buried your husband are at the door, and they will carry you out also."

[10] At that moment she fell down at his feet and died. Then the young men came in

and, finding her dead, carried her out and buried her beside her husband. [11]Great fear seized the whole church and all who heard about these events.

The Apostles Heal Many

[12]The apostles performed many miraculous signs and wonders among the people. And all the believers used to meet together in Solomon's Colonnade. [13]No one else dared join them, even though they were highly regarded by the people. [14]Nevertheless, more and more men and women believed in the Lord and were added to their number. [15]As a result, people brought the sick into the streets and laid them on beds and mats so that at least Peter's shadow might fall on some of them as he passed by. [16]Crowds gathered also from the towns around Jerusalem, bringing their sick and those tormented by evil spirits, and all of them were healed.

The Apostles Persecuted

[17]Then the high priest and all his associates, who were members of the party of the Sadducees, were filled with jealousy. [18]They arrested the apostles and put them in the public jail. [19]But during the night an angel of the Lord opened the doors of the jail and brought them out. [20]"Go, stand in the temple courts," he said, "and tell the people the full message of this new life."

[21]At daybreak they entered the temple courts, as they had been told, and began to teach the people.

When the high priest and his associates arrived, they called together the Sanhedrin—the full assembly of the elders of Israel—and sent to the jail for the apostles. [22]But on arriving at the jail, the officers did not find them there. So they went back and reported, [23]"We found the jail securely locked, with the guards standing at the doors; but when we opened them, we found no one inside." [24]On hearing this report, the captain of the temple guard and the chief priests were puzzled, wondering what would come of this.

[25]Then someone came and said, "Look! The men you put in jail are standing in the temple courts teaching the people." [26]At that, the captain went with his officers and brought the apostles. They did not use force, because they feared that the people would stone them.

[27]Having brought the apostles, they made them appear before the Sanhedrin to be questioned by the high priest. [28]"We gave you strict orders not to teach in this name," he said. "Yet you have filled Jerusalem with your teaching and are determined to make us guilty of this man's blood."

[29]Peter and the other apostles replied: "We must obey God rather than men! [30]The God of our fathers raised Jesus from the dead—whom you had killed by hanging him on a tree. [31]God exalted him to his own right hand as Prince and Savior that he might give repentance and forgiveness of sins to Israel. [32]We are witnesses of these things, and so is the Holy Spirit, whom God has given to those who obey him."

[33]When they heard this, they were furious and wanted to put them to death. [34]But a Pharisee named Gamaliel, a teacher of the law, who was honored by all the people, stood up in the Sanhedrin and ordered that the men be put outside for a little while. [35]Then he addressed them: "Men of Israel, consider carefully what you intend to do to these men. [36]Some time ago Theudas appeared, claiming to be somebody, and about four hundred men rallied to him. He was killed, all his followers were dispersed, and it all came to nothing. [37]After him, Judas the Galilean appeared in the days of the census and led a band of people in revolt. He too was killed, and all his followers were scattered. [38]Therefore, in the present case I advise you: Leave these men alone! Let them go! For if their purpose or activity is of human origin, it will fail. [39]But if it is from God, you will not be able to stop these men; you will only find yourselves fighting against God."

[40]His speech persuaded them. They called the apostles in and had them flogged. Then they ordered them not to speak in the name of Jesus, and let them go.

[41]The apostles left the Sanhedrin, rejoicing because they had been counted worthy of suffering disgrace for the Name. [42]Day after day, in the temple courts and from house to house, they never stopped teaching and proclaiming the good news that Jesus is the Christ.

About-face

Acts 9:1–31

The most effective anti-Communist of modern times is the Russian author Alexander Solzhenitsyn, a Nobel prize-winner who exposed the Soviet prison camps. Many intellectuals tempted toward communism became disillusioned when they read Solzhenitsyn's devastating accounts of life in "the Gulag Archipelago." Solzhenitsyn himself had once been a true believer, an ardent Communist, but he made one careless comment about Stalin in a personal letter intercepted by the authorities. A ten-year sentence of hard labor in the camps permanently turned Solzhenitsyn against Stalin's oppressive system.

The most surprising converts, like Solzhenitsyn, often make the best crusaders. Former alcoholics can convince others of drinking's dangers; former drug addicts give the most forceful warnings against drugs. And when the book of Acts introduces the most effective Christian missionary of all time, he turns out to be a former bounty hunter of Christians.

Acts 9 shows a glimpse of the early church even before it had a name; people called its followers "the Way," or "the brothers," or "the Nazarene sect." Its members lived in constant fear of arrest and persecution—if not from the Romans, then from the Jews. Already a leader named Stephen had been publicly stoned. And no one inspired more fear in the hearts of the early Christians than a man named Saul, who had participated in Stephen's execution.

But then came the miraculous turnabout on the road to Damascus. In a dramatic move, God stepped in and, against all odds, selected the bounty hunter Saul to lead the young church. It didn't take long to convince Saul: A blinding light and a voice from heaven knocked him out of commission for three days and changed his whole attitude toward Jesus. Such was Saul's murderous reputation, however, that the Christians in Damascus and Jerusalem accepted him only gradually.

Soon Saul (renamed Paul) was on the other side of the persecutors' whips; his former colleagues were now trying to kill *him*. He proved to be as fearless in preaching Christ as he had been in working against him. In four great missionary journeys, Paul took the news of the gospel around the shores of the Mediterranean. During those journeys he found time to write half the books of the New Testament, and in so doing laid the groundwork for Christian theology. Paul was perhaps the most thoroughly converted man who ever lived.

To Reflect On: *Have you ever had an abrupt about-face?*

ACTS 9:1–31

Saul's Conversion

9 Meanwhile, Saul was still breathing out murderous threats against the Lord's disciples. He went to the high priest ²and asked him for letters to the synagogues in Damascus, so that if he found any there who belonged to the Way, whether men or women, he might take them as prisoners to Jerusalem. ³As he neared Damascus on his journey, suddenly a light from heaven flashed around him. ⁴He fell to the ground and heard a voice say to him, "Saul, Saul, why do you persecute me?"

⁵"Who are you, Lord?" Saul asked.

"I am Jesus, whom you are persecuting," he replied. ⁶"Now get up and go into the city, and you will be told what you must do."

⁷The men traveling with Saul stood there speechless; they heard the sound but did not see anyone. ⁸Saul got up from the ground, but when he opened his eyes he could see nothing. So they led him by the hand into Damascus. ⁹For three days he was blind, and did not eat or drink anything.

¹⁰In Damascus there was a disciple named Ananias. The Lord called to him in a vision, "Ananias!"

"Yes, Lord," he answered.

¹¹The Lord told him, "Go to the house of Judas on Straight Street and ask for a man from Tarsus named Saul, for he is praying. ¹²In a vision he has seen a man named Ananias come and place his hands on him to restore his sight."

¹³"Lord," Ananias answered, "I have heard many reports about this man and all the harm he has done to your saints in Jerusalem. ¹⁴And he has come here with authority from the chief priests to arrest all who call on your name."

¹⁵But the Lord said to Ananias, "Go! This man is my chosen instrument to carry my name before the Gentiles and their kings and before the people of Israel. ¹⁶I will show him how much he must suffer for my name."

¹⁷Then Ananias went to the house and entered it. Placing his hands on Saul, he said, "Brother Saul, the Lord—Jesus, who appeared to you on the road as you were coming here—has sent me so that you may see again and be filled with the Holy Spirit." ¹⁸Immediately, something like scales fell from Saul's eyes, and he could see again. He got up and was baptized, ¹⁹and after taking some food, he regained his strength.

Saul in Damascus and Jerusalem

Saul spent several days with the disciples in Damascus. ²⁰At once he began to preach in the synagogues that Jesus is the Son of God. ²¹All those who heard him were astonished and asked, "Isn't he the man who raised havoc in Jerusalem among those who call on this name? And hasn't he come here to take them as prisoners to the chief priests?" ²²Yet Saul grew more and more powerful and baffled the Jews living in Damascus by proving that Jesus is the Christ.

²³After many days had gone by, the Jews conspired to kill him, ²⁴but Saul learned of their plan. Day and night they kept close watch on the city gates in order to kill him. ²⁵But his followers took him by night and lowered him in a basket through an opening in the wall.

²⁶When he came to Jerusalem, he tried to join the disciples, but they were all afraid of him, not believing that he really was a disciple. ²⁷But Barnabas took him and brought him to the apostles. He told them how Saul on his journey had seen the Lord and that the Lord had spoken to him, and how in Damascus he had preached fearlessly in the name of Jesus. ²⁸So Saul stayed with them and moved about freely in Jerusalem, speaking boldly in the name of the Lord. ²⁹He talked and debated with the Grecian Jews, but they tried to kill him. ³⁰When the brothers learned of this, they took him down to Caesarea and sent him off to Tarsus.

³¹Then the church throughout Judea, Galilee and Samaria enjoyed a time of peace. It was strengthened; and encouraged by the Holy Spirit, it grew in numbers, living in the fear of the Lord.

Moment of Crisis

Galatians 3:1–4:7

Paul soon became involved in a major conflict over Jew-Gentile relations that had been simmering just underneath the surface for many months. It finally broke out into the open when important church leaders came together in a conference to try to resolve the divisive issue.

All Jesus' disciples were Jewish, as were most of the converts from the day of Pentecost. But on his first missionary journey, Paul learned to his surprise that non-Jews were even more receptive to the news about Jesus. He began a policy that he would follow throughout his career: He went first to the synagogue and preached among Jews; if they rejected him, though, he turned immediately to the Gentiles.

In a twist of history, Paul gained a reputation as "the apostle to the Gentiles." Before conversion he had been a Pharisee, a strict Jewish legalist. But as he saw God work among non-Jews he became their champion. At the Jerusalem conference he boldly opposed the apostles Peter and James for their hypocrisy toward Gentiles. Paul insisted that Gentiles should have full rights in the church and need not go through Jewish rituals like circumcision. (See Acts 15 and Galatians 2 for details of the conference.)

This letter to the churches in Galatia dates from the time of the early Jew-Gentile controversy. Paul is emotionally worked up. In fact, he is downright furious at misguided attempts to shackle the church with legalism. In the first paragraph, Paul explodes with full force; he then proceeds to give a "Christian," rather than Jewish, interpretation of the Old Testament covenants with Abraham and Moses.

Legalism may seem like a rather harmless quirk of the church, but Paul could foresee the outcome of the Galatians' thinking. They would start trusting in their own human effort (keeping "the Law") to gain acceptance with God. Faith in Christ would become just one of many steps in salvation, not the only one. The bedrock of the gospel would crumble as they, in effect, devalued what Christ had done.

Paul's letter to the Galatians is, then, a protest against treason. Paul insists that faith in Christ alone, not anyone's set of laws, opens the door to acceptance by God. If a person could reach God by obeying the Law, then he, the strict Pharisee, would have done it. Galatians teaches that there is nothing we can do to make God love us more, or love us less. We can't "earn" God's love by slavishly following rules.

Paul had felt the gust of freedom that comes after liberation from a set of confining laws. He wasn't about to let that freedom slip away.

> **To Reflect On:** *The early Christians went in two directions. Some, like the Galatians, got obsessed with legalism. Others took their Christian freedom too far: They refused to follow anyone's rules. Which seems the greater danger in your circle of believers?*

GALATIANS 3:1–4:7

Faith or Observance of the Law

3 You foolish Galatians! Who has bewitched you? Before your very eyes Jesus Christ was clearly portrayed as crucified. ²I would like to learn just one thing from you: Did you receive the Spirit by observing the law, or by believing what you heard? ³Are you so foolish? After beginning with the Spirit, are you now trying to attain your goal by human effort? ⁴Have you suffered so much for nothing—if it really was for nothing? ⁵Does God give you his Spirit and work miracles among you because you observe the law, or because you believe what you heard?

⁶Consider Abraham: "He believed God, and it was credited to him as righteousness." ⁷Understand, then, that those who believe are children of Abraham. ⁸The Scripture foresaw that God would justify the Gentiles by faith, and announced the gospel in advance to Abraham: "All nations will be blessed through you." ⁹So those who have faith are blessed along with Abraham, the man of faith.

¹⁰All who rely on observing the law are under a curse, for it is written: "Cursed is everyone who does not continue to do everything written in the Book of the Law." ¹¹Clearly no one is justified before God by the law, because, "The righteous will live by faith." ¹²The law is not based on faith; on the contrary, "The man who does these things will live by them." ¹³Christ redeemed us from the curse of the law by becoming a curse for us, for it is written: "Cursed is everyone who is hung on a tree." ¹⁴He redeemed us in order that the blessing given to Abraham might come to the Gentiles through Christ Jesus, so that by faith we might receive the promise of the Spirit.

The Law and the Promise

¹⁵Brothers, let me take an example from everyday life. Just as no one can set aside or add to a human covenant that has been duly established, so it is in this case. ¹⁶The promises were spoken to Abraham and to his seed. The Scripture does not say "and to seeds," meaning many people, but "and to your seed," meaning one person, who is Christ. ¹⁷What I mean is this: The law, introduced 430 years later, does not set aside the covenant previously established by God and thus do away with the promise. ¹⁸For if the inheritance depends on the law, then it no longer depends on a promise; but God in his grace gave it to Abraham through a promise.

¹⁹What, then, was the purpose of the law? It was added because of transgressions until the Seed to whom the promise referred had come. The law was put into effect through angels by a mediator. ²⁰A mediator, however, does not represent just one party; but God is one.

²¹Is the law, therefore, opposed to the promises of God? Absolutely not! For if a law had been given that could impart life, then righteousness would certainly have come by the law. ²²But the Scripture declares that the whole world is a prisoner of sin, so that what was promised, being given through faith in Jesus Christ, might be given to those who believe.

²³Before this faith came, we were held prisoners by the law, locked up until faith should be revealed. ²⁴So the law was put in charge to lead us to Christ that we might be justified by faith. ²⁵Now that faith has come, we are no longer under the supervision of the law.

Sons of God

²⁶You are all sons of God through faith in Christ Jesus, ²⁷for all of you who were baptized into Christ have clothed yourselves with Christ. ²⁸There is neither Jew nor Greek, slave nor free, male nor female, for you are all one in Christ Jesus. ²⁹If you belong to Christ, then you are Abraham's seed, and heirs according to the promise.

4 What I am saying is that as long as the heir is a child, he is no different from a slave, although he owns the whole estate. ²He is subject to guardians and trustees until the time set by his father. ³So also, when we were children, we were in slavery under the basic principles of the world. ⁴But when the time had fully come, God sent his Son, born of a woman, born under law, ⁵to redeem those under law, that we might receive the full rights of sons. ⁶Because you are sons, God sent the Spirit of his Son into our hearts, the Spirit who calls out, "*Abba*, Father." ⁷So you are no longer a slave, but a son; and since you are a son, God has made you also an heir.

Detour

Acts 16:6–40

This chapter contains one of the Bible's most famous episodes of divine guidance: Paul's vision of a man of Macedonia. Yet the account actually shows how *uncommon* such a revelation was. It certainly startled Paul, who made an abrupt change in his travel plans. Following his normal procedure, Paul had arranged his missionary trip strategically, linking together major towns and cities in sequence. But this one time he ran into a roadblock and received an alternative itinerary.

The book of Acts follows Paul on three distinct missionary journeys. It was a good time in history to travel, for by Paul's lifetime Rome had established absolute mastery over a vast territory. Language was unified, and a rare empire-wide peace, the Pax Romana, prevailed. Moreover, Roman engineers had crisscrossed the empire with a network of roads (built so well that many still survive), and as a Roman citizen, Paul held a passport valid anywhere.

In his travels, Paul concentrated on the chief trade towns and capital cities of Roman colonies. From them, the gospel message could radiate out across the globe. If a young church showed promise, Paul would stay on, sometimes as long as three years, to direct its spiritual growth. His letters glow with affection for the friends he developed in this way. On his second and third journeys, Paul revisited many of the churches he had founded.

This chapter shows how one of Paul's favorite churches came into existence. Philippi was a leading city in the region of Macedonia, where the vision had directed him. A casual conversation with a woman by a river opened the way for Paul (women played a crucial role in many of the early churches). What took place in Philippi stands almost as a pattern for Paul's never-dull missionary visits: early acceptance, violent opposition, and providential deliverance from danger.

As this account reveals, Paul did not hesitate to use the prestige and status that came with his Roman citizenship. He was escorted from the city with proper respect, but he left behind two transformed households: one led by a woman cloth merchant, one, by a city jailer. From that unlikely combination would grow the lively church at Philippi.

> **To Reflect On:** *How have you sensed God's guidance in your life?*

ACTS 16:6–40

Paul's Vision of the Man of Macedonia

⁶Paul and his companions traveled throughout the region of Phrygia and Galatia, having been kept by the Holy Spirit from preaching the word in the province of Asia. ⁷When they came to the border of Mysia, they tried to enter Bithynia, but the Spirit of Jesus would not allow them to. ⁸So they passed by Mysia and went down to Troas. ⁹During the night Paul had a vision of a man of Macedonia standing and begging him, "Come over to Macedonia and help us." ¹⁰After Paul had seen the vision, we got ready at once to leave for Macedonia, concluding that God had called us to preach the gospel to them.

Lydia's Conversion in Philippi

¹¹From Troas we put out to sea and sailed straight for Samothrace, and the next day on to Neapolis. ¹²From there we traveled to Philippi, a Roman colony and the leading city of that district of Macedonia. And we stayed there several days.

13 On the Sabbath we went outside the city gate to the river, where we expected to find a place of prayer. We sat down and began to speak to the women who had gathered there. 14 One of those listening was a woman named Lydia, a dealer in purple cloth from the city of Thyatira, who was a worshiper of God. The Lord opened her heart to respond to Paul's message. 15 When she and the members of her household were baptized, she invited us to her home. "If you consider me a believer in the Lord," she said, "come and stay at my house." And she persuaded us.

Paul and Silas in Prison

16 Once when we were going to the place of prayer, we were met by a slave girl who had a spirit by which she predicted the future. She earned a great deal of money for her owners by fortune-telling. 17 This girl followed Paul and the rest of us, shouting, "These men are servants of the Most High God, who are telling you the way to be saved." 18 She kept this up for many days. Finally Paul became so troubled that he turned around and said to the spirit, "In the name of Jesus Christ I command you to come out of her!" At that moment the spirit left her.

19 When the owners of the slave girl realized that their hope of making money was gone, they seized Paul and Silas and dragged them into the marketplace to face the authorities. 20 They brought them before the magistrates and said, "These men are Jews, and are throwing our city into an uproar 21 by advocating customs unlawful for us Romans to accept or practice."

22 The crowd joined in the attack against Paul and Silas, and the magistrates ordered them to be stripped and beaten. 23 After they had been severely flogged, they were thrown into prison, and the jailer was commanded to guard them carefully. 24 Upon receiving such orders, he put them in the inner cell and fastened their feet in the stocks.

25 About midnight Paul and Silas were praying and singing hymns to God, and the other prisoners were listening to them. 26 Suddenly there was such a violent earthquake that the foundations of the prison were shaken. At once all the prison doors flew open, and everybody's chains came loose. 27 The jailer woke up, and when he saw the prison doors open, he drew his sword and was about to kill himself because he thought the prisoners had escaped. 28 But Paul shouted, "Don't harm yourself! We are all here!"

29 The jailer called for lights, rushed in and fell trembling before Paul and Silas. 30 He then brought them out and asked, "Sirs, what must I do to be saved?"

31 They replied, "Believe in the Lord Jesus, and you will be saved—you and your household." 32 Then they spoke the word of the Lord to him and to all the others in his house. 33 At that hour of the night the jailer took them and washed their wounds; then immediately he and all his family were baptized. 34 The jailer brought them into his house and set a meal before them; he was filled with joy because he had come to believe in God—he and his whole family.

35 When it was daylight, the magistrates sent their officers to the jailer with the order: "Release those men." 36 The jailer told Paul, "The magistrates have ordered that you and Silas be released. Now you can leave. Go in peace."

37 But Paul said to the officers: "They beat us publicly without a trial, even though we are Roman citizens, and threw us into prison. And now do they want to get rid of us quietly? No! Let them come themselves and escort us out."

38 The officers reported this to the magistrates, and when they heard that Paul and Silas were Roman citizens, they were alarmed. 39 They came to appease them and escorted them from the prison, requesting them to leave the city. 40 After Paul and Silas came out of the prison, they went to Lydia's house, where they met with the brothers and encouraged them. Then they left.

Downward Mobility

Philippians 2

Fully a decade after founding the church, Paul wrote his Philippian friends a personal letter. He had suffered much in the intervening years: beatings, imprisonment, shipwreck, hostility from jealous competitors. Surely he must have sometimes wondered, "Is it worth all this pain?" Even as he wrote this letter, he was under arrest, "in chains for Christ" (1:13). But whenever Paul's thoughts turned to Philippi, the apostle's spirits lifted.

Paul declined gifts from most churches, out of fear that his enemies might twist the facts and accuse him of being a crook. But he trusted the Philippians. At least four separate times they sacrificed to meet his needs. Just recently, they had sent Epaphroditus on an arduous journey to care for Paul in prison. Paul wrote the book of Philippians, in fact, mainly as a thank-you for all that his friends had done. Its bright, happy tone reflects the fondness he felt for his cherished friends.

If someone had bluntly asked the apostle, "Paul, tell me, what keeps you going through hard times?", he likely would have answered with words straight out of this chapter. In Philippians 2, Paul reveals the source of his irrepressible drive. First, Paul gives the example of Jesus. In a stately, hymnlike paragraph, he marvels that Jesus gave up all the glory of heaven to take on the form of a man—and not just a man, but a servant, one who poured out his life for others. Paul took on that pattern for himself: "I am being poured out like a drink offering. . . ."

Then, in a seeming paradox, Paul describes a kind of "teamwork" with God: While God is working within, we must "work out" salvation with fear and trembling. A later spiritual giant, Saint Teresa of Avila, expressed the paradox this way: "I pray as if all depends on God; I work as if all depends on me." Her formula aptly summarizes Paul's spiritual style.

Philippians gives an occasional glimpse of the apostle Paul's fatigue. But it also shows flashes of what kept him from "burnout." To him, the converts in Philippi shone "like stars in the universe." That kind of reward, and joy in their progress, kept Paul going.

> **To Reflect On:** *How can you "consider others better than yourself" without developing a bad self-image?*

PHILIPPIANS 2

Imitating Christ's Humility

2 If you have any encouragement from being united with Christ, if any comfort from his love, if any fellowship with the Spirit, if any tenderness and compassion, ²then make my joy complete by being likeminded, having the same love, being one in spirit and purpose. ³Do nothing out of selfish ambition or vain conceit, but in humility consider others better than yourselves. ⁴Each of you should look not only to your own interests, but also to the interests of others.

⁵Your attitude should be the same as that of Christ Jesus:

⁶Who, being in very nature God,
did not consider equality with God
something to be grasped,
⁷but made himself nothing,
taking the very nature of a servant,
being made in human likeness.
⁸And being found in appearance as a man,
he humbled himself
and became obedient to death—
even death on a cross!
⁹Therefore God exalted him to the highest place
and gave him the name that is above every name,
¹⁰that at the name of Jesus every knee should bow,
in heaven and on earth and under the earth,
¹¹and every tongue confess that Jesus Christ is Lord,
to the glory of God the Father.

Shining as Stars

¹²Therefore, my dear friends, as you have always obeyed—not only in my presence, but now much more in my absence—continue to work out your salvation with fear and trembling, ¹³for it is God who works in you to will and to act according to his good purpose.

¹⁴Do everything without complaining or arguing, ¹⁵so that you may become blameless and pure, children of God without fault in a crooked and depraved generation, in which you shine like stars in the universe ¹⁶as you hold out the word of life—in order that I may boast on the day of Christ that I did not run or labor for nothing. ¹⁷But even if I am being poured out like a drink offering on the sacrifice and service coming from your faith, I am glad and rejoice with all of you. ¹⁸So you too should be glad and rejoice with me.

Timothy and Epaphroditus

¹⁹I hope in the Lord Jesus to send Timothy to you soon, that I also may be cheered when I receive news about you. ²⁰I have no one else like him, who takes a genuine interest in your welfare. ²¹For everyone looks out for his own interests, not those of Jesus Christ. ²²But you know that Timothy has proved himself, because as a son with his father he has served with me in the work of the gospel. ²³I hope, therefore, to send him as soon as I see how things go with me. ²⁴And I am confident in the Lord that I myself will come soon.

²⁵But I think it is necessary to send back to you Epaphroditus, my brother, fellow worker and fellow soldier, who is also your messenger, whom you sent to take care of my needs. ²⁶For he longs for all of you and is distressed because you heard he was ill. ²⁷Indeed he was ill, and almost died. But God had mercy on him, and not on him only but also on me, to spare me sorrow upon sorrow. ²⁸Therefore I am all the more eager to send him, so that when you see him again you may be glad and I may have less anxiety. ²⁹Welcome him in the Lord with great joy, and honor men like him, ³⁰because he almost died for the work of Christ, risking his life to make up for the help you could not give me.

Mixed Results

Acts 17:1–18:4

Jesus told a parable about a farmer sowing seed, some of which fell on rocky places, some among thorns, and some on fertile ground. This chapter, which reviews events from Paul's second journey, proves that he, the first foreign missionary, encountered all those responses in quick succession.

In Thessalonica, Paul's visit sparked a riot. An angry mob chased the apostle out of town, accusing him of causing "trouble all over the world." The next town, Berea, proved far more receptive. After studying the Scriptures to test out Paul's message, many believed, both Jews and non-Jews. Yet agitators from Thessalonica soon stirred up trouble there as well. (Paul was often trailed by hostile opponents who sought to confute his work.)

In Athens, Paul faced perhaps his most daunting missionary challenge. That renowned city of philosophers subjected each new thinker to a grueling intellectual ordeal. Local philosophers, full of scorn for Paul ("this babbler"), hauled him before the council of Areopagus that oversaw religion and morals.

Confident that the new faith could compete in the marketplace of ideas, Paul stood before the skeptical audience and, in a burst of eloquence, delivered the extraordinary speech contained in this chapter. Paul gained few converts among the elite Athenians, but he next traveled to the melting pot city of Corinth and founded a church remarkable for its ethnic diversity.

A modern-day evangelist assessing Paul's career said with a sigh, "Whenever the apostle Paul visited a city, the residents started a riot; when I visit one, they serve tea."

To Reflect On: *Is your community more like Thessalonica, Berea, Athens, or Corinth? What kind of approach to the gospel would work best in your community?*

ACTS 17:1–18:4

In Thessalonica

17 When they had passed through Amphipolis and Apollonia, they came to Thessalonica, where there was a Jewish synagogue. ²As his custom was, Paul went into the synagogue, and on three Sabbath days he reasoned with them from the Scriptures, ³explaining and proving that the Christ had to suffer and rise from the dead. "This Jesus I am proclaiming to you is the Christ," he said. ⁴Some of the Jews were persuaded and joined Paul and Silas, as did a large number of God-fearing Greeks and not a few prominent women.

⁵But the Jews were jealous; so they rounded up some bad characters from the marketplace, formed a mob and started a riot in the city. They rushed to Jason's house in search of Paul and Silas in order to bring them out to the crowd. ⁶But when they did not find them, they dragged Jason and some other brothers before the city officials, shouting: "These men who have caused trouble all over the world have now come here, ⁷and Jason has welcomed them into his house. They are all defying Caesar's decrees, saying that there is another king, one called Jesus." ⁸When they heard this, the crowd and the city officials were thrown into turmoil. ⁹Then they made Jason and the others post bond and let them go.

In Berea

¹⁰As soon as it was night, the brothers sent Paul and Silas away to Berea. On arriving there, they went to the Jewish synagogue. ¹¹Now the Bereans were of

more noble character than the Thessalonians, for they received the message with great eagerness and examined the Scriptures every day to see if what Paul said was true. ¹²Many of the Jews believed, as did also a number of prominent Greek women and many Greek men.

¹³When the Jews in Thessalonica learned that Paul was preaching the word of God at Berea, they went there too, agitating the crowds and stirring them up. ¹⁴The brothers immediately sent Paul to the coast, but Silas and Timothy stayed at Berea. ¹⁵The men who escorted Paul brought him to Athens and then left with instructions for Silas and Timothy to join him as soon as possible.

In Athens

¹⁶While Paul was waiting for them in Athens, he was greatly distressed to see that the city was full of idols. ¹⁷So he reasoned in the synagogue with the Jews and the God-fearing Greeks, as well as in the marketplace day by day with those who happened to be there. ¹⁸A group of Epicurean and Stoic philosophers began to dispute with him. Some of them asked, "What is this babbler trying to say?" Others remarked, "He seems to be advocating foreign gods." They said this because Paul was preaching the good news about Jesus and the resurrection. ¹⁹Then they took him and brought him to a meeting of the Areopagus, where they said to him, "May we know what this new teaching is that you are presenting? ²⁰You are bringing some strange ideas to our ears, and we want to know what they mean." ²¹(All the Athenians and the foreigners who lived there spent their time doing nothing but talking about and listening to the latest ideas.)

²²Paul then stood up in the meeting of the Areopagus and said: "Men of Athens! I see that in every way you are very religious. ²³For as I walked around and looked carefully at your objects of worship, I even found an altar with this inscription: TO AN UNKNOWN GOD. Now what you worship as something unknown I am going to proclaim to you.

²⁴"The God who made the world and everything in it is the Lord of heaven and earth and does not live in temples built by hands. ²⁵And he is not served by human hands, as if he needed anything, because he himself gives all men life and breath and everything else. ²⁶From one man he made every nation of men, that they should inhabit the whole earth; and he determined the times set for them and the exact places where they should live. ²⁷God did this so that men would seek him and perhaps reach out for him and find him, though he is not far from each one of us. ²⁸'For in him we live and move and have our being.' As some of your own poets have said, 'We are his offspring.'

²⁹"Therefore since we are God's offspring, we should not think that the divine being is like gold or silver or stone—an image made by man's design and skill. ³⁰In the past God overlooked such ignorance, but now he commands all people everywhere to repent. ³¹For he has set a day when he will judge the world with justice by the man he has appointed. He has given proof of this to all men by raising him from the dead."

³²When they heard about the resurrection of the dead, some of them sneered, but others said, "We want to hear you again on this subject." ³³At that, Paul left the Council. ³⁴A few men became followers of Paul and believed. Among them was Dionysius, a member of the Areopagus, also a woman named Damaris, and a number of others.

In Corinth

18 After this, Paul left Athens and went to Corinth. ²There he met a Jew named Aquila a native of Pontus, who had recently come from Italy with his wife Priscilla, because Claudius had ordered all the Jews to leave Rome. Paul went to see them, ³and because he was a tentmaker as they were, he stayed and worked with them. ⁴Every Sabbath he reasoned in the synagogue, trying to persuade Jews and Greeks.

Spiritual Checkup

1 Thessalonians 2:17–4:12

Born in the midst of strife, the church at Thessalonica continued to meet hostility long after Paul was chased out of town. When he heard of their troubles, the apostle wrote this intimate letter, which provides important clues into what made him so effective as a "pastor." First Thessalonians, dating probably from A.D. 50 or 51, is our earliest record of the life of a Christian community. As such, it provides a firsthand account of Paul's relationship with a missionary church, barely twenty years after Jesus' departure.

Paul reviews his pastoral style with the Thessalonians, reminding them that while among them, he was gentle and loving, "like a mother caring for her little children" (2:7). He writes as if he has only them on his mind all day long. He praises their strengths, fusses over their weaknesses, and continually thanks God for their spiritual progress. A recent report from Timothy has indicated they are heading down the right path, but Paul urges them to live for God and to love each other "more and more."

In this letter, Paul also answers criticisms that have been leveled against him. Is he in it for the money? Paul claims that during his sojourn with the Thessalonians he worked night and day (he supported himself as a tentmaker) to avoid becoming a financial burden. Has he abandoned them? Paul takes pains to explain the reasons behind his unavoidable absence.

Unlike some of Paul's other letters, 1 Thessalonians doesn't major in theology. Rather, it reveals the gratitude, disappointment, and joy of a beloved missionary who can't stop thinking about the church he left behind. Surely one reason for Paul's success centers on his churches having made as big an impression on Paul as he made on them.

> **To Reflect On:** *What seems to please Paul most about the Thessalonians? What worries him?*

1 THESSALONIANS 2:17–4:12

Paul's Longing to See the Thessalonians

¹⁷But, brothers, when we were torn away from you for a short time (in person, not in thought), out of our intense longing we made every effort to see you. ¹⁸For we wanted to come to you—certainly I, Paul, did, again and again—but Satan stopped us. ¹⁹For what is our hope, our joy, or the crown in which we will glory in the presence of our Lord Jesus when he comes? Is it not you? ²⁰Indeed, you are our glory and joy.

3 So when we could stand it no longer, we thought it best to be left by ourselves in Athens. ²We sent Timothy, who is our brother and God's fellow worker in spreading the gospel of Christ, to strengthen and encourage you in your faith, ³so that no one would be unsettled by these trials. You know quite well that we were destined for them. ⁴In fact, when we were with you, we kept telling you that we would be persecuted. And it turned out that way, as you well know. ⁵For this reason, when I could stand it no longer, I sent to find out about your faith. I was afraid that in some way the tempter might have tempted you and our efforts might have been useless.

Timothy's Encouraging Report

⁶But Timothy has just now come to us from you and has brought good news about your faith and love. He has told us that you always have pleasant memories of us and that you long to see us, just as we also long to see you. ⁷Therefore, brothers, in all our distress and persecution we were encouraged about you because of your faith. ⁸For now we really live, since you are standing firm in the Lord. ⁹How can we thank God enough for you in return for all the joy we have in the presence of our God because of you? ¹⁰Night and day we pray most earnestly that we may see you again and supply what is lacking in your faith.

¹¹Now may our God and Father himself and our Lord Jesus clear the way for us to come to you. ¹²May the Lord make your love increase and overflow for each other and for everyone else, just as ours does for you. ¹³May he strengthen your hearts so that you will be blameless and holy in the presence of our God and Father when our Lord Jesus comes with all his holy ones.

Living to Please God

4 Finally, brothers, we instructed you how to live in order to please God, as in fact you are living. Now we ask you and urge you in the Lord Jesus to do this more and more. ²For you know what instructions we gave you by the authority of the Lord Jesus.

³It is God's will that you should be sanctified: that you should avoid sexual immorality; ⁴that each of you should learn to control his own body in a way that is holy and honorable, ⁵not in passionate lust like the heathen, who do not know God; ⁶and that in this matter no one should wrong his brother or take advantage of him. The Lord will punish men for all such sins, as we have already told you and warned you. ⁷For God did not call us to be impure, but to live a holy life. ⁸Therefore, he who rejects this instruction does not reject man but God, who gives you his Holy Spirit.

⁹Now about brotherly love we do not need to write to you, yourselves have been taught by God to love each other. ¹⁰And in fact, you do love all the brothers throughout Macedonia. Yet we urge you, brothers, to do so more and more.

¹¹Make it your ambition to lead a quiet life, to mind your own business and to work with your hands, just as we told you, ¹²so that your daily life may win the respect of outsiders and so that you will not be dependent on anybody.

Rumor Control

2 Thessalonians 2:1–3:13

If you list the topics covered in this letter, you will find an uncanny similarity to the concerns discussed in Paul's first letter to the Thessalonians. However, a sterner, more formal approach replaces the warm tenderness of the first letter. Obviously, the Thessalonians had failed to listen well the first time around.

One topic dominates 2 Thessalonians more than any other: Jesus' return to earth. Church members were disturbed by a rumor, allegedly from Paul, that the last days had already arrived. In this letter, Paul denies the report and outlines what must occur before the day of the Lord arrives.

The controversy actually traces back to a portion of Paul's first letter. Toward the end of 1 Thessalonians, he gave direct answers to questions about the afterlife. Would people who had already died miss out on resurrection from the dead? It was more than an idle question for the Thessalonians, who lived with the constant danger of persecution. On any night a knock on the door could mean imprisonment or death.

Paul had allayed the Christians' fears by assuring them that people still living when Jesus returns to earth will rejoin those who have died before them. "Therefore encourage each other with these words," he concluded (1 Thessonians 4:15–18). In the meantime, however, the Thessalonians had gone several steps beyond Paul's advice. Their speculation about the impending day of the Lord, fueled by the recent rumors, had become an obsession. Some of them had quit their jobs, and simply sat around in anticipation of that day. They were becoming, in Paul's words, "idle" and "busybodies."

Paul wrote 2 Thessalonians mainly to correct the imbalance. In the second chapter he tells of certain obscure events that must precede the second coming of Jesus. (No one is certain of Paul's exact meaning in every detail because he was building on teaching he had given the Thessalonians in private.)

Here, as elsewhere, the Bible does not focus on the last days in an abstract, theoretical way. Rather, it makes a practical application to how we should live. Paul counsels patience and steadiness. He asks his readers to trust that Jesus' return will finally bring justice to the earth, urges them to live worthily for that day, and commands them not to tolerate idleness—a good prescription for an obsession with the future in any time period.

To Reflect On: *How should we prepare for Jesus' second coming?*

2 THESSALONIANS 2:1–3:13

The Man of Lawlessness

2 Concerning the coming of our Lord Jesus Christ and our being gathered to him, we ask you, brothers, ²not to become easily unsettled or alarmed by some prophecy, report or letter supposed to have come from us, saying that the day of the Lord has already come. ³Don't let anyone deceive you in any way, for that day will not come until the rebellion occurs and the man of lawlessness is revealed, the man doomed to destruction. ⁴He will oppose and will exalt himself over everything that is called God or is worshiped, so that he sets himself up in God's temple, proclaiming himself to be God.

⁵Don't you remember that when I was with you I used to tell you these things? ⁶And now you know what is holding him back, so that he may be revealed at the proper time. ⁷For the secret power of lawlessness is already at work; but the one who now holds it back will continue to do so till he is taken out of the way. ⁸And then the lawless one will be revealed, whom the Lord Jesus will overthrow with the breath of his mouth and destroy by the splendor of his coming. ⁹The coming of the lawless one will be in accordance with the work of Satan displayed in all kinds of counterfeit miracles, signs and wonders, ¹⁰and in every sort of evil that deceives those who are perishing. They perish because they refused to love the truth and so be saved. ¹¹For this reason God sends them a powerful delusion so that they will belive the lie ¹²and so that all will be condemned who have not believed the truth but have delighted in wickedness.

Stand Firm

¹³But we ought always to thank God for you, brothers loved by the Lord, because from the beginning God chose you to be saved through the sanctifying work of the Spirit and through belief in the truth. ¹⁴He called you to this through our gospel, that you might share in the glory of our Lord Jesus Christ. ¹⁵So then, brothers, stand firm and hold to the teachings we passed on to you, whether by word of mouth or by letter.

¹⁶May our Lord Jesus Christ himself and God our Father, who loved us and by his grace gave us eternal encouragement and good hope, ¹⁷encourage your hearts and strengthen you in every good deed and word.

Request for Prayer

3 Finally, brothers, pray for us that the message of the Lord may spread rapidly and be honored, just as it was with you. ²And pray that we may be delivered from wicked and evil men, for not everyone has faith. ³But the Lord is faithful, and he will strengthen and protect you from the evil one. ⁴We have confidence in the Lord that you are doing and will continue to do the things we command. ⁵May the Lord direct your hearts into God's love and Christ's perseverance.

Warning Against Idleness

⁶In the name of the Lord Jesus Christ, we command you, brothers, to keep away from every brother who is idle and does not live according to the teaching you received from us. ⁷For you yourselves know how you ought to follow our example. We were not idle when we were with you, ⁸nor did we eat anyone's food without paying for it. On the contrary, we worked night and day, laboring and toiling so that we would not be a burden to any of you. ⁹We did this, not because we do not have the right to such help, but in order to make ourselves a model for you to follow. ¹⁰For even when we were with you, we gave you this rule: "If a man will not work, he shall not eat."

¹¹We hear that some among you are idle. They are not busy; they are busybodies. ¹²Such people we command and urge in the Lord Jesus Christ to settle down and earn the bread they eat. ¹³And as for you, brothers, never tire of doing what is right.

Out of the Melting Pot

1 Corinthians 12:12–13:13

Acts 17–18 gives important background detail on Paul and the church at Corinth. He first visited that Grecian city during one of the most stressful times of his career. Lynch mobs had chased him out of Thessalonica and Berea. The next stop, Athens, brought on a different kind of confrontation, with intellectual scoffers. Paul acknowledges that he arrived at Corinth in a fragile emotional state: "I came to you in weakness and fear, and with much trembling" (2:3).

Shortly, opposition sprang up in Corinth. Jewish leaders became abusive and hauled Paul into court. It seemed that the apostle, now reeling, would have no rest from his enemies. But in the midst of this crisis, God visited Paul with a special message of comfort: "Do not be afraid; keep on speaking, do not be silent. For I am with you, and no one is going to attack and harm you, because I have many people in this city" (Acts 18:9–10).

Those last words must have startled Paul, for Corinth was known mainly for its lewdness and drunken brawling. The Corinthians worshiped Venus, the goddess of love, and a temple built in her honor employed more than a thousand prostitutes. Thus Corinth seemed the last place on earth to expect a church to take root. Yet that's exactly what happened. A Jewish couple opened their home to Paul, and for the next eighteen months he stayed in Corinth to nurture an eager band of converts.

Corinth was a sprawling open-air market, filled with Orientals, Jews, Greeks, Egyptians, slaves, sailors, athletes, gamblers, and charioteers. And the Corinthian church reflected that same crazy-quilt pattern of diversity. When Paul wrote them this letter, he searched for a way to drive home the importance of Christian unity. At last he settled on a striking analogy from the human body. By comparing members of the church of Christ to individual parts of a human body, he could neatly illustrate how *diverse* members can indeed work together in *unity*.

Paul's analogy of the body fit so well that it became his favorite way of portraying the church. He would refer to "the body of Christ" more than thirty times in his various letters. This passage leads into one of the most famous parts of the New Testament. Paul had raised the question of how diverse people can work together in a spiritual body. He answers that question with a lyrical description of love, the greatest of all spiritual gifts.

> **To Reflect On:** *First Corinthians 13 de-scribes ideal love. Which of these characteristics do you need to work on?*

1 CORINTHIANS 12:12–13:13

One Body, Many Parts

¹²The body is a unit, though it is made up of many parts; and though all its parts are many, they form one body. So it is with Christ. ¹³For we were all baptized by one Spirit into one body—whether Jews or Greeks, slave or free—and we were all given the one Spirit to drink.

¹⁴Now the body is not made up of one part but of many. ¹⁵If the foot should say, "Because I am not a hand, I do not belong to the body," it would not for that reason cease to be part of the body. ¹⁶And if the ear should say, "Because I am not an eye, I do not belong to the body," it would not for that reason cease to be part of the body. ¹⁷If the whole body were an eye, where would the sense of hearing be? If the whole body were an ear, where would the sense of smell be? ¹⁸But in fact God has arranged the parts in the body, every one of them, just as he wanted them to be. ¹⁹If they were all one part, where would the body be? ²⁰As it is, there are many parts, but one body.

²¹The eye cannot say to the hand, "I don't need you!" And the head cannot say to the feet, "I don't need you!" ²²On the contrary, those parts of the body that seem to be weaker are indispensable, ²³and the parts that we think are less honorable we treat with special honor. And the parts that are unpresentable are treated with special modesty, ²⁴while our presentable parts need no special treatment. But God has combined the members of the body and has given greater honor to the parts that lacked it, ²⁵so that there should be no division in the body, but that its parts should have equal concern for each other. ²⁶If one part suffers, every part suffers with it; if one part is honored, every part rejoices with it.

²⁷ Now you are the body of Christ, and each one of you is a part of it. ²⁸And in the church God has appointed first of all apostles, second prophets, third teachers, then workers of miracles, also those having gifts of healing, those able to help others, those with gifts of administration, and those speaking in different kinds of tongues. ²⁹Are all apostles? Are all prophets? Are all teachers? Do all work miracles? ³⁰Do all have gifts of healing? Do all speak in tongues? Do all interpret? ³¹But eagerly desire the greater gifts.

Love

And now I will show you the most excellent way.

13 If I speak in the tongues of men and of angels, but have not love, I am only a resounding gong or a clanging cymbal. ²If I have the gift of prophecy and can fathom all mysteries and all knowledge, and if I have a faith that can move mountains, but have not love, I am nothing. ³If I give all I possess to the poor and surrender my body to the flames, but have not love, I gain nothing.

⁴Love is patient, love is kind. It does not envy, it does not boast, it is not proud. ⁵It is not rude, it is not self-seeking, it is not easily angered, it keeps no record of wrongs. ⁶Love does not delight in evil but rejoices with the truth. ⁷It always protects, always trusts, always hopes, always perseveres.

⁸Love never fails. But where there are prophecies, they will cease; where there are tongues, they will be stilled; where there is knowledge, it will pass away. ⁹For we know in part and we prophesy in part, ¹⁰but when perfection comes, the imperfect disappears. ¹¹When I was a child, I talked like a child, I thought like a child, I reasoned like a child. When I became a man, I put childish ways behind me. ¹²Now we see but a poor reflection as in a mirror; then we shall see face to face. Now I know in part; then I shall know fully, even as I am fully known.

¹³And now these three remain: faith, hope and love. But the greatest of these is love.

The Last Enemy

1 Corinthians 15:3–57

Some people in Paul's day were challenging the Christian belief in an afterlife. Death, they said, is the end. Throughout history, many people have taken such a position. In Jesus' day, a Jewish sect called Sadducees denied the resurrection from the dead. Doubters persist today, among them are Black Muslims, Buddhists, Marxists, and most atheists. Some New Age advocates present death as a natural part of the cycle of life. Why consider it bad at all?

The Corinthian church soon learned not to voice such an attitude around the apostle Paul. Belief in an afterlife to him was no fairy tale; it was the fulcrum of his entire faith. If there's no future life, he thundered, the Christian message would be a lie. He, Paul, would have no reason to continue as a minister; Christ's death would have merely wasted blood; and Christians would be the most pitiable of all people on earth.

The Bible presents a gradually developing emphasis on the afterlife. Old Testament Jews had only the vaguest conception of life after death. But as Paul points out, Jesus' resurrection from the dead changed all that. Suddenly the world had primary proof that God had the power and the will to overcome death. Chapter 15 brings together the threads of Christian belief about death. With no hesitation, Paul brands death "the enemy," the last enemy to be destroyed.

This chapter often gets read at funerals, and with good reason. As people gather around a casket, they sense as if by instinct the *unnaturalness*, the horror, of death. To such people, to all of us, this passage offers soaring words of hope. Death is not an end, but a beginning.

> **To Reflect On:** *How does a belief in the afterlife affect your life now?*

---

1 CORINTHIANS 15:3–57

3For what I received I passed on to you as of first importance: that Christ died for our sins according to the Scriptures, 4that he was buried, that he was raised on the third day according to the Scriptures, 5and that he appeared to Peter, and then to the Twelve. 6After that, he appeared to more than five hundred of the brothers at the same time, most of whom are still living, though some have fallen asleep. 7Then he appeared to James, then to all the apostles, 8and last of all he appeared to me also, as to one abnormally born.

9For I am the least of the apostles and do not even deserve to be called an apostle, because I persecuted the church of God. 10But by the grace of God I am what I am, and his grace to me was not without effect. No, I worked harder than all of them—yet not I, but the grace of God that was with me. 11Whether, then, it was I or they, this is what we preach, and this is what you believed.

The Resurrection of the Dead

12But if it is preached that Christ has been raised from the dead, how can some of you say that there is no resurrection of the dead? 13If there is no resurrection of the dead, then not even Christ has been raised. 14And if Christ has not been raised, our preaching is useless and so is your faith. 15More than that, we are then found to be false witnesses about God, for we have testified about God that he raised Christ from the dead. But he did not raise him if in fact the dead are not raised. 16For if the dead are not raised, then Christ has not been raised either. 17And if Christ has not been raised, your faith is futile; you are still in your sins. 18Then those also who have fallen asleep in Christ are lost. 19If only for this life we have hope in Christ, we are to be pitied more than all men.

²⁰But Christ has indeed been raised from the dead, the firstfruits of those who have fallen asleep. ²¹For since death came through a man, the resurrection of the dead comes also through a man. ²²For as in Adam all die, so in Christ all will be made alive. ²³But each in his own turn: Christ, the firstfruits; then, when he comes, those who belong to him. ²⁴Then the end will come, when he hands over the kingdom to God the Father after he has destroyed all dominion, authority and power. ²⁵For he must reign until he has put all his enemies under his feet. ²⁶The last enemy to be destroyed is death. ²⁷For he "has put everything under his feet." Now when it says that "everything" has been put under him, it is clear that this does not include God himself, who put everything under Christ. ²⁸When he has done this, then the Son himself will be made subject to him who put everything under him, so that God may be all in all.

²⁹Now if there is no resurrection, what will those do who are baptized for the dead? If the dead are not raised at all, why are people baptized for them? ³⁰And as for us, why do we endanger ourselves every hour? ³¹I die every day—I mean that, brothers—just as surely as I glory over you in Christ Jesus our Lord. ³²If I fought wild beasts in Ephesus for merely human reasons, what have I gained? If the dead are not raised,

"Let us eat and drink,
for tomorrow we die."

³³Do not be misled: "Bad company corrupts good character." ³⁴Come back to your senses as you ought, and stop sinning; for there are some who are ignorant of God—I say this to your shame.

The Resurrection Body

³⁵But someone may ask, "How are the dead raised? With what kind of body will they come?" ³⁶How foolish! What you sow does not come to life unless it dies. ³⁷When you sow, you do not plant the body that will be, but just a seed, perhaps of wheat or of something else. ³⁸But God gives it a body as he has determined, and to each kind of seed he gives its own body. ³⁹All flesh is not the same: Men have one kind of flesh, animals have another, birds another and fish another. ⁴⁰There are also heavenly bodies and there are earthly bodies; but the splendor of the heavenly bodies is one kind, and the splendor of the earthly bodies is another. ⁴¹The sun has one kind of splendor, the moon another and the stars another; and star differs from star in splendor.

⁴²So will it be with the resurrection of the dead. The body that is sown is perishable, it is raised imperishable; ⁴³it is sown in dishonor, it is raised in glory; it is sown in weakness, it is raised in power; ⁴⁴it is sown a natural body, it is raised a spiritual body.

If there is a natural body, there is also a spiritual body. ⁴⁵So it is written: "The first man Adam became a living being"; the last Adam, a life-giving spirit. ⁴⁶The spiritual did not come first, but the natural, and after that the spiritual. ⁴⁷The first man was of the dust of the earth, the second man from heaven. ⁴⁸As was the earthly man, so are those who are of the earth; and as is the man from heaven, so also are those who are of heaven. ⁴⁹And just as we have borne the likeness of the earthly man, so shall we bear the likeness of the man from heaven.

⁵⁰I declare to you, brothers, that flesh and blood cannot inherit the kingdom of God, nor does the perishable inherit the imperishable. ⁵¹Listen, I tell you a mystery: We will not all sleep, but we will all be changed—⁵²in a flash, in the twinkling of an eye, at the last trumpet. For the trumpet will sound, the dead will be raised imperishable, and we will be changed. ⁵³For the perishable must clothe itself with the imperishable, and the mortal with immortality. ⁵⁴When the perishable has been clothed with the imperishable, and the mortal with immortality, then the saying that is written will come true: "Death has been swallowed up in victory."

⁵⁵"Where, O death, is your victory?
Where, O death, is your sting?"

⁵⁶The sting of death is sin, and the power of sin is the law. ⁵⁷But thanks be to God! He gives us the victory through our Lord Jesus Christ.

Hope during Hard Times

2 Corinthians 4:1–5:10

It's fairly simple to figure out how Paul would answer the previous "To Reflect On" question ("How does a belief in the afterlife affect your life?"), for he kept circling back to the topic. If 1 Corinthians 15 gives the theological basis for belief in the afterlife, this passage from 2 Corinthians tells of its impact on Paul personally.

Paul blasted anyone who, as the phrase goes, "is too heavenly-minded to be of any earthly good." He did *not* prepare for the next life by sitting around all day waiting for it to happen. Paul worked as hard as anyone has ever worked, but with a new purpose: "So we make it our goal to please him, whether we are at home in the body or away from it." He sought to do God's will on earth just as it is done in heaven.

This passage shows that Paul's hope for the future kept him motivated when the crush of life tempted him to "lose heart." He wrote this letter just as an intense struggle with the Corinthian church was coming to a head, and as a result it reveals the apostle in one of his lowest, most vulnerable moments. He has barely survived hardships "far beyond our ability to endure, so that we despaired even of life" (1:8). He describes his present state as "hard pressed on every side, but not crushed; perplexed, but not in despair; persecuted, but not abandoned; struck down, but not destroyed."

In typical style, Paul uses a word picture to express his inner thoughts: "treasure in jars of clay." In his day, jars of clay were nearly as common, and as disposable, as cardboard boxes are today. Beset by difficulties, Paul felt as durable as one of those fragile jars. Yet he recognized that God had chosen to entrust the gospel, and its good news of forgiveness and eternal life, to such ordinary people as himself.

That insight seemed to give Paul renewed hope. He offers a stirring example of how a future life with God can affect a person on earth: "Therefore we do not lose heart. Though outwardly we are wasting away, yet inwardly we are being renewed day by day. For our light and momentary troubles are achieving for us an eternal glory that far outweighs them all. So we fix our eyes not on what is seen, but on what is unseen. For what is seen is temporary, but what is unseen is eternal."

> **To Reflect On:** *What kind of person would Paul call a success? A failure?*

2 CORINTHIANS 4:1–5:10

Treasures in Jars of Clay

4 Therefore, since through God's mercy we have this ministry, we do not lose heart. ²Rather, we have renounced secret and shameful ways; we do not use deception, nor do we distort the word of God. On the contrary, by setting forth the truth plainly we commend ourselves to every man's conscience in the sight of God. ³And even if our gospel is veiled, it is veiled to those who are perishing. ⁴The god of this age has blinded the minds of unbelievers, so that they cannot see the light of the gospel of the glory of Christ, who is the image of God.

⁵For we do not preach ourselves, but Jesus Christ as Lord, and ourselves as your servants for Jesus' sake. ⁶For God, who said, "Let light shine out of darkness," made his light shine in our hearts to give us the light of the knowledge of the glory of God in the face of Christ.

⁷But we have this treasure in jars of clay to show that this all-surpassing power is from God and not from us. ⁸We are hard pressed on every side, but not crushed; perplexed, but not in despair; ⁹persecuted, but not abandoned; struck down, but not destroyed. ¹⁰We always carry around in our body the death of Jesus, so that the life of Jesus may also be revealed in our body. ¹¹For we who are alive are always being given over to death for Jesus' sake, so that his life may be revealed in our mortal body. ¹²So then, death is at work in us, but life is at work in you.

¹³It is written: "I believed; therefore I have spoken." With that same spirit of faith we also believe and therefore speak, ¹⁴because we know that the one who raised the Lord Jesus from the dead will also raise us with Jesus and present us with you in his presence. ¹⁵All this is for your benefit, so that the grace that is reaching more and more people may cause thanksgiving to overflow to the glory of God.

¹⁶Therefore we do not lose heart. Though outwardly we are wasting away, yet inwardly we are being renewed day by day. ¹⁷For our light and momentary troubles are achieving for us an eternal glory that far outweighs them all. ¹⁸So we fix our eyes not on what is seen, but on what is unseen. For what is seen is temporary, but what is unseen is eternal.

Our Heavenly Dwelling

5 Now we know that if the earthly tent we live in is destroyed, we have a building from God, an eternal house in heaven, not built by human hands. ²Meanwhile we groan, longing to be clothed with our heavenly dwelling, ³because when we are clothed, we will not be found naked. ⁴For while we are in this tent, we groan and are burdened, because we do not wish to be unclothed but to be clothed with our heavenly dwelling, so that what is mortal may be swallowed up by life. ⁵Now it is God who has made us for this very purpose and has given us the Spirit as a deposit, guaranteeing what is to come.

⁶Therefore we are always confident and know that as long as we are at home in the body we are away from the Lord. ⁷We live by faith, not by sight. ⁸We are confident, I say, and would prefer to be away from the body and at home with the Lord. ⁹So we make it our goal to please him, whether we are at home in the body or away from it. ¹⁰For we must all appear before the judgment seat of Christ, that each one may receive what is due him for the things done while in the body, whether good or bad.

Paul Answers His Critics

2 Corinthians 11:16–12:10

Wherever the apostle Paul traveled, controversy trailed in his wake. The Jewish and Roman establishments viewed him as a major threat, but Paul had expected their opposition. What bothered him far more was antagonism from fellow Christians. Jealous competitors had infiltrated the Corinthian church, spreading rumors to undercut Paul's reputation. He wasn't fully Jewish, they charged. He didn't deserve the title "apostle" since he had not followed Jesus on earth. Furthermore, like many other false teachers, he was in it for the money.

In his letters to the Corinthians, Paul felt obliged to answer his critics. He confesses a reluctance to defend himself—"I am out of my mind to talk like this"—but their criticisms had gotten out of hand. Jewish? Paul was a strict Pharisee who had studied with the famous teacher Gamaliel. Apostle? True, Paul had not served as one of the twelve disciples. But he had met the risen Jesus on the road to Damascus, and was later granted an unprecedented special revelation of "inexpressible things, things that man is not permitted to tell." Exploiter? Paul had supported himself financially to avoid taking money from the church.

Thus, the self-appointed "super-apostles" had no grounds to criticize Paul. But, rather than gloating in the strength of his self-defense, Paul changes the emphasis and begins to "boast" about his weaknesses. He runs through the amazing list of beatings, imprisonments, insults, and hardships that have marked his career. And he balances off his veiled reference to the special vision with a frank account of one urgent prayer that has never been answered.

Three times Paul had asked God to remove a mysterious "thorn in the flesh." Bible scholars don't agree on the precise nature of the "thorn." Some suggest a physical ailment, such as an eye disease, malaria, or epilepsy. Others interpret it as a spiritual temptation, or a series of failures in his ministry. Whatever the ailment, Paul stresses that God declined to remove the thorn, despite all his prayers for relief, in order to teach him an important lesson about humility, grace, and dependence.

Paul never seemed to get over the wonder of the fact that God had chosen him, a former enemy, to bear the good news. He felt humbled and honored that even his weaknesses, *especially* his weaknesses, could be used to advance the kingdom.

> **To Reflect On:** *How has God spoken to you through your "weaknesses"?*

2 CORINTHIANS 11:16–12:10

Paul Boasts About His Sufferings

¹⁶I repeat: Let no one take me for a fool. But if you do, then receive me just as you would a fool, so that I may do a little boasting. ¹⁷In this self-confident boasting I am not talking as the Lord would, but as a fool. ¹⁸Since many are boasting in the way the world does, I too will boast. ¹⁹You gladly put up with fools since you are so wise! ²⁰In fact, you even put up with anyone who enslaves you or exploits you or takes advantage of you or pushes himself forward or slaps you in the face. ²¹To my shame I admit that we were too weak for that!

What anyone else dares to boast about— I am speaking as a fool—I also dare to boast about. ²²Are they Hebrews? So am I. Are they Israelites? So am I. Are they Abraham's descendants? So am I. ²³Are they servants of Christ? (I am out of my mind to talk like this.) I am more. I have worked much harder, been in prison more frequently, been flogged more severely, and been exposed to death again and again. ²⁴Five times I received from the Jews the forty lashes minus one. ²⁵Three times I was beaten with rods, once I was stoned, three times I was shipwrecked, I spent a night and a day in the open sea, ²⁶I have been constantly on the move. I have been in danger from rivers, in danger from bandits, in danger from my own countrymen, in danger from Gentiles; in danger in the city, in danger in the country, in danger at sea; and in danger from false brothers. ²⁷I have labored and toiled and have often gone without sleep; I have known hunger and thirst and have often gone without food; I have been cold and naked. ²⁸Besides everything else, I face daily the pressure of my concern for all the churches. ²⁹Who is weak, and I do not feel weak? Who is led into sin, and I do not inwardly burn?

³⁰If I must boast, I will boast of the things that show my weakness. ³¹The God and Father of the Lord Jesus, who is to be praised forever, knows that I am not lying. ³²In Damascus the governor under King Aretas had the city of the Damascenes guarded in order to arrest me. ³³But I was lowered in a basket from a window in the wall and slipped through his hands.

Paul's Vision and His Thorn

12 I must go on boasting. Although there is nothing to be gained, I will go on to visions and revelations from the Lord. ²I know a man in Christ who fourteen years ago was caught up to the third heaven. Whether it was in the body or out of the body I do not know—God knows. ³And I know that this man—whether in the body or apart from the body I do not know, but God knows—⁴was caught up to paradise. He heard inexpressible things, things that man is not permitted to tell. ⁵I will boast about a man like that, but I will not boast about myself, except about my weaknesses. ⁶Even if I should choose to boast, I would not be a fool, because I would be speaking the truth. But I refrain, so no one will think more of me than is warranted by what I do or say.

⁷To keep me from becoming conceited because of these surpassingly great revelations, there was given me a thorn in my flesh, a messenger of Satan, to torment me. ⁸Three times I pleaded with the Lord to take it away from me. ⁹But he said to me, "My grace is sufficient for you, for my power is made perfect in weakness." Therefore I will boast all the more gladly about my weaknesses, so that Christ's power may rest on me. ¹⁰That is why, for Christ's sake, I delight in weaknesses, in insults, in hardships, in persecutions, in difficulties. For when I am weak, then I am strong.

Where All Roads Led

Romans 3:10–31

Throughout his arduous and adventurous life, the apostle Paul kept one career goal constantly before him: a visit to Rome. In his day, Rome was the center of everything—law, culture, power, and learning. From that capital, a powerful empire ruled over the entire Western world.

A tiny new church had formed there, causing great excitement among other Christians. They knew that in some ways the future of the worldwide church rested on what happened in Rome. Would they simply join the host of minority sects in the outposts of the Roman Empire? If they ever expected to make a dent in the larger world, they would have to penetrate Rome.

Paul prayed for the Roman church constantly and made many plans to visit there. Since none of those plans had yet materialized, Paul wrote this letter in preparation for his long-awaited visit.

Unlike the letters to the Corinthians, Romans contains few personal asides or emotional outbursts. Paul was addressing sophisticated, demanding readers, most of whom he had never met. In the letter he sought to set forth the whole scope of Christian doctrine, which was still being passed along orally from town to town. The resulting book has no equal as a concise, yet all-encompassing summation of the Christian faith.

Romans is a book to savor slowly and carefully. The logic of Paul's argument unfolds thought by thought from the very first chapter. He is presenting the good news about God's amazing grace: A complete cure is available to all. But people won't seek a cure until they know they are ill. Thus Romans begins with, and this passage adjoins, one of the darkest summaries in the Bible. "There is no one righteous, not even one," Paul concludes. The entire world is doomed to spiritual death unless a cure can be found.

Out of the mournful notes, however, comes a bright sound of wonderful news, expressed in what some have called the central theological passage in the Bible. Paul expresses the core message of the gospel in a mere eleven verses (3:21–31).

> **To Reflect On:** *Paul uses mostly legal terminology in verses 21–31. How would you express the same truths in your own words?*

ROMANS 3:10–31

No One Is Righteous

¹⁰As it is written:

"There is no one righteous, not even
one;
¹¹ there is no one who understands,
no one who seeks God.
¹²All have turned away,
they have together become worthless;
there is no one who does good,
not even one."
¹³"Their throats are open graves;
their tongues practice deceit."
"The poison of vipers is on their lips."
¹⁴ "Their mouths are full of cursing
and bitterness."
¹⁵"Their feet are swift to shed blood;
¹⁶ ruin and misery mark their ways,
¹⁷and the way of peace they do not
know."
¹⁸ "There is no fear of God before their
eyes."

¹⁹Now we know that whatever the law says, it says to those who are under the law, so that every mouth may be silenced and the whole world held accountable to God. ²⁰Therefore no one will be declared righteous in his sight by observing the law; rather, through the law we become conscious of sin.

Righteousness Through Faith

²¹But now a righteousness from God, apart from law, has been made known, to which the Law and the Prophets testify. ²²This righteousness from God comes through faith in Jesus Christ to all who believe. There is no difference, ²³for all have sinned and fall short of the glory of God, ²⁴and are justified freely by his grace through the redemption that came by Christ Jesus. ²⁵God presented him as a sacrifice of atonement, through faith in his blood. He did this to demonstrate his justice, because in his forbearance he had left the sins committed beforehand unpunished—²⁶he did it to demonstrate his justice at the present time, so as to be just and the one who justifies those who have faith in Jesus.

²⁷Where, then, is boasting? It is excluded. On what principle? On that of observing the law? No, but on that of faith. ²⁸For we maintain that a man is justified by faith apart from observing the law. ²⁹Is God the God of Jews only? Is he not the God of Gentiles too? Yes, of Gentiles too, ³⁰since there is only one God, who will justify the circumcised by faith and the uncircumcised through that same faith. ³¹Do we, then, nullify the law by this faith? Not at all! Rather, we uphold the law.

Limits of the Law

Romans 7

One issue comes up in virtually every one of Paul's letters: "What good is the law?" To most of Paul's readers, the word *law* stood for the huge collection of rules and rituals codified from the Old Testament. Thanks to his earlier days as a Pharisee, Paul knew those rules well. And whenever he started talking about "the new covenant," or "freedom in Christ," the Jews wanted to know what he now thought about that law.

This chapter, the most personal and autobiographical in Romans, discloses exactly what Paul thought

1. When the Law is helpful. Paul never recommended throwing out the Law entirely. He saw that it reveals a basic code of morality, an ideal of the kind of behavior that pleases God. The Law is good for one thing: It exposes sin. "Indeed I would not have known what sin was except through the Law." To Paul, such rules as The Ten Commandments were helpful, righteous, and good.

2. When the Law is helpless. There's one problem with the Law: Although it proves how bad you are, it doesn't make you any better. During his days of legalism, Paul had developed a very sensitive conscience, but, as he poignantly recounts, it mainly made him feel guilty all the time. "What a wretched man I am!" he confessed. The Law bared his weaknesses but could not provide the power needed to overcome them. The Law—or *any* set of rules—leads ultimately to a dead end.

Romans 7 gives a striking illustration of the struggle that ensues when an imperfect person commits himself to a perfect God. Any Christian who wonders "How can I ever get rid of my nagging sins?" will find comfort in Paul's frank confession. In the face of God's standards, every one of us feels helpless, and that is Paul's point precisely. No set of rules can break the terrible cycle of guilt and failure. We need outside help to "serve in the new way of the Spirit, and not in the old way of the written code." Paul celebrates that help in the next chapter.

> **To Reflect On:** *What personal struggle makes you feel most "helpless?" Where do you turn?*

ROMANS 7

An Illustration From Marriage

7 Do you not know, brothers—for I am speaking to men who know the law—that the law has authority over a man only as long as he lives? ²For example, by law a married woman is bound to her husband as long as he is alive, but if her husband dies, she is released from the law of marriage. ³So then, if she marries another man while her husband is still alive, she is called an adulteress. But if her husband dies, she is released from that law and is not an adulteress, even though she marries another man.

⁴So, my brothers, you also died to the law through the body of Christ, that you might belong to another, to him who was raised from the dead, in order that we might bear fruit to God. ⁵For when we were controlled by the sinful nature, the sinful passions aroused by the law were at work in our bodies, so that we bore fruit for death. ⁶But now, by dying to what once bound us, we have been released from the law so that we serve in the new way of the Spirit, and not in the old way of the written code.

Struggling With Sin

⁷What shall we say, then? Is the law sin? Certainly not! Indeed I would not have known what sin was except through the law. For I would not have known what coveting really was if the law had not said, "Do not covet." ⁸But sin, seizing the opportunity afforded by the commandment, produced in me every kind of covetous desire. For apart from law, sin is dead. ⁹Once I was alive apart from law; but when the commandment came, sin sprang to life and I died. ¹⁰I found that the very commandment that was intended to bring life actually brought death. ¹¹For sin, seizing the opportunity afforded by the commandment, deceived me, and through the commandment put me to death. ¹²So then, the law is holy, and the commandment is holy, righteous and good.

¹³Did that which is good, then, become death to me? By no means! But in order that sin might be recognized as sin, it produced death in me through what was good, so that through the commandment sin might become utterly sinful.

¹⁴We know that the law is spiritual; but I am unspiritual, sold as a slave to sin. ¹⁵I do not understand what I do. For what I want to do I do not do, but what I hate I do. ¹⁶And if I do what I do not want to do, I agree that the law is good. ¹⁷As it is, it is no longer I myself who do it, but it is sin living in me. ¹⁸I know that nothing good lives in me, that is, in my sinful nature. For I have the desire to do what is good, but I cannot carry it out. ¹⁹For what I do is not the good I want to do; no, the evil I do not want to do—this I keep on doing. ²⁰Now if I do what I do not want to do, it is no longer I who do it, but it is sin living in me that does it.

²¹So I find this law at work: When I want to do good, evil is right there with me. ²²For in my inner being I delight in God's law; ²³but I see another law at work in the members of my body, waging war against the law of my mind and making me a prisoner of the law of sin at work within my members. ²⁴What a wretched man I am! Who will rescue me from this body of death? ²⁵Thanks be to God—through Jesus Christ our Lord!

So then, I myself in my mind am a slave to God's law, but in the sinful nature a slave to the law of sin.

Spirit Life

Romans 8

Like a gust of outside air flooding into a prison cell, one of the most refreshing passages in the Bible displaces all the despondency of Romans 7. The Holy Spirit is its theme, and Paul gives a panoramic survey of how the Spirit can make a difference in a person's life.

First, Paul sets to rest the nagging problem of sin he has just raised so forcefully. "There is now no condemnation. . . ." he announces. Jesus Christ, through his life and death, took care of "the sin problem" for all time.

Elsewhere (Romans 4), Paul borrows a word from banking to explain the process. God "credits" Jesus' own perfection to our accounts, so that we are judged not by our behavior, but by his. Similarly, God has transferred all the punishment we deserve onto Jesus, through his death on the cross. In this transaction, human beings come out the clear winners, set free at last from the curse of sin.

And, as always with Paul, the best news of all is that Jesus Christ did not stay dead. Paul marvels that the very same power that raised Christ from the dead can also "enliven" us. The Spirit is a life-giver who alone can break the gloomy, deathlike pattern described in Romans 7.

To be sure, the Spirit does not remove all problems. The very titles the Bible applies to him—Intercessor, Helper, Counselor, Comforter—assume there will be problems. But the God within is able to do for us what we could never do for ourselves. The Spirit works alongside us as we relate to God, helping us in our weakness, even praying for us when we don't know what to ask. Mainly, the Spirit teaches us the full benefits of our new identity as children of God.

The way Paul tells it, what happens inside individual believers is the central drama of history: "All of creation waits in eager expectation for the sons of God to be revealed." Somehow, spiritual victories within us will help bring about the liberation and healing of a "groaning" creation. The apostle can hardly contain himself as he contemplates these matters. Romans 8 ends with a ringing declaration that nothing—*absolutely, positively nothing*—can ever separate us from God's love. For Paul, that was a fact worth shouting about.

> **To Reflect On:** *According to this chapter, how can the Holy Spirit make a difference in your daily life?*

ROMANS 8
Life Through the Spirit

8 Therefore, there is now no condemnation for those who are in Christ Jesus, [2] because through Christ Jesus the law of the Spirit of life set me free from the law of sin and death. [3] For what the law was powerless to do in that it was weakened by the sinful nature, God did by sending his own Son in the likeness of sinful man to be a sin offering. And so he condemned sin in sinful man, [4] in order that the righteous requirements of the law might be fully met in us, who do not live according to the sinful nature but according to the Spirit.

[5] Those who live according to the sinful nature have their minds set on what that nature desires; but those who live in accordance with the Spirit have their minds set on what the Spirit desires. [6] The mind of sinful man is death, but the mind controlled by the Spirit is life and peace; [7] the sinful mind is hostile to God. It does not submit to God's law, nor can it do so. [8] Those con-

trolled by the sinful nature cannot please God. ⁹You, however, are controlled not by the sinful nature but by the Spirit, if the Spirit of God lives in you. And if anyone does not have the Spirit of Christ, he does not belong to Christ. ¹⁰But if Christ is in you, your body is dead because of sin, yet your spirit is alive because of righteousness. ¹¹And if the Spirit of him who raised Jesus from the dead is living in you, he who raised Christ from the dead will also give life to your mortal bodies through his Spirit, who lives in you.

¹²Therefore, brothers, we have an obligation—but it is not to the sinful nature, to live according to it. ¹³For if you live according to the sinful nature, you will die; but if by the Spirit you put to death the misdeeds of the body, you will live, ¹⁴because those who are led by the Spirit of God are sons of God. ¹⁵For you did not receive a spirit that makes you a slave again to fear, but you received the Spirit of sonship. And by him we cry, "*Abba*, Father." ¹⁶The Spirit himself testifies with our spirit that we are God's children. ¹⁷Now if we are children, then we are heirs—heirs of God and co-heirs with Christ, if indeed we share in his sufferings in order that we may also share in his glory.

Future Glory

¹⁸I consider that our present sufferings are not worth comparing with the glory that will be revealed in us. ¹⁹The creation waits in eager expectation for the sons of God to be revealed. ²⁰For the creation was subjected to frustration, not by its own choice, but by the will of the one who subjected it, in hope ²¹that the creation itself will be liberated from its bondage to decay and brought into the glorious freedom of the children of God.

²²We know that the whole creation has been groaning as in the pains of childbirth right up to the present time. ²³Not only so, but we ourselves, who have the firstfruits of the Spirit, groan inwardly as we wait eagerly for our adoption as son, the redemption of our bodies. ²⁴For in this hope we were saved. But hope that is seen is no hope at all. Who hopes for what he already has?

²⁵But if we hope for what we do not yet have, we wait for it patiently.

²⁶In the same way, the Spirit helps us in our weakness. We do not know what we ought to pray for, but the Spirit himself intercedes for us with groans that words cannot express. ²⁷And he who searches our hearts knows the mind of the Spirit, because the Spirit intercedes for the saints in accordance with God's will.

More Than Conquerors

²⁸And we know that in all things God works for the good of those who love him, who have been called according to his purpose. ²⁹For those God foreknew he also predestined to be conformed to the likeness of his Son, that he might be the firstborn among many brothers. ³⁰And those he predestined, he also called; those he called, he also justified; those he justified, he also glorified.

³¹What, then, shall we say in response to this? If God is for us, who can be against us? ³²He who did not spare his own Son, but gave him up for us all—how will he not also, along with him, graciously give us all things? ³³Who will bring any charge against those whom God has chosen? It is God who justifies. ³⁴Who is he that condemns? Christ Jesus, who died—more than that, who was raised to life—is at the right hand of God and is also interceding for us. ³⁵Who shall separate us from the love of Christ? Shall trouble or hardship or persecution or famine or nakedness or danger or sword? ³⁶As it is written:

"For your sake we face death all day
    long;
we are considered as sheep to be
    slaughtered."

³⁷No, in all these things we are more than conquerors through him who loved us. ³⁸For I am convinced that neither death nor life, neither angels nor demons, neither the present nor the future, nor any powers, ³⁹neither height nor depth, nor anything else in all creation, will be able to separate us from the love of God that is in Christ Jesus our Lord.

Getting Down to Earth

Romans 12

Too often theology is viewed as stuff for hermits to think about. When there's nothing else to do, *then* is the time to ask abstract questions about God. Such a notion would have exasperated the apostle Paul. To him, theology was worthless unless it made a difference in how people lived. Thus, after laying out the most thorough, concise summary of Christian theology in the Bible, he turns his attention at the end of Romans to a down-to-earth discussion of everyday problems.

Paul's own life offers a good example of how to make theology practical. In fact, he wrote the lofty book of Romans while traveling to raise funds for Jewish famine relief. By collecting offerings from Gentile Christians for the sake of Jews in Jerusalem, Paul modeled the kind of unity sorely needed by both groups. (See 2 Corinthians 8 for more details of this mercy mission.)

Romans 12 needs no special commentary or study aids. The problem lies not in understanding these words, but in obeying them. Paul is describing what love in action should look like. Once more he uses the analogy of the human body to illustrate how diverse parts can work together in unity.

"Offer your bodies as living sacrifices," Paul urged his readers. The Romans, both Jews and Gentiles, associated the word "sacrifices" with the lambs and other animals they brought to the temple for priests to kill on an altar. But Paul makes clear that God wants *living* human beings, not dead animals. A person committed to God's will is the kind of offering most pleasing to God.

> **To Reflect On:** *Use verses 9–21 as a kind of checklist. Which commands do you have the most trouble with? Which are the easiest?*

ROMANS 12

Living Sacrifices

12 Therefore, I urge you, brothers, in view of God's mercy, to offer your bodies as living sacrifices, holy and pleasing to God—this is your spiritual act of worship. ²Do not conform any longer to the pattern of this world, but be transformed by the renewing of your mind. Then you will be able to test and approve what God's will is—his good, pleasing and perfect will.

³For by the grace given me I say to every one of you: Do not think of yourself more highly than you ought, but rather think of yourself with sober judgment, in accordance with the measure of faith God has given you. ⁴Just as each of us has one body with many members, and these members do not all have the same function, ⁵so in Christ we who are many form one body, and each member belongs to all the others. ⁶We have different gifts, according to the grace given us. If a man's gift is prophesying, let him use it in proportion to his faith. ⁷If it is serving, let him serve; if it is teaching, let him teach; ⁸if it is encouraging, let him encourage; if it is contributing to the needs of others, let him give generously; if it is leadership, let him govern diligently; if it is showing mercy, let him do it cheerfully.

Love

⁹Love must be sincere. Hate what is evil; cling to what is good. ¹⁰Be devoted to one another in brotherly love. Honor one another above yourselves. ¹¹Never be lacking in zeal, but keep your spiritual fervor, serving the Lord. ¹²Be joyful in hope, patient in affliction, faithful in prayer. ¹³Share with God's people who are in need. Practice hospitality.

¹⁴Bless those who persecute you; bless and do not curse. ¹⁵Rejoice with those who rejoice; mourn with those who mourn. ¹⁶Live in harmony with one another. Do not be proud, but be willing to associate with people of low position. Do not be conceited.

¹⁷Do not repay anyone evil for evil. Be careful to do what is right in the eyes of everybody. ¹⁸If it is possible, as far as it depends on you, live at peace with everyone. ¹⁹Do not take revenge, my friends, but leave rom for God's wrath, for it is written: "It is mind to avenge; I will repay," says the Lord. ²⁰On the contrary:

"If your enemy is hungry, feed him;
  if he is thirsty, give him something
    to drink.
In doing this, you will heap burning
    coals on his head."

²¹Do not be overcome by evil, but overcome evil with good.

Unexpected Passage

Acts 25:23–26:32

Paul determined to deliver in person the relief money he had collected. Friends begged him not to go to Jerusalem, still a hotbed of persecution against the Christians. But Paul, "compelled by the Spirit" (20:22), persisted. He knew that God wanted him to carry his word to Rome, and no disaster in Jerusalem could interfere with that plan.

When Paul reached Jerusalem, true to his friends' predictions, the worst happened. He was arrested on trumped-up charges, and soon all of Jerusalem was in uproar. Forty Jewish fanatics made a solemn vow not to eat or drink until they had killed Paul. His reputation as a Christian missionary had so aroused the conspirators that it took a brigade of 470 Roman soldiers to protect him.

The last few chapters of Acts show Paul at his most fearless. He boldly confronted a lynch mob, until Roman soldiers had to drag him into barracks for his own protection. The next day, he took on the Jewish ruling body, the Sanhedrin, causing such a ruckus that the Roman commander feared they would tear Paul in pieces. In the midst of all this turmoil, Paul got a comforting vision from the Lord, who said, "Take courage! As you have testified about me in Jerusalem, so you must also testify in Rome" (23:11).

After being smuggled out of town under heavy guard and the cover of darkness, Paul arrived at last in the palace of the Roman governor. His troubles were far from over. After hearing Paul's defense, Felix sent him to prison for two years, as a political favor to the Jews. Even that did not quiet the furor. The moment the new governor Festus arrived, Jewish leaders hatched yet another death plot against Paul.

Acts preserves three of the speeches delivered by Paul on trial. Roman officials, intrigued by the most talked-about prisoner in their corner of the empire, would bring him out to perform, like a circus sideshow. As always, Paul made the best of his opportunities. This chapter records the impression he made on the most distinguished judge of all, King Herod Agrippa.

As a result of the Romans' inquisitions, Paul got his long-awaited trip to Rome—not via a missionary journey, but in a Roman ship as a prisoner of the empire.

> **To Reflect On:** *If you were prosecuted for your beliefs, what might be said in your defense speech?*

ACTS 25:23–26:32

²³The next day Agrippa and Bernice came with great pomp and entered the audience room with the high ranking officers and the leading men of the city. At the command of Festus, Paul was brought in. ²⁴Festus said: "King Agrippa, and all who are present with us, you see this man! The whole Jewish community has petitioned me about him in Jerusalem and here in Caesarea, shouting that he ought not to live any longer. ²⁵I found he had done nothing deserving of death, but because he made his appeal to the Emperor I decided to send him to Rome. ²⁶But I have nothing definite to write to His Majesty about him. Therefore I have brought him before all of you, and especially before you, King Agrippa, so that as a result of this investigation I may have something to write. ²⁷For I think it is unreasonable to send on a prisoner without specifying the charges against him."

26 Then Agrippa said to Paul, "You have permission to speak for yourself."

So Paul motioned with his hand and began his defense: ²"King Agrippa, I consider myself fortunate to stand before you today as I make my defense against all the accusations of the Jews, ³and especially so because you are well acquainted with all the Jewish customs and controversies. Therefore, I beg you to listen to me patiently.

⁴"The Jews all know the way I have lived ever since I was a child, from the beginning of my life in my own country, and also in Jerusalem. ⁵They have known me for a long time and can testify, if they are willing, that according to the strictest sect of our religion, I lived as a Pharisee. ⁶And now it is because of my hope in what God has promised our fathers that I am on trial today. ⁷This is the promise our twelve tribes are hoping to see fulfilled as they earnestly serve God day and night. O king, it is because of this hope that the Jews are accusing me. ⁸Why should any of you consider it incredible that God raises the dead?

⁹"I too was convinced that I ought to do all that was possible to oppose the name of Jesus of Nazareth. ¹⁰And that is just what I did in Jerusalem. On the authority of the chief priests I put many of the saints in prison, and when they were put to death, I cast my vote against them. ¹¹Many a time I went from one synagogue to another to have them punished, and I tried to force them to blaspheme. In my obsession against them, I even went to foreign cities to persecute them.

¹²"On one of these journeys I was going to Damascus with the authority and commission of the chief priests. ¹³About noon, O king, as I was on the road, I saw a light from heaven, brighter than the sun, blazing around me and my companions. ¹⁴We all fell to the ground, and I heard a voice saying to me in Aramaic, 'Saul, Saul, why do you persecute me? It is hard for you to kick against the goads.'

¹⁵"Then I asked, 'Who are you, Lord?'

" 'I am Jesus, whom you are persecuting,' the Lord replied. ¹⁶'Now get up and stand on your feet. I have appeared to you to appoint you as a servant and as a witness of what you have seen of me and what I will show you. ¹⁷I will rescue you from your own people and from the Gentiles. I am

sending you to them ¹⁸to open their eyes and turn them from darkness to light, and from the power of Satan to God, so that they may receive forgiveness of sins and a place among those who are sanctified by faith in me.'

¹⁹"So then, King Agrippa, I was not disobedient to the vision from heaven. ²⁰First to those in Damascus, then to those in Jerusalem and in all Judea, and to the Gentiles also, I preached that they should repent and turn to God and prove their repentance by their deeds. ²¹That is why the Jews seized me in the temple courts and tried to kill me. ²²But I have had God's help to this very day, and so I stand here and testify to small and great alike. I am saying nothing beyond what the prophets and Moses said would happen—²³that the Christ would suffer and, as the first to rise from the dead, would proclaim light to his own people and to the Gentiles."

²⁴At this point Festus interrupted Paul's defense. "You are out of your mind, Paul!" he shouted. "Your great learning is driving you insane."

²⁵"I am not insane, most excellent Festus," Paul replied. "What I am saying is true and reasonable. ²⁶The king is familiar with these things, and I can speak freely to him. I am convinced that none of this has escaped his notice, because it was not done in a corner. ²⁷King Agrippa, do you believe the prophets? I know you do."

²⁸Then Agrippa said to Paul, "Do you think that in such a short time you can persuade me to be a Christian?"

²⁹Paul replied, "Short time or long—I pray God that not only you but all who are listening to me today may become what I am, except for these chains."

³⁰The king rose, and with him the governor and Bernice and those sitting with them. ³¹They left the room, and while talking with one another, they said, "This man is not doing anything that deserves death or imprisonment."

³²Agrippa said to Festus, "This man could have been set free if he had not appealed to Caesar."

Prisoner in Charge

Acts 27

After surviving assassination plots, riots, imprisonment, and a corrupt judicial system, Paul encountered a new set of obstacles on his voyage to Rome. This chapter gives an eyewitness account of an ocean storm, the once-in-a-decade kind of storm that survivors would never forget. Dense clouds blotted out the sun and stars for many days; the entire shipload of 276 passengers and crew went without food for two weeks, and no one knew whether they would survive to see another day. No one, that is, except the apostle Paul.

Luke, a passenger accompanying Paul (note the prominent word "we"), recounts the experience in vivid detail. He depicts the frenzy onboard: sailors lashing ropes around their groaning ship, the crew heaving precious food supplies and even the ship's tackle overboard, Roman soldiers with drawn swords halting the sailors' save-our-own-necks escape attempts and preparing to slash their prisoners' throats. In the midst of all this hysteria stands the apostle Paul, perfectly calm, foretelling what will happen next. God had promised the apostle would visit Rome, a vision confirmed it, and Paul never doubted, even when the boat broke in pieces around him.

Once more, Paul reveals himself as a man of unassailable courage. The Roman centurion surely recognized it: He granted Paul extraordinary privileges and protection. By the end of the storm, everyone on the ship was following the advice of the strange, unflappable prisoner from Tarsus.

To Reflect On: *How do you normally react in a crisis?*

ACTS 27

Paul Sails for Rome

27 When it was decided that we would sail for Italy, Paul and some other prisoners were handed over to a centurion named Julius, who belonged to the Imperial Regiment. [2] We boarded a ship from Adramyttium about to sail for ports along the coast of the province of Asia, and we put out to sea. Aristarchus, a Macedonian from Thessalonica, was with us.

[3] The next day we landed at Sidon; and Julius, in kindness to Paul, allowed him to go to his friends so that they might provide for his needs. [4] From there we put out to sea again and passed to the lee of Cyprus because the winds were against us. [5] When we had sailed across the open sea off the coast of Cilicia and Pamphylia, we landed at Myra in Lycia. [6] There the centurion found an Alexandrian ship sailing for Italy and put us on board. [7] We made slow headway for many days and had difficulty arriving off Cnidus. When the wind did not allow us to hold our course, we sailed to the lee of Crete, opposite Salmone. [8] We moved along the coast with difficulty and came to a place called Fair Havens, near the town of Lasea.

[9] Much time had been lost, and sailing had already become dangerous because by now it was after the Fast. So Paul warned them, [10] "Men, I can see that our voyage is going to be disastrous and bring great loss to ship and cargo, and to our own lives also." [11] But the centurion, instead of listening to what Paul said, followed the advice of the pilot and of the owner of the ship. [12] Since the harbor was unsuitable to winter in, the majority decided that we should sail on, hoping ot reach Phoenix and winter there. This was a harbor in Crete, facing both southwest and northwest.

The Storm

[13] When a gentle south wind began to blow, they thought they had obtained what they wanted; so they weighed anchor and

sailed along the shore of Crete. 14Before very long, a wind of hurricane force, called the "northeaster," swept down from the island. 15The ship was caught by the storm and could not head into the wind; so we gave way to it and were driven along. 16As we passed to the lee of a small island called Cauda, we were hardly able to make the lifeboat secure. 17When the men had hoisted it aboard, they passed ropes under the ship itself to hold it together. Fearing that they would run aground on the sandbars of Syrtis, they lowered the sea anchor and let the ship be driven along. 18We took such a violent battering from the storm that the next day they began to throw the cargo overboard. 19On the third day, they threw the ship's tackle overboard with their own hands. 20When neither sun nor stars appeared for many days and the storm continued raging, we finally gave up all hope of being saved.

21After the men had gone a long time without food, Paul stood up before them and said: "Men, you should have taken my advice not to sail from Crete; then you would have spared yourselves this damage and loss. 22But now I urge you to keep up your courage, because not one of you will be lost; only the ship will be destroyed. 23Last night an angel of the God whose I am and whom I serve stood beside me 24and said, 'Do not be afraid, Paul. You must stand trial before Caesar; and God has graciously given you the lives of all who sail with you.' 25So keep up your courage, men, for I have faith in God that it will happen just as he told me. 26Nevertheless, we must run aground on some island."

The Shipwreck

27On the fourteenth night we were still being driven across the Adriatic Sea, when about midnight the sailors sensed they were approaching land. 28They took soundings and found that the water was a hundred and twenty feet deep. A short time later they took soundings again and found it was ninety feet deep. 29Fearing that we would be dashed against the rocks, they dropped four anchors from the stern and prayed for daylight. 30In an attempt to escape from the ship, the sailors let the lifeboat down into the sea, pretending they were going to lower some anchors from the bow. 31Then Paul said to the centurion and the soldiers, "Unless these men stay with the ship, you cannot be saved." 32So the soldiers cut the ropes that held the lifeboat and let it fall away.

33Just before dawn Paul urged them all to eat. "For the last fourteen days, he said, "you have been in constant suspense and have gone without food—you haven't eaten anything. 34Now I urge you to take some food. You need it to survive. Not one of you will lose a single hair from his head." 35After he said this, he took some bread and gave thanks to God in front of them all. Then he broke it and began to eat. 36They were all encouraged and ate some food themselves. 37Altogether there were 276 of us on board. 38When they had eaten as much as they wanted, they lightened the ship by throwing the grain into the sea.

39When daylight came, they did not recognize the land, but they saw a bay with a sandy beach, where they decided to run the ship aground if they could. 40Cutting loose the anchors, they left them in the sea and at the same time untied the ropes that held the rudders. Then they hoisted the foresail to the wind and made for the beach. 41But the ship struck a sandbar and ran aground. The bow stuck fast and would not move, and the stern was broken to pieces by the pounding of the surf.

42The soldiers planned to kill the prisoners to prevent any of them from swimming away and escaping. 43But the centurion wanted to spare Paul's life and kept them from carrying out their plan. He ordered those who could swim to jump overboard first and get to land. 44The rest were to get there on planks or on pieces of the ship. In this way everyone reached land in safety.

Rome at Last

Acts 28

The future of the Gentile church depended in large measure on what happened to Paul, God's chosen apostle to the Gentiles. Thus the last few chapters of Acts portray a kind of spiritual warfare in which God turns apparent tragedy into good. Paul gets arrested; he's sent at last to Rome. The ship wrecks; they all survive; and Paul befriends a centurion. A poisonous snake bites Paul; he shakes it off and starts a healing ministry.

Paul arrived in Rome, his ultimate destination, under guard. Undoubtedly the reputation he had gained on the voyage helped convince authorities to treat him leniently. He lived by himself under a kind of "house arrest." A soldier was always present, possibly chained to the apostle. In typical fashion, Paul put his time to good use. The very first week he called in Jewish leaders to explain to them the Christian "sect" everyone was talking about. Over the next months and years (the protective custody may have lasted as long as four years) Paul got hours of quiet solitude to work on fond letters to the churches he had left behind.

Luke details the process of Roman justice so thoroughly that some have speculated he wrote Acts as a legal brief for Paul's defense. Was Paul a violent terrorist intent on inciting revolt? Luke meticulously records that Paul had no political ambitions and consistently worked within Roman law. Most of the time, Roman law found Paul innocent. Governor Festus and King Agrippa both concluded Paul might have been freed outright had he not appealed to Caesar.

Luke breaks off the story with Paul's fate still undecided. Most scholars believe that Paul, released from this imprisonment, went on to take his message to new frontiers. Luke records nothing of those journeys, and nothing about Paul's trial or sentencing. He ends with a single memory, frozen in time: Paul, confined to his house, preaching to all his visitors. Paul could no longer choose his audience; they had to seek him. But boldly, in the heart of mighty Rome, he proclaimed a new kingdom and a new king. Before long, some of Caesar's own household staff were converting to the new faith. Christianity had made the journey, and the transition, from Jerusalem to Rome.

Tradition records that a few years later the Emperor Nero had Paul executed. The final verse of Acts serves as a fitting epitaph of the apostle's remarkable career.

> **To Reflect On:** *Do you, like Paul, strive to "make the best" of bad situations?*

ACTS 28

Ashore on Malta

28 Once safely on shore, we found out that the island was called Malta. [2]The islanders showed us unusual kindness. They built a fire and welcomed us all because it was raining and cold. [3]Paul gathered a pile of brushwood and, as he put it on the fire, a viper, driven out by the heat, fastened itself on his hand. [4]When the islanders saw the snake hanging from his hand, they said to each other, "This man must be a murderer; for though he escaped from the sea, Justice has not allowed him to live." [5]But Paul shook the snake off into the fire and suffered no ill effects. [6]The people expected him to swell up or suddenly fall dead, but after waiting a long time and seeing nothing unusual happen to him, they changed their minds and said he was a god.

[7]There was an estate nearby that belonged to Publius, the chief official of the

island. He welcomed us to his home and for three days entertained us hospitably. ⁸His father was sick in bed, suffering from fever and dysentery. Paul went in to see him and, after prayer, placed his hands on him and healed him. ⁹When this had happened, the rest of the sick on the island came and were cured. ¹⁰They honored us in many ways and when we were ready to sail, they furnished us with the supplies we needed.

Arrival at Rome

¹¹After three months we put out to sea in a ship that had wintered in the island. It was an Alexandrian ship with the figurehead of the twin gods Castor and Pollux. ¹²We put in at Syracuse and stayed there three days. ¹³From there we set sail and arrived at Rhegium. The next day the south wind came up, and on the following day we reached Puteoli. ¹⁴There we found some brothers who invited us to spend a week with them. And so we came to Rome. ¹⁵The brothers there had heard that we were coming, and they traveled as far as the Forum of Appius and the Three Taverns to meet us. At the sight of these men Paul thanked God and was encouraged. ¹⁶When we got to Rome, Paul was allowed to live by himself, with a soldier to guard him.

Paul Preaches at Rome Under Guard

¹⁷Three days later he called together the leaders of the Jews. When they had assembled, Paul said to them: "My brothers, although I have done nothing against our people or against the customs of our ancestors, I was arrested in Jerusalem and handed over to the Romans. ¹⁸They examined me and wanted to release me, because I was not guilty of any crime deserving death. ¹⁹But when the Jews objected, I was compelled to appeal to Caesar—not that I had any charge to bring against my own people. ²⁰For this reason I have asked to see you and talk with you. It is because of the hope of Israel that I am bound with this chain."

²¹They replied, "We have not received any letters from Judea concerning you, and none of the brothers who have come from there has reported or said anything bad about you. ²²But we want to hear what your views are, for we know that people everywhere are talking against this sect."

²³They arranged to meet Paul on a certain day, and came in even larger numbers to the place where he was staying. From morning till evening he explained and declared to them the kingdom of God and tried to convince them about Jesus from the Law of Moses and from the Prophets. ²⁴Some were convinced by what he said, but others would not believe. ²⁵They disagreed among themselves and began to leave after Paul had made this final statement: "The Holy Spirit spoke the truth to your forefathers when he said through Isaiah the prophet:

²⁶" 'Go to this people and say,
   "You will be ever hearing but never
         understanding;
      you will be ever seeing but never
         perceiving."
²⁷For this people's heart has become
         calloused;
      they hardly hear with their ears,
      and they have closed their eyes.
   Otherwise they might see with their
         eyes,
      hear with their ears,
      understand with their hearts
   and turn, and I would heal them.'

²⁸"Therefore I want you to know that God's salvation has been sent to the Gentiles, and they will listen!"

³⁰For two whole years Paul stayed there in his own rented house and welcomed all who came to see him. ³¹Boldly and without hindrance he preached the kingdom of God and taught about the Lord Jesus Christ.

Looking Up

Ephesians 1:15–2:13

Ironically, some of the brightest, most hopeful books of the Bible—the letters to the Philippians, Colossians, and Ephesians—came out of Paul's term of house arrest in Rome. There's a good reason: Prison offered him the precious commodity of time. Paul was no longer journeying from town to town, stamping out fires set by his enemies. Settled into passably comfortable surroundings, he could devote attention to lofty thoughts about the meaning of life.

A prisoner who survived fourteen years in a Cuban jail told how he kept his spirits up: "The worst part was the monotony. I had no window in my cell, and so I mentally constructed one on the door. I 'saw' in my mind a beautiful scene from the mountains, with water tumbling down a ravine over rocks. It became so real to me that I would visualize it without effort every time I looked at the cell door."

The letter to Ephesians gives a hint as to what the apostle Paul "saw" when he let his mind wander beyond the monotony of his place of confinement. First, he visualized the spiritual growth in the churches he had left behind. This passage opens with a burst of thanksgiving for the vitality of the Ephesian church. Then, he sought to open "the eyes of their hearts" to even more exalted sights: the "incomparable riches" of God's grace.

Ephesians is full of staggering good news. In it, Paul asks the grandest question of all: "What is God's overall purpose for this world?" He raises the sights far above his own circumstances to bigger issues, cosmic issues. And when he cranks up the volume to express God's plan of love, not one low, mournful note sneaks in.

If you feel discouraged, or wonder if God really cares, or question whether the Christian life is worth the effort, Ephesians provides a great tonic. It prescribes the "riches in Christ" available to all.

> **To Reflect On:** *What do you find most encouraging about Paul's good-news message?*

EPHESIANS 1:15–2:13

Thanksgiving and Prayer

¹⁵For this reason, ever since I heard about your faith in the Lord Jesus and your love for all the saints, ¹⁶I have not stopped giving thanks for you, remembering you in my prayers. ¹⁷I keep asking that the God of our Lord Jesus Christ, the glorious Father, may give you the Spirit of wisdom and revelation, so that you may know him better. ¹⁸I pray also that the eyes of your heart may be enlightened in order that you may know the hope to which he has called you, the riches of his glorious inheritance in the saints, ¹⁹and his incomparably great power for us who believe. That power is like the working of his mighty strength, ²⁰which he exerted in Christ when he raised him from the dead and seated him at his right hand in the heavenly realms, ²¹far above all rule and authority, power and dominion, and every title that can be given, not only in the present age but also in the one to come. ²²And God placed all things under his feet and appointed him to be head over everything for the church, ²³which is his body, the fullness of him who fills everything in every way.

Made Alive in Christ

2 As for you, you were dead in your transgressions and sins, ²in which you used to live when you followed the ways of this world and of the ruler of the kingdom of the air, the spirit who is now at work in those who are disobedient. ³All of us also lived among them at one time, gratifying the cravings of our sinful nature and following its desires and thoughts. Like the rest, we were by nature objects of wrath. ⁴But because of his great love for us, God, who is rich in mercy, ⁵made us alive with Christ even when we were dead in transgressions—it is by grace you have been saved. ⁶And God raised us up with Christ and seated us with him in the heavenly realms in Christ Jesus, ⁷in order that in the coming ages he might show the incomparable riches of his grace, expressed in his kindness to us in Christ Jesus. ⁸For it is by grace you have been saved, through faith—and this not from yourselves, it is the gift of God—⁹not by works, so that no one can boast. ¹⁰For we are God's workmanship, created in Christ Jesus to do good works, which God prepared in advance for us to do.

One in Christ

¹¹Therefore, remember that formerly you who are Gentiles by birth and called "uncircumcised" by those who call themselves "the circumcision" (that done in the body by the hands of men)—¹²remember that at that time you were separate from Christ, excluded from citizenship in Israel and foreigners to the covenants of the promise, without hope and without God in the world. ¹³But now in Christ Jesus you who once were far away have been brought near through the blood of Christ.

A Checkered Past

Ephesians 2:14–3:21

The missionary church at Ephesus was one of Paul's success stories. He first visited there, the most important city in western Asia Minor (now Turkey), on his third missionary journey. Ephesus was renowned for its religion—but not the kind of religion Paul represented. Worship of the Roman goddess Diana centered in Ephesus, and its residents took great pride in the temple devoted to her. The temple building ranked among the seven wonders of the ancient world, and inside it hundreds of professional prostitute-priestesses assisted the "worshipers."

In that unlikely place, Paul discovered a tiny Christian community already in existence. They knew something about John the Baptist, not much about Jesus, and had never even heard of the Holy Spirit. Paul spent three months preaching to Jews in the synagogue and then moved to a lecture hall where he taught Gentiles for almost two years. A burgeoning church took root, and soon word spread throughout the entire province of Asia.

Miraculous signs and wonders marked Paul's ministry in Ephesus, so impressing local sorcerers and magicians that they spontaneously held a public burning of their valuable scrolls. In the face of such religious enthusiasm, the Ephesian merchants, who made their living on profitable sales of idols, finally chased Paul out of town. (See Acts 19 for background.)

Like most early churches, the one at Ephesus struggled with Jew-Gentile differences. Believers from a Jewish background, raised on a steady diet of anti-idolatry, had huge obstacles to overcome in accepting former idol-worshipers into their church. This section of Ephesians addresses the unity issues head-on.

In keeping with the spirit of this letter, and the healthy state of the church, Paul maintains an upbeat tone. He presents Christ as the great destroyer of barriers, the one who demolishes walls of division. (The Jewish temple in Jerusalem had an actual wall that no Gentile could go beyond.) No church demonstrated the miracle of new community better than the one at Ephesus. There, idol-worshipers—as far from God as anyone on earth—had been "brought near," joining Jews, the chosen people, as full members of God's household.

To Paul, the new community formed of both Jews and Gentiles was one of the great mysteries of the ages, a culmination of God's original plan, kept secret for many centuries, but now made known. Paul can hardly contain his soaring spirit, and language, as he marvels at God's plan being fulfilled at that moment.

> **To Reflect On:** *In Paul's time, Jews and Gentiles were the two factions most given to quarreling and division. What groups divide churches today?*

EPHESIANS 2:14–3:21

14For he himself is our peace, who has made the two one and has destroyed the barrier, the dividing wall of hostility, 15by abolishing in his flesh the law with its commandments and regulations. His purpose was to create in himself one new man out of the two, thus making peace, 16and in this one body to reconcile both of them to God through the cross, by which he put to death their hostility. 17He came and preached peace to you who were far away and peace to those who were near. 18For through him we both have access to the Father by one Spirit.

19Consequently, you are no longer foreigners and aliens, but fellow citizens with God's people and members of God's household, 20built on the foundation of the apostles and prophets, with Christ Jesus himself as the chief cornerstone. 21In him the whole building is joined together and rises to become a holy temple in the Lord. 22And in him you too are being built together to become a dwelling in which God lives by his Spirit.

Paul the Preacher to the Gentiles

3 For this reason I, Paul, the prisoner of Christ Jesus for the sake of you Gentiles—

2Surely you have heard about the administration of God's grace that was given to me for you, 3that is, the mystery made known to me by revelation, as I have already written briefly. 4In reading this, then, you will be able to understand my insight into the mystery of Christ, 5which was not made known to men in other generations as it has now been revealed by the Spirit to God's holy apostles and prophets. 6This mystery is that through the gospel the Gentiles are heirs together with Israel, members together of one body, and sharers together in the promise in Christ Jesus.

7I became a servant of this gospel by the gift of God's grace given me through the working of his power. 8Although I am less than the least of all God's people, this grace was given me: to preach to the Gentiles the unsearchable riches of Christ, 9and to make plain to everyone the administration of this mystery, which for ages past was kept hidden in God, who created all things. 10His intent was that now, through the church, the manifold wisdom of God should be made known to the rulers and authorities in the heavenly realms, 11according to his eternal purpose which he accomplished in Christ Jesus our Lord. 12In him and through faith in him we may approach God with freedom and confidence. 13I ask you, therefore, not to be discouraged because of my sufferings for you, which are your glory.

A Prayer for the Ephesians

14For this reason I kneel before the Father, 15from whom his whole family in heaven and on earth derives its name. 16I pray that out of his glorious riches he may strengthen you with power through his Spirit in your inner being, 17so that Christ may dwell in your hearts through faith. And I pray that you, being rooted and established in love, 18may have power, together with all the saints, to grasp how wide and long and high and deep is the love of Christ, 19and to know this love that surpasses knowledge—that you may be filled to the measure of all the fullness of God.

20Now to him who is able to do immeasurably more than all we ask or imagine, according to his power that is at work within us, 21to him be glory in the church and in Christ Jesus throughout all generations, for ever and ever! Amen.

Christ Is Enough

Colossians 1:1–2:5

The book of Colossians may sound like Ephesians, and with good reason—fully half the verses in Ephesians appear in some form in Colossians. The two cities were neighbors, and one of the converts from Paul's stay in Ephesus had taken the gospel over to Colosse. Paul himself had never visited Colosse, and thus wrote this book to people who knew him by reputation only.

The letter opens on an optimistic note, with Paul thanking God for the Colossians' spiritual progress. Yet he also brings up for discussion a doctrinal flaw that had crept into their church. The best modern equivalent would be a "cult," one that includes some Christian principles overlaid with many other mysterious beliefs.

First-century Colosse, situated on a major trade route from the East, was a perfect breeding ground for cults. Even Jews in that area worshiped angels and river spirits. Often these cults (like many now) did not reject Jesus Christ outright; they merely worked him into a more elaborate scheme. Christ and simple forms of worship, they taught, were fine for beginners; however, for the "deep things of God," some further steps were required.

Rather than attacking each peculiar belief point by point, Paul counters with a positive theology. "Christ is enough," he declares in this first chapter. He is God, the fullness of God, the one who made the world, the reason that everything exists. All the "mystery" and treasure and wisdom you could ask for are found in the person of Jesus Christ. There is no need to look elsewhere. The masterful summation paragraph that begins at verse 15 may have been adapted for use as a hymn by the early church.

Paul tells the Colossians just what he had told the Ephesians: Before Christ, a mystery was kept hidden for many centuries. But when Christ came, everything broke out into the open. The fullness of God lived, died, and then reappeared after death—all in broad daylight. Why settle for counterfeits?

To Reflect On: *Who is trying to deceive people by "fine-sounding arguments" today?*

COLOSSIANS 1:1–2:5

1 Paul, an apostle of Christ Jesus by the will of God, and Timothy our brother,

²To the holy and faithful brothers in Christ at Colosse:

Grace and peace to you from God our Father.

Thanksgiving and Prayer

³We always thank God, the Father of our Lord Jesus Christ, when we pray for you, ⁴because we have heard of your faith in Christ Jesus and of the love you have for all the saints—⁵the faith and love that spring from the hope that is stored up for you in heaven and that you have already heard about in the word of truth, the gospel ⁶that has come to you. All over the world this gospel is bearing fruit and growing, just as it has been doing among you since the day you heard it and understood God's grace in all its truth. ⁷You learned it from Epaphras, our dear fellow servant, who is a faithful minister of Christ on our behalf, ⁸and who also told us of your love in the Spirit.

⁹For this reason, since the day we heard about you, we have not stopped praying for you and asking God to fill you with the knowledge of his will through all spiritual wisdom and understanding. ¹⁰And we pray this in order that you may live a life worthy of the Lord and may please him in every way: bearing fruit in every good work, growing in the knowledge of God, ¹¹being strengthened with all power according to his glorious might so that you may have great endurance and patience, and joyfully ¹²giving thanks to the Father, who has qualified you to share in the inheritance of the saints in the kingdom of light. ¹³For he has rescued us from the dominion of darkness and brought us into the kingdom of the Son he loves, ¹⁴in whom we have redemption, the forgiveness of sins.

The Supremacy of Christ

¹⁵He is the image of the invisible God, the firstborn over all creation. ¹⁶For by him all things were created: things in heaven and on earth, visible and invisible, whether thrones or powers or rulers or authorities; all things were created by him and for him. ¹⁷He is before all things, and in him all things hold together. ¹⁸And he is the head of the body, the church; he is the beginning and the firstborn from among the dead, so that in everything he might have the supremacy. ¹⁹For God was pleased to have all his fullness dwell in him, ²⁰and through him to reconcile to himself all things, whether things on earth or things in heaven, by making peace through his blood, shed on the cross.

²¹Once you were alienated from God and were enemies in your minds because of your evil behavior. ²²But now he has reconciled you by Christ's physical body through death to present you holy in his sight, without blemish and free from accusation—²³if you continue in your faith, established and firm, not moved from the hope held out in the gospel. This is the gospel that you heard and that has been proclaimed to every creature under heaven, and of which I, Paul, have become a servant.

Paul's Labor for the Church

²⁴Now I rejoice in what was suffered for you, and I fill up in my flesh what is still lacking in regard to Christ's afflictions, for the sake of his body, which is the church. ²⁵I have become its servant by the commission God gave me to present to you the word of God in its fullness—²⁶the mystery that has been kept hidden for ages and generations, but is now disclosed to the saints. ²⁷To them God has chosen to make known among the Gentiles the glorious riches of this mystery, which is Christ in you, the hope of glory.

²⁸We proclaim him, admonishing and teaching everyone with all wisdom, so that we may present everyone perfect in Christ. ²⁹To this end I labor, struggling with all his energy, which so powerfully works in me.

2 I want you to know how much I am struggling for you and for those at Laodicea, and for all who have not met me personally. ²My purpose is that they may be encouraged in heart and united in love, so that they may have the full riches of complete understanding, in order that they may know the mystery of God, namely, Christ, ³in whom are hidden all the treasures of wisdom and knowledge. ⁴I tell you this so that no one may deceive you by fine-sounding arguments. ⁵For though I am absent from you in body, I am present with you in spirit and delight to see how orderly you are and how firm your faith in Christ is.

A Personal Favor

Philemon

In addition to Paul's letters to churches, the New Testament includes four of the apostle's letters to individuals (Philemon, Titus, 1 and 2 Timothy). Of these, Philemon is the briefest, and also the most personal. Paul is writing a friend to ask a favor—a *big* favor, for a person's life hangs in the balance.

Like most respectable citizens of his day, Philemon owned slaves (historians estimate as many as sixty million slaves served the Roman Empire). One of these, Onesimus, had stolen from his master and run away. He went to Rome, where, along with other fugitives, he spent his days dodging soldiers and bounty hunters in that city's dark, grimy alleys. There, he encountered the apostle Paul and became a Christian. Perhaps he and Paul shared a jail cell.

As a Christian, the slave Onesimus felt the need to make restitution to his master, whom he had wronged. But the laws of the empire were merciless to runaway slaves. If Onesimus returned, his master Philemon had the legal power to sentence him to immediate execution. Or, he could brand the letter *F* (for *Fugitivus*) on his forehead with a hot iron, marking him for life.

The apostle Paul, sympathetic to the slave's cause, agreed to use his full influence on Philemon, and this brief letter, a masterpiece of persuasion and diplomacy, is the result. Every phrase in Philemon seems crafted to produce the best possible effect. Paul appeals to Philemon's friendship, his status as a Christian leader, his sense of love and compassion. Sometimes he applies blatant pressure, reminding Philemon that "you owe me your very self." He even offers to pay back Onesimus's debts.

Paul does not call for the outright abolition of slavery in this letter. Such a call, by threatening the economic base of the empire, would have brought the crushing weight of Rome down on the fledgling church. In fact, slavery would endure for another 1,800 years after this letter was written. But eventually the moral force of Christianity, and only that, proved strong enough to purge slavery from the globe. The tiny book of Philemon shows that faith had a profound impact on slavery long before its abolition.

Onesimus, his Christian conscience pricked, was assuming a grave risk by turning himself in. In Philemon, Paul asks for a second act of faith, by pleading with the slave's owner to "welcome him as you would welcome me." Onesimus was no longer "property," but rather a Christian brother. Such an attitude in that culture was social dynamite.

To Reflect On: *Do you know of any situations in which you could be a reconciler?*

PHILEMON

[1]Paul, a prisoner of Christ Jesus, and Timothy our brother,

To Philemon our dear friend and fellow worker, [2]to Apphia our sister, to Archippus our fellow soldier and to the church that meets in your home:

[3]Grace to you and peace from God our Father and the Lord Jesus Christ.

Thanksgiving and Prayer

[4]I always thank my God as I remember you in my prayers, [5]because I hear about your faith in the Lord Jesus and your love for all the saints. [6]I pray that you may be active in sharing your faith, so that you will have a full understanding of every good thing we have in Christ. [7]Your love has given me great joy and encouragement, because you, brother, have refreshed the hearts of the saints.

Paul's Plea for Onesimus

[8]Therefore, although in Christ I could be bold and order you to do what you ought to do, [9]yet I appeal to you on the basis of love. I then, as Paul—an old man and now also a prisoner of Christ Jesus—[10]I appeal to you for my son Onesimus, who became my son while I was in chains. [11]Formerly he was useless to you, but now he has become useful both to you and to me.

[12]I am sending him—who is my very heart—back to you. [13]I would have liked to keep him with me so that he could take your place in helping me while I am in chains for the gospel. [14]But I did not want to do anything without your consent, so that any favor you do will be spontaneous and not forced. [15]Perhaps the reason he was separated from you for a little while was that you might have him back for good—[16]no longer as a slave, but better than a slave, as a dear brother. He is very dear to me but even dearer to you, both as a man and as a brother in the Lord.

[17]So if you consider me a partner, welcome him as you would welcome me. [18]If he has done you any wrong or owes you anything, charge it to me. [19]I, Paul, am writing this with my own hand. I will pay it back—not to mention that you owe me your very self. [20]I do wish, brother, that I may have some benefit from you in the Lord; refresh my heart in Christ. [21]Confident of your obedience, I write to you, knowing that you will do even more than I ask.

[22]And one thing more: Prepare a guest room for me, because I hope to be restored to you in answer to your prayers.

[23]Epaphras, my fellow prisoner in Christ Jesus, sends you greetings. [24]And so do Mark, Aristarchus, Demas and Luke, my fellow workers.

[25]The grace of the Lord Jesus Christ be with your spirit.

Paul's Troubleshooter

Titus 2:1–3:8

In his early years, Paul, in a whirlwind of energy, had personally carried the message of the gospel to the far corners of the Near East. But age and poor health gradually slowed him down, and he spent many of his later years locked away in prison. Increasingly, he turned to loyal helpers to carry on his work.

The name Titus appears fourteen times in Paul's letters. The book of Galatians (2:1–5) introduces him as Paul's "exhibit A" proving that a Gentile could become a fully acceptable Christian. For more than a decade Paul relied on his trusted associate, who seemed to specialize in crisis churches. Twice Titus was dispatched on a diplomatic mission to the rowdy church at Corinth. This letter indicates he faced an equally challenging task on Crete. Paul was writing him a set of personal instructions on how to handle a difficult assignment.

Crete, an island in the Mediterranean, had an ethnically divided population. Its main knowledge of the outside world came through pirates and coarse sailors. You can get an idea of the challenges Titus faced there by reading between the lines of Paul's advice. For example, Paul's advice to the older men to "be temperate, worthy of respect, self-controlled" reveals something about their normal patterns; likewise, his charge to the women "not to be slanderers or addicted to much wine." One of the island's own poets had described Cretans as "liars, evil brutes, lazy gluttons."

Paul always kept in mind that the Christian church, as a new phenomenon, would attract close scrutiny from the outside world. In Titus, he gives advice on how each of the diverse groups in the church—older men, older women, younger women, young men, slaves—could provide the best example for that watching world. The goal: "so that those who oppose you may be ashamed because they have nothing bad to say about us."

> **To Reflect On:** *Of the advice Paul gives to the various groups, which applies most directly to you?*

TITUS 2:1–3:8

What Must Be Taught to Various Groups

2 You must teach what is in accord with sound doctrine. ²Teach the older men to be temperate, worthy of respect, self-controlled, and sound in faith, in love and in endurance.

³Likewise, teach the older women to be reverent in the way they live, not to be slanderers or addicted to much wine, but to teach what is good. ⁴Then they can train the younger women to love their husbands and children, ⁵to be self-controlled and pure, to be busy at home, to be kind, and to be subject to their husbands, so that no one will malign the word of God.

⁶Similarly, encourage the young men to be self-controlled. ⁷In everything set them an example by doing what is good. In your teaching show integrity, seriousness ⁸and soundness of speech that cannot be condemned, so that those who oppose you may be ashamed because they have nothing bad to say about us.

⁹Teach slaves to be subject to their masters in everything, to try to please them, not to talk back to them, ¹⁰and not to steal from them, but to show that they can be fully trusted, so that in every way they will make the teaching about God our Savior attractive.

¹¹For the grace of God that brings salvation has appeared to all men. ¹²It teaches us to say "No" to ungodliness and worldly passions, and to live self-controlled, upright and godly lives in this present age, ¹³while we wait for the blessed hope—the glorious appearing of our great God and Savior, Jesus Christ, ¹⁴who gave himself for us to redeem us from all wickedness and to purify for himself a people that are his very own, eager to do what is good.

¹⁵These, then, are the things you should teach. Encourage and rebuke with all authority. Do not let anyone despise you.

Doing What Is Good

3 Remind the people to be subject to rulers and authorities, to be obedient, to be ready to do whatever is good, ²to slander no one, to be peaceable and considerate, and to show true humility toward all men.

³At one time we too were foolish, disobedient, deceived and enslaved by all kinds of passions and pleasures. We lived in malice and envy, being hated and hating one another. ⁴But when the kindness and love of God our Savior appeared, ⁵he saved us, not because of righteous things we had done, but because of his mercy. He saved us through the washing of rebirth and renewal by the Holy Spirit, ⁶whom he poured out on us generously through Jesus Christ our Savior, ⁷so that, having been justified by his grace, we might become heirs having the hope of eternal life. ⁸This is a trustworthy saying. And I want you to stress these things, so that those who have trusted in God may be careful to devote themselves to doing what is good. These things are excellent and profitable for everyone.

Growing Pains

1 Timothy 1:1–2:7

The role of women in the church, social welfare programs, fund-raising techniques, a Christian's relationship to society, order of worship, materialism—the list could describe the agenda for a modern-day denominational convention. But the apostle Paul was already addressing these issues in the first century, just a few decades after Jesus' life on earth.

Actually, the problems discussed in 1 Timothy represent growing pains. For example, out of Christian compassion Christians had extended help to needy widows. But before long, some members with a "welfare mentality" saw the widows' list as an easy way to avoid financial responsibility for their families. In 1 Timothy, Paul outlines a form of "enrollment" to establish who was truly needy.

These and other problems were afflicting the church at Ephesus where Timothy now served as pastor. Paul had spent three years with the Christians in Ephesus, and the church had grown and thrived despite intense opposition from within that secular city. The letter to the Ephesians was one of Paul's happiest, containing only the barest hint of problems. But now, almost ten years after his visit to Ephesus, Paul has learned of major troubles brewing.

The time had come for older churches to get organized and to bring some order to their worship and outreach programs. Otherwise, they would drift toward endless division and disagreement. For that thankless job, Paul turned to his trusted companion Timothy.

Converted during Paul's first missionary journey, Timothy had over time gained the apostle's complete trust, despite some major differences in personality. Timothy had a reserved, timid disposition, which may have contributed to his chronic stomach trouble. Given his shyness and his half-Jewish/half-Gentile ancestry, Timothy did not seem the ideal choice for a heresy fighter in a turbulent church. But Paul was convinced he could do the job.

"I have no one else like him," Paul once wrote of Timothy. "As a son with his father he has served with me in the work of the gospel" (Philippians 2). Through disturbances, riots, and even into prison, Timothy had loyally accompanied the apostle. Six of Paul's letters begin with the news that Timothy is at his side. Despite a weak stomach and timid disposition, Timothy had proved his mettle to Paul in many ways, and Paul wrote this letter to encourage him in a difficult task.

> **To Reflect On:** *Do you have any personality traits that make Christian service seem difficult?*

---

1 TIMOTHY 1:1–2:7

1 Paul, an apostle of Christ Jesus by the command of God our Savior and of Christ Jesus our hope,

²To Timothy my true son in the faith:
Grace, mercy and peace from God the Father and Christ Jesus our Lord.

Warning Against False Teachers of the Law

³As I urged you when I went into Macedonia, stay there in Ephesus so that you may command certain men not to teach false doctrines any longer ⁴nor to devote themselves to myths and endless genealogies. These promote controversies rather than God's work—which is by faith. ⁵The goal of this command is love, which comes from a pure heart and a good conscience and a sincere faith. ⁶Some have wandered away from these and turned to meaningless talk. ⁷They want to be teachers of the law, but they do not know what they are talking about or what they so confidently affirm.

⁸We know that the law is good if one uses it properly. ⁹We also know that law is made not for the righteous but for lawbreakers and rebels, the ungodly and sinful, the unholy and irreligious; for those who kill their fathers or mothers, for murderers, ¹⁰for adulterers and perverts, for slave traders and liars and perjurers—and for whatever else is contrary to the sound doctrine ¹¹that conforms to the glorious gospel of the blessed God, which he entrusted to me.

The Lord's Grace to Paul

¹²I thank Christ Jesus our Lord, who has given me strength, that he considered me faithful, appointing me to his service. ¹³Even though I was once a blasphemer and a persecutor and a violent man, I was shown mercy because I acted in ignorance and unbelief. ¹⁴The grace of our Lord was poured out on me abundantly, along with the faith and love that are in Christ Jesus.

¹⁵Here is a trustworthy saying that deserves full acceptance: Christ Jesus came into the world to save sinners—of whom I am the worst. ¹⁶But for that very reason I was shown mercy so that in me, the worst of sinners, Christ Jesus might display his unlimited patience as an example for those who would believe on him and receive eternal life. ¹⁷Now to the King eternal, immortal, invisible, the only God, be honor and glory for ever and ever. Amen.

¹⁸Timothy, my son, I give you this instruction in keeping with the prophecies once made about you, so that by following them you may fight the good fight, ¹⁹holding on to faith and a good conscience. Some have rejected these and so have shipwrecked their faith. ²⁰Among them are Hymenaeus and Alexander, whom I have handed over to Satan to be taught not to blaspheme.

Instructions on Worship

2 I urge, then, first of all, that requests, prayers, intercession and thanksgiving be made for everyone—²for kings and all those in authority, that we may live peaceful and quiet lives in all godliness and holiness. ³This is good, and pleases God our Savior, ⁴who wants all men to be saved and to come to a knowledge of the truth. ⁵For there is one God and one mediator between God and men, the man Christ Jesus, ⁶who gave himself as a ransom for all men—the testimony given in its proper time. ⁷And for this purpose I was appointed a herald and an apostle—I am telling the truth, I am not lying—and a teacher of the true faith to the Gentiles.

Final Words

2 Timothy 2

I am suffering even to the point of being chained like a criminal. But God's word is not chained." Those words from Paul to Timothy sum up both his personal plight and his burning desire to see his life's work continue after his death.

The second letter to Timothy contains many clues about Paul's circumstances. He is imprisoned in Rome once again, but this time the treatment seems far harsher than the previous house arrest. Now he is being kept in chains, in a cold dungeon that his friends can barely locate. Paul's spirits are sagging. He feels abandoned by "everyone in the province of Asia" (1:15) and laments that at a recent trial, not a single witness came to his defense (4:16).

This letter almost certainly dates from the time of Emperor Nero, around A.D. 66–67. By then Christianity had grown from a splinter sect of Judaism into a major force with many thousands of converts, and Nero seized upon it as a scapegoat for the ills of the empire. He burned Rome to the ground and promptly blamed the Christians for the fire. Soon the crazed emperor was torturing believers by crucifying them, by wrapping them in animal skins and turning his hunting dogs loose on them, and by burning them alive as human torches to illuminate the games in his garden.

Little wonder that Paul, imprisoned in that era, exhorted Timothy on the need for boldness in the face of suffering. Paul's own life was nearing an end, and he wrote these, his last recorded words, as a legacy to pass on to Timothy and other "reliable men who will also be qualified to teach others."

Second Timothy is a moody book. Sometimes Paul makes himself vulnerable, exposing his fears and his loneliness. Other times, as in this chapter, he gives a rousing "pep talk" meant to cheer Timothy's spirits—and perhaps his own. Life was closing in on the apostle, and he strings together last-minute reminders: advice on pure living, essential nuggets of theology, inspiring analogies, one-line proverbs, warnings, common sayings. There is no particular order to this book; Paul has no time for that. He is setting down a kind of spiritual "last will and testament" for his son in Christ.

Tradition teaches that Paul was killed by Rome for his faith. But, thanks to his life and the legacy he passed on to converts like Timothy, the world would never be the same.

To Reflect On: *What issues seem to concern Paul most as he faces death?*

2 TIMOTHY 2

2 You then, my son, be strong in the grace that is in Christ Jesus. ²And the things you have heard me say in the presence of many witnesses entrust to reliable men who will also be qualified to teach others. ³Endure hardship with us like a good soldier of Christ Jesus. ⁴No one serving as a soldier gets involved in civilian affairs—he wants to please his commanding officer. ⁵Similarly, if anyone competes as an athlete, he does not receive the victor's crown unless he competes according to the rules. ⁶The hardworking farmer should be the first to receive a share of the crops. ⁷Reflect on what I am saying, for the Lord will give you insight into all this.

⁸Remember Jesus Christ, raised from the dead, descended from David. This is my gospel, ⁹for which I am suffering even to the point of being chained like a criminal. But God's word is not chained. ¹⁰Therefore I endure everything for the sake of the elect, that they too may obtain the salvation that is in Christ Jesus, with eternal glory.

¹¹Here is a trustworthy saying:

If we died with him,
  we will also live with him;
¹²if we endure,
  we will also reign with him.
If we disown him,
  he will also disown us;
¹³if we are faithless,
  he will remain faithful,
  for he cannot disown himself.

A Workman Approved by God

¹⁴Keep reminding them of these things. Warn them before God against quarreling about words; it is of no value, and only ruins those who listen. ¹⁵Do your best to present yourself to God as one approved, a workman who does not need to be ashamed and who correctly handles the word of truth. ¹⁶Avoid godless chatter, because those who indulge in it will become more and more ungodly. ¹⁷Their teaching will spread like gangrene. Among them are Hymenaeus and Philetus, ¹⁸who have wandered away from the truth. They say that the resurrection has already taken place, and they destroy the faith of some. ¹⁹Nevertheless, God's solid foundation stands firm, sealed with this inscription: "The Lord knows those who are his," and, "Everyone who confesses the name of the Lord must turn away from wickedness."

²⁰In a large house there are articles not only of gold and silver, but also of wood and clay; some are for noble purposes and some for ignoble. ²¹If a man cleanses himself from the latter, he will be an instrument for noble purposes, made holy, useful to the Master and prepared to do any good work.

²²Flee the evil desires of youth, and pursue righteousness, faith, love and peace, along with those who call on the Lord out of a pure heart. ²³Don't have anything to do with foolish and stupid arguments, because you know they produce quarrels. ²⁴And the Lord's servant must not quarrel; instead, he must be kind to everyone, able to teach, not resentful. ²⁵Those who oppose him he must gently instruct, in the hope that God will grant them repentance leading them to a knowledge of the truth, ²⁶and that they will come to their senses and escape from the trap of the devil, who has taken them captive to do his will.

Why Better?

Hebrews 2:1–3:6

Are religions all that different?" skeptics ask. "Isn't the most important thing to be sincere in whatever you believe?" Such "modern" questions have, in fact, been debated for thousands of years. The book of Hebrews was written in response to people torn between the Jewish religion and the new faith of Christianity.

Some favored sticking with the familiar routine of Judaism, which had centuries-old traditions behind it. Another advantage: The Jews enjoyed Rome's official protection, while Christians were subject to persecution. Was faith in Christ worth the risk?

Hebrews insists there are decisive reasons to choose Christ. The whole book is constructed around the word *better*. Jesus is better than the angels, or Moses, or the Old Testament way—better than anything the world has to offer. God "has put everything under his feet," says the author, quoting from the Psalms.

Yet, after recording that gust of grand theology from the Psalms, the author of Hebrews seems to pause and reconsider. Yes, it's true that Jesus is in control, but it sure doesn't look like it: "At present we do not see everything subject to him." Could a world in which Christians were being arrested, tortured, and tossed into jail really be subject to Christ?

From there, the author explains why it mattered that God descended to the world and became a human being. He did not magically remove all human problems, but rather *subjected himself* to the same hardships that any of us face. Hebrews goes further than any other New Testament book in explaining Jesus' human nature. This chapter gives two powerful reasons why Jesus came to earth:

1. By dying, he freed us from the power of death and won for us eternal life.
2. By experiencing normal human temptations, he can better help us with our own temptations.

No angel, and no God in distant heaven, could have accomplished those things. Jesus came, in effect, on a rescue mission, to free humanity from slavery. Apart from Christ, we live in constant fear of death and in constant bondage to our failures, or sins. Only Jesus can set us free. That's why he's worth the risk.

> **To Reflect On:** *According to this chapter, what "advantages" does Jesus offer you?*

HEBREWS 2:1–3:6

Warning to Pay Attention

2 We must pay more careful attention, therefore, to what we have heard, so that we do not drift away. ²For if the message spoken by angels was binding, and every violation and disobedience received its just punishment, ³how shall we escape if we ignore such a great salvation? This salvation, which was first announced by the Lord, was confirmed to us by those who heard him. ⁴God also testified to it by signs, wonders and various miracles, and gifts of the Holy Spirit distributed according to his will.

Jesus Made Like His Brothers

⁵It is not to angels that he has subjected the world to come, about which we are speaking. ⁶But there is a place where someone has testified:

"What is man that you are mindful of him,
  the son of man that you care for him?
⁷You made him a little lower than the angels;
  you crowned him with glory and honor
⁸and put everything under his feet."

In putting everything under him, God left nothing that is not subject to him. Yet at present we do not see everything subject to him. ⁹But we see Jesus, who was made a little lower than the angels, now crowned with glory and honor because he suffered death, so that by the grace of God he might taste death for everyone.

¹⁰In bringing many sons to glory, it was fitting that God, for whom and through whom everything exists, should make the author of their salvation perfect through suffering. ¹¹Both the one who makes men holy and those who are made holy are of the same family. So Jesus is not ashamed to call them brothers. ¹²He says,

"I will declare your name to my brothers;
  in the presence of the congregation I will sing your praises."

¹³And again,

"I will put my trust in him."

And again he says,

"Here am I, and the children God has given me."

¹⁴Since the children have flesh and blood, he too shared in their humanity so that by his death he might destroy him who holds the power of death—that is, the devil—¹⁵and free those who all their lives were held in slavery by their fear of death. ¹⁶For surely it is not angels he helps, but Abraham's descendants. ¹⁷For this reason he had to be made like his brothers in every way, in order that he might become a merciful and faithful high priest in service to God, and that he might make atonement for the sins of the people. ¹⁸Because he himself suffered when he was tempted, he is able to help those who are being tempted.

Jesus Greater Than Moses

3 Therefore, holy brothers, who share in the heavenly calling, fix your thoughts on Jesus, the apostle and high priest whom we confess. ²He was faithful to the one who appointed him, just as Moses was faithful in all God's house. ³Jesus has been found worthy of greater honor than Moses, just as the builder of a house has greater honor than the house itself. ⁴For every house is built by someone, but God is the builder of everything. ⁵Moses was faithful as a servant in all God's house, testifying to what would be said in the future. ⁶But Christ is faithful as a son over God's house. And we are his house, if we hold on to our courage and the hope of which we boast.

Tough Faith

Hebrews 11

The last few paragraphs of chapter 10 reveal much about the original readers of Hebrews. Converting to Christ had brought them much abuse: confiscation of property, public insult, and even imprisonment. In the early days, they accepted such persecution gladly, even joyfully. But as time went on, and the trials continued, some were beginning to lose heart.

To these discouraged people, Hebrews 11 presents a stirring reminder of what constitutes "true faith." It's tempting to think of faith as a kind of magic formula: If you muster up enough of it, you'll get rich, stay healthy, and live a contented life with automatic answers to all your prayers. But the readers of Hebrews were discovering that life does not work according to such neat formulas. As proof, the author painstakingly reviews the lives of some Old Testament giants of faith. (Some have dubbed Hebrews 11 the "Faith Hall of Fame.")

"Without faith," Hebrews says bluntly, "it is impossible to please God." But the author uses rather pointed words in describing that faith: "persevere," "endure," "don't lose heart." As a result of their faith, some heroes triumphed: They routed armies, escaped the sword, survived lions. But many others met less happy ends: They were flogged, chained, stoned, sawed in two. The chapter concludes, "These were all commended for their faith, yet none of them received what had been promised."

The picture of faith that emerges from this chapter does not fit into an easy formula. Sometimes faith leads to victory and triumph. Sometimes it requires a gritty determination to "hang on at any cost." Hebrews 11 does not hold up one kind of faith as superior to the other. Both rest on the belief that God is in ultimate control and will indeed keep his promises, whether in this life or in the next. Of such people, Hebrews says, "God is not ashamed to be called their God, for he has prepared a city for them."

> **To Reflect On:** *Think through your own life of faith. Do you more closely identify with the victorious heroes of faith or with those who "hang on at any cost"?*

HEBREWS 11

By Faith

11 Now faith is being sure of what we hope for and certain of what we do not see. ²This is what the ancients were commended for.

³By faith we understand that the universe was formed at God's command, so that what is seen was not made out of what was visible.

⁴By faith Abel offered God a better sacrifice than Cain did. By faith he was commended as a righteous man, when God spoke well of his offerings. And by faith he still speaks, even though he is dead.

⁵By faith Enoch was taken from this life, so that he did not experience death; he could not be found, because God had taken him away. For before he was taken, he was commended as one who pleased God. ⁶And without faith it is impossible to please God, because anyone who comes to Him must believe that he exists and that he rewards those who earnestly seek him.

⁷By faith Noah, when warned about things not yet seen, in holy fear built an ark to save his family. By his faith he condemned the world and became heir of the righteousness that comes by faith.

⁸By faith Abraham, when called to go to a place he would later receive as his inheri-

tance, obeyed and went, even though he did not know where he was going. 9By faith he made his home in the promised land like a stranger in a foreign country; he lived in tents, as did Isaac and Jacob, who were heirs with him of the same promise. 10For he was looking forward to the city with foundations, whose architect and builder is God.

11By faith Abraham, even though he was past age—and Sarah herself was barren—was enabled to become a father because he considered him faithful who had made the promise. 12And so from this one man, and he as good as dead, came descendants as numerous as the stars in the sky and as countless as the sand on the seashore.

13All these people were still living by faith when they died. They did not receive the things promised; they only saw them and welcomed them from a distance. And they admitted that they were aliens and strangers on earth. 14People who say such things show that they are looking for a country of their own. 15If they had been thinking of the country they had left, they would have had opportunity to return. 16Instead, they were longing for a better country—a heavenly one. Therefore God is not ashamed to be called their God, for he has prepared a city for them.

17By faith Abraham, when God tested him, offered Isaac as a sacrifice. He who had received the promises was about to sacrifice his one and only son, 18even though God had said to him, "It is through Isaac that your offspring will be reckoned." 19Abraham reasoned that God could raise the dead, and figuratively speaking, he did receive Isaac back from death.

20By faith Isaac blessed Jacob and Esau in regard to their future.

21By faith Jacob, when he was dying, blessed each of Joseph's sons, and worshiped as he leaned on the top of his staff.

22By faith Joseph, when his end was near, spoke about the exodus of the Israelites from Egypt and gave instructions about his bones. 23By faith Moses' parents hid him for three months after he was born, because they saw he was no ordinary child, and they were not afraid of the king's edict.

24By faith Moses, when he had grown up, refused to be known as the son of Pharaoh's daughter. 25He chose to be mistreated along with the people of God rather than to enjoy the pleasures of sin for a short time. 26He regarded disgrace for the sake of Christ as of greater value than the treasures of Egypt, because he was looking ahead to his reward. 27By faith he left Egypt, not fearing the king's anger; he persevered because he saw him who is invisible. 28By faith he kept the Passover and the sprinkling of blood, so that the destroyer of the firstborn would not touch the firstborn of Israel.

29By faith the people passed through the Red Sea as on dry land; but when the Egyptians tried to do so, they were drowned.

30By faith the walls of Jericho fell, after the people had marched around them for seven days.

31By faith the prostitute Rahab, because she welcomed the spies, was not killed with those who were disobedient.

32And what more shall I say? I do not have time to tell about Gideon, Barak, Samson, Jephthah, David, Samuel and the prophets, 33who through faith conquered kingdoms, administered justice, and gained what was promised; who shut the mouths of lions, 34quenched the fury of the flames, and escaped the edge of the sword; whose weakness was turned to strength; and who became powerful in battle and routed foreign armies. 35Women received back their dead, raised to life again. Others were tortured and refused to be released, so that they might gain a better resurrection. 36Some faced jeers and flogging, while still others were chained and put in prison. 37They were stoned; they were sawed in two; they were put to death by the sword. They went about in sheepskins and goatskins, destitute, persecuted and mistreated—38the world was not worthy of them. They wandered in deserts and mountains, and in caves and holes in the ground.

39These were all commended for their faith, yet none of them received had been promised. 40God had planned something better for us so that only together with us would they be made perfect.

Marathon Race

Hebrews 12

Hebrews 12 takes up right where the previous chapter left off, only the author moves the spotlight from Old Testament history to the readers themselves. He likens faith to an athletic contest in a stadium. Those who have gone before—the giants of faith from chapter 11—are like "a great cloud of witnesses" watching the rest of us run the race of faith. Therefore, "throw off everything that hinders," Hebrews coaches, and again, "strengthen your feeble arms and weak knees."

Evidently, the original readers of Hebrews had expected a short sprint, but not a grueling marathon run. They needed extra encouragement and discipline to survive a long-distance spiritual contest.

The analogy of a marathon race provides a convenient way to think about the Christian life. Why do people punish their bodies through a twenty-six-mile course? Most runners mention a sense of personal accomplishment, combined with the physical benefits of exercise. There are parallel benefits in a "spiritual marathon." Applying the discipline needed to resist temptation, and to endure hardship, leads to certain good results; namely, strong character and a clean conscience. Not to mention the eternal rewards that await all who finish the race.

True competitors set their sights on the lead runner, and as might be expected, Hebrews holds up Jesus as the ultimate standard for our faith. He endured the terrible suffering of the cross for the sake of "the joy set before him." Because of Jesus, no one can complain, "God doesn't know what it's like down here." He does know, for he, too, has been here. And for anyone tempted to grow weary and lose heart, the very best cure is to "fix your eyes on Jesus, the author and perfecter of our faith."

The chapter ends with a soaring passage that celebrates how much better is Christ's new covenant than the old one between God and the Israelites. The new covenant will culminate in a new creation and a new kingdom—one that can never be shaken.

To Reflect On: *If maturing spiritually is like a marathon race, how far along are you?*

HEBREWS 12

God Disciples His Sons

12 Therefore, since we are surrounded by such a great cloud of witnesses, let us throw off everything that hinders and the sin that so easily entangles, and let us run with perseverance the race marked out for us. ²Let us fix our eyes on Jesus, the author and perfecter of our faith, who for the joy set before him endured the cross, scorning its shame, and sat down at the right hand of the throne of God. ³Consider him who endured such opposition from sinful men, so that you will not grow weary and lose heart.

⁴In your struggle against sin, you have not yet resisted to the point of shedding your blood. ⁵And you have forgotten that word of encouragement that addresses you as sons:

"My son, do not make light of the
    Lord's discipline,
  and do not lose heart when he
    rebukes you,
⁶because the Lord disciplines those he
    loves,
  and he punishes everyone he accepts
    as a son."

⁷Endure hardship as discipline; God is treating you as sons. For what son is not disciplined by his father? ⁸If you are not disciplined (and everyone undergoes discipline), then you are illegitimate children and not true sons. ⁹Moreover, we have all had human fathers who disciplined us and we respected them for it. How much more should we submit to the Father of our spirits and live! ¹⁰Our fathers disciplined us for a little while as they thought best; but God disciplines us for our good, that we may share in his holiness. ¹¹No discipline seems pleasant at the time, but painful. Later on, however, it produces a harvest of righteousness and peace for those who have been trained by it.

¹²Therefore, strengthen your feeble arms and weak knees. ¹³"Make level paths for your feet," so that the lame may not be disabled, but rather healed.

Warning Against Refusing God

¹⁴Make every effort to live in peace with all men and to be holy; without holiness no one will see the Lord. ¹⁵See to it that no one misses the grace of God and that no bitter root grows up to cause trouble and defile many. ¹⁶See that no one is sexually immoral, or is godless like Esau, who for a single meal sold his inheritance rights as the oldest son. ¹⁷Afterward, as you know, when he wanted to inherit this blessing, he was rejected. He could bring about no change of mind, though he sought the blessing with tears.

¹⁸You have not come to a mountain that can be touched and that is burning with fire; to darkness, gloom and storm; ¹⁹to a trumpet blast or to such a voice speaking words that those who heard it begged that no further word be spoken to them, ²⁰because they could not bear what was commanded: "If even an animal touches the mountain, it must be stoned." ²¹The sight was so terrifying that Moses said, "I am trembling with fear."

²²But you have come to Mount Zion, to the heavenly Jerusalem, the city of the living God. You have come to thousands upon thousands of angels in joyful assembly, ²³to the church of the firstborn, whose names are written in heaven. You have come to God, the judge of all men, to the spirits of righteous men made perfect, ²⁴to Jesus the mediator of a new covenant, and to the sprinkled blood that speaks a better word than the blood of Abel.

²⁵See to it that you do not refuse him who speaks. If they did not escape when they refused him who warned them on earth, how much less will we, if we turn away from him who warns us from heaven? ²⁶At that time his voice shook the earth, but now he has promised, "Once more I will shake not only the earth but also the heavens." ²⁷The words "once more" indicate the removing of what can be shaken—that is, created things—so that what cannot be shaken may remain.

²⁸Therefore, since we are receiving a kingdom that cannot be shaken, let us be thankful, and so worship God acceptably with reverence and awe, ²⁹for our "God is a consuming fire."

Practice What You Preach

James 1:1–2:10

You get a sense of James's style in the first two sentences of his letter. After the sparsest of greetings, he dives directly into the topic at hand and starts dishing out advice. James lacked the education and sophistication of the apostle Paul, so you won't find his letter wandering off into abstract theology. He was a simple man, a man of the soil. He drew analogies from nature—ocean waves, wilted flowers, a forest fire, spring rains—and expressed his thoughts in pithy sayings almost like proverbs.

Since James's church in Jerusalem was one of the main targets of Jewish persecution, it's natural that his letter begins with encouragement for people undergoing trials. But it quickly moves on to a variety of topics, in each case exhorting readers to live out their beliefs. *Be humble!* James orders. *Control your tongue! Stop sinning!* James is as forthright as an Old Testament prophet. It's hard to miss his point.

One verse in the first chapter neatly summarizes the pervasive message of this book: "Do not merely listen to the word, and so deceive yourselves. Do what it says." James offers up a very pointed illustration of exactly the kind of hypocrisy he is talking about: church members who defer to the wealthy and powerful. The message hits close to home and leaves no room for ambiguity.

The illustration of preferential treatment seems as relevant today as when James first wrote it, 1,900 years ago. Modern readers face the same dilemma as the first recipients of this unsettling letter. His words are easy enough to understand, but are we doing what he says?

> **To Reflect On:** *Who do you tend to show favoritism to? The rich? Slim, attractive people? Athletes? People of your race? Those who share your religious or political beliefs? Whom do you tend to look down upon?*

JAMES 1:1–2:10

1 James, a servant of God and of the Lord Jesus Christ,

To the twelve tribes scattered among the nations:

Greetings.

Trials and Temptations

² Consider it pure joy, my brothers, whenever you face trials of many kinds, ³ because you know that the testing of your faith develops perseverance. ⁴ Perseverance must finish its work so that you may be mature and complete, not lacking anything. ⁵ If any of you lacks wisdom, he should ask God, who gives generously to all without finding fault, and it will be given to him. ⁶ But when he asks, he must believe and not doubt, because he who doubts is like a wave of the sea, blown and tossed by the wind. ⁷ That man should not think he will receive anything from the Lord; ⁸ he is a double-minded man, unstable in all he does.

⁹ The brother in humble circumstances ought to take pride in his high position. ¹⁰ But the one who is rich should take pride in his low position, because he will pass away like a wild flower. ¹¹ For the sun rises with scorching heat and withers the plant; its blossom falls and its beauty is destroyed. In the same way, the rich man will fade away even while he goes about his business.

¹² Blessed is the man who perseveres under trial, because when he has stood the test, he will receive the crown of life that God has promised to those who love him.

13When tempted, no one should say, "God is tempting me." For God cannot be tempted by evil, nor does he tempt anyone; 14but each one is tempted when, by his own evil desire, he is dragged away and enticed. 15Then, after desire has conceived, it gives birth to sin; and sin, when it is full-grown, gives birth to death.

16Don't be deceived, my dear brothers. 17Every good and perfect gift is from above, coming down from the Father of the heavenly lights, who does not change like shifting shadows. 18He chose to give us birth through the word of truth, that we might be a kind of firstfruits of all he created.

Listening and Doing

19My dear brothers, take note of this: Everyone should be quick to listen, slow to speak and slow to become angry, 20for man's anger does not bring about the righteous life that God desires. 21Therefore, get rid of all moral filth and the evil that is so prevalent and humbly accept the word planted in you, which can save you.

22Do not merely listen to the word, and so deceive yourselves. Do what it says. 23Anyone who listens to the word but does not do what it says is like a man who looks at his face in a mirror 24and, after looking at himself, goes away and immediately forgets what he looks like. 25But the man who looks intently into the perfect law that gives freedom, and continues to do this, not forgetting what he has heard, but doing it— he will be blessed in what he does.

26If anyone considers himself religious and yet does not keep a tight rein on his tongue, he deceives himself and his religion is worthless. 27Religion that God our Father accepts as pure and faultless is this: to look after orphans and widows in their distress and to keep oneself from being polluted by the world.

Favoritism Forbidden

2 My brothers, as believers in our glorious Lord Jesus Christ, don't show favoritism. 2Suppose a man comes into your meeting wearing a gold ring and fine clothes, and a poor man in shabby clothes also comes in. 3If you show special attention to the man wearing fine clothes and say, "Here's a good seat for you," but say to the poor man, "You stand there" or "sit on the floor by my feet," 4have you not discriminated among yourselves and become judges with evil thoughts?

5Listen, my dear brother: Has not God chosen those who are poor in the eyes of the world to be rich in faith and to inherit the kingdom he promised those who love him? 6But you have insulted the poor. Is it not the rich who are exploiting you? Are they not the ones who are dragging you into court? 7Are they not the ones who are slandering the noble name of him to whom you belong?

8If you really keep the royal law found in Scripture, "Love your neighbor as yourself," you are doing right. 9But if you show favoritism, you sin and are convicted by the law as lawbreakers. 10For whoever keeps the whole law and yet stumbles at just one point is guilty of breaking all of it.

Converted Coward

1 Peter 1:1–2:3

The Peter portrayed in the Gospels and the Peter seen in this letter are hardly recognizable as the same person. The Gospels show him cowering in the darkness the night of Jesus' trial and execution, and denying with an oath that he had ever known the man he had followed for three years. But in this letter Peter welcomes suffering as a badge of honor, proof of his commitment to Christ at any cost. Seeing the resurrected Jesus—especially in the poignant scene by a lake when Jesus reinstated him (John 21)—had changed Peter forever.

Most likely, Peter wrote this letter during an outbreak of persecution under Nero. At first Christians had enjoyed official toleration by the Roman Empire, despite all their talk about another "kingdom." But eventually the government grew to resent the believers' moralizing about idolatry and decadence, and the emperor turned on them as scapegoats. Leaders of the church, the apostle Paul among them, were shipped to Rome for imprisonment and execution.

Urgent questions stirred up within the embattled Christian community. Should they flee or resist? Should they tone down their outward signs of faith? Peter's readers, their lives in danger, needed clear advice. Beyond that, they also desired some explanation of the meaning of suffering. Why does God allow it? Does God care?

As this chapter shows, Peter's response focuses not on the *cause* of suffering—the "Why?"—but rather on the *results*. What can suffering produce? He answers that suffering can "refine" faith, much like a furnace refines impure metals. Suffering shifts attention from the rewards of this world—wealth, status, power—to more permanent, "imperishable" rewards in the life to come. And if Christians maintain their faith through persecution, a watching world will have to acknowledge the source of that faith, God himself.

Evidently, the early Christians heeded Peter's advice. More often than not, intense persecution led to a spurt of growth in the church. An ancient saying expresses this phenomenon, "The blood of martyrs is the seed of the church." According to tradition, Peter himself died a martyrs' death. He was reportedly crucified head downward on a Roman cross because he thought himself unworthy to die right side up like Jesus.

In this first chapter, Peter turns what could be a reason for despair into a reason for great hope. He sees the church, in all its birth pangs, as the long-awaited goal of the Old Testament prophets, indeed, the goal of all history. As he put it, "Even angels long to look into these things."

> **To Reflect On:** *When has your faith gone through a "refining fire"?*

1 PETER 1:1–2:3

1 Peter, an apostle of Jesus Christ,

To God's elect, strangers in the world, scattered throughout Pontus, Galatia, Cappadocia, Asia and Bithynia, ²who have been chosen according to the foreknowledge of God the Father, through the sanctifying work of the Spirit, for obedience to Jesus Christ and sprinkling by his blood:

Grace and peace be yours in abundance.

Praise to God for a Living Hope

³Praise be to the God and Father of our Lord Jesus Christ! In his great mercy he has given us new birth into a living hope through the resurrection of Jesus Christ from the dead, ⁴and into an inheritance that can never perish, spoil or fade—kept in heaven for you, ⁵who through faith are shielded by God's power until the coming of the salvation that is ready to be revealed in the last time. ⁶In this you greatly rejoice, though now for a little while you may have had to suffer grief in all kinds of trials. ⁷These have come so that your faith—of greater worth than gold, which perishes even though refined by fire—may be proved genuine and may result in praise, glory and honor when Jesus Christ is revealed. ⁸Though you have not seen him, you love him; and even though you do not see him now, you believe in him and are filled with an inexpressible and glorious joy, ⁹for you are receiving the goal of your faith, the salvation of your souls.

¹⁰Concerning this salvation, the prophets, who spoke of the grace that was to come to you, searched intently and with the greatest care, ¹¹trying to find out the time and circumstances to which the Spirit of Christ in them was pointing when he predicted the sufferings of Christ and the glories that would follow. ¹²It was revealed to them that they were not serving themselves but you, when they spoke of the things that have now been told you by those who have preached the gospel to you by the Holy Spirit sent from heaven. Even angels long to look into these things.

Be Holy

¹³Therefore, prepare your minds for action; be self-controlled; set your hope fully on the grace to be given you when Jesus Christ is revealed. ¹⁴As obedient children, do not conform to the evil desires you had when you lived in ignorance. ¹⁵But just as he who called you is holy, so be holy in all you do; ¹⁶for it is written: "Be holy, because I am holy."

¹⁷Since you call on a Father who judges each man's work impartially, live your lives as strangers here in reverent fear. ¹⁸For you know that it was not with perishable things such as silver or gold that you were redeemed from the empty way of life handed down to you from your forefathers, ¹⁹but with the precious blood of Christ, a lamb without blemish or defect. ²⁰He was chosen before the creation of the world, but was revealed in these last times for your sake. ²¹Through him you believe in God, who raised him from the dead and glorified him, and so your faith and hope are in God.

²²Now that you have purified yourselves by obeying the truth so that you have sincere love for your brothers, love one another deeply, from the heart. ²³For you have been born again, not of perishable seed, but of imperishable, through the living and enduring word of God. ²⁴For,

"All men are like grass,
  and all their glory is like the flowers
    of the field;
the grass withers and the flowers fall,
²⁵ but the word of the Lord stands
      forever."

And this is the word that was preached to you.

2 Therefore, rid yourselves of all malice and all deceit, hypocrisy, envy, and slander of every kind. ²Like newborn babies, crave pure spiritual milk, so that by it you may grow up in your salvation, ³now that you have tasted that the Lord is good.

Hidden Dangers

2 Peter 1:1–2:3

As 1 Peter demonstrates, leaders of the New Testament church did not consider persecution a grave threat. To the contrary, such trials purified and strengthened the church by forcing true believers to come forward and exhibit their courage and faith.

The real dangers to the church came from within. Take the matter of unity. At the Last Supper with the disciples, Jesus had prayed that believers "may be one as we are one" (John 17:11). But within a generation, the church had splintered into followers of Paul or his rivals, legalists, free-wheelers, Judaizers, doomsdayers, and dozens of different groups.

Typically, these groups would focus on a minor doctrinal issue and waste energy on meaningless debates. This letter, for example, seems directed toward Christians obsessed with the last days. Some, impatient over unfulfilled predictions of Christ's second coming, were already beginning to scoff at the whole idea.

The author of 2 Peter has strong words of correction for such splinter groups. He reminds them that the Gospel is no fairy tale, no collection of "cleverly invented stories." As an eyewitness on the Mount of Transfiguration, he had heard God give resounding approval to his Son. If that God has promised a Second Coming, then rest assured it will take place.

As in many New Testament letters, the emphasis in 2 Peter strays back and forth between what to believe and what kind of person to be. The author lays out a progressive list of qualities—faith, goodness, knowledge, self-control, perseverance, godliness, brotherly kindness, love—that will strengthen against any temptations toward disunity.

The author of this letter is an old man, soon to face death. As a final swan song, he can do no better than remind his readers of the most basic truths of the Christian life. The answer to false knowledge is true knowledge; the answer to immoral living is moral living. As he prepares to die, the author of 2 Peter appeals one last time for truth.

> **To Reflect On:** *Of the seven qualities mentioned in 2 Peter 1:5–7, which describe your life now? Which need work?*

2 PETER 1:1–2:3

1 Simon Peter, a servant and apostle of Jesus Christ,

To those who through the righteousness of our God and Savior Jesus Christ have received a faith as precious as ours:

2 Grace and peace be yours in abundance through the knowledge of God and of Jesus our Lord.

Making One's Calling and Election Sure

3 His divine power has given us everything we need for life and godliness through our knowledge of him who called us by his own glory and goodness. 4 Through these he has given us his very great and precious promises, so that through them you may participate in the divine nature and escape the corruption in the world caused by evil desires.

5 For this very reason, make every effort to add to your faith goodness; and to goodness, knowledge; 6 and to knowledge, self-control; and to self-control, perseverance; and to perseverance, godliness; 7 and to godliness, brotherly kindness; and to brotherly kindness, love. 8 For if you possess these qualities in increasing measure, they will keep you from being ineffective and unproductive in your knowledge of our Lord Jesus Christ. 9 But if anyone does not have them, he is nearsighted and blind, and has forgotten that he has been cleansed from his past sins.

10 Therefore, my brothers, be all the more eager to make your calling and election sure. For if you do these things, you will never fall, 11 and you will receive a rich welcome into the eternal kingdom of our Lord and Savior Jesus Christ.

Prophecy of Scripture

12 So I will always remind you of these things, even though you know them and are firmly established in the truth you now have. 13 I think it is right to refresh your memory as long as I live in the tent of this body, 14 because I know that I will soon put it aside, as our Lord Jesus Christ has made clear to me. 15 And I will make every effort to see that after my departure you will always be able to remember these things.

16 We did not follow cleverly invented stories when we told you about the power and coming of our Lord Jesus Christ, but we were eye witnesses of his majesty. 17 For he received honor and glory from God the Father when the voice came to him from the Majestic Glory, saying, "This is my Son, whom I love; with him I am well pleased." 18 We ourselves heard this voice that came from heaven when we were with him on the sacred mountain.

19 And we have the word of the prophets made more certain, and you will do well to pay attention to it, as to a light shining in a dark place, until the day dawns and the morning star rises in your hearts. 20 Above all, you must understand that no prophecy of Scripture came about by the prophet's own interpretation. 21 For prophecy never had its origin in the will of man, but men spoke from God as they were carried along by the Holy Spirit.

False Teachers and Their Destruction

2 But there were also false prophets among the people, just as there will be false teachers among you. They will secretly introduce destructive heresies, even denying the sovereign Lord who bought them— bringing swift destruction on themselves. 2 Many will follow their shameful ways and will bring the way of truth into disrepute. 3 In their greed these teachers will exploit you with stories they have made up. Their condemnation has long been hanging over them, and their destruction has not been sleeping.

Sounding the Alarm

Jude

The brief letter from Jude (possibly the brother of Jesus) has much in common with 2 Peter. Both of them concern danger signs in the church, and the actual wording in Jude closely parallels that of 2 Peter 2. But Jude speaks with an even shriller tone. The disease has spread. If not soon arrested, it will infect the entire body.

In its approach, Jude resembles the scary movies against drugs and drunk driving that high schools sometimes show their students. They make viewers uncomfortable, which is precisely their purpose. Jude confesses that although he would prefer to write a more joyful letter about salvation, first he must alert them to the serious threat posed by certain troublemakers.

Jude doesn't elaborate on what the troublemakers were saying, but the early church was plagued by roving teachers who claimed some special "word from the Lord." Often these false teachers, seeking a profit, told audiences exactly what they wanted to hear: God's grace is so great that you can live however you want, with no penalty. Jude makes devastatingly clear what he thinks of such ideas. He calls the imposters spies and urges believers to fight for the true faith.

Ironically, only one portion of Jude gets much attention today: the beautiful doxology at the end. Evidently, Jude's strong words are no easier to take today than when they were first given.

> **To Reflect On:** *If Jude were alive today, what issues in the world might he write about in this fiery tone?*

JUDE

Jude, a servant of Jesus Christ and a brother of James,

To those who have been called, who are loved by God the Father and kept by Jesus Christ:

²Mercy, peace and love be yours in abundance.

The Sin and Doom of Godless Men

³Dear friends, although I was very eager to write to you about the salvation we share, I felt I had to write and urge you to contend for the faith that was once for all entrusted to the saints. ⁴For certain men whose condemnation was written about long ago have secretly slipped in among you. They are godless men, who change the grace of our God into a license for immorality and deny Jesus Christ our only Sovereign and Lord.

⁵Though you already know all this, I want to remind you that the Lord delivered his people out of Egypt, but later destroyed those who did not believe. ⁶And the angels who did not keep their positions of authority but abandoned their own home—these he has kept in darkness, bound with everlasting chains for judgment on the great Day. ⁷In a similar way, Sodom and Gomorrah and the surrounding towns gave themselves up to sexual immorality and perversion. They serve as an example of those who suffer the punishment of eternal fire.

⁸In the very same way, these dreamers pollute their own bodies, reject authority and slander celestial beings. ⁹But even the archangel Michael, when he was disputing with the devil about the body of Moses, did not dare to bring a slanderous accusation against him, but said, "The Lord rebuke you!" ¹⁰Yet these men speak abusively against whatever they do not understand; and what things they do understand by instinct, like unreasoning animals—these are the very things that destroy them.

¹¹Woe to them! They have taken the way of Cain; they have rushed for profit into Balaam's error; they have been destroyed in Korah's rebellion.

¹²These men are blemishes at your love feasts, eating with you without the slightest qualm—shepherds who feed only themselves. They are clouds without rain, blown along by the wind; autumn trees, without fruit and uprooted—twice dead. ¹³They are wild waves of the sea, foaming up their shame; wandering stars, for whom blackest darkness has been reserved forever.

¹⁴Enoch, the seventh from Adam, prophesied about these men: "See, the Lord is coming with thousands upon thousands of his holy ones ¹⁵to judge everyone, and to convict all the ungodly of all the ungodly acts they have done in the ungodly way, and of all the harsh words ungodly sinners have spoken against him." ¹⁶These men are grumblers and faultfinders; they follow their own evil desires; they boast about themselves and flatter others for their own advantage.

A Call to Persevere

¹⁷But, dear friends, remember what the apostles of our Lord Jesus Christ foretold. ¹⁸They said to you, "In the last times there will be scoffers who will follow their own ungodly desires." ¹⁹These are the men who divide you, who follow mere natural instincts and do not have the Spirit.

²⁰But you, dear friends, build yourselves up in your most holy faith and pray in the Holy Spirit. ²¹Keep yourselves in God's love as you wait for the mercy of our Lord Jesus Christ to bring you to eternal life.

²²Be merciful to those who doubt; ²³snatch others from the fire and save them; to others show mercy, mixed with fear—hating even the clothing stained by corrupted flesh.

Doxology

²⁴To him who is able to keep you from falling and to present you before his glorious presence without fault and with great joy—²⁵to the only God our Savior be glory, majesty, power and authority, through Jesus Christ our Lord, before all ages, now and forevermore! Amen.

Merest Christianity

1 John 3

Shortly after World War II, the brilliant Christian thinker C.S. Lewis communicated his beliefs about the faith in a series of British radio broadcasts that were then edited into the book *Mere Christianity*. He covered the basics, the bare essentials of Christian belief. Yet even that slim book would seem overly long and complex to the apostle John, author of this letter. John used the simplest language of any New Testament writer—his three letters together employed barely 300 different Greek words—to express the gospel in its most distilled form.

An early Christian writer named Jerome tells the story of John as a very old man being carried into the church at Ephesus. The people had gathered to hear a message from the famous apostle, but he would only repeat, "Little children, love one another." When asked why, he replied, "Because it is the Lord's command, and if this is done, it is enough."

That kind of single-mindedness shines through John's letters. This passage begins with wonder, astonishment even, that God has lavished his love on us. We are his children! But then John asks the obvious question: If we are God's children, why don't we act like it? Don't children of good parents naturally want to emulate them?

John was the last surviving apostle. He lived almost to the end of the first century, and may have been in his eighties when he wrote this book. Already, elite cults such as the Gnostics had sprung up within the church, and Christians were hotly debating esoteric matters of theology and ethics. John dismissed these with a wave of his hand. To him, the proof of a person's faith was perfectly obvious: "If anyone has material possessions and sees his brother in need but has no pity on him, how can the love of God be in him?" His words are as piercingly direct as the words of the Sermon on the Mount. A person who loves God acts like it; it's that simple.

For John, the heart of the gospel really did boil down to Jesus' command, "Love one another." Those three words expressed the heart of God.

> **To Reflect On:** *If you could condense the code you live by into one sentence, what would it be?*

1 JOHN 3

3 How great is the love the Father has lavished on us, that we should be called children of God! And that is what we are! The reason the world does not know us is that it did not know him. ²Dear friends, now we are children of God, and what we will be has not yet been made known. But we know that when he appears, we shall be like him, for we shall see him as he is. ³Everyone who has this hope in him purifies himself, just as he is pure.

⁴Everyone who sins breaks the law; in fact, sin is lawlessness. ⁵But you know that he appeared so that he might take away our sins. And in him is no sin. ⁶No one who lives in him keeps on sinning. No one who continues to sin has either seen him or known him.

⁷Dear children, do not let anyone lead you astray. He who does what is right is righteous, just as he is righteous. ⁸He who does what is sinful is of the devil, because the devil has been sinning from the beginning. The reason the Son of God appeared was to destroy the devil's work. ⁹No one who is born of God will continue to sin, because God's seed remains in him; he cannot go on sinning, because he has been born of God. ¹⁰This is how we know who the children of God are and who the children of the devil are: Anyone who does not do what is right is not a child of God; nor is anyone who does not love his brother.

Love One Another

¹¹This is the message you heard from the beginning: We should love one another.

¹²Do not be like Cain, who belonged to the evil one and murdered his brother. And why did he murder him? Because his own actions were evil and his brother's were righteous. ¹³Do not be surprised, my brothers, if the world hates you. ¹⁴We know that we have passed from death to life, because we love our brothers. Anyone who does not love remains in death. ¹⁵Anyone who hates his brother is a murderer, and you know that no murderer has eternal life in him.

¹⁶This is how we know what love is: Jesus Christ laid down his life for us. And we ought to lay down our lives for our brothers. ¹⁷If anyone has material possessions and sees his brother in need but has no pity on him, how can the love of God be in him? ¹⁸Dear children, let us not love with words or tongue but with actions and in truth. ¹⁹This then is how we know that we belong to the truth, and how we set our hearts at rest in his presence ²⁰whenever our hearts condemn us. For God is greater than our hearts, and he knows everything.

²¹Dear friends, if our hearts do not condemn us, we have confidence before God ²²and receive from him anything we ask, because we obey his commands and do what pleases him. ²³And this is his command: to believe in the name of his Son, Jesus Christ, and to love one another as he commanded us. ²⁴Those who obey his commands live in him, and he in them. And this is how we know that he lives in us: We know it by the Spirit he gave us.

When To Be Hospitable

2 John, 3 John

Most early churches founded by missionaries like the apostle Paul met in private homes. Later on, Paul began sending out emissaries, like Timothy and Titus, who joined the original apostles in making "the circuit" from church to church. Christians had the practice of hosting traveling teachers in their homes, rather than making them stay in the notoriously unsafe Roman inns.

Before long, however, false teachers followed suit, bringing distortions of the original gospel and sowing confusion and discord. Soon religious racketeers joined in, seeking free food and lodging. The issue arose of what to do with the new breed of pseudo-evangelists. Should Christians offer hospitality to them, too? The letters of 2 and 3 John, the shortest letters in the New Testament, deal with this very problem.

These two letters are best read together, since each gives one side of a problem facing a young church. The book of 2 John urges Christians to use discretion in testing a visitor's message and motive. It cautions against hosting visitors who do not teach the truth about Christ. True to his nickname, the apostle of love repeats his motto, "Love one another," even in this letter of warning.

On the other hand, 3 John praises a man named Gaius for warmly welcoming genuine Christian teachers. Gaius's church was dominated by a gossipy dictator who excluded all outsiders.

In a very condensed form, John's two letters deal with heresy and church splits—two problems that have plagued the church in every age, in every place. To defend against those dangers, John stresses the need for love and discernment. Believers must know whom to accept and support, and whom to resist.

> **To Reflect On:** *Who are some modern "deceivers" or false teachers? What issues tend to provoke "church discipline" today?*

2 JOHN, 3 JOHN

2 John

¹The elder,

To the chosen lady and her children, whom I love in the truth—and not I only, but also all who know the truth—²because of the truth, which lives in us and will be with us forever:

³Grace, mercy and peace from God the Father and from Jesus Christ, the Father's Son, will be with us in truth and love.

⁴It has given me great joy to find some of your children walking in the truth, just as the Father commanded us. ⁵And now, dear lady, I am not writing you a new command but one we have had from the beginning. I ask that we love one another. ⁶And this is love: that we walk in obedience to his commands. As you have heard from the beginning, his command is that you walk in love.

⁷Many deceivers, who do not acknowledge Jesus Christ as coming in the flesh, have gone out into the world. Any such person is the deceiver and the antichrist. ⁸Watch out that you do not lose what you have worked for, but that you may be rewarded fully. ⁹Anyone who runs ahead and does not continue in the teaching of Christ does not have God; whoever continues in the teaching has both the Father and the Son. ¹⁰If anyone comes to you and does not bring this teaching, do not take him into your house or welcome him. ¹¹Anyone who welcomes him shares in his wicked work.

¹²I have much to write to you, but I do not want to use paper and ink. Instead, I hope to visit you and talk with you face to face, so that our joy may be complete.

¹³The children of your chosen sister send their greetings.

3 John

¹The elder,

To my dear friend Gaius, whom I love in the truth.

²Dear friend, I pray that you may enjoy good health and that all may go well with you, even as your soul is getting along well. ³It gave me great joy to have some brothers come and tell about your faithfulness to the truth and how you continue to walk in the truth. ⁴I have no greater joy than to hear that my children are walking in the truth.

⁵Dear friend, you are faithful in what you are doing for the brothers, even though they are strangers to you. ⁶They have told the church about your love. You will do well to send them on their way in a manner worthy of God. ⁷It was for the sake of the Name that they went out, receiving no help from the pagans. ⁸We ought therefore to show hospitality to such men so that we may work together for the truth.

⁹I wrote to the church, but Diotrephes, who loves to be first, will have nothing to do with us. ¹⁰So if I come, I will call attention to what he is doing, gossiping maliciously about us. Not satisfied with that, he refuses to welcome the brothers. He also stops those who want to do so and puts them out of the church.

¹¹Dear friend, do not imitate what is evil but what is good. Anyone who does what is good is from God. Anyone who does what is evil has not seen God. ¹²Demetrius is well spoken of by everyone—and even by the truth itself. We also speak well of him, and you know that our testimony is true.

¹³I have much to write you, but I do not want to do so with pen and ink. ¹⁴I hope to see you soon, and we will talk face to face.

Peace to you. The friends here send their greetings. Greet the friends there by name.

The Final Word

Revelation 1

Everyone agrees that Revelation is the strangest book in the New Testament, but beyond that, readers agree on little else. Revelation, with its mysterious use of numbers and symbols and messages in code, has spawned more weird theories over the centuries than any other portion of the Bible. What purpose, then, does it serve?

The best way to answer that question is to imagine the Bible without the book of Revelation. After the Old Testament come the four Gospels, which then lead into Acts and its account of missionary ventures, followed by the letters to the resulting churches. All fine so far, but one thing is missing: Where is history going? Where will it all end up?

Jesus' disciples, all Jewish, grew up hearing about a Messiah who would overturn injustice and unrighteousness and usher in a new kingdom of peace and love and justice. Such long-awaited dreams disappeared as they watched Jesus die between two thieves, but came surging back a few days later when Jesus reappeared. "Lord, are you at this time going to restore the kingdom to Israel?" were the last words on their lips just before he left them at the Ascension (Acts 1).

One would have to reach beyond all credibility to make a case that the prophets' promised kingdom of peace and righteousness has come about in the years since the Ascension. Our own century has included two World Wars, several hundred lesser wars, two atom bomb attacks, a Holocaust, the Gulag Archipelago, and numerous mass killings by half-crazed dictators. Where is the time promised by Isaiah when swords will be beaten into plowshares and the lion will lie down by the calf?

Revelation adds a two-word message: Just wait. God is not finished with this planet. The Bible stakes God's own reputation on his ability to restore this planet to its original state of perfection. Only when that happens will history have run its course.

As the book opens, the apostle John has been banished on the island of Patmos, a hard-labor colony maintained by the Roman Empire. In that bleak setting, he receives a vision remarkably similar in style to those reported by the prophets Ezekiel and Daniel. Many details of John's vision no one can claim to understand with confidence. But this first chapter establishes why the visions were given. John presents a new picture of Jesus.

Yes, Jesus is the babe in the manger, and the Good Shepherd, and the teacher of disciples, and the model of humanity, and the Son of God who died on a cross. But he is something else as well: He is the blazing supernatural creature whose very presence knocked John to the ground. He is the Creator of this world who will someday return to re-create, and make new all that humankind has spoiled.

To Reflect On: *Does your "image" of Jesus include the image given in this chapter?*

REVELATION 1

Prologue

1 The revelation of Jesus Christ, which God gave him to show his servants what must soon take place. He made it known by sending his angel to his servant John, ²who testifies to everything he saw— that is, the word of God and the testimony of Jesus Christ. ³Blessed is the one who reads the words of this prophecy, and blessed are those who hear it and take to heart what is written in it, because the time is near.

Greetings and Doxology

⁴John,

To the seven churches in the province of Asia:

Grace and peace to you from him who is, and who was, and who is to come, and from the seven spirits before his throne, ⁵and from Jesus Christ, who is the faithful witness, the firstborn from the dead, and the ruler of the kings of the earth.

To him who loves us and has freed us from our sins by his blood, ⁶and has made us to be a kingdom and priests to serve his God and Father—to him be glory and power for ever and ever! Amen.

⁷Look, he is coming with the clouds,
    and every eye will see him,
even those who pierced him;
    and all the peoples of the earth will
        mourn because of him.
                    So shall it be! Amen.

⁸"I am the Alpha and the Omega," says the Lord God, "who is, and who was, and who is to come, the Almighty."

One Like a Son of Man

⁹I, John, your brother and companion in the suffering and kingdom and patient endurance that are ours in Jesus, was on the island of Patmos because of the word of God and the testimony of Jesus. ¹⁰On the Lord's Day I was in the Spirit, and I heard behind me a loud voice like a trumpet, ¹¹which said: "Write on a scroll what you see and send it to the seven churches: to Ephesus, Smyrna, Pergamum, Thyatira, Sardis, Philadelphia and Laodicea."

¹²I turned around to see the voice that was speaking to me. And when I turned I saw seven golden lampstands, ¹³and among the lampstands was someone "like a son of man," dressed in a robe reaching down to his feet and with a golden sash around his chest. ¹⁴His head and hair were white like wool, as white as snow, and his eyes were like blazing fire. ¹⁵His feet were like bronze glowing in a furnace, and his voice was like the sound of rushing waters. ¹⁶In his right hand he held seven stars, and out of his mouth came a sharp double-edged sword. His face was like the sun shining in all its brilliance.

¹⁷When I saw him, I fell at his feet as though dead. Then he placed his right hand on me and said: "Do not be afraid. I am the First and the Last. ¹⁸I am the Living One; I was dead, and behold I am alive for ever and ever! And I hold the keys of death and Hades.

¹⁹"Write, therefore, what you have seen, what is now and what will take place later. ²⁰The mystery of the seven stars that you saw in my right hand and of the seven golden lampstands is this: The seven stars are the angels of the seven churches, and the seven lampstands are the seven churches.

Another Side of History

Revelation 12

This passage from Revelation vividly illustrates how prophetic visions can shed new light on history. John uses bizarre, cosmic symbols: a pregnant woman clothed with the sun; a seven-headed red dragon so enormous that its tail sweeps a third of the stars from the sky; a flight into the desert; a war in heaven. Commentaries suggest many possible interpretations of this chapter, but almost all of them agree that it has something to do with Jesus' birth and its effect on the universe. When a baby was born, the universe shuddered.

In a sense, Revelation 12 presents Christmas from a cosmic perspective, adding a new set of images to the familiar scenes of manger and shepherds and the Slaughter of the Innocents. What was visible on earth represented ripples on the surface; underneath, massive disruptions were shaking the foundations of the universe. Even as King Herod was trying to kill all male babies in Palestine, cosmic forces were at war behind the scenes. From God's viewpoint—and Satan's—Christmas was far more than the birth of a baby; it was an invasion, the decisive advance in the great struggle for the cosmos. Revelation depicts this struggle in terms of a murderous dragon opposing the forces of good.

Which is the "true" picture of Christmas: the account in Matthew and Luke, or that in Revelation? They are the same picture, told from two different points of view. This view of Christ's birth in Revelation 12 typifies the pattern of the entire book, in which John fuses things seen with things normally not seen.

In daily life, two parallel histories occur at the same time: one on earth and one in heaven. Revelation, by parting the curtain, allows us to view them together. It leaves the unmistakable impression that, as we make everyday choices between good and evil, those choices are having an impact on the supernatural universe we cannot see.

Revelation portrays history through sharply contrasting images: good vs. evil, the Lamb vs. the dragon, Jerusalem vs. Babylon, the bride vs. the prostitute. But it also insists that, no matter how it may appear from our limited perspective, God maintains firm control over all history. Ultimately, even the despots will end up fulfilling the plan mapped out for them by God. Pontius Pilate and his Roman soldiers demonstrated that truth. They thought they were getting rid of Jesus by crucifying him; instead, they made possible the salvation of the world.

To Reflect On: *When have you ever felt part of a "spiritual warfare"?*

REVELATION 12

The Woman and the Dragon

12 A great and wondrous sign appeared in heaven: a woman clothed with the sun, with the moon under her feet and a crown of twelve stars on her head. ²She was pregnant and cried out in pain as she was about to give birth. ³Then another sign appeared in heaven: an enormous red dragon with seven heads and ten horns and seven crowns on his heads. ⁴His tail swept a third of the stars out of the sky and flung them to the earth. The dragon stood in front of the woman who was about to give birth, so that he might devour her child the moment it was born. ⁵She gave birth to a son, a male child, who will rule all the nations with an iron scepter. And her child was snatched up to God and to his throne. ⁶The woman fled into the desert to a place prepared for her by God, where she might be taken care of for 1,260 days.

⁷And there was war in heaven. Michael and his angels fought against the dragon, and the dragon and his angels fought back. ⁸But he was not strong enough, and they lost their place in heaven. ⁹The great dragon was hurled down—that ancient serpent called the devil or Satan, who leads the whole world astray. He was hurled to the earth, and his angels with him.

¹⁰Then I heard a loud voice in heaven say:

"Now have come the salvation and the
    power and the kingdom of our
    God,
  and the authority of his Christ.

For the accuser of our brothers,
  who accuses them before our God
    day and night,
  has been hurled down.
¹¹They overcame him
  by the blood of the Lamb
  and by the word of their
    testimony;
they did not love their lives so much
  as to shrink from death.
¹²Therefore rejoice, you heavens
  and you who dwell in them!
But woe to the earth and the sea,
  because the devil has gone down
    to you!
He is filled with fury,
  because he knows that his time is
    short."

¹³When the dragon saw that he had been hurled to the earth, he pursued the woman who had given birth to the male child. ¹⁴The woman was given the two wings of a great eagle, so that she might fly to the place prepared for her in the desert, where she would be taken care of for a time, times and half a time, out of the serpent's reach. ¹⁵Then from his mouth the serpent spewed water like a river, to overtake the woman and sweep her away with the torrent. ¹⁶But the earth helped the woman by opening its mouth and swallowing the river that the dragon had spewed out of his mouth. ¹⁷Then the dragon was enraged at the woman and went off to make war against the rest of her offspring—those who obey God's commandments and hold to the testimony of Jesus.

Return to Eden

Revelation 21:1–22:5

In its "plot," the Bible ends up very much where it began. The broken relationship between God and human beings has healed over at last, and the curse of Genesis 3 is lifted. Borrowing images from Eden, Revelation pictures a river and a tree of life. But this time a great city replaces the garden setting, a city filled with worshipers of God. Nothing will pollute that city; no death or sadness will ever darken that scene. There will be no crying or pain. For the first time since Eden, the *World as It Is* will finally match the *World as God Wants It.*

John saw heaven as the fulfillment of every Jewish dream: Jerusalem restored, with walls of jasper and streets of gleaming gold. For someone else—say, a refugee in the Third World today—heaven may represent a family reunited, a home abundant with food and fresh drinking water. Heaven stands for the fulfillment of every true longing. As C.S. Lewis has said, all the beauty and joy on planet earth represent "only the scent of a flower we have not found, the echo of a tune we have not heard, news from a country we have never yet visited."

Revelation promises that our longings are not mere fantasies. They will come true. When we awake in the new heaven and new earth, we will have at last whatever we have longed for. Somehow, from out of all the bad news in a book like Revelation, good news emerges—spectacular Good News. A promise of goodness without a catch in it somewhere. There is a happy ending after all.

In the Bible, heaven is not an afterthought or optional belief. It is the final justification of all creation. The Bible never belittles human tragedy and disappointment—is any book more painfully honest?—but it does add the one key word *temporary.* What we feel now, we will not always feel. The time for *re-creation* will come.

For people who feel trapped in pain or in a broken home, in economic misery or in fear—for all those people, for all of us, heaven promises a future time, far longer and more substantial than the time we spend on earth, a time of health and wholeness and pleasure and peace. The Bible began with that promise in the book of Genesis. And the Bible ends with that same promise, a guarantee of future reality. The end will be a beginning.

To Reflect On: *What do you long for in the re-created earth?*

———————◆•◆———————

REVELATION 21:1–22:5

The New Jerusalem

21 Then I saw a new heaven and a new earth, for the first heaven and the first earth had passed away, and there was no longer any sea. ²I saw the Holy City, the new Jerusalem, coming down out of heaven from God, prepared as a bride beautifully dressed for her husband. ³And I heard a loud voice from the throne saying, "Now the dwelling of God is with men, and he will live with them. They will be his people, and God himself will be with them and be their God. ⁴He will wipe every tear from their eyes. There will be no more death or mourning or crying or pain, for the old order of things has passed away."

⁵He who was seated on the throne said, "I am making everything new!" Then he said, "Write this down, for these words are trustworthy and true."

⁶He said to me: "It is done. I am the Alpha and the Omega, the Beginning and the End. To him who is thirsty I will give to drink without cost from the spring of the water of life. ⁷He who overcomes will inherit all this, and I will be his God and he will be my son. ⁸But the cowardly, the unbelieving, the vile, the murderers, the sexually immoral, those who practice magic arts, the idolaters and all liars—their place will be in the fiery lake of burning sulfur. This is the second death."

⁹One of the seven angels who had the seven bowls full of the seven last plagues came and said to me, "Come, I will show you the bride, the wife of the Lamb." ¹⁰And he carried me away in the Spirit to a mountain great and high, and showed me the Holy City, Jerusalem, coming down out of heaven from God. ¹¹It shone with the glory of God, and its brilliance was like that of a very precious jewel, like a jasper, clear as crystal. ¹²It had a great, high wall with twelve gates, and with twelve angels at the gates. On the gates were written the names of the twelve tribes of Israel. ¹³There were three gates on the east, three on the north, three on the south and three on the west. ¹⁴The wall of the city had twelve foundations, and on them were the names of the twelve apostles of the Lamb.

¹⁵The angel who talked with me had a measuring rod of gold to measure the city, its gates and its walls. ¹⁶The city was laid out like a square, as long as it was wide. He measured the city with a rod and found it to be 12,000 stadia in length, and as wide and high as it is long. ¹⁷He measured its wall and it was 144 cubits thick, by man's measurement, which the angel was using. ¹⁸The wall was made of jasper, and the city of pure gold, as pure as glass. ¹⁹The foundations of the city walls were decorated with every kind of precious stone. The first foundation was jasper, the second sapphire, the third chalcedony, the fourth emerald, ²⁰the fifth sardonyx, the sixth carnelian, the seventh chrysolite, the eighth beryl, the ninth topaz, the tenth chrysophrase, the eleventh jacinth, and the twelfth amethyst. ²¹The twelve gates were twelve pearls, each gate made of a single pearl. The great street of the city was of pure gold, like transparent glass.

²²I did not see a temple in the city, because the Lord God Almighty and the Lamb are its temple. ²³The city does not need the sun or the moon to shine on it, for the glory of God gives it light, and the Lamb is its lamp. ²⁴The nations will walk by its light, and the kings of the earth will bring their splendor into it. ²⁵On no day will its gates ever be shut, for there will be no night there. ²⁶The glory and honor of the nations will be brought into it. ²⁷Nothing impure will ever enter it, nor will anyone who does what is shameful or deceitful, but only those whose names are written in the Lamb's book of life.

The River of Life

22 Then the angel showed me the river of the water of life, as clear as crystal, flowing from the throne of God and of the Lamb ²down the middle of the great street of the city. On each side of the river stood the tree of life, bearing twelve crops of fruit, yielding its fruit every month. And the leaves of the tree are for the healing of the nations. ³No longer will there be any curse. The throne of God and of the Lamb will be in the city, and his servants will serve him. ⁴They will see his face, and his name will be on their foreheads. ⁵There will be no more night. They will not need the light of a lamp or the light of the sun, for the Lord God will give them light. And they will reign for ever and ever.

Daybreak Books are inspirational books that encourage believers in their daily spiritual walk.

The devotional text of *A Guided Tour of the Bible* is set in 10/11.5 Folio Light. Folio was designed by Konrad Bauer and Walter Baum in 1957. The scripture text is set in 9/10.5 Palatino. Palatino was designed by Hermann Zapf in Germany in 1948. The type was set on a Mergenthaler Linotron 202/N by the Photocomposition Department of Zondervan Publishing House; Nancy Wilson, compositor; Louise Bauer, designer. Printed by Arcata Graphics of Fairfield, Pennsylvania.